Reform and Development of Powers and Functions of China's Criminal Proceedings

Weidong Chen

Reform and Development of Powers and Functions of China's Criminal Proceedings

中国人民大学出版社
CHINA RENMIN UNIVERSITY PRESS

Springer

Weidong Chen
School of Law
Renmin University of China
Beijing, China

ISBN 978-981-15-8430-5 ISBN 978-981-15-8431-2 (eBook)
https://doi.org/10.1007/978-981-15-8431-2

Jointly published with China Renmin University Press
The print edition is not for sale in China (Mainland). Customers from China (Mainland) please order the print book from: China Renmin University Press.

This Springer imprint is published by the registered company Springer Nature Singapore Pte Ltd.
The registered company address is: 152 Beach Road, #21-01/04 Gateway East, Singapore 189721, Singapore

Preface

The criminal procedure is process that criminal actions go on. Chief parties during the actions include judicial organs handling cases, suspects who may be investigated for criminal responsibility, defendants, and other litigation participants. In the process of investigating criminal responsibility of criminal suspects and defendants by the police and judicial organs, they exercise the state power, while suspects and defendants exercise personal rights. The police and judicial organs must exercise power to investigate criminal responsibility of criminal suspect and defendant in accordance with the legal procedure, meanwhile suspects, defendants, and their entrusted defenders must exercise their litigation rights in the light of procedure to safeguard their lawful rights and interests. Here, the power and rights are intertwined and even conflicting, which demonstrates obvious features of the criminal procedure, and it also symbolizes the civilization of the criminal procedure of a country. Therefore, when studying the criminal procedure we must begin with the prospective of powers and functions, paying attention to power and rights. In the research of law, powers and functions are mostly studied in the branch of jurisprudence and civil and commercial law, but rarely in the criminal procedure law. It is because of this consideration, the author has been thinking about whether the power of public security and judicial organs can be combined with the individual rights of citizens, that is to say, to study the powers and functions of criminal procedure, which constitutes the original intention of writing this book. At present, there is no unified expression about how to understand the powers and functions of criminal procedure. Some people regard the powers and functions as right and obligation itself, and some people regard it as the subordinate concept of right and obligation, which is embodied in the right of jurisdiction, prosecution, investigation, defense, etc. In this book, the author claims that powers and functions actually refer to power and right.

This book, firstly, explores the powers and functions in theory and analyzes the concept, features, and fundamental principles of it and the relationship between powers and functions, and then explores the right of jurisdiction from the perspective of jurisdiction of the court. As the judicial organ, the court exercises the power of jurisdiction. Combined with the ongoing judicial reform, this book explores how the people's court further improve its ideas and guide the realization of its power with a new idea in the process of exercising its jurisdiction. Main changes include: from one-sided crackdown on crime in the past to equal emphasis on both crackdown on crime and protection of human rights, from over emphasis on substantive justice to equal emphasis on both substantive and procedural justice, from overemphasizing the proof of verbal evidence to emphasizing the proof of physical evidence. The court also emphasizes the balance between justice and efficiency. How to exercise judicial power impartially and independently according to law has been a focus and sensitive topic in the academic circle of law for many years. This book comprehensively combs the external environmental factors that affect the judicial organs to exercise their functions and powers independently in accordance with law, responses to the relationship between independent handling of cases by judicial organs in accordance with the law and social and political effects, and puts forward that the main consideration should be the legal effect, and over emphasis on social and political effects often leads to the neglect of legal effects. Combined with the reform of judicial responsibility system, the independent exercise of judicial power after the reform is explored. The author also pays special attention to the issue of how the judicial organ can exercise the judicial power fairly without external intervention and the internal approval and supervision of presidents and heads of the court after delegating authorities to judges themselves. This is a worrying issue, which is likely to become a major hidden danger of judicial injustice in China in the future. At the beginning of the reform of judicial responsibility system, the consequences will be unimaginable if we don't have a clear understanding of this issue and take precautions. At present, it is urgent to discuss how to strengthen the all-round supervision of the jurisdiction. In this regard, the author puts forward some improving plans, for example, specialized inspection, regular selective examination, expert review, judicial precedent giving, accountability for misjudged cases, etc. Meanwhile, it is also an important part to strengthen the supervision of the president of court under new situation. In the discussion of judicial jurisdiction, the author also talks about the judicial review mechanism. This is an integral part and the due meaning of judicial power, and also the common characteristics of judicial power in the world. In China, the authority of judicial review doesn't belong to the court; the relevant powers and functions, such as the jurisdiction of arrest inspection, are entrusted to the procuratorial organ. On the premise of generally recognizing the judicial nature of the procuratorial organ, we cannot but say that this is an alternative judicial review. The problem is that, as far as the procuratorial organ concerned, its position of accusant in criminal proceedings conflicts with its neutral role in judicial review. How to ensure the legitimacy and fairness of the judicial review has become a question. For this reason, the book makes an analysis from the following four aspects: the essential characteristics of litigation form require judicial control over pretrial procedure; the nature of judicial power is the theoretical foundation of the natural rationality of judicial review mechanism; the establishment of modern constitutional state is the political foundation of judicial review mechanism; and the construction of modern criminal procedure is the system guarantee for the judicial review mechanism.

Procuratorial power marks the most complex and characteristic feature of the power of criminal procedure in China. Since the restoration and reconstruction of China's procuratorial system in the 1970s, disputes about procuratorial power have never stopped. For a long time, there has been a lot of controversy about the nature of procuratorial power in the academic circles. This book summarizes and analyzes four academic viewpoints: the theory of administrative power, the theory of judicial power, the theory of administrative and judicial power, and the theory of legal supervision power. The author believes that the research level of the concepts of procuratorial power and supervisory power is vague, which makes the academic circle fall into a long-term dispute on the nature of procuratorial power. To clarify the theoretical disputes of "procuratorial power," we must use the semantic analysis method to find out the semantic differences of the same words, concepts, and propositions, and make the differences of the actual ideological content expressed by the same words as small as possible, and confirm what questions to answer, not whether this question really exists. Some disputes are sure to be avoided or clarified and settled. The author deconstructs the procuratorial power in China from the perspective of procuratorial function, and distinguishes the functions and powers owned by procuratorial organs, that is, the connotation of procuratorial power, and then the author draws a conclusion that the concept of procuratorial power is different in broad and narrow sense: in a broad sense, the concept of procuratorial power refers to the general term of the litigation authority and power of litigation supervision granted by law to procuratorial organs, which is mainly applicable to the macro-level of the judicial system in China, and in a narrow sense, the concept of procuratorial power refers to the general term of the litigation authority granted by law to procuratorial organs, which is mainly applicable to the level of litigation structure. The nature of procuratorial power in narrow sense is administrative power in the litigation structure of our country, which can also be confirmed in the procuratorial practice of western countries, especially the common law system. However, if we discuss the nature of procuratorial power in a broad sense, and consider the litigation authority, litigation supervision power, and judicial relief power of procuratorial organs (prosecutors) as a whole, the nature of procuratorial power in a broad sense may be different. This is because, by examining the concept of procuratorial power, we can know that procuratorial power is the general term of various functions and powers entrusted to procuratorial organs by law. We can get two inspirations from it: first, the procuratorial power is the general term of the powers entrusted to the procuratorial organ. The nature of the procuratorial power is determined by the nature of the power content. As the content of the power changes, the nature of the procuratorial power may also change. Secondly, it is "law" that endows procuratorial organs with functions and powers. Here, "law" should refer to the practice method. Therefore, the functions and powers entrusted to procuratorial organs (prosecutors) by laws of different countries or regions are different, and the nature of procuratorial power is also different. It can be seen that the issue of the nature of procuratorial power is not only a theoretical (ought to be) issue, but also a practical (being) issue; in the world, it is not only a common issue, but also a personality issue.

At present, the country's judicial reform is advancing rapidly, especially reform concerning the judicial system is deepening. Recently, the CPC Central Committee issued a document to promote reform of the national supervision system, which was first piloted in Beijing, Shanxi, and Zhejiang Provinces, and was fully launched nationwide in 2018. After the state supervision organs exercise the power of filing and inquiring corruption cases, the procuratorial power faces new major issues. The author insists that after the reform of the supervision system, the procuratorial power has not changed substantially, because its powers of arrest, prosecution, supervision, and even investigation remained the same as before. What has changed is the scope of investigated cases. Therefore, we should take the reform as the background, probe into the development and change of procuratorial power, strengthen the ability of response, and build and fulfill the procuratorial power. Although the reform of the state supervision system and the judicial reform have brought great impact and influence to the procuratorial organ, from the perspective of the Constitution and the criminal procedure law, the position and attribute of the procuratorial organ as the legal supervision organ have not changed. Therefore, stripping away the investigation power of the duty crime will not reduce the position of the procuratorial organ in the national legal system. However, once the power of legal supervision is excluded, the procuratorial organ can only become the prosecutor who undertakes the function of prosecution on behalf of the state. Therefore, under the current situation, the procuratorial organ should firmly grasp the power of legal supervision, strengthen and improve the work of legal supervision. In this regard, the author has the following suggestions.

Firstly, the scope of supervision. The traditional supervision mainly focuses on the field of litigation, but with the advancement of the rule by law, especially the decision made at the Fourth Plenary Session of the 18th CPC Central Committee, the scope of procuratorial supervision is expanded, which makes the supervision of procuratorial organs expand from litigation supervision to non-litigation supervision. The decision clearly states that the procuratorial organ shall urge the administrative organ to correct any act of illegal exercise of its power or failure to exercise its power in the course of performing its duties, which enables the procuratorial organ to obtain a more clear basis for the supervision of administrative power. Some people interpret this kind of supervision as top-down supervision, which will enhance the legal status and authority of the procuratorial organ, even higher than the administrative organ in a sense. Therefore, the connotation of the legal supervision of the procuratorial organ will be further enriched. At present, the legal supervision of the procuratorial organ is still concentrated in the field of judicial power. For the supervision of administrative power, the relevant laws and regulations and reform practice are obviously insufficient. The procuratorial organ not only faces the situation of power being stripped, but also has no firm grasp of the new power entrusted. Therefore, while discussing this issue, the procuratorial organ should come up with a reform plan at an appropriate time, and the Supreme People's Procuratorate should report it to the National People's Congress for approval and then carry out a pilot project. Whether the scope of procuratorial supervision can cover the National Supervisory Committee has attracted the attention of relevant parties. At present, there is no such provision in the draft of the Supervision Law. The draft of the Supervision Law stipulates that the supervision committees will be supervised by itself, society, and party, while there is no specialized legal supervision. However, there is always a connection and restriction relationship between the procuratorial and supervision organs, which needs our careful study. In addition, the procuratorial organ broadens the scope of its supervision to the civil, administrative, and public interest cases. The author believes that at present, the number of administrative litigation cases has increased, but the corresponding administrative litigation supervision of the procuratorial organ has not been effectively followed up. The same is true to public interest litigation. The procuratorial organ should attach importance to public interest litigation and then it can be reflected that the procuratorial organ represents interest of the state. On the contrary, the author is not very in favor of the supervision of civil litigation, because this is the intervention of public rights in private rights. He always believes that there is a problem for the plaintiff or the defendant "fights against" the defendant or the plaintiff with the help of public rights. The supervision of procuratorial organs should focus on administrative litigation and public interest litigation. Of course, the supervision of civil cases of procuratorial organs is also regulated by the civil procedure law.

Secondly, the ways and means of supervision. In the past, the legal supervision has not formed the organization and procedure of handling cases, and the way of legal supervision has certain arbitrariness and irregularity. At a meeting on the promotion of procuratorial reform held in Chongqing, the author once mentioned the problem of the reform of supervision mode, which is mainly the problem of laws supervising case-handling organization. Legal supervision is not an individual act. Procuratorial supervision is implemented by the procuratorate as a whole. The decision made cannot be completed by an independent prosecutor, but by the procuratorate. At the same time, we should use investigation thinking to deal with supervision cases, to regard supervised matters as cases, to deal with legal supervision with case-handling thinking, to set up special organizations, to build special supervision procedures, and to investigate and verify the details of supervision clues.

Thirdly, enrich the means of supervision. The procuratorial organs may learn from the supervision means of the supervisory committee, such as appointment, interrogation, inquiry, etc., which are not used but should be used in legal supervision. For many years, we haven't studied deeply and thoroughly the process of regarding legal supervision as cases, the programming and standardization of legal supervision. It is necessary to establish a proper separation mechanism between the litigation function and supervision function of the procuratorial organs. The author does approve the practice of Hubei Province. Why should litigation and supervision function be separated? Many of the litigation functions demonstrate the judicial attribute, and the way of handling cases is different, while the supervisory function embodies a very strong administrative attribute. The two functions cannot be performed by one investigator, because he or she only pays attention to litigation but ignores supervision, that is to say, they mainly handle cases, rather than supervising. If separated, some specialize in handling cases, while others actively engage in supervising.

Fourthly, strengthen the effectiveness of supervision. How can legal supervision be effective? In the past, legal supervision, whether it is procuratorial advice, notice of correction of violations, or other aspects of supervision, was ignored by the people under supervision, and there is no way for the procurators. The author believes that solutions should be found. During the study of the Criminal Procedure Law, the author was inspired by the Article 263, which says: If the People's Procuratorate considers that the ruling of the People's Court on commutation or parole is improper, it shall, within 20 days after receiving the copy of the ruling, make a written correction to the People's Court. The People's Court shall, within one month after receiving the correction opinions, reconstitute a collegial panel for trial and make a final ruling. This is the latest form of supervision by the People's Procuratorate, which was added in 2012. This form is that after the procuratorate put forward supervision opinions, the supervised organs must have a special procedure to start the review of supervision opinions, unlike the previous supervision of the public security organs. In the next step, we should actively discuss with the public security organs and detention houses how to start the review procedure after supervision, which is an innovation and the necessary way for supervision. The legal consequences of further implementation of the supervision opinions should also be studied, and we are supposed to ensure the implementation of the supervision decisions made on illegal acts, and make our supervision exert substantial binding force. Once the illegal act is found and the correction opinions are put forward, the investigation and other organs as the supervised object and their relevant personnel shall response and correct, otherwise there will be corresponding adverse consequences or responsibilities, which may include: (1) for those who refuse to implement the supervision suggestions, the procuratorial organ may recommend the public security or the supervisory organ to investigate the responsibilities of the relevant personnel, and if the circumstances are minor, they shall be corrected within a time limit or given administrative sanctions, while if the circumstances are serious, they shall be dealt with as a criminal case and suggest that they be investigated for criminal responsibility. (2) Take the implementation of illegal supervision as an important reference for the quality of handling cases and the standardized assessment of law enforcement of the public security police, only in this way can the violators be urged to earnestly implement the supervision opinions or decisions. (3) When it is related to whether the case can be developed smoothly or not, the procuratorial organ may suggest the relevant organs to replace the investigators. In order to make the supervision more effective, we should try to avoid oral supervision but use written form, leaving evidence in the whole process, by which the supervision has binding force.

Fifthly, problems of the internal organs of the procuratorial organs. The central government attaches great importance to the establishment of institutions, because the establishment of institutions is closely related to the performance of the responsibilities of procuratorial organs. The author thinks, at present, that the scheme of institutional reform of Shanghai can be copied and popularized. According to the Supreme People's Procuratorate, there should be no more than 18 internal organs in provincial procuratorates. There are 17 internal organs in the Higher People's Procuratorate of Shanghai, which are divided into four parts: the first part is the judicial department, including the following: (1) The First Department of Criminal Prosecution (the Department of Arrest Inspection) sets up a number of prosecutor's offices for arrest inspection, which are responsible for inspecting the handling and guidance of arrest cases. (2) The Second Department of Criminal Prosecution (the first Department of Public Prosecution) establishes several offices for public prosecutor, and is responsible for handling and guiding public prosecution cases such as ordinary criminal cases and death penalty cases. (3) The third Department of Criminal Prosecution (the Second Department of Public Prosecution), with several public prosecutor offices, is responsible for the handling and guidance of public prosecution in special criminal cases such as duty crime, financial crime, and intellectual property. (4) The Fourth Department of Criminal Prosecution (the Supervision Department of Criminal Execution). (5) The Criminal Procedure Supervision Department shall establish several procurator offices to be responsible for the supervision of the establishment of cases, the connection of two levels of court, the supervision of the public security police station, the protest cases in the procedure for supervision upon adjudication, the investigation and verification of the major clues of the case supervision, the supervision tracking, the centralized management of the supervision documents, etc. (6) The Civil Procuratorial Department shall establish a number of procurator offices to be responsible for the supervision of civil proceedings. (7) The Administrative Procuratorial Department shall establish several procurator offices to be responsible for the supervision of administrative litigation, the supervision of administrative illegal acts and administrative compulsory measures, and the handling and guidance of administrative public interest litigation. (8) The Procuratorial Department for Juvenile Cases establishes several procurator offices to handle and guide juvenile cases. (9) The Department of Prosecution for Complaints (the Procuratorial Service Center) shall set up a number of procurator offices to perform the functions of the original Department of Prosecution and Appealing, and the Department of Litigation Supervision shall be responsible for the protested cases in the procedure for supervision upon adjudication. The second part is the Comprehensive Business Department, including the following: (1) the Business Management Department shall establish a number of procurator offices to perform the duties of the original Case Management Office. (2) The Research Office, without a change of its function, may set up the Secretary Office of the procuratorial committee to be responsible for the operation of it. The third part is the Procuratorial Auxiliary Department, including: (1) the Information Technology Department; (2) Judicial Procuratorial team. The fourth part is the Judicial Administration Department, including (1) the Political Department, (2) the Supervision office, and (3) the Security Department of Procuratorial Affairs. The author believes that these departments are well set up, but at the same time, revision suggestions are also put forward. Firstly, the departments can't be named as the First, Second, and Third Department, but named according to its function to help people have a clear acknowledgement of it. Secondly, the division of the complex supervision should be integrated. Supervision of criminal execution and supervision of criminal proceedings can be unified into supervision of criminal proceedings. Thirdly, the Civil Procuratorial Department and the Administrative Procuratorial Department should be changed into the Civil Procuratorial Supervision Department and the Administrative Procuratorial Supervision Department. This kind of setting separates the power of arrest and public prosecution, litigation and supervision, which accords with the author's idea. Shanghai emphasizes that the main purpose of setting up this department is to transfer the main body for handling cases from the named prosecutor to the prosecutor office. The internal organization is also a problem which is needed to be concentrated with the guidance of simplification, delayering, and scientification, adjusting measures according to different conditions, while avoiding imitating other levels of procuratorates or other procuratorates of the same level blindly. Internal organizations should be set flexibly according to the size of the procuratorate and the amount of cases. The above suggestions are directed against the procuratorates of provincial level, as for those of prefecture and county levels, for example, with a size of 50 officers or 30 officers, and principles are given by the central authorities but details are left to be researched.

In addition, the power of investigation of China is too much incomparable in the world. On the one hand, the criminal investigation in our country is not divided into compulsory or arbitrary. The public security organs have all rights to investigate compulsorily, with no room for negotiation. On the other hand, the investigation of our country is decided by the public security organs themselves who carry out the power of investigation. Most of the compulsory measures and compulsory investigation measures are decided by themselves, without an international judicial review system. There was a popular joke: "you must go to China to be a police man." Laws, including the People's Police Law of the People's Republic of China and the Criminal Procedure Law, empower police with huge and unrestricted power, and it mainly comes from our country's high attention to social security and social stability, and the strong control over society. In addition, this is also due to our overemphasis on fighting and punishing crime over the years, while neglecting to protect rights of the accused. However, we must face up to the fact that since the amendment of the Criminal Procedure Law in 1996, the legislators of the state have begun to restrict and regulate the investigation power continuously, especially the amendment of the criminal procedure law in 2012 has made strict restrictions on the application objects, conditions, and procedures of the compulsory measures. Time, place, audio, and video recording of the interrogation shall not force anyone to prove his guilt, the illegal evidence shall be excluded, and the complaint handling mechanism of illegal investigation behavior, all of them highlight the regulation of investigation power. This book pays special attention to the relationship between investigation and protection of human rights. Based on the basic characteristics of the restriction of investigation on human rights, and based on the norms and consensus of international conventions on investigation activities, it explores how to maximize the effective regulation of investigation rights in the Chinese context, which can be summarized in three aspects: First, strengthen the restriction, that is, according to the principle of mutual restriction, given by the law, of the police, the procuratorate, and the court, correct the past practice of only focusing on cooperation while ignoring restriction, exerting the check and balance function of procuratorate and court to investigation. Second, give full play to the special legal supervision function of the procuratorial organ in the investigation. We should not only supervise whether the investigation activities are legal, but also emphasize the supervision of the legitimate rights infringement of the criminal suspect. Third, advocate establishment of judicial control over investigation and judicial review mechanism. In China, scholars have different opinions on whether to establish judicial review system. On the one hand, we do not regard court as the center or core in litigation, but rather as a body of sharing division of responsibility and cooperating with public security organs and procuratorial organs. On the other hand, our system design determines to take procuratorate as legal supervision organs to exercise power of judicial review. In the context of comprehensively promoting the rule of law, the judicial reform puts forward the reform of the litigation system centered on trial. Therefore, it is necessary to emphasize the decisive role of court in the whole litigation process, rethink the judicial review mechanism, and explore the construction path of the system.

Different from the public power of police, procuratorate, and court, there is another form of power in criminal procedure, that is, the litigation rights of criminal suspects, defendants, and their defense lawyers. Objectively speaking, the public power of China's judicial organs has never been lacking, even very strong, while the rights of criminal suspects, defendants, and their defense lawyers are relatively weak, even vulnerable. With the continuous improvement of the criminal procedure law in recent years, especially the continuous legal reform, the protection of citizens' human rights has been greatly improved and enhanced. The protection of human rights of citizens has been improved to a great extent and it is not substantially different from international standards only in terms of system provisions, but the gap is still large in terms of judicial practice. In this book, the author evades the rights of criminal suspects and defendants, and studies the defense rights of lawyers, not because that the rights of the former are unimportant; on the contrary, these are the top priority of rights protection. It is because that the structure of this book is to analyze the forms of power and function of each participant in the process of pursuing criminal responsibility of criminal suspects and defendants. Over the years, the protection of rights of defense lawyers has been mainly focused on the so-called "three difficulties" of meeting with the suspects and defendants, reading files, and collecting evidence. After the amendment of the Criminal Procedure Law in 2012, these problems have been significantly improved, but still remain prominent. At the same time, new "three difficulties" of questioning, cross examination, and illegal evidence exclusion appear. This book has carried on omni-directional research to these new and old problems, paying attention to details and countermeasures, and it is more thorough compared with the previous discussion.

At present, in the process of in-depth implementation of the reform of criminal procedure centered on trial and the pilot program of the leniency system of confession and punishment, the importance of defense lawyers has become increasingly prominent. The Supreme People's Court and the Ministry of Justice recently put forward the implementation opinion of full coverage of criminal defense. This book does not discuss the legal aid of the duty counsels, involved in the reform, because of length and time limitation. It should be continuously researched and answers should be provided as for the question of what is the relationship between the legal aid lawyer and the duty lawyer and what is the litigation status, the litigation rights, and obligations of the duty lawyer.

The last chapter of this book studies rights of other subjects in criminal proceedings, including appraisers, witnesses, victims, and stakeholders in the special procedure of confiscation of illegal gains. The fair handling of cases is closely related to active and effective participation of the participants mentioned above. Previous studies have paid more or less attention to their obligation to testify or the litigation duty they should perform, intentionally or unintentionally ignoring their litigation rights, such as unilaterally emphasizing the fair appraisal and the obligation to appear in court of the appraisers, but lack of effective research on protecting necessary rights to ensure performance of their duties. This book puts forward relevant suggestions to protect rights from the perspective of laying particular emphasis on right protecting, with a purpose to draw attention to this issue, on one hand, and put forward suggestions for peer discussion, on the other.

It is obvious to all that the structure of power and function of China's criminal procedure is undergoing profound changes. Public right and private right are becoming more and more balanced and reasonable, with public right constantly shrinking, and private right expanding. However, where the final boundary still remains to be an unanswerable problem. At the beginning of this century, when the author was talking about this topic with an American professor during a visit to the United States, the author was deeply impressed by his answer, which said that public power and private rights are just like two people walking. The front one walks back and the one walking behind rush forward. The place they meet may be the boundary we want to reach. This humorous and wise metaphor expresses that the reasonable boundary between public power and private right is the result of resonance, debugging, and running-in of the two, which needs time and practice to be explored. In fact, the continuous revision of the Criminal Procedure Law and the promotion of judicial reform are just such a process of exploration.

Thanks to China Renmin University for publishing this book. And thanks to my students who have also provided a lot of materials, and some chapters are results of their joint research.

Beijing, China
January 2018

Weidong Chen

Contents

Chapter 1
Basic Theory of the Powers and Functions of Criminal Procedure

Since human society abandoned blood feud and relief by private force, and entered the era of national criminal procedure, the continuous differentiation of powers and expansion of rights in the realm of criminal procedure has become the main thread of the evolution of the procedural regime.

"Criminal suspects and defendants no longer play the role of procedural object, but become procedural subject that actively participates in and influences the judicial proceedings. With intensified right guarantee and continuously expanding scope of each right, the role of defendants as litigation subject has been consolidated".[1] The public power of the state in criminal procedure also undergoes an evolutionary process from inexplicit division of powers to separated investigation, prosecution and trial, presenting itself as "a self-contradictory process with constant expansion and constant decomposition".[2] In this process, the relationship between rights and powers ("an interactive relationship between individual procedural participants and national criminal justice authorities) is specifically manifested as the wane-and-wax relationship between the powers of state organs and the rights of procedural participants".[3]

The game between increasingly differentiated rights and powers shows the development vein of the criminal procedural legislation, and it will be an internal driving force for the development and progress of criminal procedure in the future. But the previous studies on the right-power relationship in criminal procedure focus on the confrontation between rights and powers, especially between the power of accusation and the right to defense.

Undeniably, in the realm of modern criminal procedure, the relationship between the power of accusation and the right to defense is a key indicator to define the procedural model, but according to the American scholar J. Griffiths, no matter it is the "crime control model" or the "due process model", the essence of which is to

[1] Chen [1].

[2] Li [2].

[3] Liu [3].

W. Chen, *Reform and Development of Powers and Functions of China's Criminal Proceedings*, https://doi.org/10.1007/978-981-15-8431-2_1

take the "battle" between the the power of accusation and the right to defense as the main content of the process, which is known as the "battle model".[4]

However, when we distract our obsessive attention from the confrontation between accusation and defense, we can find that the entire criminal procedure is essentially a "field" where different rights and powers work together; the power of accusation and the right to defense are natural protagonists, but other important rights (powers) such as the power to trial, the right of victims and other procedural participants may not be ignored. Therefore, we shall broaden our horizon when studying the rights (powers) in criminal procedure, analyze the types of rights (powers) involved in the judicial proceedings and their relationships from a more macroscopic and comprehensive perspective. Only in this way can we, while realizing specific rights (powers), avoid the imbalance and disorder of the overall procedural structure because of "seeing trees but not forests".

When we lift the veil that covers the confrontation between the power of accusation and the right to defense in the realm of criminal procedure, what emerges before us is a legal relationship framework for criminal procedure that is formed during the interaction (i.e., confrontation, cooperation, check and balance) of all rights and powers. What constitute this relationship are the procedural acts of all procedural participants, while the procedural acts are based on the specific powers and functions of criminal procedure of the acting subjects. The perspective of powers and functions helps to eliminate the prejudice and discrimination arising from different subjects of rights and powers, so as to optimize and improve the operation mechanism of rights and powers in the realm of criminal procedure by following the law of procedural operation.

1.1 Overview of the Powers and Functions of Criminal Procedure

1.1.1 Connotation

As a new concept, the powers and functions of criminal procedure are not explored in depth in previous studies. To avoid the subsequent discussions from the embarrassment of self-talk due to different understandings of this concept, we shall first interpret the connotation of the powers and functions of criminal procedure, so that the relevant studies will be based on a common object.

[4] Griffiths [4].

1.1.1.1 Concept of the Powers and Functions of Criminal Procedure

"We think, talk and discuss through concepts. Some arguments without firstly clarifying the concepts are actually meaningless, since the arguers may have different understandings of the same concepts; they are not arguing at the same level and have not formed a real confrontation. Such argument cannot add the value of knowledge, but tend to devalue it".[5]

After the concept of the powers and functions of criminal procedure came out, the first challenge in front of us is to define this concept. In the realm of criminal procedure, powers and functions are a new concept, but in the realms of jurisprudence and civil law, the research and application of this concept have yielded some results. Given this, before defining the concept of the powers and functions of criminal procedure, we shall examine the concept of powers and functions at the first place.

(1) Concept carding

The basic meaning of "powers and functions" refers to the functions that are legally prescribed or vested. Semantically, this concept is interpreted in three ways as follows: (i) authority, might; (ii) powers, functions; (iii) the elements of rights which are the specific content of rights, the role of rights or the ways to achieve them, the means that the right holder employs according to law to achieve the purposes and interests embodied in his rights, and the ways that manifest the will power of the right holder. In the past this concept did not receive much attention in the realm of criminal procedure law, but mainly examined in the realms of jurisprudence and science of civil law. The jurisprudential circle, which studies the basic theories and concepts of legal science, finds it is hard to define the concept of powers and functions, because it is unquestionably pervasive in our daily life. However, when people start to analyze this concept, everything seems so suspicious, it is mainly because this concept is intrinsically linked to other basic legal concepts such as norms, effects, obligations, subjective rights, authority and autonomy. As such, an analysis of this concept is in fact an analysis of the entire conceptual network; moreover, since all of these concepts are the basic legal concepts, a theory of powers and functions also covers the essential elements of a theory of legal nature.[6] In this sense, powers and functions could be equated to rights, and there is no significant essential difference between them.

Some people argue that powers and functions refer to the ability, which is legally justified, to create legal norms (or legal effects) through and based on the declaration of relevant effects.[7] The definition of the concept of powers and functions involves the three aspects of being possible, normative and dispositive; it is a concept closely related to rights. The jurisprudential circle usually takes powers and functions as a subordinate concept of rights; for example, a scholar even proposed the concept of "powers and functions of rights", stating that rights have three basic powers and

[5]He [5].

[6]Alexy and Wei [6].

[7]Ross [7] quoted in Alexy and Wei [6].

functions in defense, benefit and relief. "The powers and functions of rights are a unified summary of the basic interests and functions of rights, which convey the basic content and force of rights in a better way. The concept of powers and functions shall be used to express the requirements, obligations and abilities covered by rights".[8]

In the realm of civil law, the research on powers and functions focuses on the ownership and its particular relationships with powers and functions. "There are two different views on the relationships between the ownership and the powers and functions of ownership: one is the theory of collection of rights, and the other is the theory of role of rights. The powers and functions of ownership denote the rights that are held by the owner and constitute the content of the ownership; they are not independent rights in themselves, but the possibilities to realize the rights of the owner. The content of ownership refers to the powers and functions of ownership, including positive and negative powers and functions. Positive powers and functions are the content of ownership, while the negative ones indicate the claims of real rights after the ownership is infringed, and the rights of the owner to protect his ownership if it is damaged".[9]

Through interpretation of the concept of powers and functions in the realms of jurisprudence and civil law, we can find that due to the different relationships between powers and functions and rights (powers), powers and functions are sometimes the subordinate concept of rights (powers), specifically referring to the particular types of rights (powers). In some cases, powers and functions are a synonym with rights (powers), and a synthesis that uniformly denotes rights (powers). Therefore, the concept of powers and functions shall be defined as the specific qualifications and capabilities contained in rights (powers) that can produce legal effects. To be more specific, powers and functions are essentially the particular forms and methods by which rights (powers) play their role, and they are also the transitional elements that convert rights (powers) into a subjective behavior.

(2) Definition of the powers and functions of criminal procedure

In the realm of criminal procedure, the concept of powers and functions has been widely used,[10] but the in-depth studies on the concrete meanings of powers and functions remain in absence, only the term of this concept is contained. After sorting out the relevant research results, we have found that Chinese scholars on criminal procedure law generally hold two different views on the use of this term: one takes powers and functions as a subordinate concept of rights (powers) to denote the specific rights (powers) to prosecution, defense and trial; the other takes powers and functions as a synonym for rights (powers) and a neutral concept that transcends rights (powers). The first viewpoint more accords with the perception of powers and functions in the realm of civil law; if the connotative rights (powers) to investigation,

[8]Jian [8].

[9]Wang [9].

[10]Xu [10]; 11. Zhang and Liu [11]; Lv and Chen [12]; Chen [13]; Chen [14]; Wang [15]; Gu [16]; Li [17]; Xiao [18]; Gou [19]; Wang and Zhu, [20]; Gong [21]; Sheng [22]; Gong and Zheng [23]; Sun [24]; Le and Gou [25]; Zhang and Zhang [26]; Wu [27].

prosecution, defense and trial could be broken down and refined, they would be more aligned with the operational model of rights (powers) in practice.

There are special reasons for the second viewpoint to come into being. In the realm of criminal procedure, rights and powers are strictly split according to the identity of subjects: the rights (especially the procedural right) are held by the procedural participants beyond the state organs; while the powers refer in particular to the powers of investigation, prosecution, trial and enforcement enjoyed by the state organs. Moreover, in the realm of criminal procedure, there is a huge gap between rights and powers: the basic value tendency of rights is protection and manifestation, while the basic value tendency of powers is restriction and balance. Therefore, in order to eliminate the tension and conflicts caused by the innate confrontation between rights and powers during the research, we shall use the concept of powers and functions—which spans the gap between the concepts of rights and powers—to ensure the neutrality and compatibility of research.

Although the above two uses of powers and functions have reasonable grounds, if the concept of powers and functions of criminal procedure is not defined uniformly and normatively, there will be confusions and misunderstandings during the research. Based on the general meaning of powers and functions and the special institutional context of criminal procedure, the author holds that the powers and functions of criminal procedure should be defined as the concept that claims compatibility between rights and powers, and denotes all the rights and powers of criminal procedural subjects.

The above explanation is made for the following reasons: (i) The typical criminal procedural rights (powers) of investigation, prosecution, defense and trial are in essence a community constituted by a series of rights and powers. On the same occasion, the concepts of rights (powers) and powers and functions are expressed separately for fear of causing any semantic confusion. For example, the power of public prosecution, which is a core power as the power of trial in the procedural structure, is subordinate to the procuratorial power under the Chinese procedural power system. If it is taken as the powers and functions of public prosecution, the powers of the same rank will be distinguished in "superiority or inferiority", which is no good for accurately expressing the relationship between procedural rights and procedural powers. (ii) Based on the different subjects of rights (powers), the procedural subjects are divided into the subject of powers and the subject of rights for separate research. Although it helps to reflect the procedural ideas of restricting powers and protecting rights, this man-made hostile division is adverse to studying the commonalities between procedural rights and procedural powers. While coexisting in the realm of criminal procedure, procedural rights and procedural powers do have certain commonalities, such as the right (power) to appear in court – it is a power of the procuratorial organ, and a right of the defendant. The concept of powers and functions avoids being confined by the division between rights and powers, so it will not hamper the holistic research on the right of defendant and the power of prosecutor to appear in court. (iii) By analyzing the use of the term "powers and functions" in criminal procedure, we have found that this term is associated with procuratorial power in most cases, which is directly due to China's vague positioning of procuratorial power.[11] By using the concept of powers and functions, it is possible to avoid the theoretical disagreements arising from the relationship between legal supervision power (contained in procuratorial power) and other state powers such as judicial power and investigatory power. (vi) The purpose of using the concept of powers and functions is to bridge the conceptual gap caused by the mechanical distinction between procedural rights and procedural powers. If powers and functions are simply positioned as particular rights (powers), it will be unlikely to fulfill such purpose. Powers and functions shall be taken as a synthesis of rights and powers to be their neutral representation, which is premise for a value-free research on the relationship between rights and powers of different subjects in the process of criminal procedure.

1.1.1.2 Classification of the Powers and Functions of Criminal Procedure

The criminal procedural system is formed on basis of different procedural rights and powers, and the legal relationship of procedure is constituted by the procedural actions of different subjects of rights and powers. In China, the core rights (powers) in the realm of criminal procedure include the rights (powers) of investigation, prosecution, defense, trial, procedural participation and enforcement. Based on the different identities of procedural subjects, their qualifications or freedom in criminal procedure are divided into rights and powers. Such mechanical division is simple, explicit and able to show the urgency of protecting different procedural subjects, but it may lead to rigidity and lack of integrity. Thus, the concept of powers and functions of criminal procedure is introduced to change this situation. Under this concept system, the powers and functions of criminal procedure are divided into different structural systems of powers and functions based on different classification criteria.

(1) The powers and functions of prosecutor, defendant, trial and assistance

With different content, the powers and functions of criminal procedure are divided into the powers and functions of prosecution, defense, trial and assistance. Such division is made for different powers and functions to play separate roles in criminal procedure. Specifically, the powers and functions of prosecution includes the power of investigation and the power of public prosecution; the powers and functions of defense mainly refers to the right to defense; the powers and functions of trial denote the power of trial; the powers and functions of assistance include the powers of inspection and supervision, enforcement, and procedural participation of other procedural subjects. This classification breaks the distinction between rights and powers. Based on the classic structure of criminal procedure, this classification highlights the fundamental status of the powers of prosecution and trial, and the right

[11] In China there are multiple viewpoints on the attributes of procuratorial power, such as the theory of judicial power, the theory of administrative power, the theory of duality of judicial administration, and the theory of legal supervision. Chen [28].

to defense in the structural systems of powers and functions of criminal procedure, straightens up the relationship between the power of procedural supervision and the power of prosecution, splits and deconstructs the procuratorial power.

With the continuous improvement of criminal procedure, the types of powers and functions of criminal procedure have kept enriching. For example, as a result of the development of the movement of protecting the rights of victims, their right to participate in procedure has become one of the powers and functions of criminal procedure; in the amendment to China's *Criminal Procedure Law* in 2012 there is a new type of powers and functions, i.e., someone with expertise is entitled to participate in procedure. But all of this is not enough to shake the fundamental status of the powers of prosecution and trial and the right to defense in the structural systems of criminal procedural rights (powers), implying that the three parties (prosecutor, defendant and judge) still play a leading role in criminal procedure. Placing the powers and functions of prosecution, defense and trial at the same rank will help to reinforce their importance in the system of powers and functions of criminal procedure, and realize the equal adversary between prosecutor and defendant substantially.

In addition, we should note that auxiliary powers and functions, which have achieved the most fruitful results, are the focal point for developing the powers and functions of criminal procedure. For example, regarding the amendment of the criminal procedure law, an important part to be revised and refined is the protection of witnesses' right to procedural participation. Although the subject structure of prosecutors, defendants and judges, which features a three-party game, still exists in criminal procedure, we should pay enough attention to the exercise of auxiliary powers and functions of the subjects in the procedural process, and provide them with more protection.

(2) Right-based and power-base powers and functions

With different subjects and different attributes, the powers and functions of criminal procedure are divided into right-based and power-based powers and functions. This division seems to be no different from the traditional classification of rights and powers, but the introduction of social power will greatly alter the traditional relationship between criminal procedural rights and powers. To be specific, right-based powers and functions mainly refer to the procedural powers and functions of individual procedural subjects, while power-based powers and functions are either based on public power or social power. Among the three types of powers and functions, right-based and public power-based ones, as focus of the criminal procedure law study, will be free from a detailed account herein. In contrast, the newly-born social power-based powers and functions represent the development of social powers in the realm of criminal procedure, which is proved by the major breakthrough in enabling citizens to access to justice.[12] With the deepening of reform and opening-up, China's civil society has become more developed, and citizens have become active participants in criminal procedure. In addition to traditional jury system, new ways of participation such as public opinion supervision and media supervision have

[12]Cheng [29].

increased opportunities for citizens to participate in proceedings. Therefore, being taken as a component of the powers and functions of criminal procedure, the importance of social power-based powers and functions is highlighted; it will benefit their continuous development and progress.

1.1.1.3 Characteristics of the Powers and Functions of Criminal Procedure

The purpose of introducing the concept of powers and functions into the realm of criminal procedure is primarily for reversing the starting point of the adversarial research on the opposition between traditional rights and powers, which determines that the powers and functions of criminal procedure are different from the traditional criminal procedural rights and powers, but they are essentially characterized as a complex of criminal procedural rights and powers.

(1) Pluralism of subjects

In the traditional division of criminal procedural rights and powers, subjects play a decisive role: powers are enjoyed by state organs, while rights are owned by natural persons and private legal persons, showing that they are entirely different. Such simple and clear division is helpful for restriction and supervision of public power and for balance and protection of rights, but it may impress people with the confrontation between public power and rights, which is bad for accurate positioning of the relationship among judicial power, investigatory power and procuratorial power, and also bad for maintaining the balance of power between prosecutors and defendants. As a complex of criminal procedural rights and powers, the powers and functions of criminal procedure do not require designated subjects. All the procedural subjects, as long as they have certain rights and powers in proceedings, can be taken as the subjects of the powers and functions of criminal procedure and also the subjects featuring pluralism.

To a certain extent, procedural rights and powers are the basis for subjects to participate in proceedings and perform procedural acts. Therefore, all procedural subjects enjoy corresponding procedural rights and powers in the realm of criminal procedure, which determines that all procedural subjects are the subjects of powers and functions under the system of powers and functions of criminal procedure. Such a plural scope of subjects makes the concept of powers and functions of criminal procedure widely representative, includes the intricate legal relationships in criminal procedure into a unified conceptual architecture for analysis, and avoids the opposition resulting from the classification of subjects of powers and rights.

(2) Complexity of content

In the realm of criminal procedure, the content of powers and functions (as aggregate of rights and powers) features complexity, meaning that the content includes not only the public power of state organs, but also the rights of procedural participants, and the social power of citizens. There are so many doctrines about what are rights[13] and powers. For example, according to Max Weber, a German classical sociologist, power is an ability that controls the will of others despite of being opposed by them, i.e., in a social relationship, actors have opportunities to rule out resistance for carrying out their will, regardless of the basis of such opportunities.[14] Some other scholars take "power" as a force to constrain the will of others and restrain their freedom.[15] With regard to social power, it means that social subjects are able to influence and dominate the state and society with their social resources.[16] Social power has private and public attributes: from the perspective of external stipulation, particular social powers are private relative to organizations, groups, and even the state and the world at large; from the perspective of internal stipulation, social power is public relative to social members, and it is an organic collection of powers of social members.[17] The three different types of rights (powers) are incorporated into the category of the powers and functions of criminal procedure, thus making their content characterized by complexity, which require us to take a more holistic perspective when doing studies in this regard, instead of being bound by the traditional views on rights and powers.

(3) Openness of variety

In the realm of criminal procedure, with the increase in the number of participants in proceedings and the differentiation of the types of rights (powers), the system of particular powers and functions has kept expanding, and its content has been constantly enriched. The particular powers and functions of criminal procedure involve not only the traditional rights (powers) of investigation, prosecution, trial and defense, but also the emerging social power such as the increasingly important powers and functions of media and citizens in supervision of criminal procedure. Compared with the earlier integration of prosecution and trial, which features a structure of powers and functions monopolized by trial power in the case of objectification of trial objects, the current "tripod" of prosecution, defense and trial has greatly enriched the types of powers and functions of criminal procedure. Besides, since social power is becoming more and more important in the current rights (powers)-obligations structure, it is sure to occupy a vital position in the system of the powers and functions of criminal procedure. In addition, as a result of the rising "victims' rights movement",[18] the protection of victims' rights in criminal procedure has received greater

---

[13] Zhang Wenxian has systematically introduced the eight leading and most representative theories on the nature of rights: the Entitlement Theory, the Claiming Theory, the Liberty Theory, the Interest Theory, the Legal Capacity (or Power) Theory, the Possibility Theory, the Norm Theory, and the Choice Theory. These theories boast the most extensive impact. Zhang [30].

[14] Max and Gu [31].

[15] Okuda et al. [32].

[16] Guo [33].

[17] Wang [34].

[18] Liu and Liu [35].

attention, so the powers and functions of victims are also included into the category of the powers and functions of criminal procedure.

(4) Distinciton of efficacy

Owing to pluralism of subjects, complexity of content and openness of variety, the powers and functions of criminal procedure are sure to be diversified and complicated. To make it clear, regardless of the game of powers and functions, the criminal judicial verdict is based on the coercive trial power. Moreover, as provided by the criminal procedure law, different powers and functions are protected and valued to different degrees, in order to achieve a balance between punishment of crimes and protection of human rights. This determines that the powers and functions of criminal procedure have different efficacy in proceedings. The fundamental reason for differentiating the efficacy of the powers and functions of criminal procedure is to smooth the procedural operation, thereby realizing the basic values of justice and efficiency of criminal procedure. The *Criminal Procedure Law of China* is a law of authorization and a law of limitation of power, there are explicit divisions of the efficacy hierarchy of rights and powers. In the current era, human rights have become a major concern of most countries, but China has been concentrated on combating crimes and failing to pay enough attention to protection of human rights, so we need to increase the right consciousness of citizens, upgrade the efficacy hierarchy of defense right, and balance its relationship with the state power (especially prosecution power). Besides, for lack of judicial authority, China shall reiterate the dominant position and supreme authority of trial power in the system of powers and functions.

1.1.2 Subjects of the Powers and Functions of Criminal Procedure

According to the above analysis of the concept and characteristics of the powers and functions of criminal procedure, all participants in criminal procedure shall be regarded as subjects of powers and functions since they have certain criminal procedural rights and powers. In the traditional theories on criminal procedure, the criminal procedural subjects are divided into two categories: subjects of powers and subjects of rights.[19] This means that the subjects of the powers and functions of criminal procedure include both the subjects of powers (investigative organs, procuratorial offices, and courts), and the subjects of rights (criminal suspects, defendants and their close relatives, victims and their close relatives, agents of victims, parties of an incidental civil action and their agents, appraisers, deponents, and witnesses).

---

[19]The subjects of powers involve the "public security agencies, procuratorial offices, and judicial organs that are empowered by national laws to investigation, prosecution and trial in criminal procedure". The subjects of rights are the "persons who enjoy certain procedural rights and bear certain procedural obligations in criminal procedure other than the personnel of special state organs". Chen [36].

The rights and powers enjoyed by these subjects, and their role in criminal procedure are free from detailed account herein, since there are in-depth studies and discussions in this regard. The following text will, in combination of the current frontier theoretical researches on the criminal procedural subjects and practices, discuss some special subjects of the powers and functions of criminal procedure.

1.1.2.1 Detention Houses, Prisons, and Community Correction Centers

Being auxiliary organs of criminal procedure, detention houses, prisons and community correction centers had been unnoticeable in the researches on criminal procedure. But in recent years, the public started caring about extended detention, unnatural death in custody, abuse of commutation, parole and medical parole, and rapid development of community correction, thus making detention houses, prisons, and community correction centers an important object of study in the realm of criminal procedure. As result of the amendment of the criminal procedure law, quite a number of the provisions concerning detention houses, prisons and community correction centers are revised, which has further clarified their powers and responsibilities in criminal procedure.

(1) Detention houses

As a special venue of pending custody, the detention house is an important subject of procedural guarantee and playing an irreplaceable role in facilitating proceedings and protecting human rights. Currently, China has a high rate of pretrial detention, so detention house is the main venue for accommodating most criminal suspects and defendants before a judicial decision is made. More than that, as a legal venue of custody, the detention house is a key "battlefield" for investigators to collect evidence from the detainees. Due to its closed operation, detention house has never been valued by the criminal procedural law community. It was the "hide-and-seek" incident in 2009[20] that brought detention house under the spotlight, and triggered the entire society to care about the human rights protection inside detention house. In the process of revising the *Criminal Procedure Law*, the revisions to the articles involving detention house have received widespread attention. Compared to the *Criminal Procedure Law* in 1979 and 1996 where the term "detention house" only appears once, the version 2013 contains eight articles that are directly related to detention house.[21]

---

[20]Translator's note: In 2009, in a detention house in Jinning County, Yunnan Province, a 24-year-old young man, Li Qiaoming, was hurt in his head by one of his inmates while they were playing hide-and-seek, and then died after invalid rescue. Such a childish but deadly game triggered a wave of public criticism on the flawed protection of human rights of detainees.

[21]In the *Criminal Procedure Law* (2013), the term "detention house" appears ten times in altogether eight articles, i.e., articles 37, 83, 91, 116, 253, 254, 255, 257. To be specific, Article 37 provides for meeting with a lawyer in a detention house; articles 83 and 91 require that the arrestees shall be promptly transferred to a detention house after being arrested and detained; Article 116 states

The reason for highlighting the status of detention house as a subject of powers and functions in criminal procedure is to confirm its power in execution of pretrial detention. For state organs, power means responsibility; as a subject of powers and functions, detention house shall strengthen human rights protection during pretrial detention. In the revised *Criminal Procedure Law*, the contents involving detention house are as follows: the criminal suspects and defendants should be promptly sent to the detention house after being arrested and detained; the detainees involved in non-particular cases[22] are allowed to meet with a lawyer within 48 h after they are detained; and all interrogations of detainees should be done inside the detention house. Although these provisions are designed to regulate the investigative behaviors of investigation authorities, the detention house—as a statutory venue of pretrial detention—should be given corresponding powers and functions to ensure the implementation of these provisions. For example, if the criminal suspects and defendants are sent to the detention house beyond 24 h after being detained, the detention house deserves the power to ask the responsible public security organ for an explanation, otherwise it can report the matter to the prosecutor stationed in the detention house or to the higher-level public security organ.

The confirmation of the status of detention house as a subject of powers and functions will, on the one hand, help to change its positioning as a mere detention agency, and motivate it to play a greater role in safeguarding the rights of suspects and defendants; and on the other hand, make it assume more responsibilities in the realm of criminal procedure, especially in improvement of infrastructure and administrative rules and regulations, for example, facilitate a meeting with lawyer; arrange whole-process synchronous audio and video recording of interrogations; and provide necessary hardware facilities and available environment to prevent extortion of confession by torture.

(2) Prisons

Criminal procedure is a process of realizing the national punitive power; in this process investigative organs, procuratorial offices and courts shall prove the authenticity of the case through a series of lawsuits, and the ultimate purpose of applying the law is to confirm the criminal liability of the accused. With regard to China's criminal punishment system at present, freedom punishment is the main form of criminal penalty, so prisons remain the predominant agencies that execute criminal punishment. According to the provisions of the *Criminal Procedure Law*, during the execution of criminal punishment, if a prisoner has shown repentance or performed any meritorious service, the prison may submit a proposal for his/her commutation or parole to the people's court for review and adjudication. In case the prisoner is qualified for commutation or parole, the prison shall submit a written opinion to

---

that all interrogations shall be done in a detention house; articles 253, 254, 255 and 257 set out the relevant rules for a detention house in the criminal law enforcement activities.

[22]According to Article 37 of China's *Criminal Procedure Law*, the particular cases refer to the crimes of endangering national security, the crimes of terrorist activities, and the crimes of especially serious bribery.

the prison administration at or above the provincial level. In practice, the court and prison administration shall, based on the materials submitted by the prison, make the decisions for commutation, parole and temporary execution of a sentence outside prison, which shows that the opinions of prisons play a vital role in this regard.

The system of commutation, parole, and temporary execution of a sentence outside prison has played an important role in implementing the criminal policy of combining punishment and leniency, motivating offenders to turn over a new leaf to integrate into society in the future, and converting negative factors into positive factors as many as possible. But there exist some problems in the implementation of this system: some offenders exchange power or money for their freedom, evade or reduce punishment, which seriously tramples the dignity of the law and damages the credibility of law enforcement and justice. Most of the offenders that violate the provisions for commutation, parole and temporary execution of a sentence outside prison are the ones who have committed duty-related crimes, crimes of undermining the order of financial management or financial fraud, or crimes of organizing (leading, participating, shielding and conniving) the criminal gangs of underworld society nature.[23] In response to these problems, the Commission for Political and Legal Affairs under the CPC Central Committee issued the *Guiding Opinions on Strictly Regulating Commutation, Parole, and Temporary Execution of A Sentence Outside Prison, and Effective Prevention of Judicial Corruption*, requiring the enforcement agencies to strictly abide by the relevant laws and regulations.[24] While performing their powers and functions of criminal procedure as specified in the *Criminal Procedure Law*, the prisons shall regulate the commutation, parole and temporary execution of a sentence outside prison. The status as subject of powers and functions of criminal procedure means that the role of prisons as a procedural subject is recognized, and the procuratorial offices—a procedural supervisory organ—shall strengthen the supervision of prisons.

For prisons, their status as subject of powers and functions is also reflected in their role in investigation. According to Article 290 of China's *Criminal Procedure Law*, the prisons have the power of investigation for the cases taking place inside the prisons, so the content of their powers and functions should also include the investigatory power.

(3) Community correction centers

"Community correction", a method to reform offenders by employing community resources without isolating them from society, is a general term for all ways to reeducate and reform offenders in the environment of communities. As a form of non-custodial criminal punishment, community correction allows eligible offenders to be

[23] Chinese people have increased attention to the commutation, parole, and temporary execution of a sentence outside prison for the offenders of duty-related crimes, which was partly triggered by the incident that Zhang Hai, former chairman of Jianlibao Group—a pioneer Chinese sports drink producer born in 1984—employed illegal means repeatedly to have his term of imprisonment shortened from 15 years to no more than 3 years.

[24] The Supreme People's Procuratorate of China embarked on a special procuratorial campaign for commutation, parole, and temporary execution of a sentence outside prison from March 2014, in an aim to further strengthen the enforcement of criminal punishment and regulatory activities.

placed in communities where specialized state agencies, with the assistance of certain social groups, non-governmental organizations (NGOs) and volunteers, will implement correction of them within a legal time limit, so as to help them smoothly return to society upon expiration of their sentence.[25] According to the provisions of the *Criminal Procedure Law*, the offenders subject to community correction according to law are the ones who are sentenced to public surveillance, probation, parole or temporary execution of a sentence outside prison, and concurrent deprivation of political rights. This shows that the community correction centers have become a formal subject of the powers and functions of criminal procedure, so they are ought to perform the executive powers and functions in proceedings. They are not only responsible for the supervision and assessment of the offenders under correction, but also for reforming them to eliminate their risks and prevent their recidivism. Being confirmed as the subject of the powers and functions of criminal procedure, community correction centers will keep playing their role in execution of criminal punishment, improving correction effect and saving the relevant costs.

1.1.2.2 The Public and News Media

The burgeoning social power has changed the traditional "binary structure" of rights and powers, and replaced it with a "ternary structure" of rights, powers and social power, which is the same in the realm of criminal procedure. As a carrier of public opinions, social power is playing an increasingly important role in the realm of criminal procedure.

(1) The public

Criminal crime is a serious threat to social security, that's why the public has been paying great attention to the process and results of criminal procedure. According to the relevant provisions of the *Criminal Procedure Law*, the powers and functions of the public in criminal procedure include the right to participate, the right to know, and the right to supervise.

First, as far as the participation right is concerned, no matter it is the assessor system in Continental Law System or the jury system in Anglo American Law System, both of them stress the right of ordinary people to participate in criminal procedure. In China, the people's jury system indeed has some problems, but the spirit of endorsing public participation in judicial actions conveyed by this system should be valued. The people's jury system is the most direct and effective way for the public to exercise their right to participate in criminal procedure. The people's supervisor system, which is also important for the public to exercise their powers and functions of criminal procedure, facilitates the public to participate in criminal procedure, although its particular powers are different from those of the people's jury system.

Second, as far as the right to know is concerned, the principle of open criminal trial is the most concentrated manifestation of the public as subject of powers and

[25] Wu [37].

functions. According to the provisions of the *Criminal Procedure Law*, all cases shall be subject to an open trial except for the ones involving state secrets, personal privacy or minors, which ensures the public to closely participate in criminal trial. In terms of the right to know of the public, Chinese courts have been uploading the judgment documents to the website China Judgments Online, which guarantees the right to know of the public in criminal procedure. After comparing the judgments online mechanism and the principle of open trial, we find their biggest difference is "informed object": in the principle of open trial, informed object mainly denotes the trial process of the case, and the public will, by watching the whole trial process, supervise the fact finding and application of laws for the case, and confirm whether there are procedural violations in the trial. In contrast, the judgments online mechanism (all cases shall be subject to public sentencing) highlights the right of the public to know the concrete results of the trial, and supervise the substantive court proceedings.

(2) News media

News media's coverage of criminal procedure is, on the one hand, to exercise the supervision right as public media, and on the other hand provide important sources of information for the public to exercise their right to know and supervise. Compared with the traditional print media where reports are in texts and pictures, the current Internet media publish reports more intuitively and comprehensively via video and audio, which has greatly strengthened the media supervision of criminal cases, and reinforced their powers and functions in the realm of criminal procedure. Moreover, the rapidly developing "WeMedia"[26] in recent years has brought significant changes to the reporting of cases. For example, the trial of Bo Xilai, former Secretary of Dalian Municipal Committee of the CPC accused of using his position to take bribes, caused great sensation both at home and abroad in 2013; the whole process of the trial was broadcast live through official micro-blogging, showing that China's news media are doing well in delivering real-time and comprehensive case reports, and heralding that the status of news media as subject of the powers and functions of criminal procedure will be promoted. It should be noted that while confirming the status of news media as the subject of powers and functions, it is necessary to regulate and supervise the media behaviors to prevent false reports from affecting or interfering with judicial justice.

[26]WeMedia is also known as "citizen media". In July 2003, the research report WeMedia-How audiences are shaping the future of news and information by Shayne Bowman, Chris Willis, commissioned by the Media Center at the American Press Institute came out July 2003, A very strict definition: "WeMedia is a way for the general public to strengthen their digital technology and connect with the global knowledge system, a way to begin to understand how the general public provides and shares their own facts and their own news". In short, it is the carrier that citizens use to publish events they have seen and heard, such as blogs, Weibo, WeChat, forums/BBS and other online communities.

1.1.3 Research Value of the Powers and Functions of Criminal Procedure

Compared with the traditional binary opposition thought for researching rights and powers, the concept of the powers and functions of criminal procedure is more complicated in terms of concept definition, type division and subject confirmation, but this complexity contains some special value, rather than merely increasing research difficulties.

1.1.3.1 Comprehensiveness of the Perspective of Powers and Functions

The primary value of powers and functions—as complex of rights and powers—is comprehensiveness. Especially in the realm of criminal procedure, rights and powers have all along been strictly distinguished by their subjects (whether they are state organs or not). This way of thinking is simple and clear, and helpful for reflecting the value tendency of criminal procedure to restrict powers and protect rights; but it may narrow the perspective of research, making it hard to properly deal with the game relationship between rights and powers in criminal procedure. The introduction of the concept of powers and functions is able to make up for this deficiency. By studying rights and powers as an integral, we can conduct a neutral analysis of the overlapping problems in criminal procedural rights and powers. For example, from the perspective of separated rights and powers, the prosecutor will "interrogate" the defendant at the court investigation stage; the term "interrogate" clearly shows the legislative preference for powers to rights, and the superiority of prosecutor to defender. If the questioning of defendant is a kind of powers and functions, then it will be regarded as an inquiry power (right) of prosecutor and defender, which demonstrates the equal status of the two parties, and more importantly, avoids the presumption of guilt of defendant due to the ambiguous implications of "interrogation". Besides, the comprehensiveness of powers and functions is also reflected in the full compatibility of criminal procedural rights and powers. From the perspective of powers and functions, we can integrate rights, powers and social power as a whole for a more accurate analysis of the relationship between different rights and powers in criminal proceedings. For example, when the court considers the feasibility of an open trial of a case, it should listen to the opinions of both prosecutor and defender, think about the right to know of the public (which is subject of the powers and functions of criminal procedure), and balance and coordinate the tripartite interests.

1.1.3.2 Equality of the Perspective of Powers and Functions

There are differences in the efficacy hierarchy of the powers and functions of criminal procedure, all the operations of powers and functions are based on the authoritative status of judicial power, which is the root cause for the finality of criminal procedure.

In China, "appreciating powers but deappreciating rights" is a long-standing tradition in the realm of criminal procedure, thus making powers inherently superior, and the restriction of rights on powers far from sufficient. But the perspective of powers and functions helps to erase the inherent inequality between rights and powers: the efficacy relationship between rights and powers is only determined by procedural rules and legal provisions, not by the different identities of subjects. The most typical example is the procuratorial power and the right to defense. In either legal provisions or trial practices, there are circumstances where the efficacy of procuratorial power is above than the right to defense. According to Article 198 of the *Criminal Procedure Law*, when a prosecutor finds that the case to be prosecuted requires supplementary investigation, he or she may propose for adjournment, which will be approved by the court most of the times. In contrast, if it is necessary to summon new witnesses, obtain new material evidence, make a new expert evaluation or hold another inquest, the proposal for adjournment will be difficult to be approved. However, from the perspective of powers and functions, both the two practices are entitled to adjournment, and such right (power) should be equally protected.

1.1.3.3 Openness of the Perspective of Powers and Functions

The perspective of powers and functions is able to broaden the system of criminal procedural rights and powers, and conducive to introducing emerging types of powers and functions into criminal procedure. According to the principle of statutory powers, all of the state public powers in criminal procedure come out of legislative authorization. According to the principle of private rights authorization (everything is viable without legal prohibition), the types of rights in criminal procedure are ought to be extensive, but the procedural operation is a scrupulous judicial activity, since it needs to confirm the criminal liabilities of suspects and defendants. Given this, the rights in this domain, whether they are authorized or materialized, are inseparable from explicit legal provisions and guarantee. The traditional system of criminal procedural rights and powers is relatively closed, but from the perspective of the powers and functions of criminal procedure, the scope of rights and powers can be adjusted to satisfy the need for punishing criminals and protecting human rights. For example, corresponding to the powers and functions of investigative organs, procuratorial offices and courts to extend the limitation of action, the criminal suspects and defenders shall be given the powers and functions to express their opinions and apply for relief. In addition, the openness of the perspective of powers and functions allows the introduction of social power to greatly enrich the system of criminal procedural rights (powers).

1.1.3.4 Macrocosm of the Perspective of Powers and Functions

At different stages of procedure, the rights and powers enjoyed by different procedural subjects are differentiated. The previous researches, from the perspective of separation of rights and powers, are hard to fully show the overall picture of procedural operation, and incapable of macroscopic analyses on the criminal procedural structure and legal relationships. In contrast, from the perspective of the powers and functions of criminal procedure, all procedural rights and powers are a unified whole, making it available for comprehensive researches without being confined by the attributes of rights (powers). For example, Article 188 of the *Criminal Procedure Law* stipulates that "upon receipt of the notice of the people's court, the witnesses may be forced to attest in court if they do not have a just cause for refusal, except for the spouse, parents or children of the defendant". It shows that the court has the powers and functions of forcing witnesses to appear in court, while the spouse, parents or children of the defendant have the powers and functions of refusing to bear witness. This provision covers the issue of forcing witness to court, the relationship between the power of trial and the right of witnesses to participate in procedure, and more importantly, the balance between ascertainment of the facts of a case and protection of the rights of individuals; it is a concrete manifestation of the game of punishing criminals and protecting human rights in the realm of witnesses giving testimony. Therefore, when examining the scope of the relatives that refuse to testify in court, we shall think about the relationship between the right of witnesses and the power of court, the legal standpoint on discovering the facts of a case and protecting the rights of individuals within a given period, and the value tendency to punish criminals and protect human rights in this period.

1.2 Basic Principles of the Powers and Functions of Criminal Procedure

"Principles" refer to the role of the "criteria for observing and dealing with problems"[27] in legal system. On the one hand, principles are combination of specific legal provisions; on the other hand, they are guidelines for interpretation and application of specific legal rules. In the realm of criminal procedure, the basic principles of powers and functions—as complex of rights and powers—shall reflect the legal status and relationship pattern of different subjects; more importantly, they play a guiding role in improving the concrete structures and relationships of the powers and functions of criminal procedure.

The powers and functions of criminal procedure cover a wide scope, involving subjects, functions, structures, and so on. Based on different objects and domains under regulation, the basic principles of the powers and functions of criminal procedure can be divided into the status principle, functional principle, and operational principle.

[27] The Chinese Comprehensive Dictionary [38].

1.2.1 Status Principle

The subjects of the powers and functions of criminal procedure include all procedural subjects, no matter they are state organs or participants in procedure; all of them occupy a subjective status in this regard. In order to achieve the purpose of punishing criminals and protecting human rights,[28] the subjective status in powers and functions shall be properly allocated, which helps to ensure the procedural efficiency and the authority of procedural outcome.

1.2.1.1 Principle of Equality Between Prosecutor and Defender

For both prosecutor (investigative and procuratorial organs) and defender (criminal suspects and defendants), their top concern is to determine the criminal liabilities of the accused. Since human beings gave up blood feud and turned to criminal procedure for resolving their contradictions, the relationship between prosecutor and defender has become one of the important signs showing the development of criminal procedure. Firstly private prosecution in accusatory procedure (equal adversary between plaintiff and defendant), then non-separation of prosecution and trial in inquisitorial procedure (the accused being object of procedure), and finally the separation of prosecution and trial in modern adversary system and inquisitorial system (equal adversary between prosecutor and defender), the relationship between prosecutor and defender in criminal procedure has undergone a process of equal adversary, unequal adversary, and again equal adversary. But the implications of equal adversary have changed substantially: it is no longer the equal adversary between individuals, but the one between specialized state organs and individuals. Considering the dramatic differences in procedural capacity between state organs and individuals, how to balance their strength has become a major consideration for designing the modern criminal procedural system. The allocation of the powers and functions of criminal procedure—basis for the subjective status—directly determines the status of different subjects in the procedural rights (powers) structure. For these reasons, the equality between prosecutor and defender shall become a guideline for dealing with the relationship between the subjects of powers and functions. For different procedural subjects, especially prosecutor and defender,[29] the allocation of powers and functions shall be balanced; and the allocation of rights and powers for the two parties shall follow the principles of "equality of arms" and "equal protection".

[28] There are a variety of doctrines regarding the purpose of criminal procedure, such as monism, dualism and pluralism; and Chinese academic circle prefers dualism. It should be noted that no matter which doctrine is adopted, it does not affect the following discussions.

[29] The "prosecutor" here is broadly defined, including not only investigative and procuratorial organs, but also the victims and their close relatives, private prosecutors, and plaintiffs with incidental civil action.

1.2.1.2 Principle of Separation of Prosecution and Trial

From the perspective of state power, both prosecution and trial of crimes had been taken as one in the early days; however, with intensified protection of the rights of the accused, and for the purpose of ascertaining the facts of cases, the subjects of prosecution and trial were separated from each other, with different state organs respectively performing the functions of prosecution and trial. On the one hand, the separation of prosecution and trial creates necessary conditions for realizing equal adversary between prosecutor and defender. If the prosecutor is empowered to adjudicate cases, then an equal adversary between prosecutor and defender will be hard to attain, no matter how much effort is made to strengthen the right to defense, just like a contest where an athlete also acts as referee is bound to be unfair. On the other hand, the separation of prosecution and trial helps to ascertain the facts of cases. If the prosecutor concentrates on investigating cases, and the court remains neutral in reviewing and verifying the facts and evidence of the cases submitted by the prosecutor, it will avoid the paranoid perception due to oneness of subjects, as well as deviations and errors in fact-finding of the cases. It can be seen that the separation of the powers and functions of prosecution and trial not only helps punish criminals, but also protects human rights. According to this principle, the powers and functions of criminal procedure shall be respectively allocated to different procedural subjects, especially specialized state organs, according to the different characteristics of the powers and functions of prosecution and trial.

Both the *Constitution* and the *Criminal Procedure Law* of China have set out the principle for allocating the powers and functions to specialized state organs: division of labor with individual responsibility, mutual collaboration, and mutual restriction. Based on the operation of prosecution power and trial power, this principle aims at realizing checks and balances, and collaboration between different state organs. However, in criminal procedural practices, this principle has led to the drawbacks of "appreciating collaboration but depreciating restriction, appreciating division of labor but depreciating separation"; to be specific, the procedural powers are allocated to public security organs, procuratorial offices and courts as equal subjects, thus ignoring the authoritative status of trial power, and going against the establishment of judicial authority. Therefore, from the perspective of respecting the basic rules of procedure, the allocation of powers and functions to specialized state organs shall reflect the differences in efficacy hierarchy and procedural status of different powers and functions, transform the "division of labor" model to "follow the rules of procedure" model, emphasize the separation and differences between prosecution and trial in the subjective status of powers and functions, clarify their specific boundary in procedural powers and functions, and highlight the authority of the powers and functions of trial, so as to demonstrate that the separation of prosecution and trial and the equal adversary between prosecutor and defender are actually unified.

1.2.1.3 Principle of Neutral Judgment

The reason why neutral judgment is taken as the principle for the status of powers and functions is because the powers and functions of judgment play a central role in criminal procedure, and the allocation of all other procedural powers and functions revolves around those of judgment. The game between the powers and functions of prosecution and defense is to obtain a favorable closing argument, while the role of other procedural powers and functions is to facilitate the judgment-making. Neutrality means that the powers and functions of judgment enjoy the supreme authority, and the procedural subjects of other powers and functions are treated equally and protected by law.

From the perspective of the powers and functions of criminal procedure, neutrality of judgment requires the judicial organ to remain neutral between prosecutor and defender, and also between other procedural subjects. Take the witnesses for example, no matter they testify for prosecution or defense, they deserve equal protection, and their testimony may not be biased, but cross-examined and authenticated in an objective and neutral position.

1.2.1.4 Principle of Procedural Participation

The principle of procedural participation means that "any subject that may receive criminal judgment or directly impact the outcome of judgment shall have ample opportunity to participate in the proceedings, and influence the result of judgment".[30] The procedural participants are made up of two parts: the parties involved and citizens.[31] The scope of the powers and functions of criminal procedure covers rights, powers and social power. Regarding the traditional subjects of rights and powers, the legitimacy and necessity for their participation in procedure has been fully demonstrated. The perspective of the powers and functions of criminal procedure is to promote the procedural participation of the public (citizens) as subject of social power.

Since crimes are a serious threat to social security, it is the public expectation for impartial judgment of criminal cases through criminal proceedings, not only punishing the crimes that are committed, but also guarding against the potential ones in the future. In addition to investigative and judicial organs that are respectively empowered to prosecute and make judgment, the public – as an interested party – requests for the powers and functions to participate in and supervise criminal proceedings. As required by the principle of procedural participation, from the perspective of allocation of powers and functions, it is necessary to improve the public participation channels such as people's jury system and open trial system; from the perspective of guaranteeing powers and functions, it is necessary to create

[30]Chen [39].

[31]Xie and Wan [40].

realistic basis for public participation and punish those that infringe on the powers and functions in this regard.

1.2.2 Functional Principle

Under the modern criminal procedure system, the division of powers and functions is the basis for the positioning of subjects and the allocation of powers and functions. In contrast to the traditional perspective of rights and powers, the allocation of powers and functions to procedural subjects highlights macrocosm and comprehensiveness.

1.2.2.1 Principle of Separation of Powers and Check Balance

"Briefly speaking, the mechanism of separation of powers and check balance is for separating powers among different authorities, and making sure that they retain considerable defensive and confrontational strength against each other, so that rights will remain low-invasive on the whole due to mutual confrontation and mutual control".[32]

With the increasing roles of procedure, the criminal proceedings of human beings are, to a certain extent, a process where separation of powers and check balance continue deepening. From the perspective of the powers and functions of criminal procedure, the separation of powers and check balance are no longer limited in the traditional realm of powers, but extend to the relationships between all powers and rights in criminal procedure. In the realm of criminal procedure, in order to ensure that rights and powers are performed within a controllable range, there shall be check balance between rights and powers based on their separate allocation, in addition to the boundaries defined by law.

For example, both criminal suspects and defendants in their custody are protected from extortion of confession by torture; for this purpose, the *Criminal Procedure Law* provides that the investigative organs shall promptly transfer the detainees to the detention house, and the interrogation of them shall be done inside the detention house. This provision separates the power of custody from the power of detention, and also separates the power of interrogation from the power of management of the interrogated; it separately allocates the power of custody and the power of interrogation to particular investigative organs and detention houses, so as to maintain check balance between them.

As an institution of custody, detention house not only performs the powers and functions of management, but assumes the responsibility to guarantee the safety of detainees. Extorting confessions by torture will seriously harm the health and safety of detainees, and the concerned detention house will be investigated and held accountable. To prevent from such incident, the detention house opposes the extortion

[32]Li [41].

of confessions by torture by investigative organs. Now that the *Criminal Procedure Law* stipulates that the interrogation shall be done inside the detention house, it is understandable that the detention house—manager of the interrogative venue—spares no effort to record and videotape the entire interrogative process, set physical isolation of between interrogators and the interrogated, and arrange surface inspection of the interrogated, so as to prevent the extortion of confessions by torture to the utmost extent. Therefore, check balance and supervision between detention houses and investigative organs are achieved by separating the power of management of detainees from the power of interrogation. More than that, there are multiple mechanisms for separation of powers and check balance, such as the cross-examination of witnesses by experts, and they are playing an important role in the mutual restriction of all powers and functions of criminal procedure, thereby unifying the punishment of crimes and protection of human rights.

1.2.2.2 Principle of Unity of Power and Responsibility

In the traditional horizon of rights and powers, powers are executed by state organs for mandate and assignment of responsibilities. In case of any improper execution of powers, the state organs shall bear the responsibility for wrong action or inaction. Rights are the freedom of citizens, and their execution depends on the will of individuals. But this understanding is not entirely correct from the perspective of the powers and functions of criminal procedure, because both the power-based and part of the right-based powers and functions are ought to follow the principle of unity of power and responsibility. For example, Article 40 of the *Criminal Procedure Law* provide that "if the defender has collected the evidence that shows the criminal suspect was not at the crime scene, not old enough for criminal responsibility, or identified as a mental patient exempted from criminal responsibility according to law, the defender shall promptly submit the evidence to the public security organ and the people's procuratorate". It is both an obligation and mandate of the defender. According to this provision, at the stage of investigation and the stage of review and prosecution, if the defender has found the evidence proving the innocence of the criminal suspect or exemption from criminal responsibility, the defender is entitled to submit the evidence to the public security organ and the people's procuratorate, and the authorities that receive the evidence shall review it without delay and draw conclusions, which will end the proceedings in a timely manner, and prevent the lengthy prosecution from causing any unnecessary harm to the criminal suspect or defendant. Besides, all the provisions of the *Criminal Procedure Law* on the right to appeal and the right to reply in appellate period are the provisions for the unity of power and responsibility, implying that the rights may be invalid if not executed within the legal time limit. It can be seen that the principle of unity of power and responsibility regulates not only the power-based powers and functions, but also part of the right-based ones that affect the proceedings.

1.2.3 Operational Principle

The criminal proceedings are a dynamically ongoing process with participation of different procedural subjects. The operational state of various powers and functions—driving force of this ongoing process—determines the operation of criminal proceedings. From the perspective of powers and functions, we can break the division between rights and powers, and summarize the operational principles of all powers and functions in criminal procedure based on the procedural operation mechanism at the macro-level.

1.2.3.1 Principle of Human Rights Protection

The revised *Criminal Procedure Law* in 2013 includes the principle of respect and protection of human rights, highlighting the importance of human rights protection for implementing the criminal procedure system. This principle should be binding on the execution of all powers and functions in criminal procedure; moreover, the establishment and operation of all powers and functions shall reflect the requirements for respecting and protecting human rights. Before that, the focus of human rights protection was on limitation of powers and protection of rights, but there were not many detailed explanations for how to do so. In the system of powers and functions in criminal procedure, it is possible for rights, powers and social power to become sources of powers and functions that violate human rights. For this reason, in addition to the traditional mechanism for limitation of powers, there is also need for strengthening the limitation of rights and social power, so as to fully implement the principle of human rights protection. For example, open trial is an important way for the public to participate in and supervise criminal justice, but the trial of a case may involve the personal privacy or trade secrets of defendants and victims, then the power of open trial (a form of social power) shall be limited, so as to protect the right to privacy of defendants and victims. And victims also have the right of private prosecution as provided by the *Criminal Procedure Law*. However, according to the *Interpretation of Article 271 (2) of the Criminal Procedure Law*, which was adopted by the Standing Committee of the National People's Congress (NPC) in April 2014, "in the trial of a juvenile criminal case, the people's procuratorate shall listen to the views of the victim before making a conditional non-prosecution decision or a non-prosecution decision upon expiration of the probationary period. If the victim does not satisfy with the non-prosecution decision made by the people's procuratorate, he or she may appeal to the higher-level people's procuratorate, but such circumstance is not governed by Article 176 of the *Criminal Procedure Law* (victims may file a lawsuit in a people's court)". It shows that the right of private prosecution of victims is limited to protect the rights of juvenile criminal suspects who are not prosecuted.

1.2.3.2 Principle of Efficiency

Justice delayed is justice denied, meaning that efficiency of criminal proceedings is also important in addition to procedural justice and result justice. Lengthy proceedings will increase the burden of procedural participants, and waste judicial resources. Therefore, the allocation and operation of procedural powers and functions shall follow the principle of efficiency to speed up proceedings, complete the procedural tasks through the game and collaboration in the system of powers and functions within a reasonable period of time, and achieve the procedural goals. To improve the procedural efficiency from the perspective of powers and functions, it is necessary to improve the efficiency of specialized state organs in execution of powers, and also the efficiency of procedural participants in execution of rights. In the realm of criminal procedure of China, there has been a long-standing tradition to "value punishment rather than protection, value powers rather than rights", which has led to loosened time limits for execution of powers, but strict time limits for execution of rights. This situation is especially prominent in the time period provisions in the *Criminal Procedure Law* of China. The specialized state organs usually extend, recalculate or do not count into the time period, and there are short of effective sanctions for violations of the time period provisions. In contrast, there are strict time period provisions for procedural participants, e.g., limited length of time period, absent provision for extending the time period, harsh conditions for recovering the time period, and even the loss of right caused by any violation. Therefore, in accordance with the principle of efficiency, the time period provisions for various powers and functions shall be scientific and equitable, so as to smooth the operation of proceedings.

1.3 Powers-Functions Relationships in Criminal Procedure

Criminal proceedings are a platform supported by the state coercive force to realize the criminal penalty power of the state. On this platform, different subjects of powers and functions pursue the value and goals of procedure based on their role positioning and the content of powers and functions as specified by law. In criminal procedure, multiple subjects of powers and functions are unlikely isolated from each other, but intersected while performing their powers and functions; and this intersection constitutes the powers-functions relationships. From an open perspective of powers and functions, since the criminal procedure system was founded, the particular types of powers and functions have been constantly enriched and changed, it is for this reason that the powers-functions relationships in criminal procedure have gone through an increasingly complex and diverse development process.

1.3.1 Review of Powers-Functions Relationships in the Criminal Procedure of China

In primitive society, people prayed to gods to help them settle disputes, or resolve conflicts directly by force, or even led their tribe to declare war on their rival tribe. The dispute settlement through retaliation and blood feud was in essence a contest of strength between opposing parties. In contrast, in the era of criminal procedure where the dispute settlement system is based on state powers, the powers-functions relationships in criminal procedure have become increasingly complicated. A time goes by, with deepening understanding of the rules of proceedings and self-differentiation of criminal judicial power, the powers-functions relationships in criminal procedure will become more pluralistic.

1.3.1.1 Traditional Powers-Functions Relationships in Criminal Procedure

The modern criminal procedure law of China dates back to the Late Qing Dynasty (1840 ~ 1912) when the Chinese government was engaged in reforms and modification of laws by transplanting Western Laws. However, the traditional procedure system of China, which is component of the national procedural culture, still influences its powers-functions relationships in criminal procedure, especially the real state of such relationships in judicial practice beyond legislation. Therefore, it is necessity to learn about the characteristics of the traditional powers-functions relationships in criminal procedure, while will help us understand the "hidden rules" that still prevail in China's criminal procedure, and explain the differences between the real state of powers-functions relationships in judicial practice and the expected state of such relationships in the original legislative intention.

(1) In China, the primary characteristic of the traditional powers-functions relationships in criminal procedure denotes the absolute dominance of powers. In the long history of criminal procedure, the Chinese generally regard the appointment of specialized judicial officials as a sign of the emergence of the criminal procedure system. In *The Book of History: Classics of Shun*, "the Emperor said, Gao Tao, now the barbarians are invading the central land, robbing and killing everywhere, you are hereby appointed as judge to approve the execution of the five penalties". Since Gao became a specialized judicial officer, the state powers began to play a role in criminal proceedings, and judicial power—a crucial part of state powers—had been highly valued by rulers.
    At the central level, there had been generations of judicial organs and officials along with changing dynasties, but the monopolistic position of judicial power in proceedings has never been weakened, and the mindset of "valuing powers over rights" has never outdated. In ancient times, while the cases were tried, all parties concerned (including witnesses and others persons of interest) had no equality at all in court, but knelt down in front of the judge. "They were often scolded

by judge or beaten by bailiffs during the proceedings. If the criminal defendants were jailed, they would be deprived of all 'rights' and likely to be tortured for confessions. In addition to criminals, their neighbors, local acquaintances, accomplices, plaintiffs, and families of the deceased might be taken into custody or grounded after appearing in court, losing personal liberty".[33] It seems that the rights of concerned parties and other participants in proceedings were reduced to a weak position. Such pattern of overwhelming powers over rights has a far-reaching impact and still haunts the powers-functions relationships in criminal procedure of China. To truly respect and protect human rights, we shall, from the perspective of procedural culture, mitigate the impact of this tradition on investigative and judicial organs and their functionaries, and build modern powers-functions relationships based on equality between powers and rights.

(2) The traditional judicial power, which was not separated from administrative power, is unlike the judicial powers and functions in modern sense. In the days of centralized monarchy, the system of procedural powers and functions was controlled by rulers and judicial officials. The judicial power at that time was essentially different from the existing one. Throughout the traditional Chinese society, there had never been any "judiciary" independent of "administration"; and "judiciary" was no more than an "administrative" responsibility.[34] Since Gao Tao was appointed as "judge", successive dynasties had begun to set up special judicial organs and officials at the central level. After the Tang Dynasty (618–907), the "three judicial bodies" were fixed in the central judicial system,[35] but it did not mean that judicial power was an independent power, because both execution of judicial power and system design were within the scope of administration. At the local level, administrative officials had been taking charge of judicial affairs until the early twentieth century. Although there was criminal investigation minister in Song Dynasty (960 ~ 1279), and similar judicial officials at the provincial level in Qing Dynasty (1636 ~ 1912), they were under the direct leadership of administrative officials, instead of having any judicial autonomy.[36] More importantly, under the unified Imperial Examination System, the judicial officials that were selected might be non-professionals with judicial background no stronger than their administrative colleagues. Because of this, the powers-functions relationships in criminal procedure, especially the relationship between superior and subordinate judicial organs, were tainted with a strong administrative color. This kind of bureaucracy shows China's traditional powers-functions relationships in criminal procedure, especially the power relationships, are characterized by "obedience to the order of superior officers", which still has a far-reaching impact on such relationships at present. Now China is advancing the reform of the courts and procuratorates below the provincial level—a layout for localization of justice, it needs to shun

[33]Hu [42].

[34]Hu [43].

[35]Li [44].

[36]Li [45].

from "administration of justice" between lower-level and higher-level courts, and never achieves "localization of justice" through "administration of justice".

(3) In China's traditional system of powers and functions in criminal procedure, rights are an object without due respect and protection. For quite a long time powers have been dominating the system of powers and functions of China, while rights are no more than an object in this system. Although parties to a case, witnesses and other participants in proceedings are only obligated to give testimony and relevant information in court, they are sometimes interrogated with torture. In the Tang Dynasty when the system of torture was developed, in addition to defendants, plaintiffs and witnesses might be tortured,[37] showing the weak status of rights in the system of powers and functions. The objectification of rights has penetrated into China's procedural culture, which impedes its efforts in strengthening human rights protection in criminal proceedings. Such grave inequality between rights and powers runs counter to the equal adversary between the power of prosecution and the right to defense—feature of the modern criminal procedure system, and deviates from the ideas of modern criminal procedure for respecting and protecting human rights.

(4) China's traditional powers and functions of criminal procedure are less differentiated and in limited types, which is determined by the law of development of criminal procedure. In all countries, the powers and functions of criminal procedure are constantly differentiated and improved along with the developing procedure system. The modern powers of trial, investigation and prosecution, and the rights to defense and participation in proceedings are products of evolution. In addition to the general law of development, there are special reasons for China to have limited types of powers and functions and flawed powers-functions relationships in criminal procedure. For example, the mindset of "detesting proceedings" is of great impact on the development of the powers-functions relationships in criminal procedure. Chinese people on the whole expect to stay away from proceedings as possible as they can, which has held back the development of procedural powers and functions. A typical example in this regard is that a defendant usually hires a lawyer to assist him to exercise his right to defense, which was accepted by both the public and government in ancient Greece. But in ancient China, litigator or lawyer was a derogatory term and looked down upon as "suit monger".[38] As a result, China's defense powers and functions, especially those of defense lawyers, were not recognized and protected by the

[37]According to *Comments on Laws of Tang Empire*—the crowning legislative achievement of the Tang Dynasty, if the guilty of a defendant cannot be proven, then the plaintiff may be interrogated with torture; even the witness can hardly escape from being tortured. Li [44].

[38]In ancient China, litigators were usually debased as "suit mongers", since they were no better than swindlers and hooligans in most people's eyes. When they found some cases lucrative, they would instigate the victim to file a lawsuit in yamen (court), even if it was unnecessary; and then they would write a complaint for the plaintiff, turn the facts upside down during proceedings or collude with clerk and yamen runners, as long as the result of the judgment would be in their favor. Fuma Susumu, The suit mongers and lawsuit system in the Ming and Qing dynasties, 1998, *Civil Trial and Civil Contract in Ming and Qing Dynasties*, Beijing: Law Press· China.

public and state organs for a long time. This procedural culture of "detesting proceedings" has discouraged witnesses to give testimony in court. Holding a negative attitude toward proceedings, it is no wonder for Chinese people to avoid being involved in any proceedings, which is one of the reasons that China has a low rate of court attendance when trying criminal cases.

1.3.1.2 Modern Transformation of the Powers-Functions Relationships in Criminal Procedure

In the late Qing Dynasty there was a wave of "saving the nation through reform" and recovering extraterritoriality. On April 25, 1906, Shen Jiaben and Wu Tingfang, ministers to amend laws, presented a draft of the criminal and civil procedure laws to the emperor. This draft was the first modern procedure law of China, with the contents on criminal procedure as a prelude to the modernization of China's criminal procedure system. Although it was not implemented for multiple reasons, it specified the jury system and the lawyer system[39] for the first time, and provided for the rights and obligations of plaintiff, defendant, judge, witnesses and other participants in proceedings. These provisions have revolutionized the traditional powers-functions relationships in criminal procedure, clearly stipulated the contents of powers and functions and the relationships between relevant subjects. A new pattern of powers-functions relationships initially took shape, which featured centrality of trial, equal adversary between plaintiff and defendant, and valid participation of auxiliary subjects. In 1911, the *Criminal Procedure Law (Draft)* was enacted, becoming the first genuine criminal procedure code throughout the legal history of China. It consummated the powers-functions relationships in criminal procedure, exerted a far-reaching impact on the criminal law system of the Republic of China (1912–1949) and the People's Republic of China (New China), and laid the groundwork for the modern powers-functions relationships in criminal procedure of China.

Specifically, the *Criminal Procedure Law of 1911 (draft)* had improved the powers-functions relationships in criminal procedure in the following three aspects:

(1) The draft endorsed "the plaintiff to file a lawsuit directly for a case of private prosecution"; "the plaintiff is the subject of proceedings. He is the one that takes legal action against the defendant…the judge shall remain independent of both plaintiff and defendant, objectively evaluate the testimonies of both sides, ascertain the facts of the case, and make a judgment both ethical and lawful".[40] This provision established the neutral and detached status of judicial power in the powers-functions relationships in criminal procedure, thoroughly separated prosecution from trial, defined the operating basis for judicial powers and functions, and substituted the positive and powerful status of judicial power

---

[39] In the memorial presented to the emperor, Shen Jiaben and Wu Tingfang recommended some procedure laws for enforcement, and proposed to implement the jury system and the lawyer system which were common legislative practices in western countries. Wu and Zhong [46].

[40] The *Criminal Procedure Law of 1911 (draft)*, which was drawn up by Shen Jiaben and Wu Tingfang, was presented to the emperor in memorials. See the memorials in Wu and Zhong [47].

with a passive and neutral status. It is in line with the general law of passive and neutral judgment in modern criminal procedure. Although the legislation for the criminal procedural model went through some changes in the period of Republic of China and after the founding of New China, the powers-functions relationships with neutrality of judicial power has remained to date.

(2) This draft for the first time defined "procurator to initiate a public prosecution", holding that "the power to bring a lawsuit (for a criminal case) is reserved exclusively for procurator on behalf of the state". In the realm of criminal procedure, the setting of procurator transformed the traditional system of powers and functions dominated by private prosecution and trial, and transferred victim's right to criminal prosecution to procurator as subject in proceedings; this subject was independent of the judge that performed trial powers and functions, thus forming a system of powers and functions featuring independence of prosecution power and separation of prosecution from trial. During the period of the Republic of China and after the founding of New China, the specific prosecution responsibilities and functions of procuratorates and procurators were changed to a certain extent, but the system of powers and functions as defined by this draft keeps prevailing till now, featuring dominance of public prosecution and separation of prosecution from trial. The setting of procurator not only defined the subject status of procurator in the trilateral relationship of procurator, defender and judge, but more importantly, it transformed the traditional system of powers and functions where state powers had been "exercised by only one subject", thus invigorating the mutual restriction between powers in criminal procedure, and making up for the insufficient restriction of powers by rights in China where powers had long been valued over rights.

(3) This draft made a breakthrough in stipulating equality between plaintiff and defendant. It was particularly commendable that the "equality" involved not only "equal status", but "equal conditions for prosecution and defense in proceedings. Now that the procurator on behalf of the plaintiff is an expert in law, how could a defendant neither well educated nor professional defend for himself? So the defendant is allowed to hire a defender or assistant to collect favorable evidence and defend for him, which will balance the strength of the two parties".[41] This argument on equal adversary between procurator and defender is still inspirational for improving the powers-functions relationships in criminal procedure at present, particularly such relationships between prosecution and defense. By following the legislative thinking on substantive equality between plaintiff and defendant, this draft defined the powers-functions relationships in criminal procedure, which had transformed the status of procurator and defender, i.e., it confirmed the defender as a subject in proceedings, rather than an object. Moreover, this draft set out defender system, assessor system and final statement system to consolidate the weak position of defender in the powers-functions relationships. The legislative design in this draft, for the purpose of balancing

[41] The *Criminal Procedure Law of 1911 (draft)*, which was drawn up by Shen Jiaben and Wu Tingfang, was presented to the emperor in memorials. See the memorials in Wu and Zhong [46].

the powers and functions of prosecution and defense, was a symbol that China has established equal adversary between prosecution and defense, and one of the important signs for the transition of criminal procedure in modern times.

In addition, this draft also set out the norms for regulating the powers-functions relationships involved in three-trial system and open trial system, widened the scope of subjects in criminal proceedings, and comprehensively standardized the particular powers-functions relationships. The *Criminal Procedure Law of 1911 (draft)* was never put into effect due to the collapse of the Qing Dynasty, but it is undeniable that this draft—China's first special legislation for criminal procedure—was of epoch-making significance for laying the basis for the modern powers-functions relationships in criminal procedure. After that, during the period of the Republic of China and after the founding of New China, the powers-functions relationships in criminal procedure has kept developing and evolving on this basis, proving the historical value of this draft.

1.3.1.3 Powers-Functions Relationships in Criminal Procedure After the Founding of New China

After the founding of New China, numerous things were waiting to be rebuilt. In the realm of legal system, Chinese legislators first abrogated the Kuomintang's Six Codes, and then drew up six criminal procedure laws successively from 1957 to 1963 by summing up the procedural practices in revolutionary bases and learning from the Soviet legislative experiences. But a finalized criminal procedure law failed to come out for a long time due to various reasons. After the Cultural Revolution (1966 ~ 1976) came to an end, China's political and social life returned to the normal track, the legislative work of criminal procedure law was restarted. On June 26, 1979, the 2nd Session of the Fifth National People's Congress adopted the *Criminal Procedure Law of the People's Republic of China* (hereinafter referred to as the "1979 Criminal Procedure Law"), becoming the first criminal procedure law formally enacted and implemented by the New China. This law laid the foundation for the socialist powers-functions relationships in criminal procedure with Chinese characteristics, which differ from such relationships in the late Qing Dynasty in the following four aspects:

(1) The procuratorial powers and functions occupy an important position in the powers-functions relationships in criminal procedure, since they are not only responsible for prosecution, but also for supervision as authorized by the *Constitution of the People's Republic of China.* The direct reason for this circumstance is that China absorbed the Soviet criminal procedure law. The procuratorates of the Soviet Union played a vital role in supervising the operation of the national legal systems, for the purpose of ensuring their unification. After its founding in 1949, New China confirmed the status of procuratorates as a legal supervisory organ in the *Constitution* and *the Law on the Organization of the People's Procuratorate.* Based on this positioning of procuratorates, the *1979*

Criminal Procedure Law defined the procuratorates as the subject for supervising criminal proceedings, which has vigorously reinforced their status in the system of powers and functions. For example, Article 3 of this law stated that "the People's Procuratorates shall be responsible for procuratorial work, authorizing approval of arrests, conducting investigation and initiating public prosecution". According to this provision, the procuratorates were not only vested with the procuratorial powers and functions, but also the investigatory and judicial review powers and functions, far exceeding the requirements for equal adversary between prosecutor and defender. As the procuratorates were given the supervisory powers and functions (e.g., review and approval of arrests) that are independent of the parties to the case, the original pattern of neutral trial and equal adversary between prosecution and defense was broken. In front of the overwhelming procuratorial powers and functions, the defense powers and functions had no way of equal adversary. Besides, as the supervisor of proceedings, the procuratorates were also empowered to supervise the courts, which severely impaired the authority of judicial powers and functions that should be at the top of the powers-functions relationships in procedure, and incapacitated the function of trial to balance the gap in powers and functions between prosecution and defense.

(2) The relationships among investigative, procuratorial and judicial powers and functions were vaguely positioned, making it hard for mutual restriction and supervision. Article 5 of the 1979 Criminal Procedure Law stipulated that "in conducting criminal proceedings, the People's Courts, the People's Procuratorates and the public security organs shall divide responsibilities, coordinate their efforts and check each other to ensure the correct and effective enforcement of law". If investigative, procuratorial and judicial powers and functions could truly operate according to this provision, it would somewhat help China to make up for the insufficient restriction of rights to powers in the powers-functions relationships in criminal procedure. However, due to the deviations in the ideas of procedure, especially in the ideas of powers and the design of specific procedure systems, there is an apparent gap between the powers-functions relationships and the legislative intention: (i) The exercise of investigative powers and functions is not effectively supervised and restricted. The 1979 Criminal Procedure Law stipulated that the procuratorates—subject in supervision of proceedings—shall supervise the procedural behaviors of investigative organs, but both of them are on the side of prosecution with common interest demand, which obstructs supervision and restriction to effectively play their roles. (ii) The procuratorial powers and functions are over-mighty, involving investigation, examination before prosecution, and even trial of criminal cases (according to the provisions for exemption from prosecution in Article 101 of this law), which not only goes against the protection of defense powers and functions, but also encroaches on the space of judicial powers and functions. (iii) Judicial powers and functions are too proactive to remain neutral. Article 114 of this law stated that "the judge shall question the defendant after the public prosecutor reads out the indictment in the courtroom". According to this article, the judge who shall remain neutral

and objective during the trial is entitled to question the defendant in person, which seems that the judge exceeds his duties and meddles in the affairs of prosecutor. It not only mixes up the powers and functions of prosecution and trial, but also breaks the balance between the powers and functions of prosecution and defense, making the inferior position of defense powers and functions even worse, and reduced to the object of prosecution and trial.

(3) The defense powers and functions are limited to be capable of equal adversary with the prosecution powers and functions. For quite a long time, China's powers-functions relationships in criminal procedure are characterized with "valuing powers over rights", and the defense powers and functions remain in a weak position and in need of special protection from legislation and state organs. However, the 1979 Criminal Procedure Law did not contain any "preferential treatment" for the defense powers and functions, but had them limited and weakened by the specific procedural design; for example, this law did not allow defendants to hire a lawyer to defend him until the stage of trial. What's worse, the pretrial detention rate in China is extremely high, most criminal suspects are deprived of personal freedom by compulsory measures before trial. Consequently, the above provision makes it hardly for defendants to seek help from a defense lawyer, which will dwarf the defense powers and functions in adversary with the prosecution powers and functions, and destroy the realistic basis for neutrality of trial and equal adversary between prosecutor and defender.

(4) The powers and functions of other subjects in proceedings are ignored in the powers-functions relationships in criminal procedure. Although prosecutor, defender and judge play a major role in the powers-functions relationships in criminal procedure, the increasingly sophisticated and perfected criminal procedure legislation requires intensified participation of other subjects, which is important for the smooth operation of proceedings. But the 1979 Criminal Procedure Law did not pay enough attention to the powers and functions of other subjects in proceedings. Take witnesses for example, they are important subject in proceedings since they can provide important information for ascertaining the facts of a case, but the 1979 Criminal Procedure Law contained no provision for compelling witnesses to appear in court or ensuring their personal safety, that's why the court appearance rate of witness in China has remained extremely low, which has seriously affected the substantive validity of trial, because prosecutor and defender cannot question or refute the witnesses in court, and judges cannot determine the reliability and authenticity of the testimonies given by witnesses based on their performance in court.

Based on the implementation practices of the 1979 Criminal Procedure Law and the socio-economic developments, China finished the revision of this law in 1996 (the revised law is hereinafter referred to as the "1996 Criminal Procedure Law") to modify the authority criminal procedural model by taking in the adversary procedural model, limit the prosecution powers and functions, strengthen the defense powers and functions, and remove the institutional obstacles in the powers-functions relationship in criminal procedure. For example, the 1996 Criminal Procedure Law allowed criminal suspects to hire a defense lawyer during the examination before prosecution, and seek legal advice from a lawyer at the investigation stage; and improved the non-prosecution system by no longer authorizing the procuratorates to grant exemption from prosecution. However, China only made some modification and refinement to the powers-functions relationships established by the 1979 Criminal Procedure Law, instead of thoroughly transformed the guiding ideology for legislation and the mode of procedure, or substantially restructured the powers-functions relationships in criminal procedure.

1.3.2 New Developments in the Powers-Functions Relationships Established by the 2013 Criminal Procedure Law

The *Criminal Procedure Law of the People's Republic of China* went through the second revision in 2012, marking a significant change in the development of the criminal procedure law since the founding of New China. The 2013 Criminal Procedure Law contains altogether 290 articles (including 90 modified articles, 66 newly-added articles, and 1 merged article). The legislators took account of the basic national conditions of China, followed the constitutional principle of "respecting and ensuring human rights", and properly balanced the relationship between "punishment of crimes and protection of human rights", in an attempt to achieve further legalization, democratization and scientization of the criminal procedure system. It is a major achievement in the reform of the national judicial system and working mechanism, and also a breakthrough in improving the socialist legal system with Chinese characteristics.[42] Specifically, this amendment to law involves all aspects of the criminal procedure: both judicial proceedings and procedure system are modified and refined, some special procedures are added initiatively, and the criminal legislative system is improved. Consequently, China is able to optimize the criminal proceedings and procedure system, and improve the allocation of powers and functions and protection of subjects, which is sure to influence the powers-functions relationships in criminal procedure. After that, a new development trend showed up in China's powers-functions relationships in criminal procedure.

1.3.2.1 Improved Equal Adversary Between Prosecution and Defense

As early as 1911, in the memorial of the criminal procedure law (draft) presented to the emperor, Shen Jiaben made clear the significance of equal adversary between prosecution and defense and the realization approaches, that is, prosecutor and defender shall have both equal status and equality of arms to achieve substantive equality. This shows that Chinese legislators had long ago recognized that equal

[42] Chen [48].

adversary between prosecution and defense is a basic form of the powers-functions relationships in criminal prosecution. However, after the founding of New China, the procuratorial powers and functions expanded rapidly, which contained the development of equal adversary between prosecution and defense, and further suppressed the defense powers and functions which were already weak. The powers-functions relationships between prosecution and defense were seriously imbalanced, which affected the improvement of the entire powers-functions relationships in criminal procedure and went against the protection of the rights of criminal suspects and defendants. So the second amendment to the *Criminal Procedure Law* specially made the following corrections and improvements:

First, the 2013 Criminal Procedure Law has strengthened the defense powers and functions. In modern criminal proceedings, the prosecution powers and functions are usually executed by special state organs, so the defense powers and functions executed by individuals seem to be inherently disadvantageous. In order to balance the powers-functions relationships between prosecution and defense, there shall be, on the one hand, high restrictions on the prosecution powers and functions of state organs; and on the other hand, active reinforcement of the defense powers and functions of criminal suspects and defendants to build up their ability to confront prosecution. The 2013 Criminal Procedure Law has strengthened the defense powers and functions in the following two aspects:

(1) It has strengthened the right to self-defense of the criminal suspect or defendant. In China, the criminal defense rate has remained low, so the strengthening of the right to self-defense of the criminal suspect or defendant is the basis for enhancing the overall defense powers and functions in criminal procedure. In the 2013 Criminal Procedure Law, the strengthening of the right to self-defense of the criminal suspect or defendant manifests in seven aspects: (i) It clarifies the principle of respecting and protecting human rights, which is a guideline for strengthening the defense powers and functions. As a main object whose rights are infringed in criminal proceedings, the criminal suspect or defendant is the foremost beneficiary of this principle. It has elevated the importance of the criminal procedure law in protecting human rights, and provided continuous momentum and sufficient space for interpreting and refining the criminal procedure law in the future. (ii) According to Article 95 of this law, "the criminal suspect or defendant, and his legal representative, near relatives or defender have the right to apply for changing the compulsory measures. Upon receipt of this application, the People's Court, the People's Procuratorate and the public security organ shall make a decision within three days; if they do not agree to such change, they shall notify the applicant and explain the reasons for disagreement". This provision not only gives the criminal suspect or defendant the right to object the continuous application of compulsory measures, but also requires the case handling authorities to deal with his objection and give him a formal reply. (iii) No one shall be compelled to prove his guilt. This law makes it clear that self-defense is a right of the criminal suspect or defendant, rather than an obligation; he may not be forced to make any statement and exculpation

against himself. (iv) Article 86 stipulates that the criminal suspect or defendant has the right to make statements and exculpations to the procurator during the examination before prosecution. (v) Article 115 stipulates that the criminal suspect has the right of appeal and complaint for the illegal investigations to the procuratorates during the investigations of his case, so that any violation of his rights caused by the illegal investigations could be halted and eliminated as soon as possible. (vi) Article 211 stipulates that the defendant has the right to object the summary procedure that is applied. The optional right of procedure is an important content of the defense powers and functions of the defendant who is a subject in proceedings. Whether to choose the summary procedure shows that whether the defendant chooses full defense for the facts of his case during the trial, which has a great impact on his right to defense, especially the substantive right to defense, so the defendant shall be vested with the optional right of procedure. (vii) Article 240 stipulates that the Supreme People's Court shall question the defendant who is sentenced to death when reviewing the criminal case that he committed. The death penalty review procedure gives the defendant sentenced to death the last chance to defend him. If the review decision is simply made on basis of case materials without the statement of the defendant in person, he will be unable to fully execute his right to defense. The 2013 Criminal Procedure Law allows the defendant to make statements to the judges who review his death sentence case, which is highly valued for safeguarding the right to self-defense of the defendant.

(2) It has strengthened the defense powers and functions of defenders. The strengthening of the defense powers and functions of defenders (especially defense lawyer and legal aid lawyer) is of vital importance for enhancing such powers and functions of the criminal suspect or defendant, because the latter has limited legal knowledge and experience, and a large number of them remain in custody during the proceedings. If the defense powers and functions of defenders are enhanced, it will help China to improve the effect of existing defense, raise the criminal defense rate, and upgrade the quality of criminal defense on the whole. In the 2013 Criminal Procedure Law, the strengthening of the defense powers and functions of defenders manifests in seven aspects: (i) Article 33 stipulates that the criminal suspect is allowed to hire a defense lawyer at the investigation stage. With legal expertise and practice experience, a defense lawyer plays a positive role in ensuring the criminal suspect to execute his defense powers and functions. Especially at the investigation stage, if the criminal suspect in custody is able to obtain effective assistance from a defense lawyer, he will be more capable in the game with the investigative organs, and in executing his powers and functions in proceedings. (ii) According to Article 37, despite of the circumstances that the defense lawyer shall obtain the permission from the investigative organs to meet with the criminal suspect in custody when the latter is involved in the crime of endangering national security, the crime of terrorist activities, or the especially serious crime of bribery, the defense lawyer may request to meet with the criminal suspect or defendant in custody after showing his lawyer's practice license, the law firm's certificate and power of

attorney or a legal aid letter, then the detention house shall immediately arrange a meeting for them no later than 48 h; and their meeting may not be monitored. To protect the defense lawyer's right of interview will ensure the full communication between the defender and the criminal suspect during the investigation, so that the defender can learn about relevant information about the case, and the detainee can obtain legal advice and psychological comfort, which is conducive to the effective execution of the defense powers and functions. (iii) Article 39 stipulates that the defender shall have the right to request the People's Procuratorates or the People's Courts to obtain the evidence which is collected by the public security organs or the People's Procuratorates during investigation or examination before prosecution and able to prove the innocence of the criminal suspect or defendant or the pettiness of his crime, in case that he believes the evidence is not submitted. The right to apply for obtaining the evidence will make up for the incapability of the defender in collecting evidence, and ensure that all the evidence in favor of the criminal suspect or defendant will appear in court during the trial, which helps to strengthen the substantive defense powers and functions. (iv) Article 46 stipulates the defense lawyer shall have the right to keep confidential the relevant circumstances and information of his client that he is informed in his practice activities. It is an extended guarantee of the right to communicate with the criminal suspect or defendant, which will build up the mutual trust between the defense lawyer and the parties to the case, and improve the quality of defense effectively. (v) Article 47 stipulates that the defender shall have the right of appeal and complaint if the public security organs, the People's Procuratorates, the People's Courts and their staff members impede him from executing his procedural rights according to law. With this right, the defender can obtain remedy from the case handling authorities for their acts of impeding the execution of his defense powers and functions, which is an effective approach for the defense powers and functions to restrict the power-based powers and functions. (vi) According to Articles 86, 159, 170 and 240, before the investigation is concluded, and when the procuratorates examines the arrests and prosecution or when the Supreme People's Court reviews the death penalty, the defense lawyer shall have the right to directly express his opinions to the persons handling the case, while the case handling authorities shall take his request seriously, and attach his written opinions to the case file, which is of great significance for the execution of the defense powers and functions. To directly express his opinions to the persons handling the case will lay a basis for the defense lawyer to effectively execute his powers and functions. (vii) Article 196 stipulates that the judgment should be sent to the defender, which guarantees his right to know, facilitates him to have an overall grasp of the decision in a case and promptly detects the defects and errors in the judgment, so as to prepare for the possible appeal and retrial application.

Second, the 2013 Criminal Procedure Law has standardized the investigative powers and functions. The criminal cases pose serious threat to social security and feature great concealment, in order to uncover the criminal suspects and collect their fixed criminal evidence, the investigative powers and functions shall be continuously enhanced. However, the powerful investigative powers and functions seem like a double-edged sword, which cracks down on crimes on the one hand, but tends to infringe the legitimate rights and interests of the parties to the case on the other hand, especially the criminal suspects themselves. As such, in order to balance the powers-functions relationships between prosecution and defense, it is necessary to regulate the investigative powers and functions which are an important part of prosecution. The 2013 Criminal Procedure Law has standardized the investigative powers and functions in the following aspects:

(1) Article 33 (2) of this law provides that the investigative organs shall inform the criminal suspect that he has the right to entrust a defender when questioning the criminal suspect for the first time or taking compulsory measures against him.
(2) Article 54 provides that the statements of the criminal suspect or defendant that are collected by illegal means such as extortion of confessions by torture, as well as the witness's testimonies and the victim's statements that are collected by illegal means such as violence and intimidation, shall be excluded. If the collection of the material evidence and documentary evidence does not comply with legal procedures and may undermine judicial justice, it shall be corrected or reasonably explained; otherwise, such evidence shall be excluded. Article 57 provides that if the court finds that the existing evidence materials cannot prove the legitimacy of the evidence collection, the People's Procuratorate may request the People's Court to notify the concerned investigators or other personnel to explain the situation; or the People's Court may inform the concerned investigators or other personnel to appear in court to make explanations. The concerned investigators or other personnel may request initiatively to appear in court to make explanations. In terms of the 2013 Criminal Procedure Law, the inclusion of the exclusionary rule of illegally obtained evidence is one of its major achievements in protection of human rights; the primary purpose of this rule is to contain the act of extortion of confessions by torture in criminal investigation. Excluding the illegally obtained evidence will remove the inherent driving force for employing illegal means during interrogation, it is of positive value for balancing the powers-functions relationships between investigation and defense at the stage of investigation. Moreover, this rule has enhanced the defense powers and functions to confront illegal evidence collection, thereby offsetting the one-way suppression of investigation against defense.
(3) Article 83 provides that the criminal suspect shall be transferred to the detention house for custody no later than 24 h after he is arrested. Article 116 provides that after the criminal suspect is transferred to the detention house for custody, the investigators may interrogate him, but not beyond the detention house. Taking compulsory measures against the criminal suspect is an important part of the investigative powers and functions. To prevent the investigative organs from obtaining statements of the criminal suspect through illegal interrogation when he is deprived of personal freedom, the 2013 Criminal Procedure Law provides that the criminal suspect shall be promptly transferred to the detention house

after being arrested, and the interrogation of him shall be done inside the detention house. In China, the public security organs take charge of investigation of cases and administration of detention houses, i.e., investigation is yet separated from detention; in spite of this, the detention house is responsible for the personal safety of detainees, so it keeps restricting and supervising the acts of investigators to guard against extortion of confessions by torture. All the above provisions are part of the efforts to balance the powers-functions relationships between investigation and defense.

(4) Article 121 provides that investigators may record or videotape their interrogation of the criminal suspect; for the major cases that are punishable by life imprisonment or death penalty, the interrogation of the concerned criminal suspect must be recorded or videotaped. Such provision is able to avoid the extortion of confessions by torture during the interrogation. The surveys of the detention houses in lots of places across China show that synchronous sound recording or videotaping of interrogation is universalized in China's detention houses, which is good news for balancing the powers-functions relationships between investigation and defense.

(5) According to Article 150, when taking the technical investigation measures, the investigators shall strictly abide by the norms for the types, applicable objects and time limit of these measures. The investigators shall keep confidential the State secrets, trade secrets, and personal privacy known to them while taking the technical investigation measures; and the materials obtained in this process but irrelevant to the case shall be promptly destroyed. The materials obtained with the technical investigation measures can be used only for investigation, prosecution and trial of crimes, not for other purposes. In order to detect special cases more efficiently and meet the needs of investigative practice, the 2013 Criminal Procedure Law covers new content on the technical investigation measures, and sets out the norms for their time limit, applicable scope, validity of evidence, and confidentiality, since these measures are prone to cause serious violations of the privacy and other rights of the investigated objects, only by this way there will be balance between punishing crimes and protecting human rights, and also between initiative of investigation and effective adversary of defense.

(6) Article 187 provides that the police are obliged to testify in court for witnessing crimes while performing their duties. According to this provision, during the trial, the police shall be questioned by the judge and procurator, and also by the defendant and his defender, which helps to thoroughly ascertain the facts of the case; and more importantly, it demonstrates that the police are on an equal footing with other subjects in proceedings during the trial, so they are ought to be examined by the judicial powers and functions and questioned by the defense powers and functions.

Third, the 2013 Criminal Procedure Law has standardized and expanded procuratorial powers and functions. In the special powers-functions relationships in criminal procedure of China, the procuratorial organs play two roles as the subject of prosecution and the subject of procedural supervision. On the one hand, the subject of prosecution is in an adversarial relationship with defender; on the other hand, the subject of procedural supervision is obliged to supervise and restrict the acts of investigative and judicial organs that violate the procedural rights of the parties, so there is a relationship of "delivering relief and receiving relief" between prosecution and defense. For the purpose of balancing the powers-functions relationships between prosecution and defense, the 2013 Criminal Procedure Law contains the provisions for regulating the procuratorial organs' prosecution powers and functions, and strengthening their supervision powers and functions.

In this law there are two articles that regulate the prosecution powers and functions of procuratorial organs: (1) According to Article 49, in a case of public prosecution, the burden of proof to prove the guilt of the defendant is on the prosecution, i.e., on the procuratorial organs, which complies with the basic rules of procedural proof such as presumption of innocence, and makes up for the wide gap in the capability of obtaining evidence between prosecution and defense. (2) According to Article 57, in the process of a court investigation into the legitimacy of evidence collection, the People's Procuratorates shall prove the legitimacy of evidence collection, showing that the procuratorial organs shall bear the burden of proof (in line with the burden of proof distribution for the facts of a case), which balances the differences in the capability of obtaining evidence between prosecution and defense, and restricts prosecution powers and functions.

In this law there are four articles that strengthen the procedural supervision powers and functions of the procuratorial organs: (1) According to Article 47, if the defender or agent ad litem holds that the public security organ, People's Procuratorate, People's Court or their functionaries obstruct his execution of procedural rights according to law, he shall have the right to appeal to or lodge a complaint with the People's Procuratorate at the same or higher level. The People's Procuratorate shall review the appeal or complaint in a timely manner, if the circumstance is true, it shall notify the relevant authority to make correction. This is an extension of the procedural supervision function of the procuratorial organs, and also a specific mechanism for the prosecutorial organs to execute their relief function for right violations. Article 115 provides that the party and his defender, agent ad litem, or any interested party have the right to appeal to or lodge a complaint with the judicial organ if the organ or its functionaries violates their rights and interests. The authority that accepts the appeal or accusation shall handle it in a timely manner. Those who are dissatisfied with the result of handling may appeal to the People's Procuratorate at the same level; if the case is directly accepted by the People's Procuratorate, they may appeal to the People's Procuratorate at the higher level. The People's Procuratorate shall review the appeal in a timely manner, and if the circumstance is true, it shall notify the relevant authority to make correction. The above two articles provide for the supervision and correction of the acts of the case-handling authority that infringe the defender's execution of procedural rights, so as to strengthen the protection of the defense powers and functions. (2) Article 55 provides that when the People's Procuratorate receives a case report, complaint or tip-off that some investigators have collected evidence by illegal means, or finds such incident by itself, it shall verify the facts of the incident through investigation. Where the evidence is indeed collected by illegal means, correction opinions shall be put forward; where the circumstance is serious enough to constitute a crime, then criminal responsibility shall be investigated in accordance with law. To supervise the acts of illegal evidence collection is helpful to prevent their occurrence, investigate the criminal responsibility of the parties concerned, and protect the defense powers and functions. (3) According to Article 93, after the criminal suspect or defendant is arrested, the People's Procuratorate shall examine the necessity of his detention. In case there is no need to keep the criminal suspect or defendant in custody, the People's Procuratorate shall advise the relevant authority to release him or change the coercive measures against him. The relevant authority shall notify the People's Procuratorate of the handling information within ten days. Through examination of the necessity of detention, the coercive measures against the criminal suspect or defendant who do not need to be detained can be lifted in time, and the occurrence of extended detention can be prevented. To supervise the application of coercive measures by the case-handling authorities will help to provide relief channels to the detainees, and balance the powers-functions relationship between prosecution and defense.

1.3.2.2 Strengthened Judicial Powers and Functions

The effect of the judgment of criminal proceedings comes from the authority and core status of the judicial powers and functions in the procedural powers-functions relationships. All subjects of procedural powers and functions shall observe and implement the effective judgments made by the courts. Given this, strengthening the authoritative status of the judicial powers and functions is the key to guarantee the order of proceedings and the stability of the outcome of proceedings. More than that, with higher authority, the neutral and objective judicial powers and functions will be more capable of regulating other procedural powers-functions relationships. Based on the above reasons, the strengthening of the authority of the judicial powers and functions plays an important role in improving and optimizing the procedural powers-functions relationships, and there are relevant provisions in the 2013 Criminal Procedure Law:

(1) According to Article 58, after the court trial, if the evidence collection is found illegal according to Article 54 of this law or such possibility cannot be ruled out, then the relevant evidence shall be excluded. This provision confirms that the courts have the power to exclude the illegally collected evidence; it is one of the important means for the courts to impose procedural sanctions against the unlawful acts in judicial proceedings. Such judicial powers and functions, on the one hand, will strengthen the authority and decision-making power of the courts over the matters (esp. procedural matters) involved in the case during criminal proceedings—a manifestation of expanded judicial powers and functions; and on the other hand, will balance and coordinate the powers-functions

relationships between prosecution and defense, so as to form benign procedural powers-functions relationships.

(2) According to Article 182, upon receipt of the notice of the People's Court, the witness may not refuse to appear in court to give testimony without a just cause, otherwise he may be compelled to do so, except for the spouse, parents and children the defendant. The witness who refuses to appear in court without a just cause or refuses to testify after appearing in court shall be admonished; in serious circumstances, he may be detained for no more than ten days with the approval of the president of the court. This provision gives the judicial organs the power to compel witnesses to appear in court, in order to resolve the long-standing problem of low court appearance rate of witness in the criminal proceedings of China. If the witnesses could be compelled to appear in court and then questioned by the prosecutor, defender and judge, it will help to ascertain the facts of the case. In terms of the courts—organizer of criminal proceedings, their power to compel witnesses to appear in court reinforces the authority of the judicial powers and functions, and enables the judicial powers and functions to play a better role through direct questioning of witnesses. Moreover, the courts have the power to punish the witnesses who do not obey their order of mandatory appearance in court, which further strengthens the authority of the judicial powers and functions, and maintains the seriousness of the court proceedings.

(3) Article 234 provides that the judgment made by the People's Court shall deal with the seized, detained or frozen property and its interest. This provision stresses that the judicial organs have a final say over the property involved in the case, clarifies the handling procedures and the decision-making subject for the property involved in the criminal proceedings, expands the application scope of the judicial powers and functions, demonstrates their supreme decision-making power over the matters involved in the proceedings, and strengthens their authoritative status.

1.3.2.3 Expanded Procedural Participation Powers and Functions

With the increasingly sophistication and scientification of modern criminal procedure, the powers-functions relationships in criminal procedure are no longer monopolized by the traditional tripartite relationship among prosecution, defense and trial, since the powers and functions of other procedural participants have become more and more important. To be specific, the second amendment to the Criminal Procedure Law, i.e., the 2013 Criminal Procedure Law, provides for the powers and functions of other procedural participants, which can be summarized in the following five aspects:

First, the procedural powers and functions of witnesses are further guaranteed. Being an important source of information in criminal proceedings, witnesses can provide key testimony that is irreplaceable for ascertaining the facts of a case. But in China the court appearance rate of witness always remains low, in order to solve this long-standing problem, the 2013 Criminal Procedure Law attempts to enhance the importance of powers and functions of witnesses in criminal proceedings by starting with one mechanism and one system, i.e., improve the witness protection and compensation mechanism, and establish the system that witnesses must present to testify at court.

(1) Improve the witness protection and compensation mechanism. According to Article 62 of the 2013 Criminal Procedure Law, if witnesses, expert witnesses, and victims give testimony in the proceedings for the crime endangering national security, crime of terrorist activities, organized crime of an underworld nature, and drug-related crime, etc., and therefore the personal safety of them or their near relatives may be exposed to danger, the People's Courts, People's Procuratorates and public security organs should not disclose their personal information such as real name, address and work unit; conceal their appearance and real voice; prohibit specific persons from contacting witnesses, expert witnesses, victims and their near relatives; take special measures for people and house to protect their personal and property safety. According to Article 63, the witnesses shall be subsidized for transportation, accommodation, and meal expenses incurred as a result of fulfilling their obligation to testify. The subsidy for the witnesses to give testimony is counted into the operational fund of the judicial organs and guaranteed by the government finance at the same level. By protecting the witnesses and their close relatives and compensating their testimony costs, their resistance and fear of giving testimony in court can be eliminated, thereby effectively encouraging them to participate in criminal proceedings and expanding their procedural powers and functions.
(2) Establish the system that witnesses must present to testify at court. According to Article 187, if the public prosecutor, the party to the case, defender or agent ad litem has objections to the testimony of a witness which has a significant impact on the conviction and sentencing of the case, the witness shall appear in court if the People's Court considers it necessary. According to Article 188, upon receipt of the notice of the People's Court, the witness may not refuse to appear in court to give testimony without a just cause, otherwise he may be compelled to do so, except for the spouse, parents and children of the defendant. The witness who refuses to appear in court without a just cause or refuses to testify after appearing in court shall be admonished; in serious circumstances, he may be detained for no more than ten days with the approval of the president of the court. These provisions that compel witnesses to appear in court and punish those who refuse to do so are a strong guarantee for them to participate in criminal proceedings.

Second, the "persons with expertise"[43] are allowed to participate in proceedings for the first time. According to Article 192, during the court hearing, the public prosecutor, the party to the case, defender or agent ad litem may apply to the court to notify the person with expertise to appear in court to give advice on the expert opinion produced by the expert witness. As result of the rapid development of modern science and technology, there are a large number of professional issues involved in criminal proceedings; the expert opinion is hard to be screened or debated by judges and other procedural subjects without relevant professional knowledge, the only way out is to seek help from the persons with expertise to cross-examine the expert opinion. The participation of the "persons with expertise" will somewhat narrow the gap in professional skills between prosecution and defense, and help the judicial organs to make decisions more accurately.

Third, the "eligible adults" become a type of new subject in participating in proceedings. According to Article 270 of the 2013 Criminal Procedure Law, in a criminal case of a minor, if his legal representative is unreachable or unable to be present in the interrogation and trial, or if they are accomplices, other adult relatives of the minor criminal suspect or defendant, the representative of his school, unit, community-based organization in the place of his residence or minor protection organization can be notified to be present, and the entire process shall be recorded. Due to their immature mind, minors do not have comparable self-defense ability as the adult criminal suspects or defendants, so they shall be given special attention and protection. The participation of "eligible adults" in proceedings can enhance the effect of the defense powers and functions, and improve the powers-functions relationships in minor-related proceedings.

Fourth, the interested party in the procedure of property confiscation becomes the subject of procedural powers and functions. According to Article 281, the near relatives and other interested parties of the criminal suspect or defendant shall have the right to apply to participate in the pre-judgment procedure of property confiscation, or entrust an agent ad litem to do so. Article 282 provides that the near relatives and other interested parties of the criminal suspect or defendant or the People's Procuratorate may appeal or protest against the decision of the court on whether to confiscate the property. As an interested party of the property involved in a case, his participation in the pre-judgment procedure of property confiscation helps to make up for the missing defense powers and functions caused by the absence of the party with property confiscated, safeguards the legitimate rights and interests of the party with property confiscated and of the interested party, so that in the pre-judgment procedure of property confiscation there will be comprehensive procedural powers-functions relationships featuring adversary between prosecution and defense and with the judicial powers and functions playing a central role.

[43] In criminal proceedings, the "persons with expertise" include the expert witness and the person that assists the prosecutor and the defender in cross-examining the expert opinion on the professional issues involved in the case; the "persons with expertise" herein refer in particular to the latter.

Fifth, the community correction center becomes an agency that executes criminal punishment, which is in line with the current ideas of non-penalization and education-oriented punishment. The persons serving sentences that are eligible for correction and administration in community shall be the ones less likely to endanger the personal safety of others. Such practice will enable China to broaden the scope of subject of criminal punishment execution, reasonably allocate the execution agencies, and cut the cost of execution while improving the quality of correction. It can be seen that the community correction center not only helps to execute criminal punishment, but also improves the powers-functions relationships in criminal procedure.

References

1. Chen, R. (1997). *Principles of criminal trial* (p. 221). Beijing: Peking University Press.
2 Li, R. (2006a). *Basic theory of separation of powers and checks and balances in criminal procedure* (p. 11). Beijing: China Legal Publishing House.
3. Liu, T. (2005). *On the subject of criminal procedure* (p. 31). Beijing: China People's Public Security University Press.
4. Griffiths, J. (1970). Ideology in criminal procedure. *The Yale Law Journal, 79*, 359.
5. He, H. (2002). *Justice as fairness: An interpretation of J. Rawls' theory of justice* (p. 41). Jinan: Shandong People's Publishing House.
6. Alexy, R., & Wei, F. (trans.). (2013). Alf Ross' begriff der kompetenz. *Journal of Comparative Law*, Issue 5.
7. Ross, A. (1968). *Directives and norms* (p. 130). Routledge & Kegan Paul Plc.
8. Jain, C. (2008). *Restriction of power by right* (p. 248). Jinan: Shandong People's Publishing House.
9. Wang, L. (2007). *Research on property law*, vol. 1 (p. 399). Beijing: China Renmin University Press.
10. Xu, Y. (2004). Deconstruction of powers and functions of judges' command authority in criminal procedure. *People's Court Daily.*
11. Zhang, Z., & Liu, T. (2008). Diversification and specialization of powers and functions of public prosecution. *Journal of National Prosecutors College*, Issue 6.
12. Lv, D., & Chen, J. (2010). Adjustment of the relationship between the powers and functions of public prosecution and of other proceedings. *Chinese Criminal Science*, Issue 6.
13. Chen, F. (2010). Investigatory powers and functions of public prosecution and primary explorations into their practice: from the perspective of the objective obligation of prosecutors. *Legal and Economy*, Issue 8.
14. Chen, Z. (2012). Re-examination of the procuratorial powers and functions: From the perspective of "respecting and protecting human rights" as specified in the new criminal procedure law of China. *The Collected Papers on China's Eighth National Senior Prosecutors Forum.*
15. Wang, J., (2010). On the procuratorial powers and functions in the context of "supervision". *Chinese Criminal Science*, Issue 12.
16. Gu, Y. (2004). *On the initiative of judicators and forms of their powers and functions.* Master's thesis of East China University of Political Science and Law.
17. Li, J. (2000). On the nature of procuratorial power, the definition of powers and functions, and the principle of rational allocation. *Journal of Heilongjiang Administrative Cadre College of Politics and Law*, Issue 4.
18. Xiao, J. (2009). On the procuratorial powers and functions and their transition. *Legal Forum*, Issue 6.

19. Gou, H. (2008). On the perfection of lawyers' powers and functions in defense from the procuratorial perspective: Based on the revised Law of the People's Republic of China on Lawyers. *Justice of China*, Issue 1.
20. Wang, X., & Zhu, G. (2010). On the optimal allocation of the procuratorial powers and functions in China. *Journal of Political Science and Law*, Issue 5.
21. Gong, W. (1999). On the establishment of the subject of investigatory and surveillance powers and the division of its powers and functions. *Chinese Criminal Science*, Issue 5.
22. Sheng, B. (2010). On the attributes of the powers and functions of the investigatory power of duty-related crimes: Based on the reform of the procuratorial system (part 1). *Legal System and Society*, Issue 9.
23. Gong, R., & Zheng, Z. (2005). Improving the powers and functions of lawyers in defense and promoting the proper exercise of procuratorial power. *Procuratorial Daily.*
24. Sun, B. (2005). Reconstruction of the powers and functions of lawyers in defense during the criminal investigation procedure in China. *Journal of Law Application*, Issue 7.
25. Le, S., & Gou, H. (2007). Reconstruction of procuratorial powers and functions under the principle of criminal reconciliation. *The Collected Papers on China's Third National Senior Prosecutors Forum.*
26. Zhang, P., Zhang, M. (2008). Improving the allocation of the investigatory and supervisory powers and functions. *Journal of National Prosecutors College*, Issue 5.
27. Wu, G. (2009). A comparative study on the procuratorial powers and functions of China and Vietnam in the criminal investigation stage. *Journal of Guangxi University for Nationalities (Philosophy & Social Science Edition)*, Issue 3.
28. Chen, W. (2005). *The road to procedural justice*, vol. 1 (p. 163). Beijing, China: Law Press.
29. Chen, W. (2011). *Citizens' access to justice*. Beijing: China Legal Publishing House.
30. Zhang, W. (2002). *Research on the basic category of law*. Beijing: China University of Politic Science and Law Press.
31. Max, W., Gu, Z. (trans.) (2005). *Basic concepts in sociology* (p. 72). Guilin: Guangxi Normal University Press.
32. Okuda, Y., Lu, B., & Huang, B. (trans.) (2017). *General theory of law*. Shanghai: Shanghai Academy of Social Sciences Press.
33. Guo, D. (2009). *Social power and civil society* (p. 54). Nanjing: Yilin Press.
34. Wang, B. (2010). *Research on the social power issues in contemporary China: Based on the ternary framework of state, society and individuals*. Ph.D. thesis, Hebei Normal University.
35. Liu, X., & Liu, Z. (2008). On the international development trends of the protection of victims of crime. *Judicial Reform Review*, Issue 8.
36. Chen, W. (Ed.). (2008a). *Research on criminal procedure law* (p. 42). China Renmin University Press: Beijing.
37. Wu, Y. (2003). A preliminary study on community correction work. *Law Science*, Issue 5.
38. The Chinese Comprehensive Dictionary. (1979). The Chinese Comprehensive Dictionary (p. 151). Shanghai: Shanghai Chinese Classics Publishing House.
39. Chen, W. (Ed.). (2008b). *Research on criminal procedure law* (p. 101). China Renmin University Press: Beijing.
40. Xie, Y., & Wan, Y. (2002). *Principles of criminal procedure law: Cornerstone of procedural justice* (p. 311). Beijing, China: Law Press.
41. Li, R. (2006b). *Research on the basic theory of separation of powers and check balance in criminal procedure* (p. 33). Beijing: China Legal Publishing House.
42. Hu, X. (ed.) (2012a). *Prison and procedure: Research on traditional Chinese procedural culture* (p. 39). China Renmin University Press: Beijing.
43. Hu, X. (ed.) (2012b). *Prison and procedure: Research on traditional Chinese procedural culture* (pp. 12–13). Beijing: China Renmin University Press.
44. Li, J. (2002). *History of China's procedure law* (p. 69). Beijing: China Procuratorial Press.
45. Li, W. (2011). *History of China's criminal procedure law in ancient times* (p. 501). Beijing: Law Press China.

46. Wu, H., & Zhong, S. (eds.) (2012). *A century of China's criminal procedure codes (1906–2012)*, vol. 1 (p. 9). Beijing: China University of Politic Science and Law Press.
47. Wu, H., & Zhong, S. eds). *A century of China's criminal procedure codes (1906–2012)*, vol. 1 (p. 108). Beijing: China University of Politic Science and Law Press.
48. Chen, W. (ed.) (2012). *Understanding and application of the amended provisions in China's criminal procedure law* (p. 1). China Legal Publishing House: Beijing.

Chapter 2
Theory of Judicial Power and Its Transformation

2.1 Transformation of Judicial Concepts

At present, the judicial reform of China is in full swing. The criminal judicial reform firstly shakes the traditional concepts held by Chinese judicial and law enforcement personnel for years. Therefore, while researching and discussing the tendency and direction of the judicial reform, the traditional concepts in this regard shall be properly adjusted and transformed, which is a problem that must be solved. Otherwise, even a flawless system is unable to yield good results; it is because the perfect modern systems and the accompanying guidelines and management codes seem like castle in the air, if a nation has yet formed a broad and modern psychological foundation that vitalizes these systems, and if the people that implement and employ the modern systems have yet experienced modernization of psychology, thought, attitude and behavior, then there will be a destined tragedy of lopsided and failed development, and the perfect modern systems and management modes, and even advanced technologies, will become worthless waste in the hands of those old-fashioned. This transformation of concepts is not only the key to the success of judicial reform, but also an important sign that a society is turning into a law-based one. Specifically, the transformation of concepts is mainly reflected in the following aspects.

2.1.1 Transfrom from the One-Sided Value of Combating Crime to the Pluralistic Balanced Value Centered on Human Rights Protection

Looking at the historical evolution of social division of labor, the original function of the criminal judicial system is to fight against crime, that's why all countries have, for quite a long period, held that the basic value proposition of their criminal judicial systems was to crack down on crime. However, with the development of society and the progress of human civilization, the concept of protecting human rights is

W. Chen, *Reform and Development of Powers and Functions of China's Criminal Proceedings*, https://doi.org/10.1007/978-981-15-8431-2_2

increasingly valued by people all over the world, and defined as one of the value goals of criminal judicial activities in some countries. As far as China is concerned, owing to the influence of the traditional values (e.g., "selflessness") that advocate social interests, and the constraint of the mindset that the major social contradiction is the one between ourselves and the enemy, the national criminal judicial system has all along been focused on combating crime, and pays less attention to protecting the rights of criminal suspects and defendants. Nowadays, the judicial activities of modern society shall uphold justice and civilization, and the constantly developing human society shall respect human rights. Therefore, one of the goals of the reform of China's criminal judicial system is to intensify the protection of the rights of criminal suspects and defendants.

In order to highlight the importance of human rights protection in the practice of criminal justice, both judicial personnel and investigators have to change their prejudiced thinking and habits while handling cases, they should no longer treat criminal suspects and defendants as if they are "class enemies". The judicial organs should respect the basic rights of the investigated persons although they execute power on behalf of the State. In the meantime, they shall be careful to avoid going from one extreme to the other. When they strive to correct the traditional judicial concepts such as "fighting against crime comes before human rights protection", they should not place one-sided emphasis on the protection of the rights of defendants, because the criminal justice system is primarily designed to maintain social order and protect the lives and property of the public, as well as prevent and combat crime. In a word, while pursuing the civilization of justice, they should protect the legitimate rights of criminal suspects, defendants and even convicts in criminal justice activities, and always bear in mind that the fundamental task of the criminal justice system is to fight against crime and protect the people.

2.1.2 Transfrom from Laying Particular Stress on Substantive Justice to Paying Equal Attention to Substantive Justice and Procedural Justice

The so-called substantive justice means that the judgment made by the judicial organs shall reflect the spirit of fairness and justice. The so-called procedural justice means that the judicial organs shall uphold the principle of legitimacy and equality during proceedings. The core of substantive justice is the correctness of the trial result, while the core of procedural justice is the legitimacy of the trial process. If comparing the judicial system to a factory, then substantive justice examines the "product", while procedural justice examines the "manufacturing procedure" of this "product". In general, the quality of the "product" relies on a scientific and reasonable "manufacturing procedure"; and a scientific and reasonable "manufacturing procedure" is bound to bring about a qualified "product". They seem to be internally consistent, but they measure different indicators. In terms of substantive justice, the "justice" means that the "product" must be qualified no matter which "manufacturing procedure" is adopted. In terms of procedural justice, the "justice" means that a scientific and reasonable "manufacturing procedure" must be adopted regardless of "product" quality. Given this, when establishing their criminal justice system, all countries have to make explicit or implicit definitions and choices on the relationship between substantive justice and procedural justice. Of course, the practices of different countries are not uniform, and may be widely divergent. An extreme approach is to pursue substantive justice and ignore procedural justice, i.e., regardless of the procedure and the means, where there is a just outcome, there is judicial justice. It used to be one of the procedural traditions in civil law countries, and remains as the guideline for some countries to establish their criminal justice system. Another extreme approach is to place one-sided emphasis on procedural justice, even at the cost of substantive justice. This is developed on the basis of the judicial tradition of the common law countries that attach importance to the rules of procedure; the US judicial system is a typical example in this regard. In China, since the traditional concept that "values substantive justice and devalues procedural justice" remains influential among judicial personnel, great importance shall be paid to procedural justice in the reform of the criminal justice system.

Why should we pay particular attention to procedural justice?[1] This is because procedural justice is the basis for achieving substantive justice. In other words, procedural justice and substantive justice are connected with each other, and their combination is the only way to obtain ultimate justice. Without procedural justice, i.e., the legitimacy or humanity of procedure, the outcome is by no means to be just no matter how correct it is. For example, the judgment made through extortion of confessions by torture might be correct, but the cruelty of procedure will deny its substantive justice. Procedural justice is the basis for substantive justice, and they may not be split, which is the starting point for studying these two concepts.

Practical experiences have proven that mere pursuit of substantive justice will lead to disregard of and even trample on the legitimate rights of participants in proceedings, and distort the concept of judicial justice. Discovery of truth is not

[1]For a long time, when theorists are discussing the value of procedural justice and why it is ought to be insisted, they tend to arbitrarily claim that procedural justice is good for discovering the truth and thus realizing substantive justice. Such argument is arbitrary for two reasons: First, a correct outcome is not an inevitable consequence of procedural justice. For example, if extortion of confessions by torture is prohibited, and procedural justice is guaranteed, then the judgment is absolutely correct, is that right? To tell the truth, in China, extortion of confessions by torture is still a powerful weapon for some police officers to solve cases, and even the best tool to avoid unjust, false and wrong cases, although it is hard to be admitted on most occasions. Now that extortion of confessions by torture does not necessarily lead to unjust, false and wrong cases, then why it is prohibited? It is because the procedure is inhumane, brutal and unjust. It means that we should not analyze problems only on basis of outcome or truth. Second, discovering the truth has been an ideal of mankind since ancient times. Even in the era of seeking divine advice or in the era of inquisitional proceedings, judges were eager to find out the truth. No ruler, even if he was a dictator or tyrant, would expect his judicial officers to create wrong, false and wrong cases. It can be seen that the key point of human progress, reform of procedural system, and innovation of judicial concepts is not to discover the truth, but to observe the minimum moral criteria in the process of obtaining the truth.

necessarily substantive justice. Truth and justice is not the same thing: the former falls into the category of epistemology and the latter is an ethical standard and a value judgment. The category of epistemology neither considers means (which is no more than its dependency and guarantee) nor the independent value of means. From this point of view, truth is not equal to justice. According to Prof. Duff from the University of Edinburgh, substantive correctness is not equal to substantive justice, and substantive truth is an epistemological concept; doctors shall discover the truth of illness of their patients, journalists shall discover the truth of news events, and historians shall discover the truth of archaeology, but none of these phenomena has the moral restrictions like the truth in law.

One of the most critical criteria of procedural justice is equality between prosecution and defense, which is based on three elements: First, equal opportunities. Without equal opportunities, there will be no equal adversary. Although it is not a big issue in China's criminal proceedings, it may sometimes give rise to problems. For example, the evidence prepared by the prosecutor is mostly written materials, including the defendant's confession and the witness' testimony, but the witness' direct oral testimony provided by the defendant may be rejected by the judge, showing procedural injustice between prosecution and defense.[2] Second, ability of defense. Justice seems like the face of Prometheus which is capricious, but there is a final criterion, i.e., the balance shall tilt toward the weak, which is the greatest equality. The weak deserves certain privileges, while the strong shall perform certain obligations, so that those who are too weak may talk with those who are too strong on an equal footing. Without a rational and equal opportunity for a conversation, how can there be equality? The balance tilting toward the weak is an aged idea from the West, i.e., "equality of arm", which has been a criterion for justice many years. Third, effect of equal adversary. The judge shall listen to the statement of both prosecutor and defender; otherwise, there will be no equality.

As far as the procuratorial reform is concerned, in order to achieve full equality between prosecution and defense, some legal scholars propose that "prosecutors shall perform as a party". In the current substantive law, prosecutors occupy a non-party legal status. In China, the procuratorial organs are positioned as the country's legal supervisory organs in legislation. The procuratorial power is a state public power that is in parallel with legislative, administrative and judicial powers. Prosecutors

---

[2] In the court proceedings of China there used to be a fixed pattern that the prosecutor questioned witness, victim and defendant while sitting high on the prosecution stage, such superior status made people feel that the relationship between prosecution and defense was unequal, which had undermined people's trust in procedural justice. In modern times, the court seats should be in the structure of an "equality triangle" where prosecutor, defender and judge are on an equal footing, thus making substantive justice visible to all. For example, during the trial of an ordinary hit-and-run case, as the prosecutor, the procurator of Beijing Fengtai Procuratorate stepped down the prosecution stage and walked up to the witness to question and cross-examine him, and the defender had the same opportunity to question the witness. The setting of court seats and the relevant arrangements shall convey the concepts of supremacy of trial and equality between prosecution and defense. The prosecutor stepped down from the prosecution stage was to show that he would treat the defender, witness and defendant as equals, marking that the inquisitional proceedings were transforming into adversarial proceedings that feature "equality".

bear dual functions in criminal proceedings, i.e., legal supervision and prosecution. To ensure that prosecutors could give full play to their powers and powers, both the Constitution and laws of China have granted them the powers to file cases, investigate, review and prosecute, initiate and support public prosecution, non-prosecute, withdraw a case, protest, make judicial interpretation, approve arrests, take coercive measures, and supervise criminal proceedings, civil proceedings and administrative proceedings. Therefore, many legal scholars argue that the non-party status of prosecutors will affect the fairness of criminal proceedings and cause disadvantages in judicial practice. In my opinion, the proposition that prosecutors shall perform as a party is a specific issue concerning judicial system construction. This issue is about how to look at the powers of prosecutor and the rights of defender in proceedings.

Generally speaking, the proposition that prosecutors shall perform as a party is based on the thought of equal rights and powers in the procedure system. This thought is closely related to the equal status of the parties in prosecution and defense in the civil procedure system. At a deeper level, it is to emphasize the equality between state power and the rights of individual citizens, and downplay the innate advantages of state power in the procedure system. If prosecutors could perform as a party, it may be beneficial for limiting the abuse of state power. It requires establishing a mechanism to check and balance civil rights and state power on the institutional platform. In the current Chinese context, state power has always been of supreme character, so it is understandable that the "socio-political significance of prosecutors performing as a party goes far beyond the importance to ascertain the facts of the case while operating the procedure system".

To question the rationality of performing as a party is in fact to question the rationality of employing civil rights to restrict state power, and also the rationality of further restricting state power in the current Chinese context. However, while emphasizing prosecutors to perform as a party, there is possibility that the restriction of a state power is weakened, such as the power of court. In fact, the procuratorial power may be abused, which is likely to implicate the power of court. In other words, if prosecutors perform as a party, it is in essence strengthening the power of court, making it possible for the power of court to be abused. Given this, if there is no way to prevent the despotism of the power of court, we cannot argue that letting prosecutors perform as a party is more reliable. In fact, we have not yet figured out how to prevent despotism. In my opinion, the best system arrangement should contain a good network of mutual restriction between rights, between rights and powers, and between powers. In this sense, the proposition that prosecutors should perform as a party may be defective. The correct way of thinking is to pay close attention to the restriction issues in all aspects in the process of detailing the procuratorial power.

2.1.3 Transfrom from Heavy Reliance on Witnesses to Attaching Importance to Material Evidence

The judicial proof methods in human society have undergone two major changes. The first one was to change from "divine revelation"-based to "human testimony"-based; and the second one was to change from "human testimony"-based to "material evidence"-based. Correspondingly, the development process of judicial proof methods is divided into three stages: divine revelation, human testimony, and material evidence. "Divine revelation", which stands for "divine hint for evidence", requires people to pray to gods to help them decide a case, and they will take some approaches to reveal the will of gods as the basis of the judgment. The method of "divine revelation" includes "Votum" and "Ordeal". Votum requires the parties to swear before gods that their statement of the case is absolutely true. Ordeal, which is also known as God-judging, requires the parties to go through physical suffering to test the authenticity of their statement of the case.

In the period when human testimony was playing a dominant role, the statement of the parties, especially that of the criminal defendants, was undoubtedly the most important evidence. In criminal cases, the interrogation which mainly aimed at obtaining the defendants' confession became the main means of judicial proof, which laid basis for the prevalence of extortion of confessions by torture. China's feudal society had lasted for more than 2000 years, which had made the concepts of "extorting confessions by torture" and "no beating, no confession" ingrained in the mind of judicial personnel and investigators. They liked doing so because many confessions under torture were exactly true. Even if it had led to misjudged cases from time to time, like the one dubbed as "Yang Nai-wu and Hsiao Pai-tsai"[3] that is known to all Chinese, they were still in a minority. The means of torture helped to obtain evidence and solve cases more rapidly, and greatly cut the cost of investigation. The misjudged cases were left to be redressed in the future. In the Chinese society ruled by men for 2000 years, under the guiding ideology of "oral confession centrism", both officials and ordinary people took corporal punishment as a "justified" shortcut to solve cases, as long as they would not fall victim to such punishment. It can be said that the evidence system in ancient China was centered on "human testimony". Throughout the history of more than 4000 years from the establishment of the Xia Dynasty to the collapse of the Qing Dynasty, interrogation by torture had always been a statutory means for obtaining the defendants' confession, and relevant laws had explicitly provided for the conditions, methods, tools and extent of torture.

The judicial personnel in ancient China had invented some scientific methods for investigating witnesses by observing their tone, breath, eye contact, facial expression and manner, and by roundabout questioning. The application and promotion of material evidence in judicial activities is attributed to the development of science and technology. Material evidence is objective existence, but it is unlikely to appear in

[3]Translator's note: It was one of the four great disputed cases in the late Qing Dynasty. Hsiao Pai-tsai was framed to kill her husband in collusion with Yang Nai-wu. Both of them were tortured to plead guilty. They were waiting four years to be proved innocent.

court by itself to prove the facts of a case. It means that material evidence must be interpreted by people, and those who interpret material evidence must have certain scientific knowledge. Therefore, material evidence is inseparable from science and technology. In most cases, material evidence can prove nothing without science and technology. It is for this reason that we call material evidence and its related inspection and appraisal conclusions "scientific evidence". For a long time in the history of human society, the material evidence technologies had featured decentralized development, and they were randomly applied in judicial activities. It was after the eighteenth century that the science and technology related to material evidence started developing systematically, and material evidence became increasingly important for judicial proof. The nineteenth century was widely regarded as a prime time for the development of scientific proof methods.

Since the twentieth century, the science and technology dedicated to judicial proof has kept progressing with each passing day. The judicial proof of human society has entered the era of "scientific evidence" mainly based on material evidence. Owing to complicated social life and rapid development of science, the objects of judicial activities have been upgrading their sci-tech content, and the environment of judicial activities is increasingly high-tech. As such, in order to achieve judicial justice and improve judicial efficiency, we must rely on science and technology, and improve the sci-tech level of judicial proof methods. In a nutshell, judicial proof shall no longer rely on witnesses but on material evidence. But currently in China, some investigators cannot cut out the so-called "witness complex". In the process of investigating into a case, they like to obtain "the evidence from the mouth of people", rather than discover and collect the possible material evidence on the crime scene. Sometimes they may miss the opportunity to collect the valuable material evidence, and then fail to prove the facts of the case with eligible evidence, or even lead to the occurrence of misjudged cases.

2.1.4 Pay Attention to Coordinating the Relationship Between Justice and Efficiency

Justice and efficiency are an economic and social issue of common concern to all countries at present, and they also represent the value tendency or goal model of criminal procedure reform. Lots of important theoretical and practical issues in criminal law are ascribed to the two issues: procedural justice and procedural efficiency. According to the Hungarian scholar Arpad Erdei, in this day and age, almost all the reforms of criminal trial procedure have two goals: one is to find new approaches and paths to implement a fast, simple and successful procedure, in other words, to make criminal proceedings more efficient; the other is to protect the rights of the participants in proceedings, which is required by justice.

In a macroscopic view, the entire criminal procedure is nothing more than the unification of justice and efficiency, and efficiency is a requirement and means to achieve justice. But there is sharp contradiction between the two issues all the time. How to balance the two issues and coordinate their relationship is a problem that must be faced in the criminal procedure reform. Chinese traditional procedure law studies focus on procedural justice, especially substantive justice, while the studies of procedural efficiency remain in its initial stage. The relationship between procedural justice and procedural efficiency and their coordination have yet drawn interest of legal researchers. Therefore, conducting an in-depth study of the above two issues by employing a systematic approach and proceeding from the criminal procedure as a whole is not only necessary for updating our judicial concepts, but also necessary for developing China's criminal procedure law study.

When dealing with the relationship between justice and efficiency, attention shall be paid to the following three aspects:

First, justice and efficiency are the two goals we are going after, but they are not the same. Justice is the eternal theme of the procedure system, and also the main goal of the trial procedure reform. Justice is the first and foremost goal, while efficiency is the goal that we need to take into account. As an indispensable element of the judicial system, justice is the paramount criterion. Just like J. Rawls had commented, without justice, a just society will be in vain no matter how convenient and livable it is.

Second, efficiency cannot be ignored while justice is highlighted. Focusing on efficiency is a helpless choice. If manpower and material resources are inexhaustible, and if the number of cases keeps decreasing instead of increasing, we can pursue justice ceaselessly as we like. But the reality is frustrating, the judicial resources are limited and the number of cases never stops increasing, e.g., the number of criminal proceedings remains at a high level, which forces us to make sure of efficiency. It is the most basic and logical choice, although not the best choice.[4]

Third, justice and efficiency cannot be separated. Even if summary procedure is applied, the minimum justice shall be guaranteed, such as the defendant's right to final statement. For another example, in order to fully protect the defendant's

[4]According to the provisions of China's *Criminal Procedure Law*, the first-instance trial procedure of a criminal case includes general procedure and summary procedure. But in practice, 80% of cases are subject to general procedure. There are a considerable number of cases where general procedure is applied, although they are more appropriate to be subject to summary procedure (the facts are clear, the evidence is sufficient, the methods of crime are basically the same, and the defendant has confessed everything, even if they are committed for multiple times and the money involved is in large amount), simply because the defendant may be sentenced to more than three years in prison (According to Article 174 of the *Criminal Procedure Law,* the People's Court may apply summary procedure to the cases of public prosecution where the defendants may be lawfully sentenced to fixed-term imprisonment of not more than three years, criminal detention, public surveillance or punished with fines exclusively, where the facts are clear and the evidence is sufficient, and for which the People's Procuratorate suggests or agrees to the application of summary procedure). Consequently, in the process of court hearings, the two parties of prosecution and defense have to be questioned, give testimony and cross-examined one by one over the facts that they have no objection, and wait for a dozen or even dozens of testimonies to be read out, the entire process wastes time and energy and seems like going through the motions. Moreover, there is an apparent contradiction between the relative lack of judicial resources and the increasing number of cases. Take Beijing Haidian District Procuratorate and Court for example, they accepted more than 3,000 criminal cases in the year 2001, but the number of personnel handling the cases was less than 100.

procedural rights, in a court trial, the presiding judge shall ask the defendant whether he agrees to apply summary procedure, and inform him of the legal consequences if he pleads guilty. The application of summary procedure shall be upon the defendant's consent, which is the minimum requirement. Summary procedure may not be applied if anyone, either the defendant or the defender, does not agree to it. Moreover, after summary procedure is applied, general procedure may be restored for the whole or part of the case trial if the public prosecutor, the defendant or the defender makes such request. As I've said, impartiality, justice and efficiency are not separate.

2.2 Judicial Organs Shall Execute Power Independently According to Law

It is agradual and tortuous process for China to establish and stick to the principle that judicial organs shall execute power independently according to law. China first established this principle in the Constitution in 1954, then totally repudiated it amid the Anti-Rightist struggle[5] launched in 1957, and finally deleted it from the Constitution in 1975. It was a process where the principle that judicial organs shall execute power independently according to law was gravely undermined. After the end of the Cultural Revolution, the Chinese leadership and legislators began to learn from their mistakes, and re-established this principle in the Constitution in 1982.[6] With the deepening of the reform and opening-up in the 1990s, Chinese jurisprudential circle brought in the concept of "judicial independence" and conducted more in-depth comparative studies in this field. In recent years, China has been advancing a new round of judicial reform. The 3rd and 4th Plenary Sessions of the 18th CPC Central Committee proposed to guarantee the independent execution of judicial power and procuratorial power according to law. But there are still different views on how to comprehend this principle in both theory and practice, which directly affects the depth and breadth of the judicial reform. For this reason, it is necessary to keep probing into the essential connotation of this principle, and in the meantime to clarify the mistaken ideas in cognition.[7]

[5]Cohen [1].

[6]Li and Liu [2].

[7]Considering the nature and characteristics of the procuratorial power, the "judicial organs" as mentioned in this principle only refer to the People's Courts.

2.2.1 *Judge Independence is the Essence of Judicial Organs' Independent Execution of Power According to Law*

2.2.1.1 Scientific Connotation of Judge Independence

The core value of judicial organs' independent execution of power according to law is to guarantee the judge independence, which should be understood from four aspects as follows:

(1) Substantial independence of judge. When handling a case, a judge must abide by the law, follow his conscience, and shut off all distractions. Trial is a rational activity in need of reasoning. The judge shall decide a case through rational thinking on basis of evidence and his own experience. In this regard, Article 38 of the German judges law (Deutsches Richtergesetz) requires all judges to take an oath before a public trial to swear allegiance to the basic law, perform the duties of a judge according to law, decide a case with best knowledge and conscience, and respect only facts and justice, regardless of the identity and status of the parties to the case.

(2) External independence of judge. It means that all judges are free from the interference of the legislative and administrative organs, as well as other groups and individuals when handling a specific case. Such independence is sometimes known as "judicial independence" in a narrow sense or "court independence". It includes the following aspects of content: (i) Judges are independent of the legislative body. The legislative body may not give instructions to judges when they are trying a specific case. In principle, the legislative body is empowered to supervise the trial in an abstract manner. Even if it is supervising the trial in a concrete manner, the scope of the supervision shall be strictly limited; and it should be ex post facto supervision, rather than interim and specific instructions. (ii) Judges are independent of the administrative organs. Judicial power shall restrict administrative power, which is an important manifestation of law-based governance. Due to its innate fragility, judicial power is extremely vulnerable to the intrusion of overwhelming administrative power. Therefore, judges shall be independent of the administrative organs in terms of human, financial and material resources, especially independent of local administrative organs, so that they can shun from the illegal interference by the administrative organs, and have exclusive jurisdiction over cases and ultimacy of judgment. (iii) Judges are independent of political parties and other organizations and individuals. From a global perspective, it is a common practice that no political party is allowed to interfere with the trial of specific cases. The ruling party shall, both politically and organizationally, guarantee independent execution of judicial power according to law, and prevent it from any illegal interference for local interests. In addition, the freedom of media coverage may not impede the independence of judge.

(3) Internal independence of judge. It means that judges are an independent subject of trial (including the collegiate bench) at court; they are exempted from the

interference of the president of the court or the chief judge of a division, and free from the non-procedural instructions of the courts at higher levels. Judges shall handle cases impartially and according to law. After all, law is paramount for trying cases in contrast to all superior-subordinate relationships.

(4) Identity independence of judge. It means that the position and term of a judge shall be guaranteed so that he can be exempted from administrative interference. According to Article 1(1) of the *IBA Minimum Standards of Judicial Independence*, which was adopted by the 19th Annual Meeting of the International Bar Association held in New Delhi in 1982, judges shall have identity independence and substantial independence. An independent identity is a prerequisite for realizing judge independence. Without identity independence, the genuine independence of judge will be in vain, let alone judicial impartiality. Therefore, establishing the identity independence of judges is an important guarantee for establishing their authority and realizing judicial impartiality.

2.2.1.2 Judge Independence is the Core and Foothold of Judicial Organs' Independent Execution of Power According to Law

In order to obtain an accurate understanding of the value of judge independence, we need to analyze the relationship among judicial independence, court independence and judge independence. Regarding the tripartite relationship, there are different views and opinions in academic circle, and a variety of practices in different countries. Some scholars argue that judicial independence includes court independence and judge independence, so there is no need to specially mention court independence and judge independence which is the proper meaning of judicial independence. Others hold that court independence is synonymous with judicial independence, and they are in fact the same thing. In the western world, some countries put judicial independence at the first place, while others directly take judge independence as a constitutional and legal principle. In China, both constitution and laws provide for court independence, but deny judge independence. These different viewpoints and legal provisions directly affect the construction of judge system and the realization of judicial justice of each country. In my opinion, judicial independence, court independence and judge independence are three issues with different focus; no one can replace the other or equate with the other. Judge independence is the core and the foothold of court independence, while judicial independence and court independence are important guarantee and prerequisite for realizing judge independence.

Judicial independence is a mechanism for the state power distribution. In feudal society, legislative, judicial and administrative powers were at the hands of hereditary rulers. The enlightenment thinkers that were dissatisfied with this autocracy brought forth the idea of "separation of powers, checks and balances", arguing that judicial power should remain independent so as to restrict administrative and legislative powers.

According to Montesquieu, freedom exists only in the countries where power is not abused, but it is age-old truth that power holders are apt to abuse power.

The people with power never stop using it until they reach the boundary of power. Considering the nature of thing, to prevent the abuse of power, we must restrict one power with another one. If judicial power is not separated from legislative and administrative powers, freedom will be in vain. If judicial power and legislative power are combined into one, the lives and freedom of citizens will be arbitrarily treated, because judges are legislators at the same time. If judicial power and administrative power are combined into one, judges will be as powerful as oppressors.[8]

Based on the above idea, judicial independence is gradually accepted by capitalist countries. As for the distribution of state power, judicial independence is merely an abstract concept. The transformation of judicial independence from the abstract to the concrete is undertaken by specific organizations and individuals, so the court becomes the carrier for realizing judicial independence, and judicial independence is then transformed into court independence. As an organization that executes the state judicial power, the court shall have an independent status and self-own material resources to resist against the illegal interference of the legislative and administrative organs, so as to effectively implement the principle of rule of law. The nature of judicial power determines that it is a process for making a rational judgment of specific disputes.

As an organization, the court is incapable of rational thinking, but providing an organizational guarantee to resist against the illegal interference of legislative and administrative organs. But the court's function of judicial adjudication is performed by individual judges. In other words, judges are the subject that realizes judicial independence, and the abstract judicial independence is manifested by judge independence. So it can be said that that judicial independence is a principle for state power distribution and an abstract concept. Court independence is the first step to concretize judicial independence; and the function of court is to resist against the illegal interference of legislative and administrative organs, as well as other political parties and organizations. It is judge independence that finally realizes judicial independence. Therefore, judge independence is the core of judicial independence, and the manifestation of judicial independence from the abstract to the concrete. If there is only judicial independence but judge independence, then judicial independence is unable to exist at all. If judicial independence is concretized as court independence, then it is no more than a kind of nominal independence. The various disadvantages arising from judicial non-independence are bound to spread; for example, China's judicial organs are subjected to the illegal interference of legislative and administrative organs, local party and government agencies, and some individual officials, it is attributed incomplete judicial independence. If judicial independence is an important guarantee for judicial justice, then judge independence is the concrete realization of judicial justice.

[8]Montesquieu [3].

2.2.1.3 "Handling Cases According to Law" is the Essence of Judge Independence

In reference to the constitutions, basic laws and judicial practices of many countries, their emphasis on judge independence is in essence to require judges to decide cases "only by obeying the law" and "in good conscience". Just like Karl Marx had commented, "Judges are the kings of the legal world. They have no superiors except the law". Take some legal provisions of different countries for example, Article 97(1) of the Basic Law of Germany stipulates that judges shall perform their functions and powers independently and only obey the law. Article 76 of the Constitution of Japan stipulates that judicial power belongs to the Supreme Court and the inferior courts as established according to law…All judges' independent performance of functions and powers in good conscience is only bound by the Constitution and laws. In the Constitution of the Republic of Korea, Article 101(1) stipulates that judicial power belongs to the courts made up of judges; and Article 103 stipulates that judges shall try cases independently in accordance with the Constitution and laws in their conscience. In the Constitution of the Russian Federation, Article 118(1) stipulates that the judicial power in the Russian Federation is executed only by the courts; and Article 120(1) stipulates judges are independent and subject only to the Constitution of the Russian Federation and federal laws. Among all countries, the United States is the one most affected by the separation of powers. Section 1 of the Constitution of the US stipulates that "the judicial power of the United States shall be vested in one supreme court, and in such inferior courts as the Congress may from time to time ordain and establish. The judges, both of the supreme and inferior courts, shall hold their offices during good behavior, and shall, at stated times, receive for their services a compensation, which shall not be diminished during their continuance in office". The US Constitution does not provide that judges must decide cases according to law, but on the eve of drawing up the Constitution, those who supported judicial independence explained why they were in favor of independent judiciary: independent judiciary is able to restrict the overly centralized powers of the legislative and administrative organs; they agreed with Montesquieu that judges shall be free from outside interference, so that their judgment could reflect an accurate interpretation of legal provisions.[9] In the US Constitution, the provisions for judges' devotion to their duty and for their compensation have an ultimate goal of protecting them from being subject to external legislative and administrative forces, and ensuring their independent execution of power according to law. Besides, one of the core contents in the US doctrines of judicial independence is that judges shall execute their power independently according to law.[10] In addition, relevant international conventions also make it clear that judges are restricted only by law and free from

[9]Liao [4].

[10]ABA, *An independent judiciary*, p. 11. In reference to the famous case of Marbury v. Madison (1803) in the US, we can find that judicial independence plays a role of restricting political power, but the judges need to refer to the facts to make an independent judgment, which is a core content of judicial independence.

interference by external factors. For example, Article 22 of the *Basic Principles on the Independence of the Judiciary* provides that the judiciary shall remain impartial when handling cases, and make a judgment based on facts and in accordance with legal provisions, instead of being restricted or directly or indirectly affected by improper influence, incitement, pressure, threat or interference, regardless of where they come from or for whatever reason. In short, the core value of judicial independence, which is a criterion of justice, is to emphasize the judge independence, i.e., "judges" execute power independently and "according to law".

2.2.1.4 Theoretical Basis of Judge Independence

(1) Epistemological basis

From the perspective of dialectical-materialist epistemology, cognition is the subject's active reflection of the object. The dialectical development process of human cognition is an infinitely repetitive process from perceptual cognition to rational cognition, and then rational cognition will return to perceptual cognition, so that our cognition gradually approaches to truthful cognition. Marxist epistemology tells that the subject of cognition must be a person with thinking ability, and that person must make a rational judgment through personal perception; otherwise, cognition will be out of the question. Judicial activities are in essence a process of cognition and judgment. The judges will, through investigation, cross-examination, analysis and reasoning of the evidence provided by the parties to the dispute, form a kind of conviction in their heart; after this conviction ascends from perceptual knowledge to rational knowledge, the judges will make a specific decision in the end. Since the court is an organization without thinking ability, it cannot function as the subject of judgment. In this sense, if we emphasize only court independence and do not implement it into judge independence, we will break away with Marxist epistemology. As required by epistemology, judicial judgments must be based on the personal experience of judges; it is the judges that preside over trials in person that are able to make correct judgments. There are circumstances where examination and approval are made by authorities at different levels, judges do not make judgments or judgment-makers do not try cases, they are contrary to the scientific law of Marxist epistemology, and also an undesirable consequence due to the failure to establish the independent status of judges. In short, judge independence is a concrete manifestation of Marxist epistemology in judicial activities.

(2) Judge independence is determined by the nature of judicial power.

Judicial activities are a mechanism for resolving disputes and a ruling process for realizing social justice, which determines judicial power to have two natures as being neutral and personally experienced. The neutrality of judicial power indicates that judges may not have bias against any party to the dispute or have any conflict of interest with either party. An important guarantee for neutrality is the independence of judges. Although independence and neutrality are different concepts, the former is an essential condition for judges to maintain neutrality and impartiality. The second nature of judicial power is being personally experienced. Some scholars argue that judges need to "closely observe" the parties that make statements and the witnesses that give testimony, so that the judgments made on this basis would be closer to the facts and more convincing.[11] Since judicial power has such nature, the one that makes independent judgments shall be the judges rather than the court as a whole. "The system of independent trial in courts excludes the individual judges from making independent judgments, which is bound to generalize specific issues, so that all judges cannot make specific judgments of specific cases, but make general judgments based on general experiences and general circumstances, which will result in less objective and accurate judgments".[12] Therefore, judge independence is an inevitable requirement of the nature of judicial power.

(3) Judge independence is an inevitable requirement of judicial justice

Impartiality is the life of justice, and it is achieved only through the impartial decisions made by the judges. The American scholar J. N. Frank describes an ideal judge as an upright arbiter who uses intelligent discretion to make fair judgments for the parties.[13] In order to make judgments independently, judges shall have an independent status. Just like Karl Marx had commented, "Judges are the kings of the legal world. They have no superiors except the law". Based on their expertise, judges are responsible for interpreting the law when it is applied to a specific occasion. If the judicial power is subordinated to or at the mercy of others, the cases, which are irrelevant to the judges, will become their own cases. If someone in power gives orders or instructions to judges, then they have to obey the will of the powerful in addition to observing the law. When the will of the powerful conflicts with the universal will of the law, a problem will arise as to which the judges should be obedient. At this time, the judgment of the case is associated with the reverence for the powerful, and the reverence for the powerful affects the career of the judges. "To control one's life is tantamount to control his will". To dominate the judges is to dominate their judgment of the case, and the judges may deviate from the law for fear of the powerful. In a word, judge independence is an important guarantee for achieving judicial justice and resisting judicial corruption.

(4) Judge independence is an inevitable requirement of the judge responsibility system

The judge responsibility system is an important part of the judge system. The most basic legal idea is that where there is right, there is responsibility. Under the condition that the court independence system is implemented, the court executes the right to trial as a whole, the result of trial seems like a product, and the entire court shall be responsible for the product quality. However, "everybody's business is nobody's

[11]He [5].

[12]Liu [6].

[13]Frank [7].

business". Under such a system, a case is passed on to different levels for approval, i.e., it shall be approved by the chief judge of a division, the president of the court, the court's judicial committee, and even a higher court. Consequently, once a misjudged case occurs, all of the parties involved are responsible, but no one is held accountable. If an independent adjudication system for judges is established, then judges will decide a case on their own, it goes without saying that the judges themselves shall bear the responsibility for misjudged cases. This system will help judges get rid of dependence on others, strengthen sense of responsibility, improve professional quality, and speed up the improvement of the judge system.

2.2.2 *Misunderstandings of the Principle of Independent Execution of Power by the Judicial Organs According to Law*

2.2.2.1 Judicial Independence and Separation of Powers

"Judicial independence" is an unavoidable concept when talking about the principle of independent execution of power by the judicial organs according to law. In China, some state organs argue that to promote "judicial independence" is to follow the political path of "separation of powers" in Western countries. It sounds like that judicial independence is a product of the Western political system of "separation of powers" and not applicable in China. In fact, judicial independence is first and foremost a principle for judicial activities, rather than a privilege deriving from the political system of "separation of powers" in the West. Therefore, it is reasonable for us to absorb and learn from the contents of "judicial independence" that conform to the judicial rules.

(1) Judicial independence is primarily a judicial principle

Judicial independence was born in the West in the Age of Enlightenment. It was first elaborated in full by Montesquieu. Judicial independence is a proposition that upholds separation and check of powers, which is against the practice in the feudal society where legislative, administrative and judicial powers were at the hands of the monarch. According to Montesquieu, separation of powers is mainly a political system that guarantees the freedom of people. He said there are three kinds of powers in a country, i.e., legislative power, administrative power and judicial power. If judicial power and administrative power are held by the same person or the same authority, freedom will be in vain; if judicial power is not separated from legislative power and administrative power, freedom cannot exist either; if judicial power is merged with legislative power, the lives and freedom of citizens will be trampled upon, since judges themselves have the power to suppress others.[14] Regarding the domination of things, in order to prevent the abuse of power, we must check power by power.[15]

As an important connotation of the thought of separation of powers, the concept of "judicial independence" mentioned here constitutes the theoretical basis for the reform of political system. It was taken by the bourgeois revolutionists as a crucial part of their revolutionary slogan or guiding ideology, and significantly influenced the subsequent reform of the national political system. After the bourgeois revolution won victory, a new political system based on the theory of separation of powers was established. The legislative, administrative and judicial powers were separately executed by the parliament, the president (cabinet) and the court, so that the three subjects of power could restrict each other.[16] As a major achievement of the political change, judicial independence was embodied in this political system. In short, the theory of judicial independence was initially proposed as a mechanism for state power distribution, and aimed at achieving the separation, check and balance of powers; that's why the judicial independence in this sense has a strong political implication.

Judicial independence was born on basis of the theory of "separation of powers", but it does not mean that judicial independence is unreachable without "separation of powers", since they can be separated. Judicial independence requires formal independence, which in essence means independence of powers and functions, i.e., legislative, administrative and judicial functions cannot be mixed or replaced with each other, instead of remaining equal and mutually checked as required by "separation of powers". Therefore, as long as legislative, administrative and judicial functions are distinguishable and irreplaceable in operation, the formal requirements of judicial independence will be available. In other words, as long as the improper influence of administrative and legislative organs on judicial organs is ruled out, the system either for separation of powers or for unity of legislature and administration will meet the formal requirements of judicial independence.

In fact, no matter it is a country with separation of powers of the one with unity of legislature and administration, its judicial activities are influenced by both legislative and political forces, including legitimate and illegitimate influences, only to varying degrees. "The justice completely independent of politics does not exist". "In a country, especially in a Western country, various political forces are influencing the justice with explicit or implicit ways and means".[17] For example, successive US presidents are eager to appoint and dismiss the justices of the Supreme Court, so that they can designate members of their own party to preside over the Supreme Court and influence its judicial activities. It is a blunt truth that the US administrations never make secret of it. When the US presidents are about to appoint the justices

---

[14] Montesquieu [8], p. 184.

[15] Montesquieu [8], p. 183.

[16] La Constitution de l'an I (1793), which was formulated during the Great French Revolution, included the content about separation of powers. The thought of separation of powers presented by Montesquieu also had a great influence on the American constitution makers and became an important nation-building theory in the United States.

[17] Jiang [9].

of the Supreme Court, the foremost criterion for the candidates is their "political acceptability" and "ideological appropriateness".[18] In this sense, we are ought to dilute the relationship between judicial independence and separation of powers, and then gradually dilute its political implication.

It is rather a bias if judicial independence is comprehended only from a political perspective. Although judicial independence was born as a product of the political arrangements upon the bourgeois revolution, with the establishment of bourgeois regimes, judicial independence was no longer a purely political arrangement, but more like a basic principle of justice and the core thought guiding the operation of justice, and its essence is to ensure that judicial organs independently execute judicial power in accordance with law. This epitomizes the characteristics of justice itself and the rules of justice, which China should follow while advancing the independent execution of powers by judicial organs according to law.

(2) Judicial independence can exist beyond separation of powers.

The essence of the principle of judicial independence is that judges execute their power independently according to law and this should become a value consensus. There is no necessity for us to still look at this principle with any ideological "colored spectacles". Judicial independence can be divided into external independence, internal independence, identity independence and substantial independence. External independence means that judicial power is independent of legislative and administrative powers.

Judicial independence is closely related to the separation of powers, because the theory of separation of powers first provides the institutional possibility for judicial independence, i.e., it guarantees its external independence. But it cannot be assumed that judicial independence can only exist under the framework of separation of powers, and the two are tied together. Undeniably, according to the theory of separation of powers, legislative power, administrative power and judicial power are on an equal footing and mutually restricted. Under this institutional framework, judicial power can be independent of legislative and administrative powers, and gain a wide range of independence.

The external requirement of judicial independence lies not in the "separation of powers", but in the separation of powers and functions. The socialist countries, although they do not implement the separation of powers, follow the basic principle of separation and restriction of powers for distributing state powers. Judicial power is derived from legislative power, after that, it will become relatively independent. In fact, it is difficult for legislative power to interfere with judicial power, which is determined by the characteristics of legislative power itself. Judicial power and administrative power are both derivatives of legislative power and they are on an equal footing. Under the framework of powers, either the interference of administrative power on judicial power or such interference under the theory of separation of powers is not that prominent. For this reason, judicial independence in socialist countries is institutionally guaranteed; we cannot take for granted that the principle of judicial

[18] Song [10].

independence is only applicable in capitalist countries that implement the separation of powers.

In fact, in socialist countries such as Vietnam and Cuba, their constitutions have provided for the principle of judicial independence. For example, Article 122 of the *Constitution of the Republic of Cuba* stipulates that judges shall execute judicial power independently and they are subject only to law. Article 130 of the *Constitution of the Socialist Republic of Vietnam* stipulates that both judges and jurors shall try cases independently and they are subject only to law. It can be seen that "judicial independence is not an exclusive product of capitalist countries or linked up with separation of powers".[19] While China is promoting judicial independence, some people worry that judicial independence is to deny the system of people's congress, which is an unnecessary misinterpretation of judicial independence, because they are bundling judicial independence with separation of powers and it is more likely that they still are affected by a certain ideological concept.

In both capitalist and socialist countries, the goal of justice is to pursue impartiality. Judicial independence as an important guarantee for achieving impartiality must be available in all countries. It is exactly because of this, judicial independence has become a value consensus that is widely recognized across the world and written into the international legal documents. In the 1980s and 1990s, a series of specialized international legal documents that stipulate the principle of judicial independence were adopted, including *the IBA Minimum Standards of Judicial Independence (1982), the Universal Declaration on the Independence of Justice (1983), the United Nations Basic Principles on the Independence of the Judiciary (1985), the Madrid Principles on the Relationship between the Media and Judicial Independence* (1994), and *the Beijing Statement of Principles of the Independence of the Judiciary in the Lawasia Region (1995)*.

(3) Judicial independence is compatible with the system of people's congress

Despite of all efforts, China still finds it hard to practically implement the principle of judicial independence, the main reason is that this principle has been observed with a political and ideological perspective. The *Constitution of China* stipulates that the country implements the system of people's congress and the structure of "the People's Government, the People's Court and the People's Procuratorate". If we advocate judicial independence based on separation of powers, it is tantamount to embark on an erroneous path of changing our political direction, and destroy the fruits of victory of Chinese people's social revolution led by the CPC. Given, upon the founding of the People's Republic of China, the disputes over judicial independence were tainted with a strong political color and taken as a contradiction between "ourselves and the enemy". Some scholars have pointed out that the principle of judicial independence is a bourgeois legal principle and incompatible with the socialist legal system.[20] The essence of judicial independence is to "oppose the Party's leadership in trial work, tamper the nature and tasks of the People's Court, and replace the proletarian legal

[19]Chen [11].

[20]Kang [12].

viewpoints and system with those of the bourgeoisie", "if the Party has no say in a particular trial, it is to abolish its leadership".[21]

Of course, we should look at this issue dialectically. Judicial independence, as a basic principle to guide the judiciary, is in line with the rules of justice, and no country can exclude this principle. However, it should be noted that judicial independence is a collection of systems, so there may be differences in system construction, which conforms to the reality of countries around the world. The judicial independence in China is the one in the Chinese context, i.e., it is the judicial independence divorced from the theory of separation of powers, removing the "cover" of the principle of judicial independence and retaining its core. That's why this judicial independence has no impact on China's existing political system. Moreover, China implements the system of people's congress and the structure of "the People's Government, the People's Court and the People's Procuratorate". Under this institutional framework, the People's Courts are the subject executing judicial power, which accords with the international norms. But the judicial power of the People's Courts and legislative power are not equal; the former is a lower-rank power, which is essentially different from the situation in western capitalist countries. However, it is only a difference in the political system, and it does not mean that China has no judicial independence. In fact, judicial independence exists in both western countries that implement separation of powers and China that implements the system of people's congress. Despite of different approaches, the two types of judicial independence pursue the same goal of law-based judgment and social justice. They are ought to be fairly treated. Therefore, we have no reason to shun from the concept of "judicial independence", but ensure that the People's Courts and the People's Procuratorates independently execute their functions and powers according to law by satisfying the essential requirements of judicial independence and combining with China's judicial reality.

It is of great significance to highlight judicial independence in China. In practice, there are close ties between the Party and the judiciary, between the people's congress and the judiciary, and between the administration and the judiciary. Such close ties should be avoided becoming a hindrance to judicial justice. The essence of judicial independence is that the concept of judging cases according to law provides a basic criterion for handling the relationship between the Party and the judiciary, and between the people's congress and the judiciary, i.e., there is a bottom line for the Party's leadership and the system of people's congress, and the judicial organs are unimpeded in executing their judicial and procuratorial powers independently and impartially according to law. The root cause for the past lessons is that we had bias against judicial independence and failed to make sure of it. Therefore, the Third Plenary Session of the 11th CPC Central Committee drew lessons from history and clearly stated that "the procuratorial organs and judicial organs must maintain their due independence". Later, Article 4 of the *Organization Law of the People's Courts* and Article 9 of the *Organization Law of the People's Procuratorates*, which were adopted at the Second Session of the 5th National People's Congress, respectively reaffirm that "the People's Courts conduct trials independently and they are

[21] Rou and Hefang [13].

subject only to law" and "the People's Procuratorates execute their procuratorial power independently according to law and they are free from any interference by other administrative organs, groups and individuals". Moreover, Articles 126 and 131 of the *Constitution (1982)* reiterate the principle of independent execution of functions and powers by the People's Courts and the People's Procuratorates according to law. All the above legal provisions are embodiments of the principle of judicial independence in the Chinese context.

2.2.2.2 Judicial Independence and the Party's Leadership

(1) The two are not contradictory

In the early days after the founding of the People's Republic of China, there were voices that implementing judicial independence in China was to deny the CPC's leadership. Such voices are still heard nowadays although China has achieved great success in its legal system construction. For example, at the first Central Political and Judicial Work Conference held in 1981, some delegates pointed out that "if we implement judicial independence, how can we uphold the Party's leadership? Some people contend that the courts should try cases independently and only obey the law, they may not be interfered by any organ, social group or individual. In this case, how will the courts follow the leadership of the Party? How can they remain responsible to the the National People's Congress and its Standing Committee?"[22] Such point of view has never vanished since then.

This is why the current judicial reform is difficult to achieve major breakthroughs regarding the issue of judicial independence. Many Party members believe that judicial independence will deny the Party's leadership over judicial work. In fact, the emphasis on judicial independence in China does not deny the Party's leadership, but realizes the scientific transformation of the Party's leadership style. The disadvantages of traditional leadership style, which features approval of cases by the Party committee, have been exposed and become the crux of many problems. Given this, if the Party's leadership style fails to keep pace with the times and realize the scientific transformation, it will cause more negative effects. In order to transform the Party's leadership style, the key requirement is to ensure judicial independence, i.e., to ensure that the judicial organs independently perform their functions and powers and make it the core standard of the Party's leadership.

Moreover, as far as the connotation of judicial independence is concerned, it has no implications that oppose the CPC's leadership. The essence of judicial independence requires the judicial organs to "handle cases according to law", which includes two meanings: First, other organs, social groups and individuals may not interfere with the judicial organs' handling of cases according to law, so as to ensure that the judicial organs can independently apply laws and resolve disputes; Second, judicial independence also requires that the independence of the case-handling authorities should be

[22]See Ref. [14].

"law-based", i.e., judicial independence is within the legal framework, and the judicial organs must independently execute their functions and powers according to law. This shows that judicial independence is the unity of "independence" and "restriction" of the judicial organs. The two meanings of judicial independence are integrated; none of one can be ignored, otherwise, it may mislead both the understanding and practice of judicial independence.

In China, it is the CPC that has led the people in enacting the Constitution and laws, so the Constitution and laws reflect the will and interests of the Party and the people. In view of this, as long as the judicial organs execute their powers independently according to law, the leadership of the Party could be achieved. The "restrictive" nature of judicial independence indicates that all cases shall be handled pursuant to law, i.e., pursuant to the laws enacted by the people under the Party's leadership. It can be said that handling cases according to law is to realize the will and interests of the Party and the people, rather than deny the Party's leadership. It is already acknowledged by lots of scholars. "In a certain sense, laws embody the guidelines and policies of the ruling party. The party organizations also play a leading and supervisory role inside the judicial organs. Therefore, the judicial organs handle cases strictly according to law can demonstrate the Party's leadership".[23] "Obeying nothing but law is the implementation of the will of the proletariat and the obedience to the Party's leadership, rather than separation from the Party's leadership. Regarding the argument that 'independent trial' is inconsistent with the Party's leadership, it is in fact incompatible with the system of 'approval of cases by Party Secretary'.[24] It should be noted that "secretary approval" and the Party's leadership are two different issues. Recognizing the Party's leadership does not mean that the "secretary approval" approach must be adopted; conversely, negating the "secretary approval" approach is not necessarily to negate the Party's leadership. Therefore, these two issues may not be mixed with each other.

(2) Respecting judicial independence is the best way to realize the Party's leadership

Currently, the Party's leadership style to the judicial work is problematic and controversial; the root cause for this is that the Party is not "leading" the judicial organs but "acting" as the judicial organs. It causes more harm than good from the Party's own point of view. The Party does not have infinite energy and abilities,[25] so it is unable to penetrate into all aspects of society or lead all kinds of tasks impartially. Therefore,

[23] Li and Liu [15].

[24] Liao [16].

[25] Some scholars have pointed out that "the Secretary for the Political and Judiciary Committee is usually a part-time job, since he has to take charge of the political and legal work while dealing with other matters. But the political and judiciary work is so complicated that it involves the public security organs, People's Procuratorates and People's Courts. How can the Secretary have plenty of energy to attend to each and every aspect of a matter? To be honest, he can hardly have time to read the case files, let alone personally participate in the case investigation. It is more often to see that he examines and approves several cases concurrently once in a month or two. In that case, how can the Secretary remain keen and penetrative and free from making any bureaucratic acts? Liao [16].

the Party's leadership should be focused, rather than "going about several tasks at a time". Moreover, the trial of cases by the Party Committee and the approval of cases by the Party Secretary will transfer judicial responsibilities and risks. Objectively speaking, the judicial work itself contains certain risks. No country or society can avoid the occurrence of misjudged cases. What we can do is to seek justice as objectively and prudently as possible under the judicial system. Once a misjudged case occurs, the judicial organs are due to bear certain responsibilities. But the current leadership style of the Party makes it undertake the judicial responsibilities which are ought to be borne by the judicial organs, and objectively bear unnecessary risks, which may undermine the Party's leading authority.

Judicial power is the most secure power among all state powers. The judiciary is a mechanism for solving disputes, so its intervention of social life is always passive. Only when there is a dispute or lawsuit, judicial intervention will become available. "The judiciary...has no influence over either the sword or the purse; no direction either of the strength or of the wealth of the society; and can take no active resolution whatever". "The judiciary to be the weakest and most impartial of the three branches", its expansion is limited and restricted, and it is the least interfering and harmful.[26] Comparatively speaking, judicial power is on the whole a passive power.

According to Montesquieu, judicial power does not exist to some extent.[27] The multiple procedural subjects in a judicial activity are able to restrain judicial power. More importantly, judicial activities must follow their own rules and be strictly subject to law. As long as all the rights, duties and responsibilities are prescribed by law, judicial activities shall observe such provisions. Because of this, the judiciary is the "least dangerous branch" of a country, and it cannot be the vanguard of system reform; instead, it can only reflect the results of system reform.[28]

In other words, the judiciary does not constitute an impact on the national political system, it merely reflects the results of the national political reform. Therefore, based on the rules of judicial activities, as long as the will and interests of the Party and the people could be manifested through legislation, the purpose of the Party leading judicial activities can be substantially achieved. There is no need for the Party to adopt the current leadership style; instead, paying respect for judicial independence is a more scientific and sustainable way of leadership. There are two core elements of this leadership style: The first is to ensure the Party's leadership, but the Party can only be the leader of legal and policy-making affairs. The second is to respect the independent execution of powers by the judicial organs according to law and refrain from interfering with the handling of cases by the judicial organs. Since the formulation and modification of laws and policies shall follow certain procedures, the judicial organs boast better stability and a higher level of rule of law as compared with individual Party leaders. Therefore, respect for judicial independence is to improve the rule-of-law level and standardization of the Party's leadership style, and make it more scientific and sustainable.

---

[26]Hamilton et al. [17].

[27]Montesquieu [8], p. 188.

[28]Bickel [18], in Su [19], p. 433.

At the beginning of the founding of the People's Republic of China, Comrade Liu Shaoqi made it clear that "the independent trial by the courts is right and stipulated by the Constitution, neither the Party Committee nor the government should interfere in their trial of cases". "Do not say that political legal organs should absolutely follow the leadership of the Party Committees at all levels. How can the former still follow the latter's leadership when it breaks the law? If the decision of local Party Committee is inconsistent with the law or the Central Government's policy, which one should we follow? In this case, we should obey the law and follow the policy of the Central Government".[29]

In September 1979 when the reform and opening up was launched not long ago, the CPC Central Committee issued the *Instructions on Resolutely Ensuring the Practical Implementation of the Criminal Law and the Criminal Procedure Law* (known as the Document No. 64), which proposed that "in order to strengthen the Party's leadership over judicial work, the most important thing is to ensure the implementation of laws, give full play to the role of the judicial organs by making the People's Procuratorates independently execute their procuratorial power and the People's Courts independently execute their judicial power, and protect them from the intervention by other administrative organs, groups and individuals. The enactment of national laws and the establishment of the judicial organs are attributed to the Party's leadership. Anyone who does not respect the law and the functions and powers of the judicial organs will undermine the Party's leadership and prestige". This document also stated to "abolish the system for examining and approving cases by the Party Committees at all levels".

In 1986, Comrade Deng Xiaoping pointed out that "we must leave matters that fall within the scope of the law to judicial institutions; it is not appropriate for the Party to concern itself with such matters". "If the Party intervenes in everything, it will not help the people understand the importance of the rule of law".[30] This shows that the CPC has always had a clear understanding of its leadership in judicial work. This rational knowledge shall become a consensus for guiding the current judicial system reform.

2.2.3 Chinese Mode of Judicial Organs' Independent Execution of Powers and Its Deviation

2.2.3.1 Institutional Mode

Article 126 of the *Constitution of China* states that "the People's Courts exercise judicial power independently in accordance with the provisions of law, and not subject to interference by any administrative organ, public organization or individual". This is the constitutional expression of the principle of independent execution of functions

[29]See Ref. [20].

[30]See Ref. [21].

and powers with Chinese characteristics. This principle can be expounded from the four specific modes as follows:

First, the principle of independent execution of functions and powers with Chinese characteristics according to law only includes the independence of courts as a whole. Regarding the provision in Article 126 of the *Constitution of China*, there are different interpretations as to whether this principle has any implication of independence of judges. The general opinion in the academic circle is that Article 126 merely provides for the independence of courts as a whole, but not endorse the independence of judges. Although the independence of courts as a whole is underscored, such independence only involves external independence rather than internal independence of courts, i.e., independence of judges. Therefore, when trying cases in the court, each judge shall submit to the leadership of the court as a whole.

Second, the relationship between the independent execution of functions and powers with Chinese characteristics according to law and local governments. In accordance with China's Constitution and relevant organizational laws, the president of the Supreme People's Court is elected by the NPC, while the vice president, the chief judge and the deputy chief judge of a division, and judges are appointed and dismissed by the Standing Committee of the NPC; the president of local People's Courts at all levels is elected by the local people's congresses at all levels, while the vice president, the chief judge and the deputy chief judge of a division, and judges are appointed and dismissed by the standing committees of local people's congresses at all levels. In China, the creation of courts is determined by the system of people's congress which is the fundamental political system. As the institutional arrangement of China's current Constitution, the system of people's congress is of both legality and legitimacy. But it should be noted that due to some problems in the operation of the system of people's congress, such as local people's congresses at all levels are under the influence of local party committees and governments, the People's Courts are strongly "localized" and they are difficult to resist against the improper interference by local Party and government organs.

Third, the relationship between the independent execution of functions and powers with Chinese characteristics according to law and the Party's leadership. Upholding the Party's leadership is a basic constitutional practice in China. The Party's leadership of judicial work is a basic principle and a summary of China's long-term revolution and practices. At the beginning of the founding of the People's Republic of China, Dong Biwu, then President of the Supreme People's Court, stated that the Party is the core of all work and that all work of the People's Courts is carried out under the leadership of the Party.[31] However, regarding the specific ways of the Party's leadership of judicial work, there are different perceptions and practices in different periods. Prior to the founding of the People's Republic of China, the practice of "intra-party approval" had been prevailing. Arrests, trials, and especially the death penalty, decided by the People's Courts must be approved by the Party Committees at the same level. The particularly important cases required the approval of the Party

[31] See Ref. [22].

Central Committee.[32] After the reform and opening up was initiated, in view of the shortcomings of the "intra-party approval", the CPC Central Committee issued the *Instructions on Resolutely Ensuring the Practical Implementation of the Criminal Law and the Criminal Procedure Law* on September 9, 1979, declaring to abolish the approval of cases by the Party Committees at all levels. Later, the Commission for Political and Legal Affairs was formed to coordinate the handling and joint investigation of cases, and instruct the handling of individual cases, which has become the Party's specific leadership style of judicial work. In short, regardless of the specific leadership style, let the Party lead the judicial work will remain a basic principle.

Fourth, the relationship between the independent execution of functions and powers with Chinese characteristics according to law and the three organs. To understand the principle of independent execution of functions and powers by the judicial organs according to law in China, there is need to learn about the relationship among the three organs: the courts, the procuratorates and the public security organs. According to Article 135 of the *Constitution of China*, "the People's Courts, the People's Procuratorates and the public security organs shall, in handling criminal cases, divide their functions, each taking responsibility for its own work, and they shall coordinate their efforts and check each other to ensure the correct and effective enforcement of law".[33] From the perspective of division of functions and procedural collaboration, this principle has certain positive significance. But the "law in practice" is far from the "law on paper", and the independent execution of functions and powers with Chinese characteristics according to law is characterized by "non-independence". This is mainly manifested in two points: The first is that the courts are the weakest branch among the three organs, while the public security organs are a powerful government department, thus making the courts incapable of effectively restricting the public security organs, but subject to their improper interference. The procuratorates, with the power of legal supervision, can easily veto the effective judgment made by the courts. The second is the convergence of functions among the three organs, i.e., the functional goals of the courts also focus on cracking down on crimes, and ignore the protection of human rights and the restrictions on public security organs and procuratorates.

2.2.3.2 The Deviation of Independent Execution of Functions and Powers by Chinese Judicial Organs According to Law

China's judiciary lacks independence, such shortcoming is already known to both legal practitioners and scholars. It is beyond question that such shortcoming has undermined the impartiality and authority of the judiciary. Therefore, building an impartial, efficient and authoritative socialist judicial system has become the goal of

---

[32] Fan [23].

[33] The author has commented on this principle from the perspective of investigation and prosecution. Chen and Hao [24].

China's judicial reform.[34] Specifically, the lack of independence of the judiciary has two major characteristics, i.e., the localization of the judiciary and the administration of the judiciary, which have become the "chronic diseases" that affect the independent execution of functions and powers by the judicial organs.

First, the localization of the judiciary makes the courts dependent on local Party and government organs. This is mainly reflected in the following three aspects: (1) Since the judicial organs are created by the people's congresses at the same level, they are obliged to report their work to the congresses and take orders from them, thus making them like "local government organs". The judicial organs deal with the conflicts of interest and their decisions will redistribute interests; that's why "localized" judicial organs usually give priority to safeguarding local interests. (2) Failure to balance the relationship between the Party's leadership and independent execution of judicial power. On the one hand, in line with the principle of the Party assuming the responsibility for cadres' affairs, the people's congresses or their standing committees cannot appoint the president of the local courts, the chief judge of a division, members of the trial committee and judges without the consent of the Party Committees or the Party Committee Organization Departments at the same level, in this way the matters of personnel appointment and removal are at the mercy of local authorities. On the other hand, under the premise that the Party's leadership is a basic principle, following the leadership of local Party Committees (including the Commissions for Political and Legal Affairs) has evolved into intervention of the handling of individual cases. (3) In China, it is the government that holds the financial power, the funds of local People's Courts at all levels are budgeted by the People's Governments at the same level, reviewed by the People's Congresses at the same level, and then allocated by government departments. There were plans for reforming such funding system in the previous judicial reform, but the problem failed to be settled completely. The funding system for political and legal affairs has strengthened the dependence of the judicial organs on local governments. Localization makes it impossible for the judicial organs to get rid of the influence of local Party and government organs, but become their subsidiary. On the one hand, localization of the judicial organs facilitates the interference of local Party and government organs, especially when administrative jurisdictions overlap with judicial jurisdictions. On the other hand, localization of the judicial organs has deprived them of weapons to resist against external interference, and enabled local Party and government organs to interfere with judicial matters.

Second, the administration of the judiciary has made judges dependent on the court as a whole. In China, one of the root causes for the administration of the judiciary is that the independence of individual judges is not recognized, it is the independence of the court as a whole that is recognized. This sort of judicial independence emphasizes the role of the court as a whole in the operation of judicial power, but distrusts individual judges and even requires tight control of them. As a result, the administrative management of individual judges and the administrative operation of judicial power have become an inevitable choice. As far as the former is concerned, judges are treated as ordinary "civil servants", since their salary, promotion and disciplinary

[34] Chen [25].

penalty have no difference from those of ordinary "civil servants". Moreover, judges also have administrative levels; the judges who assume certain positions must have the corresponding administrative level. Therefore, judges are on the whole attached to the court as a collective, which fundamentally deprives their independence and provides external guarantee for the administrative case handling. Regarding the administrative operation of judicial power, the systems for case examination and approval, case instruction upon request, and collective decision-making by the trial committee are practically implemented. The adoption of the administrative case handling model helps to strengthen the control of judges that handle individual cases. To a certain extent, it can be taken as an internal control mechanism to improve the quality of case handling. Taking an administrative approach to handle cases also helps bring extra-legal factors into judicial judgment, thereby giving play to the role of the judiciary in ensuring social harmony and stability and escorting economic development. Besides, the collective decision-making approach is also good for avoiding the risks in handling cases to a certain extent. Although the administrative case handling model has the above positive aspects, it fundamentally denies the independence of judges, which is inconsistent with the essential attributes of judicial power. "When the parties to a case make a statement or the witnesses give testimony, the judges have to 'closely observe' them to decide the credibility of their speech. It is the judgment made on the basis of 'close observation' is closer to reality and more convincing".[35]

2.2.4 *China Reconstructs the Principle of Independent Execution of Power by the Judicial Organs by Focusing on Independent Execution of Power by Judges*

2.2.4.1 Necessity and Feasibility

(1) Necessity

Starting from the reform of the way of trial in the 1990s, the judicial reform of China has generally experienced five periods of development. Each round of reform will bring about several documents and reform measures. There are multiple ways to evaluate the effect of judicial reform. From the perspective of system and mechanism construction, China's judicial reform is of positive significance in enriching and perfecting the originally imperfect legal system. From the perspective of completion of reform tasks, the reform of the judicial system is quite a success, as the official statistics have shown that each round of the reform rounded up satisfactorily.[36]

---

[35] He [5].

[36] The Ministry of Justice of China completes all the tasks of the judicial reform, https://news.sina.com.cn/o/2013-01-09/182525996269.shtml; Hu Yunteng, Mar 18, 2013, On several rounds of China's judicial reform, *People's Court Daily* ("with the vigorous support and cooperation of competent departments, and with the joint efforts of the national courts, the 12 reform tasks

In 2012, China released the *White Paper on Judicial Reform* for the first time to summarize the results of the judicial reform. Presently, as the judicial reform continues to advance, an in-depth analysis of the judicial reform tasks reveals that they actually focus on system construction. In this sense, as long as the system construction is completed, the judicial reform tasks seem to have completed, and the reform does not care about whether the system constructed by it could operate smoothly and produce good effect. In fact, the results of the judicial reform did not run smoothly in practice: the old problems are still pending, while new problems have kept coming out. It is an important reason why China has continued promoting the judicial reform.

We can think about it further as to why is it difficult to implement a good system in practice. Take criminal justice for example. The *Criminal Procedure Law 1996* (revised) of China is of progressive significance for its objective treatment of historical issues. But the results of its implementation were disappointing, and many problems were exposed just one year after it was put into effect.[37] The *Criminal Procedure Law 2012* (revised), in terms of the number of provisions, construction of systems and improvement of rules, marked a breakthrough in history. But the individual scholars still worry about whether the new criminal procedure law could change the current status of criminal justice in China. They are lack of confidence in this regard. Why is it so? The operating environment of the *Criminal Procedure Law* of 1996 and 2012 has no remarkable difference; and in particular, the judicial system upon which the operation of the *Criminal Procedure Law* depends has not changed much. In short, if the judicial system is not adjusted accordingly, no matter how flawless the rules are, they can hardly escape from an unfortunate outcome.

To this day, the judicial reform has once again been put on the agenda. The system problems must be resolved through reform; otherwise, the effect of the judicial system may not work out. Lenin had pointed out that if we don't solve the general problems first, but rush to solve the individual problems, then we are bound to "encounter" these general problems anytime and anywhere. When reforming the judicial system, the primary issue is the independent execution of power by the judicial organs according to law. P. Gewirtz has stated that for those who have a foresight of China's current judicial reform, they will understand that a fundamental motive of the reform is to strengthen judicial independence. This is a matter of course.[38]

---

deployed by the Party Central Committee have been basically completed, and so have the 43 reform tasks that were deployed to assist other departments"); *The seven judicial reform tasks led by the Supreme People's Procuratorate have been basically completed*, https://gov.finance.sina.com.cn/chanquan/2011-12-23/112719.html; China has completed 3/4 of the 60 reform tasks for judicial system and working mechanism, https://news.ifeng.com/gundong/detail_2012_09/03/17295288_0.shtml; China's White Paper on Judicial Reform, issued on Oct 9, 2012, pointed out that "currently, the tasks of this round of judicial reform have been basically completed, as relevant laws have been amended and improved".

[37] Chen [26].

[38] Gewirtz [27].

(2) Feasibility

According to the different social and economic forces that promote the judicial reform, the scholars in Taiwan have divided the judicial reform into four types, i.e., establishing the rule of law, deepening the rule of law, simplifying the rule of law, and transforming the rule of law. (i) The "establishing the rule of law" judicial reform is compatible with the reform of the political system and is part of the system transition. The goal of the reform is to build a mechanism to maintain the new order with justice as the core after the withdrawal of political power and the liberation of social power. The former Soviet Union and the Eastern European countries are typical examples in this regard. (ii) The "deepening the rule of law" judicial reform is to consolidate and implement the core goal of judicial protection of human rights on the basis of established judiciary. The Latin American countries, and the Southern European post-authoritarian or post-fascist countries are typical examples in this regard. (iii) The "simplified the rule of law" judicial reform is usually seen in the countries in Europe, America and Western Europe. The primary task of their reform is to alleviate the burden on the judiciary. (iv) Japan is the typical example that carries out the "transforming the rule of law" judicial reform. The goal of the reform is to expand the scope of justice and make it easier for people to access to judicial assistance.[39] It can be seen that the judicial reform in China is the "establishing the rule of law" judicial reform.

The judicial reform in China is attributed to the reforms of the political and economic systems and the resulting changes in the social structure. The goal of the judicial reform is to transform the judiciary from a political tool into a neutral judge. China's judicial reform has a highly distinctive point, i.e., the reform is carried out under the overall planning of the Party Central Committee, and is compatible with the political and economic system reforms. It is an important content of the entire national system transformation. Therefore, the goal of "establishing the rule of law"[40] under the leadership of the Party Central Committee has become an inexhaustible driving force for the judicial reform, and also provided an opportunity for the judicial system reform.

The 18th National Congress of the CPC proposed to "further deepen the reform of the judicial system"; the Third and Fourth Plenary Sessions of the 18th CPC Central Committee made further deployment for comprehensively deepening the judicial system reform. To ensure the independent exercise of the judicial power in accordance with the law is one of the core contents of this reform. The *Decision on Some Major Issues Concerning Comprehensively Deepening the Reform* (hereinafter referred to as the "Decision"), adopted at the Third Plenary Session of the 18th CPC Central Committee, stated to "promote the rule of law" and set out three major tasks in judicial reform, i.e., "ensuring the independent exercise of the judicial and

[39] Su [19], pp. 417–419.

[40] The *Decision on Some Major Issues Concerning Comprehensively Deepening the Reform*, adopted at the Third Plenary Session of the 18th CPC Central Committee on November 12, 2013, put forward the statement of the construction of "rule of law in China", which can endorse that China's judicial reform is the "establishing the rule of law" judicial reform.

procuratorial power in accordance with the law", "improving the mechanism for the use of judicial power", and "improving the judicial system to protect human rights". The judicial reform in the past decade focused on the construction of legal system and simulated the "rule of law" to wait for the timing of system reform, while the judicial reform plan proposed by the 18th National Congress has created the social and political background and also provided impetus for realizing the system reform. As mentioned in the Decision, "ensuring the independent exercise of the judicial and procuratorial power in accordance with the law", "unify the management of staffs, funds and properties of courts and procuratorates below the provincial level and explore ways to establish a judicial jurisdiction system that is appropriately separated from the administrative divisions", "reform the judicial committee system, improve the responsibility system of handling cases by the presiding judge and the collegiate bench, by which the judges hand down verdicts and the collegiate bench is responsible for carrying them out"; "clarify the functions of the courts at all levels, and standardize their supervision through the judicial hierarchy". All of these proposals are actually revolving around focal point, i.e., "judicial independence". It can be seen that the new social and political background and the situation of judicial reform have provided an opportunity to promote Chinese judicial organs to exercise their power independently.

2.2.4.2 Significance in Emphasizing the Judge Independence in Exercise of Power According to Law

This book holds that China should reconstruct the principle of independent exercise of power by the judicial organs according to law with judge independence as the core. It conforms to the basic rules and requirements of justice—the most pivotal reason why we support this point of view. Moreover, while China is carrying out the judicial reform that aims at "establishing the rule of law", placing emphasis on the independence exercise of power by judges according to law has the following advantages:

First, constructing the principle of judicial independence with Chinese characteristics with judge independence as the core helps to downplay the political color of judicial independence. As mentioned earlier, judicial independence is closely related to the theory of separation of powers in the process of its creation, thus making it take on a strong political color. This is the biggest institutional obstacle for China to promote the principle of judicial independence. In fact, overemphasizing the political color of judicial independence is a misunderstanding, and we shall treat this issue rationally. Nevertheless, under the current social and political situation, the perception of judicial independence among officials and legal professionals differs greatly from that of the public.[41] Especially officials, they are still suspicious of judicial independence. Under such circumstance, to downplay the political color of judicial independence and highlight the independent exercise of power by judges according

[41] Chen [28].

to law not only satisfies the essential requirement for judicial independence, but also avoids the doubts about political correctness brought by judicial independence. Therefore, it is a practical and feasible way of reform to construct the principle independent exercise of power by the judicial organs according to law with judge independence as the core.

Second, constructing the principle of judicial independence with Chinese characteristics with judge independence as the core helps to underscore the independence of individual judges in the process of the judicial reform. According to the general theory, the judicial independence in China is fact the independence of the People's Court as a whole, which shows that the independence of individual judges is suppressed in the process of system construction. The emergence of the administrative case handling model was in response to this thinking. However, the judicial reform has been breaking the original recognition of the independence of the People's Court as a whole, and constantly expanding the power of judges by giving them greater independence to handle specific cases. The theory of the independence of the court as a whole is inapplicable in this regard. Judicial independence, with judge independence as the core, not only conforms to the independent trial by the People's Courts as defined in the Constitution, but also pays full attention to judge independence. Besides, judge independence imposes requirements on the court as a whole, and more importantly, it requires judges who handle specific cases to independently exercise their power according to law, which will guarantee the independence of individual judges to a certain extent and provide theoretical support for China's judicial reform.

Finally, constructing the principle of judicial independence with Chinese characteristics with judge independence as the core helps to ensure the organic unity of "independence" and "restriction", so as to avoid the arbitrariness caused by excessive power. In addition to the doubts about the political nature of judicial independence, there is a concern that after the judicial independence is established, the powers of courts and judges may become out-of-control like unbridled horses, not only failing to guarantee judicial justice, but also undermining the foundation of the entire judicial system. But the principle of judicial independence with judge independence as the core can effectively coordinate the relationship between "independence" and "restriction". When handling cases, the judges can only apply the law as the basis for adjudication, none of the factors beyond the case are allowed to influence the trial. This objectively constitutes the basis for the independence of judges and enables them to exclude improper interference by various forces. Besides, the independent exercise of power according to law is also a "ban" on judges, meaning that their independence is not unlimited, but bound by "law". The independent exercise of power according to law is both the basis and boundary of judge independence. Therefore, judicial independence, with judge independence as the core, combines "independence" and "restriction"; such knowledge can resolve the concern that judicial independence may lead to arbitrary judgments by judges.

2.2.5 *Judges Must "Handle Cases According to Law"*

In China, after the thought of socialist rule of law was put forward, there is a popular viewpoint that the judiciary should pursue the unity of legal effect, political effect and social effect, and take this as a requirement to guide justice. This viewpoint seems reasonable, but if we conduct an in-depth analysis of it, we will find it is contrary to the requirements of the principle of independent exercise of power by the judicial organs according to law.

(1) Political and social effects objectively exceed legal effect due to the unity of political, social and legal effects of justice

To stress the unification of the political, social and legal effects of justice will objectively lead to one-sided pursuit of the political and social effects of justice, and imposition of the political and social effects upon the legal effect. The unification of the three effects is no doubt a blessing, and it is not unreachable, because the laws that are enacted under the leadership of the CPC and manifest the will and interests of the Party and the people. Under normal circumstances, handling cases according to law will achieve the unification of the political, social and legal effects of justice.[42] But there are circumstances that these effects are not consistent. Take some high-profile cases for example, the cases of Liu Yong, Yao Jiaxin, Li Changkui, Xu Ting and Peng Yu that sparked widespread discussion have one thing in common: their political effect (especially social effect) is inconsistent with their legal effect, and even in conflict with each other. Such situation must be properly handled. These cases show that while pursuing the unification of the political, social, and legal effects of justice, we may ignore the objective reality of justice, which has no practical significance for guiding justice. In other words, if we emphasize the unification of the three effects when handling similar cases, it is tantamount to deny the legal effect of justice and replace the legal effect with the political and social effects.

Under the current judicial system in China, this kind of risk is prone to become a reality, and in fact it has already a reality. On the one hand, in order to maintain the political and social effects of justice, local Party Committees intervene in judicial organs' handling of cases according to law, thereby impairing judicial independence. On the other hand, under this system, it is inevitably for the judicial organs to take care of the political and social effects of justice. As a result, "failing to observe the law" and "difficult to observe the law" is an established fact. The unity of the political, social and legal effects of justice has evolved, and the legal effect has begun to yield to political and social effects, making the independent exercise of judicial power a luxury. Currently, lots of wrong, false and misjudged cases are related to the excessive pursuit of social and political effects at the expense of legal effect. Take the case of Zhao Zuohai in Henan province for example, the concerned judicial organs were anxious to solve this case and meet the public expectation, so they

[42] When the three effects are unified, there is no need to specially emphasize the political and legal effects of justice. As long as the legal effect of justice could be achieved, other effects are sure to be achieved.

failed to handle the case independently according to law. The case of Li Changkui happened in Yunnan province was another typical example. No to mention whether the case was properly handled, its trial procedure was criticized. After an effective ruling was made in second instance, Yunnan High Court started a retrial procedure to commute Li's death sentence with reprieve to immediate execution. Social justice might be maintained, but the court impressed the public that it was not independent and shorn of its prestige. It can be seen that emphasizing the unity of the three effects can only make the justice go nowhere and become a vassal of other social forces. From a development perspective, this is by no means a long-term plan for judicial development.

(2) Basic ideas for dealing with political (social) factors in the judicial process

The relationship between justice and politics and between justice and society is an eternal topic that people have been thinking about ever since the birth of justice. Justice was born in politics, and it is everywhere in politics—an overview of the relationship between justice and politics from a historical perspective. We should admit that in different historical periods of any country, justice is an integral part of national politics and an important tool for safeguarding the interests of the ruling class. During the period of slavery and feudalism, the control of judicial power was the foremost thing for the king. And the judicial power had always been taken as a part of the power of the monarch, the corresponding judicial subjects in judicial activities were following the orders of the monarch, and the final judicial decision was still made by the monarch. But in modern society, whether it is a common law system country or a civil law system country, justice is a vital part of its social and political life. In common law system countries without a written constitution, justice is an integral part of their political life and an extremely important power restricting the legislative and administrative powers.[43] In civil law countries with a written constitution, justice is explicitly defined in the constitution, which more clearly demonstrates that justice is a vital part of their political life.[44] In socialist countries, justice is also a well-deserved part of politics, which is defined in the constitutions of these countries. For example, the *Constitution of the Soviet Union* stipulates the judicial power and composition of judicial organs; and the constitutions Cuba, Vietnam and North Korea also have similar provisions.

The relationship between justice and politics is a long-lasting topic, because observations from different angles may lead to different conclusions. If we only examine the relationship between justice and politics from the above angles, the conclusion is sure to be one-sided. Justice is no doubt a part of politics, but the entire history of justice is also the history of separating from politics to achieve independence. It can be seen in the transition from the ancient times where justice was controlled

---

[43]For example, the Federal Court of the United States has the power to review the constitutionality of federal laws, which objectively empowers the judiciary to counteract legislative and administrative powers.

[44]The constitutions of Germany, France, Italy, Japan and Russia also have provisions for the judiciary and the judicial system.

by the king to the modern times where justice has become increasingly independent. Justice is amid political struggles, but the independence of judiciary, at least from the perspective of macro architecture, provides the possibility to avoid excessive political interference in judicial affairs. Moreover, from a micro perspective, the depoliticization of individual cases is precisely the goal pursued by the judiciary. Justice can be stripped from politics because of its own basic rules. It is an important reason why justice can be used as a means of dispute resolution (including political disputes in Western countries such as Britain and the United States). Therefore, respecting the rules of justice should become a criterion for balancing the relationship between politics and justice, and respecting the rules of justice requires to avoid excessive political interference in individual cases. "In the countries ruled by law, the depoliticization of justice is not only a political principle and social habit, but also a consensus in academia".[45] Scholars often use the United States as an example to demonstrate justice and politics are closely related, but ignore the other aspect of their relationship, i.e., justice should be free from external political interference in specific cases as much as possible.[46] "Judicial elections, impeachment, and Congress legislation have much to do with parties, but once the judges, especially the federal court judges, are appointed, they will only obey the law and largely get rid of the control and influence of parties.[47] Even the scholars who strongly support the proposition of politicizing justice do not deny that judges should avoid or restrict their personal political preferences when making decisions.[48]

Moreover, in dealing with the relationship between justice and politics, "as long as a politicized judicial decision can stand the test and inference of judicial procedures and judicial logic, then this politicization is a choice that is both legalized and acceptable",[49] "we must have both correct political awareness and sound legal awareness", "pay attention to both the legal effect and the political effect", "however, consideration of and attention to political issues must not exceed legal and valid norms".

We should be good at realizing political intentions and displaying the political functions of justice within the framework of law, i.e., realize the political functions of justice by accurately grasping the spiritual essence of the law, correctly interpreting the purpose of the law, properly filling the legal loopholes, correctly using discretionary power, and reasonably conducting value judgments and benefit measurement,[50] all of which center on "legitimacy". This is consistent with the

---

[45] Zhou Yongkun, *Why justice must be depoliticized*, https://wenku.baidu.com/view/41a247f78662caaedd3383c4bb4cf7ec4afeb6cd.html.

[46] President Lincoln frankly said that he would choose those who supported his policy to be judges, but he also admitted that he had no idea what these persons were going to do. This indirectly shows that there is a certain distance between politics and justice. See Ball [29]. Republican President Eisenhower felt regret that he appointed Earl Warren of the same party as the Chief Justice. See Pach and Richardson [30].

[47] Feng [31].

[48] Zhou [32].

[49] Zhou [32].

[50] Jiang [9].

essence of judicial independence. It shows that judicial independence or handling cases according to law should become the technical standard for dealing with the relationship between justice and politics in individual cases.

(3) Rational understanding of the relationship among the political, social and legal effects of justice

Through the analysis of the relationship between justice and politics, we can deduce the following conclusion: even we pursue the political effect of justice, it is achieved with the aid of legal effect. Regarding the relationship among the legal effect, political effect and social effect, legal effect is a pathway to achieve political effect. This shows that the direct effect pursued by the judiciary is still the legal effect, although it may eventually achieve the political or social effect. Therefore, when dealing with the relationship among the political, social and legal effect of justice, we should directly pursue the legal effect, rather than the political or social effect. But currently in China, too much emphasis is placed on the unity of the political, social and legal effect of justice. This is actually a misunderstanding. As to the issue of properly handling the relationship among the legal effect, political effect and social effect of justice, we should coordinate their relationship when they are inconsistent, there is no need to do so when they are consistent. Under normal circumstances, if the legal effect of justice is realized, its political and social effects will be naturally realized.

As mentioned earlier, justice is based on the laws that reflect the will of the Party and the people, if the requirements of the laws are fulfilled, then the interests of the Party and the people will be realized, and the corresponding political and social effects will be achieved. But this kind of "unity" requires the consistency based on the realization of the legal effect, i.e., the political and social effects are a side effect after the legal effect is achieved. In the case of inconsistency among the three effects, the pursuit of the unity of the legal, political and social effects will become a delusion, which seems like imposing the political and social effects on the legal effect, and interfering with judicial independence. The aforementioned cases are the best proof in this regard.

Some people may think that when the political and social effects of justice are inconsistent with its legal effect, the pursuit of legal effect may lead to poor political and social effects and jeopardize social and political stability. In most cases, both political and social effects can be achieved upon the realization of legal effect, and it is rare to see any inconsistency among the three effects. In China, the reason for the conflict among the three effects is mainly due to the inherent characteristics of the social interest structure in the transitional period; it is a social problem, not a judicial problem. The resolution of social problems requires adjustments in many aspects such as legislation and administration, and they cannot be solved by simply sacrificing justice. The direct task of the judiciary is to handle cases according to law, and obey only the law. Its role in maintaining social and political stability is only the outcome of independent exercise of power according to law, and it cannot be the direct or sole purpose of the judiciary. Moreover, sacrificing justice will destroy the last line of defense for safeguarding social equality and impartiality, meaning that its harm is fundamental and hard to recover. We cannot sacrifice long-term fundamental interests with immediate interests. Of course, the inconsistency among the three effects may also be a problem with the justice itself, i.e., the due legal effect of justice fails to be achieved, but what we should do is to standardize the judicial acts and implement the judicial responsibility, rather than take it as an excuse for inviting external forces to intervene in justice.

Therefore, we should change the concept of unifying the legal, political and social effects of justice as soon as possible. We can only pursue the legal effect of justice. But the realization of the legal effect usually facilitates the realization of the expected political and social effects, which is a natural outcome of the legal effect. When the legal, political and social effects of justice are inconsistent, the legal effect shall be the only choice, and the political and social effects can never be imposed on the legal effect. Only in this way can we ensure judicial independence and reestablish judicial authority.

2.2.6 Reform of the External Guarantee for Independent Exercise of Power According to Law in the Context of Judicial Reform

2.2.6.1 Transform the Functions of the Commission for Political and Legal Affairs

(1) Development of the Commission functions

The Commission for Political and Legal Affairs was once abolished in the past, it was after 1990 that the Commission for Political and Legal Affairs under the CPC Central Committee and the local Commissions at various levels were gradually reestablished. "After its restoration, the Commission for Political and Legal Affairs keeps following the principle of separation of Party functions from those of government, providing the macro-guidance and coordination for the political and legal work, and playing the role as the adviser and assistant to the Party Committee. Its subsidiary offices mainly conduct investigations and researches, refrain from undue interference in the work of various organs, and facilitate the governments at all levels to take up their responsibilities as leader of the public security and judicial organs, so as to ensure that the courts and procuratorates can independently exercise trial power and procuratorial power, and all political and legal departments can fully perform their functions".[51] All of these functions of this Commission were defined by the CPC Central Committee,[52] and recognized by the leaders at that time.[53] Since then the

---

[51] *Circular of the CPC Central Committee on Maintaining Social Stability and Strengthening Political and Legal Work*, Apr 2, 1990.

[52] Lin [33].

[53] Qiao Shi's Thought on Democracy and Legal System, in *Qiao Shi's new book discloses some details of the withdrawal and restoration of the Commission for Political and Legal Affairs*, https://china.caixin.com/2012-06-21/100403122.html.

functions of this Commission have been constantly expanded. In 1994, according to the document issued by the CPC Central Committee, this Commission had three new functions of "research and discussion of the major and complicated cases that are controversial", "organization and promotion of the work for comprehensive management of social security", and "research and guidance of the construction of political and legal teams and the leading body of political and legal departments".[54] After this round of power expansion, this Commission has the authority to intervene in case handling. The latter two functions have included the public security, procuratorates and courts and their work into the scope of comprehensive governance of social security, and gained the power over personnel in local political and legal departments. In 1995, after going through the second round of power expansion, this Commission altogether has ten functions.

In judicial practice, the functions and offices of the Commission for Political and Legal Affairs continue to increase, which has strengthened its intervention in judicial work. Consequently, the Party's leadership over political and legal work has returned to the previous model of intervening case handling. For example, this Commission can release various norms and minutes of meeting. Although these documents are not laws, they are still the valid basis for adjudication.[55] In addition, this Commission also intervenes in case handling by means of coordination, i.e., when there is a case with insufficient evidence or different understanding, the public security, procuratorial and judicial organs may report it to this Commission; after investigating the case, this Commission will convene a coordination meeting, put forward preliminary opinions, and develop the minutes of a meeting to be issued to the concerned organs.[56]

(2) Transformation of the Commission functions

The Commission for Political and Legal Affairs is mainly criticized for its intervention of case handling. This Commission was reestablished to serve as the "adviser" and "assistant" of the Party Committee, mainly engaged in providing macro guidance and free from interfering with the concrete work of the case handling organs. It is obviously a scientific and reasonable definition. However, with the development of practice, this Commission has gradually obtained the authority to intervene in the handling of individual cases, and increasingly deviated from its original functions.

The circumstance that the Commission for Political and Legal Affairs interferes in case handling first impairs the basic rule of justice. The operation of judicial power

---

[54] *Plan for the Functions, Internal Offices and Staffing of the Commission for Political and Legal Affairs under the CPC Central Committee* ([1994] Doc. No. 9).

[55] For example, in 2003, the Commission for Political and Legal Affairs under Beijing Municipal Party Committee issued the *Minutes of the Conference on Handling Minor Injury Cases*, which stipulated that regarding the minor injury cases caused by civil disputes, if the suspect has pleaded guilty, demonstrated repentance and actively compensated for the loss, and the victim agrees not to investigate the criminal responsibility of the suspect, then the case can be withdrawn, not prosecuted or exempted from criminal punishment. In 2003, the Commission for Political and Legal Affairs under Hebei Provincial Party Committee made the *Decision on Political and Legal Organs to Create a Good Environment for Improving the Socialist Market Economic System*, which contained many items in violation of national laws.

[56] Hou [34].

requires following the principle of judicial experience, while the intervention of this Commission violates this principle. An important consequence resulting from this is that many misjudged cases are closely related to the involvement of this Commission. And it is also against Article 135 of China's Constitution which stipulates that the People's Courts, the People's Procuratorates and the public security organs shall, in handling criminal cases, divide their functions, each taking responsibility for its own work. The judicial restrictions on other powers have been downplayed or even eliminated, making the credibility of the judicial organs widely questioned. More than that, the intervention of this Commission in case handling has a negative impact on the Party's leadership.

In view of this, some scholars call for the abolition of the Commission for Political and Legal Affairs,[57] some scholars argue that the "decision-making power" of this Commission should be eliminated,[58] while some scholars suggest that the "unspoken rules" for the coordination of cases by this Commission should be annulled.[59] In this regard, we believe that the existence of this Commission has its historical and practical necessity. As an adviser and assistant of the Party Committee, this Commission can play an active role in implementing the Party's leadership in judicial work. Especially in the context of the ongoing judicial reform, let this Commission, especially the Commission under the CPC Central Committee, coordinate the formulation of judicial reform policies, it helps to unify the steps of reform and integrate resources to guarantee the smooth progress of judicial reform. But the retention of this Commission does not mean that it is empowered to go beyond the judiciary. We should refer to the positioning of this Commission when it was restored in the 1990s, redefine it as an adviser and assistant of the Party Committee, and do not give it more powers. The most important thing is to prevent this Commission from intervening case handling. At the National Political and Legal Work Video Conference held in 2013, Meng Jianzhu, Secretary of the Commission for Political and Legal Affairs under the CPC Central Committee, pointed out to further innovate the leadership style of the Party Committee and the Commission, do a good job in dealing with major events, controlling and planning for the overall situation, straighten out the relationship among the Party Committee, the Commission, and other political and legal departments, support the procuratorates and courts to exercise their powers independently according to law. In the context of "further deepening the reform of the judicial system" which was presented at the 18th National Congress of the CPC, the above speech pointed out the direction for transforming the role and functions of the Commission. It is confirmed that the Commission should no longer intervene in case handling, which conforms to the basic rule of justice and helps to maintain judicial authority.

---

[57] Cui [35, 36], Wang and Sun [37].

[58] *Prof. Chen Guangzhong Proposes to Abolish the "Decision-making Power" of the Commission for Political and Legal Affairs*, May 20, 2010, https://fxxb.legal-theory.org/?mod=info&act=view&id=207.

[59] Yan [38].

2.2.6.2 Unified Management of Staffs, Funds and Properties

To manipulate the judiciary, the first thing to do is to control its human and financial resources. Once the local Party Committees and governments control the human and financial resources of the judiciary, then the entire judicial system will lose its independence when intervened by the local Party Committees and governments. As Hamilton had described that having control over someone's life is equal to having control over his thoughts.[60] In recent years, it is common to see the local Party Committees and governments interfere with the judicial work, which has not only caused a large number of misjudged cases, but also shamed the judiciary. In this regard, there has been a broad consensus in the academic and practical circles that the judiciary must be delocalized.

The 16th National Congress of the CPC held in November 2002 required to advance the judicial reform. Some achievements were made since then, but the reform was not thorough and some problems are left to date.[61] The *Decision on Some Major Issues Concerning Comprehensively Deepening the Reform*, which was adopted at the Third Plenary Session of the 18th CPC Central Committee, planned to "reform the judicial administration system, unify the management of staffs, funds and properties of courts and procuratorates below the provincial level". By separating the management of staffs, funds and properties of the judicial organs from the local authorities, the local Party Committees and governments will have no means to interfere with the judicial work. But the Decision only pointed out the direction of the reform on a whole, there are still problems in how to understand and implement the plan.

(1) Whether the unified management of staffs, funds and properties is vertical management

Many scholars and practitioners generalize the "unified management of staffs, funds and properties" of the judicial organs with "vertical management". It should be pointed out that the "vertical management" confuses the essence of the management of staffs, funds and properties. First, the issue of "staffs, funds and properties" of the judicial organs, which is to be solved according to the above Decision, is a judicial administrative affair, rather than a judicial affair. Judicial affairs should be handled in line with the rules of justice, it has nothing to do with management. Especially for the People's Courts, there is no possibility of vertical management. Second, the management power for judicial administrative affairs is a state power or the Party Central Committee's authorization, not a local power. This is compatible

[60]Hamilton et al. [39].

[61]In 2002, the report to the 16th National Congress of the CPC proposed to reform the staffs, funds and properties management system of the judicial organs. There were explorations in this regard, but the progress was slow. In 2009, the Ministry of Finance issued a document which divided the judicial funding into four categories: personnel expenses, public expenses, infrastructure construction expenses, and business equipment expenses; the former three expenses are borne by the financial department at the same level, while the last expenses are borne by the central, provincial and the same-level financial departments by jurisdiction and responsibility.

with the unitary system of China. The reason why the management power for judicial administrative affairs is at the local level is due to the "authorization" of the Central Government or the Party Central Committee, not that the localities themselves have such power.[62]

The ultimate goal of the judicial system reform is to return all management powers for judicial administrative affairs to the State, i.e., let the State uniformly manage the judicial administrative affairs. It is still difficult for the State to uniformly manage the judicial administrative affairs in one step,[63] which is proved by China's reform practices in the past. Therefore, we have to find the balance between authorized management and unified management, i.e., to authorize provincial courts and procuratorates to uniformly manage the staffs, funds and properties of local courts and procuratorates below the provincial level. This reform thinking also reflects the progressive pattern of China's judicial system reform.

(2) Whether the unified management of staffs, funds and properties violates the Constitution

In accordance with the provisions of the Constitution and relevant organizational laws of China, the presidents of the People's Courts are elected by the people's congresses at all levels and are responsible to them; while the vice presidents and judges are appointed and removed by the standing committees of the people's congresses at all levels. Will the unified management of staffs, funds and properties of the judicial organs violate the Constitution and relevant organizational laws? In this regard, it should be noted that the primary cause of judicial localization is the local Party Committees' control over judicial personnel. In China, the president of a local court should be nominated and appointed by the Party group of the higher court and the local Party Committee, otherwise, the people's congress cannot start the process of appointment, and the local Party Committee usually has a greater decision-making power. This is the primary cause for China's judicial localization. Therefore, the

---

[62] The process of setting up the procuratorial organs after the founding of New China can illustrate this point. Initially, a vertical leadership system for the procuratorates was set up, but later it was replaced by a dual leadership system. In his report to the Central People's Government Commission in September 1951, the Deputy Chief Procurator of the Supreme People's Procuratorate Li Liuru explained the reasons for the decentralization of judicial administration to the localities: "China used to be a semi-feudal and semi-colonial society, and its economic development was extremely uneven…People living on a vast territory were lack of access to transportation. The People's Procuratorates are either imperfect or not yet established. For the time being, the only way out is to follow the unified policy of the Central Government, it will authorize the local governments to guide and assist the People's Procuratorates in the locality…".

[63] In the article *Deepening the Reform of the Judicial System*, Meng Jianzhu, Secretary of the Commission for Political and Legal Affairs, pointed out that "considering China's basic national conditions that it will remain in the primary stage of socialism for a long time, it is difficult for the Central Government to uniformly manage the staffs, funds and properties of the judicial organs. It is advised that the judicial management system should be reformed step by step: first, the staffs, funds and properties of the local courts and procuratorates below the provincial level shall be uniformly managed by the provincial government; second, the local courts and procuratorates at all levels, and specialized courts and procuratorates are funded by the provincial department, with the Central Government providing part of the funds".

path of reform is to submit the personnel nomination proposal to the provincial Party Committees which will choose the candidates, and then the local people's congresses and their standing committees at all levels will make the decision of appointment. In this way, it can solve the "unconstitutional (illegal)" problem of judicial localization and ensure the effects of the reform.

(3) Whether the unified management of staffs, funds and properties will strengthen the intervention from superior

The current reform thinking is to prevent the local Party Committees and governments from intervention in the judiciary by emphasizing the unified management of judicial administrative affairs. But the problem is how can the higher judicial organ that controls staffs and funds avoid themselves from unduly interfering with the lower judicial organ in handling cases? Are we going to an extreme of strengthening judicial administration while delocalizing the judiciary? Such concerns indeed exist. One of the two major factors affecting the independent exercise of power by the people's courts is the administration of justice, which includes the administration of judicial management. Therefore, the process of judicial delocalization may strengthen the intervention of the higher judicial organs, we must be fully aware of it and provide corresponding system response. We should promote democratization of judicial management and follows the rules of justice, rather than adopt the traditional centralized approach to manage judicial administrative affairs. Strictly speaking, the judicial administrative affairs should be managed by professionals, which is the ultimate goal of the reform. The judicial reform is a gradual and progressive process, now it is aiming at promoting democratization of judicial administrative affairs at the current stage, i.e., give full play to the role of judges in judicial management, choose the representatives from the judges to participate in the decision-making process, and make judicial administrative decisions on the basis of democracy. Since the management power for the judicial administrative affairs tends to become a state power, the democratization of judicial management should be a key content of the reform.

(4) Unified management of staffs, funds and properties and supervision by the people's congress

In the process where the judicial organs keep getting rid of local control through the unified management of staffs, funds and properties, whether the local people's congress will reject the court work report so as to realize its intervention of the judicial work, it has become a matter of grave concern in the reform for the unified management of staffs, funds and properties. And such incident has happened more than once.[64] The essence of this problem lies in the nature and binding force of the rejection made by the local people's congress. The basic rule for the court operation requires individual judges to take responsibility for their cases, while the president

[64]In 2001, the work report of Shenyang Intermediate People's Court was not approved by the people's congress at the same level. In 2007, the work report of Hengyang Intermediate People's Court was rejected by the local people's congress.

of the court neither bears the responsibility for the case nor for any political consequence. As to the provision that the People's Courts shall be responsible to the organs of powers (people's congresses) which is covered in the Constitution and relevant organizational laws, it should be clarified that "taking responsibility" does not mean that the courts have to assume political responsibility; instead, they are under the supervision by the organs of powers. We'd better interpret the relationship between the courts and the people's congresses from the perspective of supervision, which is more in line with China's national conditions. On this basis, if the local people's congress rejects the court work report, the president of the court does not have to assume the political responsibility. Specifically, if the local people's congress rejects the court work report, it should be regarded as the supervision and recommendation of the court work in the past, and the expression of dissatisfaction with its work; if it rejects the future work plan of the court, then the plan shall be revised, improved and resubmitted for approval.

2.2.6.3 Separation of Judicial Jurisdictions from Administrative Divisions

In China, a major problem in the current judicial reform is that the judicial organs are restricted by local authorities. The apparent cause for such restraint is that the staffs, funds and properties of the judicial organs are controlled by the people's congresses and governments at the same level, but in essence, it is due to the overlapping of judicial jurisdictions and administrative divisions. "The current judicial jurisdictions and administrative divisions are overlapped, the judicial organs and administrative organs at the same level stem from the organs of power at the same level, which is extremely convenient for local power organs, administrative organs and judicial organs to cooperate beyond the law in protecting local interests, thus forming local protectionism".[65]

"With the expansion of local power and the growth of local interests after the reform and opening up, local protectionism has developed to a very serious extent. Quite a number of local leaders take courts at the same level as their subordinate departments to interfere with the judicial activities, and even blatantly oppose the implementation of the Constitution and laws with local policies". "It can be said that the localization of judicial power is an important cause for the serious problems of failure to observe the law, weak law enforcement and miscarriages of justice in many places".[66] Therefore, resetting the judicial jurisdictions and separating them from the administrative divisions should become an important measure of judicial reform. Many scholars have combed and demonstrated this idea, but so far it has failed to materialize".[67]

---

[65]Liu [40].

[66]Liu [41].

[67]Long [42].

In November 12, 2013, the Third Plenary Session of the 18th CPC Central Committee adopted the *Decision on Some Major Issues Concerning Comprehensively Deepening the Reform*, which proposed to "explore ways to establish a judicial jurisdiction system that is appropriately separated from the administrative divisions". In February 2015, the Supreme People's Court issued the *Opinions on Comprehensively Deepening the Reform of the People's Court—The Fourth Five-Year Reform Outline of the People's Court (2014–2018)*, which clarified the reform timetable and specific plan, and stated that "by the end of 2017, a scientific, rational, well-connected and truly impartial judicial jurisdiction system will initially take initial shape". In October 2014, the Fourth Plenary Session of the 18th CPC Central Committee adopted the *Decision on Certain Major Issues Concerning Comprehensively Advancing the Law-Based Governance of China*, which put forward to "explore ways to establish the People's Courts and People's Procuratorates across administrative divisions to handle trans-regional cases", becoming an important content and major measure of China's judicial system reform.

(1) Motivation: localization of judicial power

In the *Explanation of the Decision on Certain Major Issues Concerning Comprehensively Advancing the Law-Based Governance of China*, Xi Jinping, General Secretary of the CPC Central Committee, pointed out that the purpose of establishing the People's Courts and People's Procuratorates that are across administrative divisions is to "exclude interference with the trial and procuratorial work, and ensure that the courts and procuratorates could exercise their judicial and procuratorial powers independently and impartially according to law".[68] The logic and main axis of this round of judicial reform is to define the central authority status of the judicial organs and carry out the judicial "delocalization".[69] The so-called judicial localization is a variant in justice, meaning that the judicial organs and their staffs are improperly interfered by local relevant departments or local interest groups during the exercise of their powers, which makes the judicial power unable to be exercised independently and impartially.[70]

The judicial organs are originally a central authority, i.e., no matter where the court is located, it is a national court, and it enforces the national laws. However, under the influence of judicial localization, judicial personnel started taking sides in the local people or enterprises, harming the legal rights and interests of non-local people or enterprises, undermining judicial unity, jeopardizing judicial justice, and dissolving judicial authority. The judicial localization is largely due to the high degree of overlap between judicial jurisdictions and administrative divisions, as well as the localization of the staffs, funds and properties of the courts.

First, the high degree of overlap between judicial jurisdictions and administrative divisions is the root cause for judicial localization. According to Article 30 of the *Constitution of China*, "(1) The country is divided into provinces, autonomous

---

[68] Xi [43].

[69] Chen [44].

[70] Zhang [45].

regions, and municipalities directly under the Central Government; (2) Provinces and autonomous regions are divided into autonomous prefectures, counties, autonomous counties, and cities; and (3) Counties and autonomous counties are divided into townships, nationality townships, and towns. Municipalities directly under the Central Government and other large cities are divided into districts and counties. Autonomous prefectures are divided into counties, autonomous counties, and cities". In China, judicial jurisdictions are not defined in laws, so the courts are set up on the basis of administrative divisions. From a vertical perspective, the administrative division involves four levels: state, province, city divided into districts, and county; correspondingly, the court is also divided into four levels: supreme, high, intermediate, and primary. From a horizontal perspective, usually the court established in a certain administrative division only accepts the cases within this division. Therefore, where there are administrative divisions, there will be corresponding courts, and the scope of administrative divisions determines the scope of the court jurisdictions in principle.[71] Within each provincial administrative division, a high People's Court shall be established; within each prefecture-level administrative division, an intermediate People's Court shall be established; and within each county-level administrative division, a People's Court shall be established. For example, Haidian District People's Court, which is in the area governed by Haidian District People's Government, accepts the cases within the district. Judicial localization is based on the overlap or correspondence of judicial jurisdictions and administrative divisions, which provides "institutional soil" for local Party Committees and government organs to interfere in the exercise of judicial power.

Second, the localization of staffs, funds and properties is the incentive for judicial localization. Many scholars have explained why judicial localization inevitably occurs is that the courts in China are set up corresponding to administrative divisions; judicial jurisdictions and administrative divisions are overlapped, so that the personnel appointment and dismissal and financial supply of the courts are respectively controlled by the power organs and administrative organs at the same level, and the courts are subject to the substantial control by the local Party Committees.[72] In the *Constitution of China*, Article 101 stipulates that "local people's congresses at or above the county level elect, and have the power to recall, presidents of people's courts and chief procurators of people's procuratorates at the corresponding level. Article 128 stipulates that "the Supreme People's Court is responsible to the National People's Congress and its Standing Committee. Local people's courts at various levels are responsible to the organs of state power which created them". According to Article

---

[71] The judicial interpretations made by the Supreme People's Court on the court jurisdictions after the change of administrative divisions have confirmed this point of view. *The Reply of the Supreme People's Court on the Issue of Commuting the Original Sentence after the Revocation of the Court of Original Trial and the Change of Jurisdiction Area (Fa [1962] No. 3); The Reply of the Supreme People's Court on the Issue of Commuting the Original Sentence after the Change of the Jurisdiction Area of the Court of Original Trial (Fa [1962] No. 7); The Reply of the Supreme People's Court on the Issue of Reviewing and Commuting the Original Sentence that has Taken Effect after the Change of the Jurisdiction Area of the People's Court (Fa [1998] No. 81).*

[72] Jiao [46], Hao and Gan [47].

35 of the *Organization Law of the People's Courts*, "the president of local people's courts at all levels is elected by the local people's congresses at all levels, while the vice president, the chief judge and the deputy chief judge of a division, and judges are appointed and dismissed by the standing committees of local people's congresses at all levels". It is quite similar to Article 11 of the *Judges Law*, "local courts are created by the organs of power at the same level, local judges are appointed and removed by the people's congresses at the same level, and local judges are managed by local Party Committees and government organs". The appointment, dismissal, staffing, promotion, salary and future of the judges—the subject of trial—are all controlled by local authorities. Apparently, the exercise of judicial power is to be intervened by local authorities. Besides, Article 3 of the *Interim Measures for the Financial Management of the People's Courts* stipulates that the principle of financial management of the people's courts is "hierarchical management, hierarchical funding". It makes the finances of courts completely subordinate to and dependent on local finances, while the local fiscal revenue and expenditure entirely relies on the operation of local economy and taxation. Due to their reliance on local finances, local courts have to take care of local interests when trying cases, which in turn nurtures local protectionism. As Hamilton had described that having control over someone's life is equal to having control over his thoughts.[73] The national courts set in different areas are subject to local Party Committees and governments, it is hard for the courts to remain independent if local institutions or individuals intend to interfere with the case handling.

Therefore, "with the in-depth development of the socialist market economy and the emergence of administrative litigations, the number of the cases that are across administrative divisions and even across borders has been on the rise, and the amount involved is increasing, which has drawn attention from the competent departments and leaders in the areas where the courts are located, and they even employ powers and relationships to intervene in case handling, as if they are the team playing in their 'home field', which is not conducive to equal protection of the legitimate rights and interests of non-local parties, guaranteeing independent trials in the courts, supervising the governments' law-based administration, and maintaining fair law enforcement".[74]

The local courts which should implement the national laws are in fact protecting the local interests during the trial. Judicial localization is only an appearance, "the essence is the local interests formed by local separatism and local pattern".[75] The pressure of performance evaluation has aggravated the situation of local competition. As early as in 1998, the staffs with the courts had started discussions on how to resolve the shortcomings of judicial localization,[76] one of the countermeasures that they had proposed was to set up courts out of administrative divisions. At the National Court Work Conference held in 2002, Xiao Yang, then president of the Supreme

[73] Hamilton et al. [39].

[74] See Ref. [48].

[75] Liu [49].

[76] Jiang [50].

People's Court, proposed to "adjust the settings of the people's courts by breaking the old model that is based on administrative divisions".[77] Unfortunately, none of the previous judicial reforms has made it. In the context of comprehensively deepening the reform, it is quite urgent and necessary to explore the ways to set up the courts across administrative divisions so as to eliminate local interference, strengthen the unified exercise of judicial power, and highlight the basic attribute of central authority of the judicial power.

(2) Reference: foreign experiences in separating judicial jurisdictions from administrative divisions

Looking at the judicial practices in foreign countries, the separation of judicial jurisdictions from administrative divisions has indeed played a good role in preventing judicial localization and ensuring judicial independence. The system of judicial jurisdiction was initially established for breaking the judicial control of the manor by feudal lords. As early as the thirteenth and fourteenth centuries, the UK unified the legal system within the scope of its sovereignty by setting up circuit courts. This kind of jurisdiction system was also introduced into the US. The layout of the circuit courts in the US is not based on administrative divisions, which has objectively maintained judicial independence. Moreover, the setting of a specific judicial jurisdiction in a particular state of the US does not overlap with the administrative division. Some large states in the US are generally divided into separate judicial districts, while the courts are located in a given administrative area. For example, Alabama is divided into three judicial districts: Northern, Central and Southern; each of which is further divided into several branches, while each branch has jurisdiction over several counties, and the court is located in one of its administrative areas. The northern district is divided into seven branches, of which the northwestern branch governs the three counties of Colbert, Franklin and Lauderdale, but the court is located in the northwestern city of Florence. According to the rules established by the Judicial Conference of the United State in 1978, four factors shall be taken into account when setting up a new federal jurisdiction, i.e., case load, judicial management, geographic location, and community convenience.

In Germany and France that implement the civil law system, the courts are set up in judicial districts, and the location of the courts has nothing to do with the administrative divisions. It is mainly due to historical reasons and the court layout is subject to adjustment along with social development to facilitate litigation.[78] "The courts in Germany and France are set up according to the judicial districts which are completely separated from the administrative districts, mainly for ensuring judicial independence".[79] The ongoing judicial reform in Russia in recent years has made it an important task to maintain the judicial independence and prevent the judiciary

[77]Xiao [51].

[78]Zhou [52], p. 95.

[79]Zhou [52], p. 115.

from the interference by local authorities, and the measure that it adopts is not to set up judicial jurisdictions on basis of administrative divisions.[80]

(3) Based on domestic resources: cross-administrative division courts are already available in China

"The road to rule of law in China must be based on the country's domestic resources, and paying respect to the tradition and practice of Chinese legal culture".[81] Any system design or innovation should be based on the national conditions of a country for fear of unintended consequences, and the judicial reform cannot copy other countries' experiences mechanically. When talking about cross-administrative division courts, many scholars like to draw on the experiences of foreign countries, and demonstrate the rationality of cross-administrative division courts from the perspective of separating judicial jurisdictions from administrative divisions in most countries. It is certainly a good idea, but in my opinion, when exploring the ways to establish the cross-administrative division courts in China, it is more important to evaluate whether the existing systems are available for doing so. In fact, although the judicial jurisdictions and administrative divisions are highly overlapped in China, there are already practices that have them separated, which has laid the foundation for it to implement relevant reforms.

a. Special courts established for industry needs

The special courts are typical cross-administrative division courts. According to the *Organization Law of the People's Cour*ts (1979), "the special people's courts are made up of military courts, railway transport courts, water transport courts, forest courts, and other special courts". However, this law was amended in 1983, after that this article only stated that the special people's courts include military courts and other special courts. In practice, there have been military courts, railway transport courts, maritime courts, forest courts, mining area courts,[82] oilfield courts, and farming courts.

The military courts are a type of special court stipulated in China's *Organization Law of the People's Courts*. The military courts are divided into three levels. From a higher level to a lower one, they are Chinese People's Liberation Army (PLA)

---

[80]Li [53].

[81]Su [54].

[82]The "mining area courts" mainly included Datong Mining Area People's Court and Yangquan Mining Area People's Court in Shanxi, and Jingxing Mining Area People's Court in Hebei. Since the cities where these mining areas are located have become administrative areas, these mining area courts are no longer special courts. At present, Gansu Mining Area People's Court is the only court of this kind in China (Yang Fan, Lv Sisi, Where will the special courts go–exploration into the establishment of a jurisdiction system separated from administrative divisions, *Collective Papers of the 26th Academic Symposium of National Courts: Research on Judicial System Reform and Civil and Commercial Law Application*, https://cpfd.cnki.com.cn/Article/CPFDTOTAL-GJFG201504001010.htm). In March 2012, Gansu Mining Area People's Court was formally identified as a national court and subject to vertical management under Gansu Higher People's Court as an intermediate court.

Military Court, Military Unit Court at the level of military region, and Corps-level Military Unit Court. The trial work of military courts at all levels is supervised by the Supreme People's Court, and the trial work of military courts at lower levels is supervised by military courts at higher levels. The President of the PLA Military Court is submitted to the Standing Committee of the NPC by the President of the Supreme People's Court for appointment and dismissal.[83]

The railway courts were first built in March 1954, and then called the special courts along the railway. They were revoked in September 1957 in accordance with the State Council's *Decision on Revocation of Railway and Water Transport Courts.* With China's reform and opening up and economic construction in full swing, on July 25, 1980, the Ministry of Justice and the Ministry of Railways jointly released the *Notice on the Establishment of Railway Courts at All Levels*, planning to set up a high court of railway transport in Beijing (revoked in May 1987), an intermediate court of railway transport at the location of the railway bureau, and a railway transport court at the location of the railway sub-bureau. Around 1980, preparations were made for establishing the National Railway Transport Court, and it started trying cases since May 1, 1982. With the adjustment of the railway management system, the railway court system has also changed. The staffs, funds and properties of railway courts are borne by railway bureaus. Such model of enterprises running courts has been criticized since then.[84]

On July 8, 2009, the *Notice on the Reform of the Management System for the Public Security Organs, Procuratorates and Courts Handing Railway Transport Cases and Approval of Their Special Staffing* was released, requiring the public security organs, procuratorates and courts that are involved in railway transport cases to be incorporated into the national judicial system, and the railway courts as a whole are to be managed by the Party Committees and higher people's courts in the provinces (municipalities and autonomous regions) where they are located. At present, China has completed the reform of the railway court management system, making all of these courts included into the national judicial system. Consequently, the primary railway transport court is the provincial primary court, and the railway transport intermediate court is the intermediate court. As far as railway-related cases are concerned, the jurisdiction of the railway transport courts is the same as that of their corresponding railway bureaus (Table 2.1).

The maritime courts originated from the water transport courts. In May 1984, the Supreme People's Court and the Ministry of Transport jointly issued the *Notice on the Establishment of Maritime Courts*, showing the intention to set up special maritime courts. In June of the same year, six maritime courts including Shanghai Maritime Court were established. In the early days, it was the Ministry of Transport that took charge of the staffs, funds and properties of maritime courts,[85] while the Supreme

---

[83]The military court system of China is under reform, and it is not closely related to the theme of this book, please find relevant details in Zhang [55, 56].

[84]Shen and Zhao [57].

[85]*The Notice of the Supreme People's Court and the Ministry of Transport on the Establishment of Maritime Courts*, May 24, 1984.

Table 2.1 Railway transport court system

	High court		Intermediate court of railway transport		Primary court of railway transport
Railway transport court	Before 1987	After 1987	Inter-provincial jurisdiction	Beijing	Beijing, Tianjin, Shijiazhuang
				Shanghai	Shanghai, Hangzhou, Hefei, Nanjing, Xuzhou
	High court of railway transport	Local high court		Nanchang	Nanchang, Fuzhou
				Guangzhou	Guangzhou, Zhaoqing, Huaihua, Changsha, Hengyang
				Chengdu	Chengdu, Chongqing, Guiyang, Xichang
				Lanzhou	Lanzhou, Wuwei, Yinchuan, Xining
			Provincial jurisdiction	Harbin	Harbin, Qiqihar, Wudanjiang, Jiamusi
				Changchun	Changchun, Jilin, Tonghua, Baicheng, Tumen
				Shenyang	Shenyang, Jinzhou, Dalian, Dandong
				Taiyuan	Taiyuan, Datong, Linfen
				Jinan	Jinan, Qingdao
				Zhengzhou	Zhengzhou, Luoyang
				Wuhan	Wuhan, Xiangyang

(continued)

Table 2.1 (continued)

	High court		Intermediate court of railway transport		Primary court of railway transport
				Kunming	Kunming, Kaiyuan
				Nanning	Nanning, Liuzhou
				Xi'an	Xi'an, Ankang
				Hohhot	Hohhot, Baotou, Tongliao, Hailar
				Urumqi	Urumqi, Hami, Korla

People's Court decided the establishment and jurisdiction of maritime courts.[86] The standing committees of the municipal people's congresses in the places where the maritime courts are located decided the creation of maritime courts, and appointed and dismissed their judges.[87] As an intermediate court, the maritime courts have jurisdiction over the first-instance maritime cases and maritime business cases, but do not accept criminal cases and other civil cases. The appeals to the judgments and rulings of the maritime courts are under the jurisdiction of the high people's courts where the maritime courts are located.

There are ten maritime courts nationwide. In June 1999, the six maritime courts established before the others were transferred to the Party Committee, people's government, and the high people's court at the provincial level in the place where they are located for joint management, and thoroughly broke away from the Ministry of Transport.[88] The jurisdictions of the maritime courts are mainly divided according to the water area, which features separation from administrative divisions and an extremely broad expanded scope. To facilitate litigations, the maritime courts have set dispatched courts. For example, Dalian Maritime Court has five dispatched courts in Jinzhou, Bayuquan, Donggang, Changhai and Harbin (Table 2.2).[89]

In the late 1970s, China set up several forest courts in the state-owned forest zones in the northeastern region and Inner Mongolia. Later, China successively established about 150 forest courts, and many of them are located in the northeastern region.

[86] *The Decision of the Supreme People's Court on Several Issues Concerning the Establishment of Maritime Courts*, Nov 28, 1984; *The Notice of the Supreme People's Court on Adjusting the Jurisdictions of Wuhan and Shanghai Maritime Courts*, Jul 28, 1987.

[87] *The Decision of the Standing Committee of the NPC on the Establishment of Maritime Courts in Coastal Port Cities*, Nov 14, 1984.

[88] Tan [58].

[89] Introduction to Dalian Maritime Court, https://www.dlhsfy.gov.cn/en/index.php?m=content&c=index&a=lists&catid=106.

Table 2.2 Maritime court system

	High court	Intermediate court (first instance)
Maritime court	Local high court	Dalian, Tianjin, Qingdao, Shanghai, Ningbo, Xiamen, Wuhan, Beihai, Guangzhou, Haikou

Table 2.3 Forest court system

	High court	Intermediate court		Primary court
Forest court	Local high court	Heilongjiang province	Heilongjiang Intermediate Forest Court	Fangzheng, Shanhetun, Xinglong, Yabuli, Suileng, Tongbei, Zhanhe, Weihe, Dongfanghong, Dongjingcheng, Hailin, Dalinlin, Mu, Leng, Suiyang, Chaihe, Linkou, Bamiantong, Qinghe, Yingchun, Heli, Hebei, Huanan, Shuangyashan
		Jilin province	Changchun Intermediate Forest Court	Hongshi, Baishishan, Fusong, Jiangyuan, Linjiang
			Yanbian Intermediate Forest Court	Dunhua, Helong, Wangqing, Baihe, Hunchun
		Gansu rovince	Gansu Intermediate Forest Court	Zhuoni, Diebu, Zhouqu, Wenxian

There are 17 primary forest courts in Jilin province alone, and more than 30 primary forest courts in Heilongjiang province.[90] The staffs, funds and properties of forest courts are managed by the forestry departments.[91] Since 2007, the forest courts and procuratorates were gradually separated from the forestry departments and incorporated into the national judicial system, marking that these courts will become increasingly standardized.[92] At present, the staffs, funds and properties of forest courts are under the control of the provincial courts and procuratorates (Table 2.3).

The oilfield courts are a type of special court set up in large and medium-sized state-owned oilfields. China once had Shengli Oilfield People's Court and

[90] Yang and Huang [59].

[91] *The Notice on Establishing and Perfecting Forestry Organizations and Institutions as Public Security Organs, Procuratorates and Courts in Key Forest Regions*, Dec 1, 1980.

[92] *The Notice of the State Commission Office of Public Sectors Reform on the Matters Concerning the Establishment of Forestry Public security Organs, Procuratorates and Courts* ([2007] SCOPSR No. 19).

Shengli Oilfield Intermediate People's Court, which were respectively restructured into Dongying District People's Court and Dongying District Intermediate People's Court.[93] In 2009, the two levels of Liaohe oilfield court—the only one of this kind of court—were transferred to Liaoning Higher People's Court for management, and they were respectively renamed Liaohe People's Court and Liaohe Intermediate People's Court, with the jurisdictions made up of the production area, management area and living area in Liaohe Oilfield, involving 13 prefectures and 32 counties (banners and districts) in Liaoning province and Inner Mongolia.[94]

The courts of the Xinjiang Production and Construction Corps (XPCC) were established as result of the continuous development of the XPCC.[95] In December 1998, the Standing Committee of the NPC decided to set up the XPCC courts to be the outpost tribunals of the High People's Court in Xinjiang Uygur Autonomous Region (XUAR), and several intermediate people's courts, as well as some primary people's courts in the reclamation areas where ranches are concentrated.[96] The legal status of the XPCC courts was formally established. Now the XPCC court system has altogether 43 people's courts at three levels. The XPCC courts execute the judgments made by the High People's Court except for the second instance of cases involving death penalty. The XPCC courts are under the supervision and guidance of the Supreme People's Court and the High People's Court of the Autonomous Region, and at the same time supervise and guide the trial work of the intermediate and primary courts.[97]

In February 1982, the 19th Meeting of the Standing Committee of the 5th Heilongjiang Provincial People's Congress approved the request of Heilongjiang Provincial High People's Court to set up the courts in agricultural reclamation areas. Consequently, an intermediate reclamation court (in Harbin city) and 8 primary reclamation courts were set up gradually.[98] These courts accept all sorts of cases within the jurisdiction of the reclamation bureaus.

On August 31, 2014, the Tenth Meeting of the 12th NPC Standing Committee adopted the decision on the establishment of intellectual property courts in Beijing, Shanghai, and Guangzhou. According to the *Provisions of the Supreme People's*

---

[93]Translator's note: As the location of China's third largest oilfield, Dongying city of Shandong province was officially founded in 1983, which was the background for the oilfield courts to be rebuilt.

[94]Introduction to Liaohe Intermediate People's Court, https://lnlhzy.chinacourt.gov.cn/article/detail/2011/03/id/3612303.shtml.

[95]The organizational system of the XPCC was once revoked in 1975 and not restored until the end of 1981. Two years later, the XPCC public security organs, procuratorates, courts and prison administrations were also restored. The three levels of the XPCC courts exercise the judicial power as ordinary courts, with the capital cases reviewed by the High People's Court of the Autonomous Region.

[96]*The Decision of the Standing Committee of the NPC on the Establishment of the People's Courts and People's Procuratorates of the Xinjiang Production and Construction Corps*, Dec 29, 1998.

[97]Introduction to the courts of the XPCC, https://xjbtfy.chinacourt.gov.cn/article/index/id/MygpMzAwBCPCAAA.shtml.

[98]Introduction to the intermediate reclamation court of Heilongjiang province, https://hljnkzy.hljcourt.gov.cn/public/detail.php?id=2039.

Court on the Jurisdiction of the Intellectual Property Courts in Beijing, Shanghai, and Guangzhou, the three courts have jurisdiction as courts of first instance over the intellectual property cases within the cities where they are located. It should be noted that Guangzhou Intellectual Property Court also has cross-regional jurisdiction over certain intellectual property cases in Guangdong province.

Each special court is set up for a specific purpose, e.g., the railway courts ensure the stability of railway transport, the forest courts maintain the order of forest zones, and the oilfield courts guarantee the production of oilfields. In the early days of these courts, they were subordinate to certain government organs or enterprises. Although some early special courts might have jurisdiction across administrative divisions, they were more closely connected with relevant units. In a sense, they were sectoral courts, rather than the ideal specialized courts, which only had a negative impact on the impartial judgment of cases. Along with economic and social development, the State has gradually incorporated these courts into unified national management, so that they can separate from government organs or enterprises to become genuinely special courts. This has paved the way for establishing the courts that are across-administrative divisions.

(4) The people's courts of non-administrative divisions established due to the trial grade system

At the beginning of their establishment, the special courts had corresponding management departments. Under the court system of China, there is a type of court that is set up because of the trial grade system. They have no corresponding administrative divisions or management departments, and most scholars regard them as the people's courts across administrative divisions.

The courts of China implement the system of two instances at four levels.[99] The intermediate people's courts are set up in provinces, autonomous regions (prefectures), district-based cities, and municipalities directly under the Central Government as courts of second instance for the primary people's courts. In the four municipalities directly under the Central Government, 14 intermediate courts have been set up, which have jurisdiction over 94 primary courts. The intermediate courts at this level do not need to dock with any corresponding Party Committee, government organ or people's congress. To a certain extent, they are courts without administrative divisions.

Besides, through the reform of county administrated by province, there have been districts and counties not governed by prefecture-level cities. The layout of the courts of second instance in these districts and counties is a kind of innovation. On October 18, 1999, with the consent of the Supreme People's Court, the State Commission Office of Public Sectors Reform (SCOPSR) approved the establishment of Hanjiang Intermediate People's Court in Hubei Province, which is directly under the administration of Hubei Provincial High People's Court and under the supervision of Hubei Provincial People's Congress, with a jurisdiction covering three cities as Tianmen, Qianjiang and Xiantao directly administrated by Hubei

[99] Liu [60].

Province.[100] In 2014, Henan Province established the First Intermediate People's Court to undertake the first instance of major cases, the second instance of appellate cases, and trial supervision of the primary courts in seven counties (cities) of Gongyi, Ruzhou, Dengzhou, Yongcheng, Gushi, Luyi and Xincai. Moreover, Jiyuan Intermediate People's Court, established in 2003, was renamed Henan Provincial Second Intermediate People's Court, with a jurisdiction covering four counties (cities) of Jiyuan, Lankao, Huaxian and Changyuan.[101] The First Intermediate People's Court and the Second Intermediate People's Court of Hainan Province are the courts of the same type.[102]

Some prefecture-level cities do not have municipal jurisdictions, so the local primary courts have nothing to do with administrative divisions. This is the case in Dongguan and Zhongshan cities in Guangdong Province, Jiayuguan City in Gansu Province, and Sansha City in Hainan Province. Take Zhongshan City as an example, according to the *Reply of the Supreme People's Court on the Agreement to Revoke and Establish the Primary People's Courts in Dongguan and Zhongshan Cities* (Fa [2007] No. 187), Zhongshan People's Court was revoked in October 2007 and split into Zhongshan First People's Court and Zhongshan Second People's Court. The jurisdiction of Zhongshan First People's Court is made up of 15 districts and towns (including Torch Hi-tech Industrial Development Zone).[103] The jurisdiction of Zhongshan Second People's Court includes 9 towns in the north of Zhongshan City.[104] These two courts are free from the restriction by administrative divisions. The primary courts such as Science City People's Court of Sichuan Province and Sanya Suburban People's Court of Hainan Province are also without administrative divisions.[105]

In addition, the people's courts of development zones are also separated from administrative divisions. Although they are under management of the administrative committees at the same level, the courts of development zones are created by the standing committees of the people's congresses of the prefecture-level cities. These courts have no corresponding administrative divisions, and their establishment is for

[100]Introduction to Hanjiang Intermediate People's Court of Hubei Province, https://hjzy.hbfy.gov.cn/DocManage/ViewDoc?docid=3b70f040-aa6d-11e1-8a71-4c1fcc467667.

[101]Ten Party Committees of the counties administrated by Henan Province are directly led by Henan Provincial Party Committee, https://newpaper.dahe.cn/hnsb/html/2013-11/29/content_993858.htm?div=-1.

[102]Introduction to the First Intermediate People's Court of Hainan Province, https://hnyzy.hicourt.gov.cn/.

[103]Introduction to Zhongshan First People's Court, https://www.zscourt.gov.cn/Article/index/id/18264.html.

[104]Introduction to Zhongshan Second People's Court, https://www.zsdefy.gov.cn/?con=article&ac_id=147.

[105]Science City People's Court of Sichuan Province has jurisdiction as a court of first instance over the criminal, civil and commercial, and administrative cases in Science City. It is subject to the supervision of the Standing Committee of the People's Congress of Mianyang City, and the guidance from Mianyang Intermediate People's Court. Sanya City Suburban People's Court has no corresponding administrative divisions; it is responsible to Sanya People's Congress, the Standing Committee of Sanya People's Congress and Sanya Intermediate People's Court.

implementation of the trial grade system (as in the case of setting up an intermediary court in a municipality) or for rational allocation of cases (as in the case of splitting Zhongshan People's Court into Zhongshan First People's Court and Zhongshan Second People's Court). These courts are not established to evade local interference. They are not genuinely "cross-administrative division courts", but more like "outpost tribunals" of a high court. These courts and the aforementioned special courts are already incorporated into the national judicial system, which enables the Supreme People's Court to exercise its power to set up lower courts, and leaves institutional space for the establishment of people's courts across administrative divisions.

Both the special courts and the courts without corresponding administrative divisions are free from the fetters of administrative divisions, they have independent sources of funding and appointment and dismissal of judges, which helps to prevent the interference from local authorities and provides a useful reference for building the courts across administrative divisions and for reforming the court system.

(5) Explorations: the pilot plan for cross-administrative division courts

In December 2014, the 7th meeting of the Central Leading Group for Comprehensively Deepening Reforms adopted the *Pilot Plan for Establishing the Cross-administrative Division People's Courts and People's Procuratorates*. Under the guidance of this plan and in reference to the experiences in operating the railway transport courts, Shanghai Third Intermediate Court and Beijing Fourth Intermediate Court were established, becoming the first batch of the people's courts across the administrative divisions in China. Without the interference of the Party Committees and government organs at the same level and free from the restrictions of administrative divisions, these newly-built cross-administrative division courts seem relatively detached. Such major institutional innovation is of the milestone significance.

a. Implementation process and effect of the pilot plan

It is feasible to rebuild the railway transport courts into the people's courts across administrative divisions. First of all, in the case of the railway transport courts, their jurisdiction and administrative divisions are inherently separated, which accords with the reform idea for of setting up the courts across administrative divisions and provides a "framework" of the reform. Secondly, after the railway transport courts are incorporated into the national unified judicial system, they have been subject to the provincial-level unified management and with the professional quality of their judges gradually improved, but they have failed to handle plenty of cases. Before the above-mentioned pilot plan was implemented, many areas have made the railway transport courts assume the task of designated jurisdiction or centralized jurisdiction, which has provided the basis for the reform. Thirdly, the railway transport courts have jurisdiction over criminal cases and corresponding procuratorates, so their replacement by cross-administrative division courts will facilitate the integration of judicial resources and reduce reform costs, and it is more operable. The following analysis will be based on the samples of Shanghai Third Intermediate People's Court and Beijing Fourth Intermediate People's Court.

Shanghai Third Intermediate People's Court was established on the basis of Shanghai Railway Transport Intermediate Court. Shanghai Intellectual Property Court was established at the same time to collaborate with Shanghai Third Intermediate People's Court, thus forming a pattern of "one court with three branches".[106] During the process of implementing the pilot plan, Shanghai Third Intermediate People's Court took three indicators ("cross-regional", "susceptible to local interference" and "major") as the criteria for the handling cases that are across administrative divisions. Regarding its jurisdiction of criminal cases, it is defined that this court handles the criminal cases that seriously endanger the safety of food and drugs, infringe intellectual property rights, and destroy the environmental resources; the criminal cases investigated by the public security organs affiliated to the Customs; and the criminal cases in the field of transportation. Regarding its jurisdiction of administrative cases, this court has gradually undertaken the concentrated jurisdiction of the grassroots administrative cases in Shanghai. Regard its jurisdiction of civil and commercial cases, it is initially defined that this court handles (i) the major civil and commercial cases involving environmental resource protection and food and drug safety; (ii) the enterprise bankruptcy cases; (iii) and the contract dispute cases involving inter-region transportation.[107] Since its establishment, Shanghai Third Intermediate People's Court has accepted 1,019 administrative cases, of which 610 were accepted in 2015 and 409 in the first half of 2016. Among the people suing the government cases, almost 40% of them were against Shanghai Municipal Government.[108]

Beijing Fourth Intermediate People's Court, which was established on the basis of Beijing Railway Transport Intermediate Court, has jurisdiction over the following cases: (i) the administrative cases in which the county people's governments in Beijing are under accusation; (ii) the financial loan contract dispute cases, insurance dispute cases, foreign-related and Hong Kong, Macao and Taiwan-related commercial cases that used to be accepted by Beijing Municipal Intermediate People's Court; (iii) the major cross-regional environmental resource protection cases, major food and drug safety cases; (iv) the cases of public prosecution filed by Beijing People's Procuratorate Fourth Branch; (v) other special cases under the jurisdiction of Beijing Municipal High Court; and (vi) the criminal and civil cases under the jurisdiction of the former Beijing Railway Transport Intermediate Court.[109] Beijing Fourth Intermediate People's Court has accepted 1,892 all sorts of cases in the past year since its establishment, among which 1,700 were closed, registering a case closing rate of 99.44% within the time limit for trial. The administrative cases, civil and commercial

[106]Wei [61].

[107]Wu [62].

[108]The cross-administrative division procuratorates in Beijing and Shanghai have achieved staged results since they were established more than a year ago, https://www.spp.gov.cn/zdgz/201608/t20160819_164067.shtml.

[109]Beijing Fourth Intermediate People's Court and Beijing People's Procuratorate Fourth Branch were formally established, https://epaper.bjnews.com.cn/html/2014-12/31/content_555222.htm?div=-1.

cases, criminal cases, and enforcement cases respectively accounted for 73.8%, 20%, 1.6% and 4.6%.[110]

b. Problems in the pilot plan

The pilot plan has achieved stage results, but we should be fully aware of the remaining problems and difficulties, and endeavour to have them addressed.

First, the courts across administrative divisions are not worthy of the name. The courts covered in the pilot plan only cross the areas within the municipalities. They are far from being the genuine "cross-administrative division courts", although they are classified as such. They are ought to handle the cross-administrative division cases, but in fact they are accepting the cases under jurisdiction of the original courts in a centralized manner. The only good news is that no judicial resources are wasted, because there is only expanded scope of jurisdiction of the original courts, instead of any newly-built courts. The courts covered in the pilot plan concentrate on the trial of administrative cases; the cases with district or county governments as the defendants have been subject to cross-regional trial, but the cases with the municipal governments as the defendants are still restricted by administrative divisions. In addition, the pilot reform failed to give full play to the advantages of the railway transport courts. For example, Shanghai Third Intermediate People's Court and Beijing Fourth Intermediate People's Court, which were respectively established on the basis of Shanghai Railway Transport Intermediate Court and Beijing Railway Transport Intermediate Court, are typical examples of cross-administrative division courts. Under the jurisdiction of Shanghai Railway Transport Intermediate Court, there are five primary courts in Shanghai, Xuzhou, Hefei, Nanjing and Hangzhou. It is a pity that the inter-provincial cases handled by the cross-administrative division courts are those only related to railway transport. Take the case of Shanghai for example, Xuzhou Railway Transport Court and Nanjing Railway Transport Court have centralized jurisdiction over the local administrative cases; if they could accept all the administrative cases in Jiangsu, Anhui, Zhejiang and Shanghai, the purpose of establishing cross-administrative division courts will be achieved.

Second, some specific approaches in the current pilot plan are not clear enough. The positioning of the cross-administrative division courts is definite, i.e., to try the cases across administrative divisions free from the local interference. But some existing practices are confusing: (i) The exclusive jurisdiction and designated jurisdiction are mixed. This is partly due to the addition of the cross-administrative division courts to the original railway transport courts. In order to ensure that the people's courts across administrative divisions can truly assume their due responsibilities and play their due role after their establishment, their specific jurisdiction must be clearly defined. Is the list of cases under their jurisdiction? Are there any omissions? The jurisdiction of these courts cannot be divided or designated at will. (ii) The primary

[110]Beijing Fourth Intermediate People's Court achieved initial success in handling the cases across administrative divisions, https://legal.people.com.cn/n1/2016/0105/c188502-28011904.html.

courts and intermediate courts are not compatible. At present, it is only the intermediate courts that are covered in the pilot plan, thus making the effect of this plan hardly complete.

(6) Outlook: China's approach to separate judicial jurisdictions from administrative divisions

a. Cross-administrative courts as a complement to the court system

Any reform shall be both swift and steady. All the policies and guidelines demonstrate that the CPC Central Committee has all along been prudent about the cross-administrative division justice. The Third Plenary Session of the 18th CPC Central Committee proposed to "explore ways to establish a judicial jurisdiction system that is appropriately separated from the administrative divisions". The Fourth Plenary Session of the 18th CPC Central Committee went a step further by proposing to "explore ways to establish the people's courts and people's procuratorates across administrative divisions to handle cross-regional cases". Both the sessions suggested "exploring" for fear of the reform being pushed too hard. Xi Jinping pointed out to establish the people's courts and people's procuratorates across administrative divisions, and eventually "form a litigation pattern where ordinary cases are tried in administrative division courts and special cases tried in cross-administrative division courts".[111] It can be seen that the current judicial system reform is not to subvert the existing court system based on administrative divisions; instead, it moderately adjusts the existing court system by transferring the cross-regional and easily intervened "special" cases from the general courts them to the cross-administrative division courts. Considering the achievements of the pilot plan to date, the cross-administrative division people's courts may be in the followings forms after the reform.

In terms of court setting, a relatively simple and feasible approach is to build a provincial cross-administrative division courts on the basis of the existing 18 railway transport intermediate courts and 61 railway transport primary courts; where there is no railway transport intermediate court, the relevant setting needs to be completed in advance. This approach is in line with the current provincial level management, but the problem is that the handling of inter-provincial cases may require the Supreme People's Court to designate jurisdiction, which violates the principle of certainty of jurisdiction. The solution to this problem is to establish three levels of cross-administrative division courts by integrating the resources of special courts.[112] For example, build several primary courts in Beijing, Tianjin and Hebei to try the cases in the entire BTH region, establish one or two intermediate courts in this region, and then set up a high court in a relatively large region such as the North China region.

[111] Wei [61].

[112] Some special courts are products of a specific historical period. At present, the maritime courts may need to be retained due to the particularity of the maritime cases, but their jurisdiction has been loosened, since not all maritime cases must be handled by these courts. Likewise, the cases involving railway transport, forest and farm reclamation are not that special. It is possible to vacate the specialized functions of these courts and rebuild them into cross-administrative division courts.

In this way, a complete set of inter-regional court system characterized by central authority and compatible with the ordinary court system can be formed separately.[113]

The cases under jurisdiction shall be explicitly defined by law, at least they shall be the cases that cross administrative divisions, affect people's vital interests, or they are prone to be interfered by administrative agencies or other local authorities. In light of the Fourth Five-Year Outline released by the Supreme People's Court,[114] the cases that are accepted by the cross-administrative division courts should be those involve the major administrative affairs, environmental resource protection, enterprise bankruptcy, food and drug safety and other cases that are subject to local influence, and those for which a public prosecution is initiated by a cross-administrative division procuratorate; moreover, the antitrust cases and major financial fraud cases also fall into this scope.

b. Cross-administrative division courts in an ideal state

The author prefers an intact system of cross-administrative division courts by expanding (or merging) the jurisdictions of the original courts: the jurisdiction of a primary court should cover two or more counties or districts; and that of an intermediate court should cover three or more prefecture-level cities.[115] The system of "four independent and three non-independent judicial districts" is also recommended. The "four independent judicial districts" are made up of the central judicial district, the high judicial district, the appeal judicial district and the primary judicial district; among them, the high judicial district, the appeal judicial district and the primary judicial district do not conform to the administrative divisions, i.e., their jurisdictions feature a larger territory and a higher level than the provinces, prefecture-level cities and counties. The "three non-independent judicial districts" are based on further division of the high judicial district, the appeal judicial district and the primary judicial district, which is convenient for holding hearings at multiple locations and for citizen to file a lawsuit.[116] The author insists on the setting of cross-administrative division courts for the following reasons[117]:

First, the establishment of cross-administrative division courts is an inevitable requirement of the judiciary as the central authority. China implements a unitary

---

[113]Wu [63].

[114]*The Opinions of the Supreme People's Court on Comprehensively Deepening the Reform of the People's Courts—The Fourth Five-Year Outline for the Reform of the People's Courts (2014 ~ 2018) (Fa [2015] No. 3).*

[115]Liu [40].

[116]Zhao and Zou [64] (The primary judicial district may consist of two to four county-level administrative districts. There is only one primary court in each primary jurisdiction. The appeal judicial district is composed of about 20 county-level administrative districts, including about five primary judicial districts. There is only one appeal court in each appeal judicial district. The appellate courts are allowed to set up branches to meet the need for holding hearings at multiple locations. The high judicial district is generally set up across provincial administrative districts, and composed of about 280 county-level administrative districts, including about 14 appeal judicial districts. Each high judicial district has a high court, and branch courts can be set up according to local conditions.).

[117]Chen [65].

system with the judicial power as the central authority. Regarding the judicial system reform, Meng Jianzhu, Secretary of the Commission for Political and Legal Affairs under the CPC Central Committee, once pointed that China will remain in the primary stage of socialism for a long time, it is difficult to unify the management of the staffs, funds and properties of the judiciary by the Central Government. So the judicial management system should be reformed progressively. The first thing to do is transfer the staffs, funds and properties of the local people's courts and people's procuratorates below the provincial level to the provincial unified management. The funds of local people's courts and people's procuratorates, special people's courts and people's procuratorates at all levels are pooled by the provincial finance, and supplemented by the central finance.[118] It can be seen that the unified management at provincial level is a contingent policy based on the current national conditions, and the management at central level is an inevitable trend in the future. Since the judiciary is the central authority, it is necessary for separating judicial jurisdictions from the current administrative divisions. At present, the establishment of many courts without corresponding administrative divisions has verified the feasibility of setting up the courts of this kind.

Second, the cross-administrative division courts are the common choice of all countries in the world. Judicial localization, as an important problem that plagues judicial organs' independent exercise of power in accordance with law, also exists in western countries and has been criticized by the public. However, with the continuous implementation of the judicial system reform, this problem has been properly resolved in the countries either implement the unitary system or the federal system. For example, the UK, France, the US and Germany have established independent judicial districts. China can learn from the practical experiences of western countries when exploring the ways to build the judicial organs across administrative divisions. In China that implements the unitary system, the judicial power is set from top to bottom, there is only one judicial system in the country, and the establishment of central and local judicial organs and the allocation of judicial jurisdictions are stipulated in both the Constitution and the organic laws for the national judicial organs. Therefore, the judicial organs at all levels exercise jurisdiction under the premise of unified state regulation.

Third, the cross-administrative division courts are a practical need to optimize the allocation of judicial resources. For the courts of the same level in China, some of them have to handle a large number of cases, while others have no enough work to do. Since the judicial regions zoning system has the function of allocating judicial resources and facilitating people to file lawsuits, the well-planned cross-administrative division courts should not only resist local protectionism in judicial activities, but also optimize the allocation of judicial resources.[119]

[118] Meng [66].

[119] Yi and Wang [67].

(7) Brief summary

The separation of judicial jurisdictions from administrative divisions is a complicated issue, since it involves institutional setup, transport convenience, and creation of judicial organs. However, compared with the reform prospects, the pains of reform are generally tolerable. Moreover, the military system, railway system and aviation system in China are not set up according to administrative divisions, they are useful experiences for the judicial system reform. Many problems are in fact surmountable. Of course, we should admit that the biggest problem in this reform lies in its constitutionality. According to China's Constitution, "local people's congresses at or above the county level elect, and have the power to recall, presidents of people's courts and chief procurators of people's procuratorates at the corresponding level", "local people's courts at various levels are responsible to the organs of state power which created them", "people's procuratorates at various local levels are responsible to the organs of state power which created them and to the people's procuratorates at higher levels". The *Organization Law of the People's Courts* and the *Organization Law of the People's Procuratorate* also set up the people's courts and procuratorates at all levels based on administrative divisions. In order to separate judicial jurisdictions from administrative divisions, two ways of thinking are recommended: one is to amend the Constitution and related organizational laws; the other is to find a compromise method under the current legal framework. Looking at the situation at the present stage, it may be difficult to fully separate judicial jurisdictions from administrative divisions in the short run. In fact, the unified management of staffs, funds and properties of the judiciary has indirectly achieved the relative separation of judicial jurisdictions from administrative divisions, cut the connection between judicial personnel and local authorities, and objectively avoided the influence of local Party Committees and government organs. The judges of local people's courts at all levels are managed by the Party Committees of the provinces, autonomous regions, and municipalities directly under the Central Government, nominated by the provincial high courts, and appointed and dismissed by the people's congresses at all levels. In this way, the personnel management power of judges is stripped from the local authorities, which can prevent the judges from losing their independence because of local personnel control, and solved the problem of judicial localization to a certain extent.

In addition, to promote this reform, it is necessary to distinguish and clarify the concepts of "jurisdiction" and "the place where the crime was committed". Someone has suggested that the separation of judicial jurisdictions from administrative divisions would violate the provisions of the *Criminal Procedure Law of China* regarding jurisdiction (Article 24 of this law provides that "a criminal case shall be under the jurisdiction of the people's court in the place where the crime was committed"). If the jurisdiction is inconsistent with the administrative division, it will lead to a "illegal" consequence that the case is to be handled by the people's court not in "the place where the crime was committed". For example, if a cross-district (A and B) court is set up in district A, then a crime committed in district B is available to be handled by the court in district A. The viewpoint that this practice "violates" the relevant regulations is fundamentally untenable. The reason why this viewpoint still exists is due to the traditional concept that judicial jurisdictions are identical with administrative divisions. According to the existing provisions, "the place where the crime was committed" appears to be consistent with the administrative division, such consistency is caused by the overlap of judicial jurisdictions and administrative divisions, not that judicial jurisdictions are based administrative divisions. In other words, "the place where the crime was committed" is not a concept of administrative divisions, but that of judicial jurisdictions. As long as the crime is committed in a judicial jurisdiction, it can be handled by the court possessing the judicial power of this jurisdiction.

2.2.6.4 Judges' Independent Exercise of Power According to Law and Reform of Judge System

(1) Judges' independent exercise of power according to law and selection of judges

In most countries the judges are appointed by the highest legislative or executive organ, instead of through election. In order to prevent local authorities from interfering in judicial activities, and also prevent them from affecting the independent trial by judges (they may succumb to such interference out of gratitude or fear if they are appointed by local authorities), all western countries, almost without exception, empower the central government to appoint judges. For example, the US Constitution stipulates that the President cannot directly appoint the federal court judges after his nomination is approved by the Senate. In the UK, the Lord High Chancellor, who has legislative, executive and judicial duties, is nominated by the Prime Minister and appointed by the King. The judges of the court of appeal, high court, and circuit court are recommended by the Lord High Chancellor and appointed by the King. The magistrate is appointed by the Lord High Chancellor. In Japan, the president of the Supreme Court is appointed by the Emperor based on the nomination of the Cabinet, and other judges of the Supreme Court are appointed by the Cabinet, and their appointment and dismissal are attested by the Emperor; the president of the High Court is nominated by the Supreme Court and appointed by the Cabinet.[120]

In China, with the advancement of the reform of the unified management of staffs, funds and properties of the judiciary at the provincial level, the establishment of a judge selection committee at the provincial level should become the consensus of the reform. The selection committee should nominate the judges from a professional perspective, and the personnel, discipline inspection and supervision departments should check the political accomplishment, integrity and self-discipline of the candidates. The members of the selection committee shall be broadly representative, i.e., there should be experienced judges, prosecutors, lawyers, legal scholars, and other representatives from all sectors of society. Moreover, in order to ensure of a fairness result, the entire selection process should remain transparent.

[120] Wang [68].

(2) Economic guarantee for judges' independent exercise of power according to law

In order to guarantee the independence of judges and their integrity, foreign laws generally provide for their economic guarantee. As Hamilton had described that the most helpful tool to maintain the independence of judges is to provide them a fixed salary in addition to a fixed position.[121] This economic guarantee system is made up of three parts: (i) A high salary. For example, the Lord High Chancellor of the UK earns a higher annual salary than that of the Prime Minister. In Japan, the salary of the President of the Supreme Court is the same as that of the cabinet ministers and the speaker of parliament. (ii) The salary may not be cut. As stipulated in Article 3 of the US Constitution, the judges of the Supreme Court and the lower courts shall continue to hold office if they behave properly. And they should get remuneration for their services within the prescribed period, and this remuneration may not be reduced during their continued tenure. (iii) A generous pension. Foreign laws generally stipulate that judges are entitled to a generous pension after retirement. Take Japan for example, it is provided by law that judges will receive favorable treatment after their retirement.

In China, to improve the treatment of judges, it is possible to increase their salary to twice that of the civil servants at the same level in the near future. After the specialization of judges is realized, their salary should be three times that of the civil servants at the same level; and the renumeration of judges at the same level of courts differs only because of their years of work. It is the principle that the judges at the same level of courts shall be treated equally. This is conducive to attracting excellent talents to enter the profession of judges and resisting corruption, and helpful for the exchange between judges from different regions and avoiding the localization of appointment of judges.

(3) Judges' independent exercise of power according to law and their disciplinary punishment

In order to guarantee the independence of judges, countries under the rule of law generally provide that the judges may not be dismissed or punished without statutory circumstances and legal procedures. The first measure is to separate disciplinary power from appointment power, i.e., administrative agencies have the power to appoint judges, but they cannot have them dismissed. For example, the federal court judges in the US are appointed by the President, but they are impeached by the Congress. Japanese judges are nominated and appointed by the Cabinet, while their impeachment is organized by the Congress. The second measure is that judges are free from disciplinary punishment without statutory circumstances and legal procedures. In the US, the judges are impeached only when they are found having committed crimes, not including any dereliction of duty. That is to say, the judges should not suffer impeachment due to negligence in making a judgement. The judges' disciplinary violations are exclusively handled by a special committee of the circuit court

[121] Hamilton et al. [39].

of appeal; this committee may impose vigilance and suspension of work on the concerned judges, instead of depriving of their qualifications. In Japan, according to Article 2 of the *Judge Impeachment Act*, the reasons for impeachment of judges include their obvious violations of duties or serious remiss performance of their duties, and apparent acts of undermining the judge authority. The impeachment of judges shall be investigated by a prosecution committee and allowed for prosecution.

The *Judges Law* of China stipulates that the judges may not be dismissed or punished without statutory circumstances and legal procedures, and also provides for the reasons for their dismissal and disciplinary punishment. The shortcoming is that the provisions for the disciplinary punishment of judges (including dismissal in a broad sense) lack specific procedural guarantees, and the statutory circumstances are too generalized. By learning the system settings in foreign countries and following the requirements of its own judicial reform, China may set up a special disciplinary committee for judges at the provincial level to ascertain where the responsibility lies. Of course, in order to protect the rights and interests of judges, efforts shall be made to ensure the transparency and fairness of the operation of the disciplinary committee.

(4) Judges' independent exercise of power according to law and their job security

The lifelong tenure of judges is an important condition for guaranteeing their independence. In the opinion of Hamilton, steadiness and consistent respect for the human rights granted by the Constitution is a necessary quality of the judiciary, and it cannot be possessed by the temporarily appointed judicial officers. A short tenure will affect the independence of judges in some ways no matter how or by whom they are appointed.[122] Based on this, Germany and France implement the lifelong tenure system and the retirement system for judges. Some states in the US implement the lifelong tenure system, and some implement the tenure system (it is close to the lifelong tenure system since the judges may serve consecutive terms). The judges in Japan have a term of office of ten years, but they can be reappointed consecutively unless there is any good cause. In addition, judges should enjoy judicial immunity, i.e., they are exempted from being investigated by law for their speech and acts during the trial unless they have committed any illegal or improper act maliciously.

To guarantee the duties of judges is of vital significance for guaranteeing their independence. At present, the term of office of judges in China is 5 years, which is the same as that of civil servants. This is too short for the profession of judges, which is not conducive to the stability of this vital profession, nor is it consistent with the usual practice in the world. The near-term goal of the current reform is to extend the term of office of judges to 10 years, and allow them to be re-elected as long as they have not made any major mistake. In the long run, it is necessary for China to implement a lifelong tenure system for judges.

[122] Liao [69].

2.2.7 *Reform of Internal Guarantee for Independent Exercise of Power According to Law in the Context of Judicial Reform*

2.2.7.1 Key Points in the Internal Guarantee Reform

The reform of the people's courts has always been the focus of China's judicial reform, which is determined by the position of the people's courts in the entire judicial system. The adjudicatory power of the people's courts is a power of judgment of finality, symbolizing that the judiciary is the last line of defense for maintaining social justice. Because of this, Francis Bacon in his work *Of Judicature* commented that an unfair trial is more to blame than multiple unfair actions, because these unfair actions merely contaminate the water flow, whereas the unfair trial destroys the water source. As far as the current judicial environment is concerned, the primary factor affecting judicial justice is non-independence of the judiciary. Judicial independence includes not only external independence but also internal independence, the latter refers to the independence of subjects in exercising judicial power within the entire judicial system. The reform of the people's courts is to eliminate the factors that affect judicial independence from within. As mentioned before, judicial independence is the integration of "independence" and "restraint". From the perspective of bearing responsibilities or risks, independence is a prerequisite for restraint (responsibility), and without independence there is no such thing as restraint (responsibility). In this context, independence is the prerequisite for defining power and responsibility. However, the current situation is that the subjects of adjudicatory power are not identified, which has resulted in unidentified subjects of responsibility in trial, and substitution of the adjudicatory power by the administration and management powers of the president of the court and the chief judge of a division. In other words, the subjects of responsibility are not consistent with the subjects of power. In this regard, the author once stated that the judicial injustice is not caused by judicial corruption in most cases, but that the current judiciary is not really responsible. Therefore, adjusting the relationship between the various subjects within the people's courts, and clarifying the subjects of power and responsibility have become the core content of the internal reform of the people's courts.

In fact, the internal reform of the people's courts, especially the reform of the trial organization, has always been an important part of the entire judicial reform, which can be proved by a series of judicial reform documents issued by the people's courts. For example, the*First Five-Year Outline for the Reform of the People's Courts (1999–2003)*,[123] the *Second Five-Year Outline for the Reform of the People's Courts (2004–2008)*, and the *Third Five-Year Outline for the Reform of the People's Courts (2009–2013)* have made it the key content of the reform to establish an organization form of trial that conforms to the rules of trial work, define the responsibilities of the president

[123]The Supreme People's Court released *Several Provisions on the Work of the Collegiate Panel of the People's Court*, which was a result of the judicial reform at this stage. See the academic evaluation of these provisions in Chen and Liu [70].

and vice president of the court, the chief judge and deputy judge of a division, and strengthen the trial responsibilities of the collegiate bench and the sole judge. But it should be noted that in the reform process, the scope of responsibilities and operating procedures of the trial committee and the functions of the collegiate bench were changed for several times. For example, the *First Five-Year Outline* followed the reform idea of "returning power to the collegiate bench", and required that "except for the major and difficult cases which are submitted to the trial committee for discussion and decision upon the consent of the president of the court, all other cases shall be tried and judged by the collegiate bench, neither the president of the court nor the chief judge of a division is allowed to change the decision of the collegiate bench personally". In contrast, the *Second Five-Year Outline* underscored to "strengthen the judicial responsibilities of the president and vice president of the court, the chief judge and deputy judge of a division", but at the same time "reform and improve the management of judicial trial". Consequently, the decision-making power was partly or mostly taken back from the collegiate bench and the sole judge, which objectively restored the system of examining and approving cases by the president of the court and the chief judge of a division. To this day, such phenomenon still exists and the functions of the collegiate bench are yet strengthened.

The *Decision of the CCCPC on Some Major Issues Concerning Comprehensively Deepening the Reform*, adopted at the Third Plenary Session of the 18th CPC Central Committee in November 2013, proposed to "improve the mechanism for the use of judicial power", "reform the judicial committee system, improve the responsibility system of handling cases by the presiding judge and the collegiate bench, by which the judges hand down verdicts and the collegiate bench is responsible for carrying them out". As such, keep advancing the reform of the internal operating mechanism of the people's courts will remain a difficult issue amid the judicial reform.

2.2.7.2 Specific Measures for Reforming the Internal Operating Mechanism of the Courts

(1) Empower judges to handle cases independently

The first measure to ensure the internal independence of the judiciary is to define the power of judges to handle cases according to law and construct a case handling system with judges as the subject of power, which will be a solution to eliminate the administrative case-handling model—one of the failings of the previous reforms. As a new round of judicial reform is about to start, some people's courts have embarked on the explorations in this regard. For example, Foshan Intermediate People's Court and Shenzhen Futian People's Court, both in Guangdong Province, have recently launched a reform model of the "presiding judge responsibility system". Take Shenzhen Futian People's Court for example, "after the reform, the cases are firstly filed and then distributed to the presiding judge who will decide their second distribution after initial combing of these cases. The major, difficult and complex cases are presided over by the presiding judge, the simple cases are tried by ordinary judges alone but under the guidance and supervision of the presiding judge; where there are significant differences in the cases, they will be taken as difficult cases and transferred to the collegiate bench to go through general procedures presided over by the presiding judge". "The presiding judge is responsible for the entire team of judges and the final outcome of the cases. In the past, the presiding judge was approving cases by listening to the reports without taking part in court hearings or collegial discussions in person, now he has to try his best to attend the hearings at the collegiate bench.[124]" Similarly, in Foshan Intermediate People's Court, there is a fixed collegiate bench constituted by the presiding judge and two judges, and the presiding judge has to participate in all court trials in person.[125]

The above reform is an important exploration to transform from the independence of the court as a whole to the independence of judges, and also an important step towards "responsibility justice".[126] The core of the "presiding judge responsibility system" is that the presiding judge, both professional and experienced, shall attend the court hearings in person, rather than making decisions by listening to the work reports of other judges, which is a combination of trial and judgment. It can be seen that the thinking of the current reform is different from the traditional one, and the current reform pursues an ultimate goal of judicial professionalism and judge independence.

It should be noted that this reform has not touched the core content of judge independence. The principle of judge independence does not call for the independence of some judges, while denies the independence of others. In fact, this principle is to recognize and guarantee the independence of every judge when handling cases. Only in this way, it is possible to fundamentally eliminate the administrative case handling model. The above reform practice only gave the "presiding judge" the authority to handle cases independently, so not every judge is entitled to doing so. This kind of reform has the risk of administerization of the "presiding judge", making him become more president-like, not participate in the trial of cases, but has the power to approve cases. In view of this, future reforms should identify judges as the responsibility subject in independent handling of cases, and directly give each of them the authority to independently handle cases according to law. Now that the Third Plenary Session of the 18th CPC Central Committee required to "improve the responsibility system of handling cases by the presiding judge and the collegiate bench", the Supreme People's Court has proposed to implement the presiding judge system, which confirms the independence of judges when handling the case and accords with the basic rules of judicial independence. The core of the presiding judge system is that the presiding judge has independent trial power and is fully responsible for the case; meanwhile, the collegiate bench responsibility system shall be implemented, with the duties and responsibilities of each member of the collegiate bench explicitly defined and trial power returned to the presiding judge and collegiate bench, which

---

[124] Yuan [71].

[125] Zhao [72].

[126] Jiang [73].

will make sure of "clarified powers and responsibilities, consistency between powers and responsibilities".

(2) Clarify the roles of the president of the court and the chief judge of a division

In addition to directly giving judges the authority to independently handle cases according to law, how to coordinate the relationship between the president of the court, the chief judge of a division and the judge is also the key to the success of the reform. Both the president of the court and the chief judge of a division are judicial management personnel inside the court, they are of an administrative nature; unless they personally participate in the trial of cases, they should not participate in the adjudication of cases or publish opinions that determine the facts of the cases or applicable laws. In China, the selection of the president of the court and the chief judge of a division is related to their capabilities; however, if we expect to establish a prudent case review and approval system by relying on more professional and highly skilled judges, it is to mix up judicial administration with adjudicatory function and erode the adjudicatory function. Looking into the prospect of the reform, it is necessary to clarify the boundaries between the judicial administrative and supervisory powers of the president of the court and the chief judge of a division and the adjudicatory power the judges, and establish a power list system.

(3) Define the responsibilities of the trial committee

There is need to set up a trial committee, which embodies the idea of judges' autonomy and brings into play the collective wisdom of judges. However, the system that trial committee discusses cases is contrary to the rules of judicial operation. Therefore, the relationship between the purpose of the trial committee and the rules of judicial operation shall be coordinated during the reform. In the future, the functions of the trial committee shall be gradually transformed. Considering the status and role of the trial committee in China, the author suggests that on the one hand, the scope of the cases discussed by the trial committee should be gradually narrowed, and there shall be a consensus that the trial committee can only discuss and study the legal application of cases and refrain from discussing the facts of the cases; on the other hand, the trial committee may be transformed into a case-handling organization to directly join in the trial and adjudication of major or complex cases, rather than limited to discussion of cases.

2.2.8 Judicial Organs Exercise Their Power Independently According to Law and the Restraint of Judges

Under the current legal system and the judicial environment and taking into account the professional ethics of judges, is it possible to give rise to the abuse of judicial power if we highlight the independence of judges? How can we make the public believe that the judicial power will be properly exercised? This is a worrying problem.

Without enough restriction and supervision, corruption may be bred among judges and becomes uncontrollable. With regard to this possible negative effect, it is necessary to take precautions in the course of judicial reform, and make a system response in advance. Therefore, while emphasizing the independence of judges, we need to build a new supervision and restriction mechanism that conforms to the rules of judicial power operation. In this regard, the author believes that system construction should be strengthened in the following four aspects:

First, improve the professional ethics of judges. In China there is a tradition that ignores the professional ethics of judges. Correspondingly, special attention has been paid to the administrative control of the power of judges when they handle cases, so as to prevent them from making decisions arbitrarily and improve the working quality of case handling. With the development of a new round of judicial reform, the issue of judicial de-administration has become the focus of reform. In this situation, we must abandon the traditional mindset of administrative control and improve the professional ethics of judges, in order to transform the pattern of power control from external control to internal self-discipline.

Second, build disciplinary and withdrawal mechanisms for judges. Disciplinary punishment should be an important guarantee mechanism for judges' professional ethics. In this regard, an organization like a judges disciplinary committee should be built to supervise and punish the judges' violations of laws and regulations. The more common practice in world is to set up a special organization or institution to take charge of disciplinary supervision and punishment of judges. For example, the Judicial Disciplinary Punishment Committee located in Nevada of the US, with members made up of judges and prosecutors, deal with the complaints of violations of laws and regulations by judges and prosecutors within its jurisdiction and impose punishment upon the violators when necessary. In the UK the Judge Complaints Committee is one of the key institutions that are in close contact with the Judge Selection Committee. "The Judge Complaints Committee provides support services to the Secretary of State for Justice and the Lord Chief Justice for them to perform their duties in handling complaints and disciplinary punishment, so as to ensure that the punishment of judges can be carried out in a unified, fair and efficient manner".[127] The establishment of a special organization to perform the functions of supervision and disciplinary punishment against judicial personnel is conducive to determining whether the relevant subjects need to bear responsibility from a professional and neutral standpoint, and forms a functional complementarity and win–win situation with the Judge Selection Committee. In China, the reform of unified management of staffs, funds and properties by the courts at the provincial level has been advancing, we can take this opportunity to build a unified judicial disciplinary punishment committee with the provincial courts as the unit. This committee should consist of senior judges, prosecutors, scholars and the general public, and develop into an organizational mechanism that draws participation of legal professionals (as the subject) and certain public figures. It is responsible for punishing the judges that make law-bending judgments in violation of laws and their professional ethics, and

[127] Jiang and Yang [74].

following the principle of "power coming with responsibility, supervision of use of power, accountability for dereliction of duty, and investigation into violation of law", so as to achieve the balance between the independent exercise of judicial power and effective supervision and restriction.

Third, develop a strict and reasonable responsibility mechanism that complies with the rules of justice. Considering the special nature of judicial adjudication, how to scientifically define the standards that hold someone accountable and delineate the levels of responsibility has become the basic content of the responsibility system. It is advised to explore the establishment of a responsibility investigation mechanism based on the rules of judicial adjudication, strictly limit the scope of disciplinary punishment and accountability, and delineate levels of responsibility according to the severity of the behaviors, especially the determination of "misjudged cases". We must strictly distinguish between intentional behaviors and negligent behaviors, distinguish between gross negligence and general negligence, and draw the line between fault and differences in general legal knowledge.

Fourth, strengthen citizen participation in judicial activities. The current judicial reform is trying to make the judicial activities open to the public as much as possible, so as to facilitate people's supervision of judges in performing their duties. Citizen participation in justice[128] is a means of reform for supervising and restricting the behaviors of judges. Especially in the actual judicial environment of China, citizen participation in justice may be more effective than other supervision and restriction mechanisms. In recent years, citizen participation in justice as an important mechanism to monitor and restrict the judicial power has received increasing attention. For example, the judicial reforms of Japan and South Korea in recent years emphasize citizen participation in justice. In connection with this, China has not only constructed a people's assessor system during the trial stage, but also established a people's supervisor system during the prosecution process,[129] which is of great significance for promoting judicial justice. Therefore, the people's assessor system and the people's supervisor system should be reformed and improved to ensure the orderly and substantial participation of citizens in justice.[130]

2.3 Study on Professionalization of Judges and Reform of the Judge Selection System

Through decades of judicial reform, China has gradually improved the professionalization of judges. However, the overall quality of the judicial team is still uneven. The spread of judicial corruption and the low quality of handling cases remain serious. The people's anticipation for fairness and justice has multiplied the embarrassment

[128] Chen [75].

[129] Chen [76].

[130] Chen [77].

of the judiciary. The construction of the judicial contingent has become a bottleneck restricting China's comprehensive promotion of ruling the country by law and modernization of the rule of law. How to guarantee the homogeneity, specialization and elitism of the judicial contingent has become the key to the success of China's judicial reform. For this reason, the Third Plenary Session of the 18th CPC Central Committee once again brought the issue of professionalization of judges to the reform agenda.

2.3.1 Professionalization of Judges and Reform of the Judge Selection System

The professionalization of judges means that "judges take the exercise of the state judicial power as a specialized profession, and they possess unique professional awareness, professional skills and professional status"[131]; and judges perform their duties as general civil servants, and more importantly they hold special positions and implement a special function—adjudicatory function—in a special way.[132] When any citizen becomes a judge, he should remain relatively alienated from political affairs, economic activities and emotional social thoughts for a long period of time, devoting himself into the trial work in a neutral and diligent manner, and avoiding obtaining benefits from undertaking other operations while serving as a judge. The state should provide mature and effective guarantees and binding norms for the professional conducts of judges as the institutional basis, including professional qualification system, professional training system, professional security system, and professional responsibility and ethics mechanism.[133]

2.3.1.1 Necessity and Positive Significance of Professionalization of Judges

(1) Necessity of professionalization of judges

The professionalization of judges is a product of social development to a certain degree and the result of the division of labor in a society. But in essence, the professionalization of judges is determined by the characteristics of the judiciary itself, which could be understood from the following three aspects:

First, judicial power is a power of judgment for resolving disputes. In fact, it is a reply to the historical facts that occurred in the past, and it ascertains the true facts with certain means and paths by relying on the evidence; and then applies laws correctly on this basis. Therefore, those who undertake the judicial work shall have

---

[131]*Announcement of the Supreme People's Court*, Apr 2002.

[132]Li [78].

[133]Tan and Wang [79].

a unique knowledge structure, profound legal knowledge background, professional skills, superb way of thinking, rich judicial experience, and a lofty character.

Second, the adjudicatory power exercised by judges is of vital significance. The result of judgment concerns the personal rights and property rights of citizens, as well as the limitation and deprivation of their right to life. Therefore, such power cannot be exercised by anyone at will, but by professionals with both professional belief and quality, and all countries in the world have chosen judges as the subject to exercise the adjudicatory power.

Finally, the professionalization of judges is determined by the unique functions and roles of the judiciary. There are many ways to resolve disputes in modern society, but the judicial approach is the last way to do so. The disputes that go through the judicial procedure are often more complex and significant problems that ordinary people cannot resolve on their own. The resolution of such disputes is not only related to people's rights, but also to social stability and harmony. Not everyone is capable of performing such special function and role, it should be the one that has received special training and possesses special skills that is capable of doing so.

(2) Value of professionalization of judges

The value of professionalization of judges is mainly reflected in the following aspects:

First, the professionalization of judges helps judges resist the interference of various non-legal factors on judicial justice, and ensure that judges can impartially reproduce the justice of the law with his keen judgment on the facts and insight of the law. The professionalization of judges makes them form a high-quality elite group. With internal homogeneity, high quality and lofty character, all the members of this group jointly resist the external interference with judicial independence. Moreover, there is also institutional guarantee for the professionalization of judges. That's why judges have formed an autonomous group which is more powerful than individual judges. The rule-of-law experiences in western countries tell us that judicial justice comes from the independence of the judiciary (the core of which is the independence of judges), and the independence of the judiciary is partly attributed to the promotion by the professional group of judges. "Independent justice is inseparable from a high-quality and powerful judicial group, which is a prerequisite for counteracting the influence of other social forces, otherwise the so-called independence will be no better than a prop on the stage, it seems to be indispensable, but useless in real life".[134] "The successful experiences of a society ruled by law show that the strength of the group of legalists comes from its internal unity and solidarity; such unity and solidarity is not due to the same origin of the members of this group, but because of the consistency of their knowledge background, training methods and professional interests". "Legalists who have a high degree of consistency in these aspects naturally constitute a so-called interpretive community. This community has a recognized reputation, which has strengthened power, and the proper use of power has boosted its prestige, so it is enough for this community to respond to the society's expectation

[134] Xia [80].

for the rule of law and justice, and then help to spread the consciousness of rule of law in society and improves the modernization of the society as a whole".[135]

Second, the professionalization of judges helps to form a group of highly professional and elite judges. Laws are abstract rules; in order to apply these abstract rules to our practical life, and turn the due concept of justice contained in law into justice declared by society, we must have highly qualified judges with professional knowledge, proficient legal skills and high moral character. Justice comes to the world through the incarnation of justice. "If judges lack an accurate and comprehensive understanding of the law, it is impossible for them to apply the legal rules correctly to substantive cases, it is also hard for them to handle cases strictly in accordance with legal procedures, and it is even difficult to form faith in the law. If judges are not able to make correct judgement based on the evidence, or expound the reasons for making such judgement, then it will be difficult to guarantee judicial justice and the quality of judgment".[136] The purpose of the professionalization of judges is to cultivate a group of professional and elite judges and make them embodiment of social justice.

Third, the professionalization of judges is conducive to realizing the value of judicial authority. When the worship of personal authority yields to the worship of rational authority, our society will transit from a brutal authoritarian one to a modern one ruled by law. As Max Weber has commented, we are in the era of rational authority; the most fundamental sign of rational authority is the worship of legal authority.[137] Laws without authority will no longer be laws, becoming as insignificant as air vibration in the eyes of Lenin. How can we continue worshiping the law if it has no authority at all? A society worshiping violence or personal authority is bound to be dangerous. Harold J. Berman once said "the law must be faith, otherwise it will exist in name only". This is the most basic characteristic of a society ruled by law. Where does the authority of the law come from? Of course, the backing of the national coercive force is the last line of defense for the legal authority. More importantly, the legal authority comes from the inherent character of the law—the distribution of justice. According to the Norwegian scholar Freede Castberg, the demand for justice in society is rooted in our spiritual instincts, as strong as our thoughts demand for logical relations.[138] The authority of law is attributed to the impartial judgments made by professional judges, fair legal procedures, and people's belief in the law. The authority of law is specifically manifested in two aspects: one is the process and results of justice—the judgement should reflect impartiality, which is the premise of judicial authority; the other one is the execution of impartial judgments, which is a necessary requirement for judicial authority.[139] The core of establishing judicial authority lies in a group of highly qualified and elitist judges. With a strong belief in the law, ideas of social justice and professional skills, these judges can resolve disputes impartially

[135] He [81].

[136] Wang [82].

[137] Quoted in Liu [83].

[138] Quoted in Bodenheimer [84].

[139] He [85].

and declare fairness and justice to the society through the form of judgements. And the judgements must reflect fairness and justice so as to be executed by the parties voluntarily, and then the ambiguous justice implicit in the legal provisions can be clearly conveyed to the society through execution of the judgements. It can be seen that professional judges have established and guided the judicial authority with their profession, it is because "for all parties to a social conflict, their understanding and perception of the internal spirit of their country's legal system is always under the ultimate guidance of judicial decisions, while the operational process of judicial power is in essence loaded with the longing and expectation of social members for their country's legal system".[140] This is not only limited to theoretical analysis, but proved by the successful practices in some countries. According to Ji Weidong's account, "(Japan) launched the judicial reform after the Second World War, mainly for building up its judicial independence and authority, one of the means for achieving this purpose is to organize strict judicial examinations and select legal professionals, so as to enhance people's trust in the legal profession, especially the judges, thereby improving the judicial authority.[141]

Last, the professionalization of judges is conducive to realizing the value of procedural efficiency. "Justice and Efficiency" are the two century themes raised by the Supreme People's Court. Judicial justice is precisely the ultimate goal of the judicial profession. Judicial justice itself materializes the pursuit for judicial efficiency, since "justice delayed is justice denied". Nevertheless, in the face of the increasingly overstocked cases, action delays and low judicial efficiency in China, efficiency under the premise of justice has also become one of the goals of the country's judicial reform endeavor. Through comparison of the number of judges and per capita judge ratio between China and overseas, one can easily see that the low procedural efficiency currently confronting China does not lie in the limited number of judges, but the low degree of professionalization or specialization of judges despite the huge number in stock. Hence taking the road of excellentizing judges through the professionalization of judges, raising the bar for the judge profession, strengthening the occupational training system for judges, separating the order of rankings among judges, judicial assistants and administrators, and practically paving out a road of professionalization of judges with high proficiency and competence will be very helpful to increasing procedural efficiency and reducing procedural cost.

2.3.1.2 Professionalization of Judges and Reform of the Judge Selection System

From the existing reform program, there are currently four channels of achieving the professionalization of judges. First, classified management of the court staff. That is, the personnel inside the court are classified as judges, judicial assistants and judicial administrators, for whom separate management systems are implemented. For

[140]Lv and He [86].

[141]Ji [87].

judges, a management system different from that for civil servants should be implemented. A separate order of ranking for the judge profession should be established to help link the grades of judges to their administrative rankings. Second, specified number of judges. That is, the best judges are included into the list of the specified number of judges and equipped with trial support personnel such as judicial assistants and court clerks so that the human resources of the court are concentrated at the front line of case handling. Third, reform of the judge selection system. Fourth, refinement of the judge performance assessment system. Fifth, refinement of the on-the-job training mechanism of judges.

Regarding these reforms, the judge selection system constitutes a very important fundamental task. The judge selection system, as the first pass for promoting the professionalization of judges, determines the overall level of specialization and standardization of the judge population from the source. All possible reforms, whether it be classified management of the court staff or performance assessment of judges or reform of the training mechanism of judges, are based upon a robust judge selection system; the effecting of specified number of judges is also braced upon the judge selection system. In reality, as some Chinese authors observed, among other means available, judge selection is a more important means of improving the competence of judges. The significance of judge selection lies in the fact that "first, a good selection system will pick out a 'virtuous person' so that people in the society capable of and talented in judicial judgment will have the opportunity of becoming a judge; second, a good selection system will also inspire judges already in office to work harder, pay more attention to gaining judicial knowledge, become more determined to devote their lifetime to judicial adjudication and keep abreast of the times, thereby upgrading the overall level of judges."[142] In this regard, reform of the judge selection system is of great significant to upgrading the specialization and standardization level of judges in China.

2.3.2 *Overseas Practices in Judge Selection*

2.3.2.1 Models of Judge Selection System

Most countries under the rule of law nowadays have a strict judge selection system in place targeted at securing the occupational integration, specialization and excellentization of judge selection. However, subject to the divergent historical traditions, political systems and legal systems, the judge selection system they adopt also differ from one country to another. Overall, modern judge selection systems can be categorized into three different types. The first type is empirical judge selection, as represented by the common law countries and characterized by the emphasis on the experiences of judges. The second type is bureaucratic judge selection, as represented by the civil

[142]Su [88].

law countries and characterized by the emphasis on the professional expertise of the judges. The third type is mixed judge selection, as represented by Japan.

(1) Empirical judge selection

In the Anglo-American law countries, judges are normally selected following the principle of "experienced", "excellent" and "elderly". In an Anglo-American law country, a citizen desiring to become a judge has to first receive university education to obtain a J.D. Degree of Law and prepare himself for becoming a lawyer in future, then work as a lawyer to gain occupational experience in judicial practice and stay in that profession for a long time before he is qualified to be selected and appointed as a judge.

In the United States, although no explicit qualification is defined for judges, by convention, except judges of the peace in some of the states, judges are normally qualified by the following criteria: citizenship of the United States, J.D Degree of Law, having passed the lawyers' qualification examination, and generally having worked as a lawyer for at least six years.

In the United States, courts are set up at both the federal and state levels. Each judicial system has its own management system. It is but a common thing that the superior court selects judges for the subordinate courts in different ways or judges are initially appointed and reappointed in different ways. There, judge selection, as an important part of this process, is also subject different qualifications and procedures. In the United States, judges of the federal courts are selected through nomination by the president, review by the federal board of judges affiliated with the bar association, consultation and consent by the Upper House, approval by the Upper House by a simple majority vote, and appointment by the president. Judges of courts below the state supreme court are typically selected in one of the following ways: (i) election, which includes two different forms. One involves the nomination by the state governor and partisan election in accordance with the Constitution; the other involves non-partisan election (also known as general election) which is held together with the election of the state governor and senators. (ii) appointment, which, with the exception of very few states where judges are appointed by the courts themselves, involves the appointment by the state council or state governor from a list of candidates provided by the judicial nominating commission. (iii) Missouri Compromise, which as a compromise between the election and appointment regimes is highly acclaimed by the American Law Institute and many states.[143] When a judge of a federal court system is nominated by the president, an important contribution is the critical role played by the 15 members of the Federal Judicial Committee of the American Bar Association (ABA), which evaluates the competence of all federal judges nominated by the president. This committee normally completes this work within six to eight months. They then rate the candidates and submit the ratings to the attorney-general in the following description: WQ (well qualified), Q (qualified), and NQ (not qualified). The president will determine a formal list of nominees based on these ratings. There is very narrow chance for an ABA-unqualified candidate to be

[143] Source: https://www.your-missourijudges.org/missouri-plan/. Quoted in Yao [89].

nominated. According to statistics, no single unqualified candidate had been nominated over the period 1965 to 1975. Members of the ABA are generally reluctant to recommend lawyers without court experience; they would also insist that a candidate have 12 to 15 years of working experience in law. Besides, the opinions of the chief grand justice of the supreme court also count.[144]

In the United Kingdom, a citizen desiring to become a judge has to first receive three years of university education in law to obtain a Bachelor of Law degree, then file an application and pass the examination. If he passes the examination, he will study at one of the four law schools affiliated with the Law Society for one year; after passing the examination, he will obtain a lawyer's degree awarded by the law school; after one year's internship, he will become a regular lawyer. A lawyer is not qualified for being nominated as a judge unless he has worked in this profession for a sufficient length of time (generally, with the exception of judges at a magistrates' court, a judge of a local court has to have at least seven years' experience of working as a court lawyer; a judge of an appeal court has to have at least 10 years of working as a court lawyer; a judge candidate of an appealing court has to have at least 15 years of working in this profession).

In the United Kingdom, almost all judges originate from lawyers; judges of the High Court of Justice mostly come from court lawyers. The rigid restrictions on the qualification, experience, performance and personality of judge candidates make it an extremely lucky thing for any person who is appointed as a judge before the age of 40.[145] A person is qualified to enter the judicial circle only after working as a lawyer for many years. The transposition from a lawyer to a judge marks the summit of an occupation rather than the start of a new occupation. In the United Kingdom, obviously, the appointment of most of the judges represents an honor or reward to senior lawyers for their good performance in professional expertise and personal reputation, as well as a trust of the judicial circle in these lawyers.[146] In the United Kingdom, judges are appointed and all power to judicial appointment rests with the Queen, although such appointment is guided by the recommendations of the Prime Minister or Lord Chancellor. In fact, for a long time in the past, the power to appoint judges has actually been held by the Lord Chancellor. In order to promote judicial independence and strengthen judicial transparency, in 2005, the United Kingdom adopted the Constitutional Reform Act 2005, which involved a number of reforms centering round the power of the Lord Chancellor. The initiative in the appointment procedure was transferred to the newly established Selection Commission; the Lord Chancellor no longer holds the initiative except making contentious decisions on the suggestions of the Committee. To ensure that the Commission is neutral, transparent and authoritative, the Act identified it as a non-departmental public body with

[144] See Song [90], pp. 139–152.

[145] See Zhou [52], p. 143.

[146] See Zhou [52], p. 143.

members impartially selected *pro rata* among judges, jurists, government officials with no political inclination, and the public.[147]

When a superior court selects a judge for a subordinate court, what is highlighted is the performance of the judge candidate. This also represents one of the features of the judge selection system in the United States. In summary, a judge is selected out of the list of candidates based on three criteria: legal knowledge and experience, professional expertise, and personality. In terms of knowledge, experience and expertise, the requirements include: (i) appropriate legal knowledge, judicial experience and occupational achievements; (ii) thinking and analytical ability; (iii) good judgment; (iv) decisional ability; (v) ability to communicate with various people; and (vi) ability to maintain the authority of the court and protect the dignity of the court. In terms of personality, the requirements include: (i) integrity; (ii) impartiality; (iii) understanding the public and society; (iv) good personal conduct; and (v) politeness and mercy.[148] In addition to experience and ability, the selector will subconsciously guarantee the political-social balance of the British courts—by investigating the party affiliation of the candidates, especially in the selection of judges of the Higher Court of Justice, where the Lord Chancellor would normally discuss with the judges to ensure that the selected ones will stay in good cooperation with the judicial department.[149]

(2) Bureaucratic judge selection

In a civil law country, new judges are selected by emphasizing their professional knowledge before taking office, "posing an almost cruel professional requisite upon them". Judges as a law professional are separately cultivated and are generally not selected from lawyers. That is what people call the binary system of judge selection, also known as the career or bureaucratic judge system.[150]

In Germany, law professions are integrated. All law professionals have to receive the same legal training whether they want to work as a judge, a state attorney, a lawyer in private practice, a state-employed civil service official, or a legal expert in a company's personnel or legal department. A citizen desiring to work in the law profession has to walk a lengthy and rough road. First, he has to receive regular university education for a minimum of three years and a half, which takes an average of five years to complete and is generally more focused on theoretical studies. At the end of the regular education, the student has to take a bar examination. If he passes the examination, he will be called a referender and will start a two-year internship. During this period, the referender will be required to work in five different fields, at a civil court, a criminal court, a procurator's office, a type of administrative body, and a private law firm. He will select five workplaces from a list of approved legal businesses or government departments. At each of these five places, the referender

[147] Source: https://www.judiciary.gov.uk/related-offices-and-bodies/judicial-appointments-commission/. Quoted in Yao [89].

[148] See Chen [91].

[149] See Yao [89].

[150] See Chen [91].

will spend three to nine months. During the internship, the referender will be treated as a civil servant and paid by the government. At the end of the two-year internship, he will take a second bar examination, which lasts a few days and comprises various written tests. Then he will be orally tested by a panel of four people selected from different sectors of law. After passing the second national bar examination, this person will be called an assessor and will work in any sector of law.

If an assessor having passed the second bar examination desires to work as a judge, he has to apply with the state department of justice. If his application is accepted, an interview will be organized by the personnel department of the state department of justice. If he passes the interview, his grade of the second bar examination, personality appraisal and other personal information will be collected by the personnel department of the state department of justice. All the materials will be examined and evaluated by the head of the personnel department. If the personnel department considers he is qualified, it will deliver a letter of recommendation to the minister of justice for decision along with all the materials. The minister of justice will issue a notice of appointment to the successful applicant along with the initial work assignment. The new judge will be sent to a regional court (court of first instance). A first appointee will have a three-year probation. Upon expiry of the probation and if he proves satisfactory, he will be appointed a lifetime judge. An unsuccessful applicant may join in the lawyer profession first and reapply in one or two years.[151]

In Germany, although the procedure and standard for judge selection are not totally identical among all states, the difference is modest. In the individual states, new judges are selected primarily by the department of justice. In most of the states, are appointed by the head of the department of justice, but there are still some states where judges are jointly appointed by the department of justice and the judge selection commission. The judge selection commission is composed of councilmen, department of justice officials and lawyers. This commission selects judges mainly by the following criteria: (i) passion for work and ability to work under pressure; (ii) acceptance of judicial mission; (iii) ability to try and mediate; (iv) ability to solve disputes and make decisions; (v) ability to cooperate; (vi) social cognition to consider and understand other people's social life relationships with no prejudice and in their positions; (vii) sense of justice to pursue and make lawful, reasonable judgments within the framework of the constitution that are immune to his own personal value; and (viii) exercise of power and responsibility.[152]

In France, to become a judge of a general court, in addition to completing four years of university courses in law and obtaining a Bachelor of Law degree, one has to pass a government examination and receive a 31-month professional training at the National School of the Judiciary, which includes lessons and internships at businesses, administrative bodies and law firms and practical work at courts. Then he needs to pass two examinations and, if he passes them, receive a 6-month subdiscipline training.

[151] See Bing [90], pp. 152–169.

[152] See [Germany] Isermann [92].

In France, judges of courts at all levels are appointed. The appointment of judges of the supreme court and presidents of the appeal courts is proposed by the Supreme Council of Magistracy of the country. This council is chaired by the president or minister of justice as the chairman. Its members include five judges, one procurator and four representatives outside the judicial system. The Supreme Council of Magistrature proposes the candidate judges of the supreme court and presidents of the appeal courts, who are then appointed by the president. Other judges are appointed by the minister of justice, but the Supreme Council of Magistrature will provide opinions on the appointment of other judges proposed by the minister of justice according to the conditions under the Court Organic Act. Among the administrative court series, except judges of the supreme administrative court that are administered and appointed by the minister of justice, all other judges are appointed by the government.[153]

(3) Mixed judge selection

In Japan, law professions are integrated. Judges, procurators and lawyers are collectively called "housou" and appointed by the same standard. As Mr. Ji Weidong observed, "in the initial stage of modern legal system, Japan attached great importance to the qualities of judges and procurators, by starting right with qualification examination." In its transformation toward the modernization of rule of law, Japan established a strict judge examination and appointment system. In today's Japan, a citizen desiring to work in the law profession has to obtain a Bachelor of Law degree from a regular university and then take the extremely strict national bar examination. If he passes the examination, he will receive another tough examination given by a commission, composed of a bar examination review committee appointed by the minister of justice. The very few winners having passed the second examination will be appointed as legal trainees under the jurisdiction of the supreme court. After two years of study at the legal training and research institute, the legal trainee will take a third bar examination, if he passes this examination, will be qualified as a judicial apprentice. Only after spending at least to years gaining rich experience as a judge in reserve (hanjiho), procurator, lawyer or law professor can a judicial apprentice be appointed as a judge (hanji) authorized to try various cases by himself. After three strict bar examinations, only a sixtieth of the candidates have a chance of eventually becoming a judge.

In Japan, judges are selected from a broader spectrum, covering both judicial practitioners such as judicial assistants (when required to work as judge of a summary court, judges (those who have worked as a judge of a subordinate court), procurators, lawyers, those working in a judicial or law post, and scholars of legal theory research such as university law professors or associate professors.

Meanwhile, the qualifications required for judges are not totally identical among different grades of court. Typically, the higher the grade of a court, the higher the qualifications are required for the judge. For example, to become a judge of the supreme court, one has to possess high knowledge, legal accomplishments, be older

[153]See Wang [93].

than 40, and have worked for more than 20 years as president or judge of the high court, judge of a summary court, procurator, lawyer, or university law professor or associate professor. By comparison, the qualifications for judges of the high court, local courts, or family courts are roughly equal to those for a judge of the supreme court, except that the candidate's work experience is reduced from 20 to 10 years. To become a judge of a summary court, one needs to be have worked for at least three years as judicial assistant, procurator, lawyer, court investigator and/or other specified judicial or law posts after judicial internship; or for at least three years as university law professor or associate professor; or as president or judge of the high court.[154] The president of the supreme court is nominated by the Cabinet and appointed by the Emperor. Other judges of the supreme court are appointed by the cabinet, and their appointment is attested by the emperor. The president of the high court is nominated by the supreme court and appointed by the Cabinet. Besides, those having worked in judicial affairs and other posts, as long as they have the knowledge and experience needed for holding a position in a summary court, may also be appointed after an examination given by the judge selection commission for summary courts.

2.3.2.2 Comparison Among Different Models of Judge Selection

(1) Similarities among different models of judge selection

These three different models of judge selection share the following similarities:

First, the requirement of professional knowledge during judge selection. All three models, whether in a civil law country or in an Anglo-American law country or in Japan, require that a newly appointed judge have rich professional knowledge, which constitutes the premise and basis for a judge to enforce law accurately and impartially. Judges are selected actually under the premise of a basic idea, namely, to what kind of a person the judicial power is conferred. The answer to this question can help distinguish between a judge and a general civil servant. The complexity of modern social relations has made law—which adjusts social relations—a multifarious technical rule that cannot be resolved with the concept of natural justice, but can only be mastered through constant learning and practice. As Hamilton noted, "There are so many kinds of problems arising from human weakness that the vast ocean of cases must be studied assiduously for a long time before they can be seen. Therefore, only a few people in the world have enough knowledge of the law to become judges."[155] In view of the occupational characteristics and social position of judges, each country requires that their judges have exquisite professional knowledge of law. Only by receiving systematic higher education can judges familiarize themselves with the basic contents of the legal system and become able to reason, analyze and judge in a logical way of law. Legal examinations are a means of directly testing legal competence of individuals. In the civil law countries and some regions, two

[154] See Wang [93].

[155] [US] Hamilton et al. [17], pp. 395–396.

rounds of bar examinations are to be taken; in the Anglo-American law countries and regions, judges must be selected from lawyers, and strict qualification examinations apply to any person who wants to become a lawyer.[156]

Second, concerns about professional experience during judge selection. Although the Anglo-American law countries are more concerned about the experience of a newly appointed judge in legal practice than the civil law countries, the requirement of practical experience for a newly appointed judge is negligible for none of the three models of judge selection. As law has always been an applied science rather than a theoretical one and deals with human's social relations rather than natural knowledge, one can never truly understand law without profound understanding of the society. As the great U.S. jurist Wendell Holmes noted, "The life of the law has not been logic: it has been experience".[157] Hence, in the Anglo-American law countries and some other regions, only lawyers having practiced a substantial period of time are qualified to be selected as a judge, and the exact period of time also differs depending on the grade of the court. In the civil law countries and regions, a candidate has to receive internship training for a very long time before he is qualified as a judge; it is also a rigid rule that judges must be promoted level by level.

Third, requirement of personality for a newly appointed judge. Ever since the ancient times, judges have been considered the embodiment of justice. Exquisite knowledge and expertise are the necessary, but not sufficient, conditions to ensure judicial justice in substance or procedure. Only those combining ethics with knowledge can become a judge. The requirement of lofty characters for a newly appointed judge is an indispensable important part for all three models. As Japanese researcher Ooki Masao commented, "A judge can never show justice without conscience", "...Their qualifications not only include legal knowledge, but more specifically, extensive education and honest quality".[158] Without the intrinsic excellent qualities of the judges, no impartial judge can be produced even under the most perfect system.

Fourth, level-by-level promotion of the judges. All three models of judge selection require that a newly appointed judge work at a court of first instance before he can be promoted level by level based on his performance. This regime of promotion can ensure that the grade of the court agrees with the competence of the judge, and judges of a higher court know all details of the work of judges of a lower court. This not only helps ensure the consistency of judgments and step-by-step practice of the judges, but also incorporates a competition that guarantees the honor of judges of the higher court.

Fifth, neutralization and professionality of the judge selectors. From the development of the legal systems overseas, many countries and regions have gradually set up or reformed their legal selection systems, typically targeted at neutralization and specialization. Generally speaking, judges are qualified based on, above anything else, their professional competence, covering the professional knowledge of law,

---

[156] See Yao [89].

[157] [US] Holmes [94].

[158] [Japan] Masao [95].

ability of factual judgment, ability of legal interpretation, skill of court trial, and level of document writing. Hence, the selectors themselves must possess the professional ability of law to give correct and reasonable comments. Selectors are given a neutral position to avoid exposing the appointment of judges to potential influences of other organizations, entities or individuals, thereby consolidating the impartiality and transparency of judge selection and ensure judicial independence.[159]

(2) Differences among different models of judge selection

In a manner of speaking, there are still some differences among these models of judge selection. More specifically: first, judges in the Anglo-American law countries are selected from lawyers, whereas judges in the civil law countries and Japan are appointed by the country from law graduates after two rounds of national bar examination and special training. Second, the Anglo-American law countries are more concerned about the judicial experience of newly appointed judges, whereas the civil law countries and Japan are more concerned about their professional knowledge. Third, the civil law countries and Japan are more concerned about the integration of law professions, whereas the Anglo-American law countries typically implement separate selection mechanisms and appointment systems for lawyers, procurators, and judges.

These differences among the models of judge selection are caused by many factors. Among them, the greatest contributors to these differences are:

First, different historical traditions. In the Anglo-American law countries, as judges and lawyers played a decisive part in the common law and equity law, the common law is also called the "judge-made law". The unique role played by judges and lawyers in modern legal construction has won them high respect and admiration. This adds to the natural connection between judges and lawyers and it also lays foundation for the selection of judges from lawyers. In the civil law countries, as following the succession of Roman law, university professors played a great part in interpreting and creating law, the laws in these countries are also called the "professor-made law". University professors are extremely prestigious, whereas judges are not so highly recognized as they are deemed tools for law application. This has given rise to the phenomenon of "professor-created judges" and, consequently, "university-produced judges".

Second, different legal traditions. The Anglo-American law countries are countries of precedent law, which requires that judges should not only interpret law, but also create law. "An ideal judge is not only a wise expert in adjudicating disputes, but also a person who creates and develops legal norms and guides society forward."[160] As the great U.S. jurist Benjamin N Cardozo observed, "This is the way of the great judges of equity, who built the system of equity by constantly resorting to the theory of just reason and conscience, without sacrificing the consistency and certainty of law."[161] As the "a judge is a lawmaker" proposition in the common law system

---

[159]See Yao [89].

[160]Wang [96].

[161][US] Cardozo [97].

requires judges to not only study existing legal knowledge, but also discover and create law over constant practice, one can never become a judge unless and until after constant practice. This determines that judges have to be selected from those having worked as a lawyer for a long time. The civil law, on the other side, is focused on the making of law. Under this system, judges are only a "Declarant of the Oracle" (by William Blackstone), who are obliged to interpret and apply law in strict accordance with the statute law and are not allowed to create law. This determines that judges must be skilled at applying the provisions of law. To test the knowledge obtained in this form, the best way is an examination. Hence, selecting judiciaries through strict examinations has become a common practice for the civil law countries.

2.3.3 *Problems with the Current Judge Selection System in China and Countermeasures of the Present Judicial Reform*

2.3.3.1 Problems with the Current Judge Selection System in China

Compared with the judge selection systems overseas, the judge selection system in China is confronted with the following problems:

(1) Low requirement of professional experience in law

The current "Judges Law" of China prescribes that a person can be appointed as a judge if he has worked in the law profession for at least two years in the case of a graduate from an undergraduate course in the law speciality of an institution of higher education or in the case of a graduate from an undergraduate course in a non-law specialty of an institution of higher education who possesses the professional knowledge of law, and such a graduate can be appointed as a judge of a higher people's court or the supreme people's court if he has worked in law for at least three years; a person can be appointed as a judge if he has worked in law for at least one year in the case of a person holding a Master of Law degree or Doctor of Law degree; such a graduate can be appointed as a judge of a higher people's court or the supreme people's court if he has worked in law for at least two years. From the prescriptions of the "Judges Law", although professional experience of law is required by the "Judges Law", as a general practice, a university graduate is directly recruited by the court (subject to a bar examination after the implementation of bar examination system). Then, he will work for a maximum of three years as law clerk or judicial assistant before he is qualified to be promoted as a judge, subject to the consent of the president of the court and the approval of the judicial council. He can even become a chief justice of the supreme court at an age younger than 30. For the special profession of justice, professional experience in law is strongly neglected. The lack of professional experience in law is evident compared with the other countries.

(2) Serious deficiency in the judge selection system

Compared with the judge selection systems overseas, the following problems exist in the current judge selection system in China. First, the judge selection system is multivariate, which is negative to establishing a uniform standard for judge qualification and results in the localization of judges. Under the current system, judges in China are nominated by the related department and elected or appointed by the organ of power. Within this framework, the judges of courts at all levels are appointed by the organ of power at the same levels. As a consequence, a uniform appointment or election standard is nonexistent. The majority of the judges are appointed by the local organ of power, turning national judges into local ones. This heavily compromises the country's judicial unification, causing judges to lack independence and their competence to degrade. Second, no uniform standard exists for the selection of judges, resulting in the under-homogenization among judges. Last, a special mechanism of judge selection is absent. Judges are selected by the standard and procedure for general civil servants. This is against the scientific law of the judge selection system and diverges from the general trend of world's judge selection.

(3) Lack of a level-by-level promotion mechanism for judges

Whatever the model of judge selection, judges are promoted level by level in most countries. Here in China, judges are promoted in an administrative format; the transfer of judges between a superior and a subordinate court is also implemented in an administrative style. This practice of promoting or transferring judges in an administrative style and determining the competence of a judge by the grade of the court where the judge was first appointed is jokingly referred to as "determinism by birth". Of course, the competence and ability of a judge is not necessarily connected with the grade of a court. A context where judges of a superior court do not know about the work of judges of a subordinate one, and where judges do not have a sense of competition and do not possess an experience of starting with the grassroots court is not good for improving the competence of judiciaries.

2.3.3.2 Current Judicial Reform with Respect to the Judge Selection System

Regarding the problems with the judge selection system in China, on November 12, 2013, the Third Plenary Session of the 18th CPC Central Committee passed the "Decision of the CPC Central Committee on Several Major Issues concerning Comprehensively Deepening Reform", which called on promoting the construction of China under the rule of law and put forward five reform tasks, including efforts to "establish a judicial personnel management system fitting their professional characteristics, improve the system for unified recruitment, orderly exchange and level-by-level promotion of judges, procurators and the police, improve the classified management system of legal personnel, and guarantee the job security of judges, procurators and the police". After that, the Leading Group of the Central

Committee for Comprehensively Deepening Reform adopted the "Framework Opinions on Several Issues concerning the Pilot Reform of the Judicial System" and other documents. The Supreme People's Court also published the "Opinions on Comprehensively Deepening the Reform of the People's Court" (i.e., the Fourth Five-Year Outline for the Reform of the People's Courts), which defined the concrete reform measures for promoting the normalization, specialization and professionalization of the judge selection system in China. This series of decisions pointed the direction for the reform of the judge selection system in China.

Reform measures with respect to the judge selection system in China mainly include the following:

First, raising the bar for the selection of newly appointed judges, including raising the minimum age of newly appointed judges and setting different qualifications for different grades of court. Further detailed exploration has been implemented in some pilot places. For example, under the reform program of Shanghai, in addition to the provisions prescribed by the "Judges Law", a newly appointed judge should also possess the following qualifications: (i) over 28 years of age; (ii) having passed the national bar examination and obtained the qualification for law profession; and (iii) having worked as judicial assistant for at least five years and being a grade 3 or higher grade judicial assistant. A person is qualified to be appointed as judge of a higher court only if he is a grade 2 or a higher grade judge; a person is qualified to be appointed as judge of an intermediate court only if he is a grade 3 or a higher grade judge. Under the pilot reform program of Shenzhen, technically, a person is qualified to become a newly appointed judge only if is a graduate from an undergraduate course in the law specialty of a full-time institution of higher education, has passed the national bar examination and obtained the qualification for law profession; a person is qualified to be appointed as judge of a grassroots court only if he has worked in the legal sector for at least four years; a persons is qualified to be appointed as judge of an intermediate court or procurator of a prefecture-level city procuratorate only if he has worked in the legal sector for at least six years; a person is qualified to be appointed judge of a higher court or procurator of a provincial procuratorate only if he has worked in the legal sector for at least ten years. In the case of a person holding a Master of Law degree, the length of his working experience in the legal sector may be reduced by one year; in the case of a person holding a Doctor of Law degree, the length of his working experience in the legal sector can be reduced by two years.

Second, specifying that any newly appointed judge must work at a grassroots court; judges of the superior court must technically come from a subordinate court. The "Decision" of the Fourth Plenary Session of the 18th CPC Central Committee explicitly prescribes that newly appointed judges shall be uniformly recruited by the higher people's court and shall all work at a grassroots court; judges of a superior people's court shall generally be selected from outstanding judges of a lower-level people's court. This was reiterated in the "Fourth Five-Year Outline)" of the People's Court.

Third, setting up a judge selection committee. The "Framework Opinions on Several Issues concerning the Pilot Reform of the Judicial System" issued by the Political and Judiciary Commission under the CPC Central Committee proposed that a judge selection committee should be set up at the provincial level as a judge selection function after the implementation of the unified management of human, financial and material resources at the provincial level. The "Fourth Five-Year Outline" of the People's Court also proposed that "a Judge Selection Committee, with the participation of judge representatives and social related personnel, will be set up separately to establish an open, fair and just elective procedure to ensure that outstanding legal personnel with good conduct, rich experience and higher professional level become candidates, such that the judge selection mechanism and the statutory appointment and removal mechanism can be effectively linked". In practice, local courts have also set up their respective judge selection committees and established the working mechanism of the judge selection committee.

Fourth, perfecting the system of selecting excellent law professionals as judges. According to the reform plan, judges will be selected from excellent lawyers or law researchers, as well as law professionals working in the legislative, procuratorial and law enforcement sectors.

From these reform measures, the reform of the judge selection system in China targets some of the drawbacks in the existing system, which is very significant to perfecting the judge selection system in China.

First, the current reform program emphasizes the "experience" and "professionality" of judges. Raising the age bar of newly appointed judges is intended to increase the life experience of judges. The diversity of social life facing the judicial practice not only calls for professional competence, but also needs support from social life experience. The minimum length of professional experience in law for judges and the rigid requirement for newly appointed judges to work at grassroots law posts are intended to increase the judicial experience and professionality of the judges. The selection of judges from excellent lawyers, law researchers, and professionals at lawmaking, procuratorate and law enforcement sectors also helps upgrade the professionality and experience of the judge population.

Second, setting up a judge selection committee helps unify the standard for selecting judges and mitigate the localization or administrativization of judge selection. As the judge selection committee is specifically responsible for selecting judges, this allows selecting judges by a standard different from that for civil servants and addressing the particularity and regularity the judge profession. Furthermore, a judge selection committee at the provincial level, as an important grip for the unified management of human, financial and material resources at the provincial level, helps mitigate the localization of judge selection. This ensures that judges belong to the country instead of any particular place and better guarantees that judges will handle cases independently according to law.[162] Besides, setting up a judge selection committee also helps mitigate the closedness and administrativization of judge selection. According to the reform arrangement of unified management of human, financial and material resources at the provincial level, if a provincial court holds the decisional power toward the promotion and appointment of all legal workers at all levels of courts within the province without necessary supervision

[162]See Shao [98].

or restriction, the "side effect" can be far greater than the potential negative effect caused by the localization of judicial power. Especially under the current situation of China, "administrativization has been commonly intensified in all trades; the administrativization trend of courts is becoming serious with every passing day. Courts and court staff are ranked according to the 'official-oriented' hierarchy of administrative organs. Judges are labeled with different ranks, resulting in a subordination between higher and lower ranks. Between the president and vise president, between the vice president and the chief judge, and between the chief judge and the judge is a relationship of leading and being led or dominating and being dominated".[163] In such a context, it becomes very important to strengthen the democratization of judge selection. Setting up a judge selection committee is in a way positive to promoting the democratization of judge selection, since the composition of a judge selection committee is widely representative, involving both well experienced judge representatives as well as social representatives such as lawyers and law researchers. This precludes the possibility of turning judge selection into a sole decision of one or two leaders. In Shanghai, for example, the Judge Selection Committee of Shanghai is composed of 15 members, including eight expert members who are mainly experts from law schools of Shanghai, and seven special members from related functions of the city. Although members of the selection committee also include those from provincial judicial organs or judicial administrations, members from non-judicial organs will help balance and restrict the selective power of the provincial judicial organs.

Last, the current reform program emphasizes the openness of judges, which helps mitigate the bureaucratization mood of judges. The traditional way of judge selection in China is essentially a bureaucratic model of selection. That is, more emphasis is placed on selecting judges from court workers and cultivating judges from judges. While this way of cultivating judges allows the inheritance of knowledge and experience, there exists a very important problem. That is, the lack of independence for the judges themselves. On the chain of level-by-level promotion, judges are more like civil officials. They lack the awareness and character of being independent and are more likely to turn to their superior for instructions when faced with any problem. The emphasis of selecting excellent professional law talents from outside into the workforce of judges breaks the closedness of the judge profession and helps change the lack of independence for judges. As these outcomers are not too much connected with judges inside the court system and are therefore less exposed to constraints, they are more likely to make independent, objective judicial judgments.

[163] See Zhang [99].

2.3.4 Possible Problems Facing the Current Reform of the Judge Selection System in China and Countermeasures

2.3.4.1 Possible Problems Facing the Current Reform of the Judge Selection System

As mentioned earlier, the reform measures currently adopted by the judge selection system in China are of great significance to improving the specialization and professionalization of judges. However, we still need to see that while these reform measures have solved some problems, they have also brought some new problems.

First is the lack of backup resources for judges in the economically underdeveloped regions in Midwest China. According to the current reform ideas, the threshold for newly appointed judges should be raised, including the age threshold and the length of time required to engage in legal work. For example, in Shanghai, a newly appointed judge must be over 28 years of age, and have worked in the law profession for 5 years. In Shenzhen, a newly appointed judge must have engaged in the law profession for more than 4 years. This method of raising the threshold for newly appointed judges may be feasible in economically developed areas such as Shanghai and Shenzhen, but whether it is also feasible in remote, economically underdeveloped regions in Midwest China remains a big problem. In the economically underdeveloped region in Midwest China, legal talents are extremely scarce. These regions are short of legal talents cultivated by themselves and also lack the ability to attract adequate numbers of legal talents from outside. Even the undergraduate background requirement prescribed by the "Judges Law" for newly appointed judges could be too high a threshold to cross. Because of this, Article 9 of China's "Judges Law" allows the relaxation of academic qualifications for judges in certain areas to be "graduates of law majors in colleges and universities". Under such circumstances, it is debatable whether raising the threshold for newly appointed judges can be implemented in economically underdeveloped regions in Midwest China.

Next is the lack of attraction of courts to legal talents and the outflow of talents. In reality, even in economically developed regions, raising the threshold for newly appointed judges and requiring all newly appointed judges to work at grassroots courts can still lead to two problems: one is the lack of ability of courts to attract talents; the other is the potential outflow of talents. Raising the threshold for newly appointed judges and requiring all of them to work at grassroots courts will make the growth prospect of legal talents upon entry into the court appear not so optimistic. For professional legal talents looking for a job, compared with the grueling, prolonged and uncertain journey toward the enrollment as a judicial assistant and the selection to a higher-level court, working as a lawyer or otherwise pays better. More importantly, there usually is a chance of making great improvement in three years after entry into the lawyer sector or other professions. This could stop many excellent legal talents at the door of courts, exposing the talent reserve of courts to serious deficiency. In some areas, as courts are not attractive enough themselves, they are even faced with the embarrassment of having nobody to sign up for the judge recruitment.[164] Today, when judge selection system reform is being promoted, whether this phenomenon will further intensify is worth further observation. For judicial assistants and other professionals inside the court, in a situation where the income is not handsome, promotions take time and are difficult to realize, staying out of court may become a better option. The greatest consequence is the outflow of talents from grassroots courts. For example, as disclosed by media, more than 500 persons in the court system of Beijing have either resigned or transferred to other professions over the past five years. The outgoing talents are mostly those working at grassroots courts who are well experienced and highly able to handle cases. In China, as intermediate and grassroots courts are responsible for handling the overwhelming majority of cases, they are intrinsically faced with the undercapacity for cases and insufficient ability to handle cases. With the advancement of the specified number of judges system reform and the judge selection system reform, if the outflow of talents from grassroots courts further intensifies, the undercapacity of judges for cases and high pressure for judges in handling cases will become even more austere. This, in turn, will prompt even more judges to leave. The selection of judges of a superior people's court from excellent judges of a lower-level court can also lead to the outflow of excellent judges from grassroots courts. Selecting excellent judges step by step to a higher court where there is no need to handle large quantities of cases will disconnect professional talents from the front line of case handing and cause the configuration of legal talents to become illogical.

Still next is the administrativization inside the courts. According to the requirements of the reform plan, all newly appointed judges must work at a grassroots court, and judges of a superior people's court must be selected from excellent judges of a lower-level court. In a manner of speaking, the intention of such a reform plan is good. Yet we cannot deny that such a reform plan has some problems, too. For example, this may lead to the functional inseparation between a grassroots court and a superior court. This does not favor the specialization and professionalization; the administrativization inside the court system may also be exacerbated as a result of position or job promotion.[165] Most importantly, the level-by-level selection of judges has the potential of resulting in the administrativization inside the court system. First, the reason behind judges' interest in selection and in entering a court at a higher level signifies the strong administrativization for courts in China. In Here, entering a court at a higher level usually means not having to handle cases at the front line, thus freeing oneself from the hardship of handling cases. Above that, this also means possessing more authority, political status and promotion opportunities. Although it is prescribed by law that the relationship between superior and subordinate courts is that of supervising and being supervised, in actual practice, this relationship of supervising and being supervised will usually evolve into a relationship of leading and being led. Entering a court at a higher level, to some extent, signifies the authority

[164] See Ren [100].

[165] See Hua [101].

to lead the subordinate courts or subordinate departments. In China, where administrativization is quite serious, promotion of the administrative ranking and political status is directly linked to various material and spiritual benefits. It also affects job promotion in future. In a such situation, judges may opt to pursue a promotion at the sacrifice of their independence. Second, although the current reform requires the unified management of human, financial and materials resources at the provincial level, it is still uncertain whether the presidents of grassroots courts or intermediate courts would totally lose their right of discourse in the unified management of judges. In reality, in the context of the current legal system in China, it is hardly possible to fully isolate the influences and roles of the presidents of grassroots courts or intermediate courts in the unified management of judges. This signifies that the administrativization inside grassroots and intermediate courts may still persist and become even worse, since as required by the current reform, all newly appointed judges must work at a grassroots court and be subjected to level-by-level selection. Third, despite unified management at the provincial level, setting up a judge selection committee at the provincial court can still lead to the administrativization inside the court. Undoubtedly, unified management at the provincial level will strengthen the position and role of the higher court in judge selection, and this will lead to the administrativization at the higher court level at the same time. Although the current reform requires setting up a selection committee at the provincial level, as will be discussed later, the functional positioning and operating mechanism of the selection committee itself has yet to be defined. Hence it is unclear whether the initiative will be able to overcome the exacerbated administrativization caused by the unified management at the provincial court.[166]

Last is the institutional design of the judge selection committee. The institutional design of the judge selection committee represents a pioneering step in the present judicial reform. Yet, different opinions exist regarding how to construct the judge selection committee system in China. Whether the judge selection committee system is designed scientifically and rationally directly determines whether the judge selection committee will be able to play its desired role. In brief, the construction of a separate judge selection committee is confronted with the following problems. First is where to set up the judge selection committee. Second is whom the judge selection committee will select. That is, whether the judge selection committee will select only newly appointed judges or whether chief judges and court presidents included too? Third is the functional positioning of the judge selection committee. That is, whether the judge selection committee is a deciding organ or a proposing organ? Fourth is the composition and proportion of the members of the judge selection committee.

2.3.4.2 Possible Countermeasures

The problems confronting the judge selection system reform in China should be treated rationally. On the one hand, China should upgrade the specialization and

[166]See Su [88].

professionalization of judges. The direction of reform is definitely correct. On the other hand, attention should also be paid to two problems. One is the current judicial reality of China, which features unbalanced economic development among different areas, assymmetry between court development and court allocation, and considerable divergence between Mideast and East China. The other is the scientific rationality of the reform measures themselves. That is, precautions should be taken to prevent creating new problems while solving problems, especially the possibility of creating new problems without solving any existing problem.

As to raising the threshold for newly appointed judges, in view of the imbalance and considerable divergence in economic development and legal system development among different areas, a grace period would be necessary for particularly difficult areas, during which a lower threshold is implemented for selecting newly appointed judges.

Of course, regarding the reform plan of raising the threshold for newly appointed judges and allocating them to grassroots courts for level-by-level selection, we should acknowledge its important benefit of upgrading the competence of judges and replenishing the case handling capacity at the front line. As to the potential insufficient stock of talents for courts, outflow of talents and administrativization of courts, they are not all the result of the reform measures themselves, but the result of the lack of associated institutional reform. In the case of allocating all newly appointed judges to grassroots courts, for example, the essence of the problem lies in the remuneration of judges rather than the allocation of newly appointed judges to grassroots courts. Judges of grassroots courts are exposed to very great stress in handling cases, yet their income is not so substantial and is not directly proportional to their stress in handling cases. Furthermore, Judges in China are managed according to the order of ranking for civil servants and are administratively ranked. Judges of grassroots courts are of a relatively low ranking. Although judges of grassroots courts may sometimes be more professionally competent and capable, their administrative ranking is incomparable to judges of the superior court. To make things worse, as the relationship between superior and subordinate courts in China has already been dissimilated into an a hierarchical relationship on the administrative dimension, this further intensifies the administrative hierarchy between judges of superior and subordinate courts. When linked to the administrative ranking of judges, their remuneration cannot be raised, either. In such a situation, it is only natural that judicial assistants and other reserve talents for judges would oppose to handling cases at a grassroots court. Hence, toward the problems confronting this reform measure, viable countermeasures should include the following: First, further increase the remuneration of judges, especially judges of grassroots courts, and ensure that the remuneration of a judge of a grassroots court is at least not lower than a judge of a court at any other level. Second, further put into effect reform measures of the order of ranking for judges that different from that for civil servants. Judges should not be managed in the same manner as civil servants. Instead, the administrative ranking of judges should be canceled; the remuneration of judges should not be linked to the administrative ranking, administrative position or the hierarchical level of the court. Third, straighten up the relationship between superior and subordinate courts and between judges of superior and subordinate courts.

The relationship between superior and subordinate courts and between judges of superior and subordinate courts is simply a relationship of supervising and being supervised in business rather than that of leading and being led. One important task is to achieve a functional transformation of the supreme court and the higher courts, reduce their administrative business and their instruction on the business of subordinate courts, and centralize their function on the trial of cases. In the meantime, it is also necessary to limit the number of judges of the supreme court and higher courts, dispatch the case-handling capacity down to grassroots and intermediate people's courts, and centralize judges to the front line of case handling.

Regarding the potential administrativization in the level-by-level selection of judges, on the one hand, as mentioned earlier, the administrative management pattern of judges should be changed. At a time when judges have their professional dignity, satisfactory professional remuneration and good professional guarantee whether working at a grassroots court or an intermediate court or a higher court, they will remain rational toward any level-by-level selection; the administration in the level-by-level selection of judges will be naturally weakened. On the other hand, setting a judge selection committee at the provincial court offers a good opportunity for solving this problem to some extent. Hence, by setting up a judge selection committee, there is good chance to preclude the potential administrativization in the level-by-level selection of judges.

In terms of setting up a judge selection committee, given that this system is still in the pilot phase, we suggest paying attention to the following problems. First is the relative independence of the judge selection committee. Currently, courts are particularly eager to have the judge selection committee set up inside them so that it will always be under their control. But if that were the case, the power of selection and proposal would both fall on the courts, which wouldn't be good for the decentralization of powers. If the committee were set up at the politics and law committee, this would comply with the spirit of the Party administering cadres, but could easily lead to its intervention in cases. If the committee were set up at the People's Congress, as judges and procurators are appointed by the People's Congress, this would also involve over-centralization of powers. Another view holds that an independent selection committee not affiliated to any department should be established. In our opinions, it would be appropriate if the current judicial reform pilot projects try each of these options. That is, different provinces may implement different options. After trial and comparison, a decision will be made according to whichever option best ensures the independence of the selection committee and the scientificity of its operation. Second is the functional positioning of the judge selection committee. Will the judge selection committee function as a proposing organ or a deciding organ? Regarding this question, considering that China is under the regime of the People's Congress system, the function of the judge selection committee can only be proposing rather than deciding. According to this functional positioning, the roles of various organs in judge selection will be: the party committee as the personnel management organ; the selection committee as the proposing organ for selection, which is responsible for listing judge candidates for selection; the provincial court will nominate potential judges; the People's Congress and its standing committee as the decider as to who will finally be selected. Third is the scope of functions of the judge selection committee. In this regard, we suggest that the judge selection committee not only select judges, it also select presidents and chief judges. This does not contradict with the spirit of the Party's leadership or the Party administering cadres, since the selection committee only proposes and does not decide. If the proposal for the selection of judges and chief judges were not included, and the appointment of court presidents and chief judges were still at the disposal of the organization department under the local Party committee, the localization of judicial power would not be truly eliminated. Fourth is the composition of the judge selection committee. Regarding the composition of the judge selection committee, on the one hand, the proportions of court presidents and chief judges should be limited. Higher priority should be given to well experienced judges and procurator representatives, as well as social representatives such as lawyers and law researchers. On the other hand, the functions and roles of persons inside the court system and those outside the system should be treated equally. Otherwise persons outside the court system would only be a companion rather than a candidate. Additionally, the generation mechanism of the judge selection committee should also be designed in a scientific manner. Measures should be taken to ensure that members of the judge selection committee are not recommended or appointed by the court itself, hence guaranteeing that the committees remain a substantial level of independence and neutrality.

2.4 Research on the Reform of the Judicial Accountability System

Since the Third Plenary Session of the 18th CPC Central Committee proposed that "We will reform the judicial committee system, improve the accountability system of handling cases by the presiding judge and the collegiate bench, by which triers shall render judgment and judges shall be accountable, promoting the reform of the judicial accountability system, speeding up the reform of the judicial accountability system has become an important part of judicial reform. The related Central Committee departments and the Supreme People's Court have successively launched a series of reform measures. Toward how to speed up the reform of the judicial accountability system, there exist different understandings in theory as well as some misunderstandings in practice. The following section intends to discuss this issue, with a view to benefiting the current reform of the judicial accountability system.

2.4.1 Subject of Judicial Power

In the proposal "triers shall render judgment and judges shall be accountable", "triers shall render judgment" actually reveals who will be the subject of judicial power.

For the purpose of this text, "judicial power" is used in its narrower sense. That is, it relates only to trial power and does not cover the procuratorial power of the procuratorate. Judicial power in its narrower sense, namely, trial power, is the power to try and judge cases, encompassing both trial and judgment. Determining the scope of the subject of judicial power is of crucial importance to determining the subject of judgment and the subject of judicial accountability. Hence, how to understand "triers shall render judgment" becomes the core element for promoting the reform of the judicial accountability system.

"Triers shall render judgment" is a reform measure aimed at the disorder in the operation of trial power in the traditional judicial practice of China, in which the handling of cases does not only involve the sole judge and the collegiate bench, but also the court president (including the vice president in charge), chief judge and judicial committee. All of them have a say over the case and the the potential of affecting or deciding how the case will be handled. Court presidents or chief judges, in addition to affecting the judgment of a case in an implicit form such as making private prearrangements, may also affect or decide how the case will be handled by reviewing the case; the judicial committee may decide how a case will be concluded by discussing the case submitted. In this operation of judgment power, the real trier of the case is extremely confusing. Sometimes it might be the sole judge or the collegiate bench, at other times it might be the court president or chief judge (on the basis of judicial supervision power), and sometimes it might be the judicial committee (on the basis of trial power as generally accepted). This decentralizes the judgment power. Once there is a misjudgment for a case, it will be hard to determine who is in charge of the case at all. Consequently, nobody is held accountable or the power belongs with one person while the accountability rests with another. Additionally, the involvement of all subjects inside a court into the handling of cases also imposes other subjects in between the actual person in charge of the case (the sole judge or collegiate bench) and the parties concerned. This would not only lead to improper influences of external factors on the judgment of the cases, but also impair the trust of the parties concerned in justice and their acceptability to the judgment. Besides, the involvement of the subjects in the handling of cases would also offer a hotbed for nourishing power rent-seeking.[167] It was right in view of this situation that the judicial reform put forward the proposal that "triers shall render judgment and judges shall be accountable", identifying the subject of accountability by determining the triers of cases.

This being said, a question arises as to who should become the triers of cases? According to the proposal of the judicial reform, "triers shall render judgment" means that "triers" are the subject of judgment power. Obviously, how to understand the term "triers" becomes the key to determining who will try cases.

Regarding how to understand the term "triers", different people hold different opinions. By reference to "triers", Chinese authors generally mean the judge that presides over or attending the "court trial" of a case; neither court presidents (or vice presidents in charge) nor chief judges nor judicial committees are a "trier" of a case.

[167] See He [102].

But some author also argue that "trial" does not mean "court trial" alone; reading case files, listening to reports of the handling judge and discussing the case are also regarded as a process and form of "trial". In terms of the internal relationship of the court, "triers shall render judgment and judges shall be accountable" is defined as "the discourse of the subjects over the judgment of a case should be based upon whether they have tried the case (of course, not limited to 'court trial'); each subject should be responsible for what it has done to affect or decide the judgment".[168] According to this logic, although the court president, chief judge or judicial committee does not preside over or attend the court trial, as long as they try their best to know about the facts of the case by reading case files, listening to reports of the handling judge and/or viewing videos of the court trial, they are also the "trier" here and, consequently, can affect or decide the judgment of the case.

In a manner of speaking, the definition of "trier" does not constitute a problem in the western countries, since judges are independent and trial power belongs with judges. The triers of cases are of course the judges in charge the specific cases under the law. The complexity of the situation in China lies in the general assumption that trial power is exercised by the people's court; judges are merely the exercisers of the trial power; judges are not independent; court presidents, chief judges and judicial committees all have a share of trial power and are de facto triers. As mentioned earlier, this leads to the confusion of whoever is the subject of judgment at all. It is unclear whether cases are decided by the sole judge/collegiate bench or the court president/chief judge or the judicial committee. And this is precisely an important driver for the need of judicial reform. If the term "triers" were understood in a broader sense, "triers shall render judgment" would become no more than a reform slogan without any sense, since it would not change the current reality of judgment of cases being affected or decided by a range of subjects. Evidently, this interpretation is both questionable and inconsistent with the Central Committee's spirit of judicial reform.

It is unreasonable to assume that, although court presidents, chief Judges or judicial committees do not preside over or attend the court trial, they can still become a "trier" by reading case files, viewing videos of the court trial or listening to reports, and are therefore authorized to affect or decide the judgment of the case handled by the sole judge or collegiate bench. First, although court presidents, chief judges or judicial committees can conduct investigation personally by reading case files, viewing videos of the court trial or listening to reports, which sounds something like a "trial", this cannot be considered a "trial" in its contemporary description. In its contemporary description, the core element of "trial" is the personal experience. Specifically, "trial" means: (i) the trial is made straightforward in words; (ii) the trial is made mainly in the form of court trial; (iii) the trial is made in a centralized manner; (iv) the trier is not replaced; (v) facts are ascertained at the court; and (vi) triers shall render judgment and judges shall be accountable. "The trial is made straightforward in words" represents the main form of personal experience; "the trial is made mainly in the form of court trial" represents a key venue for personal experience; "the trial is made in a centralized manner" and "the trier is not replaced" are

[168]Gu [103].

the guarantee measures for personal experience; "facts are ascertained at the court" and "triers shall render judgment and judges shall be accountable" are the destination of personal experience.[169] That is to say, the "trial" in its contemporary description covers the requirements for the subject, venue, form and result. It is open, transparent and closed enough to ensure the participation of both parties and to minimize any potential undue influence from external factors. While reading case files, viewing videos of the court trial and listening to reports are conducted by the court president, chief judge or judicial committee personally, first, their fact-finding about the case is not based or is not completely based on primary evidence. Although this finding can be true, the chance of it being a wrong is even greater. Second, this "trial" lacks the procedural legitimacy. It is usually and primarily conducted outside the court without involving the parties concerned, thus lacking openness and transparency. This form of investigation is essentially infringing upon the defendant's right to a fair trial, hence cannot be considered a "trial" in its contemporary description. In a manner of speaking, the contemporary description of trial" is built on the premise of abandoning this form of investigation. Next, more importantly, if we confess that this is also a form of trial and allow court presidents, chief judges or judicial committees to affect or decide the judgement of cases on this ground, it mean that the open, transparent, scientific trial conducted by a sole judge or collegiate bench is but a trial in form or on show, whereas the secret, non-participatory, non-scientific investigation conducted by the court president, chief judge or judicial committee is a trial in essence. This will cause the trial in China to evolve, wholly and radically, into a trial in writing or in secret. Such a behind-the-scene justice will not only give an impression that justice can be intervened by invisible subjects, but also open the gate for various out-of-court factors to affect the judgment of cases, eventually exposing justice to the interference of external factors. What's even worse, this behind-the-scene justice also infringes upon the defendant's right to a fair trial. In a word, this formula of judicial action of trial by the sole judge/collegiate bench + review by the court president/chief judge or decision by the judicial committee will overwhelm the public impression of judicial action and its fairness in general, and compromise the fairness and acceptability of the trial. Objectively, this is precisely the essential reason why the current judicial reform emphasizes the personal experience in trials, the consistency between the subject of judgment and the subject of trial, and the unchangeability of the subject of trial. As such, "triers" in the "triers shall render judgment" actually refer to the sole judge or the collegiate bench or other trying organ assigned to be directly responsible for a case after its attribution to the court. This is a counterpart subject to the court president, chief judge or judicial committee that does not participate in the court trial. Its external difference from the court president, chief judge or judicial committee generally lies in the fact that it presides over or attend the court session personally; its essential difference is the fact that it experiences the judicial action on the scene. Of course, if the court president, chief judge or judicial committee is directly responsible for the trial of a case as a judge, they are undoubtedly a "trier" in this description, too.

---

[169] See Zhu [104].

So far, from the practice of reform, it is already a consensus that the court president and chief judge are not a trier of cases and may not examine and approve cases. According to the "Several Opinions of the Supreme People's Court on Improving the Judicial Accountability System of the People's Court" (the "Opinions on Judicial Accountability System"), a judgment document of a case tried by a sole judge shall be directly signed by the sole judge himself; a judgment document of a case tried by a collegiate bench shall be signed by the handling judge, other members of the collegiate bench, and the presiding judge; where the presiding judge is the handling judge, such document shall be finally signed by the presiding judge; in view of the particularity of cases to be decided by the judicial committee and the need to carry through the opinions of the judicial committee, such cases shall still be subject to the checking and signing procedure.

Here, an important problem is how to look at the requirement that cases shall be decided by the judicial committee. Some suggest that the judicial committee or the function of the judicial committee to discuss cases should be canceled; others tend to reserve the judicial committee but at the same time downplay its function of deciding the facts of cases and reserve or principally highlight its function to decide the application of law. Regarding the judicial committee, one has to see that under this formula of trial power of "trial by the judge/collegiate bench + decision by the judicial committee", limiting the function of the judicial committee to primarily or only discussing the application of law of a case makes no radical change to the identity and role of the judicial committee as not being a "trier". Undeniably, of course, a judicial committee is in generally made up of judges well experienced in case handling; it does play an important part in controlling the handling of cases or ensuring the quality of cases. Especially under the current legal system of China, reserving the judicial committee and giving play to its role with respect to specialty is still necessary. To this end, the current reform ideas are: First, narrow down the scope of and the matters covered by the discussion of the judicial committee. That is, the judicial committee will only discuss major, complicated cases involving the national diplomacy, security and social stability, and the application of law of major, difficult, complicated cases. Second, strengthen the personal experience of the judicial committee. That is, where a case is to be decided by the judicial committee, members of the judicial committee should review the material submitted by the collegiate bench for discussion in advance to inform themselves about the different opinions of the collegiate bench on the application of law and the underlying reasons, retrieve the audio and/or video record of the court trial or view the related files where necessary. Third, let the judicial committee try cases themselves. That is, major, difficult, complicated cases may be directly tried by a collegiate bench comprising the court president, vice president and the judicial committee. In a way, these reform ideas are an eclectic choice accounting for the current reality of China. Of course, in the long run, things will eventually come around to the third measure. That is, the judicial committee will be transformed into a true "trier" that directly tries and judges cases. On the one hand, some major, difficult, complicated cases may be directly tried by the judicial committee; on the other hand, where deemed by the judge or collegiate bench responsible for a case that such case should be tried by the review committee, it may apply for changing the subject of trial; where examination finds it necessary for the case to be tried by the judicial committee, the trier of the case should be changed to the judicial committee, which should try the case again according to the legal trial procedure and make a judgment. Only in this way can the proposal "triers shall render judgment and judges are held accountable" be truly effected. In judicial practice, some places have implemented pilot projects where cases are directly tried by members of the special committee. This reform idea is applaudable and further exploration will be worthwhile for the concrete implementation mechanism in a reproducible, promotable form. An important point of this is to define the extent to which cases are directly tried by the judicial committee and the procedure by which the subject of trial is changed.

2.4.2 Concept Definition and Principle for Setting Trial Accountability

As the legal canon goes, "All power tends to corrupt and absolute power corrupts absolutely".[170] To limit the potential misuse and corruption of absolute power, the exerciser of power must be exerted the accountability appropriate to such power. Regarding the restriction of power, President Xi Jinping clearly pointed out that "we should improve the power operating mechanism and supervision system and ensure that power is accompanied with accountability, power is used under supervision, dereliction of duty is held responsible, and violation of laws is investigated". While trial power has its particularity, from both the experience of the other parts of the world and the practice in China, it is necessary to set and identify the accountability of judges. Of course, the setting of trial accountability should follow the basic rule of the operation of trial power.

2.4.2.1 Concept Definition of Trial Accountability

The concept of trial accountability is by no means clear in terms of either theory or practice. For a long time, no adequate attention has been paid to this problem. Briefly, trial accountability is the legal accountability to be borne by the subject of trial for trying and judging cases. Broadly speaking, in addition to the accountability for illegal trial, trial accountability also covers trial defections such as fact defections, evidence defections, law defections and document defections, as well as occupational disciplines. As far as trial defections are concerned, we ordinary people are not sages, hence it is simply inevitable that cases are handled with defections, yet these defections can be made right in the litigation process. Indiscriminately pursuing accountability will greatly handicap the liberty of the case handlers and cause them to refuse to do what should be done and push off the accountability to others, which

[170][UK] Dalberg-Acton [105].

is very adverse to handling cases well.[171] What's more, the accountability for such defections is markedly lighter than that for illegal trial. Hence, although these defections should be restricted, it is still inappropriate to include them into the scope of trial accountability. In the same way, it is also inappropriate to include issues relating to the lifestyle and professional ethics of judges into trial accountability. As a result, "trial accountability" is used in this text in its narrower sense. That is, it is defined by the accountability of a judge for the quality of case handling within its capacity when performing his duty of trial.

2.4.2.2 Principles for Setting Trial Accountability

Although the exercise of trial power as a public power is subject to the supervision and restriction of trial accountability as are the other public powers, as trial accountability itself is a judicial power involving both the power to try and judge cases, its attribute is different from any administrative power, and the accountability of this power should also possess its own particularity. That is, it should be based on exemption as the principle and accountability as an exception. The particularity of the imputation of trial accountability should be understood from the following perspectives:

First, during the process of litigation, under the principle of evidence judgment, judges can only rely on evidence for ascertaining the facts of cases. However, the evidence submitted by the parties afterwards may not always reflect the real facts of the case, and not all evidence provided by the parties can serve as basis for finalizing the case. Judges not only need to investigate and verify the trueness, relevance and legitimacy of the evidence, in some cases where evidence is absent or facts are fuzzy, they also need to use their life experience and normal logic to make judgment. This is just an example of how fuzzy and difficult it is for judges to ascertain the facts of cases.

Second, judges as the finder and trier of facts act as a terminator of litigation disputes. Hence, whether or not the facts are clear, the trier has to give a judgment within the limited term of litigation. Such a judicial judgment mechanism determines the relative nature of the correctness of the judgment made by the judges. On the one hand, subject to the limited term of litigation, if judges are to judge cases with fuzzy facts or inadequate facts within a limited period of time, the accuracy and correctness of the judgment will inevitably be compromised. On the other hand, concluding a case within a limited term of litigation is where a judge's duty lies and judges are not allowed to refuse to try a case by excuse of inadequate evidence or fuzzy facts. Regarding the judge's fact findings for the case under the evidence conditions and litigation conditions at that time, except under a few particular circumstances, it is not feasible or legitimate to hold the judge liable regardless of whether these findings are proved to be correct later on. Hence, the accountability related to a judge's trial power cannot be determined simply based on whether the judgment proves to be correct. In fact, it is also impractical to define a judgment made by judges simply

---

171 See Chen [106].

by whether it is correct or incorrect. The law gives judges discretionary power in the process of litigation, within which whatever judgment they make should be construed as "correct". Consequently, instead of understanding the correctness of a judgment partially, we should acknowledge and accept the "multiple correct solution" of the judgment and even, within a reasonable extent, maintain a level of tolerance to inconsistent judgments toward the same case. Only in this way can we sweep away the worries of judges when trying cases so that they will make decisions on a case-to-case basis and become better prepared for realizing individual justice.

Third, excessively tight trial accountability could increase the occupational stress and trial burden of judges. This would not only lead to the outflow of judge talents, but also force judges to avoid trial and evade accountability by means such as reporting to the leader, submitting the case to the judicial committee for discussion and decision, remanding the case for retrial or withdrawing the case. Particularly, excessively tight or loose trial accountability could both impair the judges' ability to exercise their trial power independently according to law.

It is right because of these reasons that in setting the trial accountability of judges, almost all countries in the world have followed the judicial law of "immunity as the principle and accountability as an exception".[172] From Articles 23, 25 and 28 of the "Opinions on Judicial Accountability System", we can see that China's reform of its judicial accountability system also uses "immunity as the principle and accountability as an exception" as the principle for setting trial accountability.

2.4.3 Compositional Elements and Immunity Conditions of Trial Accountability

2.4.3.1 Compositional Elements of Trial Accountability

In order to ensure that judges exercise their trial power independently and objectively, each country is substantially prudent in specifying the trial accountability of judges. China should also make proper considerations when establishing the details of accountability. As the core determinant for scoping trial accountability, setting scientifically rational compositional elements of trial accountability constitutes the basis for balancing the independent exercise of trial power and the regulation of judicial acts. By compositional elements, it means the preconditions for the legal effect to taken place. The realm of accountability includes both the subjective and objective aspects, which can be further divided into four contents, namely, act, mentality, damage, and causality.[173] As a legal liability, the compositional elements of trial accountability is unexceptionally composed of both subjective and objective aspects. The objective aspect of trial accountability relates to the concrete, objective

[172]He [102].

[173]Zhou [107].

act against the legal provisions or leading to misjudgment, the damage as a consequence, and the causality. The subjective aspect of trial accountability relates to the intentional or negligent attitude held by the trier toward the act of illegal trial and the consequence of such act.

Regarding the compositional elements of trial accountability, the academic world is primarily concerned about the subjective aspect of trial accountability. What worries academic researchers is that the "consequence only" principle of accountability ascertainment may ignore the subjective mentality of a trier about his own misconduct, which disagrees with the law of justice. Administration of justice is to ascertain facts having taken place in the past. Due to the limitations of various conditions, it is impossible for a trier to ascertain all past facts without any mistake. Where a misjudgment occurs despite fulfilling the duty of care, the judge cannot be held accountable for such case. In this regard, we suggest that when setting the compositional elements of trial accountability, especially when "misjudgments" are concerned, attention should be paid to the following aspects: First, whether a mistake is made intentionally or negligently; second, whether the negligence is gross or general; and third, whether the accountability relates to an error or a general discrepancy in legal understanding.[174] The "Opinions on Judicial Accountability System" basically follows this principle of ascertaining judicial accountability. In its Article 25, the acts covered by trial accountability are categorized into intentional and gross negligence. The first is "intentionally violates the law"; the second is "causes a misjudgment that leads to serious consequences because of gross negligence".

"Intentionally violates law during trial activities" means that the trier makes an illegal judgment by intentionally not following the provisions of law in procedure or in substance. "Intentionally" is the key of this clause. According to related law theory, "intentionally" means "knowing" that his conduct will entail a harmful consequence and "wishing" or "letting" this harmful consequence to take place.[175] However, in ascertaining trial accountability, once during the trial activity, a judge knowingly violates the law, he is already infringing upon the fairness of trial. The harmful consequence has already taken place. Hence there is no need to consider his own awareness of his conduct itself. As far as "knowingly" is concerned, a judge needs to possess a substantial understanding about the provisions of law to be observed and the substantive or procedural law to be applied. Specifically, all illegalities in act, such as taking bribes, bending the law for personal gains, destroying evidence material or concealing case facts, or substantive or procedural errors that obviously disagree with the common sense of a legal person in terms of the application of law should be ascertained as "knowingly".

"Causes a misjudgment that leads to serious consequences during trial activities" means that a trier makes a misjudgment out of carelessness or overconfidence and such a misjudgment leads to serious consequences. In the theory of crime, "negligence" is typically categorized into two types. As defined by Article 15 of the "Criminal Law", one is "should have foreseen that his act would possibly entail

---

[174]See Chen [108].

[175]See the ascertainment of "intentional" in criminal intent in Gao and Ma [109].

harmful consequences to society but fails to do so through his negligence"; the other is "having foreseen the consequences, readily believes that they can be avoided, so that the consequences do occur". Accordingly, the accountability for trial negligence can also be categorized into two types. One is the judge "should have foreseen" that there is some error in his judicial act, such as failure to finalize the case on basis of a probabilistic conclusion that should have been made according to existing evidence material, omission of important evidence or clues leading to wide disagreement between the conclusion and the objective facts of the case, or applying legal provisions that are already nullified, but "fails to do so" through its own subjective reasons; it also includes failure to perform some judicial acts when he should have done, leading to serious consequences". The other is "having foreseen that his judicial act would lead to a misjudgment, readily believes that they can be avoided, so that the consequences do occur, such as violating the related proving standard, objective logic or common sense, artificially expanding the proving power of an evidence, discounting the evidence or clues provided by the defending party, and readily believing that they can be avoided".

Trial is an activity of understanding facts that have already taken place once again. When ascertaining the facts of a case, it is impossible for the trier to put everything back as they were. What he can do is merely restore and represent the objective facts step by step through existing evidence of the case and select a conclusion with the greatest possibility after comprehensive consideration of the evidence of the whole case. The law respects the triers' freedom to ascertain facts through conviction. Although the resulted conclusion may not be totally dependable, it is because of this reality that the accountability system cannot be overcritical over or hold the trier liable for such mistakes. To achieve a balance between them, the "Opinions on Judicial Accountability System" defines the extents of the accountability for negligence during trial: First, the negligence must be "gross". Second, it must have led to a "misjudgment". Third, "serious consequences" must have been entailed as a result of such misjudgment.

By "gross negligence", it means a combination of subjective and objective errors. That is, it involves a subjective mentality first, along with an external act dominated by the subjective will of the actor.[176] More specifically, a gross negligence involves both the subjective and objective aspects. That is, the actor's violation of his duty of care is extremely unreasonable and may lead to serious damage to others. When trial accountability is concerned, a negligence cannot be deemed "gross" unless a trier fails to perform his duty of care that should have normally been performed by other triers, through negligence or overconfidence, and such failure leads to a consequence that could affect the trial result substantially, such as the loss of evidence or a wrong type of document. Negligence liability is generally not based on the act itself as the necessary and sufficient condition for accountability, but on certain actual consequences as the precondition. Although during trial activities, an act qualified as a "gross negligence", such as omission of key evidence or applying nullified legal provisions, will generally lead to a "misjudgment", there are still incidences where the result of judgment of a

[176]See Ye [110].

case involving gross negligence is error-free. For example, although the text of the law applied is already nullified, the concrete provisions involved are still existent in other laws. Consequently, no substantive misjudgment is resulted. If a misjudgment does not occur, this act can be made right through an appellate procedure or trial supervision procedure, and no trial accountability will be called to account.

Overall, the setup of the compositional elements of trial accountability in China agrees quite well with the current judicial conditions of the country. On the one hand, in judicial activities, illegal judgment is still not completely eradicated. Under a judicial reform that grants greater independence to judges, supervising how their power is exercised and setting a related accountability system should be a must. On the other hand, for purpose of ensuring that judges exercise their trial power objectively and independently, strictly limiting the subjective and objective aspects of the compositional elements of trial accountability and precluding incidences of improper accountability is also key to the scientific operation of the system.

2.4.3.2 Circumstances and Conditions of Immunity from Trial Accountability

To secure the regular operation of public power, in addition to setting the scope of power and the power-restricting measures, a society under the rule of law should also set the accountability corresponding to each exercise of power. However, accountability systems are a double-edged sword. While a strict accountability system is definitely able to confine power into the cage of system, it can also deprive power of its ability to evolve and mobilize. Hence, a immunity mechanism of trial accountability, as an indispensable part of the system, should be added so that the two mechanisms will complement and depend on each other to better lead the judicial accountability system in China toward further improvement.

Immunity from trial accountability, also known in the academic world as immunity from judges' accountability, means the right enjoyed by a judge to be exempted from control or legal liability for what he does, what he says and what he decides in the course of justice.[177] The earliest example of immunity from judicial accountability originated from Britain. As the kings of the feudalism would often displace judges from their position, to challenge the imperial authority and safeguard democracy and liberty, a set of systems related to the protection of the professional position of judges was gradually developed.[178] After that, the United States also established through judicial precedents, assuming that judges should also enjoy judicial immunity, as long as they do not act without obvious lack of jurisdiction, even if their act is taken wrongly, made maliciously, or beyond their authority.[179] Besides, many international treaties and rules also reflect the spirit of immunity from trial accountability. One example is Article 44 of the "Minimum Standard of Judicial Independence" adopted

[177]See Tan and Sun [111].

[178]See Wang [112].

[179]Jan Green [113].

at the 19th annual conference of the International Bar Association in New Delhi in 1982, which prescribes that judges shall enjoy immunity from proceedings and testimony for their acts or omissions in the exercise of their judicial functions. Another example is Article 16 of the "Basic Principles on the Independence of the Judiciary" adopted at the 7th United Nations Congress on the Prevention of Crime and the Treatment of Offenders in 1985, which prescribes that "Without prejudice to any disciplinary procedure or to any right of appeal or to compensation from the State, in accordance with national law, judges should enjoy personal immunity from civil suits for monetary damages for improper acts or omissions in the exercise of their judicial functions".

With the sustained progress of modern rule of law, immunity from trial accountability has also gained continued improvement and development. People's understanding of the theory behind immunity from trial accountability has also deepened continuously. More specifically, the theoretical ideas behind immunity from trial accountability mainly include the following: First, the idea of judicial independence. The immunity system of trial accountability was initially established to protect judges as an independent profession from the restrictions of imperial authority. Rule of law is a social management regime continuously pursued by modern countries and regions. To realize rule of law, an impartial, efficient and authoritative judicial system has to be possessed and relied upon, and such an impartial judicial system is definitely independent. This is because only an independent judicial system is able to incubate independent, detached, neutral judges, who are expected to terminate disputes and uphold justice according to prior regulations and procedures of law. Meanwhile, as judicial power is a form of judgment power, whether it is just is reliant on the independent reasoning of the judges themselves. Only under the condition of judicial independence and judiciary independence can the judgments made by judges possess a procedural coat of justice. Second, theory of bounded rationality of human cognition, which holds that "human behaviors are conscious and rational, yet this rational cognition is a bounded one instead of a boundless one".[180] The reason behind the bounded rationality of human being lies in their constantly changing habitat and their bounded ability to cognize the objective world subjectively. Hence, judges are also constrained by their bounded rationality when ascertaining facts of a case according to the evidence and making conviction and sentencing to the criminal suspect or defendant. Such a rational judgment may be deemed completely correct at the time of decision, but over time, people may change this intrinsic observation. If the accountability for these "misjudgments" were imputed to the judge, it would be obviously be unfair. For this reason, granting judges immunity from trial responsibility also means giving judges the liberty to make the best of their rationality, discover the facts of cases to the furthest extent and realize judicial justice.

When we look at the immunity system of trial accountability across different countries in the world, we can discover that each country has an immunity system of trial accountability unique to themselves. In the United Kingdom, for example, absolute immunity for judges was established by the "Appellate Jurisdiction Act"

[180]Chen [114].

dated 1876 and the "Supreme Court Act" dated 1981. All acts and words of judges in the course of justice, including even any malicious act of judges, are covered by the immunity. In the United States, immunity was first established in the form of absolute immunity as practiced in the United Kingdom. However, as in actual practice, problems kept arising out of absolute immunity, finally, in 1984, the supreme court of the United States modified the scope and boundary of judge immunity through judicial precedents, which excluded non-judicial acts or obviously administrative acts from judges' immunity and provided procedural immunity for criminal cases.[181] Correspondingly, most civil law countries implement a relative immunity system. "Where during the exercise of its judicial function a judge entails damages to a party concerned because of its own fault, such judge will be held civilly liable and will compensate such party, provided always that such decision of compensation should not be effected unless and until all other possible reliefs available under the law are exhausted".[182]

In China, the judicial reform also includes the circumstances where judges' accountability should be exempted. Article 28 of the "Opinions on Judicial Accountability System" prescribes that where a case is overruled after retrial according to the trial supervision procedure, a judge shall be exempted from trial accountability in any of the following circumstances: (1) the judge holds a different understanding about the concrete text of a law, regulation, rule or judicial interpretation and can give a reasonable explanation within his professional knowledge; (2) the judge holds discrepancy or doubt about the judgment of the basic facts of the case and can give a reasonable explanation according to the rule of evidence; (3) a party waives or partly waives or partly waives his claim of rights; (4) change occurs in the fact of the case already established because of the fault on a party concerned or other objective causes; (5) the decision is changed as a result of new evidence; (6) modifications are made to the applicable law or policy; (7) other legal documents on which the decision is based have been canceled or altered; or (8) other circumstances where a judge should be exempted from accountability when exercising his judicial function.

Among these eight circumstances, the last five are well comprehensible. As to the third circumstance, if a party concerned waives or partly waives his claim of rights, the judicial proceeding or judicial phase will be simplified to one degree or another. The judge's ascertainment of the facts of the case will be affected and constrained by such party's waiver of his right of action and may thus become considerably inconsistent with the reality of the case. As such, if the existing, effective judgment is retried and amended and the judge is errorless within his obligation, he may be exempted from trial accountability.

The first and second circumstances relate to two trial duties of how judges ascertain facts and how they apply the law. In terms of judges' duty of ascertaining facts, when trying to resolve disputes or judging cases, a judge should first conduct fact-finding of the case, namely, the they should ascertain the evidence supporting the facts of the case. Depending on the ability of the parties to obtain evidence, their

[181] See Yan [115].

[182] Liu [116].

skill of debate in litigation, the rule of evidence, the term of trial, and the logic and experience of the judges themselves, judges may use different judgment and selection standards when ascertaining evidence. Incidences may occur from time to time where different fact-findings are made over the same case. Hence, as long as the judge making such fact-finding can give a reasonable explanation why he adopted the evidence and consequently admitted the evidence as true within his professional knowledge. In terms of judges' duty of applying law, the same problem also exists. Judges' understanding of law can be inconsistent. Although judges are affected by roughly same law education, qualification examination of the law profession and the professional community of law, existence of this difference is not only a manifestation that judges are handling cases independently, neutrally and objectively, but also the ultimate result of their interpreting the lively, changing, concrete practical cases with technical and sometimes even conservative law. As such, as long as the judge can give a reasonable explanation within his professional knowledge, he may also be exempted from trial accountability.

2.4.4 Subject and Procedure of Accountability Investigation for Misjudgments

The accountability investigation for misjudgments is the procedural guarantee for effecting the judicial accountability system. In order to secure the successful operation of the judicial system, judges should be well remunerated to ensure that they exercise the power vested in them by law; delinquent judges should also be punished to prevent judicial corruption and realize judicial justice.[183] The reform of the judicial accountability system clearly calls for establishing a separate disciplinary system for judges, with special focus on improving the disciplinary organization and perfecting the disciplinary procedure. Only with a professional, neutral subject of accountability investigation for misjudgments according to a scientific, rational legal procedure is it possible to make impartial, objective decisions, protect the rights of judges, and realize the substantive objective of the reform of the judicial accountability system.[184]

2.4.4.1 Subject of Accountability Investigation for Misjudgments

The core value of the judicial accountability system is to ensure the independent exercise of trial power. The subject of investigating the accountability for misjudgments should be highly independent so that judges' exercise of trial power are not be subjected to the pressure from political factors and the social public.[185] The subject of

---

[183] See Ma and Yi [117].

[184] See Wang [118].

[185] See Jiang and Wu [119].
See Hu [120].

accountability investigation should be independent from any administrative, judicial or lawmaking organ; nor can it have any interest relationship with any judge who violates the professional or ethic obligation of a judge or any subject of complaint.[186] Besides, the setup of the subject of accountability investigation should be higher than a general local court so that it is sufficiently empowered to perform its duty and avoid the intervention from local power. In western countries, disciplinary actions against judges are generally determined by a high-level institution to show the prudence of the disciplinary decision. In the United States, for example, if a federal judge is in breach of the discipline, his act will be investigated by the commission of inquiry. If the inquiry assumes that the judge should be warned or his work should be suspended, these assumptions are subject to the decision of the Congress; decisions to disqualify the judge should be passed by both the Senate and the House of Representatives. In France, punishment of judges is exercised by the Supreme Council of Magistrature.

The "Judges Law of the People's Republic of China" prescribes that judges are obligated to take facts as the basis, and laws as the criterion when trying cases, to handle cases impartially, and not to bend law for personal gain. Nevertheless, judges are not vending machines. They are human beings with their own personalities, their interest pursuits and initiatives. The judgment made by judges are the inference of past facts according to existing evidence and the product of their subjective cognition. Given the limitation of subjective cognition, whether a judge should be held accountable for handling a case should be appraised objectively and scientifically according to the concrete context in which the case is handled. Hence, a separate organ should be set up so that determination is made by separate persons as to whether a judge should be held accountable.

Having a separate organ to exercise the disciplinary function against judges helps adopt a uniform standard and scale for evaluating the behavior of judges. In view of the judge disciplinary systems overseas, many developed countries under the rule of law have a separate judge disciplinary organ in place. Funds needed for maintaining the regular operation of this organ are generally separately budgeted. For example, in the United States, the Nevada Commission on Judicial Discipline is an institution specifically established to deal with complaints and disciplinary actions related to law violations by judges and procurators. In the United Kingdom, the justice complaint commission provides support services for the Secretary of State for Justice and Lord Chancellor in performing their function of dealing with complaints and disciplinary actions.[187] In Germany, a court of judicial duties is in place at both the supreme general court and the state courts to decide judicial disciplines, punishments and other matters. Members of the disciplinary authorities must be qualified with sufficient professional knowledge and rich judicial experience. Ascertaining the subjective faults of judges by senior peers helps ensure the professionality of disciplinary decisions and avoid insiders being evaluated by outsiders. The disciplinary organ should comprise a diversity of subjects from the professional community of law to preclude unit protectionism; deputies to the NPC and public personnel should also

[186]See Chen [121].

[187]See Chen [122].

be involved to reflect democracy and ensure that disciplinary decisions are objective, impartial, and more credible.[188] In view of these, the disciplinary committee should comprise veteran judges and procurators, as well as researchers and social public to form an organizational mechanism represented by law professionals with modest involvement of the social public and take disciplinary actions against judges who make illegal judgments or practice favoritism against professional ethics or the law.

In China, arrangements for a disciplinary committee have been made in related documents. For example, Article 56 of the "Opinions on Comprehensively Deepening the Reform of the People's Court" issued by the Supreme People's Court in 2015 explicitly pointed out that a judge disciplinary committee will be set up at both the national and provincial level. In order to put into effect the accountability system for judges and procurators in handling cases, the Supreme People's Court and the Supreme People's Procuratorate issued the "Opinions on Establishing the Disciplinary System for Judges and Prosecutors (for Trial Implementation)" in 2016, defining the composition of the disciplinary committee in greater details. According to this document, the disciplinary committee should comprise persons with high political qualities, high professional competence and good professional integrity; members of the disciplinary committee should include deputies to the NPC, CPPCC members, legal experts, representatives of lawyers, and representatives of judges. Representatives of judges should account for a minimum of 50% of the total number of the committee members and should be selected from the people's courts at different levels. The head of the disciplinary committee should be nominated from well experienced, highly respected senior law professionals and determined by the provincial (autonomous region, municipality) Party committee.[189] In a manner of speaking, China's idea of setting up a disciplinary committee is appropriate. Setting up a disciplinary committee at the provincial level agrees well with the initiative of unified management of human, financial and material resources at the provincial level. Furthermore, setting up a disciplinary committee at the provincial level will be even more conducive to ensuring the independence of this organ; the member composition of the disciplinary committee can also reflect the democracy of disciplines and prevent disciplinary actions against judges from being decided solely by leaders. Such an institutional design will allow the disciplinary committee to make disciplinary decisions more independently and objectively and improve the credibility of the disciplinary actions.

2.4.4.2 Procedure of Accountability Investigation for Misjudgments

Besides setting up a separate judge disciplinary committee, the establishment of a precise, rational accountability investigation mechanism in line with the rule of judicial operation is also dependent on an open, impartial judge disciplinary procedure.

---

[188] See Cheng and Wang [123].

[189] See Article 4 of the "Opinions of the Supreme People's Court and Supreme People's Procuratorate on Establishing the Disciplinary System for Judges and Prosecutors (for Trial Implementation)".

Judges, as subjects that exercise their trial power independently, protect the social justice. Hence, when judges become the object of a disciplinary action, they should also be entitled to equally impartial treatment so that their rights and interests are protected, too. When ascertaining and investigating the accountability of judges in handling cases, the judge disciplinary committee should follow the principle of due process, not only to ensure that the judge who violates rule and law is punished in time, but also to guarantee their rights to defend, prove, apply for reconsideration, and petition. Worldwide, many countries have established their own highly operable, strongly efficient judge disciplinary systems, with separate laws specifying the procedural norms such as the initiating conditions for judge disciplines, the right of statement of the judges concerned, and the mechanism of making disciplinary decision. In the current "Judges Law" of China, the object, scope and form of disciplinary actions are specifically prescribed. The working rules and disciplinary procedures of the disciplinary committee have yet to be separately established through a separate system so that they both absorb advanced practices and experiences from other countries and address the judicial reality of China. A complete judge disciplinary procedure should cover the following three parts: investigation, trial decisions, and relief.[190]

In the investigation stage, the supervisory department of the people's court can be used as the main accountability discovery and investigation department as provided in previous laws. The supervisory department of the people's court should investigate and verify, and take necessary, proper protective measures for, any judge suspected of violating his judicial functions. During the investigation, the judge concerned should have the right to know, defend and prove. The supervisory department of the people's court should record the opinions, defenses and proofs of the judge concerned faithfully and indicate in the investigation report whether they are adopted. If after investigation the supervisory department of the people's court deems it necessary to ascertain whether intentional or gross negligence is constituted, the committee should report the case to the court president for decision and submit it to the judge disciplinary committee for consideration.[191]

In the trial stage, the related people's court should be responsible for providing proof. The supervisory department of the people's court should send personnel to inform the judge disciplinary committee of the facts of the illegal trial of the judge concerned and the proposed treatment and the basis thereof, and provide proof supporting his acts and subjective faults of his illegal trial. Whether the trial act of a judge is an intentional violation of law or a gross negligence essentially lies in whether the formation of his inner conviction and the application of law are legal and legitimate. Hence, the judges concerned should be given the rights to state, defend and prove during the trial. From the provisions concerning judge disciplinary committees throughout the world, although they differ in concrete procedural design, almost all of them address the protection of the procedural rights of judges such as defense and

---

190 See Zhan [124].

191 See Articles 34, 25 and 36 of the "Several Opinions of the Supreme People's Court on Improving the Judicial Accountability System of the People's Court".

proof. For example, in France, the judicial disciplinary procedure covers both the prosecuting and defending parties. Judges may employ a defender; they may also call witnesses or expert witnesses. Investigation is separated from trial. The "Supreme Council of Magistrature" attending the investigation is not allowed to participate in the defense. Court trials should be open except for very special, substantially reasonable decisions. In China's Taiwan, the "court of duties" tries judge disciplinary cases and conducts verbal debates, highlighting the judicial nature of the disciplinary system.[192] Throughout the trial, in addition to protecting the procedural rights of the judges concerned, necessary, proper protective measures should also be taken for them. At a time when the Internet is highly developed, investigating a judge upon receipt of a report will not only heavily impair the independence of judges in performing their duties according to law, it will also offer a good chance for those waiting to maliciously slander judges. On July 28, 2016, the General Office of the CPC Central Committee and the General Office of the State Council issued the "Provisions on Protecting Judicial Personnel to Lawfully Perform Statutory Duties", which details the security mechanisms for the various rights and interests of judicial professionals, broadens the security coverage of the judicial profession, and protects the legitimate rights and interests of judges and procurators while strengthening their responsibility in handling cases. This helps eliminate the worries of individual judges, protect the judgment of cases from various interference, and defend the authority of judicial justice and rule of law.

After the trial, the disciplinary committee should, subject to the approval of the majority of the members (at least two thirds), make a proposal as to whether the judge should be held responsible, exempted from accountability or subjected to disciplinary actions according to the facts or circumstances ascertained and relevant provisions.[193] As prescribed by Article 10 of the "Opinions on Establishing the Disciplinary System for Judges and Prosecutors (for Trial Implementation)", where the disciplinary committee determines that a judge's violation of his trial functions is true and constitutes an intentional or gross negligence that leads to misjudgment of the case with serious consequences, the people's court should make a disciplinary decision in accordance with the "Judges Law of the People's Republic of China" and other relevant provisions and give corresponding punishments: (1) in the case of suspension, delayed promotion, disqualification from the judge ration or removal from office, resign in charge or dismiss, such punishment shall be made by the organization and personnel department according to the authority and procedure of cadre management; (2) in the case of a disciplinary punishment, such punishment shall be given by the discipline inspection and supervision department according to the relevant provisions and procedures; or (3) in the case of a suspected crime, the law-breaking clues shall be transferred by the discipline inspection and supervision department to the relevant judicial organ for treatment according to law. Any removal of a judge from his office shall be made by the National People's Congress according

[192]See He [125].

[193]See Articles 7 and 8 of the "Opinions of the Supreme People's Court and the Supreme People's Procuratorate on the Establishment of a Disciplinary System for Judges and Prosecutors".

to the statutory procedure or submitted to the Standing Committee of the National People's Congress for decision.

A normative legal provision should cover not only rights, responsibilities and consequences, but also a related relief procedure. Otherwise it will become a mere scrap of paper. Setting up a relief procedure is both the necessary requirement for procedural justice and an important means for securing the rights of judges. In the reform of the judicial accountability system, in order to protect the rights of the judge population, the investigation procedure for misjudgments should provide proper relief approaches for judges concerned and grant them the rights to apply for reconsideration and petition. Articles 9 and 11 of the "Opinions on Establishing the Disciplinary System for Judges and Prosecutors (for Trial Implementation)" prescribes that where a judge concerned raises an objection to the review opinions of the disciplinary committee, the disciplinary committee shall review the objection and its reasons, make a decision and reply to the judge concerned; if the judge concerned refuses to accept the disciplinary decision of the relevant people's court, he may apply with the people's court for reconsideration, and has the right to petition to the people's court at a higher level.

2.4.5 Supervision and Restriction of Trial Power

Although the current process of deepening judicial reform in all respects highlights "returning power to judges" to realize the important goal of "triers shall render judgment", this does not necessarily mean that the power of judges is unrestrained. Besides ensuring that judges are subject to the restrictions of professional ethics when performing their functions, in order to secure the normalized operation of jurisdiction and discriminate the limits of power among different subjects, special attention should also be paid to the internal and external supervision and restrictions over the trial power of judges. Only in this way can we achieve the consistency between power and responsibility when constructing the judicial accountability system and ensure that the reform of judicial accountability will be put into effect.

2.4.5.1 Internal Supervision

The internal supervision of trial power mainly relates to trial management power and trial supervision power trial management power is the power to organize, coordinate, and supervise trial activities. Typically, trial management power corresponds to internal administrative affairs, including the management of the trial procedure and the management of the trial process. For the former, these include procedural matters such as whether avoidance or publicity is permitted; for the latter, these include matters related to services of the parties concerned or public services like inquiries on cases and complaints. The subjects conferred with trial management power are generally persons and organizations inside the court conferred with leadership or management functions, including the court president, presiding judge, and trial management office. Trial supervision power is the power to supervise the correctness of judgments. Trial supervision power corresponds to the judgments made by judges. The subjects conferred with trial supervision power are generally the court president and chief judge.

In the reform of the judicial accountability system promoting "triers shall render judgment and judges shall be accountable", a disputed topic is how to look at the trial management power and trial supervision power of the court president and chief judge. Regarding this topic, there exist different understandings. Some suggest that, now that triers shall render judgment, this definitely means the preclusion of the court president or presiding judge from intervening in the handling of cases. Others hold that triers shall render judgment does not necessarily deny the trial management power and trial supervision power of the court president or chief judge.

We should see that "trial management power" and "trial supervision power" do not have clear legal basis. They are actually terms spontaneously derived out of practice, and this practice is synchronous with the reform of trial power. In 1999, to address the administrativization of judicial power in judicial practice where cases were reviewed level by level and numerous cases were judged through discussion by the judicial committee, the "First Five-Year Outline for the Reform of the People's Courts" (1999) put forward the reform of "returning power to the collegiate bench". It specified that "except major or difficult cases submitted by the collegiate bench for the judicial committee to decide through discussion, all other cases shall be tried and judged by the collegiate bench". Unfortunately, this reform, although in line with the judicial principles, has given rise to problems in judicial practice such as inconsistent judgments over the same cases, disputes remaining after conclusion of cases, non-transparent trial processes, and judicial corruption. To solve these problems, attempts have been made in judicial practice to separate trial power from trial management power.[194] At the seminar of grand judges on innovating and enhancing trial management held in Jianggangshan in 2010, the Supreme People's Court further clarified that "trial management is to make proper arrangements for the trial work, strictly regulate the judicial process, scientifically evaluate the quality and efficiency of trials, and effectively integrate judicial resources through organization, leadership, instruction, evaluation, supervision, and restriction, to ensure the justice, integrity, and efficiency of the judiciary". This lays foundation for straightening up the relationship between trial power and trial management power.[195] Following that, in November 2010, the Supreme People's Court set up an office specifically responsible for trial management. Local courts also started setting up their own trial management offices. As far as the trial management during this period is concerned, overall, a more generalized concept was adopted. That is, it included the various management activities endogenous to the operation of trial power inside the courts, and the various management

[194] See Jiang [126].

[195] See Hu and Fan [127].

activities exogenous to the operation of trial power.[196] More specifically, the trial management in this description included both tracking the process of cases and evaluating the quality of cases, as well as the power to review and issue cases, and to confirm, change, amend, and make objections to, the judgment opinions.[197] That is to say, over this period, the review of cases by the court presidents or chief judges and their interventions in the judgment results were made in the name of trial management power. The 18th National Congress of the CPC inaugurated a new round of judicial reform. The decisions of the Third and Fourth Sessions of the 18th National Congress of the CPC also made comprehensive deployments for judicial reform. The reform of the judicial accountability system promoting "triers shall render judgment and judges shall be accountable" represents an important part of judicial reform. The treatment for the review and approval of cases and intervention in cases by court presidents and chief judges became part of the reform once again. In such a background, the Supreme People's court distilled an exceptionally particular trial supervision power out of trial management power. This is centrally reflected in the "Opinions on Comprehensively Deepening the Reform of the People's Court" (2014–2018) (the "Fourth Five-Year Outline"). Article 29 of the "Fourth Five-Year Outline" is headed by "Perfecting the court president and presiding judge trial management mechanism"; Article 30 is headed by "Perfecting the court president and presiding judge trial supervision mechanism"; Article 31 is headed by "Perfecting the trial management system". In a manner of speaking, this is the first time for the people's court to clearly distinguish between the trial management power and trial supervision power of court presidents and chief judges.

From the long way to the separation among trial management power, trial supervision power and trial power described above, we can see that trial management power and trial supervision power are both necessary; they are also a choice when no better ways are available.[198] The separation among trial management power, trial supervision power, and trial power is none other than a tradeoff between the independence of judges in handling cases and their subjection to supervision. As the competence of judges continues to upgrade and their independence continues to increase, the limits and operation of trial management power and trial supervision power will become more scientific and more consistent with the basic law of justice. As such, in the current situation, rather than discussing whether it is necessary for the trial management power and trial supervision power of court presidents and chief judges to exist, it would be more appropriate to clarify to what extent and by what means the trial management power and trial supervision power of court presidents and chief judges should be exercised to preclude court presidents and chief judges from directly intervening in or deciding the judgment results of cases like before.

In a manner of speaking, it is right under the guidance of this idea that the "Opinions on Judicial Accountability System" separated among trial management power,

---

[196] See Shen [128].

[197] See Hu and Fan [127].

[198] Wan and Yang [129].

trial supervision power, and trial power, and put forward new procedural and substantive requirements concerning the operation of trial management power and trial supervision power. Regarding the procedural elements for the exercise of trial management power and trial supervision power, the "Opinions on Judicial Accountability System" requires that traces are "followed" and "documented" throughout the procedure. To prevent intervening in justice in the name of administrative, the "Opinions on Judicial Accountability System" specifies that the objects of trial supervision power can only be procedural matters and shall not cover substantive matters. Regarding trial supervision power, to prevent trial supervision power from evolving into trial power in practical operation, the "Opinions on Judicial Accountability System" identifies the special rules to be followed by court presidents and chief judges in exercising trial supervision power. First, it defines the type of cases for which the court president or chief judge may ask the trier to submit the progress and evaluation result. That is, cases involving mass disputes that may affect social stability, difficult, complicated cases having great social influences, cases that potentially conflict with the judgment of similar cases by own court or a superior court, and cases involving illegal judgment by judges as reported by related organizations or individuals. Second, it defines the effectiveness of trial supervision power of court presidents or chief judges. Trial supervision power of court presidents and chief judges does not directly change the judgment result of cases; whether the supervision opinions of the court presidents or chief judges are correct can only be determined by the judicial committee or professional judge meeting. This way, by tying trial supervision power with the functions of the judicial committee or professional judge meeting, the shade of administrative interference in supervision can be avoided.[199] Besides, by enjoying trial supervision power, court presidents or chief judges are also burdened with potential liability risks arising out of improper supervision. Hence, they have to enhance the awareness of supervision.

2.4.5.2 External Supervision and Restriction

Of course, in addition to the internal supervision forms of trial management and trial supervision, attention should also be paid to external supervision and restriction. These external supervision and restriction, in a way, can be of greater significance. They also represent the main development trend of the supervision and restriction for judges.

(1) Judicial openness and judgment reasoning system

Judicial judgment is a complicated, professional, and to some extent mysterious activity. In the past, judgments made by judges have not been open enough; the judgment documents have been too heavily formatted to show good reasoning. These have unexceptionally compromised the credibility of the judgments made by judges

---

[199] He [130].

in exercising their functions.[200] The purpose of judicial openness is to pursue both procedural justice and substantive justice. It is an effective solution for exposing how judges judge cases to the supervision by the public and allowing the particular act of judges in exercising their functions to be understood, known, and accepted by the public through special approaches. Judicial openness not only covers the course of litigation and process of litigation. Judgment openness is at the core of judicial justice. Hence, it is even more necessary to pay special attention to the reasoning part of any judgment document. To make judicial activities necessarily and sufficiently open, the concrete system and approaches should be constructed from judicial process, judicial result, and judicial reason and appeal. Not only the stance and legal basis of the judges of the court should be indicated, the opinions, viewpoints, reasons and appeals of the subjects of the litigation should also be appropriately made open. This helps ensure that judgments are duly made with good reasoning and consolidate the legality and legitimacy of judgments. During this process, how the judges evaluate evidence, how they apply legal provisions, and how they the opinions of the parties to the litigation are all presented and indicated. All subjects, including the social public, have a chance to know and view the process and result of the exercise of trial power by judges. This reform idea not only allows supervising the operation of judicial power, it is also an indispensable option for protecting the credibility of the judgments made by judges.

(2) People's assessors system

The people's assessors system, as an important approach for public participation in justice in the modern society under the rule of law, is considered an effective way of external supervision and restriction over the trial power of the court. Especially in a background of comprehensively deepening judicial reform, the people's assessors system has made remarkable achievements. In 2015, the Supreme People's Court and the Ministry of Justice issued the "Pilot Program on the Reform of the System of People's Assessors" (the "Program on Assessors System"), which launched steps for further improving the conditions and procedures for the selection and appointment of people's assessors and, aiming at the phenomena of "assessment without trial" and "trial without discussion", broadened the extent to which assessors assess trials and perfected the related assessing mechanism. More importantly, it properly distinguished the functions and powers between assessors and judges, specifying that the functions and powers of assessors are limited to participating in the trial of fact-finding problems. In addition to further improving the people's assessors system, these core reform steps of the "Program on Assessors System" also pose some restriction on judges' exercise of judgment power, broadening the spectrum of the supervision mechanism from the horizon of public participation in justice.[201]

In order to substantially ensure that the people's assessors system can effectively play its positive role in supervising and restricting trial power, special consideration

[200] See Research Group of Hubei Higher People's Court [131].

[201] See Ye [132].

should be given to the following aspects: First, we should identify the potential liabilities of the different subjects of judgment, including judges and assessors, gradually develop a differential judicial accountability system involving different subjects of power, thereby precluding potential poor disciplinary effect resulted from unclear subjects of accountability. Second, the people's assessors should be jointly responsible for ascertaining the facts of the case with the judges. If they disagree, facts of the cases should be ascertained according to the opinions of the majority, but the opinions of the minority shall be documented, too. If the judge holds a substantially different opinion from that of the majority of the assessors and he believes that the ascertainment of the facts by the opinion of the majority of the assessors is against the rule of evidence and will potentially lead to misapplication of law or misjudgment of the case, the case should be submitted to the court president to decide whether it should be discussed by the judicial committee. This risk-aversion solution based on the division of functions and powers can minimize the possibility of judges misusing their power despite other people's objections. Third, attention should be paid to perfecting the security system of people's judgments for fulfilling their duty. Failure of the reformers to ensure that people's assessors obtain security conditions for fulfilling their duty appropriate to their power will burden the people's assessors with a lot of doubts and worries when fulfilling their duty, making it impossible to motivate their enthusiasm for participating in the trial and giving their opinions. Hence, we should prohibit punishing the assessors without good reason, hold confidential the personal information of people's assessors, provide pertinent security measures and personal security mechanisms for the people's assessors, and identify the consequences of infringing upon the people's assessors' regular fulfillment of their duty. This way, the enthusiasm of the people's assessors for participating in the court trial will be motivated. Continuously enhancing their consciousness of subject, consciousness of duty and consciousness of judgment during the trial of cases will ultimately make a substantial difference to the judgment activities of the judges.

(3) Restriction from parties concerned

In a manner of speaking, the parties concerned are the persons immediately affected by the act of the judge and the judgment he makes. These parties are therefore more concerned about the legality and legitimacy of the act of the judge and the judgment he makes, and are therefore strongly desirous of pursuing relief against the act of the judge and the judgment he makes. Hence, in terms of restricting the judges, one force that can never be neglected is the force of the parties concerned.

To solve this problem, we should strengthen the right of action of the parties concerned. Perfecting the relief mechanism of the parties concerned in litigation also constitutes an important part of restricting judges. On the one hand, we should improve the right relief mechanism, including appeal, accusation and reconsideration, that is dependent on the case handling organ. Such relief mechanism is too dependent on the case handling organ for the judicial organ to be brave enough to correct its own mistake by "scraping the poison off the bone". Consequently, the effect of the relief may not be very satisfactory. A possible way is to modify such mechanism through processualization so as to solve the effectiveness of right relief through an open, transparent, due procedure. On the other hand, we should give play to the role of trial-level relief. This trial-level relief should not be limited to the substantive aspect, but also cover the procedural aspect. As such, in China, a particularly critical task for trial-level relief is to establish a procedural appeal system, under which improper trial by a judge at a lower court is relieved by the court at a higher level. So far, in the case of criminal proceedings, for example, the unlawful act of a trial organ (e.g., violation of jurisdictional requirements) can also be relieved through the appeal system. Nevertheless, as under such an institutional arrangement, procedural right relief is dependent on substantive relief, this is not good for the relief of procedural rights.[202] What's worse, the number of unlawful judicial acts for which which relief is available is also limited.[203] For other judicial acts, no relief can be provided. For example, no relief can be obtained through trial for the sealing up, seizure, freezing, unlawful arrest, or infringement upon the defense counsel's right to defend, by the trial organ. For this reason, we should, on the one hand, establish a separate procedural appeal system that allows the parties concerned to obtain separate relief for unlawful judicial acts against the contentious procedure; on the other hand, broaden the scope of unlawful judicial acts for which relief can be obtained.

2.5 Theoretical Basement of Judicial Inspection System

2.5.1 The Essential Nature of the Forms of Action Requires Judicial Control of the Pretrial Procedure

Order exists in any social group, and a certain social relationship is formed in human interactions. Such relationship is sustained by order, which, propelled by various conflicting interests, drives the society forward, Therefore, the existence of any society must be premised on the existence of a contradictory resolution mechanism, and the development of the early private remedies of mankind to the modern public remedies shows the continuous progress of mankind's understanding of the dispute resolution mechanism, in which the inherent characters of such mechanism are the distribution of justice, the reduction of costs and the improvement of efficiency. The distribution of justice comes on top of these three, while costs and efficiency play the role of increasing and decreasing the value of the mechanism. The manifestation of the earliest simple concept of justice in human history is "a tooth for a tooth, an eye for an eye, and blood for blood" and its essence embodies the demand

---

[202]It has to be noted that there is an exception here, namely, an appeal against a ruling is comparative to a procedural appeal.

[203]According to Article 227 of the "Judges Law" of China, irregular judicial acts for which a relief is available are all some of the acts are serious against the law and affect impartial trial such as violations of rules for open trial or jurisdiction. Even an appeal is up to one against a ruling, as the coverage of the ruling is quite limited, the irregular judicial acts for which a relief is available are still very limited.

for remedial justice. However, due to its excessive social cost, the simple justice remedial mechanism of revenge of the state has been replaced by a rational form of action, a landmark progress in the search for dispute resolution mechanisms in the development of human civilization. The basic characteristic of procedure is that the settlement of a dispute must require the presence of a neutral third party, who represents rationality and justice and decides for both parties to the dispute. In this context, the concept of "natural justice" has emerged. "Natural justice" includes two basic principles: first, no one should be the judge in his or her own case; and second, the views of both parties should be heard. These two basic principles demonstrate the essential feature of procedure, namely the intervention of a neutral third party. The concept of natural justice was later firmly established in the British Law, and the promulgation of the Magna Carta of England in 1215 replaced "natural justice" with the modern procedural concept of "due process of law". Instead of changing the intrinsic character of natural justice, due process of law further sublimates and manifests it. Modern criminal proceedings, as an important form of action, still contains the essential attributes of proceedings, that a neutral third party (judge) is required for making decisions for the parties to the procedure (the accuser and the defendant). Where there are a conflict of interests and a dispute, there must be a neutral judicator. The criminal pretrial procedure, as an important stage of criminal procedure, must have the essential attributes of procedure and play the role of a neutral dispute settler between the accuser and the defendant, otherwise, in the criminal pretrial procedure, disputes arising from serious confrontations between the accuser, who represents state power, and the defendant, who represents civil rights, cannot be justly resolved, and the characteristics of procedure will therefore lose their basis of existence, resulting in a predatorial behavior. Based on this concept, modern countries have generally introduced judicial review mechanisms in pretrial proceedings, which, on the one hand, guarantee the achievement of justice and, on the other hand, reduce the costs of proceedings (according to the American scholar Dworkin's,[204] such costs include direct costs and error costs, i.e., moral costs). Thus, it is safe to say that it is the very nature of the form of action that dictates the introduction of control over judicial power in criminal pretrial proceedings. The Decision of the Fourth Plenary Session of the 18th CPC Central Committee clearly states that it is necessary to "promote the reform of the trial-centered procedural system to ensure that the factual evidence in the investigation and prosecution of cases can stand the test of the law. The rules for the evidence adjudication shall be comprehensively implemented, evidence shall be collected, fixed, preserved, reviewed and used in strict accordance with the law, the system for the appearance of witnesses and expert witnesses in court should be improved, and court hearings should be ensured to play a decisive role in ascertaining the facts, concluding evidence, protecting the right to appeal and making fair verdicts." At this point, the goal of "trial centrism" has been formally established, which has an imperative role to play in the construction of China's judicial review mechanism, and we should seize the opportunity of reform

[204]Bayles [133].

to explore the construction of a criminal judicial review mechanism that is in line with our national situation.

2.5.2 *The Nature of the Judicial Power is a Theoretical Cornerstone of the Natural Rationality of Judicial Review Mechanisms*

Criminal pretrial procedure is an important stage of criminal proceedings, which necessarily takes the form of procedures and determines the need to introduce a neutral judicator at this stage. So, who should assume this role of neutral judicator? The nature of the judicial power determines itself to be the optimal choice for this role. There are many views regard to the nature of judicial power, and different people have different views. However, scholars at home and abroad have reached a consensus over the essential characteristics of judicial power. In our view, judicial power is by its very nature a jurisdiction. It presupposes the existence of a dispute, and it has made itself a just third-party judicator. The nature of the jurisdiction dictates that judicial power must have the external characteristics of an impartial judicator.

By its external characteristics, the American scholar Golding has divided judicial power into a number of following basic elements: (1) the existence of a particular conflict or dispute of interest; (2) the involvement of two or more specific parties (parties to the dispute) in said dispute; (3) the submission of the dispute (case) by one of the parties to the organs, organizations or persons with judicial power (judicator); (5) a hearing in which the parties to the dispute shall participate simultaneously and influence the conclusions of the judicator by words; (6) if the dispute involves a question of fact finding, the parties to the dispute shall submit evidence to the judicator and call witnesses; if the dispute only involves a question of law, the parties to the dispute shall request legal arguments; (7) the judicator shall formulate and pronounce a verdict conclusion to resolve the dispute between the parties; (8) the judicator shall make a verdict over the dispute on the basis of the claims, evidence and opinions of each party and apply to that fact the relevant principles and rules established by substantive law; in the case of a legal dispute only, the disputed legal question shall be decided in accordance with legal principles, rules, precedents or relevant theories.[205] We believe that judicial power shall have the following external characteristics:

First, the existence of judicial power presupposes the existence of a dispute. The interpretation of a dispute by the Supreme Court of the United States is that an actual case or dispute is one in which there is a genuine and opposing interest between the two parties, and if there is no actual case or dispute between them, the Federal Court will dismiss the case for there is nothing to be decided. As some scholars in China[206] have pointed out, the decision of justice is based on the existence of a

[205]Golding [134]. Quoted in Chen [135].

[206]Alton [136].

conflicted interest between two or more parties.[207] Judicial power exists for the sake of disputes, and it is only in the process of resolving disputes that judicial power can reveal its own significance.[208] And such disputes cannot be resolved by settlement, arbitration or other non-procedural means between the parties.

Second, the two parties file an application (proceeding) and a third party intervenes as a judicator to preside over the settlement of the dispute. When the interests of the parties to a dispute already involves the interests of the society as a whole (i.e., social order and security) but the parties cannot resolve the dispute through self-imposed non-violent or non-procedural method, the intervention of a third party as a judicator becomes necessary. When revenge of the state and private remedies was substituted with public remedies, many historians regarded it as a magnificent achievement in the development of human civilization. The judicial adjudication is a typical form of public remedy activity. It participates in the dispute resolution process as the judicators exercising judicial power on behalf of the State, which is the main sign of the dispute resolution moving towards public remedies. The intervention of the judicial adjudication is the last method of dispute resolution as well as the last embankment of rights protection.

Third, the third parties intervening as judicators must be neutral, rational and passive. The third party intervenes and reallocates or remedies or penalizes the rights of the parties to the dispute. For such a verdict to be authoritative and convincing, it requires not only coercive support but also impartiality from the judicators. Such impartiality is reflected not only in the impartiality of the outcome but also in that of the adjudication process. According to Taylor, "Because people usually have no idea what the right outcome is, they focus on the evidence to ensure that the process is fair. We have said it that when it is unclear what the right outcome is, people are concerned about procedural justice. Similarly, when it is uncertain what the appropriate outcome is, neutrality is valued."[209] The British proverb states that "justice must not only be done, but must be seen to be done.". Consequently, the neutrality of the judicator is required. Based on the spirit of the times, the American scholar Golding interpreted "natural justice" as nine criteria, of which the first and second one requires that the judges have no interest in the case itself, while the third and fourth criteria require them to treat parties to the procedure fairly. "Among the philosophies and systems that guarantee the achievement of justice, 'neutrality' is prominent."[210] An important characteristic of the judicial power is neutrality. The judiciary is the last line of defense for the rights of social subjects and it has to make an authoritative and final decision on social conflicts. For this particular reason, only through abiding by neutrality will judicial power be able to assume this heavy responsibility. Once the judicial power has a certain value orientation and interest bias with one party to the conflict, the impartiality of the judgement will be called into question. Therefore, the judge must remain neutral in the procedure, and pay equal attention to the claims and interests of

---

[207] Chen [137].

[208] Sun [138].

[209] Quoted in Yasuhei [139].

[210] Chen and Wang [140].

both the accuser and defendant.[211] It can be seen that the neutrality of the judicator is an important guarantee of the impartiality of the judgment, and under adversary system, the preparation of the procedures between the two parties is compared to a "game". If the judicator also plays as a party to the game, then what justice can there be in the rules of the game, and who will truly obey the result of that judgement?

We can conclude from the above three elements of the operation of the judicial power that, as an adjudication, when a dispute over a right (conflict of interest) requires a final remedy through public power for the realization of the right, the judicial power should intervene in the parties to the conflict as a neutral judicator to provide a final protection for the parties whose rights have been violated. As the American scholar Long Fuller has said, "The purpose of the rule of law is to settle disputes peacefully, not violently, but the peaceful resolution of disputes cannot be achieved through agreement, consultation or the enactment of laws alone; there must be some institution capable of determining the rights of each party in the specific context in which the dispute occurs."

The criminal pretrial procedure is the stage at which the accuser and the defendant actively prepare for the court trial, and the state power actively intervenes. In order to control crime and maintain peace, the accuser, backed by the state power, actively collects evidence, and may take all kinds of coercive measures against suspects and defendants, which are directly related to the suspect's personal, liberty and property interests; Meanwhile, the defense, on the basis of civil rights, appears powerless in the face of strong state power, but the gains and losses in their personal, property and liberty interests also force them to strive for evidentiary materials in their favor. This will inevitably lead to confrontation and conflict between the two parties, which are often acute and of vital interest. Therefore, in general, it is impossible to settle the conflict by agreement. Such insoluble nature of interest, which is in essence a natural contradiction between the control of crime and the protection of human rights, requires the intervention and impartial adjudication of a neutral third party as a protector of rights. According to the concept of impartiality, the role of the third-party judicator cannot be played by either of the parties (the accuser or the defendant), and the nature of the judicial power determines itself to be the optimal choice for this role. Thus, the existence of a criminal pretrial dispute and the intervention of the judicial power as a judicator have become one of the theoretical cornerstones of judicial power control in the criminal pretrial procedure.

2.5.3 The Establishment of a Modern Constitutional State is the Political Basis for the Emergence of Judicial Review Mechanisms

The history of criminal process clearly reflects the development and transformation of the state concept, from private prosecution in the early days of mankind to judicial

---

[211] Chen [141].

tyranny in feudal autocracy countries, and to human rights protection in modern constitutional states.[212] One of the most obvious signs of a modern constitutional country is the establishment of some basic principles of the rule of law. The principle of "separation of powers" is reflected in the law as "supremacy of law" and judicial review (i.e., the restriction of the judicial power on the legislative and administrative powers). As the American scholar Thomas Friedman has put it, "Judicial review system is the basis for the department of justice to play its central role in the American system of government, and the role of the department of justice—along with the respect towards the judgment of the department, the outcome of which we might disagree—is the foundation of the rule of law in America." When discussing the "meaning and general application of the rule of law" in his book Introduction to the Study of the Law of the Constitution, Dicey, the famous British constitutionalist, points out that the advantage or the supremacy of the rule of law consists of at least three interrelated meanings: (1) people cannot be subjected to property or physical prejudice unless they follow the due process of law and prove that they have violated the law before a common court. The first meaning of the rule of law is to prevent "governments under the rule of men" from exercising discretionary powers that "broadly" and "arbitrarily" restrict human rights; (2) All persons are equal before the law. (3) The Constitution of the United Kingdom is the cumulative result of the judgments of individual cases of all British courts and is therefore the result, rather than the source, of the protection of human rights by the courts. Dicey emphasized that the primary condition for the rule of law is the exclusion of the arbitrary power of the government, primarily the administrative power. The British scholar Stevie believes that, "the system of criminal proceedings has a certain constitutional significance: its practical operation provides a standard for testing the degree of justice within a society and in the relations between individuals and the state." "Criminal procedure process is not only about justice between the parties—it is also a direct embodiment of the ideal of the 'rule of law' that the law binds not only the individual, but the State." This constitutional significance is particularly evident in pretrial activities. It can be seen that the concept of the modern rule of law is mainly reflected in the denial of feudal autocracy, as well as utilizing judicial power to check and restrict the arbitrariness and tyranny of legislation and administration through the separation of powers, so as to achieve the rational and limited operation of power, thus protecting human rights.

In terms of its more profound origins, the rule of law has its roots in natural law philosophy and the social contract theory of the ancient Roman age. Based on the natural law philosophy, the early Enlightenment thinker, Locke, argued that everyone was entitled to natural rights, and individual rights were not the gifts from the country; they were born and existed prior to the country and the country must respect and protect these pre-existing rights. When the administrative or legislative power tries to turn its rule into a tyranny and to enslave or destroy its people, people have recourse to their last resort, that is "God". By exercising the right to resistance or revolution, the people are able to defend natural law in a positive process against

[212]Radbruch [142], p. 120.

oppression and the negation of natural law. Montesquieu shared Locke's view that human freedom was the highest goal to be achieved by the country, and he focused on designing a political system in which freedom could be enjoyed and protected by the most feasible and effective method. According to Montesquieu, some justice precedes the positive law. "If there is no justice or injustice except what is required or prohibited by positive law, then it means all radius distances are unequal until one draws a circle." In order to achieve justice and rationality, he emphasized the separation as well as the check and balance of powers. He pointed out that everyone with power tends to abuse it, and to use it to the limit, which is a lesson that will never alter. In order to prevent the abuse of power, it is crucial to restrict power with power.

The idea of separation of powers later became the philosophical basis for the British Bill of Rights and the American Declaration of Independence. "At certain stages in its development, the interpretation by the Supreme Court of the United States of certain provisions in the British Bill of Rights, particularly the due process clause, was also influenced by Locke's theory."[213] In the case of Savinge and loan Association Topeba, the Supreme Court of the United States explained that, under any free government, people have certain rights that are not controlled by the state. If a government does not recognize these rights and believes that the life, liberty and property of its citizens should at all times be subject to the autocratic handling and unrestricted control of the most democratic of rulers, then such a government is ultimately an autocratic one. The restriction of such power of the government is the fundamental nature of all free government (which implies the preservation of individual rights), otherwise a social contract would not exist; of course, all genuine governments would respect these rights.[214] This means that the power of government (administrative power) must be limited and that even the most democratic government (administrative power) cannot restrict the basic personal freedoms of individual citizens through discretion and it must be subject to external power. Madison, known as the "Father of the Constitution" of the United States, noted, "If men were angels, there would be no need for government. If angels rule mankind, then neither external nor internal control over the government is required. To create a government in which people rule people, the greatest difficulty is that you first have to empower the government to control the ruled; on the other hand, it is necessary to enable the government to control itself."[215] According to Mr. Zhu Chaoliang, a scholar from Taiwan, the concept of rule of law in the common law system lies in the domination of law or the supremacy of law, which is a concept of the rule of law formed after the expansion of the autonomy of private law under the influence of individualism and liberalism. The Constitution is the guarantee of civil rights signed by the people (Congress and the administration) on the basis of a social contract. In accordance with the principle that where there is right there is remedy, and the separation and the check and balance of powers. When there is a dispute among the people over the violation of civil rights in

[213]Crant [143].

[214]Bodenheimer [144].

[215]Madison [145].

the way the rulers rule, the court will judge as an impartial third party who is above the administrative organs and the people in order to uphold the dignity of human rights guaranteed by the Constitution. The court is therefore called the keeper of the Constitution or the protector of civil rights, and it is not the ruling organ that herds or govern people. The entire ruling bureaucracy and the people should be subject to the judgement of the courts, creating a form of state power with "judicial supremacy".

The above arguments fully demonstrate that, although it is necessary for the administrative power to exercise a certain degree of discretion in the light of the need to safeguard social order and security, it must be exercised in accordance with legal procedures, must be limited, and its coercive disposition must be reviewed by a relatively neutral judicial body in order to enable citizens to enjoy effective legal remedies. "In the view of modern countries, there is a possibility of conflict between the country (to a certain extent by the government) and the individual, and to prevent the arbitrariness of state power during the conflict, it must be judged and judicated by a neutral judicial organ, the court, so as to prevent the expansion and erosion of state power over individual rights. In modern society, the courts are often perceived as the strongest and last measure to counterbalance the state power and protect the rights of citizens, and only after the due process review by the courts can the state exert compulsory sanction on its citizens."[216]

In criminal pretrial proceedings, which are the stage where the state fully exercises its coercive power, in order to control the crime, the prosecutor often takes various coercive measures against the person being prosecuted, which are directly related to the fundamental human rights of citizens guaranteed by the Constitution. Therefore, it must be decided by the courts as the "guardians of rights". As the German scholar Professor Joachim Herrmann has said, "According to today's German legal science, the power of the country must be restricted and, meanwhile, the citizens must be entitled to the right to have it reviewed by a court; in this dual method, the citizens are protected not only against coercive measures of state power, but also against non-coercive violations of their rights at any time, including by the state power."[217] Not only civil law countries, but also common law countries, which are based on the concept of due process, are gradually placing emphasis on judicial review in criminal pretrial proceedings. "In common law countries, in accordance with the concept of due process and the informal, non-judgmental fact-finding procedures, there is a great potential for error, distrust and mischief, often resulting in a serious deprivation of the individual rights of citizens by the government. Therefore, when faced with a conflict between an individual and a state, the power of the government to inquire and detain suspects should be limited, and the exercise of the power to prosecute officials must be controlled by the judicial power."[218]

---

[216] Xie [146].

[217] Herrmann [147].

[218] Cole [148].

2.5.4 Modern Criminal Procedural Structure is an Institutional Guarantee of the Existence of Judicial Review Mechanisms

Criminal procedural structure is determined by the purpose of the procedure and by the interrelationship of the three parties, namely, the prosecution, defense and judicator, reflected in the main process and the basic approach of procedure.[219] Characterized in accordance with this, the historical pattern of criminal procedure has gone through impeachment, inquisitorial, modern criminal procedural pattern (doctrine of function and power, and adversary system), and the revised doctrine of function and power, and adversary system (hybrid) criminal procedure pattern. Radbruch once said, "In the development of criminal proceedings, two factors have always been at play: the increased demand for the protection of the state against criminals, which leads to the transformation of medieval criminal procedure into inquisitorial procedure; and the increased requirement for the protection of the innocent against the state, which results in the transformation of inquisitorial procedure into modern criminal procedure starting in 1848."[220] The impeachment procedural structure exists mainly in medieval slave society and some countries in the early years of feudal society, and it is the earliest procedure pattern that emerged in human history, embodying the concept of justice in natural law. Its basic characteristic is that no complaint, no trial, and the prosecution of a crime is entirely implemented by the parties involved. The judge plays as the judicator while the accuser and the defendant are on an equal footing and enjoy equal procedure rights. Both of them are the subjects of the procedure, and are in a position to lead the procedure process. In the event of doubt, the case is resolved through the trial by ordeal. The value of impeachment procedure lies in the fact that "to a considerable extent, medieval crime was an offence against the individuals involved, and the idea of the private law nature of this crime logically corresponds to the idea of civil procedure in criminal procedures".[221] The advantage of this procedure pattern is that it clearly distinguishes among the three functions of accusation, the defense and trial, and that the court operates based on "no complaint, no trial". This effectively prevents the possible situation of treating the accused as the object of the procedure if the judge enjoys the integrated power of prosecution and trial.

Under the structure of impeachment procedure, "if the victim is not courageous and powerful enough to propose a private prosecution, or if the perpetrator has sufficient courage and friends to swear an oath of innocence with the assistance of a sworn guarantor, the crime cannot be punished. This criminal procedure had to be abolished because of recidivism and the late medieval knights who conducted road robberies. The fact that a large number of violations go unpunished has led the state power to suddenly realize that the prosecution of crimes requires the participation

---

[219] Li [149].

[220] Radbruch [142], p. 122.

[221] Radbruch [142], p. 120.

not only of the victims but also the state itself". Through the Constitution Criminalis Carolina of 1532, inquisitorial procedures were introduced in Germany. The structure of inquisitorial procedure was originated during the Roman Empire and prevailed in the continental European countries during the absolute monarchy period in the late Middle Ages. The main features of inquisitorial procedure are: the application of the principle that trial can be conducted without complaint; as an instrument of feudal regime, the court possessed unrestricted power, with the integrated power of trial and procedure; the defendant was not the subject of criminal proceedings but its object, having no right in the criminal procedure but, on the contrary, an obligation to confess; the presumption of guilt; the defendant's confession is made the king of evidence, and he is thus rightly obliged to prove his own guilt; court trials are held in secret, and there is no remedy procedure for wrongful verdicts of the court. "The merit of the inquisitorial process is that it makes people realize that the prosecution of crimes is not a private matter for the victim, but the responsibility of the state. Its disadvantage is that the task of prosecuting the crime is entrusted to the judge, thus integrating the judge with the parties to the case." "If in the past, the accusatorial procedure was carried out among the plaintiff, the accused and the judge, then the inquisitorial procedure only involves the judge and the accused only. The accused is helpless in the face of a prosecutor who has the absolute power as a judge. The proverb for inquisitorial procedure is: "If the accuser becomes a judge, he needs God as a lawyer." The criminal pretrial procedure is generally observed as a form of action. If such procedure concerns the compulsory sanctions of the constitutional right of the personal interests of the accused, and it is decided by the police and procuratorial organs without the intervention of a judge, it is precisely a reflection of the proverb summarized by Mr. Radbruch that "If the accuser becomes a judge, he needs God as a lawyer", which applies to the inquisitorial procedure. Therefore, a key factor in the shift from the inquisitorial criminal procedure to the modern criminal procedure lies in the separation of the prosecution and trial where the control over judicial power is introduced into the pretrial proceedings. It makes the criminal pretrial procedure an important form of procedure rather than the inquisitorial criminal punishment procedure. And this is also one of the significant hallmarks that distinguishes inquisitorialism from modern criminal procedure.

"When the more enlightened human age removed the inquisitorial process, the whole solid edifice of the inquisitorial procedure was on the verge of a collapse."[222] Modern criminal procedure began with the introduction of prosecutors and the separation of accusation and trial. It has been established based on the dual values of crime control and human rights protection, but the inherent contradiction between the two has led to the different focuses on crime control and human rights protection in different countries, which results in the formation of two distinctive procedural patterns, namely, doctrine of function and power and adversary system.

The foundation of the doctrine of function and power is: its rule of law is the idea of ruling by the law, which transforms the police state into a nation of law. In its view, the main purpose of law-making is to regulate the ruling power of the

[222]Radbruch [142], p. 122.

sate rulers so that they do not arbitrarily violate civil rights. Ruling by the law is to directly restrict the governing of the rulers and indirectly protect civil rights. The Constitution and the law are, without exception, the basis (or instrument) for the rulers' rule over the people. It considers that people should be ruled and dominated as long as the ruler acts "according to the law". Therefore, not only the administrative organ is the ruling organ of the people, but also the court. The difference is that the former is the active ruling organ while the latter is regarded as the passive one. This results in an "administrative superiority" type of state power. The value of the criminal proceedings of the doctrine of function and power is that "crime control" is the most major function of national criminal procedure. If a country's criminal procedure fails to effectively control the crime, it will cause the collapse of social system and public order as a result of the proliferation of crime. Unless "all guilty people must be punished", it will lead to people despising criminal norms and the disintegration of society. Therefore, the value of criminal procedure shall lie in that "all guilty people must be punished". As long as a large number of cases can be quickly dealt with by limited manpower, and criminal procedures are effective in producing a guilty verdict to control the crime, it is the best criminal procedure that accords with the crime control mode here. Hence, the handling of criminal cases must concentrate on the processing speed and the finality of the verdict that all guilty people must be punished. To this end, full reliance is placed on the impartiality and objectivity of the judicial organ. It is believed that the judicial organs involved in criminal proceedings, including prosecutors and judges, all have the dual function of "discoverer of the facts" and "protector of civil rights".

Mr. Zhu Chaoliang, a scholar in Taiwan, attributes the shortcomings of the procedural pattern of doctrine of function and power to: (1) incomplete investigation. In order to prosecute the crime if the accused who is guilty quickly and effectively and to achieve the effectiveness of the crime investigation, normally the focus of the investigation activities must be on the collection of evidence of the crime of the accused while only a fishing type of collection is conducted for collecting evidence in favor of the accused. As a result, it is difficult to expect that the prosecutor will thoroughly collect evidence in favor of the accused; therefore, it is questionable whether it is effective to solely rely on prosecutor's objective obligation to collect such evidence. (2) Undetached trials. The public trial procedure becomes a procedure in which the court confronts the accused, rather than a procedure in which non-prosecutor confronts the accused; when someone acts as both the player and the referee, it is naturally difficult for the court judgment to be detached. (3) Ineffective defense. (4) The accused has no place in the investigation. (5) The accused shall prove his or her own innocence.[223]

With the rise of the due process revolution in the 1960s, criminal procedural goals of the civil-law countries that they overly pursued the "guilty verdict" and "efficiency" shifted to the value of crime control and human rights protection. The most typical example is the amendment of the Italian Criminal Procedure Law, in which the adversarial factors are gradually increased, the judges intervene the criminal pretrial

[223]Zhu [150].

proceedings as neutral third parties and the control of the judicial power over the prosecuting authorities is enhanced. With the increase in the number of adversarial factors, the strengthening of the control over judicial power is a remedy measure for the accused party who are naturally disadvantaged and it is an important safeguard for achieving a balance between prosecution and defense. As some scholars have put it, "With the development and improvement of the human rights protection system, it is absolutely necessary to strengthen the judicial control over coercive measures in order to prevent the abuse of coercive power by the prosecution organs. Especially considering the intensified procedural confrontation, the requirements on judicial control are increasing; and the negative impact of the possible "becoming adversary" (role bias) caused by such an increase also requires enhanced judicial control to prevent it."[224]

The concept of the rule of law is based on the principle of the "where there is right there is remedy" and the "principle of the separation of powers and check and balance". When a dispute arises among the people over the way the ruler rules in violation of their civil rights, the court will judge as an impartial third party who is above the government in order to uphold the dignity of the constitutional protection of human rights. Thus, the court is called the guardians of the Constitution or protectors of civil rights. The adversary system view of criminal procedure is established upon the value that it is equally important to guarantee the individual rights and control crime in the society. It believes that, while crime control is important, it does not justify the violation of civil rights; otherwise, the innocent is punished, which renders the guarantees of constitutional rights null and void. In addition to norms and order, we also need justice, which is the true meaning of a democratic state. And the distinction between "order" and "justice" is more important than that between democratic and authoritarian systems.[225] In the interests of procedural justice, even if there is a situation in which the guilty are exempt from punishment, it is an unavoidable matter in the perfectly equitable balance of fundamental human rights. Therefore, the value of common law's insistence on due process of law lies in the fact that procedural justice is a fundamental human right of the individual and the only way to obtain a balance with the values of public order. It is under the value of due process of law that common law countries have constructed the "isosceles triangle" procedural structure. "The core idea of the concept of due process of law is 'restraining power by procedure', which requires the state to follow fair and lawful procedure in disposing of citizens' rights and interests, and to prevent the arbitrariness of state power. In criminal procedure, the essence of the principle of due process is to prevent the state from abusing its right of criminal prosecution and violating the human rights of its citizens by setting up procedural mechanisms to ensure that the state follows an impartial procedure in investigating criminal activities."[226]

It can be seen that the control of judicial power in criminal pretrial procedure is an inevitable requirement of due process of law, an imperative guarantee of the principle

[224] Long [151].

[225] Huang [152].

[226] Xie [146].

of separation of prosecution and trial as well as the balance between the prosecution and defense. It is also an important and indispensable pillar in the structure of modern criminal procedure, a touch stone of the difference between inquisitorial procedure and modern criminal procedure, and a landmark in the development of criminal procedure in the direction of democracy and civilization.

References

1. Cohen, J. A. (1969). The Chinese communist party and "Judicial Independence": 1949–1959. *Harvard Law Review, 82*(5).
2. Li, B., & Liu, Z. (2002). Several issues of judicial independence. *Chinese Journal of Law*, Issue 3.
3. Montesquieu. (1991). *The spirit of laws* (Vol. 1, pp. 154–156), Beijing: The Commercial Press.
4. Liao, H. (1999). A historical investigation into the debates on the American judicial independence. *Science of Law*, Issue 1.
5. He, W. (1997). Two problems in China's judicial management system. *China Legal Science*, Issue 6.
6. Liu, R. (1999). Civil justice and its system guarantee. *Frontiers of Law*, Issue 3.
7. Frank, J. N. (1935). *Law and the modern mind* (p. 157). NY: Tudor Publishing Company.
8. Montesquieu. (2006). *De L'esprit Des Lois* (Vol. 1) (L. Sun, P. Sun, & R. Fan, Trans.). Xi'an: Shaanxi People's Publishing House.
9. Jiang, B. (2009). A correct understanding of the relationship between justice and administration. *QiuShi Journal*, Issue 24.
10. Song, B. (Ed.). (1998). *Judicial systems and judicial procedures in the United States and Germany* (pp. 145–147). Beijing: China University of Politic Science and Law Press.
11. Chen, G. (2013). Principle of judicial independence with Chinese characteristics from the perspective of comparative law. *Journal of Comparative Law*, Issue 2.
12. Kang, S. (1958). Reactionary nature of "judicial independence". *Political and Legal Studies*, Issue 2.
13. Ruo, Q., & Hefang. (1957, December 24). Do not tamper the nature of the People's Courts—refute the fallacies of Jia Qian and others on "independence of trial" and "in dubio pro reo". *People's Daily.*
14. *Selected Works of Peng Zhen* (p. 416). (1991). Beijing: People's Publishing House.
15. Li, B., & Liu, Z. (2002). Several issues about judicial independence. *Chinese Journal of Law*, Issue 3.
16. Liao, J. (1979). Independent trial and handling of cases by Party Secretary. *Modern Law Science*, Issue 1.
17. Hamilton, A., Madison, J., & Jay, J. (1980). *The federalist papers* (F. Cheng, et al., Trans.) (p. 191). Beijing: The Commercial Press.
18. Bickel, A. M. (1962). *The least dangerous branch.*
19. Su, Y. (2005). Judicial reform affected by two judicial concepts—social background and legal basis for the judicial reform in Taiwan. In Z. Mingjie (Eds.), *Reform of the judiciary—review and prospect of China's judicial reform* (p. 433). Beijing: Social Sciences Academic Press.
20. *Selected Works of Liu Shaoqi* (Vol. 2, p. 450). (1985). Beijing: People's Publishing House.
21. *Selected Works of Deng Xiaoping* (Vol. 3, p. 163). (1993). Beijing: People's Publishing House.
22. *Selected Works of Dong Biwu* (pp. 458–461). (1985). Beijing: People's Publishing House.
23. Fan, H. (Ed.). (1988). *Dictionary of political system reform* (pp. 305–306). Beijing: China Material Press.

24. Chen, W., & Hao, Y. (1999). Study on the integrated model of investigation and prosecution. *Chinese Journal of Law*, Issue 1.
25. Chen, W. On the building of an impartial, efficient and authoritative judicial system. *Journal of Renmin University of China*, Issue 6.
26. Chen, W. (Ed.). (2005). *Research report on the operation of China's criminal procedure system*. Beijing: China Fangzheng Publishing House.
27. Gewirtz, P. (2002). Independence and accountability of courts (M. Ge, Trans.). *Global Law Review*, Issue 1.
28. Chen, X. (2005). Judicial independence in the Chinese context. In Z. Mingjie (Eds.), *Reform of the judiciary—review and prospect of China's judicial reform* (pp. 140–151). Beijing: Social Sciences Academic Press.
29. Ball, H. (1980). *Courts and politics-the federal judicial system* (p. 59). New Jersey: Prentice-Hall, Ing and Englewood Cliffs.
30. Pach, C. J., Jr. & Richardson, E. (1991). *The president of Dwight D. Eisenhower* (p. 141). Lawrence: University Press of Kansas.
31. Feng, L. (2005). Political parties and justice: Relevance and distance—another interpretation of American judicial independence. *Peking University Law Journal*, Issue 4.
32. Zhou, Z. (2013). Politicization: An aspect of justice. *Law Science*, Issue 3.
33. Lin, Z. (Ed.). (2004). *Functions and macro-political and legal work of the party committees and the commissions for political and legal affairs at all levels*. Beijing: China Changan Publishing House.
34. Hou, M. (2003). Political and legal governance in the context of judicial reform—A case study of the grassroots commission for political and legal affairs. *ECUPL Journal*, Issue 5.
35. Cui, M. (2000). On the reasonable allocation of judicial power. *Public Security Science Journal*, Issue 3.
36. Cui, M. (2008). Three suggestions for optimizing the allocation of judicial power. In *Criminal justice forum* (Vol. 1, p. 31). Beijing: China Renmin University Press.
37. Wang, J., & Sun, Y. On the authority of the judiciary and the authoritative judiciary. *Law Review*, Issue 4.
38. Yan, L. (2010). The unspoken rules as the "injustice coordination meeting" of the local commission for political and legal affairs should be abolished. *Law Science*, Issue 6.
39. Hamilton, A., Madison, J., & Jay, J. (1995). *The federalist papers* (F. Cheng, et al., Trans.). Beijing: The Commercial Press.
40. Liu, T. (1999). Resetting the judicial jurisdictions and strengthening the awareness of national unity. *Law Science*, Issue 2.
41. Liu, H. (2002). Thoughts on the reform of the management system of the People's Courts. *Law Science*, Issue 2.
42. Long, Y. (1996). Explorations into the separation of administrative power and judicial power. *Administration and Law*, Issue 2.
43. Xi, J. (2014, Oct 28). *The explanation of the decision on certain major issues concerning comprehensively advancing the law-based Governance of China.*
44. Chen, W. (2014). Judicial "delocalization": Logic, challenges and countermeasures of China's judicial system reform. *Global Law Review*, Issue 1.
45. Zhang, W. (2003). *Judicial reform: Analysis and development* (p. 126). Beijing, China: Law Press.
46. Jiao, H. (2000). From the localization of courts to the dual-track system for setting up the courts. *Journal of Chinese Academy of Governance*, Issue 1.
47. Hao, Z., & Gan, G. (2006). On the judicial justice and the reform of the jurisdictions of administrative litigation. *Journal of Henan Normal University (Philosophy & Social Sciences Edition)*, Issue 6.
48. *Tutoring reader of the decision on certain major issues concerning comprehensively advancing the law-based Governance of China* (pp. 59–60). (2014). Beijing: People's Publishing House.

49. Liu, Z. (2003). Criticism of China's judicial local protectionism—also on the reform thinking of "nationalization of judicial power". *Chinese Journal of Law*, Issue 1.
50. Jiang, H. (1998). Pros and cons of judicial localization and reform. *People's Judicature*, Issue 2.
51. Xiao, Y. (2002, Dec 22). *Report at the 18th National Court Work Conference.*
52. Zhou, D. (Ed.). (2000). *Foreign court organization and judge system* (p. 95). Beijing: People's Court Press.
53. Li, W. (2004). Thoughts on the judicial jurisdiction system. *Henan Social Sciences*, Issue 4.
54. Su, L. (2004). *The rule of law in China and its domestic resources* (p. 6). Beijing: China University of Politic Science and Law Press.
55. Zhang, J. (2016). Thinking about the reform of the military court system. *Law Science*, Issue 2.
56. Zhang, Z. (2016). Evolution and reform of China's military trial system. *Journal of Xi'an Politics Institute of PLA*, Issue 2.
57. Shen, Y., & Zhao, L. (2016, Sep 30). *Looking into the road of railway court reform from the "Cao Dahe Case"*. https://www.infzm.com/content/29520?dooc.
58. Tan, X. (2015). Domestic resources for the judicial system reform—explorations and enlightenment of the maritime courts. *Chinese Journal of Maritime Law*, Issue 1.
59. Yang, F., & Huang, B. (2011). On the reform of the establishment of forest courts. *Journal of Law Application*, Issue 7, p. 85.
60. Liu, Z. The creation and evolution of the system of two instances at four levels. *Chinese Journal of Law*, Issue 4, pp. 41–57.
61. Wei, J. (2014, Dec 29). China's first people's court and people's procuratorate across administrative divisions were set up in Shanghai. *People's Court Daily.*
62. Wu, X. (2016). Thinking on the establishment of the courts across administrative divisions based on the practices of Shanghai Third Intermediate People's Court. *People Rule of Law*, Issue 1, p. 12.
63. Wu, Z. (2015). Several key issues in the reform of cross-administrative division courts. In W. Zaicun (Ed.), *Exploration and practice of the reform of cross-administrative division courts* (pp. 5–7). Beijing: Law Press China.
64. Zhao, X., & Zou, B. (2013). Reflections on the reform of China's judicial districts. *Social Sciences in Yunnan*, pp. 134–138.
65. Chen, W. (2014). Research on judicial organs' independent exercise of power according to law. *China Legal Science*, Issue 2.
66. Meng, J. *Deepening the reform of the judicial system.* https://theory.people.com.cn/n/2013/1126/c40531-23655604.html.
67. Yi, P., & Wang, Y. *A study on China' judicial regions zoning system separated from administrative divisions—based on the empirical analysis of a southern province.* https://cpfd.cnki.com.cn/Article/CPFDTOTAL-GJFG201504001009.htm.
68. Wang, D. (1999). Promoting judicial reform with the guarantee of judge independence as the core. *Studies in Law and Business*, Issue 1.
69. Liao, H. (1999). A historical investigation of the debates on the judicial independence in the United States. *Science of Law*, Issue 1.
70. Chen, W., & Liu, J. (2003). On centralized hearing and strengthening the function of the collegiate panel. *China Legal Science*, Issue 1.
71. Yuan, D. (2013, Jul 24). Investigation of the professionalization of China's judge team Reform (Part 2). *Legal Daily.*
72. Zhao, L. (2013, Aug 29). The pilot reform of independent trial in Foshan—What is ahead of this boldest court reform. https://www.infzm.com/content/89909.
73. Jiang, H. (2013). Anticipation for the de-administration oriented judicial reform. *Chinese Cadres Tribune*, Issue 7.
74. Jiang, H., & Yang, Y. *How does the British judge selection committee work.* https://rmfyb.chinacourt.org/paper/html/2014-07/04/content_84213.htm?div=-1,2014-07-12.
75. Chen, W. (2011). *Citizens' access to justice.* Beijing: China Legal Publishing House.

76. Chen, W. (2012). Plight and outlet of the people's supervisor system. *Tribune of Political Science and Law*, Issue 4.
77. Chen, W. (2015). Citizen participation in justice: Theory, practice and reform—An investigation centering on criminal justice. *Chinese Journal of Law*, Issue 2.
78. Li, C. (2000). On the judicial value of the professionalization of judges. *People's Congress Studying*, Issue 6.
79. Tan, B., & Wang, Z. (2001). On the modernization of judges: Specialization, professionalization and homogeneity—Also on the modernization of Chinese judge contingent. *China Legal Science*, Issue 3.
80. Xia, Y. (Ed.). (1995). *Towards the age of rights* (p. 214). Beijing: China Legal Publishing House.
81. He, W. (1998). *Judicial ideas and system* (pp. 7–8). Beijing: China Legal Publishing House.
82. Wang, L. (2000). *Research on judicial reform* (p. 447). Beijing: Law Press China.
83. Liu, Z. (1998). *Max Weber: A wise man of the "Age of Gods"* (pp. 242–243). Hebei University Publishing House.
84. Bodenheimer, E. (1998). *Jurisprudence: The philosophy and method of the law* (p. 160). Beijing: China University of Politic Science and Law Press.
85. He, R. (1999). On judicial authority and judicial reform. *Law Review*, Issue 5.
86. Lv, S., & He, X. (1999). On the nationalism tendency in the operation of judicial power. In X. Chunying, & L. Lin (Eds.), *Law-based governance of the country and judicial reform* (p. 399). Beijing: China Legal Publishing House.
87. Ji, W. (1994). Positioning of legal profession—the practice of reforming power structure in Japan. *Social Sciences in China*, Issue 2.
88. Li. S. (2004). A probe into the system of judge selection. *Law Science*, Issue 3.
89. Yao, L. (2015). Comparison and enlightenment: The reform and optimization of judge selection system in China. *Modern Law Science*, Issue 7.
90. Song, B. (Ed.). (1998). *Judicial systems and judicial procedures in the United Kingdom and Germany*. Beijing: China University of Politic Science and Law Press.
91. Chen, Y. (1998). A comparison of the judge system between two major legal systems. *Tribune of Political Science and Law*, Issue 5.
92. Isermann, E. (2003). Das Richtersystem in Deutschland—am Beispiel Niedersachsen (N. Zhao, Trans.). *German Studies*, Issue 4.
93. Wang, Q. (2010). Investigation and reference of judge selection systems outside China: A focus on the judge selection systems in the United States, United Kingdoms, Germany, France and Japan. *Legal Forum*, Issue 5.
94. Holmes, O. W. Jr. (2006). *The common law* (H. Ran, & Z. Yao, Trans.) (p. 1). Beijing: China University of Political Science and Law Press.
95. Masao, O. (1999). *Comparative law* (Y. Fan, Trans.) (p. 318). Beijing: Law Press.
96. Wang, Y. (1993). *The foreign criminal procedure* (p. 64). Beijing: Peking University Press.
97. Cardozo, B. N. (1998). *The nature of judicial process* (L. Su, Trans.) (p. 86). Beijing: The Commercial Press.
98. Shao, C. (2014, Dec 24). Judge and procurator selection: Ready to come out. *Democracy and Law Times*.
99. Zhang, W. (2014). Comprehensively promoting legal reform, accelerating the construction of the rule of law in China: The jurisprudential interpretation of the spirit of the Third Session of the 18th CPC Central Committee. *Law and Social Development*, Issue 1.
100. Ren, Z. (2015, April 17). Judges are wanted, courts are worried, things are changing. *Southern Weekly*.
101. Hua, X. (2015, Nov 16). Registration for the 2016 Beijing test: Large vacancy for judicial assistant. *Southern Weekly*.
102. He, X. (2015). The goal, value and path of the judicial accountability system. In *A guide on the opinions on judicial accountability system of people's courts*. Beijing: People's Court Press.
103. Gu, P. (2014). On the establishment of the operative mechanism of judicial authority of people's court. *China Legal Science*, Issue 5.

104. Zhu, X. (2015). Judicial experience. *Peking University Law Journal*, Issue 4.
105. Dalberg-Acton, J. E. E. (2001). *Essays on freedom and power* (J. Hou, et al., Trans.) (p. 342). Beijing: The Commercial Press.
106. Chen, W. (2016). Characteristics and difficulties of the current judicial reform. *Hunan Social Sciences*, Issue 2.
107. Zhou, Y. (2010). *Jurisprudence: Global perspective* (pp. 244–246). Beijing: Legal Press.
108. Chen, W. (2014). Legality, democracy and restriction: Three key-words the judicial reform should focus on. *Law Science Magazine*, Issue 10.
109. Gao, M., & Ma, K. (2000). *The criminal law* (p. 109). Beijing: Peking University Press, Higher Education Press.
110. Ye, M. (2009). Construction of the theory of gross negligence. *Chinese Journal of Law Science*, Issue 6.
111. Tan, S., & Sun, L. (2009). On judge responsibility exempt system. *Journal of Political Science and Law*, Issue 10.
112. Wang, L. (2001). *Research on judicial reform* (p. 471). Beijing: Law Press.
113. Jan Green, K. G. (1995). Rethinking judicial immunity for the twenty-first century. *Howard Law Journal*, Fall.
114. Chen, Y. (2001). *Research on immunity* (p. 98). Beijing: China Legal Publishing House.
115. Yan, J. (2016). Problems and construction of criminal responsibility immunity for judges in China. *Journal of Inner Mongolia Radio & TV University*, Issue 3.
116. Liu, C. (2016). Study on the judge exemption liability system in China. *Legal System and Society*, Issue 5, (Part 2).
117. Ma, J., & Yi, Z. (1999). On the disciplines to the dereliction of duty of judges and public procurators. *Hebei Law Science*, Issue 4.
118. Wang, Z. (2015). "Whoever hears a case should take responsibility for it": The reconstruction of the judicial system about judges as the responsible. *Journal of Fujian Police College*, Issue 5.
119. Jiang, G., & Wu, Y. (2016). Opinions on improving the judge disciplinary system in China and the amendment to Chapter XI of the "Judges Law of the People's Republic of China". *Journal of Jianghan University (Social Science Edition)*, Issue 2.
120. Hu, Y. (2011). Judicial error and judicial accountability and the legitimacy of accountability investigation for misjudgments. *Journal of Law Application*, Issue 3.
121. Chen, Y. (2010). On the compatibility between immunity and rule of law and the establishment and improvement of an immunity system for public officials. *Political Science and Law*, Issue 12.
122. Chen, W. (2016). Establishing a unified judiciary disciplinary committee. *People Rule of Law*, Issue 6.
123. Chen, G., & Wang, Y. (2016). Discussion on several issues related to the judicial accountability system. *China University of Political Science and Law Press*, Issue 2.
124. Zhan, J. (2016). Difficulties and outlets of the judge disciplinary system in China. *Law Review*, Issue 2.
125. He, Z. (2014). On the ethics of prosecutors in Taiwan. *Journal of National Prosecutors College*, Issue 1.
126. Jiang, A. (2010). The reform of the two powers: Microsamples of the trial operation mechanism in China. *Legal Information*, Issue 12.
127. Hu, Y., & Fan, Y. (2011). Study on the operating mechanism of trial power and trial management power. *People Rule of Law*, Issue 15.
128. Shen, D. (2014). *Speech at the 2010 National Forum on Trial Management of Courts, Trial Management Office of the Supreme People's Court: Research and Reference on Trial Management* (p. 26). Beijing: Law Press.
129. Wan, Y., & Yang, C. (2016). On the trial supervision power of the president of the court. *The Ideological Front*, Issue 4.
130. He, X. (2015). How to hold the ox nose of judicial accountability system. *People's Court Daily*, 2015–09–23, Ed. 005.

131. Research Group of Hubei Higher People's Court. (2014). Research on the problem of judicial credibility. *Journal of Law Application*, Issue 12.
132. Ye, Q. (2016). Premise and mechanism consideration for improving the judicial accountability system. *People Rule of Law*, Issue 6, p. 14.
133. Bayles, M. D. (1996). *Principles of law: A normative analysis* (W. Zhang, et al., Trans.) (p. 27). Beijing: Encyclopedia of China Publishing House.
134. Golding, M. (1975). *Philosophy of law* (pp. 108–120). Englewood Cliffs, N.J: PRENTICE—Hall.
135. Chen, R. (1997). *Principles of criminal justice* (p. 1). Beijing: Peking University Press.
136. Alton, S. R. (2002). From Marbury v. Madison to Bush v. Gore: 200 years of judicial review in the United States (S. Guo, Trans.). *Law Review*, Issue 5.
137. Chen, R. (2000). The nature of judicial power. *Law Review*, Issue 5.
138. Sun, W. (2002). *A jurisprudential interpretation of judicial power* (p. 37). Beijing, China: Law Press.
139. Yasuhei, T. (1998). *Procedural justice, procedure, justice and modernization.* Beijing: China University of Political Science and Law Press.
140. Chen, G., & Wang, H. (2001). *On the Idea of Neutrality in Criminal Proceedings, a thesis of 2001 Annual Conference of Procedural Law.*
141. Chen, W. (2002). The reflection and reconstruction on the of procuratorial power. *Law Review*, Issue 2.
142. Radbruch, G. (1997). *Introduction to law* (J. Mi, & L. Zhu, Trans.) (p. 120). Beijing: Encyclopedia of China Publishing House.
143. Crant, J. A. (1931). National law background of due process. *Columbia Law Review, 56.*
144. Bodenheimer, E. (1999). *The philosophy and method of law* (Z. Deng, Trans.) (p. 56). Beijing: China University of Political Science and Law Press.
145. Madison, J. (1980). *The federalist papers* (p. 47). Beijing: The Commercial Press.
146. Xie, Y. (2003). Principle of judicial review from the perspective of criminal procedure. *Peking University Law Journal*, Issue 7.
147. Herrmann, J. (1995). *German criminal procedure code, the introduction in the Chinese version.* Beijing: China University of Political Science and Law.
148. Cole, G. F. Rights of the criminally accused. *Collected Translations of Legal Science*, Issue 4.
149. Li, X. (1992). *On the criminal litigation structure* (p. 7). Beijing: China University of Political Science and Law.
150. Zhu, C. A prosecutor's position in criminal procedure. *Tokai University Law Review*, Issue 15.
151. Long, Z. (1998). An examination of the adversarial factors in criminal procedure in china and its reasonable limits. *Jianghai Academic Journal*, Issue 2.
152. Huang, D. (1995). *Study on criminal procedure law* (p. 175). Taibei: San Min Book Co., Ltd.

Chapter 3
Theories of Procuratorial Powers and Its Reconstruction

3.1 The Nature of Procuratorial Power

For a long time, the nature of the prosecutorial power has undergone quire some controversy in the academic world, which can be summarized into four academic views from the perspectives of administrative power, judicial power, administrative-judicial duality and legal supervision power. After careful analysis, I believe that the above academic views contain thoughtful insight, but since the prosecutorial power, supervision and other conceptual issues and research level are ambiguous, many scholars have fallen into the quagmire of self-talk on the nature of procuratorial power. To clarify the theoretical disputes over "prosecutorial power", "it is necessary to apply semantic analysis approach to identify semantic differences in the same words, concepts, propositions, and to minimize the differences in the actual content of the ideas expressed in the same words, to ascertain what questions are to be answered, what questions are not, and whether the question really exists. Some of the disputes can be avoided or clarified and resolved".[1]

3.1.1 Procuratorial Power: Connotation, Development and Conceptual Definition

"Prosecutorial power is a generic term for the various powers conferred by the law on the procuratorial organs",[2] which makes it appear to be a simple concept. However, since China's procuratorial organs are endowed with complex and diverse powers, in different contexts and conditions, the connotation of the powers of the procuratorial organs is very likely to alter slightly, so that the meaning of the procuratorial

[1]Zhang Wenxian [1].

[2]Zhang Zhihui [2].

W. Chen, *Reform and Development of Powers and Functions of China's Criminal Proceedings*, https://doi.org/10.1007/978-981-15-8431-2_3

power will also change. Thus, in order to accurately define the concept of prosecutorial power, a distinction should firstly be made between the powers vested in the prosecutorial organs, that is, the connotation of prosecutorial power.

The definition and partition of the power of the procuratorial organ have been a hot topic of discussion in academic and theoretical circles. There are three types of procuratorial function theories that the academic world advocates: first, it is believed that the power of the procuratorial organs lies in and only in legal supervision, which can be called "the monism of legal supervision"; second, it is assumed that the power of the procuratorial organs only refers to the procedural functions, which can be called "the monism of procedural function and power"; third, it is thought that in criminal proceedings, the power of the procuratorial organs includes not only the procedural power to prosecute crimes, but also the legal supervision power to supervise the implementation of laws, which can be called "dualism". In general, prior to the amendment of the Criminal Procedure Law, it was generally recognized in the academic world that the power exercised by the procuratorial organs included both procedure and procedural supervision. In our view, as far as the procedural and procedural supervision functions and powers of the procuratorial organs are concerned, all the procedural powers stipulated by the law and exercised by the procuratorial organs themselves are specific manifestations of their procuratorial procedural power, including the investigation of self-investigating cases, the approval of arrests and the initiation of public prosecutions. Accordingly, powers which are not directly exercised by the procuratorial organs or by themselves, that is to say, supervision by the enforcement of powers on other organs or individuals, may be classified as acts of procedural supervision, such as the case-filing supervision and the supervision of the legality of investigative, judicial and execution activities. With the amendment of the Criminal Procedure Law in 2012, the new law has given new content to the procuratorial power and function and further developed the procuratorial function. The procuratorial function has evolved from the original procedural and procedural supervision functions to the present three functions including procedural, procedural supervision, and judicial remedy function.

Although the procuratorial organs exercise both procedure and procedural supervision, it is worth noting that the positioning of the powers of the procuratorial organs (procuratorial power) in the procedural is not the same as its positioning in the judicial system. This is because the procedural powers of the procuratorial organs are related to the main tasks undertaken by the procuratorial organs in criminal proceedings in China. Therefore, the positioning in the procedural structure only reflects the procedural rights of the procuratorial power and excludes the procedural supervision; under the judicial system with Chinese characteristics, the broad concept of judicature includes not only procedural activities, but also procedural supervision and non-procedural activities, so that the procuratorial power in the judicial system includes both procedural and procedural supervision functions and powers. Procedure and judicature, while closely linked, are district in their concepts. Procedure is the legal procedural mechanism for the handling of individual cases, while judicature is the specialized activity of the state's judicial organs in the application of the law; the main object of procedural activity is the parties to the proceedings, while the main object of judicial activity is the judicial organs and judicial officers; the basic structure of procedure is the prosecution, defense and trial, while the basic structure of judicature is procedure and procedural supervision as well as relevant non-procedural activities. Thus, in the procedural structure, "trial-centrism" is justified, but in the judiciary structure, it is not.[3]

It can be seen that the concept of procuratorial powers encompasses both broad and narrow distinctions. The concept of procuratorial power in the broad sense refers to the generic term of the powers conferred by law on the procuratorial organs, such as the procedural power and procedural supervision, and is mainly applicable to the macro level of our judicial system; the concept of procuratorial power in the narrow sense refers to the generic term of the procedural power conferred by law on the procuratorial organs, and is mainly applicable to the level of procedural structure.

3.1.2 Basic Analysis of the Nature of the Procuratorial Powers

3.1.2.1 Several View Currently Existing in the Academic World

The first view is that of the administrative power, which believes that the procuratorial power is the administrative power.[4] There are two reasons for this: first, the organizational structure and action principles of the procuratorial organs are administrative in nature. One of the basic principles of the organization and activities of the procuratorial organs is the "integration of procuratorial work", in which the organs integrate as a whole. It is specifically embodied in the "hierarchical structure" and the "power of direction" of the superior; the superior prosecutor has the "power of direction" of commanding and supervising the subordinate prosecutor, while the subordinate has the obligation to obey, which is a typical administrative relationship; transfer of duties system: the superior has the right to personally handle the cases and matters that belong to the subordinate prosecutor, at the same time, the superior prosecutor is entitled to transfer the cases and matters of the subordinate prosecutor to other subordinate prosecutors; the system of official substitutions: even if the prosecutor involved in the proceedings is replaced halfway, it has no impact on the effectiveness of the case in procedural law; the chief agent system, in Germany, Russia and other countries, prosecutors of procuratorial organs at all levels are the agents of the chief procurator in the external exercise of powers. Secondly, the separation of legislative, administrative and judiciary powers and checks and balances are the basic structure of Western political system. In this structure, the procuratorial power does not belong to legislative power, nor is it a judicial power that has the function of judicating in

[3]Wu Jianxiong [3].

[4]Long Zongzhi [4].

accordance with the law and is guaranteed constitutional independence. The prosecutor is the "spokesman" of the government in the proceedings and is the organ that exercises supervision and checks on the third power on behalf of the second (administrative) power.[5]

The second view is that of the judicial power, which considers that the prosecutor and judge are homogeneous but differ in functions. The two roles are equivalent and the prosecutor performs important functions in the judicial area like the judge.[6] The reason is the "proximity" of the procuratorial power to the power of trial and the "similarity" of the prosecutor to the judge. The prosecutor is considered as the guardian of the law and for both the prosecutor and the judge, the finding of facts and the determination of the law should act with the same objective in mind. These are strong evidence that the two can be mentioned in the same breath. The particularly evident example is that, after the conclusion of the investigation, based on the results of the investigation, the prosecutor's decision on whether to prosecute the suspect or not is very similar to that of the judge. Some scholars even point out that compared to the power of non-procedural judge, the prosecutor acting as a criminal prosecutor is closer to the judicial power. With regard to the influence of the prosecution on the trial, some scholars even point out the proximity between the prosecutor and the judge is like the interrelated gear of the clock. The so-called independent judicial power is only possible and the improper intervention of administration in criminal justice can only be prevented when the prosecutor acts like the judicial officer, and the corresponding safeguards are provided.[7]

The third view is that of administrative-judicial duality, which believes the procuratorial power to be both administrative and judicial in nature. The reasons for this are: on the one hand, the organizational system and activity principle of the integration of procuratorial organs eminently embody the administrative characteristics of the procuratorial power; procuratorial organs directly organize prosecutors to carry out investigation, and have a strict organizational structure and supervision-command relationship. Meanwhile, it highlights the effectiveness of actions, which also shows an obvious administrative character. On the other hand, the public prosecution power of procuratorial power examines evidence material, decides on whether to prosecute and upholds the prosecution in court. The review of prosecutions is very similar to the decisions of judges as both of them are acts applying the law and are aimed at upholding the law and the public interest; the prosecutor has relative independence in procedural activities; the prosecutor and the judge enjoy the same or similar job security, and in this sense the prosecutorial power also belongs to judicial power.[8]

The fourth view is that of legal supervision, which considers the essential attribute of the procuratorial power to be legal supervision. The procuratorial power combines an administrative and judicial character in certain aspects of its content and operation mode, and its judicial character is quite pronounced. However, both of its

---

[5]Chen Weidong [5].

[6]Long Zongzhi [4].

[7]Chen Weidong [5].

[8]Liu Lixian, Zhang Zhihui et al. [8].

administrative and judicial characteristics are the partial, subordinate, secondary and non-essential features of the procuratorial power. Normally, the procuratorial organs of socialist countries have not only the powers and functions of the Western procuratorial organs, but also the power to supervise administrative law enforcement and judicial activities. As a result, the procuratorial power in socialist countries has a more obvious and extensive legal supervision character.[9]

3.1.2.2 Positioning of the Nature of the Procuratorial Power in the Procedural Structure

In order to understand the nature of the procuratorial power in the procedural structure, it is first necessary to understand the essential attributes of the procuratorial organ (prosecutor) and its functions in the proceedings. As mentioned above, the judicial power view is that prosecutors and judges are homogeneous but performs different functions and are equivalent in nature. The prosecutor performs important functions in the field of justice as a judge, on the grounds of the "proximity" of the procuratorial power and the power of trial and the "similarity" of the prosecutor to the judge. The prosecutor plays as the guardian of the law, and both the prosecutor and the judge should act with the same objective as the law when investigating the facts and making legal judgement. Therefore, it is argued that the procuratorial organ (the public prosecutor) is a judicial organ and exercises judicial power. In the author's view, just as the idea of attributing the birth of the procuratorial organ to the liberal rule of law "is to some extent an over-optimistic and romantic conjecture", the essence of the prosecutor as an organ of prosecution is submerged in the proclamation of the "judicial office" and the "guardian of the law" proposed by the optimists. German prosecutors, who were born out of the idea of a free rule of law, were no exception.

The German concept of "guardians of the law" and statutory prosecution principle give prosecutors the duty to maintain the authority of the law as well as to comply with its provisions, respectively. Although the starting point for this is that the prosecutor was created as an "independent office" to preserve the unity of legal system, and a strict statutory prosecution principle is applied to prevent the abuse of prosecution power by the prosecutor. But laws are made and recognized by the state, and "in the history of legislation, the guardians of the law have guarded the interests of the state, while the protection of individual interests only remains at the level of interpretation".[10] Similarly, by virtue of the application of the statutory principle, the "impartiality and objectivity" of the procuratorial can only be achieved by upholding the implementation of the law, that is, its essence is to fulfill the law and, consequently, its justice, which, to a certain extent, is only concerned with the merit of the law rather than the contribution of the prosecutor. At the same time, the prosecutor is also essentially a state prosecutorial organ, whose inherent mission is to punish crimes

[9]Liu Lixian, Zhang Zhihui et al. [9,10].

[10]Zhen Zhen [11].

without exception under the statutory principle, and whose starting point is to protect state (public) interest under the prosecution principle of the state. Such a prosecutorial role defines the prosecutor's tendency to ignore or abandon the rights and interests of the individual citizen being prosecuted in the process of prosecution. The power of government gains control over the prosecution and even the courts by exerting influence over legislation and criminal policy. What is hidden under the complement of the "guardian of the law" is the attempt of the government power to interfere the administration of justice, and the consequences of the supervision of judges naturally lead to "an opportunity for the government to impact the administration of justice".[11] The demotion of the procuratorial organ to "an established control organ" during the Germany Nazi period is a clear example of this.

In author's view, it is inaccurate to say that the German procuratorial organ is a judicial organ, and "at least up to the present, there is still quite some controversy over the position of the procuratorial organ, and one might even say that it is an uncertain and developing topic".[12] In the process of rebuilding the judicial system in Germany after the Second World War, the question of the legal positioning of the prosecutor was again the subject of heated debate, with the prevailing view that "since the prosecutors are restrained by the power of direction and their decision do no possess the final legal effect, their function, status, and organization are still clearly distinguishable from those of the judges".[13] "The profound contradiction between "the prosecutor as the most objective official in the world and the procuratorial organ as a hierarchical bureaucracy" still exists and "has not been thoroughly resolved".[14]

Part of the reason why procuratorial organs are recognized as judicial offices is that the "concept of it being an objective organization" is still recognized and believed in, and the prosecutors can be given greater security and legitimacy to its objective obligations as the judicial office. However, no matter how the procuratorial organ is defined, there will be no change in its hierarchical structure or in its prosecutorial duties as a prosecutorial body, such as investigating and prosecuting. Therefore, the author believes that in the course of litigation, especially under the trend of "trial-centrism" litigation reform, the grasp of the procuratorial organs (prosecutors) and their intrinsic attributes should not be based on their role as "judicial officers", but rather on the their essence as prosecution organs, and the nature of their power should be positioned as administrative power.

In addition, in terms of the power of the procuratorial organ (prosecutor) in the procedural structure, it includes the investigation of self-investigating cases, the approval of arrests and the initiation of public prosecutions. However, as the last line of defense of the social justice, the judicial power should be characterized by its intrinsic attributes of finality, neutrality and independence.[15] Contrarily, the procuratorial power in the procedural structure does not possess such attributes: first, the

[11]Wei Wu [12].

[12]Wei Wu [13].

[13]Long Zongzhi [14].

[14]Li Min [15].

[15]Chen Weidong [5].

power of public prosecution, as a right of petition and prosecution, requires the active and effective investigation of crimes and the maintenance of social order. In order to ensure that public prosecution organs fulfil their duties of prosecuting crimes, protecting social order and upholding the law, countries around the world have generally adopted an organizational method of integrated public prosecution in order to concentrate their efforts and achieve effectiveness. Second, the legislation also gives the procuratorial organs investigative power to serve the public prosecution in order to fulfil the requirement of its effectiveness. The above two powers do not possess the characteristics of finality, neutrality and independence; in addition, their requirements for effectiveness are quite different from the passivity of the judicial power, while such effectiveness is inherent in the administrative power. Third, "the people's procuratorates approve and decide on the arrest during the investigation", which constitutes the Chinese model of arrest review system. The quantitative analysis shows that the widespread application of arrest in criminal proceedings in China contradicts the legal elements of arrest, which adversely affects the fair trial and effective defense; the qualitative analysis shows that the widespread application of arrest is rooted in the fact that the procuratorial organs that enjoy the power to approve and decide on the arrest are in fact prosecution organs. Meanwhile, their implementation of substantive standards, review procedures and the guiding principle of "fast arrest and fast prosecution" determines that they are very different from the judicial power that is passive-neutral, final and independent.[16] Therefore, it can be learnt that the procuratorial power in the procedural structure belongs to administrative power.

3.1.2.3 The Nature and Position of the Procuratorial Power in the Judicial System

In the context of Western "separation of powers" theory, "justice is by and large equivalent to procedure".[17] Procedure generally refers to the activities of the courts applying the law to the trial of cases, and the investigative or procuratorial organs participating in the investigation of the procedure belong to either administration or the courts. Judicial activity is centered on the trial. The judicial organs refer only to the trial authorities, and its judicial system is a monist justice model structured around different levels and types of courts.[18] In the narrow sense, the nature of prosecutorial power is administrative power in the Chinese procedural structure, and this is also confirmed by the procuratorial practice in the West, particularly in common law countries. However, when powers and functions of the procuratorial organs (prosecutor), such as the procedural power, the procedural supervision power and the judicial remedy power, are discussed as a whole in the broad conceptual sense, the nature of the procuratorial power is likely to change. This is because, through the concept of procuratorial power, we can see that it is a generic term for

---

[16]Liu Jihua [17].

[17]Chen Guangzhong, and Cui Jie [18].

[18]Wu Jianxiong [3].

the various powers conferred on the procuratorial organs by law. From this concept we can draw two revelations: first, the procuratorial power is a general term for the functions and powers of the procuratorial organs, and its nature is determined by the nature of its functions and powers. The alteration in the functions and powers may also lead to the change in the nature of procuratorial power. Secondly, the subject that confers the powers on the procuratorial organs is the "law", which in this case obviously refers to the law as it is. As a result, the functions and powers given to the procuratorial organ (prosecutor) by the laws of different states or subjects differ, as does the nature of its procuratorial powers. This shows that the subject of the nature of the procuratorial power is both a theoretical (ought to be) and a practical (being) issue; it is both a common issue and a personalized issue throughout the world.

Unlike Western countries, in addition to vesting a procedural power in the procuratorial organs, the legislation of China also gives those organs the functions of procedural supervision and judicial remedy. The reasons for such a provision are mainly based on the following factors: first, China adopts "Unitary Power Model" to distribute powers, and the state power lacks natural supervision and checks and balances as in the "Separation of Powers" model in Western countries, so special supervisory organs are needed to prevent the abuse of power. Secondly, for historical reasons, at the early days of the People's Republic of China, China accepted a great deal of law science and legal thoughts from the Soviet Union, including the ideas of Lenin, the classic Marxist writer, on procuratorial power. In Lenin's view, the procuratorial organs should ensure the strict implementation of the provisions of Soviet law by the organs of the Council of People's Commissars of the Soviet Union, as well as by local authorities, so that the legal system is truly uniform throughout the Republic and the Federation. The Soviet procuratorial organs were thus entrusted with powers in three fields, namely, general supervision, procedural supervision and legal uniform supervision. Against this backdrop, the procuratorial organs in China were also given the corresponding procedural supervision power. Thirdly, during the period of full restoration of the legal system after the "Great Cultural Revolution", and in the light of the fact that the legal system had been undermined, the state was in a chaos and the rights of the people could not be guaranteed, the legislature believed that, without the establishment of special legal supervision bodies, there would be no reliable institutional guarantee for the implementation of laws and the unity of the legal system.[19] Fourthly, with the needs of contemporary judicial practice and the continuous progress of judicial reform, the way in which the procuratorial organs objectively performs its procedural and supervisory functions is also changing. For example, the prosecutor's decision to approve arrest procedures moves towards a tripartite structure; the introduction of systems such as that of the Chief Prosecutor emphasizes the independence of the prosecutor in the handling of individual cases. These changes are moving towards "de-administration" and gradual "judicialization". In the legislature's view, in accordance with the national situation of China, it is appropriate and feasible for the judicial remedy function to be exercised by the procuratorial organs.

[19] Wang Guiwu [20].

Thus, it can be seen that, with the continuous incorporation and improvement of the functions of procedural supervision and judicial remedy in the functions of the procuratorial organs in China, such functions have begun to take on judicial characteristics: their functions are not only to prosecute and combat crimes at the procedure stage, thereby maintaining social stability; they should also be impartial within the judicial system, receive impeachments and appeals from the public, investigate and punish corruption among state officials, and correct the improper words and behaviors of judicial officials, so as to achieve stability in the legal system. Although there is still a considerable gap between the finality, independence and neutrality of the procuratorial power and those of the judicial power, under the model of China's constitutional system of "people's government, court and procuratorate", though the term "judicial organs" is not directly used in the constitutional text, in terms of the institutional arrangement, the Constitution equates the people's court and the people's procuratorate as judicial organs outside the administrative organs; furthermore, the important documents of the Party Central Committee have repeatedly clarified this basic view in accordance with the spirit stipulated in the Constitution and positioned the people's court and the people's procuratorate as judicial organs, thus constituting a judicial structure in which the trial and prosecution are parallel. Under such constitutional "practice", the people's procuratorate and people's court are jointly defined as judicial organs. Therefore, the conclusion that judicial power includes the power of trial and procuratorial powers, and judicial activity includes procedural activity and procedural supervision activity is consistent with the specific connotations of Chinese socialist justice. From this point of view, the author believes that, at the level of the judicial system, the attributes of procuratorial power in the broad sense should be defined as judicial power.

3.1.3 The Relationship Between Procuratorial and Supervision Powers

The term "supervision" essentially means control power in political science, that is, to achieve the control over power. There are generally two ways to control power: restrict power by power or restrict power by right. Since this section focuses on the nature of the procuratorial power and its relationship with the supervision power, the term supervision is used here to exclusively refer to restrict power by power and, accordingly, supervision power refers to the power used to restrict power.

The exploration of the relationship between procuratorial power and supervision power can be described as a theoretical issue arising under the Chinese system and context. It is very necessary and valuable for research. After careful analysis, it is not difficult to find that the connotations of the two are overlapped. According to the above, the procuratorial power in a broad sense contains the function of procedural supervision, including such functions as case-filing supervision, and supervision of whether the investigation activities, trial activities, and execution activities are legal.

The procuratorial power in the sense of supervision not only coordinates and restricts power through a reasonable procedural structure, but also has the responsibility of legally supervising procedural activities and correcting illegal behaviors in such activities. That is to say, the procuratorial power follows the principle of coordination and mutual checks among public security organs, procuratorial organs and courts in criminal proceedings, gives full play to its role as the central link in the restriction and coordination, and ensures that the proceedings proceed in accordance with the law. At the same time, the procuratorial power must correct errors in the procedure and ensure the correctness and impartiality by supervising the investigation activities of public security organs, trial activities of courts, and execution of penalties in prisons.[20] Of course, in addition to the above-mentioned procedure and supervision functions, by "intensifying the punishment and prevention of duty-related crimes", the procuratorial organs are also implementing the legal system supervision, or legal supervision, over public power at the level of the national political system.

China adopts "Unitary Power Model" to distribute powers, and the state power lacks natural supervision and checks and balances as in the "Separation of Powers" model in Western countries, so special supervisory organs are needed to prevent the abuse of power. Therefore, supervision power has become an inherent requirement of the constitutional government system of the socialism with Chinese characteristics and constituted an important feature of China's judicial system. In fact, this procuratorial supervision system that supervises litigation is similar to the ruling and ruling supervision (disciplinary inspection) within the party's leadership system as well as the administrative management and administrative supervision in the administrative management system. But the supervision of the procuratorial organ is not only a procedural supervision, but also a legal system supervision (legal supervision), because the procuratorial organs of China have been given the historical mission of guaranteeing and maintaining the unity of the legal system since the beginning of their establishment.

There are a lot of controversies and debates in the academic world over the relationship between procuratorial power and legal supervision (power). While some scholars see the two as parallel powers, others believe that they can be merged into one. The author believes that, in China, procuratorial power is a legal concept (written into the legal provisions), and meanwhile it is a concept in the procuratorial theory, which refers specifically to the general term of the various powers conferred by law on the procuratorial organs and the definition defers in broad and narrow senses. Legal supervision (power), on the other hand, is not so much a power or a function as it is a position, or an expected objective. The procedural supervision function of procuratorial organs can only be applied in the procedural structure. However, in the sense of supervision, for investigations of duty-related crimes of state officials, the initiation of civil public welfare litigation, and the supervision of public security investigations and court trials as well as the handling of impeachment and appeals from the public, the role and impact of the procuratorial power go far beyond the scope of the proceedings. From this, it can be seen that, although the procuratorial

[20] Wu Jianxiong [3].

organs have many functions, such as procedure, supervision and remedy, from the perspective of the positioning of the legislatures in China, the primary objective of the procuratorial organs is to unify the legal operation with the legal system, as well as guarantee the legal system supervision (legal supervision) of the impartial judicial operation. This legal supervision is precisely what China's Constitution positions and expects of the procuratorial organs.

3.2 Realization of Procuratorial Supervision

Article 129 of the Constitution states, "The people's procuratorates of the People's Republic of China are state organs for legal supervision." The Criminal Procedure Law and the Organic Law of the People's Procuratorates of China have also emphasized this procuratorial positioning. And based on this constitutional positioning, the supervision of people's procuratorates over criminal proceedings has been included in the key regulation and control, and a series of system construction and regulations have been made. According to this, the procuratorial supervision function is important power and function that the procuratorial organ has in criminal proceedings. According to the provisions of the Criminal Procedure Law of China and relevant judicial interpretations, in theory, it is generally believed that the procuratorial supervision power and function mainly include four aspects: case-filing supervision, investigative supervision, trial supervision and implementation supervision.

3.2.1 Case-Filing Supervision Power and Function

In China, case-filing is considered to be an independent procedure stage and the starting point of criminal proceedings. Supervision of case-filing activities is an important part of China's procuratorial supervision. In general, case-filling supervision is studied as the content of investigative supervision in a broad sense. In order to better clarify the problems of the case-filing supervision power and function themselves, this book will juxtapose the case-filing supervision power and function and the narrowly-defined investigative supervision power, and study them separately.

3.2.1.1 Overview of Case-Filing Supervision Power and Function

Case-filing supervision power and function include two important contents, namely, supervision over the situation where cases that should be filed are not filed, and the supervision over situations where cases that should not be filed are filed. The former refers to the supervision of acts that the investigative organs (departments) do not file a case for investigation when they should have. Such supervision is to require the investigative organs (departments) to file the case. The latter, in turn, refers to the supervision of the acts of the investigative organs (departments) that they file a case for investigation when they should not have done so. Such supervision requests the investigative organs (departments) not to file the case or withdraw the case.

It should be said that the case-filing supervision power and function, as established in our criminal procedure law, only include supervision over the situation in which cases that should be filed are not filed. This is mainly reflected in the provisions of Article 111 of the Criminal Procedure Law of China, that is, "Where the people's procuratorate considers that a case should be filed for investigation by a public security organ but the latter has not done so, or where a victim considers that a case should be filed for investigation by a public security organ but the latter has not done so and the victim has brought the matter to a People's Procuratorate, the People's Procuratorate shall request the public security organ to state the reason for not filing the case. If the People's Procuratorate considers that the reasons for not filing the case given by the public security organs are untenable, it shall notify the public security organ to file the case and upon receiving the notification, the public security organ shall file the case." However, the "Rules for Criminal Procedure of the People's Procuratorate (for Trial Implementation)" (hereinafter referred to as the "Rules of the Supreme Procuratorate"), as amended in 2012, clearly clarifies the supervision of the situation in which cases that should not be filed are filed. This is reflected in the provisions of article 553, paragraph 1, of the Rules of Supreme Procuratorate, which stipulates that, "The people's procuratorate shall receive and examine any case submitted to it by the parties involved who believes that the public security organs have filed a case that should not be filed." Therefore, it is generally considered that the current case-filing supervision power and function of China contain the content of the above two aspects.

In addition, it should be noted that the case-filing supervision established by the criminal procedure law of China is aimed at the public security organs and does not specify whether it includes the self-investigative departments of the procuratorial organs. The supervision of the such departments is provided by "Rules for Criminal Procedure of the People's Procuratorate (for Trial Implementation)", which stipulates in Article 563, "If the investigative supervision departments of the people's procuratorate or the public prosecution department find that investigative department of the procuratorate does not file the case that should be filed for investigation or conducts investigation of the case that should not be filed for investigation, it shall recommend the investigative department to file the case for investigation or withdraw the case; if the recommendation is not accepted, it shall be reported to the chief procurator for decision." It shows that the supervision of the self-investigating department of the procuratorial organs also includes the supervision over the situations in which the department fails to file the case that should be filed or it files a case that shouldn't be.

The case-filing supervision power and function were not stipulated in the 1979 Criminal Procedure Law and were first included in it when it was amended in 1996. However, at that time, the case-filing supervision power and function only included the supervision over the situation where the cases that should be filed and investigated were not filed. The legislative drafting department explained the reasons for the establishment of case-filing supervision power and function as that "this Article is added in the light of the fact that in practice, some public security organs fail to file cases that should be filed, and the public have no way to file a complaint and the crimes are not effectively combated".[21] After that, the case-filing supervision power established by the 1996 Criminal Procedure Law was inherited by the 2012 Criminal Procedure Law, but the latter also failed to include in it the supervision of the situation where cases that should not be filed were filed.

However, the problems in judicial practice with regard to case filing are not limited to the inaction of the investigative organs, but also include excessive actions by them, such as the active intervention of the investigative organs in civil and economic cases, or the active exercise of investigative powers for the purpose of retaliation or undue interests, which has led to an extremely negative social impact. Based on this, in 2010, the Supreme People's Procuratorate and the Ministry of Public Security jointly issued the Provisions on the Supervision of Criminal Case Filing (for Trial Implementation), which established for the first time that the procuratorial organs shall supervise the situation in which the public security organs file the cases that should not be filed for investigation. Subsequently, after the amendment of the Criminal Procedure Law in 2012, the Rules for Criminal Procedure of the People's Procuratorate (for Trial Implementation) amended by the Supreme People's Procuratorate clearly includes the situation in which cases that should not be filed for investigation are filed within the procuratorial supervision. As a result, the connotation of the case-filing supervision power of China's procuratorial organs becomes more comprehensive.

3.2.1.2 Problems in the Operation of Case-Filing Supervision Power and Function

Case-filing supervision power and function have played a certain role in practice, but its effect is quite limited.[22] In fact, its impact in practice is not ideal, especially because of the internal quality evaluation of the procuratorial organs, which makes it difficult to distinguish the authenticity of the cases as there may be some false reports.[23] In addition, although the number of cases filed and supervised by the national procuratorial organs has been increasing year by year, the proportion of cases filed and supervised by the procuratorial organs is undoubtedly very low when compared horizontally with the number of cases filed by the public security organs, not to mention the number of stash cases of the public security organs.

The operation of the case-filing supervision power and function in practice is not ideal, and from the view of the system, some system design is unscientific and

---

[21] Criminal Law Office of the Legislative Affairs Commission of the Standing Committee of the National People's Congress [22].

[22] For relevant empirical research, please refer to Zuo Weimin and Zhao Kainian [23].

[23] Some scholars have conducted a research two municipalities in a province, which shows that the implementation situation of case-filing supervision power and function is worse in practice. Ji Meijun and Shan Min [24].

unreasonable, which restricts the performance. First, there are limited sources of information for the case-filing supervision. In order perform such supervision, the procuratorial organs must have the right to know and be aware of the existence of improperly filed or unfiled cases, otherwise, they will not be able to exercise case-filing supervision power. In China, the sources of information available to the procuratorial organs for case-filing supervision are limited and dysfunctional. From the legal point of view, the ways of the procuratorial organs exercising such power are by "discovering" the existence of improperly filed or unfiled cases, or by receiving accusations, reports or appeals. In particular, the procuratorial organs "find" the improperly filed or unfiled cases mainly through the examination and approval of arrests or review of prosecutions. Whether the procuratorial organs find improperly filed or unfiled cases, or receive accusations, reports and appeals, it reflects a part of the information of case-filing, rather than the whole of it. In other words, the above-mentioned sources of information simply cannot guarantee that the procuratorial organs have comprehensive and accurate information about the case. In addition, the above-mentioned sources of information are lagging in nature and cannot provide timely remedies for improperly filed or unfiled cases, and it inevitably causes unnecessary losses or damage to the subjects concerned. The limited sources of information available to the procuratorial organs have made it more difficult for them to conduct case-filing supervision. For example, in practice, investigative organs treat some criminal cases as public security cases in order to reduce the incidence of criminal cases or to reduce the workload and difficulty of their work. With regard to these practices of substituting penalty for punishment and failing to file a case that should be filed, it is hard for the procuratorial organs to be actively aware of the existence of misconduct, and the relevant subjects of the case may not object to it, making it difficult for the procuratorial organs to initiate the case-filing supervision.

Second, the safeguard measures for the case-filing supervision are inadequate. According to the provisions of the Criminal Procedure Law and the Rules for Criminal Procedure of the People's Procuratorate (for Trial Implementation), in the case of improperly filed or unfiled cases, the people's procuratorate may, firstly, request the investigative organs to clarify the reasons for filing or not filing the case. After that, if it considers that the reasons for filing or not filing the case cannot be established, it shall immediately notify the investigative organs to file or withdraw the case. However, the implementation of the above-mentioned measures is not coercive, and when the procuratorial organs require the investigative organs to state the reasons, and notify them to file or withdraw the cases, the execution is not guaranteed. If the investigative organs do not implement the measures, the procuratorial organs will have no better countermeasure. It is for this reason that we find that the request of the procuratorial organs for the case-filing supervision are not always met. For example, between 1998 and 2010, 7.1% of the country's case-filing supervision remained unimplemented.[24] Even if such request is implemented, it may be a mere "response". For example, for cases that should be filed by the investigative organs but are not filed, in order to deal with the supervision of the procuratorial organs,

[24]Liu Jihua [25].

upon the receipt of the Notice of Request to State the Reasons for Not Filing a Case from the procuratorial organs, the investigative organs will usually add a case file, in which the time for filing the case is ahead of the actual date. Moreover, after the cases are filed, the investigative organs may not take active investigative measures, that is they "file the case but do not investigate it", resulting in a prolonged delay in the case. This phenomenon is prevalent. According to statistics, only around 30% of the cases filed and supervised by the procuratorial organs can eventually enter the arrest, prosecution and trial stage, while about 70% of the cases are never proceeded.[25] The research of the practice departments also shows that the main reason for the ineffective case-filing supervision is that there is no provision for the punishment and remedy measures when the public security organs still refuse to file the case; and for those who accept the case-filing supervision but do not actively fix it, the procuratorial organs lack the corresponding strong countermeasures.[26]

In fact, the problems in the operation of China's case-filing supervision power and function not only lie at the system level, but also at the structure level. And the problems at the structure level are even more critical, fundamentally constraining the exercise of the various procuratorial supervision powers and functions of the procuratorial organs, including the case-filing supervision. At the heart of these structure problems is the question of the relationship between the procuratorial organs and the police. In the field of procuratorial supervision, such relationship fundamentally determines whether the procuratorial organs implement "internal" supervision as the commanding supervisor of the investigative organs, or simply carry out "external" supervision as their external supervisor.

In China, in accordance with Article 135 of the Constitution and Article 7 of Criminal Procedure Law, the investigative and procuratorial organs divide responsibilities, coordinate their efforts and check each other. The general view is that the dividing responsibilities means that the two organs exercise their powers within the limits of the law and are not allowed to replace each other or exercise functions outside their remit. Coordination, as determined by the unity of behavior and objectives, refers to that the two organs shall collaborate with each other in criminal proceedings on the basis of the dividing responsibilities, and that they shall not sabotage each other's activities. Checking each other means that, in criminal proceedings, there must be a restraining relationship between the two organs in order to prevent the abuse of power and the violation of the law.

As a general principle governing the relationship between the two organs in criminal proceedings, "dividing responsibilities, coordinating their efforts and checking each other" seems to be consistent with scientific principles on the surface. However, as it focuses too much on the principle, there are no specific measures to regulate the relationship between the two, and more importantly, because of its own limitations and non-scientific constraints, many serious problems have arisen in judicial practice. As explained in the traditional litigation theory, investigation and prosecution

[25] Yuan Ming, Hu Yaoxian and Tao Jianwang [26].

[26] Beijing Haidian District People's Procuratorate, "The Prosecution-Police Relations Project Group" [27].

are independent stages of proceedings, which invisibly lead to an equal relationship between the public security organs and the procuratorial organs, or even to an actual investigation-centered pattern. In practice, because of the overemphasis on the independence of each party, the phenomenon of wrangling is inevitable; and too much emphasis is placed on dividing responsibility that coordination with each other decreases, and even if there is coordination, it is mostly abnormal one, such as some cases in which the procuratorial organs approve the arrest without fully examining the case, resulting in their failure to appropriately restrict the public security organs. In some places, the relationship between the public security organs and the procuratorial organs has become "uncomfortable" because of restrictions, resulting in a stalemate between them, such as when the procuratorial organs return the case files to the public security organs for additional investigation during the review and prosecution process, in practice, the public security organs strangely return the case files "as they are". The purpose of restriction is to prevent and correct mistakes that could or have been made, but it turns out to be a case of mutual wrangling, and in some places, the procuratorial organs are reluctant to exercise restraint and turn a blind eye to the violations of the law by the investigative organs, either because of the good relations between the two or for the sake of their own reputation. All of these were not expected by the legislator.

It should be said that the principle of "dividing responsibilities, coordinating their efforts and checking each other" is ideal in theory and it would be perfect to actually achieve it, but because it is too idealistic and lacks reasonableness in procedural system, it is relatively challenging to achieve in practice and even leads to chronic problems. The use of such principles to regulate the relationship between the two is clearly a cause for disregarding the unity of the direct interests of the procuratorial and the investigative organs in criminal proceedings. It should be noted that the public security organs and the procuratorial organs have the same purpose in criminal prosecution activities, and that the relationship of mutual restraint based on the dividing responsibility has inevitably led to internal friction, and the relationship of checking each other has not prevented the recurrence of illegal conducts such as violations of procedure, abuse of power and infringement of citizens' legal rights.

Both the Constitution and the Criminal Procedure Law of China have made it clear that the procuratorial organs are legal supervisory organs. However, under this alienated institutional arrangement of dividing responsibilities, coordinating their efforts and checking each other between the two organs, the procuratorial organs have neither organizational control nor functional leadership over the investigative organs, which makes the procuratorial organs unable to exercise their case-filing supervision power and function and the investigative supervision functions mentioned below. It is precisely because the procuratorial organs are unable to control the investigative organs that they lack information about the illegal conducts of the investigative organs, And it is precisely because the procuratorial authorities are unable to control the investigative organs that the various supervisory acts of the procuratorial organs cannot be accepted or implemented by the investigative organs. In view of this, the strengthening of the supervision function of the procuratorial organs over the investigative organs in China will require a change in the positioning of the relationship between the two.

3.2.1.3 Reform Approach of Case-Filing Supervision Power and Function

Based on the above analysis, the author believes that the reform of China's case-filing supervision power and function should be directed towards the investigation and prosecution integration reform, building a system that meets the requirements of such integration on the basis of reshaping the investigation and prosecution relationship.

It should be said that the investigation and prosecution integration reform is in line with the basic development of the prosecution function. The procuratorial organs are the prosecuting authorities and dominate the prosecution, which determines their superior position over the investigative organs. The investigative organs shall submit to and serve the procuratorial organs and this should be the basic relationship between the two. The relationship of mutual restraint between the two organs, especially the restriction of the investigative organs on the procuratorial organs, will inevitably lead to the decentralization of the prosecuting power and the weakening of the state's function of prosecuting crimes. Thus, the equal relationship between the two, and in particular, the restriction placed on the procuratorial organs by the investigative organs unavoidably leads to an internal drain on the resources of the prosecution. Particularly with the strengthening of the separation of prosecution and trial, the increasing neutrality of judges, the enhanced prosecution responsibility of the prosecutors and the improvement of the rules of evidence, there will certainly be higher requirements for the accusation evidence, that is its legality, validity and comprehensiveness of the investigative evidence. The strengthening of the prosecution function therefore requires a reform of the traditional model of the investigation and prosecution relationship and the shaping of an integrated relationship between the two. On the one hand, the investigation and prosecution integration model is based on giving full play to the respective functions of the investigative and procuratorial organs, rationalizing and optimizing the allocation of their judicial resources and reducing the costs of litigation by appropriately streamlining the litigation process, thus effectively speeding up the process; on the other hand, by placing the prosecutor at the central position at this procedural stage, the possible separatist tendency of the investigative organs in criminal proceedings can be prevented, thus greatly enhancing the effectiveness of the prosecution function. In addition, for prosecutors, as a representative of the public interest, and the judicial police, who supports the prosecutor in the performance of their prosecutorial tasks, their value orientation and procedural interests are unanimously in favor of the maintenance of social order and the stability of public security.[27] This is determined by the nature of the prosecution function shared by both parties. It is this unity of values and procedural interests that

[27] Huang Dongxiong [28].

inevitably requires a high degree of centralization and unity between the investigation and prosecution during the whole process of criminal proceedings.

Moreover, the investigation and prosecution integration reform can curb illegal investigation and protect human rights by strengthening the control of the procuratorial organs over the investigative organs. At present, investigative organs have almost unlimited investigative power and enjoy full autonomy in such areas as custody, residential surveillance, bail pending trial, custody, search and seizure, technical investigation, etc. The overall procedural awareness of the police in China is weak and they lack the respect for the rights of the accused, which easily leads to the violation of the personal and legal rights of the accused. In this context, rather than emphasizing external supervision of the investigative organs, it is better to strengthen command and supervision of them and to achieve simultaneous control over investigative powers.

There are three patterns of investigation and prosecution relationships in the world.

1. The dominant type

Typical countries adopt this model are Germany and France. These countries placed great emphasis on the high degree of centralization and unity of criminal justice and focus on the pursuit of procedural efficiency in the process of inquiry and prosecution. Therefore, in order to prevent possible separatist tendencies in the investigative organs, investigative command and investigative supervision powers are centralized to the procuratorial organs, and investigative powers are exercised jointly by both parties under the unified leadership of the procuratorial organs. Throughout the investigation, the procuratorial organs occupy the leadership position. Some states even provide that the procuratorial organ is an investigative organ, that is, the procuratorial power includes the investigative power.

2. Guidance and participation type

Typical country adopts this model is the United States. The United States does not have well-organized national police and procuratorial institutions, but only local, state and federal police and procuratorial systems. As a result, they perform their own duties in a decentralized and independent manner and are accountable for their own. However, this does not mean that the prosecutors are inactive in the criminal investigation activities. Although their main function is to prosecute on behalf of the state in criminal cases, they are also entitled to participate in investigations. Of course, in most cases, prosecutors do not conduct investigation by themselves, but direct and supervise the investigation by professional investigators. In some cases, however, such as in sparsely populated areas or small towns, or in some metropolitans, the procuratorial organ will conduct its own inquiry if the public requests. In the United States, some procuratorial organs have their own specialized investigators; and some often transfer detectives from local police stations to form investigation teams. Thus, although on the surface the relationship between the procuratorial and police organs in United States is rather loose, the role of prosecutors in guiding and participating in police investigation and evidence collection cannot be ignored.

3. Assistance type

Basically, the country that adopts this model is Japan. According to the relevant provisions of Japan's Criminal Procedure Law, the first investigation is generally carried out by a judicial police officers, and only when it is necessary can the prosecutor investigate on his or her own, direct the judicial police to assist him or her in the investigation or give the necessary general instructions. That is to say, while the prosecutors' investigative powers are secondary, they still have general direction and command power over judicial police officers, which is mainly reflected in the following aspects: (1) prosecutors may give necessary general instructions to judicial police officers in investigations carried out within their jurisdiction. (2) Prosecutors may give necessary general command to judicial police officers for investigations that require assistance within their jurisdiction. (3) Prosecutors may, if they deem it necessary in the case of a self-investigation, direct judicial police officers to assist the investigation. (4) In the first three cases, judicial police officers shall be subject to the directions or command of the prosecutors. Despite the different approaches of the different models mentioned above, a common trend is that the prosecutor dominates the entire investigation and prosecution process. And the prosecutor and the judicial police, who perform investigative functions, do not have an equal and independent relationship. On the contrary, it is a legal relationship of leading and being led, commanding and being commanded, and supervising and being supervised, that is, the so-called "the superior orders and the subordinate follows" relationship,[28] in which the investigative power has become a subsidiary power in the service of prosecutorial power and is no longer a decentralized and independent force.

It can be seen that the construction of an investigation and prosecution integration model should be the direction of the development of investigation and prosecution relations in China. As far as case-filing supervision is concerned, the construction of the investigation and prosecution integration model is reflected in the control of the filing and withdrawal of the cases. Specifically, first, case-filing control should be implemented. In order to prevent police authorities from failing to file cases in which criminal responsibility should be investigated and from improperly filing cases, a filing record system should be established. The case filed by the public security organs shall be reported to the procuratorial organs for the record, and the procuratorial organs have the power to review so as to prevent the substitution of case-filing and investigation with penalties. For the abuse of law and indulgence of crimes of investitive organs, procuratorial organs have the right to investigate and order the investigative organs to file a case, thus bringing the power to decide on the prosecution of criminal cases under the unified control of the procuratorial organs. Second, control over the withdrawal of cases shall be implemented. If the investigative organs decided to withdraw the cases that are filed, it shall report to the procuratorial organ for the record. If the procuratorial organ does not approve the withdrawal, it shall order the investigative organ to continue the investigation, which shall be carried out without delay. Thirdly, in addition to the control of the filing and

[28]Huang Dongxiong [29].

withdrawal of cases, it should also be provided that the procuratorial organs have the power to investigate all criminal cases (in fact, they already enjoy supplementary investigative power), and that if the investigative organs do not comply with the command and supervision of the procuratorial organs, the latter may directly file or withdraw the cases. In addition, the command and supervision of the procuratorial organs over the investigative organs and investigators must be guaranteed. In Japan, in the event that a judicial police officer does not obey the direction or command of the prosecutor without just cause, the chief of the procuratorial organs may appeal to the Public Safety Commission for disciplinary action or dismissal. The establishment of corresponding safeguards shall also be considered in China.

3.2.2 *Investigative Supervision Power and Function*

Investigative supervision is the supervision of criminal investigations by the people's procuratorate. The investigative supervision here refers to a kind of investigative supervision in the narrow sense of the term and does not include the case-filing supervision power and function of the procuratorial organs. As a whole, the investigative supervision power consists of two types of contents: general supervision of the entire investigation activity and the supervision of coercive measures taken by the investigative organs through the examination and approval of arrests.

The investigative supervision power and function are important elements of the procuratorial supervision power and function. In China, the emphasis on procuratorial supervision of investigative powers is determined by our special judicial system. Unlike the extraterritorial control of the investigative power by the judicial power, the structure of criminal proceedings in China is an assembly line type, with three organs, public prosecution, procuratorial and legislative organs, being responsible for a division of labor and each administering a section. The court is usually not involved in the investigation stage, and the adjudication power cannot control the investigative power as well. However, it is well known that the nature of the investigative power itself dictates that it needs to be checked and balanced by external forces, otherwise it will become a "wild horse on the loose". Therefore, on the basis of China's system of procuratorial supervision, it is only natural that the procuratorial power should exercise procuratorial supervision over the investigative power. This has bridged the gap in the external control of China's investigative power, and also constitutes a pattern of procuratorial control over investigative power with Chinese characteristics.

It should be said that procuratorial supervision of investigation activities in China has played an important role in safeguarding the legitimate rights of citizens and promoting the proper implementation of the law. The supervision of investigations by the procuratorial organs not only provides an effective check on the investigative powers of public security, but also ensures that the public security organs can exercise their powers within the limits of the law. Moreover, the procuratorial organs and the public security organs are both organs of prosecution, which is conducive to achieving a balance of power between the prosecution and the defense on the basis of the procuratorial organs' supervision of the legality of the investigation activities of the public security organs. Of course, it should also be seen that there are also problems with the investigative supervision in China, and how to correctly understand the investigative supervision power and function and their future development direction is a major theoretical issue that requires our serious consideration.

3.2.2.1 Difficulties Facing General Investigative Supervision and Its Reform

The so-called general investigative supervision is investigative supervisions other than the special form of supervision in which arrests are reviewed and approved. There is a significant difference between general investigative supervision and special supervision such as examination and approval of arrest. Examination and approval of arrests are the supervision of the investigative organs in the form of excreting the decisive power of examination and approval of arrest. Such supervision is achieved on the basis of the division of investigative powers into implementation and decision-making powers and the exercise of decision-making power by the procuratorial organs. However, in general investigative supervision, procuratorial organs do not enjoy the right to make substantive decisions on investigative acts, but rather exercise independent procuratorial supervision powers in addition to their investigative powers.

In China, general investigative supervision has abundant contents. According to Article 565 of the Rules for Criminal Procedure of the People's Procuratorate (for Trial Implementation), investigative supervision is mainly carried out in the following areas: (1) the use of torture or other illegal methods to extort confessions from criminal suspects; (2) the use of violence, threats and other illegal methods to collect witness testimony or victim statements, or the use of violence, threats and other methods to prevent witnesses from testifying or to order others to give false testimony; (3) forging, concealing, destroying, exchanging, changing or altering evidence without authorization, or helping the party to the case destroy or falsify evidence; (4) favoritism, and indulging or harboring criminals; (5) intentionally creating wrong, false or erroneous cases; (6) Taking advantage of his or her position in the investigation to obtain illegal benefits; (7) illegally detaining others or depriving others of freedom with other methods; (8) Illegally searching others' body or home or invading others' home; (9) illegally taking technical investigative measures; (10) during the investigation, cases that should not be withdrawn are withdrawn; (11) to seal up, seize or freeze property irrelevant to the case at hand, or to fail to terminate the sealing, seizure and freeze of property as required; (12) to embezzle, misappropriate, privately divide, replace, or use in violation of relevant provisions the property that has been sealed up, seized or frozen and its interest; (13) the bail deposit that should be refunded is not refunded; (14) in violation of the provisions of the Criminal Procedure Law concerning the decision, execution, modification or withdrawal of coercive measures; (15) The investigator that should withdraw from the case but do not withdraw; (16) the suspects shall be informed of their procedural rights in accordance with the law, but are not informed, which affects the exercise of their procedural rights; (17) the parties concerned, the defender or the prosecutor are prevented from exercising their procedural rights in accordance with the law; (18) the interrogation of the suspect shall be recorded or filmed in accordance with the law is not recorded or filmed; (19) the suspect's family shall be notified in accordance with the law after the custody, arrest or surveillance of the residence of the suspect, but they are not notified; (20) other violations of the relevant provisions of the Criminal Procedure Law during the investigation. This shows the importance that China attaches to investigative supervision.

The question is, has the effectiveness of investigative supervision in judicial practice lived up to our expectation at the legislation? If the answer is no, what are the reasons for it and what is the future direction of the general investigative supervision? These are the questions that need to be answered.

1. Assessment of the effectiveness of the implementation of general investigative supervision

Although general investigative supervision has played a certain positive role in judicial practice, it is undeniable that its effectiveness in judicial practice in China is unsatisfactory.

First, although the procuratorial organs will implement investigative supervision, the cases in which such supervision is carried out are only a small part of the numerous cases handled by the public security organs. According to the statistics of scholars, between 1998 and 2000, the national procuratorial organs submitted tens of thousands of corrective opinions each year, but the proportion is relatively low compared with the millions of cases filed and investigated by public security organs each year. Between 1998 and 2010, 56,322,950 criminal cases were filed by public security organs nationwide, and 190,366 cases were investigated and supervised by the procuratorial organs, representing only 0.3%.[29] This does not mean that more than 99% of the cases are free from problems in the investigation. No one with any knowledge of China's investigative practice would come to such a conclusion. For example, the study found that, outside the scope of investigative supervision, illegal investigation activities by investigative organs, including illegal interrogation, illegal custody, imprisonment, bail and search still exist in some areas.[30] This illustrates the limitations of investigative supervision that the supervision over the vast majority of investigative acts of investigative organs is not or cannot be implemented, that is to say, the scope of control over investigative powers is limited.

Second, the implementation of general investigative supervision by the public security organs is inadequate. In theory, the supervision of investigations by the procuratorial organs should be fully accepted and carried out by the public security organs, as the procuratorial organs supervise the illegal or improper conducts of the investigative organs from an objective and fair standpoint. In practice, however, not all investigative supervision is accepted by the public security organs. Between 1998

[29] Liu Jihua [25].

[30] Zuo Weimin and Zhao Kainian [31].

and 2010, the national correction rate for investigative supervision was 85.3%,[31] which, although very high, is sufficient to show that not all investigative supervision by the procuratorial organs is accepted. In other words, a significant proportion of violations and improper investigations remain uncorrected, which means that, for suspects, their rights are not remedied in these cases.

Finally, there is a "walk through" by the procuratorial organs in respect of general investigative supervision. According to scholars, in practice, investigative supervision in some places has shown a declining trend year by year.[32] In practice, another phenomenon that corresponds to this one is the phenomenon of "walk through" in general investigative supervision. After the implementation of the Criminal Procedure Law in 2012, the author has found in the research process that, the investigative supervision departments often only focus on the special form of investigative supervision through the examination and approval of arrest, and they do not pay attention to the general investigative supervision. The reasons for this concern various aspects, but for the staff of the investigative supervision departments, who are constrained by the limited energy for handling the case, it is difficult to have enough energy for general investigative supervision after properly handling the review of arrests. However, in practice, the middle and high level procuratorial departments often have assessment requirements for the amount of general investigative supervision. Therefore, in order to be able to cope with the assessment of the superior, the subordinate procuratorial organs will often take the form of misrepresentation and falsification of general investigative supervision. Moreover, even if there is real investigative supervision, it may be a mere formality.

As can be seen from the above, general investigative supervision has very limited control over the investigation stage in China. This also leads to many drawbacks. In practice, the public security organs enjoy discretionary power on all coercive investigation methods other than arrest, including detention, search, seizure, wiretapping, etc. And the use of these coercive investigation methods is directly related to citizens' fundamental rights to personal freedom, property and privacy. These unrestricted powers of the public security organs are the greatest cause of serious infringement of citizens' personal freedom and other fundamental rights during the investigation stage. The legislative design of the investigative organs being unrestricted in a power vacuum has created a super-inquisitorial investigation structure, which is incompatible with the democratization and open reforms in the field of criminal procedure and the trend towards the rule of law and the legitimization of criminal procedure in China. Therefore, there is an urgent need to reform investigative supervision in China and to achieve effective control over investigation activities by investigative supervision.o

2. Analysis of the causes of the "failure" of general investigative supervision

In China, the main reasons why general investigative supervision cannot achieve effective control over the investigation stage are as follows:

---

31 Liu Jihua [25].

32 Zuo Weimin and Zhao Kainian [31].

First, there is sufficient cooperation but insufficient supervision between the procuratorial and investigative organs. Although procuratorial organs have the status of legal supervision and assume investigative supervision power and function, in criminal proceedings, the investigation and prosecution both exercise the function of prosecution and undertake the task of prosecuting crimes, so they are intrinsically and inextricably interlinked. Therefore, it becomes difficult for the prosecutor to get rid of the psychological burden of prosecuting crimes, and they are often "too soft-hearted" in supervising the investigative organs, and the supervision of the investigation organs often become a mere formality.

Second, the general investigative supervision of the procuratorial organs has a lagging nature. As everyone knows, the general investigative supervision of the procuratorial organs is not simultaneous, but rather an ex post facto supervision, which means general investigative supervision is often conducted only after the illegal investigation are carried out and is thus delayed. This lag in supervision has brought multiple negative consequences. First, the lagging nature of general investigative supervision leads to poor information access to supervision. Unlike simultaneous supervision, which can obtain a large amount of information on investigation activities in a timely and effective manner, ex post facto supervision can only obtain information on illegal investigation activities and restore such illegal activities through other methods. These methods of obtaining information are often not as effective as simultaneous supervision. Secondly, the lagging nature of general investigative supervision leads to untimely remedies for the accused, and the supervision of the illegal investigative acts will not produce positive effect. On the one hand, it is often difficult for the procuratorial organs to provide timely and effective remedy to the accused after the illegal investigation has taken place, and the remedy needs of the right of the accused cannot be satisfied; on the other hand, after the illegal investigation has taken place, its purpose has often been achieved. The subsequent supervision usually does not negate the effect of the illegal investigation activities, and the punishment for them is limited, which cannot fundamentally curb the occurrence of such activities.

Besides, the procuratorial organs have limited access to information for general investigative supervision, so such supervision is usually a mere formality. As mentioned above, since the general investigative supervision by the procuratorial organs is an ex post facto supervision, information on the illegal investigation can only be obtained by other means. In practice, general investigative supervision is often initiated at the request of the accused. In the absence of a request from the accused, the procuratorial organs have no effective ways of knowing the existence of illegal investigation acts and will not take the initiative to intervene. Moreover, even if the accused has requested for general investigative supervision, the lack of sufficient factual and evidentiary information often makes it difficult for the procuratorial organs to exercise effective supervision. For example, criminal suspects and others reflect to the procuratorial organs that the police, in their investigation activities, have extorted confessions through torture, deception, inducement and other illegal acts, and request the procuratorial organ to supervise. However, the procuratorial organ often needs the criminal suspect to provide corresponding evidentiary material, while the criminal suspect has limited ability to obtain evidence, especially at the investigation stage when his personal freedom is restricted. Therefore, the criminal suspect often fails to provide the corresponding evidentiary material, and without such evidence, normally, the procuratorial organ will not easily believe it, nor will they initiate general investigative supervision. Even if they do, it will be very difficult for them to obtain evidence.

Lastly, the effectiveness of supervision by the procuratorial organs is inadequate. In China, general investigative supervision is mostly a kind of "soft supervision", that is, the procuratorial organs cannot directly order the investigative organs to do or not to do certain acts. They cannot directly correct the illegal investigation activities of the investigative organs and they can only suggest the investigative organs to correct their own mistakes. As to whether or not the investigative organs accept the procuratorial supervision and whether or not to correct it is up to the investigative organs to decide. Even if the investigative organs do not accept the investigative supervision and disregard the supervision of the procuratorial organs, the procuratorial organs have no other sanction measures to guarantee the implementation of investigative supervision.

In fact, it can be concluded from the above reasons that, fundamentally speaking, the root cause of the failure of general investigative supervision in China is that such supervision in China is in fact an "external supervision". In this mode of supervision, the procuratorial organ is not responsible for or specifically performs a certain procedural power, but inspects and supervises the criminal procedure as a procedural observer and an outsider.[33] That is to say, as far as general investigative supervision is concerned, the procuratorial and the public security organs share different powers, with the former being the legal supervision power and the latter the investigative power, rather than the powers of investigative leadership, decision-making, command and supervision and the investigation implementation that belong to the same power. Such a supervision model will inevitably divide the power and function relationship between the investigative and procuratorial organs and make the procuratorial organs more of an external party, so that they cannot simultaneously intervene in the investigation activities as leaders, decision-makers or commanders, but can only "observe" the execution of the investigation process as an external observer. This fundamentally limits the effectiveness of general investigative supervision.

3. Transformation of general investigative supervision

The Fourth Plenary Session of the 18th CPC Central Committee has proposed a request to promote the reform of the trial-centered procedural system, "Promote the reform of the trial-centered procedural system and ensure that the factual evidence in the investigation and the review and prosecution of the cases can stand the test of law. The evidence adjudication rule shall be fully implemented, and evidences should be collected, fixed, preserved, examined and used in strict accordance with the law. The system for the appearance of witnesses and experts in court should

[33] Wan Yi [34].

be improved, and it should be ensured that court hearings play decisive roles in ascertaining the facts, concluding evidence, protecting the right to appeal and making fair adjudication." For the pretrial stage, a central issue in promoting the reform of the trial-centered procedural system is to require strict control of evidence and to improve the quality of investigative evidence, which include both procedural and substantive quality requirement, so that the facts of the cases can withstand the test of history. There is no doubt that enhanced investigative supervision and increased procuratorial involvement in investigations should be the focus of the reform. In this context, there is an urgent need to discuss how to achieve the transformation of general investigative supervision.

As stated above, the fundamental reason behind the various reasons for the failure of general investigative supervision in China lies in its "external supervision" model. Clearly, in order to effectively address this problem, an "outside-in" shift in general investigative supervision should be achieved.

For the realization of this transformation, theoretically, the following conditions should be met: first, the separation of the subject of the investigative power from the subject of the general investigative supervision power. The object of general investigative supervision is investigation activities; if the subject of the investigative power and the subject of the general investigative supervision power are the same, then supervision is only an empty talk. Secondly, the general investigative supervision power should be superior or decisive in relation to the investigative power. This is primarily to ensure that the general investigative supervision power is a sufficient deterrent to the investigative power. The purpose of general investigative supervision is to correct and avoid illegal acts, so if the general investigative supervision power is a parallel or equal power to the investigative power, then the effectiveness of supervision will be greatly undermined, and the purpose of supervision will not be achieved. Finally, the general investigative supervision power should be synchronized with the investigative power and should be fully, actively and comprehensively involved in the investigation activities, rather than passively and reactively involved after the activities are implemented.

It should be said that the investigation and prosecution integration model is the optimal model that meets these conditions and is most conducive to achieving a shift in general investigative supervision from an external to an internal supervision model. Under the investigation and prosecution integration model, the prosecutor leads the entire investigation and prosecution process, and all legal acts of the investigative organs are brought under the lead, command and supervision of the procuratorial organs. The relationship between the prosecutor and the police officer with investigative functions is not equal and independent, but rather a relationship of leading and being led, commanding and being commanded, supervising and being supervised, that is, the so-called "the superior orders and the subordinate follows" relationship.[34] The investigators must accept the supervision of procuratorial organs, otherwise they will be subject to adverse consequences in terms of promotion, reward,

[34]Huang Dongxiong [35].

etc. The positioning of the prosecutorial-investigative relationship in the investigation and prosecution integration model determines that this model is most conducive to strengthening the supervision of investigation activities. Moreover, as explained in the section on case-filing supervision, form a worldwide perspective, although the relationship between investigation and prosecution is not identical, there is a common tendency to emphasize investigation and prosecution integration and emphasize the prosecutors' command and supervision over investigation activities.

As far as general investigative supervision is concerned, the core of the construction of an investigation and prosecution integration model is the realization of the full and dynamic supervision of investigative powers. To this end, the system should be designed in such a way that, on the one hand, the procuratorial organs should be given command and sanctioning powers over the investigative organs. It is envisaged that the procuratorial officers may be appointed in the procuratorial organs as assistants to the chief prosecutor, responsible for directing the investigation activities of the criminal police, who shall be subject to the general and specific command of the procuratorial officers. On the other hand, effective measures must be formulated to ensure that prosecutors exercise command and supervision over investigators. As mentioned earlier, in Japan, in the event that a judicial police officer does not obey the direction or command of the prosecutor without just cause, the chief of the procuratorial organs may appeal to the Public Safety Commission for disciplinary action or dismissal. The establishment of corresponding safeguards shall also be considered in China. If an investigator does not follow instructions, the prosecutor may request the chief of the public security organs to dismiss and replace the investigator. Of course, the investigation and prosecution integration mode should not only be established between the public security organs and the procuratorial organs. For self-investigating cases of the procuratorial organs, the direction and guidance of the procuratorial supervision department to the investigation department should also be established.

It should be noted that the strengthening of general investigative supervision does not exclude judicial control over investigation activities. In fact, under the investigation and prosecution integration model, it is all the more necessary for the judge to intervene in the investigation and to exercise full control over the investigation activity. In particular, the judge intervenes in the investigation process as a third party, supervises and regulates the entire process and makes the final decision on the legitimacy and legality of the investigation activities and the related coercive measures. For example, coercive investigative measures involving personal freedom and property shall be reviewed by the judge for approval, in order to prevent the abuse of the state's criminal judicial power by investigators and prosecutors in violation of human rights. There are similar legislative precedents in other countries in this regard. In France, for instance, the examining magistrate exercises full legal control over investigation activities and has the power to decide on major issues in the investigation as well as on issues involving legal measures; in common law systems, the judge exercises legal control over the investigation through the power to authorize legal measures and to decide on the selection of evidence at trial and other procedural issues.[35] In addition, in the process of strengthening general investigative supervision, the participation of the accused in the investigation process should also be strengthened. As Professor Merryman has said, "the inequality of rights of action and the secrecy of the written procedure often contribute to the danger of authoritarian tyranny".[36] In this regard, in order to strengthen the power of the defense, the lawyers should be allowed to fully engage in the investigation process and they should be entitled to the right to be present during the interrogation of the suspect.

3.2.2.2 The Dilemma Facing by the Power and Function to Examine and Approve Arrests and Its Reform

Article 88 of Criminal Procedure Law stipulates that, "After a People's Procuratorate has examines a case with respect to which a public security organ has submitted a request for approval of arrest, it shall decide according to the circumstances of the case either to approve the arrest or disapprove the arrest. If it decides to approve the arrest, the public security organs shall execute it immediately and inform the People's Procuratorate of the result without delay. If the People's Procuratorate disapproves the arrest, it shall give its reasons therefor, and if it deems a supplementary investigation necessary, it shall at the same time notify the public security organ of the need." This is the power and function of the examination and approval of arrest that China's procuratorial organs have, and it is generally considered to be an important approach for the procuratorial organs to supervise the investigation activities. The examination and approval of arrest by the procuratorial organs constitute a model of examination and approval of arrest with Chinese characteristics. In judicial practice, the power and function to examine and approve arrests has played a positive role. For example, in the case of Wang Moulei of Hebei, the arrest approval department of the procuratorial organs found illegal evidence at the time of arrest, and by excluding illegal evidence, a case of injustice and wrongful conviction was avoided.[37] However, in China, the power and function to examine and approve arrests also face some problems both in theory and in practice that fundamentally constrain the development of the power and function to examine and approve arrests.

1. Theoretical dilemmas facing the power and function to examine and approve arrests

China's laws give the procuratorial organs the power to examine and approve arrests, and the legislation is intended to ensure that arrests are strictly monitored and that unlawful acts by the public security organs in their investigation activities are corrected. However, this has inevitably turned the investigative supervision power of the procuratorial organs into judicial adjudication power, and they have assumed

[35] Xu Jingcun ed. [35].

[36] John Henry Merryman [37].

[37] Supreme People's Procuratorate work report (2015).

an adjudication function in the investigative supervision process. This is the biggest theoretical challenge facing our procuratorial organs in their power and function to examine and approve arrests.

It is well known that in criminal proceedings, arrest is one of the most severe coercive measures of deprivation of personal freedom of the suspect, which may result in the loss of personal freedom of the suspect for months or even years and is no less than the penalties imposed for some minor offences. This is the precise reason that arrest is regarded as an interference with fundamental rights, and that the power to approve arrest is also seen as an important composition of the judicial power and is part of the judicial reservation. The examination and approval of arrests by the procuratorial organs in the name of investigative supervision is, in fact, the exercise of judicial functions by the procuratorial organs. This function should in no way be implemented by the procuratorial organs. As a legal supervisory organ, the function of the procuratorial organs is to "observe and supervise"; whereas as a public prosecution organ, the procuratorial organ enjoys a mere right to apply for adjudication. These two are fundamentally different from the adjudication power to judge a particular subject.

Moreover, from the worldwide perspective, the power and function to examine and approve arrests are all wielded by judges. In the United States, police are required to transport suspects arrested on "reasonable grounds" to the nearest federal magistrate judge or state magistrate "without undue delay" for the judge's decision. In the United Kingdom, police officers must make a prior application to a magistrate to arrest a suspect and state their proper and reasonable grounds. After the arrest and before the charges, the police may hold a suspect in custody for up to 36 h in order to obtain the evidence necessary to bring charges, and if an extension is necessary, it must be approved by the Magistrate's Court; after charges are brought, the suspect in custody must be sent to the Magistrate's Court without delay, who will decide on custody or bail. If an arrest is made without a warrant, the warrant shall be applied as soon as possible and presented to the arrested, who shall be handed over to the magistrate within 24 h and a copy of the indictment shall be sent to the arrested. The same holds true for civil law countries. In Germany, in accordance with Article 125 and 126 of its Criminal Procedure Law, at the request of the prosecutor or if the public prosecutor cannot be contacted and there is a delay with regard to the danger, the warrant of arrest is legally issued prior to the public prosecution by a local court judge with territorial jurisdiction or in the place of residence of the accused. After executing an arrest, the judicial police must hand over the arrested suspect to the judge who has jurisdiction over the case without delay. In Japan, the arrest warrant doctrine is practiced, and although the arrest of a flagrante delicto is an exception to the warrant doctrine, the judge can examine the arrest immediately afterwards. Custody pending indictment after the arrest is, in principle, the responsibility of the judge of the local court or summary court where the prosecutor's office is located. In particular, arrests carried out by the judicial police are reviewed by the prosecutor and brought before a judge within 72 h, who will decide accordingly on the question of custody. In the case of an arrest carried out by a prosecutor, the application for custody must be submitted to the judge within 48 h. Custody following the indictment is, in principle, decided by the court that accepts the case. In Taiwan, China, after the 1997 amendment of the Criminal Procedure Law, the judge became the sole authority to decide on custody, reflecting the absolute reservation principle of judges. As can be seen from the above, the court generally has the power to decide on the initial determination of custody and on the extension of its duration in countries and regions throughout the world.

2. Practical dilemmas facing the power and function to examine and approve arrests

The exercise of the power to examine and approve arrests by the procuratorial organs in the name of investigative supervision is controversial in theory. In addition, it also faces many problems in judicial practice, which not only constrain the functioning of the examination and approval, but also fails to effectively guarantee the legal rights of the accused.

First, the prosecutor is not neutral enough. In criminal proceedings in China, the people's procuratorate, as an organ of public prosecution, is responsible for prosecuting. The division of labor inevitably requires that it must aim at achieving penalties for crimes, especially as the amendment of the Criminal Procedure Law and the advancement in judicial reform have placed increasing emphasis on the burden of proof on the procuratorial organs. This will certainly strengthen the procuratorial organs' tendency to prosecute. In the meantime, our Constitution confers on the people's procuratorate the nature of a legal supervisory organ, but in criminal proceedings it has not been able to maintain the objective, neutral and detached status that the supervisors should have. Because it is a party to the procedure, it unavoidably has an accusatory streak. This is best demonstrated by the fact that, in judicial practice, there used to be cases where procuratorial organs deliberately concealed the evidence of the innocence of the accused from being presented at the trial. It can be seen that the prosecution function has hindered the performance of the so-called supervision function of the procuratorial organs.[38] In fact, the procuratorial organ has been reduced to a mere prosecution organ, and its activities in criminal proceedings can be fully included in the prosecution function. That is the reason why, although the procuratorial organs can play a certain role in ensuring that the custody power of the public security organs is carried out in accordance with legal procedures (such as the procedure for applying for the approval of the arrests and for applying for the extension of the custody period, etc.), due to the inseparable link between the public security organs and the procuratorial organs in their duty to prosecute, it is difficult for the procuratorial organs to get rid of the psychological influence of prosecuting crimes and they are prone to making decisions unfavorable to the suspects. They may detain those who should not be detained and grant extensions of the custody period that should not be extended. In addition, the procuratorial organs, based on the investigation centralism, rely on the evidence collection activities of the public security organs for the performance of their prosecution function, and based on their own role, they will inevitably, for utilitarian purposes, indulge the public security organs in the

[38] Chen Weidong, Liu Jihua [39].

unlawful application of custody, which is an extremely effective coercive measure for obtaining confessions.[39]

Second, the administrative operation of the power and function to examine and approve arrests. As noted above, the power and function to examine and approve arrest are adjudication power by themselves, which requires it to operate in a judicial manner. Moreover, since the power and function to examine and approve arrests are intended to supervise the investigation activity of the investigative organs, it should not exclude the participation of the accused that the supervision is intended to protect. In fact, in the experience of extraterritorial countries or regions, the exercise of the power to examine and approve arrests has been premised on the full participation of the accused. In the United States, for example, the court should organize an antecedent trial to review the decision to approve an arrest. During the antecedent trial, both the police and the defense are required to take part in the hearing, and both parties may argue on issues such as whether custody or release on bail is applicable. In France, the Criminal Procedure Law applies court hearings for decisions on custody, and the examining magistrate is obliged to inform the person under review of the preparation of his or her defense and of the choice to hire or appoint lawyers. During the trial, there must be arguments from both sides, the prosecutor and the person under the review must be heard and, if necessary, the lawyer shall also be heard. In Germany, the procedure for custody decision is more prudently regulated, with the use of interrogation by a judge. During interrogation, the judge must inform the suspects of their relevant procedural rights, give them an opportunity to present their defense and decide whether or not to continue the custody.

However, as for the judicial practice in China, despite the emphasis on the openness of the procedure in the process of amending the Criminal Procedure Law in 2012, the written and closed characteristics of the power and function to examine and approve arrests are still not fundamentally resolved. Arrests continue to be reviewed and approved in writing by the procuratorial organs without a hearing in court for the opinions of the defense. Although article 86, paragraph 2, of China's Criminal Procedure Law stipulates that, "The people's procuratorate may question witness and other litigation participants and listen to opinions of defense lawyers during the course of examining and approving the arrest. It shall hear the opinion of the defense lawyers if they have so requested." However, normally it is entirely up to the procuratorial organs to decide whether or not to question witnesses and to hear the opinion of the lawyers. In particular, the low defense rate of the lawyers and the limited involvement of the defense lawyers at the investigation stage have made it impossible to fundamentally change the nature of the administrative operation of the examination and approval of arrest in China. The administrative operation of the power and function to examine and approve arrests is inconducive to curbing illegal and improper investigations. Since the unlawful behaviors of the investigative organs are barely presented in the case file, it is difficult for the procuratorial organs to detect illegal or improper investigation activities through the examination and approval of

[39] Chen Weidong and Lu Erqi [40].

the arrests by reading the files and excluding the participation of the accused. Moreover, the supervision mode of the examination and approval of arrests is intended to safeguard the legitimate rights and interests of the accused and to curb improper investigative conducts. However, the accused, who are most qualified to speak about the infringement of their rights and interests, are often excluded from the process. Therefore, it is doubtful to what extent the rights of the accused can be safeguarded.

Lastly, it is difficult for the procuratorial organs to supervise themselves. In China, the procuratorial organs also have investigative powers in respect of duty-related crimes, and it has been questioned whether their investigative supervision departments can conduct supervision over self-investigating departments. In order to resolve the doubts and criticisms raised by the internal investigative supervision departments of the same procuratorial organs regarding the supervision of self-investigating departments through the examination and approval of arrests, in 2009, the Supreme People's Procuratorate introduced a reform in which the power to examine and approve arrests in self-investigating cases was promoted a level higher, that is, when the subordinate procuratorial organs need to arrest criminal suspects regarding self-investigating cases, the investigative supervision departments of the procuratorial organs at a level higher shall examine and approve the arrest. Nonetheless, since the superior and subordinate procuratorial organs belong to the same system and are inextricably linked in terms of their functions, it is doubtful whether the function of examining and approving arrests performed by the procuratorial organs at a level higher can serve the purpose of supervising the self-investigating departments of subordinate procuratorial organs in handling the cases. This kind of self-supervision within the procuratorial organ system has proved to be ineffective in practice. For example, six months after the implementation of the reform of promoting a level higher (March 2010), the national non-arrest rate of duty-related crimes was 6.9%, an increase of 3% compared with 3.9% in 2008, and the non-arrest rate in some regions rose to 8%[40]; from January 2010 to June 2011, the national non-arrest rate of duty-related crimes was 8.5%, an increase of 4.4% compared with that of 2009.[41] Despite a marked increase in the non-arrest rate after promoting the arrest power one level higher, the arrest rate remains very high. Obviously, a look at the judicial practice in China shows that this does not reflect the high quality of self-investigating cases, but rather reveals the inadequacy of self-supervision in the examination and approval of arrests of duty-related crimes.

The lack of neutrality of the procuratorial organs, the administrative operation of the power and function to examine and approve arrests, and the lack of self-supervision by the procuratorial organs have all objectively led to extremely serious consequences, that is, the accused has completely become the object of the prosecution, and the investigative supervision of the procuratorial organs to examine and approve arrests has also evolved into a tool for prosecuting the accused. This fundamentally reverses the role that the examination and approval of arrest should play.

[40] Wang Xinyou [41].

[41] Li Na [17].

According to statistics, between 1990 and 2009, 94.84% of the defendants of criminal offences were arrested with the approval from the procuratorial organs.[42] Such a high arrest rate is sufficient to demonstrate that the procuratorial organ's examination and approval of arrests fail to constrain the investigation and protect the legitimate rights of the accused. On the contrary, its functioning has led to serious adverse consequences for the accused. In addition to the adverse consequences and loss of benefits result from custody, which include the deprivation of personal freedom, the impairment of physical health, mental anguish, family alienation, damage to the reputation, economic loss, etc., the accused also face deprivation of education and jobs, family disintegration and enormous difficulties in reintegrating into the society. Besides, the accused may also be subjected to various forms of violence in custody.[43]

2. The reform road of the power and function to examine and approve arrest in China

Since the power and function to examine and approve arrests are essentially adjudication power, there is no doubt that the most desirable reform scheme would be to assign the power and function to examine and approve arrest to the courts, over which a consensus has been reached in the academic world. Of course, it should also be recognized that the reform of the power and function to examine and approve arrests is a structural reform that requires comprehensive arrangement and gradual progress. At present, the transfer of the power to examine and approve arrests to the courts faces some resistance against reform. Against this backdrop, a transitional mechanism should be explored to achieve the effective functioning of the examination and approval of arrests and, when the time comes in the future, such power can be transferred to the courts. Based on this, the author believes that a useful improvement scheme is to promote the judicial reform of the power and function to examine and approve arrests, and to realize its appropriate judicialization.

The so-called appropriate judicialization of the examination and approval of arrest is in fact the establishment of a mechanism for the examination and approval of arrest that operates transparently with the full participation of the party requesting the examination and approval of arrests and the accused. In fact, the appropriate judicialization of the examination and approval of arrests is to create a reasonable procedural structure. Specifically, this appropriate judicialization is made up of following elements: first, the subjective element. That is, this judiciary mechanism of examination and approval of arrests should have a relatively independent prosecutor as the final adjudicator, with the participation of both the party requesting the examination and approval and the accused. Secondly, the physical element. That is, judicial examination and approval of arrests should take place "in court". Thirdly, procedural elements. Judicial examination and approval of arrests should be consistent with the requirements of procedural justice as well as respect the right of the accused to participate in the procedure and ensure their full participation.

---

[42]Liu Jihua [43].

[43]Liu Jihua [44].

It should be said that, following the amendment of the Criminal Procedure Law in 2012, China has taken a step forward in the reform of the appropriate judicialization of the examination and approval of arrests. The 2012 Criminal Procedure Law added that the people's procuratorate may interrogate criminal suspects when examining and approving arrests, and that the criminal suspects should be interrogated in the following cases: there is a doubt as to whether they meet the conditions for arrests; the criminal suspect requests to make a statement to the procurator in person; there may be significant violations of the law in the investigation and the criminal suspect is a minor. The process of examining and approving arrests has gradually transformed from the traditional written trial to a verbal trial, and the process of approving arrests has become increasingly litigious. The Rules for Criminal Procedure of the People's Procuratorate (for Trial Implementation) further include the other two situations in which a criminal suspect must be interrogated, namely in cases of great difficulty and complexity and where the criminal suspect has limited capacity, including blind, deaf, mute or mentally ill persons. In addition, for criminal suspects who are not required to be interrogated in person, the Rules require that their views on the arrest measures must also be heard in writing, that is, Article 306 of the Rules provides that if a criminal suspect is not interrogated during the review of an arrest, a letter shall be served on the suspect for his or her opinion, which shall be completed by the suspect and then promptly recollected for review and attached to the file. If the review finds that the suspect should be interrogated, the interrogation shall be conducted promptly. The above two provisions have expanded the scope of interrogating criminal suspects in person and achieved full coverage of the hearing of criminal suspects' opinions. Meanwhile, the Criminal Procedure Law and the Rules for Criminal Procedure of the People's Procuratorate (for Trial Implementation) have required the implementation of systems, such as in which the defense lawyer shall be heard and in which witnesses and other procedural participants can be interrogated when it is necessary. With the above improvements, the reform of the procedural structure for the examination and approval of arrests procedures has taken an important step forward and is of great value in ensuring that the opinions of both parties can be heard when making decisions on the examination and approval of arrests and that arrest measures are correctly applied.

However, it should be noted that the above-mentioned reforms still have certain limitations, and that further progress should be made in the future to promote the judicial transformation of the examination and approval of arrests, so as to truly realize its judicialization. In particular:

First, a special prosecutor with independent decision-making power shall be appointed to examine and approve arrests. This is a prerequisite for ensuring that the power and function to examine and approve arrests operate independently and impartially. At present, China is advancing the reform of the accountability system for prosecutors, and an important element of the reform is the clarification of the powers and responsibilities of prosecutors. This should be used as an opportunity to change the three-tier system for examining and approving arrests and to make it clear that the power to examine and approve arrests falls within the function and power of the prosecutor that handles the case, who will decide independently and autonomously whether or not to approve the arrest and assume the responsibility for the case that this entails.

Second, a hearing procedure for examining and approving arrests shall be established. It should be said that the establishment of a hearing procedure for examining and approving arrests is a key initiative to ensure the judicialization of examination and approval of arrests. This requires that: firstly, during the process, the examination and approval of the arrest must be conducted not by unilateral interrogation, but by a hearing and only oral form of hearing, rather than written form shall be conducted; secondly, during the process, the party requesting the examination and approval of the arrest must also participate in the hearing procedure and express themselves in response to the rebuttal from the accused; and thirdly, the decision to examine and approve the arrest must be taken on the basis of a full hearing of both parties.

Third, remedy procedures for the decisions to examine and approve arrest shall be constructed. Considering the future transformation of China's examination and approval of arrest procedures, the author believes that the remedy of the procuratorial organs' decisions to examine and approve arrests can be explored, that is, when the accused refuse to accept the decision of the procuratorial organ to approve the arrest, they may appeal to the people's court, and the court will appoint a special judge to be responsible for the appeal. If necessary, the hearing procedure can also be conducted to review whether the procuratorial organ's decision to approve the arrest is legal and justified.

3.2.3 Trial Supervision Power and Function

The criminal trial supervision power and function refer to the power and responsibility of people's procuratorate to conduct legal supervision on the whether the trial activities of the people's courts comply with legal procedures, and whether their criminal judgments and verdicts are correct. The trial supervision power and function are an important composition of the legal supervision of the people's procuratorate. In China, the trial supervision power and function of the procuratorial organs are actually composed of two parts: first, the power and function of the people's procuratorate to supervise the legality of trial activities of the people's courts, that is, the supervision of trial activities; and second, the power and function of the people's procuratorate to supervise the legality of the judgments and verdicts made by the people's court, that is, adjudication supervision.[44]

For a long period of time, China supports, or at least does not object the trial supervision power and function of procuratorial organs. This is highly relevant to the inadequate legislative preparation during the drafting of China's Criminal Procedure Law. Of course, this is also the result of China's construction of its procuratorial system based on the legal supervision theory of the Soviet Union. With the continuous improvement of the modernization of China's criminal procedure and the further

[44]Chen Guangzhong ed. [45] and Cheng Rongbin ed. [46].

deepening of theoretical research, the power and function of the procuratorial organs' trial supervision are reflected on in theory. Especially after the Fourth Plenary Session of the 18th CPC Central Committee, the issue of the reform of the trial-centered procedural system was raised. The emphasis on trial-centrism inevitably involves the positioning and relationship adjustment of trial, investigation and procuratorial functions. In this context, how to transform the trial supervision power and function is also an important part of promoting the reform of trial-centered procedural system.

3.2.3.1 Overview of Trial Supervision Power and Function

In China, the adjudicative supervision power and function of the procuratorial organs are reflected in relevant provisions of Articles 217 and 243 of the Criminal Procedure Law. Article 217 provides that, "If a local People's Procuratorate at any level considers that there is some definite error in a judgment or order of the first instance made by a People's Court at the same level, it shall present a protest to the People's Court at the next higher level". Article 243, paragraph 3, stipulates that, "If the Supreme People's Courts finds some definite error in a legally effective judgment or order of a People's Court at any level, or if a People's Procuratorate at a higher Level finds some definite error in a legally effective judgment or order of a People's Court at a lower level, it shall have the power to present a protest to the People's Court at the same level against the judgment or order in accordance with the procedure for trial supervisions." According to the above-mentioned provisions, depending on the supervision objects, the adjudicative supervision powers and functions of the procuratorial organs can be divided into supervision powers and functions over adjudication that has taken effect and those over adjudication that has not taken effect. The former aims at judgements and verdicts that have not taken effect in the first instance, while the latter aims at those that have taken effect in the second instance. The adjudicative supervision power and function of the procuratorial organs are in fact the power and function to initiate remedial proceedings, and the performance of the procuratorial organs' supervision power will lead to the initiation of second instance or retrial proceedings, that is, the procuratorial organs' adjudicative supervision power is realized through the initiation of second instance and retrial procedure.

With regard to the powers and functions of the procuratorial organs to supervise trial activities, as early as 1979, Criminal Procedure Law of China expressly provides that, "The procurators appearing before the court shall have the right to submit a corrective opinion to the court if they find violations of the law in trial activities." Under this provision, the procurators appearing in court may submit a corrective opinion in court. But when the Criminal Procedure Law was amended in 1996, the supervision of trial activities by the procuratorial organs in court was highly controversial. In particular, with the introduction of the procedure model of adversary system in criminal proceedings, new demands have been made on the structure of criminal proceedings and the adjustment of the functions of prosecution and trial. The academic community is concerned that in the reform of the criminal trial methods in China, the imbalance between the prosecution and the defense has already occurred due to the strong power of the prosecution and the weak power of the defense. Under such circumstances, the trial supervision of the court by public prosecutors on behalf of the people's procuratorates will inevitably threaten the neutrality of judges and damage the already imbalanced relationship between the prosecution and the defense as well as the already skewed procedural structure. In the light of this, a trend towards weakening in-court supervision by the procuratorial organs emerged during the 1996 amendment of the Criminal Procedure Law. First, Article 169 of the 1996 Criminal Procedure Law stipulates that, "A people's procuratorate which finds any violation of the procedures prescribed by the law in trial activities of a people's court shall have the right to put forward its opinion for making correction to the people's court." This provision has changed the expression of Article 112 of the 1979 Criminal Procedure Law and weakened the procuratorial organs' power to supervise trial activities: first of all, the subject of the supervision of trial activities can only be the people's procuratorates and no longer the procurators who appear in court, which means that in-court supervision is abolished and in fact becomes a kind of ex post facto supervision. Secondly, the content of the supervision of trial activities has changed from "violations of the law" to "violation of the procedures prescribed by the law", which means that the content of the supervision of trial activities is mainly procedural violations and substantive violations are not included. Secondly, judicial interpretations promulgated after the 1996 amendments further clarify that the supervision of trial activities by the procuratorial organs can only take place after the court hearing. In accordance with Article 43 of the Provisions of the Supreme People's Court, the Supreme People's Procuratorate, the Ministry of Public Security, the Ministry of State Security, the Ministry of Justice, and the Legislative Affairs Commission of the Standing Committee of the National People's Congress on Several Issues Concerning the Implementation of the Criminal Procedure Law issued on January 19, 1998 (hereinafter referred to as the "Provisions of the Six Ministries"), the people's procuratorates shall submit corrective opinions on court hearings that violate legal procedures and submit them after the court hearings. The 1999 People's Procuratorate Criminal Procedure Rules also stipulate that if the procurators attending the court hearings find that the court trial violates legal procedures, they shall report to the chief procurator of this Court in a timely manner after the adjournment. The people's procuratorates shall submit corrective opinions on court hearings that violate procedures and submit them after the court hearings.

This post-court supervision model of trial activities established in the 1996 Criminal Procedure Law and relevant judicial interpretations were inherited by the 2012 Criminal Procedure Law and the judicial interpretation enacted afterwards. In terms of the Criminal Procedure Law itself, the 2012 Criminal Procedure Law makes no new adjustment regarding the procuratorial organs' supervision power and function of trial activities. But Article 580 of the Rules for Criminal Procedure of the People's Procuratorate (for Trial Implementation), as amended in 2012, maintains the provisions of the 1999 People's Procuratorate Criminal Procedure Rules, and specifies that the people's procuratorates shall submit corrective opinions on court hearings that violate procedures and submit them after the court hearings.

It should be noted that the procuratorial organs' trial supervision power has undergone some development in the course of the 2012 amendment of the Criminal Procedure Law. This is mainly reflected in the supervision of the procuratorial organs in death penalty review cases and in the supervision of special procedures. With regard to the former, the legal supervision of the procuratorial organs in death penalty review cases has been formally established in the Criminal Procedure Law, that is, article 240, paragraph 2 of the Criminal Procedure Law stipulates that the Supreme People's Procuratorate may submit its opinions to the Supreme People's Court when the latter reviews a case involving death penalty sentence. The Supreme People's Court shall notify the review results of the case to the Supreme People's Procuratorate. This is regarded as an extension of the procuratorial organs' trial supervision power and function.[45] With regard to the latter, the 2012 amendment of the Criminal Procedure Law adds a part on special procedures, which poses new challenges and opportunities for the procuratorial organs.[46] One of its important element is the development of the trial supervision power and function of the procuratorial organs, which is extended to the confiscation of illegal gains in the cases of the escape and deaths of the criminal suspects and the defendants, and to the compulsory medical treatment of mental patients who are not criminally responsible under the law.

With regard to the supervision by the procuratorial organs of the confiscation of illegal gains, it is not explicitly stipulated in the 2012 Criminal Procedure Law, but rather in the Rules for Criminal Procedure of the People's Procuratorate (for Trial Implementation). Article 536 of this judicial interpretation specifies, "When the people's procuratorate finds that the people's courts or judges have violated the legal criminal procedure when they try cases of confiscation of illegal gains, it shall submit to the people's courts a corrective opinion. If the people's procuratorate finds that the people's court at the same level has made an error in the first instance decision in accordance with the procedure for confiscation of illegal gains, it shall lodge a protest with the people's court at the next higher level within five days. If the Supreme People's Procuratorate or a provincial people's procuratorate considers that a lower-level people's court has made errors in the judgment made in accordance with the procedure for the confiscation of illegal gains that has taken effect, a protest shall be lodged to a people's court at the same level in accordance with the trial supervision procedure." From this we can see that the procuratorial organs' trial supervision power and function in the confiscation procedure of illegal gains include both the power to supervise trial activities and the power to supervise decisions on the confiscation of illegal gains that has taken or not taken effect.

The supervision of the procuratorial organs over compulsory medical treatment procedures is regulated by Article 289 of the Criminal Procedure Law, which states

---

[45] Although the nature of the procuratorial organs' participation in the death penalty review process is theoretically controversial, the practical departments generally regard it as a manifestation of the procuratorial organs' performance of their legal supervision function. Chen Guoqing [46] and Chen Fukuang, Deng Siqing [47].

[46] For the evaluation and analysis of the challenges and opportunities for the procuratorial organs following the 2012 amendment of the Criminal Procedure Code, please see Chen Weidong, Du Lei [48].

that people's procuratorates shall supervise the decision and implementation of compulsory medical treatment. It should be noted that, although compulsory medical treatment is rendered by way of a "decision" rather than a "judgement or verdict", it is in the nature a security measure procedure.[47] In this procedure, the judge exercises the power of trial and performs the function of judicial review; therefore, the supervision of compulsory medical treatment procedures by the procuratorial organs also falls within the scope of trial supervision. With regard to the procuratorial organs' trial supervision power and function over compulsory medical procedures, Article 550 of the Rules for Criminal Procedure of the People's Procuratorate (for Trial Implementation) makes further elaboration, "If the people's procuratorate finds that the people's courts or judges have violated the legal procedure when hearing compulsory medical treatment cases, it shall submit a corrective opinion to the people's court. If the people's procuratorate considers the decision of the people's court to compel medical treatment or its decision to reject an application for compulsory medical treatment to be inappropriate, it shall submit a written corrective opinion to the people's court within twenty days after receiving a copy of the decision." It can be seen that trial supervision of compulsory medical treatment also includes both supervision of trial activities and supervision of decisions.

3.2.3.2 Erosion of Trial Supervision Power and Function on the Structure of Criminal Procedure

In the process of advancing the procedural structure reform and creating a trial-centered procedural system, one imperative issue is the repositioning and reform of the trial supervision power and function. The reason for this is that the trial supervision power contradicts the basic concepts of the modern criminal procedural structure and trial-centralism, and has become a system barrier constraining the modernization of China's criminal procedural system. Specifically, the erosion of the trial supervision power in the criminal procedural structure is reflected in the following aspects.

1. The supervision power and function break the stability of the procedural structure

In criminal procedure, three major functions, prosecution, defense and trial, constitute the basic elements of the criminal procedural structure. Theoretically, it is generally believed that the equality of prosecution and defense and the neutrality of the trial are the prerequisites and foundations for the stability of the criminal procedural structure. The most stable structure is the isosceles triangle, with the prosecution and defense functions at the base and the trial at the apex. In this structure, the court, which exercises the power of trial, is a power subject in a position of detached neutrality between the prosecution and the defense. Its detached neutrality ensures that it is not influenced by the state's will to prosecute crimes and that it can achieve its purpose of protecting human rights.

[47] Chen Weidong [48].

However, in China's current criminal judicial system, the procuratorial organs' trial supervision power and function enable it to go beyond the mere function of prosecuting and have an advantage over the defense and the trial supervision functions. From the standpoint of prosecution and trial, the procuratorial organs can supervise and correct unlawful acts committed by court judges. Both the court activities of the judges and their adjudication acts will be subject to the supervision of the prosecutor. Supervision is different from restriction. Restriction is two-way and exercised by both parties, whereas supervision is one-way, which means supervisors unilaterally supervise those being supervised. Placing court judges under the supervision of the prosecutors of the procuratorates means that the prosecutors of the procuratorates will take precedence over court judges and become the "judge above the judge". On the one hand, the neutrality of court judges can hardly be guaranteed under the supervision of the prosecutors of the procuratorates, which leads to isosceles triangle of criminal procedure losing its balance; on the other hand, the status of the judge of the court as a judicator ceases to exist, so the isosceles triangle of criminal procedure loses a fulcrum. From the point of view of prosecution and defense, since the prosecutors of the procuratorates, in addition to their prosecution functions, also exercises trial supervision, the position of the prosecution and the defense is not equal anymore, as the prosecution can supervise the trial, while the defense can only restrain the trial. Thus, when the prosecutor exercises both prosecution function and trial supervision power and function in criminal proceedings, the isosceles triangle structure of prosecution, defense and trial that should have existed is broken.

2. The erosion of the trial supervision power and function in trial power and function, leading to a lack of separation between prosecution and trial

The separation of prosecution and trial functions is regarded as the cornerstone of the modern criminal procedure rule of law, and an important symbol of the transformation from inquisitorial criminal procedure to modern criminal procedure. According to this principle, the prosecution function and the judicial function should be performed by separate bodies; the prosecution is a prerequisite for the trial and if there is no prosecution, there is no such thing as a trial; the judge's adjudication shall be limited to the scope of the prosecutor's prosecution. The significance of the separation of the functions of prosecution and trial is to prevent the accused from becoming a complete object of criminal proceedings.

Instead, the prosecutor's role as trial supervisor is emphasized in criminal procedure, including in the second instance, retrial, death penalty review procedure, and special procedure. By emphasizing the prosecutor's role as a legal supervisor, the procuratorial organ is in fact endowed with the power and function of trial. In this regard, the procuratorial organs can not only judge whether the judges' trial activities are lawful or not, but also whether there is any error in the judges' adjudication. This makes the prosecutor, rather than the judge, the de facto final arbiter of the case. This not only makes the procuratorial organs share the power of trial that should be vested in the courts, but also creates the problem of the lack of separation between the prosecution and the trial. As some scholars have pointed out, it allows the prosecution, in addition to its prosecution function, to take precedence over the trial and to supervise the latter. The prosecution power and the adjudication power have been combined, at least to a certain extent.[48] As a result of this lack of separation of prosecution and trial functions, the inquisitorial nature of the criminal procedure has become more obvious, and the accused has gradually been reduced to the object of criminal procedures.

3. Trial supervision power and function undermine the judiciary authority and is contrary to the trial-centered spirit.

In China, in promoting the reform of the trial-centered procedural system, it is necessary to respect the status and role of the trial function and give full play to its impact on reviewing the investigation and prosecution of cases as well as its final hearing of the cases. This is decided by the adjudication feature of the power of trial and its final dispute resolution function. In order to respect the status and role of the trial function, it is certainly necessary to respect the courts and judges who perform such function. Thus, the promotion of a trial-centralism in China is essentially to establish the judicial authority of the courts.

In China, there are many ways to establish judicial authority, which are subject to various limitations, while the design of a convincing justified procedure is the most direct method to establish judicial authority.[49] An important aspect of justification of procedure is to ensure the exclusivity, independence, neutrality and finality of court decisions, which is also the prerequisite and foundation for ensuring the trial-centralism; otherwise, promoting the reform of the trial-centered procedural system is just empty talk. The practice of giving the procuratorial organs the trial supervision power and function in China has affected the establishment of the judicial authority of the courts in all the above aspects: The procuratorial authorities' trial supervision power has evolved into a power of trial, which divides and weakens the court's power of trial; the procuratorial organs' trial supervision power has put the adjudication acts and results of the judges under the legal supervision of the procuratorial organs, which affects the independence and neutrality of the court's adjudication; in particular, the trial supervision power and function can make the prosecutor a "judge above the judge" and jeopardize the finality of the judge's adjudication. These all cast a shadow over the judicial authority of the court and undermines the establishment of the trial-centered system.

3.2.3.3 Reconsideration of the Trial Supervision Power and Function

From the foregoing discussion, it is clear that the emphasis on the trial supervision power and function in criminal proceedings is not in conformity with the basic rules of criminal procedure and is not conductive to the modernization of criminal procedure. So, what should we know about the trial supervision power and function of the procuratorial organs? Is it impossible to ensure the restrictiveness and impartiality of

[48] He Weifang [49].

[49] Wang Jiancheng and Sun Yuan [50].

the power and function of trial in absence of the trial supervision power and function in criminal procedure? These are questions that need to be answered. In fact, the "trial supervision power and function" enjoyed by the procuratorial organs can be incorporated into the scope of the public prosecution power and function, and this does not undermine the impartiality of the operation of the power of trial.

1. The trial supervision power and function can be included in the scope of the public prosecution power and function

The supervision scope and method of trial supervision power and function of China's procuratorial organs can both be incorporated into the public prosecution function.

First of all, in terms of the scope of supervision of the procuratorial organs' trial supervision power and function, such supervision can be totally incorporated into the public prosecution function, which can be achieved through the operation of public prosecution function. With regard to the scope of supervision of the procuratorial organs' power and function to supervise trial activities, Article 577 of the Rules for Criminal Procedure of the People's Procuratorate (for Trial Implementation) gives specific enumeration, including violations of jurisdictional provisions, time limits for hearings and time limits for service of process.[50] In these matters, the procuratorial organ, as a participant subject affected by the judge's decision, is without doubt entitled to act in the name of a participant subject to express opinions and request remedies for trial activities that affect the fairness of the proceedings and jeopardize the interests of the procedural subject, without the need to resort to the so-called "supervision". By the same token, the supervision of judgements, verdicts and decisions by the procuratorial organs does not go beyond the scope of the public prosecution power and function. As the public prosecutor, the procuratorial organ

[50]In accordance with Article 577 of the Rules for Criminal Procedure of the People's Procuratorate (for Trial Implementation), the supervision of trial activities mainly reveals and corrects the following violations: (1) acceptance of a criminal case by a people's court in violation of jurisdictional provisions; (2) people's courts' violation of legal deadlines for hearings and service of process in court cases; (3) the composition of the court does not comply with the provisions of the law or those who violate the law fail to recuse themselves; (4) violation of legal procedures in court cases; (5) violation of the procedural rights and other legal rights of the parties to the proceedings or and other participants of the proceedings; (6) the court's decision on a procedural issue during a hearing violates the law; (7) the court of second instance decide on remand for retiral in violation of the law; (8) intentionally destroy, alter, conceal, forge, or swap evidence or other procedural materials, or settle a case on the basis of evidence that has not been investigated or cross-examined in accordance with due process of law.; (9) relevant evidence that should be investigated and collected but is not collect; (10) bend the law for personal gain, intentionally violate the facts and the law to make perverted adjudication; (11) accept or take property or other interests from the parties to the proceeding, their close relatives or a lawyer entrusted by them or others; (12) take coercive measures in violation of the law or when the legal time limit for coercive measures has expired, the person is not released, and the measures are not rescinded or changed; (13) the bail deposit that should be refunded is not refunded; (14) to seal up, seize or freeze property irrelevant to the case at hand, or to fail to terminate the sealing, seizure and freeze of property as required; (15) to embezzle, misappropriate, privately divide, replace, or use in violation of relevant provisions the property that has been sealed up, seized or frozen and its interest; (16) Other actions that violate the trial procedures prescribed by the law.

surely has the right to apply for remedy against the outcome of the public prosecution. It is not necessary to go beyond the scope of the procuratorial organs' public prosecution power and function and include such matters in the trial supervision power and function. In fact, as far as the accused are concerned, they also have the right to express their opinions and raise objections to the illegal conducts of the judges in the trial activities. All of these are regarded as part of the defense power and function of accused rather than the supervision of the court. The accused may seek remedies against the judge's trial activities as participant subjects of the procedure. Does the procuratorial organs have a greater urgency to obtain remedy than the accused to the extent that it has to resort to the name of supervision? Moreover, these elements should not be defined as trial supervision power and function from the standpoint of the equivalence between the prosecution and the defense.

Secondly, from supervision methods the procuratorial organ takes to exercise its trial supervision power, these methods also have no substantive difference in nature from the public prosecution function. In the so-called "supervision" of the courts by the procuratorial organs, the defense also enjoys statutory remedies. For example, the people's procuratorates' supervision of the judgments and verdicts of the people's courts is manifested in their protest power, that is, if the people's procuratorate considers that the judgement or verdicts of the people's court have been erroneous, they shall lodge a protest. As a matter of fact, the defendant has the same protest power against judgments and verdicts that have not taken effect at first instance (the grounds of protests naturally include various procedural violations in the court's trial activities). The legal consequences of a protest by the procuratorial organs are the same as those of an appeal by the accused, and both entail a second instance procedure, notwithstanding the question of whether or not to proceed to trial. However, there is no substantive distinction (even if the procuratorial organs' protest against the adjudication that has taken effect is merely a procedural proposal, which is similar to those in most civil law countries). Can we say that the defendant is "supervising" the court? In an adversarial trial, the protest of the procuratorial organs and the corrective opinion of court's possible erroneous procedure (which is actually an objection) are in fact a procedural right, one that has no different legal effect from that of an appeal and procedural objections by the defendant. Moreover, as for the "corrective opinion" form of supervision by the procuratorial organs, it is also essentially a public prosecution function. This is because such supervision does not have the effect of changing the acts or decisions of the court, but is merely a form of procedural advice and opinion, which is of the same nature as the right of the accused and their defender to object the court.[51]

2. Positioning trial supervision power and function as public prosecution power and function will not undermine the impartiality of the operation of the power of trial

The repositioning of the trial supervision power and function as a public prosecution power and function will not reduce its restriction on the power of trial, nor will it undermine the impartiality of the operation of the power of trial. First of all, redefining

[51]Liu Jihua [52].

the trial supervision power and function as a public prosecution power and function does not reduce the restrictions on the power of trial. In fact, such redefinition is merely a repositioning, which does not reduce the restriction on the power of trial.

Secondly, the redefinition of the trial supervision power and function as a public prosecution power and function will not diminish the effect of restricting the power of trials. As mentioned above, the trial supervision power and function of procuratorial organs is essentially a procedural supervision and does not directly alter the judges' trial acts or their adjudication results. There is no essential difference between the operation mechanism of the trial supervision power and function and the public prosecution power and function. Therefore, defining it as the public prosecution power and function is merely returning to its original purpose rather than diminishing its effectiveness. In fact, the return of the trial supervision power to the public prosecution power may be more conducive to its role as a restriction on the courts' adjudication. For example, trial supervision by the procuratorial organs in the name of legal supervisors may be resented and resisted by the courts, while it might be more acceptable for courts if they object and restrict the operation of adjudication powers as the participant subject in the proceedings. To a certain extent, this may be a better way to exercise restriction over the adjudication. Moreover, for the procuratorial organs themselves, calling themselves trial supervisors will lead to increased psychological pressure on the prosecutor, which makes it difficult for them to face the judge rationally. On the contrary, by taking off the aura of "supervisors", the procuratorial organs will be able to unburden themselves and offer more specialized opinions and recommendations from the finding of facts of the cases and application of law, which will further contribute to the exercise of restriction on the power of trial. In addition, the current trial supervision power and function, particularly with regard to trial activities, is only an ex post facto supervision, which does not timely and effectively suppress improper trial activities and cannot bring timely and effective remedy to the prosecution and the defense. Contrarily, if the procedure is designed in accordance with the public prosecution power and function and the prosecution is allowed to raise objections in time, and the problem can be solved effectively. It can be seen that rather than reducing the restriction effect of the public prosecution power on the adjudication power, the repositioning of the trial supervision power and function as the pubic prosecution power and function will increase such effect.

Lastly, in practice, the experience of extraterritorial states has shown that when the procuratorial organs do not participate in proceedings and perform public prosecution functions in the name of trial supervision, the impartiality of the adjudication is not affected. In common law countries, the public prosecutor, who investigates crimes on behalf of the public interest, is a party to the proceedings and exercises the prosecution power of the administrative power. The judge (including the jury) is the judicator in the procedure, who exercises the judicial power of the state. In criminal proceedings, the judge is the absolute authority and the public prosecutor has no right to exercise legal supervision over the judge's trial activities and, on the basis of the "prohibition against double jeopardy", the prosecutor is forbidden from lodging appeals or protests against court decisions. In civil law countries, the prosecutor is generally referred to as a "standing judge", which is the expression of the special status of the prosecutor in the doctrine of function and power. In Germany and France, while the procuratorial organ has the right to appeal or protest against the court decisions that have taken or not taken effect, this is only a procedural right of action enjoyed by one of the parties to the proceedings, and the defendant enjoys such rights as well. This right of the public prosecutor is therefore not regarded as a special legal supervision, that is, unlike China's current view of protest as a form of one-way procuratorial supervision. In France, for example, as a plaintiff, the procuratorial organ has various ways to appeal against the adjudication and decisions already made by the court, that is to lodge an appeal. However, it is also the right of other parties to the procedure, and there is no essential difference between the two. In Japan, the prosecutor (public prosecutor) is a party representing the state in criminal proceedings and have no trial supervision power enjoyed by the procuratorial organs. In both common law and civil law countries, there is no provision on the trial supervision power and function of the procuratorial organs, but meanwhile, these countries do not suffer from inadequate restriction on the power and function of trial and unfair adjudication due to the lack of procuratorial organs' trial supervision power and function.

3. The repositioning of the trial supervision power and function as public prosecution power and function helps to resolve the theoretical oddity of who supervises the supervisors

An important reason why the academics have questioned the supervision powers of the procuratorial organs is that, from the comprehensive nature of legal supervision, it is inappropriate to empower the trial prosecutor the function of legal supervision. The reason for this is that, if we consider the prosecutor in criminal proceedings as the specific subject that exercises legal supervision power, a difficult question will arise: who will supervise the supervisors? If legal supervision is exercised by the prosecutor, who is a party to the proceedings, this will lead to the prosecutor being in a "detached" position in which they are not subject to supervision and put them above the judicial power. By the very nature of legal supervision, all acts in criminal proceedings should be included in the scope of being supervised. If self-supervision is difficult to achieve, then self-supervision by the prosecutor therein will also lead to the one-sidedness of legal supervision, thus depriving legal supervision of its intended function. In practice, the trial supervision system constructed under the theory of legal supervision also fails to achieve its desired results, and the prosecutors, as legal supervisors, also break the law, handle cases in violation of the law, use their power for personal gains, use cases for money and so on. The dilution of the procuratorial organs' trial supervision power and function and the strengthening of their public prosecution restriction function can not only give better play to the role of the procuratorial organs in restricting adjudication, but also help solve the self-supervision problems that they face.

In addition, the repositioning of the trial supervision power and function as public prosecution and function power will also solve the problem of the procuratorial organs being both an athlete and a referee. It is often argued that there is a conflict between public prosecution and trial supervision powers and functions, with the former aiming to prosecute crimes and the latter to supervise the legality of the acts and results of the judge' adjudication, which is essentially a sharing of the judges' judicial power. In fact, the exercise of these two powers and functions by the prosecutors will involve them as both the athletes and referees. This leads to confusion in the prosecutor's role, which contradicts the basic laws of psychology. This inherent role conflict can be eliminated by diluting the trial supervision power of the procuratorial organs, so that they can concentrate more on performing their public prosecution power and function.

3.2.3.4 The Reform Thinking of Trial Supervision Power and Function in China

Based on the above discussion, the author believes that the overall direction of China's future trial supervision power and function should be redefining trial supervision power and function as public prosecution function, diluting its trial supervision aspect and reconstructing these trial supervision powers and functions according to the methods and characteristics of the public prosecution power and function. Specifically:

1. The power and function to supervise trial activities is transformed into a procedural objection power

As already mentioned, the supervision of trial activities has experienced a circuitous history and, ultimately, through the refinement by judicial interpretations, the power to supervise trial activities is designed to be an ex post facto supervision rather in-court supervision. The purpose of this legislative design is to diminish the adverse influence of the trial supervision of the procuratorial organs on the lawful and independent adjudication of judges and reduce the skepticism towards their power to supervise trial activities in court. However, this legislative design, which is designed to ensure the "legal supervision" status of the procuratorial organs, has some drawbacks. As we all know, trials are conducted in an immediate manner, and it is important to provide timely and effective remedies to trials that are conducted in violation of the legal procedures. Otherwise, providing remedy after the entire trial is over will not only lead to untimely remedies of rights, but will also lead to a waste of procedural resources and a decrease in the procedural efficiency due to invalid procedural acts. As a matter of fact, the above-mentioned problems can be effectively solved by transforming procuratorial organs' power and function to supervise trial activities into the pubic prosecution power and function and designing the procuratorial organs' power to restrict trials in accordance with the operation rules of the public prosecution power. For this reason, the author believes that the power and function of the procuratorial organs to supervise trial activities should be diluted or abolished and, on this basis, they should be given the procedural objection power. The prosecutor may object in court to a violation of the legal procedure, and the court shall rule on the validity of the prosecutor's objection and grant remedy. If the prosecutor is unsatisfied with the decision of the court, he or she shall also be allowed remedy by other ways, such as protests. Of course, based on the equality of the prosecution and the defense, the accused shall also be given the procedural objection power.

2. Transformation of the retrial protest power and function into a procedural power

Worldwide, with the exception of the Russian procuratorial organs, which still have the retiral protest power, the majority of national procuratorial organ's applications for retrial are similar to other applicants for retrial, which do not necessarily lead to a trial, and some states do not even grant the procuratorial organs the application power. In France, for example, in accordance with Article 623 of its Criminal Procedure Law, only the Minister of Justice, the convicted or in the event of his or her incapacity, the agent ad litem of the convicted, or in the event of the death or disappearance of the convicted, the spouse, children, or other direct lineal relatives and the legatees that receive bequests including partial bequests, or persons expressly entrusted by the convicted have the right to apply for a retrial. As for the reform of the retiral protest power of China's procuratorial organs, the author believes that it should be reconstructed in accordance with the essence of the public prosecution power and function, and clarify that the retrial application power of the procuratorial organs, like that of other subjects of proceedings, is a mere right of action. The two are equal and do not go beyond the power of trial of the trial organs. In terms of system design, on the one hand, the provision in the Criminal Procedure Law that a retrial protest by the procuratorial organs will necessarily entail retrial proceedings should be abolished, and on the other hand., the practice of setting different matters for retrial on the basis of the distinction between retrial protests and appeals by the procuratorial organs should be abolished and the matters for retrial should be set uniformly.

3. Construct the participation of prosecutors in the death penalty review process in accordance with the positioning of the public prosecution power and function

An important element of the 2012 amendment of the Criminal Procedure Law is the clarification of the participation of the procuratorial organs in the death penalty review process. According to article 240, paragraph 2, of the Criminal Procedure Law, the Supreme People's Procuratorate may submit its opinions to the Supreme People's Court when the latter reviews a case involving death penalty sentence. The Supreme People's Court shall notify the review results of the case to the Supreme People's Procuratorate. According to the brief provisions of this paragraph, the nature of the procuratorial organs' power and function to participate in the death penalty review process is ambiguous. On the one hand, the phrase that the Supreme People's Procuratorate may "submit its opinion" to the Supreme People's Court suggests that the procuratorial organs are clearly exercising procedural function here rather than procuratorial supervision function. Looking at the provisions of the Criminal Procedure Law as a whole, the supervision function of the people's procuratorates is often expressed in the phrase "to submit corrective opinions". From this point of view, the Criminal Procedure Law seems to emphasize that the procuratorial organs' power to participate in the death penalty review process is public prosecution power and function rather than procuratorial supervision power and function. On the other hand, however, the Criminal Procedure Law provides that the Supreme People's Court shall "inform" the Supreme People's Procuratorate of the results of the review of the death penalty. The word "inform" used here again clearly excludes the position of the Supreme People's Procuratorate in the death penalty review process from one of the subjects. Unlike the ambiguous legislative positioning in the Criminal Procedure Law, the Rules for Criminal Procedure of the People's Procuratorate (for Trial Implementation) clearly position the function of the procuratorial organs in death penalty review process as procuratorial supervision and systems are specifically designed in accordance with the principle of procuratorial supervision. Moreover, the supreme procuratorial organ has set up a special procuratorial office for death penalty review.[52] However, the practice of defining the functions of the procuratorial organs in the death penalty review process as procuratorial supervision function not only restricts the scope of their involvement, but also faces a challenge common to all supervision functions. In this regard, the author believes that, with the litigation development of the death penalty review process, constructing the procuratorial organs' power to participate in the death penalty review process in accordance with the public prosecution power and function should be the future trend. In particular, the procuratorial organs should enjoy at least the following procedural powers and functions in the death penalty review process: (1) the power to express their opinions, including the power to express their views orally or in writing to the Death Penalty Review Chamber of the Supreme People's Court; (2) the procedural objection power, that is, the power to object the Supreme People's Court's conducts of the trial in death penalty review process that violate the law; (3) the right to request a reconsideration of the death penalty review decisions of the Supreme People's Court, that is the Supreme People's Procuratorate may request a reconsideration of the death penalty review decisions of the Supreme People's Court, including decisions approving or disapproving the death penalty.

4. Construct the participation of the procuratorial organs in special procedures in accordance with the position of the public prosecution power and function

The participation of the procuratorial organs in special procedures here refers primarily to its role in unjudged property confiscation procedures and compulsory medical treatment procedures. The procuratorial organs' supervision in unjudged property confiscation procedure is not expressly stipulated in China's Criminal Procedure Law, but is prescribed by the Article 536 of the Rules for Criminal Procedure of the People's Procuratorate (for Trial Implementation). According to this article, the people's procuratorate performs its supervision function in the same manner in the unjudged property confiscation procedure as it does in ordinary procedures. Therefore, the above-mentioned reform thinking of the power to supervise trial activities and retiral protest power is also applicable here.

[52]Zhao Yang [53].

With regard to procuratorial supervision in the context of compulsory medical treatment, Article 289 of the Criminal Procedure Law simply stipulates that people's procuratorates shall supervise the decision and implementation of compulsory medical treatment. Article 550 of the Rules for Criminal Procedure of the People's Procuratorate (for Trial Implementation) specifies the methods that the people's procuratorates use to supervise the trials of compulsory medical treatment, that is the supervision of the trial activities and decisions of compulsory medical treatment. With regard to the former, paragraph 1 of the Article stipulates that when a people's procuratorate finds that a people's court or a judge has violated the procedural provisions of the law in hearing a case of compulsory medical treatment, it shall submit a corrective opinion to the people's court. Thus, the supervision power and function of the procuratorial organs in trial activities of compulsory medical treatment are identical to those in ordinary procedures, and its reform thinking is similar as well, that is to transform it into a procedural objection power. With regard to the latter, paragraph 2 of the article provides that if the people's procuratorate considers the decision of the people's court to compel medical treatment or its decision to reject an application for compulsory medical treatment to be inappropriate, it shall submit a written corrective opinion to the people's court within 20 days after receiving a copy of the decision. Unlike the method the procuratorial organs use to supervise adjudication in ordinary procedures, they supervise the compulsory medical treatment decision by submitting written corrective opinions, rather than protests. This form of supervision exacerbates the disadvantage that the procuratorial supervision power and function of the procuratorial organs override the adjudication power and function. In fact, in the compulsory medical treatment procedure, the procuratorial organs also perform the prosecution function, assuming the role of the prosecutor, and its function and power cannot go beyond those of the prosecutor. Therefore, the supervision power and function of the procuratorial organs over compulsory medical treatment decisions should be transformed into a procedural restriction power and function over compulsory medical treatment decisions, and the power to restrict the power of trials should be given to the procuratorial organs. Of course, it should be noted that, subject to the limitations of China's criminal procedure legislation, compulsory medical treatment is a "decision" rather than a "verdict". This determines that, under the existing legal system, the procuratorial organs can only lodge a reconsideration of the compulsory medical treatment decision, but not a protest.

3.2.4 Execution Supervision Power and Function

As the name implies, execution supervision refers to the supervision of the legality of the people's procuratorate's criminal execution activities such as execution of case adjudications, execution of coercive measures and execution of compulsory medical treatment decisions. From an overall perspective, in accordance with the provisions of China's Criminal Procedure Law and the relevant judicial interpretations, the execution supervision power and function consist of three aspects. In other words, they supervise the execution of adjudication, the execution of coercive measures and the execution of compulsory medical treatment decisions.

The execution supervision power and function are a manifestation of the people's procuratorates' function as the legal supervisory organ of the state, and is also an important part of China's procuratorial supervision. Traditionally, not enough attention has been paid to the execution supervision power and function. In recent years, a number of problems have come to light in the course of criminal execution activities, which have highlighted the lack of supervision and restriction of criminal execution power in these activities. The issue of execution supervision is receiving increasing attention. Moreover, after the amendment of the Criminal Procedure Law in 2012, there has been some development of execution supervision power and function. In judicial practice, the implementation of execution supervision is not ideal. Against this backdrop, how to theoretically understand and position the execution supervision power and function is also an important topic that we need to ponder over.

3.2.4.1 New Developments in Execution Supervision Power and Function

With the 2012 amendment of the Criminal Procedure Law as an opportunity, the execution supervision power has gained some development in both legislation and practice. At the legislative level, the legislation has adjusted the execution supervision power and function in many aspects, such as the content of the power and function and the supervision methods. First of all, the content of the execution supervision power becomes richer. In terms of the content of the power and function, the criminal procedure law and relevant judicial interpretations have included the execution supervision of death penalty, supervision of property-oriented penalty, supervision of community correction, supervision of compulsory medical treatment, simultaneous supervision of commutation of sentences and paroles, supervision of residential surveillance in designated residences, review of the necessity of custody[53] into the scope of the execution supervision power and function, whose content has been enriched.

Secondly, from the perspective of the physical places where they functions, traditionally the execution supervision power and function functioned mainly in regulated places such as prisons and detention houses, but after the amendment, the

---

[53]It is important to note that in accordance with the provisions of the Rules for Criminal Procedure of the People's Procuratorate (for Trial Implementation), the review of the necessity of custody is carried out by the "three branches of government", that is, the investigation department is responsible for the review of the necessity of custody at the investigation stage; the trial department is responsible for the review of the necessity of custody at the trial stage. If during the inspection of the regulated places, the procuratorial department of regulated places finds that there is no need for further custody, it may request the release of the suspect and the defendant or propose to alter coercive measures. However, the Supreme People's Procuratorate has changed this practice by issuing the Provisions on the Handling of Cases Involving Examination of the Necessity of Custody of People's Procuratorates (for Trial Implementation). The power to review the necessity of custody is fully delegated to the criminal execution procuratorial departments.

execution supervision power and function have been extended beyond such places to the supervision of property-oriented penalties, supervision of the execution of community correction, on-site supervision of death penalty, supervision of residential surveillance in designated residences and so on.

Third, from the perspective of the objects, the execution supervision power and function in China has developed from unitary punishment execution supervision power and function into pluralistic supervision power and function, and the execution supervision of coercive measures, compulsory medical treatment and others are all included in the scope of execution supervision.

Finally, in terms of its operation modes, China's execution supervision power and function have developed from ex post facto supervision to simultaneous supervision to a certain extent. This is mainly reflected in the supervision of temporary service of sentence outside prison, commutation of sentences and paroles. As far as the supervision of temporary service of sentence outside prison is concerned, in the past, such decision was copied to the procuratorial organs only after a decision had been made by the relevant organs, which is an ex post facto supervision. The 2012 amendment of the Criminal Procedure Law has strengthened this supervision by requiring that when prisons and detention houses request temporary service of sentence outside prison, they shall copy the request to the people's procuratorate at the same time. The people's procuratorate may submit its views in writing to the approving or deciding organs. This expands the supervision of the people's procuratorate from ex post facto supervision to interim and simultaneous supervision. In the same way that procuratorial organs supervise temporary service of sentence outside prison, the 2012 Criminal Procedure Law requires procuratorial organs to conduct interim and simultaneous supervision of the commutation of sentences and paroles. If the execution organ requests the commutation of sentences and paroles, it shall send the copy of the recommendation to people's procuratorate, who can submit written opinion to the people's court.

At the practical level, there have also been some new developments in the execution supervision power and function. With regard to the content, while re-education through labor has traditionally been an important part of the execution supervision power and function, on December 28, 2013, the Standing Committee of the National People's Congress adopted a decision on the abolition of the re-education through labor system, and such system was formally abolished. Correspondingly, supervision of re-education through labor is no longer a part of the execution supervision power and function. The disappearance of the supervision of re-education through labor means that the content of the execution supervision power and function are purified and more concentrated on the supervision of criminal execution activities. Moreover, changes in the legislation and practice of the content of the execution supervision power and function have also led to corresponding adjustments in its subject matter, namely, the main subject of the execution supervision power and function has been changed from the procuratorial department of the regulated places to the criminal execution procuratorial department. Traditionally, the execution supervision power was vested in the procuratorial department of regulated places, which is why the execution supervision and execution prosecution are also known as supervision of regulated places and prosecution of regulated places. However, with the development of the execution supervision power and function, the title of the procuratorial department of regulated places has become inappropriate and cannot scientifically and comprehensively reflect the nature and content of the criminal execution power and function.[54] Therefore, at the end of 2014, with the approval of the Office of Central Institutional Organization Commission, the "Procuratorial Office of Regulated Places" used by the Supreme People's Procuratorate for more than thirty years was officially renamed the "Criminal Execution Procuratorial Office", which means that the subject of the execution supervision power and function was changed to the "Criminal Execution Procuratorial Office".[55] In addition, it should be noted that, in order to overcome various problems associated with stationed procuratorates, the practice has also explored multiple new methods of procuratorial work, such as itinerant procuratorial inspection and procuratorial inspection patrol. Itinerant procuratorial inspection in the context of criminal execution usually refers to a form of execution supervision in which procuratorial personnel are not necessary or are not available to be stationed in regulated places, designated residences for residential surveillance or community correction activities as the number of detainees or inmates is relatively small, but they will supervise the aforementioned execution or regulatory activities from time to time. Meanwhile, the so-called procuratorial inspection patrol refers to the inspection by the procuratorial departments of regulated places of procuratorates at or above the prefecture (city) level of whether the execution of punishment and regulated activities in prisons and detention houses under the supervision of procuratorates at lower levels within their jurisdictions are lawful. At the same time, the performance of legal supervision duties by the procuratorial organs assigned and stationed to the regulated places will also be inspected. This is a form of procuratorial work first proposed by the Procuratorial Office of Regulated Places of the Supreme People' Procuratorate (now the Criminal Execution Procuratorial Office) in its Opinions on the Work of Procuratorial Tour by Procuratorial Departments of People's Procuratorates at Higher Levels.[56]

3.2.4.2 The Implementation of Execution Supervision Power and Function

In China, criminal execution is characterized by its unilateral and closed features, and has limited supervision and restriction on criminal execution. Therefore, the supervision of criminal execution activities by the procuratorial organs as the legal supervisory organs of the state has positive effect on compensating for the lack of supervision of criminal execution power. Judicial practice has also shown that the procuratorial supervision of criminal executions has played an imperative role in

[54] On the reasons for the change of the title of the Criminal Execution Procuratorial Office, see Yuan Qiguo [55].

[55] Xu Yingyan [56].

[56] Yuan Qiguo [57].

supervising and correcting illegal execution actions. For example, in 2012, procuratorial organs nationwide issued 110,656 corrective opinions on violations of the law in the execution of punishment and regulated activities, corrected 52,068 cases of improper execution of commutation of sentences, paroles and temporary service of sentence outside prison, and corrected 1,894 cases of extended custody.[57] In 2013, procuratorial organs nationwide supervised and corrected 42,873 cases of violations of the law in the execution of punishment and in regulated activities, 432 cases of extended custody, and 16,708 cases of improper execution of commutation of sentences, paroles and temporary service of sentence outside prison.[58] In 2014, procuratorial organs nationwide supervised and corrected 23,827 cases of improper execution of commutation of sentences, paroles and temporary service of sentence outside prison.[59] In 2015, for applications for commutation of sentences, paroles and temporary service of sentence outside prison that did not comply to the legal condition or procedure, the procuratorial organs nationwide supervised and corrected 20,062 such cases. It supervised and corrected 2,727 cases of inappropriate verdicts or decisions. The number of persons serving community correction sentences who were released from custody was 7,164, while the number of those who were not corrected was 3,614; for those who disappeared in serious violation of the supervision provisions or the conditions of temporary service of sentence outside prison, 1,063 persons were sentenced to imprisonment. 331 improperly filed amnesty cases and 23 improper verdicts were corrected.[60]

While overall criminal execution supervision plays an important role, from a microscopic point of view, its effectiveness is limited in practice. First, although there is a high number of cases in which the procuratorial organs have carried out procuratorial supervision on criminal executions, this does not mean that they have discovered or remedied all the illegal execution acts, and the proportion of these unknown acts is also unclear. Second, on the whole, the procuratorial organs have been relatively effective in the procuratorial supervision on criminal executions, but considering that China has more than 3,000 procuratorial organs below the municipal level, the average workload of criminal execution procuratorial supervision per procuratorial service does not appear to be significant. Thirdly, from the statistical data, the execution supervision work of the procuratorial organs fluctuates considerably. For example, 110,656 corrective opinions were issued in cases of violations of the law in punishment execution and regulated activities, while by 2013, the number dropped to 42,873, less than half the number in 2012. This shows the precariousness of the procuratorial organs' performance of its execution supervision function, which may affect their performance of such function. In practice, any failure to remedy rights constitutes skepticism to the effectiveness of the criminal execution supervision power and function. For example, following the implementation of the 2012 amendments to the Criminal Procedure Law, a lawyer was prevented from

[57] See Report on the Work of the Supreme People's Procuratorate (2013).

[58] See Report on the Work of the Supreme People's Procuratorate (2014).

[59] See Report on the Work of the Supreme People's Procuratorate (2015).

[60] See Report on the Work of the Supreme People's Procuratorate (2016).

meeting his client in a detention house, and he reported it the resident prosecutor. The resident prosecutor considered that there must be a reason for the denial of the meeting, but in view of his ignorance of the case, he advised the lawyer to contact the case officer. After some negotiation, the resident prosecutor asked the lawyer for the telephone number of the case officer, after which he informed the lawyer that the case officer did provide the detention house with formalities such as denial to the meeting, but as to whether the reasons were valid, the resident prosecutor could not reply to the lawyer because he did not know the facts of the case.[61]

From the above, it can be seen that there are limitations in the execution supervision power and function, and the supervision over illegal conducts cannot be fully achieved. From an objective point of view, in practice, the execution supervision faces problems in multiple aspects, both in practice and in the design of the system. As a result, the effect of the execution supervision function of the procuratorial organs is limited. In summary, these problems faced in system and in practice mainly include:

1. Incomprehensive execution supervision

Criminal execution supervision does not cover all criminal execution activities. This is mainly reflected in the execution supervision of property penalties and qualification penalties.[62] China's Criminal Procedure Law does not contain any special provisions on the supervision of property penalties, except for Article 265, which stipulates that the people's procuratorates shall supervise the execution of criminal punishments by executing organs to see if the execution conforms to law. The Rules for Criminal Procedure of the People's Procuratorate (for Trial Implementation), which serve as a guideline for the procuratorial organs in the conduct of criminal proceedings, clarify in Article 658 that, the people's procuratorate shall legally supervise people's court's execution activities of fine penalty, property confiscation penalty and confiscation of unlawful gains or other properties involved in the case in the execution of judgments and verdicts that have taken effect. However, there is no clarification as to how the supervision of property penalties is to be achieved, even in the law and at the level of judicial interpretations, there is no clear definition of the internal subject of execution supervision of the property penalties. As with the supervision of property penalties, Article 259 of the Criminal Procedure Law only provides that the qualification punishment shall be enforced by a public security organ and the supervision of it is not clarified. Meanwhile, Article 657 of the Rules for Criminal Procedure of the People's Procuratorate (for Trial Implementation) only stipulates a general provision on the supervision of qualification penalties and lacks the establishment of a supervision subject, supervision mechanism and so on. Due to the above-mentioned gaps in legislation, the people's procuratorates implement execution supervision based only on judicial interpretations or internal regulations, and the scope of the effectiveness is confined to the internal procuratorial organs and has no binding effect over the

[61] See Research Report on the Implementation of the New Criminal Procedure Law (First Quarter of 2013), https://www.sqxb.com/WorksNewsInfo.php?SysID=66. Accessed: August, 26, 2016.

[62] Shan Min [58].

other organs and departments, which makes the execution supervision of procuratorial organs "words without weight", and has also lowered its standard and status. In addition to the lack of legislation in China's criminal procedure law, the judicial interpretations of provisions are inattentive and the people's procuratorates have traditionally paid little emphasis on the execution supervision of property penalties, qualification penalties and other punishment execution problems outside the regulated places, which contributes to the long-term drifting of execution supervision of property penalties and qualification penalties outside the execution supervision scope of the people's procuratorates. At the national level, execution supervision of property penalties is largely absent, as is that of qualification penalties.

2. Poor execution supervision mechanisms

The poor execution supervision mechanism is reflected in many aspects: first, the inattentive or unreasonable legal provisions and the unclear or unreasonable provisions, including the subjects and procedures of execution supervision, impact the effectiveness of execution supervision. For example, Article 660 of the Rules for Criminal Procedure of the People's Procuratorate (for Trial Implementation) provides that the people's procuratorates may supervise the delivery execution activities of the people's courts, public security organs, detention houses and so on. However, there is no more detailed and feasible provisions on how to conduct the delivery execution supervision. Second, procuratorial organs have poor information channels to carry out execution supervision. The prerequisite for the procuratorial organs to implement execution supervision is to be aware of the existence of illegal execution acts or regulatory activities. However, procuratorial organs and the supervised organs belong to different departments, so the information communication mechanism between the two is not smooth, and the procuratorial organs cannot simultaneously access the information on the execution actions or regulatory activities of the execution organs. This leads to the fact that the execution supervision conducted by the procuratorial organs is mainly a passive supervision rather than an active one; moreover, execution supervision is incomprehensive as well. From an objective point of view, poor information channels and so on are an important factor in limiting the effectiveness of the execution supervision, which are also a challenge facing almost all current execution supervision work of the procuratorial organs. For example, with regard to the execution supervision of the property penalties, the procuratorial departments of regulated places do not have a complete picture of the decision of the criminal property penalties and they cannot obtain information on the execution activities of property penalties of the court's execution department. This is one important reason for the ineffectiveness of the execution supervision of the property penalties.[63] Another example is that in the execution supervision of compulsory medical treatment decisions, neither the Ankang Hospital nor the general psychiatric hospital, which acts as a representative, has formed an information communication mechanism with the procuratorial organs, and even within the procuratorial organs, such mechanism is not established. It is precisely because they are unaware of the existence of cases

[63] Shang Aiguo [62].

of compulsory medical treatment execution, some procuratorial organs did not carry out execution supervision activities on compulsory medical treatment for a long time after the 2012 Criminal Procedure Law came into force.[64] Third, the methods used by procuratorial organs for the execution supervision are not sufficiently effective. According to the provisions of China's criminal procedure law, the procuratorial organs' main approaches of execution supervision are procuratorial recommendations and the illegal act correction notice. However, whether it is a procuratorial recommendation or an illegal act correction notice, it is only procedural supervision, which does not have the effect of mandatory execution, and cannot directly change the execution acts. Whether or not execution supervision will be adopted depends entirely on the will of the execution organs. Moreover, the procuratorial organs have no protest power against the court's decision on punishment alteration execution, but only the power to issue corrective opinions. The effectiveness of the procuratorial organs' supervision of punishment alteration execution has also been impacted.[65]

3. Lack of motivation in execution supervision

The effectiveness of execution supervision depends largely on the subjective initiative of the execution supervisors. However, in China, the motivation of the execution supervisors to implement execution supervision is low. First of all, the execution supervisors are not fully aware of the importance of the execution supervision work. Traditionally, the execution supervision function has long been marginalized, and is not the core of the procuratorial supervision. Besides, there is also insufficient internal awareness of the importance of this work in procuratorial organs. Moreover, the execution supervisors do not attach much importance to this function. In particular, the execution supervisors appointed are often not the backbone of the procuratorial system, but rather procurators that have resigned from the leading post and are those "who are old, weak, ill or disabled". This directly contributes to their lack of motivation on implementing execution supervision. Second, execution supervisors are often reluctant or afraid to supervise the punishment execution. Supervision often implies a negative evaluation of the execution actions of the execution organs, which is unfavorable to the execution organs and may affect their overall performance. As a result, execution supervisors are often unwilling to supervise out of the consideration to "look after" the execution organs. Moreover, the execution organs often have some ability to restrain the procuratorial organs, especially that they can refuse to execute the procuratorial recommendation or the illegal act correction notice of the procuratorial organs. In order to preserve their relations with the execution organs or to maintain images of the procuratorial organs, execution supervisors often inactively implement execution supervision. Finally, there is a homogenization problem in stationed procuratorial works. The stationed procuratorial office is an important form of supervising the execution and regulatory activities in prisons. At present, 94.4% of regulated places in China have already implemented stationed

[64] Nantong People's Procuratorate Research Group [60].

[65] Shan Min [62].

procurators.[66] However, an important problem with stationed procurators is their homogeneity. Stationed procuratorate is generally set inside the regulated places, and the stationed procurators and the management personnel of the regulated place get along with each other day and night. In particular, the office expenses, sites, facilities, living quarters and others of the stationed procuratorates are also generally dependent on the regulated places. Therefore, the stationed procurators have a high degree of confusion in their roles and mix their supervision duties with the management duties of the management staff of the regulated places. The supervision initiative and independence are lost and, as a result, there is a problem of ineffective supervision such as stationing without residence, stationing without inspection, and superficial inspection.[67]

4. Limited execution supervision resources

Limited execution supervision resources are also an important factor affecting the effectiveness of such supervision. According to statistics, as of 2013, there were 3,118 procuratorial departments of regulated places nationwide, staffed with 13,173 procuratorial staff.[68] This means that there is an average of only 4.2 persons in each procuratorial department of the regulated places, which clearly shows the shortage in procuratorial human resources. For example, in a local procuratorial department of the regulated places, there are 47 staff members, but they are assigned with stationed procuratorial works of seven detention houses and three prisons as well as the procuratorial work of community correction in nine districts and counties. In addition, they are responsible for reviewing the necessity of custody, the execution supervision of residential surveillance in designated residences, execution supervision of property penalties, execution supervision of compulsory medical treatment decisions and other supervision works.[69] Of the country's execution procurators, 71.9% are procurators assigned to station at the regulated places, which means that there is only about one procurator implementing other supervision work. In addition to supervision in regulated places, procuratorial organs are also responsible for the execution supervision of residential surveillance in designated residences, execution supervision of property penalties, execution supervision of compulsory medical treatment decisions, execution supervision of delivery and other works. It is obviously difficult for these procurators to fulfil their statutory duties of execution supervision. Even in the case of stationed procuratorial works, the workload is enormous and the shortage of human resources is acute. At the national level, as of 2013, there were 2,686 detention houses and 666 prisons that needed to be supervised by the procuratorial departments of regulated places. On average, there are only 2.5 people in each stationed procuratorial office. In addition to their stationed procuratorial duties, these procurators are also responsible for the supervision of nearly 600,000 criminals scattering in counties, streets and communities who are on temporary service of sentence

[66]Zhou Wei [67].

[67]Li Guoan, Qi Yunshun and Chen Wei [34].

[68]Zhou Wei [69].

[69]Nantong People's Procuratorate Research Group [70].

outside prison. Moreover, the procuratorial departments of the regulated places are also responsible for the supervision of the legality of the custody of the criminal suspects and the defendant, as well as the simultaneous supervision of the commutation of sentences, paroles and medical paroles of the persons serving sentences.[70] From this, it can be that the contradiction between the heavy workload of execution supervision and the shortage of human resources for it is striking. Apart from the relatively small size of the executive supervisors, it is often the case that they are procurators who have resigned from the leading post due to their "age, weakness, illness and disability", so they have some problems in terms of work capacity and motivation, which aggravates the problem of the inadequate human resources for execution supervision.

3.2.4.3 Reflection on the Role of the Procuratorial Organs in the Criminal Execution Supervision

In view of the various problems in China's execution supervision, most theories advocate that in the existing execution supervision model, the information construction, the information obtaining capacity of the execution supervision department and so on shall be strengthened. In practice, reform has largely been carried out along these lines of work. For example, the procuratorial organs strengthen the construction of "two networks and one line", that is strengthening the construction of surveillance network between the procuratorial offices of the procuratorial organs stationed in regulated places and the detention houses, the information system network, and a branch network linking the stationed procuratorial office to the private network of the procuratorial system. While this resource-investment response model may be effective, it is worth reflecting on whether it can fundamentally address the problems of execution supervision.[71]

China's execution supervision model is based on a system of allocating the execution power with Chinese characteristics. In China, the power to execute punishment is vested in the courts, public security organs, prisons, detention houses, juvenile correctional institutions, community correction institutions, and other institutions. Among them, the courts are responsible for the execution of death penalties (to be executed immediately), fines and the confiscation of property; the public security organs are responsible for control, detention, deprivation of political right, deportation and other penalties; prisons are responsible for the execution of death sentences

[70]Zhou Wei [71].

[71]It needs to be noted that the supervision of the execution of criminal coercive measures reflects the relationship between investigation and prosecution, and the investigation and prosecution integration reform discussed above is also applicable to the reform of the execution supervision of coercive measures, while the function of reviewing the necessity of custody essentially belongs to the function of judicial remedy performed by the procuratorial organs, which should be judicially reformed in accordance with judicial laws. Therefore, the reflection on the role of the procuratorial organs in criminal execution, discussed below, is mainly concerned with the role of the procuratorial organs in the execution of penalties, including the enforcement of decisions on compulsory medical treatment.

with a two-year suspension of sentence, life imprisonment and fixed-term imprisonment; detention houses are entrusted with the execution of the remaining three months of the sentence; community correction institutions are responsible for the execution of community corrections. Under this system of allocation of execution powers, the procuratorial organs, which perform the function of public prosecution, have neither the power to deliver the execution of punishment nor the power to request the alteration of punishment. The punishment delivery execution power is performed by the court and the punishment alteration power is exercised by the execution organs. From this it can be seen that apart from the execution supervision power, the procuratorial organs enjoy no substantive participation power in the entire process of execution supervision. This also determines that the execution carried out by the procuratorial organs can only be a form of external supervision, rather than an internal supervision based on the functional command-and-supervision relationship.

Under the external execution supervision model, the procuratorial organs can only play the role of an external supervisor. In the absence of a functional command and supervision relationship, it is difficult for procuratorial organs to exercise control over execution organs. On the one hand, the procuratorial organs do not have control over the initiation of all the execution activities or punishment alterations, and they cannot obtain information about such activities or alterations. The ex post facto, untimely, and incomprehensive nature of supervision is inevitable. On the other hand, the functions of procuratorial supervision and the punishment execution are two independent functions, and the procuratorial organs and the execution organs are not in a command-and-being-commended relationship, which determines that even procuratorial organs exercise execution supervision, it will be difficult for them to order the execution organs to follow their supervision, so the effectiveness of execution supervision will be greatly diminished. Moreover, since the procuratorial organs do not substantively participate in the punishment execution, they do not enjoy the central power in the execution or alteration of punishment. Their supervision function, which has a very high legal status, is not a crucial one in the punishment execution, but a marginal power. As a marginal role in the punishment execution, in order to protect their own image and maintain relations with the execution organs, the procuratorial organs' involvement in the execution process is extremely limited, so is their effectiveness.

It should be said that it is the deviated positioning of the role of the procuratorial organs that fundamentally affects the effectiveness of the execution supervision. In the external execution supervision mode, although the "two networks and one line" information construction and other investments can strengthen the procuratorial organs' ability to collect information, the reform approach faces a number of difficulties. On the one hand, the cost of such reform method is huge. The network construction and maintenance are relatively expensive, especially when some modern scientific and technological equipment needs to be introduced, and the investment is enormous. On the other hand, even with such a large investment, it is still unknown whether a better supervision effect can be achieved. The introduction of modern equipment can indeed ensure real-time supervision and whole supervision, but in terms of judicial practice in China, this kind of procuratorial informatization construction is to a large extent only an "image project", which has not brought an ideal effect. The reason for this is, in fact, the role played by the procuratorial organs in the execution process. It is because the procuratorial organs do not share substantive punishment execution power in the process of execution, and they do not have a functional command-and-supervise relationship with the execution organs, that their supervision opinions are not respected or adopted by the execution organs. Due to such functions and roles, execution supervisors are less motivated to carry out execution supervision, have a low sense of responsibility, and in many cases, they are reluctance to supervise, "turning a blind eye" and "playing the good guy". Of course, both the academic and practical worlds have recognized the lack of effectiveness of the execution supervision methods. Therefore, it is recommended to make the execution supervision opinions of the procuratorial organs compulsory by the law. However, under current external execution supervision model, making the execution supervision opinions of the procuratorial organs compulsory by law contradicts the positioning that procuratorial supervision can only be an external procedural supervision. In fact, the logic behind this idea is to change the role of the procuratorial organs in criminal execution. As can be seen from the above, in order to tackle the various problems faced in China's execution supervision, the fundamental solution is to alter the role of the procuratorial organs in criminal execution.

Theoretically speaking, the procuratorial organs should have the power to control the execution of punishment.[72] This is determined by the link between criminal prosecution activities and criminal execution activities. Procuratorial organs perform prosecution function in criminal proceedings, the purpose of which is to realize the power of punishment of the state, and the achievement of such purpose is dependent on the execution of punishment. If the procuratorial organs are unable to control the punishment execution power, they will inevitably create an artificial separation between the prosecution function and punishment execution function, which will be inconducive to the ultimate realization of prosecution function. Moreover, criminal execution activities are, in a certain sense, an extension of criminal prosecution activities. Criminal execution activities are the result of the procuratorial organs' criminal prosecution activities. In this sense, the criminal execution power constitutes a backward extension of the criminal prosecution power.

From the experience of civil law countries, most of them also give the procuratorial organs the power to command criminal execution activities. In Germany, Article 451 of the German Criminal Procedure Law (Execution Organs) provides that, "The execution of punishment shall be carried out by the procuratorate as the execution organ on the basis of a certified copy of the main text of the judgment issued by the clerk of the Secretariat, accompanied by a certificate of executability, ...". Under German law, the execution officer of the punishment is the procuratorial organ, while prisons and other judicial administrative organs play as assisting organs to the procuratorial organs' exercise of execution power. In France, Article 707 of the Criminal Procedure Law stipulates that, "After the adjudication becomes final, it

[72] Zhang Zhihui [73].

shall be enforced on the application of the procuratorate"; Article 709 states, "The procurator and the Chief Procurator of the Republic have the right to directly request the assistance of the public power to ensure the execution of the judgment." In Japan, Article 472 of the Criminal Procedure Law stipulates, "The execution of the adjudication shall be commanded by the prosecutor of the procuratorial office corresponding to the court that issues it. However, it does not include occasions stipulated in the proviso to article 70, paragraph 1, and the proviso to article 108, paragraph 1, and other occasions when, by the nature, a court or judge shall command. The prosecutor of the procuratorial office corresponding to the appellate court shall command the adjudication of the appeal or the execution of the adjudication of the lower-level court as a result of the withdrawal of the appeal. However, when the procedures are recorded in a lower court or in a procuratorial office corresponding to that court, the prosecutor of the procuratorial office corresponding to that court shall command." Moreover, in Japan, the prosecutor also has the power to suspend the punishment execution. Article 482 of the Japanese Criminal Procedure Law states, "In the case of a person sentenced to penal servitude, imprisonment or detention, if one of the following circumstances applies, the punishment execution can be suspended according to the command of the prosecutor of the procuratorial office corresponding to the court that pronounced the punishment or the prosecutor of the place of jurisdiction of the current location of the person subject to the punishment..." This execution system arrangement in civil law countries helps prosecutors to directly "command" rather than merely "supervise" the execution, and has increased the control of the procuratorial organs over criminal execution activities. The relationship of "execution government office" and "assisting organ" between the procuratorial organs and other organs such as prisons clarifies the power relationship between them in criminal execution activities. It helps to solve the problems of "failure to command" and "ineffective mobilization" of the procuratorial organs.[73]

As can be seen from the above, China's punishment execution system, in which the courts, public security organs and prisons control the punishment execution, excludes the substantive participation of procuratorial organs as criminal prosecution organs in the criminal execution activities, artificially severing the link between criminal prosecution activities and criminal execution activities. This does not comply with the rules of criminal procedure, nor does it enable the procuratorial organs to effectively command and supervise criminal execution activities. In the future, the role of the procuratorial organs in criminal execution should be transformed so that they are positioned as command supervisors of criminal execution activities. And the reform of China's criminal execution supervision system should be promoted on this basis.

[73]Wan Yi [74].

3.2.4.4 The Reform of Execution Supervision Power and Function in China

The above mainly discusses the role of the procuratorial organs in the punishment execution and the execution of compulsory medical treatment decisions. From long term, radical changes in these problems of execution supervision require a redefinition of the role of the procuratorial organs from an external supervisor to an internal command supervisor. Specifically, the legal status of the procuratorial organs as the command supervisor of the punishment execution and the execution of compulsory medical treatment decisions should first be clarified. The procuratorial organs should be defined as the real subjects of the punishment execution and the execution of compulsory medical decisions, while institutions such as prisons, public security organs and detention houses should be defined as the assisting subjects to procuratorial organs' exercise of execution power, and they are subject to the unified command and supervision of the procuratorial organs. It needs to be noted that the command and supervision here reflect only a functional relationship, rather than organizational, personnel and other aspects of subordination or management relations. Of course, there are exceptions to the procuratorial organs' role as the execution command supervisor, that is, when the nature determines that the execution shall be commanded and supervised by the judge or court, or in other cases, as otherwise provided by law, the judge or court shall command the execution.

Secondly, a delivery execution system should be established, and the procuratorial organs should be endowed with the delivery execution power. Delivery execution is the starting point of criminal execution activities and a very important link in the control of criminal execution activities by the procuratorial organs. At present, there is no formal delivery execution system in China's criminal execution system. The execution is often initiated by the court's delivery and there is no space for the participation of the procuratorial organs. Such system design is not scientific, does not conform to the rules of criminal execution activities and is inconducive to achieving the supervision and restriction effect of the procuratorial organs in criminal execution activities. To this end, a delivery execution system should be established in China and the delivery execution power should be vested in the procuratorial organs. The system could be designed in such a way that the punishment shall be delivered and executed by the procuratorial organs, which, in turn, shall prepare a letter of command and attach an adjudication document.

Lastly, the procuratorial organ should be given the power to request the alteration of punishment. In China, in accordance with the provisions of the Criminal Procedure Law, temporary service of sentence outside prison shall be decided by the court or approved by the prison administration organs at the provincial level or above or by the public security organs at the municipal level (with districts) or above; in the case of commutation of sentences or paroles, the execution organ submits a proposal and the court rules on it. It can be seen that the people's procuratorates do not have a substantive role to play in the process of deciding on temporary service of sentence outside prison or approving the commutation of sentences or paroles. The law stipulates that the procuratorial organs enjoy supervision power, and in the course of the

2012 amendment of the Criminal Procedure Law, emphasis was placed on the simultaneous supervision. However, as mentioned above, such supervision is essentially an external supervision, the effectiveness of which cannot be guaranteed. And in practice, the simultaneous supervision stipulated in law is subject to the smoothness of the coordination mechanism between procuratorates and courts, prison administration organs and public security organs, and many other factors. Therefore, it is difficult to implement simultaneous supervision. In this regard, we should learn from the experience and practices of civil law countries and give the procuratorial organs the power to request the alteration of punishment. Specifically, the procuratorial organs should submit an application for temporary service of sentence outside prison before the delivery execution; after the delivery execution, the procuratorial organs review the opinion of temporary service of sentence outside prison proposed by the prisons and the detention houses. If they believe that such request shall be granted, they shall submit the application for it to the relevant organs. In the case of commutation of sentences or paroles, the prison where the punishment is executed shall, in the light of the specific circumstances arising during the execution, submit an opinion on the commutation of sentence or parole. The procuratorial organ will review the opinion and if it finds that the conditions are met, they shall submit an application to the court for commutation of sentence or parole.

As for the supervision of the execution of criminal coercive measures, as mentioned above, it reflects the relationship between the investigative and procuratorial powers. In China, supervision of the execution of criminal coercive measures is incomprehensive and is mostly limited to detention and supervision of post-arrest custody. After the 2012 amendment of the Criminal Procedure Law, execution supervision of residential surveillance in designated residences was added, but supervision of the execution of other coercive measures was not included in the scope of execution supervision. In addition, procuratorial organs are also faced with the aforementioned problems of inadequate supervision mechanisms and ineffective supervision. The root cause of these problems lies in the unscientific positioning of the relationship between investigative and procuratorial powers, the solution to which is to conduct investigation and prosecution integration reform, whereby the procuratorial organs command the investigative organs in their investigation activities, including the supervision of the execution of coercive measures.

In the case of the review of the necessity of custody, reform should be based on the nature of this power. From the worldwide perspective, the application of coercive measures that restrict personal freedom, including the subsequent review of custody, is a matter of judicial reserve and is generally reviewed and judged by the courts. In other words, the procuratorial organs in China have in fact assumed part of the judicial remedy function. Although in practice the procuratorial organs are the ones to review the necessity of custody, such review should be based on the judicial nature of the power to review the necessity of custody. Therefore, the main future development of the power to review the necessity of custody is to strengthen its judicial nature and to transform it into a judicial power.

It should be pointed out that, looking at the system construction of China's execution supervision power, it can be found that such power reflects mainly the proactive action of public power organs, neglecting the participation of the person subject to the criminal execution, who has limited effect in it. And there is also insufficient effective means of remedy in the case of criminal execution in violation of the law. The persons who are subject to criminal execution are the relative persons of the criminal execution acts so they have a better knowledge of the existence of improper or illegal criminal execution acts and have a stronger demand for the remedy of right. Therefore, they should be the core force to supervise and restrain the criminal execution power. The current practice in China of focusing on the dominant execution supervision power of the public power organs is inconducive to the supervision and restriction of criminal execution, and even less useful for the remedy of civil rights. Execution supervision is aimed at correcting violations of the law and safeguarding the legal rights of the persons subject to execution. How can a criminal execution supervision that has no participation from the persons subject to the criminal execution and fails to provide them with a remedy of their rights can state that it is protecting their legal rights? In this regard, the author believes that in the future, one of the development direction of China's criminal execution supervision is to strengthen the initiative of the persons subject to criminal execution in the process of execution supervision and construct a remedy mechanism for their legal rights. In this respect, the complaint handling mechanism for detainees, which has been explored on a pilot basis in judicial practice,[74] may be a useful path to reform. Its aim is to provide persons subject to criminal execution with an unobstructed mechanism for the remedy of rights.[75] Of course, this mechanism of remedy of right should be extended to all areas of criminal execution and should not be limited to criminal execution activities in detention houses. Moreover, in the future, the courts' judicial adjudication shall play a positive role in remedying the rights and interests of the persons subject to criminal execution and a judicial remedy system for them should be constructed.

In addition, the current criminal execution supervision in China is a form of supervision and restriction between the public power organs of the state. There are some unsolvable drawbacks in this model of supervision and restriction, namely, sufficient cooperation but insufficient supervision among the public power organs, that is homogenization and other problems. It is therefore necessary to explore other forms of supervision and restriction in order to compensate for the insufficient supervision and restriction of the public power organs. In this regard, the participation of citizens shall be emphasized. Public participation in the supervision of criminal execution activities is an important step in overcoming these challenges. In this respect, the author has explored in practice an inspection patrol system in places of custody, in

---

[74]The complaint handling mechanism for detainees is a pilot reform that the author and judicial practice departments have jointly propelled. Since the pilot project was launched in August 2010 in Wuhu City, it has achieved desirable pilot results and has been gradually promoted to other regions.

[75]For a study of the complaint handling mechanism for detainees, see Chen Weidong and Sun Hao [76].

which the public inspects the places of custody and offers corrective recommendations and ideal pilot results have been achieved.[76] In the future, it is necessary to refine and improve this system and extend it to other execution areas such as prisons.

3.2.5 *Methods of Procuratorial Supervision*

The procuratorial supervision method, that is, the procuratorial supervision approach, refer to the specific method or approach by which the procuratorial supervision power can be applied to the object being supervised. The procuratorial supervision method is the specific guarantee that ensures the exercise of the legal supervision power and the completion of legal supervision tasks.[77] It determines the effect of procuratorial supervision to a certain extent. It can be seen, the procuratorial supervision method in the operation of the procuratorial supervision power and function has a very important status, and the study of such method is of great importance to strengthen the prosecutorial supervision function.

3.2.5.1 Specific Methods of Procuratorial Supervision

Depending on the different objects and contents of supervision, the procuratorial supervision methods vary. In China, procuratorial supervision is usually divided into case-filing supervision, investigative supervision, trial supervision and execution supervision. Procuratorial supervision in these different supervision functions is explored in turn below.

1. Methods of case-filing supervision

To sum up, in general, the methods for case-filing supervision of the public security organs can be divided into five levels of supervision, and these five levels have a progressive relationship. Specifically: (1) The first level is to require the public security organ to explain the reasons for not filing a case or filing a case. For the supervision of cases that should be filed but are not filed, according to Article 111 of the Criminal Procedure Law, where the people's procuratorate considers that a case should be filed for investigation by a public security organ but the latter has not done so, or where a victim considers that a case should be filed for investigation by a public security organ but the latter has not done so and the victim has brought the matter to a People's Procuratorate, the People's Procuratorate shall request the public security organ to state the reason for not filing the case. With regard to the supervision of cases that should not have been filed but are filed, article 555, paragraph 2, of the Rules for Criminal Procedure of the People's Procuratorate (for Trial Implementation) stipulates that, where there is evidence that a public security organ may have illegally

---

[76] For inspection patrol system in places of custody, see Chen Weidong [77].

[77] Wang Shouan [78].

used criminal means to intervene in a civil or economic dispute, or that it may have filed the case to take revenge, extort money or seek other unlawful benefits, if it has not yet been approved for arrest or transferred for review and prosecution, the public security organ shall be required, with the approval from the Chief Procurator, to state in writing the reasons for filing the case. The first level of supervision is in fact mainly an inquiring approach, the purpose of which is to inquire and grasp the basis on which the public security organs do not file a case or file a case. (2) The second level is to notify the public security organs to file or withdraw the case. In accordance with the provisions of Article 111 of the Criminal Procedure Law and article 558, paragraph 1, of the Rules for Criminal Procedure of the People's Procuratorate (for Trial Implementation), after the review of the reasons for not filing a case or filing a case, the procuratorial authorities are required to notify the public security organs to file a case or withdraw a case if they find that the reasons are invalid. Generally speaking, the public security organs should file or withdraw a case after receiving the notice to file or withdraw the case. If the public security organs accept the supervision, there will not be a third level of supervision. (3) The third level is to issue an illegal act correction notice. According to article 560, paragraph 2, of the Rules for Criminal Procedure of the People's Procuratorate (for Trial Implementation), if the public security organs do not file a case or lodge a reconsideration or withdraw the case after the review within 15 days of receiving the notice to file a case or to withdraw a case, the people's procuratorate shall issue an illegal act correction notice. (4) The law does not specify the specific method of the fourth-level case-filing supervision, but only stipulates that if public security organ still fails to correct the violation after the procuratorate issues the illegal act correction notice, the case shall be reported to the people's procuratorate at the next higher level for consultation and should be handled by the public security organ at the same level. (5) The fifth-level supervision is the issuance of a reminder for case-filing supervision case. According to article 560, paragraph 3 of the Rules for Criminal Procedure of the People's Procuratorate (for Trial Implementation), if the investigation is not completed within three months after the public security organ has filed a case, the people's procuratorate may issue a reminder to the public security organ for the case-filing supervision case, and the public security organs are required to provide timely feedback to the people's procuratorates on the progress of their investigations. Such case-filing supervision is directed at cases in which the public security organs accept case-filing supervision but do not take further investigation action.

In addition, there is a special situation in case-filing supervision, that is, the case-filing supervision of major crimes committed by the state personnel under the jurisdiction of public security organs. In such cases, if the public security organ does not file a case after the procuratorial organ has notified it, the procuratorial organ may, with the approval of the procuratorate at or above the provincial level, directly file the case for investigation.

As for the initiation of the confiscation of illegal gains and compulsory medical treatment procedure, according to Articles 530 and 545 of the Rules for Criminal Procedure of the People's Procuratorate (for Trial Implementation), the case-filing supervision method is relatively simple and is mainly directed at cases in which a special procedure should be initiated but is not, and there are two levels of supervision: first, the public security organ is required to state in writing the reasons for not initiating the special procedure; second, on this basis, if the reasons for not initiating the special procedure by the public security organ are considered invalid, the public security organ should be notified to initiate the procedure.

Of course, the case filing supervision by the procuratorial organs is directed not only at the public security organs, but also at the internal self-investigating departments of the procuratorial organs. According to Article 563 of the Rules for Criminal Procedure of the People's Procuratorate (for Trial Implementation), the supervision of the internal case-filing activities of the procuratorial organs is different from that of the public security organs. In general, they can only recommend the investigating department to file the case for investigation or withdraw the case; if the recommendation is not accepted, it shall be reported to the Chief Procurator for decision.

2. Methods of investigation supervision

With regard to the specific methods of investigative supervision, article 13, paragraph 2, of the Organic Law of the People's Procuratorates only specifies that if the people's procuratorate finds investigation activities of the public security organs are in violation of the law, it shall notify the public security organs to correct the violation. Article 566 of the Rules for Criminal Procedure of the People's Procuratorate (for Trial Implementation) contains more detailed provisions, which include the following: (1) oral corrective opinions. This form of investigation supervision is mainly applicable in cases of minor illegal investigation. Usually oral corrective opinion is proposed by the procurators to the investigators or the head of the public security organs, and if necessary, it can be proposed by the head of the department. (2) Issuance of an illegal act correction notice. This type of supervision applies to serious violations of the law, and shall be reported to the Chief Procurator for approval. (3) Transfer to the relevant departments for criminal responsibility. This kind of supervision applies to the situation that may constitute a crime. In addition, in the investigation supervision, there is a special type of supervision, namely, supervising cases in which the public security organs request the approval of arrests by applying the form of examination and approval of arrests.

For the supervision of self-investigating cases of procuratorial organs, according to Article 573 of the Rules for Criminal Procedure of the People's Procuratorate (for Trial Implementation), for the less serious illegal investigation, the investigation supervision department or the public prosecution department can directly submit corrective opinions to the investigation department of this court; for the more serious cases or cases in which criminal responsibility needs to be pursued, it should be reported to the Chief Procurator for decision; if higher-level procuratorates find violations in the investigation of lower-level procuratorates, the latter should be notified to correct.

3. Methods of trial supervision

As mentioned earlier, trial supervision includes supervision of trial activities and supervision of court judgements, verdicts and their decisions. The supervision methods vary in accordance with supervision contents. Specifically: (1) supervision method of court trial activities. According to Article 203 of the Criminal Procedure Law and Article 580 of the Rules for Criminal Procedure of the People's Procuratorate (for Trial Implementation), if a People's Procuratorate discovers that in handling a case a People's Court has violated the litigation procedure prescribed by law, it shall have the power to suggest to the People's Court that it should set it right.. With regard to the specific supervision methods of trial activities, in accordance with Article 581 of the Rules for Criminal Procedure of the People's Procuratorate (for Trial Implementation), it should be conducted in the way in which investigation acts are supervised, that is to say, the supervision of trial activities includes the oral corrective opinions, issuance of an illegal act correction notice, transfer to the relevant departments for criminal responsibility and so on. In special criminal proceedings, the procuratorial organs supervise trial activities in the same way as in ordinary proceedings. According to article 536, paragraph 1, and article 550, paragraph 1, of the Rules for Criminal Procedure of the People's Procuratorate (for Trial Implementation), if the procuratorial organs find people's courts or judges have violated procedures prescribed by the law in cases of confiscation of illegal gains or compulsory medical treatment, corrective opinions shall be submitted to the people's court. (2) Supervision of court judgements, verdicts and their decisions. The procuratorial organs supervise court judgements, verdicts and decisions primarily by protests. Protest is used as a form of supervision in second instance and retrial cases, as well as in cases of confiscation of illegal gains. In addition to protests, there is also a special form of adjudication supervision in compulsory medical treatment procedures, namely, the submission of a written corrective opinion. In other words, according to article 550, paragraph 2, of the Rules for Criminal Procedure of the People's Procuratorate (for Trial Implementation), if the people's procuratorate considers the decision of the people's court to compel medical treatment or its decision to reject an application for compulsory medical treatment to be inappropriate, it shall submit a written corrective opinion to the people's court within 20 days after receiving a copy of the decision.

4. Methods of execution supervision

In execution supervision, the supervision methods include general supervision and special supervision. General supervision is mainly the submission of corrective opinions. This is also the most frequent supervision methods applied in the whole process of execution supervision. Corrective opinions include oral and written corrective opinions, of which the former is aimed at minor violations of the law, while the latter at serious violations of the law that do not constitute crimes. For example, under Article 646 of the Rules for Criminal Procedure of the People's Procuratorate (for Trial Implementation), in cases of temporary service of sentence outside prison decisions, if the procuratorial organs consider that the temporary service of sentence outside prison is inappropriate after the review, they may submit a written corrective opinion to the organ which decides or approves the temporary service of sentence outside prison. Because of the complexity of the content of execution supervision, there are some special forms of supervision for different types of execution activities. For example, according to article 619 of the Rules for Criminal Procedure of the People's Procuratorate (for Trial Implementation), for those that meet the conditions of the review of the necessity of custody, the procuratorial organs may submit a written recommendation to the relevant authorities for release or for the alteration of the coercive measures; Article 637 provides that, when the death penalty is carried out, the procurators supervising the execution on the spot shall make a recommendation to the court to immediately suspend the execution of death penalty if legal circumstances are met; Article 644 stipulates that, upon receipt of a copy of the written opinion of the prison or detention houses on temporary service of sentence outside prison, if legal conditions are not met or the legal procedure is violated, the procuratorial organ may submit a written procuratorial opinion to the deciding or approving organ; Article 639 prescribes that if the criminal intentionally commits a crime during the suspension period of the execution of the death penalty, and the court still gives the criminal a commutation of sentence after the procuratorial organ prosecutes, the procuratorial organ may lodge a protest with the court; Article 651 stipulates that, in cases of commutation of sentences or paroles, the procuratorial organ shall send representatives in court to present opinions. This is another method the procuratorial organs use to supervise execution activities.

To summarize the above-mentioned methods the procuratorial organs apply for case-filing supervision, investigation supervision, trial supervision, and execution supervision, general methods of procuratorial organs implementing supervision include: oral corrective opinions, written corrective advice, protests, and pursing criminal responsibility for crimes. The special methods of supervision by the procuratorial organs include: stating the reasons for filing a case or not filing a case (initiating special procedures), notification to file a case or withdraw a case, reminder for case-filing supervision cases, examination and approval of arrests, written recommendation for release or alteration of coercive measures, recommendation of immediate suspension of the execution of death penalties, and issuance of written procuratorial opinions, etc.

It should also be noted that, in addition to the above-mentioned supervision methods prescribed in the Organic Law of the People's Procuratorates, the Criminal Procedure Law and judicial interpretations, in judicial practice, a number of other supervision methods has been explored.[78] These methods include the inquiry of judicial staff malfeasance and proposed replacement of handling persons established by Central Document No.21. Meanwhile, Several Opinions on Further Utilizing the Role of NPC Deputies and Strengthening the System Construction of NPC Standing Committee ([2005] Zhongfa No. 9) of the Leading Party Member's Group

[78]Zhang Buhong [5].

of Standing Committee of the National People's Congress stipulates that Supreme People's Procuratorate reports to the Standing Committee of the National People's Congress for retrial by the Supreme People's Court. In addition, the Regulations of the People's Procuratorate on Procuratorial Recommendations (for Trial Implementation), issued by the Supreme People's Procuratorate in 2009, prescribe the supervision method of procuratorial recommendation. When procuratorial recommendations are applied to law enforcement and judicial organs, they are recommendations to the relevant organs to resolve issues such as tendencies and emerging problems in law enforcement and judicial activities, rather than a recommendation for individual cases.[79]

3.2.5.2 Effectiveness of Procuratorial Supervision Methods

As for the effectiveness of procuratorial supervision methods in China, it can be investigated from different angles:

From the effect and content of procuratorial supervision, the procuratorial supervision methods in China are effective in the initiation of procedures, permission of specific procedural acts, and recommendation on whether to take/not take a specific act, etc. By the effect of the initiation of procedures, it means that procuratorial supervision can trigger the initiation of procedures. For example, a protest by the procuratorial organs can lead to the initiation of second instance or retrial proceedings. Another example is that in cases of commutation of sentences or paroles, according to Article 263 of the Criminal Procedure Law, if a People's Procuratorate considers that the order on commutation of sentence or on parole made by a People's Court is improper, it shall submit a written recommendation to the People's Court for correction. The People's Court shall form a new collegial panel to handle the case and render a final order. This means that the corrective opinions submitted by the procuratorial organs have the effect of initiating proceedings for commutation of sentences or paroles. Furthermore, under the provisions of Article 256 of the Criminal Procedure Law, in the course of the temporary service, where the people's procuratorate deems temporary service of sentence outside prison as inappropriate, it shall send its written opinion to the organ that has decided or approved the temporary service of sentence outside the prison. Upon receipt of the written opinions of the people's procuratorate, the said organ shall re-examine the decision. Here, the written opinion of the procuratorial organs also have the effect of initiating the re-examination procedure of the temporary service of sentence outside prison. The effect of permission of specific procedural acts means that the operation of the procuratorial supervision power and function results in permitting or not permitting a specific procedural act by the relevant organ. This mainly refers to that in situations where examination and approval of arrests are needed, the procuratorial organs' approval or disapproval of arrests is an important basis on which the public security organs can take arrest actions. As for the effect of recommendation on whether to take/not take a specific

[79]Zhu Xiaoqing and Zhang Zhihui [80].

act, it refers to the procuratorial supervision of the legality of case-filing, investigation, trial and execution activities, and proposal of opinions on correcting illegal conducts of relevant organs. Meanwhile, according to the circumstance of the cases, it also offers recommendations towards the tendencies and emerging problems in judicial practices as well as recommends and urges relevant organs to take or not to take a certain act. For example, for illegal investigation acts during the investigation, oral or written corrective opinions can be issued to urge the investigative organs to take or not to take certain actions. It should be noted here that the corrective opinions in the case of commutation of sentences, paroles and temporary service of sentence outside prison all have the effect to initiate corresponding procedures, so they are different from the supervision method of submitting corrective opinions here, which only has the effect of recommending whether to take or not to take certain acts.

From the point of view of the coerciveness of binding effect of the procuratorial supervision methods, some of China's procuratorial supervision methods have a strong binding effect while some do not. The former is a rigid procuratorial supervision method, while the latter is a flexible one. The so-called rigid procuratorial supervision methods are those that have a substantive binding effect on the procedural conducts of relevant organs because of their own characteristics. These procuratorial supervision methods will inevitably lead to the initiation or circulation of procedures. For example, the protest of the procuratorial organs can trigger the initiation of the second instance or retrial procedures and has the effect of initiating the second instance or retrial procedures. Such rigid effect is conferred by the law on specific supervision methods, and the relevant organs have the corresponding obligations. The aforementioned supervision methods that have the effect of initiating procedures and permitting certain procedural acts are rigid procuratorial supervision methods. The flexible supervision methods, on the other hand, do not have the effect prescribed by the law of compelling the initiation or permission of a specific procedure. They are the methods that can only be implemented relying on the correctness of their own opinions, the authority of procuratorial organs, and the cooperation of the case-handling organs. For example, the procuratorial organs make recommendations to the relevant organs on the release of detainees or the alteration of coercive measures in cases where the conditions for the review of the necessity of custody are met. Such a recommendation does not necessarily lead to the release of the detainee or the alteration of the coercive measure, but only to the review and verification by the relevant organs, which only release the detainee or alter the coercive measures if they consider the opinion to be correct; if they consider the opinion to be incorrect, then there will be no release of the detainee or alteration of coercive measures and the supervision opinion of the procuratorial organs will not be implemented. Flexible supervision methods are mainly those that only have the effect of recommending whether to take or not to take certain acts.

From the perspective of whether the procuratorial supervision method is substantively decisive, such methods in China are mainly a procedural supervision, which only has a procedural significance. By procedural significance, it means that procuratorial supervision itself does not have substantive disposition or substantive decision-making power, nor is it final. Only by initiating corresponding procedures or by making corrective opinions or recommendations can the relevant organs be urged to correct the wrong conducts, and change the wrong adjudications or decisions. In other words, supervision means inspection and urge, rather than final disposition. It is precisely because of the procedural supervision feature of the procuratorial organs that their supervision does not take precedence over the administrative and judicial functions. This is because even if there is an injustice or judicial error, the procuratorial organs cannot exceed their duties and correct it by their own. They can only supervise the case-handing organ to correct it.[80]

3.2.5.3 Problems and Reforms in the Operation of Procuratorial Supervision Methods

There are some problems in the operation of the procuratorial supervision methods, the most important of which are their positioning, setting and effectiveness. For example, in the trial supervision, how to position the retiral protest of the procuratorial organs, and whether should it have the effectiveness of appeal exceeding that of the parties to the proceedings? Should the illegal conducts of courts or judges in a trial be corrected by supervision or restrained by objection? For example, if the procuratorial organ considers a commutation of sentence or parole decision to be inappropriate, should it be corrected by a protest or by a corrective opinion? In addition, when reviewing the necessity for custody, should the procuratorial organs use "recommendation" method or other methods? For recommendation on whether to take/not take a specific act, how should the effectiveness of this type of supervision be determined? In judicial practice, some organs do not pay attention to or even ignore the recommendations or corrective opinions of the procuratorial organs, which seriously undermines the motivation and authority of the latter in legal supervision.

The positioning, setting and effectiveness of procuratorial supervision methods are fundamentally determined by the nature and positioning of the specific procuratorial supervision power and function. And the positioning, specific setting and effectiveness of the procuratorial supervision methods should also reflect the nature and positioning of the specific procuratorial supervision power and function. Therefore, in the long run, in order to solve the problems in the operation of China's procuratorial supervision methods, it is necessary to combine the nature and positioning of specific procuratorial supervision powers. Such nature and positioning discussed above should be the basis for the fundamental reform of the procuratorial supervision methods. Specifically: firstly, in the case-filing supervision and general investigative supervision, the procuratorial supervision methods need to be adjusted according to the shift in the relationship between investigation and prosecution towards investigation and prosecution integration, as well as the procuratorial organs' command and supervision over investigation actions. In the case-filing supervision and general investigative supervision, the procuratorial organs no longer conduct their supervision mainly by flexible supervision methods of recommending on whether to take/not

[80]Long Zongzhi [81].

take a specific act. Instead, they adopt a command and supervision method, and the investigation must be subject to the prosecution's command. Secondly, as for the review of the necessity of arrests and custody, since it is essentially a kind of judicial power and function exercised by the procuratorial organs under the current system, its final outcome should not be a recommendation to the relevant organs to release or alter the coercive measures. Rather, it should decide to release or to alter the coercive measure, which must be implemented by the relevant organs. Thirdly, in the trial supervision, the trial supervision method should be adjusted to the restriction of prosecution power. The procuratorial organs should not supervise a court or a judge's conduct that violates the law in a trial by issuing corrective opinions, but should do so by filing objections; the procuratorial organs' retrial protest power is only a kind of public prosecution power and function, which cannot compel initiation of retrial proceedings; for compulsory medical treatment decision, procuratorial organs shall also restrict it through prosecution power and function, that is, exert restriction by exercising reconsideration power and function rather than submitting corrective opinions. Lastly, in the execution supervision, as mentioned above, the procuratorial organs should have the power to command and supervise the execution of punishment. Thus, if the procuratorial organs find that a violation of the law has occurred in general execution acts, they may directly command and supervise the relevant execution organs to correct it, and the execution organs must be subject to such command and supervision. In addition, in the process of commutation of sentences or paroles, the procuratorial organs in fact play the function of public prosecution, and in the event that the decision on commutation of sentence or parole is improper, the procuratorial organs shall supervise by way of a protest.

Of course, under the current system, as far as the current judicial practice is concerned, the public power lacks supervision and retraction over the process of case-filing, investigation and execution. Placing emphasis on the supervision function of the procuratorial organs is a last resort. So, how to perform the supervision functions of the procuratorial organs in the case-filing, investigation and execution is an issue to be considered. One important question is how to strengthen the effectiveness of the procuratorial supervision methods, mainly how to strengthen the effectiveness of supervision method of recommending on whether to take/not take specific acts. In this regard, the author believes that it is of the utmost importance to strengthen the implementation procedures of this type of supervision and to ensure that the supervision of the procuratorial organs is carried out in practice. This will not only increase the effectiveness of this type of supervision, but will also help solve the problem of the implementation of procuratorial supervision. To be specific, first, it should be made clear that the organs being supervised must initiate a reconsideration process after it has undergone procuratorial supervision, that is to say, a review of the relevant acts and decisions. Second, it should clarify that the organs being supervised have an obligation to respond to the procuratorial organs within a certain period of time. In the current system, some procuratorial supervision have made it clear that the organs being supervised are required to inform the procuratorial organs within a certain period of time of relevant disposal situation, some do not. In the future, it should be made clear in all cases of procuratorial supervision that the organs being supervised have the obligation to respond within a certain period of time. Moreover, the legal consequences of the organs or persons being supervised refusing to accept the supervision should be made clear. Lastly, it should clarify that in the event of deprivation of life or that it causes or may cause significant damage to personal freedom, physical health and so on, the supervision by the procuratorial organs has the effect of suspending the relevant acts. For example, in the course of on-site supervision of the death penalty, if the procuratorial organ finds that there are circumstances in which the death penalty should not be carried out and recommends an immediate suspension on the execution, the recommendation should have the effect of suspending the execution of the death penalty.

3.3 New Development of Procuratorial Powers and Functions

Is the procuratorial power a judicial power? A wide and in-depth debate was launched regarding this question in the theoretical and practical world in the late twentieth century, and this major discussion about the nature of China's procuratorial power has continued to this day.[81] In this academic debate, we have clearly stated that the judicial power should be final, neutral, independent and passive. And because of the lack of these characteristics, in its essence and ultimate sense, the procuratorial power in the procedural structure should be administrative power. And the powers and functions it contains have no judicial characteristics.[82] However, following the 2012 amendment of the Criminal Procedure Law, it can be seen that the new law has given new powers to the procuratorial organs, and their powers and functions have also been further expanded. Procuratorial powers and functions have developed from the original procedural power and function and procedural supervision power and function to the current procedural power and function, procedural supervision power and function and judicial remedy power and function. The procuratorial power also objectively contains part of the content that is judicial in nature.

The establishment of the judicial remedy power and function of the procuratorial organs is a product of the partial judicialization of the procuratorial power and function, which expands the scope of judicial remedy power and function from the aspects including subject, object, and operation. Article 47 of the Criminal Procedure

[81] Recently, there are many articles studying the nature of procuratorial powers, including, Lian Yuqiang [82] and Song Yinghui and Lin Lin [83] and Zhou Yezhong and Ye Zhengguo [53].

[82] Chen Weidong [85].

Law stipulates the power of the procuratorial organs to review[83] and handle[84] appeals and accusations made by a defenders and agent ad litem against the public security, procuratorial and judicial organs and their staff for obstructing the exercise of procedural rights in accordance with the law; Article 115 prescribes that the procuratorial organs shall have the power to review and handle dissatisfaction of the parties to the case and defenders, agents ad litem and interested persons with the judicial organs' handling of the corresponding illegal investigation acts.[85] It is obvious that the new powers of "review and handle" conferred by the law on the procuratorial organs are not covered by the original scope of procuratorial power. It is neither procedural power and function nor procedural supervision power and function. A specific analysis of the attributes and connotations of this power and function will show that they have unique properties and characteristics that are different from those of administrative and procedural supervision, including passivity of initiation, substantiality of decision, relative independence, limited effectiveness, and relative neutrality. It is also because of these characteristics that the judicial remedy of procuratorial organs acquires the character of a judicial power.

Due to the principle of the relevant laws and regulations, the exercise of the judicial remedy power and function by the procuratorial organs is still characterized

[83] It is noteworthy that in the first draft of the Criminal Procedure Law drafted by the legislature, instead of the word "review, "investigate and verify" were used, which is clearly more proactive and stronger compared with "review". This wording, however, was questioned by other judicial organs, which argued that if the procuratorial organs conducted an in-depth investigation and verification into the matter in question, the relationship between the three organs of the public security, procuratorial and judicial organs, which is based on dividing responsibilities and checking each other, would be affected. Therefore, the legislature then replaced it with a more moderate word "review", which, although it did the right thing, brought into question the effectiveness of the measure. New Issues. See Chen Weidong ed. [86].

[84] Article 47 of the Criminal Procedure Law stipulates, "A defender or agent ad litem shall be entitled to a petition or bring a complaint to the people's procuratorate at the same or the next higher level if he/she is of the opinion that the relevant public security organ, people's procuratorate, people's court or its staff members have hindered his/her exercise of the litigation rights. The said people's procuratorate shall review the petition or complaint in a timely manner, and notify relevant organs to make correction if the authenticity of petition or complaint is confirmed.".

[85] Article 115 of the Criminal Procedure Law provides that, "The party concerned, his/her defender, the agent ad litem or an interested party shall be entitled to file a petition or complaint to a judicial organ if he/she is of the opinion the judicial organ or its staff members have any of the following acts: (1) To fail to order release from, or termination of, or alteration to, a compulsory measure upon expiry of the statutory time period; (2) To fail to return the bond for bail with restricted freedom pending trial that shall be returned; (3) To seal up, seize or freeze property irrelevant to the case at hand; (4) To fail to terminate the sealing, seizure and freeze of property as required; or (5) To embezzle, misappropriate, privately divide, replace, or use in violation of relevant provisions the property that has been sealed up, seized or frozen. The organ that has accepted the petition or complaint shall handle the petition or complaint in a timely manner. The party lodging the petition or complaint may appeal to the people's procuratorate at the same level if he/she has objections to the handling results. For a case accepted directly by a people's procuratorate, the party concerned may appeal to the people's procuratorate at the next higher level. The people's procuratorate shall review the appeal in a timely manner and shall notify the relevant organ to make correction if the appeal is found to be true."

by a series of problems, such as unclear subjects that exercise the power, irregular review procedures, non-compulsory notification of corrective measures, and unclear feedback procedures. In addition, compared with the judicial remedy procedure in the courts, there are also system problems in the exercise of remedy power by the procuratorial organs, including the problems of lack of neutrality and independence, and inadequate execution of decisions. In order to solve these problems, in the future, we should take judicialization as the direction of improvement, and continue to promote the improvement in the mechanism and operation procedure where the procuratorial organs exercise the remedy power and function from various aspects including the review process, notification of correction procedures and feedback procedures.

3.3.1 The Establishment of the Judicial Remedy Power and Function of the Procuratorial Organs

3.3.1.1 Theoretical Controversy Over the Power and Function of Procuratorial Organs

Powers and functions, that is, functions are determined by the power, which also means that "if there is power, there must be responsibility, and the power and function must be consistent". Generally speaking, as far as the public power organs are concerned, their functions are as great as the scope and degree of powers conferred by the law. The definition and division of procuratorial powers and functions have been the hotspot of academic discussion, and the purpose of the debate is to solve the problem of the positioning of the procuratorial organs, and to reconcile the contradiction that the procuratorial organs perform as the public prosecution organs and as the legal supervisory organs. The discussion on the positioning of the procuratorial organs has been centered around the theory of public prosecution and supervision power. There are three types of procuratorial function theories that the academic world advocates: first, it is believed that the power of the procuratorial organs lies in and only in legal supervision, which can be called "the monism of legal supervision"; second, it is assumed that the power of the procuratorial organs only refers to the procedural functions, which can be called "the monism of procedural function"; third, it is thought that in criminal proceedings, the power of the procuratorial organs includes not only the procedural power to prosecute crimes, but also the legal supervision power to supervise the implementation of laws, which can be called "dualism".[86] According to the scholars who hold the view of "monism of legal supervision", since the Constitution stipulates that the people's procuratorates are the legal supervisory organs of the state, and exercise procuratorial power on behalf of the state, it determines that the sole function of the procuratorial organs in China is legal supervision,

[86]Zhang Jue [87].

and the procuratorial function is a legal supervision function".[87] This statement, however, seems to confuse the relevant concepts. It should be considered that the term "legal supervision" refers mainly to the positioning of the nature of the procuratorial organs, which is not at the same logical level as their powers or functions. The positioning of the nature answers question of "what the procuratorial organs are" and the positioning of the functions answers the question of "what they do".[88] This view of "monism of legal supervision" is obviously influenced by the Soviet theory of procuratorial supervision, and it does not conform with the "trial centrism" in which the power of trial is supreme that our modern rule of law emphasizes.

Scholars who hold the view of "monism of procedural function believe that the procuratorial organs have assumed the procedural function in the criminal proceedings. None of the Western countries regard the procedural supervision as the function of procuratorial organs, but the difference between the powers and functions of the procuratorial organs in China and those of the Western countries is indistinctive. It is inappropriate to forcibly interpret the specific functions of the procuratorial organs, such as examining and approving the arrests, reviewing prosecutions and lodging protests, as procedural supervision. It is asserted that "it is a misunderstanding in China's traditional theoretical study of criminal procedure that there is no independent trial supervision function apart from the procedural function, and the functions of procuratorial organs in criminal trial procedure are divided into procedural function and supervision function. This has not brought any special effect but given rise to many maladies".[89] This view points out the shortcomings of the "monism of legal supervision", but focuses too much on the "should" side of the procedural function of the procuratorial organs and ignores procuratorial organs' supervision functions stipulated in the positive law, which is inappropriate as well.

The scholars who hold the view of "dualism" consider that "legal supervision and public prosecution are the two components and two basic functions of the procuratorial power in China: if the public prosecution function is strengthened, the effect of legal supervision will surely appear. The public prosecution is the approach, the legal supervision is the purpose, and the achievement of the unity of the legal system is the effect".[90] The problem with this view is that this argument only pursues conceptual unity, rather than the right way to solve the problem. The clarification of procuratorial functions is of great significance for clearing the boundaries between the value of criminal procedures and the public power. A general compromise between these two concepts has no substantive meaning to our study of the nature, positioning and scope of the procuratorial function.

Based on the scope of powers conferred on the public procuratorial organs, the content of their functions and the relevant provisions of the Constitution and the law on their positioning, the following criteria are used to distinguish between the procedural function and procedural supervision function of the procuratorial organs: first,

[87]Zhang Zhihui ed. [88].

[88]Wang Jiancheng and Wang Yiming [89].

[89]Liu Jihua [90].

[90]Fan Chongyi [91].

whenever the law provides, the procedural powers exercised by the procuratorial organs themselves are all concrete manifestations of their procuratorial functions, including the investigation of self-investigating cases, the approval of arrests, and initiation of public prosecutions; secondly, functions that are not directly exercised by the procuratorial organs themselves, that is to say, acts of supervising by using the powers exercised on other organs or individuals can be categorized as procedural supervision acts, such as case-filing supervision, the supervision of the legality of investigation activities, trial activities, and execution activities. The procedural function of the procuratorial organs are related to the main tasks they undertake in the criminal proceedings in China, namely, to prosecute crimes and protect public interests, which makes the positioning of the procuratorial organs in the procedural structure a mere procedural function; and judging from the current constitutional and legal positioning of state legal supervision organs, the procuratorial function in the judicial system is also characterized by a procedural supervision function and a non-procedural function.

As far as the procuratorial function under the power and function concept is concerned, its connotation and scope should be clear. From the macroscopic perspective of the judicial system, the powers of the procuratorial organs are governed by the Constitution, the Criminal Procedure Law, the Organic Law of the People's Procuratorates and other laws. These powers are expressed in clear legal provisions, and as for the scope of their specific functions, they are divided into procedural functions and procedural supervision functions through typified conclusion, which is also the general consensus of the academic circles. However, following the adoption of the 2012 Criminal Procedure Law, articles 47 and 115 of the Law endows the procuratorial organs with a new remedy power. The function to which this power refers cannot be subsumed under the procedural function, and it is distinctly different from the ordinary procedural supervision function; instead, it is more in the nature of a judicial remedy. The addition of this "judicial" remedy function to the procuratorial organs "has led to the reversal of the previous reference to the two major procuratorial functions".[91]

3.3.1.2 Background to the Establishment of the Procuratorial Organs' Judicial Remedy Power and Function

Due to the lack of effective remedy approaches for parties to the case and defenders, agents ad litem, interested persons and other persons in criminal proceedings regarding illegal conducts of public power organs in China, especially at the pretrial stage of criminal proceedings, frequent procedural violations arise. Therefore, legislatures consider add this procedure mechanism that is relevant to the protection of civil rights in the amendment of the Criminal Procedure Law. This mechanism is in nature an adjudication power, that is, the accusations or appeals lodged by one party against the other should be heard and judged by a third-party institution with

[91] Ge Lin [92].

certain neutrality or independence. This type of procedural mechanism has a certain jurisdictional nature and belongs to the judicial remedy power. As a general rule throughout the world, the judicial remedy power is generally exercised by the court, even at the pretrial investigation stage, and disputes arising in this stage are also adjudicated by the courts. However, under China's current judicial system and procedural mechanism, it is not feasible for the court to uniformly exercise judicial remedy for pretrial disputes. There are several reasons for this.

First of all, the Constitution of China has established a procedural system in which the public security, procuratorial and judicial organs divide their responsibilities and perform their respective duties, so the procedural structure is a linear one where each organ is responsible for their own. Although we now propose a "trial-centered" procedural system reform, in practice, the enclosed linear structure of the procedural stage is difficult to break at this stage. One of the problems arising from this situation is that the people's courts are unable to intervene and exercise judicial power in the process of investigating, reviewing and prosecuting cases, for if the court exercises its judicial power at the stage of investigation, review and prosecution, it would appear to be in violation of the criminal procedural principle of "dividing responsibilities, coordinating their efforts and checking each other".

Secondly, direct involvement of the court in pretrial disputes will undermine its neutrality. An important reason for excluding the court from pretrial proceedings in China's criminal procedure system is to prevent the judge from prejudging the case. The correctness of the substantive judgement is the key to guaranteeing judicial impartiality. Meanwhile, the neutrality of the judge, as the final arbiter of the substantive judgement, is the foundation and key to ensuring the impartiality of the judgment. If the judge intervenes in the dispute before the trial, this will inevitably lead to the formation of the corresponding prejudgment, which will affect the neutrality of the judge and even the trial court, and this is an implicit infringement of the right of the accused to a fair trial.

Third, with the needs of judicial practice and the continuous deepening of judicial reform, there has also been changes in the procuratorial organs' methods of objectively exercising the procedural power and function and procedural supervision power and function, which to a certain extent makes them "qualified" to exercise judicial power. For example, the process of procuratorial decision to approve arrest is moving towards a tripartite structure; the introduction of systems such as that of the chief prosecutor system emphasizes the independence of the prosecutor in the handling of individual cases. These changes are moving towards "de-administration" and gradual "judicialization", and corresponding judicial attribute are progressively added to the original procuratorial power, including, for example, the neutrality of the prosecutor, the procedural structure of the adversarial hearing, the passive method of the initiation of the function and power, and the substantive decision-making power.

Taking these circumstances into account and combining the actual practice of criminal procedure, the legislature considers that, in the light of China's national conditions, it is appropriate and feasible to vest the power and function of judicial remedy in procuratorial organs. Articles 47 and 115 of the 2012 Criminal Procedure Law are formulated based on this, which is a symbol of the formal establishment of the procuratorial organs' judicial remedy power and function, transforming the functions of the procuratorial organs from the original procedural function and procedural supervision function into the current triad of the procedural function, procedural supervision function and judicial remedy function.

3.3.2 *Connotation of the Judicial Remedy Power and Function of Procuratorial Organs*

The judicial remedy power means that when any person's constitutional and legal rights are violated, they have the right to institute legal proceedings in independent and unbiased courts to have them justly decided by the court after a proper hearing.[92] When studying the nature of the judicial power, we have stated that the judicial power has the following characteristics: (1) finality. Judiciary is the last line of defense of the state to solve social conflicts and protect the rights and interests of social subjects. The principle of the rule of law assumes the authority of this activity and has designed judicial procedures to guarantee the correctness of its decisions in accordance with the rules, forbidding any subject other than the judicial organs to challenge the adjudication that has taken effect. Therefore, it has finality. (2) Neutrality. Justice is the last line of defense to protect the rights and interests of social subjects, and it has to make an authoritative and final adjudication on social conflicts. It is because of this that judicial power can only carry out this task through neutrality, which must be strictly observed by the judiciary. (3) Independence. If the judicial power is not independent from external interference, the authority of the judiciary as the final judicator will be eliminated. Therefore, judiciary must be independent. (4) Passivity. In order to ensure the neutrality and impartiality of the judicial power in judging conflicts, the principle of no complaint no trial must be adhered. Only when a conflicted dispute is brought to the attention of the courts can the judiciary adjudicate the claims of the parties to the dispute in accordance with the law.[93] The same is true for the judicial remedy power of the procuratorial organs as a judicial power, but these power and function are distinct from those of different types and natures, including the judicial remedy power exercised by the trial organs. In order to study the content of these power and function in detail, we will look specifically at the distinction between these powers and functions in order to clearly elucidate their uniqueness.

---

[92]Miao Lianying [93].

[93]Chen Weidong [94].

3.3.2.1 Distinction Between the Judicial Remedy Power and Function and Administrative Remedy Power and Function

The concept of administrative remedy is controversial in China. In the early scholars' discussion, administrative procedure is equivalent to administrative remedy, and the letters and visits system is also seen as an administrative remedy.[94] The application of this concept has not yet been clarified and systematized. Along with the development of legal science system and theoretical research, for the concept of administrative remedy, the academic world basically forms three different views: first, it considers that "an administrative remedy is a "legal remedial mechanism" whereby the relevant state organ reviews, in accordance with the law, whether an administrative act is lawful and reasonable, and eliminates or modifies the unlawful or improper administrative act".[95] Second, it is believed that "administrative remedy refers to a means of defense and a way of appeal when the rights and interests of citizens are infringed, or are likely to be infringed, by administrative organs; it is also a legal system for restoring jeopardized civil rights and remedying their interests by settling administrative disputes, correcting, stopping or rectifying administrative infringements. Thus, administrative remedy is a legal remedy against a negative consequence of the operation of administrative power".[96] Third, it is believed that administrative remedy "refers to a legal system in which an administrative relative person files an appeal in accordance with the law after his or her lawful rights and interests are infringed by the illegal or negligent acts of an administrative organ, and an administrative organ with supervision power provides remedy in accordance with legal procedures. This kind of remedy is carried out by the administrative organ, thus is abbreviated as administrative remedy".[97]

As far as the first viewpoint is concerned, it regards the administrative remedy as the correction of administrative acts, which contains the public power organs' (legislative, judicial, administrative) initiative to correct unlawful or improper administrative acts, corrections based on the application of the person involved, as well as indirect remedies aiming at non-applicable unlawful or improper administrative acts. The latter two views are based on the premise of the violation of civil rights, and believe that administrative remedy is the remedy for the violation of rights. The difference between the two is that the second view limits the subject of the remedy to administrative organs.[98] In the current context of legal research, administrative remedy is generally in accordance with the concept given by the third view, and is limited to the remedy given by the administrative organ, as opposed to the judicial remedy by the judicial organ.[99] This is also the view adopted in this book,

94 Shen Kaiju and Fan Baocheng [95].

95 Ye Bifeng [96].

96 Zhang Shuyi [97].

97 Guo Depei ed. [98].

98 Lin Lihong [99].

99 For example, the "exhaustion of administrative remedies principle", as used in the study of comparative law, means that "the relative person must exhaust all feasible administrative remedies before

which considers that, unlike the administrative remedy function, the judicial remedy function has the attribute of judicial power.

The implementation subject of judicial remedy is the "judicial organ", which generally means the trial organs in China, but in the matters provided for in Article 47 and 115 of the Criminal Procedure Law, the procuratorial organs may also be the subject to exercise judicial remedy power; the implementation subject of administrative remedy is an administrative organ, generally either the administrative organ that performs the administrative act or a superior administrative organ that exercises leadership and management over that organ. In terms of the nature of the implementation subject, while both remedy powers are aimed at correcting erroneous decisions made by public powers, there is a big difference in the natures of the "correcting". The administrative acts of administrative organs to correct obviously belong to the "self-regulatory" category; And the integrated administrative structure leads to a relationship of "leading and being led, commanding and being commanded" within the administrative organs, and the subordinate administrative organs must follow the orders of their superiors, while the superior administrative organs also have the responsibility to supervise the subordinates. While a subordinate administrative organ makes illegal or inappropriate administrative act, the superior has the power and responsibility to command the subordinate to correct it. This integrated structure also belongs to "self-regulatory" category to some extent. However, this is not the case with judicial remedy. Judicial organs that implement judicial remedies have no direct relationship of leadership with the administrative organs. Their remedy through judicial adjudication or decision is a form of "external supervision" or "external restriction".

In order to guarantee the effectiveness of "external supervision", it is first necessary to ensure that it is "external". The leadership and command relationship between the persons being supervised and supervisors should be cut off to ensure the neutrality and independence of the external supervisors. The review subject of judicial remedies must be neutral and it should be ensured to be neither party to the dispute or the conflict, so that it can review the dispute or conflict without bias; at the same time, the judicial review subject must also be characterized by independence, which means that it will not be influenced by external factors in the process of reviewing dispute or conflict and the process of making review decisions. Other organizations and individuals must not interfere with the review of the review subject. The successive judicial reforms that have been implemented have focused on the neutrality and independence of the judiciary, particularly in the current round of judicial reform, the central government is now pushing forward the reform of "de-administration" and "de-localization" of the judicial organs, such as reducing factors of interference by local governments in the judicial organs in their regions through the provincial centralized management of judicial human resources, funds and property, and reducing factors of interference by local human resource and administrative departments in judicial personnel through the provincial selection system of judges and

seeking judicial remedies through the courts", limiting administrative remedies to this concept. Xing Hongfei [100].

prosecutors. These measures have further strengthened the neutrality and independence of the judicial organs from the administrative organs in order to guarantee the impartial exercise of the judicial remedy power.

As a form of internal supervision, administrative remedies are actually oriented towards correction rather than remedy. The imposition of internal restriction and regulation ensures the rationality and legality of administrative acts, which in turn maintains and strengthens the legitimate status of the administrative organs. This leads to the exercise of administrative remedy following active principle that "all wrongs must be corrected". On the one hand, when the administrative organ finds errors in itself or when it finds errors in the administrative act of its subordinates, it must adopt active measures to correct the error; on the other hand, when the relative person applies, there is possible error in administrative act and the corresponding organ should also review the administrative act. However, judicial remedy, which has a stronger nature of external supervision, is different. Regarding almost all disputes, the review subject of judicial remedy adopts the principle of "no complaint, no remedy" (except in trial control procedures). Its passivity is obvious. The review subject cannot initiate the remedy proceedings on its own initiative, but must take the appeals, accusation, etc. of the parties concerned as the prerequisite.

In addition, the resolution of the dispute or conflict to which the judicial remedy is directed must be made in accordance with the procedure prescribed by law, and it has a stronger need to clarify procedural requirements than administrative remedies. Moreover, the decisions taken by the review subject of judicial remedies have a certain legal and final effect, which may have an impact on the substantive rights and obligations of both parties. It is substantively decisive and final.

3.3.2.2 Distinctions Between Procuratorial Organs' Judicial Remedy Power and Function and Procedural Supervision Power and Function

The judicial remedy power of the procuratorial organs may involve procuratorial organs' review and correction of wrong conducts of public security organs, judicial organs and their staff in the course of proceedings. There is a certain similarity between it and the procedural supervision power and function. Some scholars believe that the procuratorial organs' judicial remedy power is a manifestation of their legal supervision power, which is the remedies offered by the procuratorial organs as the legal supervisors for relevant organs' violations of the procedural and substantive rights of the parties to the case, defenders, agents ad litem or interested persons. In fact, this is not the case. Although procuratorial organs' judicial remedy power and function and procedural supervision power and function are very much alike,[100] the

[100]The similarity between the procuratorial organs' judicial remedy power and procedural supervision power is reflected in the fact that both are aimed at correcting the unlawful conducts by judicial organs or their staff; both are of a delayed nature, that is, premised on the occurrence of unlawful conducts; and both have a certain degree of neutrality, that is, they all present their opinions from an

two intrinsically belong to two different powers and functions, and the two cannot be confused with each other.

First of all, the initiation of judicial remedy power of the procuratorial organs are passive, whereas procedural supervision is proactive power and function. In other words, procedural supervision can not only be initiated in passive way such as accepting appeals and accusations, but also by the procuratorial organs' active initiation. According to Article 111 of the Criminal Procedure Law, for example, "Where the people's procuratorate considers that a case should be filed for investigation by a public security organ but the latter has not done so, or where a victim considers that a case should be filed for investigation by a public security organ but the latter has not done so and the victim has brought the matter to a People's Procuratorate, the People's Procuratorate shall request the public security organ to state the reason for not filing the case. If the People's Procuratorate considers that the reasons for not filing the case given by the public security organs are untenable, it shall notify the public security organ to file the case and upon receiving the notification, the public security organ shall file the case.." From this, it can be seen that there are two ways to initiate supervision when the procuratorial organ finds that the public security organ does not file a case for investigation that should be filed for investigation: passive initiation of supervision upon applications and procuratorial organs' own initiation of supervision when they actively discover violations. In addition, these two types of initiation are also included in the supervision of investigation, trial and execution. The initiation of judicial remedies by the procuratorial organs is more passive in nature, as the remedy procedure normally will not be initiated if the participants in the proceedings or interested persons do not lodge appeals or accusations. Procuratorial organs can only proceed to handle the matter when a participant in the proceedings or an interested person reports to them on the unlawful acts of the relevant organs and their staff, and requests them to review and handle it. In other words, the procuratorial organs can only passively wait for the appeal or accusation of the participant in the relevant proceedings, but cannot initiate the remedy procedure on the basis of active discovery or review of relevant procedural acts. Thus, the initiation of the remedy power and function of procuratorial organs is passive. This characteristic is one of the key factors in assuming that the remedy power of the procuratorial organs has the attributes of judicial power, and it is because of this attribute that the procuratorial organs' remedy power can break away from an administrative and proactive exercise approach and adopt a passive judicial operation approach.

Secondly, the judicial remedy of the procuratorial organs is of a substantive decisive nature, whereas the procedural supervision is more of an advisory nature. The procuratorial organs often carry out supervision by offering procuratorial recommendations in exercising their procedural supervision power and function, which are procedure power and function and are not substantively decisive. At the beginning of China, procuratorial organs were given general legal supervision power and function, that is, abstract and general supervision acts that supervise, safeguard and

objective and neutral standpoint, rather than on the premise of their own interests in the proceedings; etc.

protect the unity of national law are not procedural.[101] The 1979 Criminal Procedure Law and the Organic Law of the People's Procuratorates abolished this power and function and limited the scope of supervision to procedural supervision, which means that the supervision power and function of the procuratorial organs can be exercised in the course of proceedings and must be exercised in accordance with certain procedural norms. It is a specific and procedural supervision act of a procedural nature. However, unlike the judicialized mode of operation, the exercise of this supervision power and function by the procuratorial organs does not lead to a final substantive decision, still less to directly lead to a change in the content of substantive rights and obligations. When the procuratorial organ discovers unlawful acts committed by other judicial organs and their staff, it can only issue corrective opinions, and those organs shall conscientiously correct it. And judicial remedy itself is an integral part of the procedure, in which the procuratorial organs can directly make remedy decisions regarding the infringement of the rights of the participants in the proceedings.[102] In particular, the procuratorial organs may, through their review, qualify the procedural action that is the subject of the appeal or accusation. If the action is confirmed to be unlawful, a notice of violation may be issued against the organ and its staff. Although not as absolutely enforceable as a judicial decision, the notice of violation still can have direct effect on the organ and its staff, and the relevant organ and individual must follow and execute it.

Procedural supervision is a kind of recommendatory power, in which the procuratorial organ supervises the main subject of the procedure. It belongs to the one-way procedural structure of both sides; whereas the remedy power and function tend to operate in a judicial way, and the participants in the remedy process include not only the procuratorial organ itself, but also the two equivalent subjects of the person who lodges the appeal or accusation, and the organ or individual that the appeal or accusation is lodged against. It belongs to the tripartite procedural structure.

3.3.2.3 Distinctions Between the Judicial Remedy Power and Function of Procuratorial Organs and Those of Trial Organs

In the past, judicial remedy power referred only to the power and function of trial of the people's courts in criminal proceedings, that is, conducting judicial remedy through the trial of cases and making adjudications. However, after the adoption of the new Criminal Procedure Law, judicial remedy power and function in criminal proceedings have been extended in many aspects, including the subject, object and mode of operation. Judicial remedy power and function are exercised not only by the people's courts but also by the procuratorial organs, as provided for in Article 47 and 115 of the Criminal Procedure Law. In general: (1) in terms of the subject, the organs entitled for judicial remedies include not only the people's courts, but also the procuratorial organs; (2) in terms of the object, different from the scope of the object

[101] Dai Yuzhong [102].

[102] Chen Weidong and Cheng Yongfeng [103].

of the judicial remedy power and function of the people's courts, under the provisions of the new Criminal Procedure Law, procuratorial organs shall provide remedies to the procedural infringement caused by public security organs, judicial organs and their staff in the course of criminal proceedings, which to a certain extent fills a gap in the area where the people's courts have difficulty in functioning; (3) in terms of operation mode, according to the law, the procedural process for the procuratorial organs to exercise remedy power includes three steps of receipt of appeals and accusations, review, and notification of correction. This is not a standardized form of judicial review in the traditional sense, but rather a relatively simple procedural process, and thus the operation methods of judicial remedy power and function are also expanded to some extent.

There are also certain similarities between the procuratorial organs' method to exercise their judicial remedy power and function and that of the court. However, as a new type of procuratorial power and function, the judicial remedy power and function of procuratorial organs have unique characteristics. Although we believe that the procuratorial organs' judicial remedy power and function belong to judicial powers, its independence, neutrality and effectiveness degrees are different to those of the courts. The fundamental reason for this difference lies in the subject of the power and function – the administrative tendency of the procuratorate. In other words, although the procuratorial organs' remedy power and function have an attribute similar to that of judicial power, it is subject to the internal administrative organization system and control model of the procuratorial organs and its judicial character has certain limitations.

First of all, procuratorial organs' exercise of judicial remedy power and function lacks strict independence and is only "relatively independent" compared with the trial organs. When we discuss the question of the independence of exercising powers, we are actually referring to the independence of the subject that exercises the power. The essence of judicial independence lies in the independent exercise of the function and power in accordance with the law, free from interference by administrative organs, social groups and individuals, which in a horizontal manner enables judicial organs to maintain their independence within the system. China's Constitution clearly stipulates that the relationship between the people's courts at higher and lower levels is that of supervisor and supervisee. Therefore, people's courts at higher levels may not arbitrarily interfere in the individual trials of people's courts at lower levels, which, in turn, vertically guarantees the independence of people's courts at all levels within the system.[103] Thus, both vertically and horizontally, the judicial independence of the trial organs is relatively well established, and the court can also exercise its judicial power in a relative independent manner. Article 131 of the Constitution explicitly states that "people's procuratorates shall, in accordance with the law, exercise procuratorial power independently and are not subject to interference by administrative organs, public organizations, or individuals", horizontally guaranteeing the independence of procuratorial organs, which is similar to that of the courts. Vertically, however, Article 132 of the Constitution makes it clear that

[103]For specific studies on the judicial independence issue, see Chen Weidong [104].

people's procuratorates at higher levels "direct" the work of those at lower levels; Article 3 of the Organic Law of the People's Procuratorates stipulates that "the chief procurator exercises unified leadership over the work of the procuratorates". In other words, within a procuratorial organ, there is a relationship of leading and being led between the procuratorial organs at higher and lower levels; within a procuratorate, the relationship between the Chief Procurator and the prosecutors is also one of leading and being led. This means that local people's procuratorates at all levels are not independent from the those at higher levels, nor are the prosecutors independent from the Chief Procurator. Their work methods and work content may be under the direct "leadership" of the people's procuratorates at higher levels and the Chief Procurator. In order to change the status quo of the procuratorial organs that they are not vertically independent, and to promote reform of the judicial system, the Fourth Plenary Session of the 18th CPC Central Committee pointed out that "members of the judicial organs shall not violate the regulation to interfere in cases being handled by other internal members, and a record-keeping system and an accountability system shall be established for the handling of cases by internal members of the judicial organs", "improve the Chief Prosecutor case handling accountability system, and ensure that whoever handles the case is responsible for the case". The Opinions on Deepening Procuratorial Reform, issued by the Supreme People's Procuratorate, also contain detailed provisions on this matter, which is constructing the mode in which prosecutors independently handle cases from the frame structure. Although to a large extent the independence of the procuratorial organs and the prosecutors has been strengthened, it must be recognized that, due to the limitation imposed by the administrative and directive nature of its main functions, it is also difficult for procuratorial work to achieve absolute independence, and the judicial remedy power and function of the procuratorial organs only have a relative and limited independence.

Secondly, the judicial remedy power exercised by procuratorial organs is not as effective as that exercised by trial organs, as it is in a state of "being limited". It has been argued above that the judicial remedy power and function of the procuratorial organs are different from the procedural supervision power and function, as they are substantively decisive and decisions made on this basis can directly change the substantive rights and obligations of the parties involved. However, such substantive effects remain largely different from the coercive effect of a court's judicial rulings. The adjudications of the courts, whether they are judgements, verdicts or decisions, are compulsorily enforceable and guaranteed by the state's coercive power. However, in the provisions of the Criminal Procedure Law relating to judicial remedies by the procuratorial organs, after reviewing the appeal or accusation, if the procuratorial organ concludes that there is a violation of the law, it can only notify the relevant organs to correct it. That is to say, the compulsory provisions of the law only require that "the procuratorial organs shall correct the legal violations", but leave open the question of what the procuratorial organs should do when the relevant organs refuse to correct the violation. Should they leave it alone or take tougher measures? In the absence of any disciplinary powers granted to the procuratorial organs, and in accordance with the general principle of "the division of responsibilities and boundaries shall not be crossed" of the three organs, the effectiveness of this law is indeed a cause for concern.[104] It can be seen that, although the procuratorial organs are expressly authorized by law to review and dispose procedural legal violations, they lack corresponding sanction approaches as a guarantee of enforcement, and their decisions do not have the rigid effect of binding the other party.[105] In other words, although the law provides that certain supervision powers of the procuratorial organs may be exercised by way of "notification", and the corresponding authorities "shall" execute it, such execution lacks corresponding execution force. Moreover, even if the organ does not execute the notice, there is no subsequent mandatory system to ensure it. After all, the remedy power of the procuratorial organs does not belong to the absolute sense of the term "judicial power", and it is difficult to ensure the effectiveness of the implementation of this power and function by giving them coercive execution force. One of the key points we should study is how to improve the procedural structure of the system to ensure the effectiveness of its implementation.

Thirdly, the procuratorial organs, as the subject of judicial remedies, are also less neutral than the trial organs. The procedural structure of the judicial remedy should be that "both parties to the proceedings shall present, and the opinions on five penalties shall be heard". There should not only be a prosecutor and an accused, but also a neutral judicator to hear the case and adjudicate. The principle of the neutrality of the court is thus derived from this. Through ensuring the neutrality of the exercise of judicial power, its reasonable, impartial and independent operation can be guaranteed. A judge can neither be a party to either the prosecution or the defense, nor have an interest in the parties, and the judge must not proactively intervene in the dispute. In criminal proceedings, the neutrality of the trial organs' remedy power and function is reflected in the fact that judges must remain unbiased, must not take sides in the cases, and meanwhile, opinions of both the prosecution and the defense shall be fully heard; on this basis, a fair adjudication shall be made. It can be inferred from the original meaning of the judicial remedy power and function that the procuratorial organs should also maintain a certain degree of neutrality in the exercise of such power. When adjudicating the judicial acts that the appeals or accusations refer to, on the basis of neutrality and unbiasedness, the procuratorial organs should review the information or material provided by both sides and fully hear their opinions to make an impartial judgement. However, it should be noted that the primary power and function of the procuratorial organs are not judicial remedy but criminal prosecution, and the requirements of neutrality of the procuratorial organs in judicial review is fundamentally in conflict with its procedural powers and functions, in particular the prosecution power and function. In the "trial-centered" procedural structure, the primary objective of the procuratorial organs, as the prosecutor, is to complete the prosecution. Such positioning in the procedural structure seriously affects the neutrality of the procuratorial organs in assuming remedy power and function. In addition, procuratorial organs are at the same time an investigative organ and a prosecution organ, and may therefore also be the organ accused of directly committing violations. In response to this conflict, the legislature has provided for

[104] Chen Weidong ed. [99].

[105] Zhan Jianhong [106].

the possibility of lodging appeals and accusations with the people's procuratorate at a higher level, that is, overcoming the contradiction that the accused party is the same subject as the remedy organ through internal administrative supervision of procuratorial organs.[106] Although this option is more realistic and has a certain degree of operability, it is not entirely reassuring whether the higher-level procuratorial organs can enforce the law impartially when reviewing the conduct of the lower-level organs. In our view, the key to resolving this problem is to achieve a relative separation among different powers and functions of the procuratorial organs on the basis of an accurate delimitation of them.[107] Judicial remedy power and function are endowed to a specific procuratorial department, which no longer assumes procedural power and function but exclusively focuses on judicial remedies, thereby strengthening the neutrality of the procuratorial organs in the conduct of judicial remedies.

In the light of the foregoing, the remedy power and function of the procuratorial organs have essentially acquired a "judicial" attribute. However, since the procuratorial organs are still primarily responsible for procedures, and their internal management model still tends to be administrative operation, their remedy power and function are not strictly judicial in nature.

3.3.3 Significance of the Establishment of the Procuratorial Organs' Judicial Remedy Power and Function

3.3.3.1 Improve the Judicial Protection of Civil Rights

In today's society, the protection of human rights has been regarded as the embodiment of the core values of a modern state, and the degree of civilization of a state is highly relevant to the importance it attaches to human rights. In China, respect for and protection of human rights have been written into the Constitution and the Criminal Procedure Law. While undertaking the task of prosecuting and punishing criminals and maintaining social stability, the people's courts, the people's procuratorates and the public security organs are also charged with the responsibility of respecting and safeguarding human rights to achieve the unity between the punishment of crimes and the protection of human rights. How to achieve the unity of the two is a major problem lying in front of the organs handling the case. The theory of procedural justice provides a theoretical system for balancing the protection of human rights and the prosecution of crimes, that is, satisfying the needs of human rights protection and criminal prosecution by recognizing the real value of the procedure, designing an impartial and proper procedural system and strictly implementing it. As an important part of procedural justice, judicial remedies in the course of proceedings are a necessary system design of procedural law to ensure that the participants

[106]Long Zongzhi [107].

[107]Chen Weidong [108].

to the proceedings can receive prompt and appropriate procedural remedies, thereby guaranteeing substantive justice and the realization of human right values.

The inherently expansive and aggressive nature of state power has made it the greatest threat to human rights, and since the First World War, states' interventions in socio-economic life are becoming more and more frequent, and both capitalist and socialist countries are gradually moving towards the development dimension of nationalism. The power of the government is growing and the restrictions on the civil rights are increasing. At the legislative level, the state has enacted a series of laws restricting civil liberties, systematically and leanly controlling the society and interfering rights in the form of laws. As for administration, public power permeates every corner of citizens' lives and may at any time, intentionally or unintentionally infringe the legitimate rights of citizens. Only justice can provide a fairer remedy for the legitimate rights of citizens. Since an independent, neutral and passive judicial power is unlikely to directly infringe the civil rights, it is entrusted with the heavy task to be the most powerful state power to protect civil rights and become the most important guardian of civil rights and liberty.[108]

It is common practice in all countries to realize the purpose of protecting human rights through judicial remedies, and in order to achieve this purpose, states are also making efforts to expand the jurisdiction of judicial power. It is with this in mind that Articles 47 and 115 of China's Criminal Procedure Law have been newly introduced, which stipulate judicial settlement of the corresponding procedural disputes.

3.3.3.2 Promote the Active Exercise of Powers of Defense Layers

As we all know, the lawyer's exercise of the power in defense faces "three difficulties", and "five difficulties". Criminal defense is the hardest business in the whole lawyer service industry. For a long time, defense lawyers have seemed to be on the opposite side of the public power, both because of the different nature of the prosecution and the defense, and because of the inappropriate perception by the public power organs of the meaning of the lawyer system. Regardless of the underlying causes of this confrontational situation, the reality is that the primary negative impact of this current situation lies in that the public power organs – whether public security organs, procuratorial organs or people's courts – have intentionally or unintentionally posed undue restrictions on the lawyer's power in defense, thus contributing to the widespread phenomenon of the "difficulty in defense".

Article 47 and 115 of the Criminal Procedure Law begin by listing these undue restrictions in a general sense. The first is the obstruction by public power organs of the defenders' exercise of "procedural rights" in accordance with the law, including the meeting and communication right, the right to review the files, and the right to inquire and obtain evidence; the second is the unlawful infringement by a public power organ on the lawful personal and property rights of a criminal suspect or defendant, including the failure to alter or rescind coercive measures, failure to return

[108] Gao Xinhua [97].

bail deposit, and improper handling of seized, detained or frozen property. Besides, Articles 47 and 115 clarify the judicial remedy modes for the defender in the above-mentioned cases, stipulating that the procuratorial organs are responsible for the review and handling of illegal infringement of public power organs, which to a certain extent, guarantees the legitimate rights of defense lawyers and parties to the case, and reduces the lawyers' worries about exercising the power in defense in accordance with the law. It objectively promotes the active exercise of the power in defense by defense lawyers, and reduces the prevalence of "difficult in defense" situations.

3.3.3.3 Promote the Deep Reform of Procuratorial System

The remedy power of the procuratorial organs has judicial characteristic, and is a symbol of the judicialization of the exercise of procuratorial power. Since 2008, a new round of judicial reform has been under way in China, and the reform of procuratorial organs themselves has been launched as well. After many years of procuratorial reform, procuratorial organs have made great progress in terms of their working mechanism, organizational structure, supervision mechanism, cadre management mechanism and other aspects. It is also playing an increasingly important role in China's judicial system. However, the administrative operation mode of the procuratorial organs has, to a certain extent, limited the reform of procuratorial organs themselves. Therefore, to continue to promote the procuratorial reform, especially to achieve the optimal allocation of the powers and functions of the procuratorial organs, it is necessary to expand the way in which the procuratorial power can function by judicial process design, compensate for the limitations of the existing procuratorial power and function by the characteristics of judicial power, and gradually realize the judicialization of the exercise of procuratorial power.

The establishment of the judicial remedy power and function of procuratorial organs is an important example of the judicialization of the exercise of procuratorial power. The remedy power and function of procuratorial organs have certain specific attributes of the judicial power, including passive initiation, relative independence, relative neutrality, substantive decisive nature, etc. The degree of judicialization of these attributes is limited by the inherent functions and organizational structure of procuratorial organs. However, the existence of these attributes still determines the nature of the remedy power and function of procuratorial organs, that is, its judicial nature. The judicial nature of the remedy power and function of procuratorial organs should also be the guiding principle for the improvement of such power and function, in order to further deepening the reform in aspects including the independence and neutrality of procuratorial organs.

3.3.4 Exercise and Improvement of the Procuratorial Organs' Judicial Remedy Power and Function

Although it is of great importance to empower the procuratorial organs with judicial remedy power and function, due to the inattentive relevant provisions of the Criminal Procedure law and of the judicial interpretation, natural conflict between the judicial remedy power and function and the public prosecution power has led to the fact that such power and function have not produced desired effect in judicial practice. In Province Z, for example, between January 2013 and February 2015, the province accepted 34 cases of "remedies for obstructing the defense in the exercise of procedural rights", "remedies for obstructing the representatives in the exercise of procedural rights" "remedies for illegal coercive measures against suspects and defendants", and "remedies for illegal coercive measures against properties related to the case". 22 cases were reviewed, 12 corrective opinions were submitted and 11 units involved corrected it.[109] From a quantitative point of view, the number of judicial remedy appeals and accusations received by the procuratorial organs is insignificant compared to the province's annual average of nearly 90,000 criminal cases in the first instance and the second largest number of arrest and prosecution cases in the country; From the specific operation of judicial remedies, the 65% review rate and 50% correction rate also suggest that there may well be problems in the operation of the system in judicial practice.

In order to solve the problems in the operation of the system and to strengthen the effective exercise of the judicial remedy power and function of the procuratorial organs, the author would like to propose several theoretical improvement directions. We believe that the improvement of the judicial remedy power and function of the procuratorial organs should start from their connotation, and take the positioning of "quasi-judicial" power and function as a criterion for improving the procedures for their operation. After the promulgation of the new Criminal Procedure Law, in order to better implement the provisions of the new law, the Supreme People's Procuratorate amended and promulgated Rules for Criminal Procedure of the People's Procuratorate (for Trial Implementation). In the Rules, contents relevant to the remedy power and function of the procuratorial organs include provisions in Article 5, which are relevant to division of criminal operations within the people's procuratorates, provisions in Article 57, which are related to the appeals or accusations to the people's procuratorate by defenders and agents ad litem against public security organs, people's procuratorates, people's courts and their staff for obstructing the exercise of their procedural rights in accordance with the law, and provisions in Article 574, which are relevant to the appeals or accusations to the people's procuratorate by parties to the case, defenders, agents ad litem and interested persons against the organ handling the case and its staff for the acts stipulated in Article 115 of the Criminal Procedure Law. We must affirm the importance of the above provisions for the system construction of the procuratorial organs' judicial remedy power and

[109]Wang Lifei [106].

function. Its further refining of the provisions in the criminal procedure law has to a certain extent streamlined the framework for the operation of power. However, these refined provisions are still cursory, lacking provisions on the specific procedures in the remedy process, and do not adequately embody the judicial nature of the procuratorial organs' remedy power and function. Therefore, we advocate that, on the basis of the existing provisions, the judicial remedy power and function system should be improved through the judicial system framework.

3.3.4.1 Subject that Exercises Judicial Remedy Power

It has been argued that since the matters that determine the initiation of remedy procedure are at different stages of the procedure, in accordance with the principle of convenience and efficiency in the allocation of public power, the remedy power may be allocated to investigative supervision, review of arrests, public prosecution, trial supervision and execution supervision.[110] We should note that, if a mode in which procuratorial subjects at different procedure stage exercise the power is constructed only from the "convenience" and "efficiency" of the allocation of public power, the base of the remedy will undergo fundamental changes. The remedy power and the supervision power are placed side by side, but compared with supervision power, which has a relatively weak execution power and execution system, the remedy power should go beyond the strange circle of "no one to supervise the supervisors". In the allocation of powers, although by taking only the convenience and efficiency of the exercise of power into account and ignoring the purpose of legislation, the complexity of institutional setting can be avoided, the result can only be the failure to realize legal effects.

Judicial power must be exercised in a centralized manner, which is inherent in the principles of judicial independence and neutrality. The internal decentralization of judicial power (or the so-called dividing responsibilities) will inevitably lead to an embarrassing situation of delayed efficiency and inability to exercise power; and the professionalism of the judiciary requires such power and function to be exercised independently by specialized organs. The exercise of judicial power by an organ that has already taken the power would inevitably lead to inefficiency or idle resources, and would also constitute a violation of judicial independence and judicial professionalism. The same applies to the establishment of judicial remedy power of the procuratorial organs. Only by establishing a special judicial remedy department, which is directly responsible for the remedies of the rights of participates to the proceeding, can we better respond to the skepticism that the dual role of procuratorial organs cannot ensure their neutrality, and realize the appropriate separation of internal functions and the relative restrictions of power, thereby solving the above difficulties.[111]

---

[110] Xiang Zeyuan [111].

[111] Zhan Jianhong [112].

Specifically, it can be discussed in the following two aspects. First of all, there should be a consolidation of powers and functions within the procuratorial organs, with the establishment of a specialized department for review and remedies, and the remedy power and function of procuratorial organs at different stages shall be effectively allocated to create a professional division of labor. Second, since judicial remedies should not be exercised as actively as supervision powers, a special distributary system should be set up. At the acceptance stage, the case management department classifies the appeals and accusations, transferring those falling within the scope of supervision powers to the supervision department, and assigning those within the scope of judicial remedies to the new organ for review.

3.3.4.2 Review Process

The core of the procuratorial organs' exercise of judicial remedy power and function lies in the review process. The aforementioned data show that the current review rate of the procuratorial organs for judicial remedies is still at a relatively low level, so importance must be attached to the reform and improvement of the review process of judicial remedy. The judicial review process, in the strict sense of the term, should involve the participation of three parties, and the reviewers and decision makers should adjudicate in an independent and objective manner. Both parties to the dispute shall be fully heard on the spot, and this is the foundation and basis for the decision. It should be noted, however, that not all judicial review requires the application of the principle of direct speech, and that judicial hearings in written form are abundantly available in judicial practice. Taking into account the rational allocation and application of judicial resources, judicial procedures where judicial remedy power and function are exercised completely by speech trial may lead to low efficiency, which in turn may affect the conduct of the main judicial proceedings. Therefore, we advocate that we should distinguish between different situations and improve the review process of the procuratorial organs' remedy power and function by focusing on written review and supplementing it with hearing procedures.

Where the content of the appeal and accusation is relatively clear and it is comparatively easy to obtain evidentiary material, a written trial procedure may be adopted. Procuratorial organs exercise their judicial remedy power mainly in two situations: first, the public security organs, people's procuratorates, people's courts and their staff obstruct the exercise of legal procedural rights of the parties to the case; and second, investigation measures taken by the judicial organs and their staff do not comply with the law, and violate the legal rights of the parties to the case. Generally speaking, since both cases involve errors in the conduct of the officials handling the case, and such conduct is generally documented in the internal records of the relevant organs, it is sufficient for procuratorial organs to ascertain the facts in dispute by obtaining information such as transcripts or audio and video recordings, and therefore it is adequate for the trial to be conducted in writing. The effectiveness of the written trial must be based on the active cooperation of the departments concerned, and therefore it is necessary to communicate well with the relevant organs. The relevant regulations should also clearly stipulate the obligation of the subjects under investigation to cooperate with the procuratorial organs in their review.

In cases where the judicial act is of a serious nature and the characterization of the act is unclear, the procuratorial organ shall organize a hearing procedure for the person who lodges appeal and accusation and the relevant case handlers. Under the auspices of the procuratorial organ, both parties are required to make statements, present evidence and cross-examine the evidence, and the procuratorial organ will make a decision. On the burden of proof, in criminal proceedings, the disparity between the suspect and the accused and the "armed" public security organs, procuratorates and courts is too distinct, and the party to the case is so likely to be under the control of the public power party. Therefore, as required by the principle of equity, a reversion of burden of proof model shall be established. To be specific, it shall be up to the party applying for remedy to provide clues or information on violations committed by the case-handling organs and their staff, while it shall be up to the party against whom the accusation and appeal are lodged to provide evidence that the violation does not exist or cannot be constituted.

3.3.4.3 Notification of Correction Process

After hearing the appeals and accusations, if the procuratorial organ considers the situation to be true, it shall notify the relevant organ or department to correct it. Since the law does not endowed the notification of correction with the coercive executability, it is impossible to guarantee the effectiveness of the correction of illegal acts. Therefore, we believe that it is possible to supplement this lack of effectiveness with procedural restrictions by refining the implementation scheme for notification of corrections.

To be specific, the following aspects can be taken into account. First of all, the content of the illegal act correction notice should include a description of the violation situation, the factual and legal basis for confirming the violation as well as the specific corrective measures to be taken so that the relevant organs are aware of the violations appealed and accused and know how to correct it. Secondly, in the service of the illegal act correction notice, for minor violations and clear corrective measures, the postal service is used, but an acknowledgement of receipt is required, which will be sent back by the relevant department after the implementation of corrective measures. If the violation is serious or corrective measures are more complex, special personal service is required. Relevant judicial support staff will send the illegal act correction notice directly to the person in charge of the relevant department or its superior organs, and properly explain the review result and the corrective measures to be implemented to the person in charge. Again, for those who refuse to sign the illegal act correction notice or refuse to correct the relevant violations, it can be revealed to the public by service by publication, so as to exert deterrent effect on the units that violate the law, and improve the authority of judicial remedy power and function of the procuratorial organs.

3.3.4.4 Feedback Procedure

Feedback procedure is also an important part of the procuratorial organs' exercise of judicial remedy power and function. After the results of the review of the appeal and accusation are issued, regardless of whether the violation is confirmed or not, the results of the review should be communicated to the person lodging the appeal and accusation in writing. If it is confirmed that the situation is true and the relevant department has been notified of the correction, the result of the correction shall be reported back to the person lodging the appeal and accusation in writing again after the relevant department has corrected the violation.

3.3.5 Summary

The Decision of the Fourth Plenary Session of the 18th CPC Central Committee requires to ensure the independent and impartial exercise of procuratorial power in accordance with the law, promote the unified management of human resources, funds and property of local courts and procuratorates below the provincial level through reform of the judicial management system, and explore the establishment of a judicial jurisdiction system that is appropriately separated from administrative divisions. The Decision states that the system for ensuring the independent and impartial exercise of procuratorial power in accordance with the law should be perfected, the party and government offices as well as leaders and cadres at all levels should be prevented from interfering in judicial activities, and punishment for interference in the handling of judicial cases should be implemented; the judicial system should be improved and the system for the management of human resources, funds and property of the judicial organs should be reformed, and the separation of judicial administrative affairs and procuratorial powers of the procuratorial organs should be explored. Procuratorial independence and procuratorial neutrality are the direction of the reform and development of the judicial system. Moreover, promoting the independence of the procuratorial organs can effectively guarantee the fair exercise of their judicial remedy power, so as to promote the system construction of their judicial remedy.

The establishment of the procuratorial organs' judicial remedy power and function is a product of the judicialization of the exercise of procuratorial powers, and is a major innovation in promoting the scientific and systematic allocation of such power and function. As the procuratorial reform progresses, more attention should be paid to the judicial remedy power and function of the procuratorial organs. The exercise of judicial power should guarantee the independence, neutrality and objectivity of the organ exercising it, and the judicial remedy power and function of procuratorial organs should also be constructed in accordance with this path. The procuratorial organ has its core power and function lying in procedure, and its primary positioning should be public prosecution organ. The development of its remedy power and function cannot negate this positioning, nor can it affect the effective functioning of its procedural power and function. It is therefore essential to distinguish and separate precisely the various powers and functions of the procuratorial organs in order to optimize the allocation of the procuratorial power and function.

3.4 Reform of Procuratorial Powers Under the Background of Procuratorial System Reform

November 7, 2016, the Central Commission for Discipline Inspection website released the news that the General Office of the CPC Central Committee recently issued the Pilot Project Scheme on Carrying out the Reform of National Supervision System in Beijing Municipality, Shanxi Province and Zhejiang Province (hereinafter referred to as "the Pilot Project"), marking the official launch of the reform of the national supervision system. On December 25, 2016, the 25th Session of the Standing Committee of the 12th National People's Congress voted to adopt the Decision on Launching Pilot Work on the Reform of National Supervision System in Beijing Municipality, Shanxi Province and Zhejiang Province (hereinafter referred to as the "Pilot Decision"), authorizing Beijing Municipality, Shanxi Province, Zhejiang Province and the counties, cities and municipal districts under their jurisdiction to set up supervisory committees, which exercise supervision functions and powers.[112] This reform is considered to be a key political reform of general importance, triggering a major adjustment in the state power structure and having a significant impact on procuratorial power. In this context, it is necessary to discuss the future direction of changes in procuratorial power.

3.4.1 Overview of the Reform of the Supervisory Committee System

3.4.1.1 The Necessity of the Establishment of Supervisory Committees

1. Integrate anti-corruption resources

At present, China's anti-corruption efforts and resources present a diversified situation, mainly including discipline inspection committees, which exercise execution powers, government supervisory committees, which exercise administrative supervisory powers, and the procuratorial departments, which exercise investigative powers in respect of duty-related crimes, the latter being the anti-corruption, anti-graft and

---

[112]Central Commission for Discipline Inspection website, General Office of the Central Committee of the Communist Party of China Issue the Decision on Launching Pilot Work on the Reform of National Supervision System in Beijing Municipality, Shanxi Province and Zhejiang Province, https://www.ccdi.gov.cn/xwtt/201611/t20161107_89267.html. Accessed: Jan 23, 2017.

corruption prevention departments set within the procuratorates. This pluralistic form of power allocation has led to two major problems in the fight against corruption: first, fragmentation of anti-corruption efforts and lack of a comparatively unified and independent supervisory function, which makes it difficult to form a synergy in the fight against corruption. In reality, anti-corruption functions dispersed among the party, political and judicial organs "are overlapped and have unclear boundaries",[113] and "lack standardized and efficient linkage and coordination mechanism".[114] The main manifestation of this is the lack of a central and pivotal organ among the anti-corruption organs; second, gradually, the party's discipline inspection departments and the government's supervisory departments are showing the situation of "one leg long, and one leg short",[115] making it difficult to achieve full coverage of anti-corruption targets.[116] Under such circumstances, the national supervision system must be adjusted and changed accordingly. Otherwise, there will be great incoherence as well as gaps in supervision and areas beyond the reach of supervision.

---

[113]There is overlap and duplication in the functions of these institutions, such as the existence of corruption prevention institutions in the procuratorates and within the government, and the fragmentation of functions reduces efficiency of resources. The consolidation of these functions can lead to greater efficiency and authority, as well as reduced administrative and judicial costs.

[114]At present, a large proportion of corruption cases are first taken over by the discipline inspection commission. After the inquiry, if it is suspected of a crime, it will be handed over to the judicial organs to file the case for investigation. There are two problems with this model of case linkage: first, the disciplinary inspection commission can use some disciplinary means in the course of investigating and prosecuting cases, and it can also collect some evidence (which, because of the special nature of the duty-related crimes, is mostly verbal evidence), but this evidence must be subjected to a second hearing before being included in the criminal procedure process. And there is a high risk of variability in the process, resulting in delays or even interruptions in the proceedings; secondly, after being transferred to the procuratorial organs, case-filing and investigation shall be initiated, which is a duplication of inquiry and is a waste of judicial resources. After the reform of the supervision system, the procuratorial organs may directly initiate the review and prosecution of cases transferred to them by the supervisory departments after they have been filed, which will be conducive to the realization of "no overlapping" functional linkage.

[115]The "long-leg" is the discipline inspection commission system. After the 18th National Congress, the party proposed a comprehensive and strict governance, and increased anti-corruption efforts. The Ministry of Supervision and the Central Commission for Discipline Inspection operate jointly and their business department was established with the first discipline inspection and supervision office and the second discipline inspection and supervision office of the Central Commission for Discipline Inspection. The discipline inspection departments have also explored new ways and means of combating corruption and have carried out some reforms of the discipline inspection system. The skillful application and development of these systems has led to the incoherent problem of "one leg long, and one leg short". The Ministry of Supervision, on the other hand, is only a government department and is limited by the function given by the Administrative Supervision Law, which is to supervise government organs and the personnel they appoint. In other words, it can only supervise within the governmental sphere, and the supervision approaches are extremely limited, which makes it the "short leg". "Legal duties must be performed and laws cannot be performed without authorization", Ma Huaide's interpretation of the National Supervisory Committee, https://www.infzm.com/content/120901. Accessed: Jan 27, 2017.

[116]In accordance with the Administrative Supervision Law, the objects of administrative supervision are state administrative organs, their civil servants and other persons appointed by them. This scope

The important task of the reform of the supervision system is to integrate all the anti-corruption efforts and resources to form a new systemic anti-corruption system. The Pilot Decision states, "The relevant functions of the supervisory departments (bureaus), corruption prevention bureaus and departments of people's procuratorates that deal with corruption and bribery, dereliction of duty and malfeasance and the crime prevention in the pilot areas shall be integrated into the supervisory committee." The newly-established supervisory committee and the discipline inspection organs jointly operate to form an efficient mechanism to supervise corruptions and are entitled to inquire discipline violations, legal violations and duty-related crimes and to decide on disciplinary, administrative penalties and the transfer for judicial punishment, respectively. The Pilot Decision also states, "The supervisory committee of the pilot area shall, in accordance with its management authorization and the law, supervise all public officials exercising public power in the area." From this, it can be seen that the newly established supervisory committee has expanded the scope of supervisory objects and successfully connected with the supervision of the discipline inspection commission, realizing the full coverage of the inspection of public officials exercising public powers.

2. Make the anti-corruption the rule of law

Since the 18th CPC National Congress, the Party Central Committee has made great achievements in the fight against corruption by "fighting tigers and swatting flies" with the force as powerful as a thunderbolt. It has gained time and experience in dealing with both the symptoms and the root causes of corruption. The reform of the supervision system focuses on "tackling the root causes", with the intention of institutionalizing anti-corruption achievements and making them the rule of law, as well as putting power in the cage of the system.[117] "A sound supervision system is a guarantee and a manifestation of the modernization of the country's governance capacity."[118] The establishment of a centralized, unified, authoritative and efficient supervision system, as proposed in the Pilot Project, is not only an urgent requirement for the modernization of China's governance, but also an inevitable consequence of its historical development.

The reform of the supervision system will promote the further development of the anti-corruption work in China, and it will demonstrate the Party's principle of operating within the framework of the Constitution and the law.[119] The newly established supervisory committee is different from the discipline inspection departments of the

is far narrower than the scope of public officials defined in the Civil Service Law and makes it difficult to supervise public officials such as the legislatures, the judicial organs, political parties and main private sectors. On the other hand, the objects of discipline inspection are party members, and their scope generally covers the former. However, given the available corruption data, not all corrupted persons are member of the Communist Party, and there is a very high percentage of corruption among non-party members. Thus, neither the current administrative supervision nor the disciplining inspection can provide full coverage of the supervision of public officials.

[117] In Chairman Xi Jinping's words, "You cannot keep the cat inside the cattle pen".

[118] Wang Conghu, Zhai Jiguang, et al. [113].

[119] Hao Tiechuan [112].

past[120] and is an "organ of the rule of law". It emanates from the highest organs of state power and the forthcoming National Supervision Law, which will regulate their functions and procedures, will make it possible to prevent and control corruption "in accordance with the law". The nature of the NPC-constituted supervisory committee as a state organ, on the one hand, enhances the status of the supervisory committee, and on the other hand, it solves issue of the legality of the inspection by the discipline inspection commission. At the same time, part of the supervisory functions exercised by the discipline inspection commission can also be transferred to the supervisory committee, thus incorporating part of the supervisory powers that formally belonged to the discipline inspection commission into the tract of the rule of law. The high status of the supervisory committee, the full coverage of the supervision system and the integration of anti-corruption effort all mean that the fight against corruption has entered a new stage of system reform.[121]

3.4.1.2 Basic Positioning of Supervisory Committees

1. Power structure of supervisory committees

The Pilot Decision states, "The supervisory committee in the pilot area shall be elected by the people's congress at its own level." The reform of the state supervision system has changed the pattern of power in the country and can be described as a "major political reform that concerns the whole situation". The newly-established supervisory committee, along with the government, the court and the procuratorate, will be produced by the National People's Congress, accountable to it and supervised by it; in the system of state organs, the power structure of "one government, one committee, a court and a procuratorate" will be formed under the governance of the people's congresses at all levels. In the past, the supervision of both the party's discipline inspection organs and the government's administrative supervisory organs was self-supervision and internal supervision within the party and government systems, which makes it difficult to solve the problem of "darkness under the lamplight". The reasonableness and effectiveness of the supervision were controversial as well. The anti-corruption department of the procuratorate is only an internal department, whose anti-corruption ability is subject to many limitations. "One of the reasons the procuratorial organs have been criticized for exercising their power to investigate duty-related crimes is their ineffective anti-corruption efforts."[122] The

[120]Although the CCDI has stronger anti-corruption capabilities, it is, after all, a party organ rather than a state organ, and its ability to exercise its supervision function is questionable.

[121]On January 15, 2017, at the 6th China Law Enforcement Forum on the theme "Comprehensive and Strict Governance of the Party and Law Enforcement", Professor Chen Guangzhong spoke about the recently launched reform of the supervision system. Chen Guangzhong, Reform of the supervision system requires the initiation of a systematic project to amend the law, https://china.caixin.com/2017-01-17/101044638.html. Accessed: Jan 17, 2017.

[122]At the end of 2014, Qiu Xueqiang, Deputy Chief Procurator of the Supreme People's Procuratorate, admitted in an interview with Xinhua News Agency that the anti-corruption bureau had

current anti-corruption force, in addition to being relatively decentralized, also lacks authority and independence. This is because, for one thing, the discipline inspection commission and the administrative supervisory department are lower in the administrative hierarchy or hierarchical status than the party committee and government at the same level, which makes the subject of supervision not fundamentally "symmetrical" or "superior" vis-à-vis the object of supervision so the authority of the supervision is greatly diminished; secondly, supervision subjects are often subject to local constraints, either personnel or financial, and lose their independence.[123]

After the reform, the supervisory committee is directly elected by the National People's Congress, the aim of which is to enhance the authority and independence of the supervision organs, and it is conducive to the realization of extracorporeal supervision and allogeneic accountability. In terms of legal status, the supervisory committee is ostensibly parallel to the "one government, one court and one procuratorate". However, considering that its own job is supervision and the objects of its supervision include the "one government, one court and one procuratorate", it has been argued that "this, in a sense, makes it a comprehensive supervision force above the 'one government, one court and one procuratorate'".[124] This means not only that the constitutional and political status of the supervision organs has been improved, but also that their supervision authority and independence have been enhanced.

2. Nature of the supervisory committee

The mechanism of direct election of the supervisory committee by the National People's Congress has elevated the previous "administrative discipline inspection supervision" to "state supervision". The supervisory committee has become a specialized state organ parallel to the government and judicial organs. What kind of state organ is it then? How should it be precisely positioned? First of all, it does not belong to the party organs, but jointly operates with the party's discipline inspection organs. From past experience, it's usually "two crews working under the same name"[125];

problems in the system, "Since the establishment of the General Bureau Against Corruption and Bribery of the Supreme People's Procuratorate in 1995, a number of problems affecting the effectiveness of the handling of cases have gradually come to light. In particular, the problems of irrational institutional set-up, decentralized forces, too many cases and too few personnel, lack of coordination and outdated equipment have become increasingly prominent and are not fully adaptable to the new situation in the fight against corruption."

[123] In practice, the personnel, financial and material resources of the supervision organs are controlled by local governments, and these organs lack the necessary independence in the work, which affects the authority of the supervision. As far as the procuratorial organs are concerned, although judicial reform has been carried out in recent years with regard to the "centralized provincial management of human resources, funds and property", their independence in exercising functions and powers in accordance with the law continues to be greatly challenged, particularly by the interference of local politics and law committees in the handling of cases. Xi Zhigang [25].

[124] Wang Conghu, Zhai Jiguang, et al. [116].

[125] The Central Government has clearly proposed that after the supervisory committee and the discipline inspection commission jointly operate, in areas where the functions of the discipline inspection commission could not be fulfilled or could not be implemented, such functions can now be implemented through the supervisory committee in the name of state organs in accordance

secondly, it does not belong to the administrative organs as well. An important purpose of this reform is to ensure that the supervisory committee, while absorbing and retaining the administrative supervisory function, is separated from the governmental hierarchy in order to ensure the independence of the supervision function. Lastly, it is not a judicial body and does not possess some of the characteristics of a judicial organ, such as "neutrality, finality and passivity".[126] Although the duty-related crime investigation department of the procuratorate has been transferred to the supervisory committee, this does not mean that the supervisory committee has acquired judicial attribute; in fact, the supervisory committee only has inquiry power, and does not possess investigative power in corruption cases that are suspected of crimes and can only transfer the cases to judicial organs. Moreover, they do not enjoy the power to review the prosecution.

The general objective of the Central Government in carrying out this reform is to establish a centralized and unified anti-corruption organ and to form an authoritative and efficient state supervision system.[127] The basic positioning of the supervisory committee is that it is an independent state supervisory organ, with the attribute of being a specialized state anti-corruption organ, and is distinguished from the disciplinary, administrative and judicial organs. It is very important to accurately define the nature of the supervisory committee, which not only has to do with its legal and political status, but also involves the key issues of "procedural positioning, effectiveness of evidence and linkage of functions", so it needs to be strictly grasped.

3.4.1.3 Functions of the Supervisory Committee

Under Article 2 of the Pilot Decision, the supervisory committee exercises three basic functions of supervision, inquiry and disposition, and is entrusted with 12 inquiry measures to guarantee the effective performance of its supervisory functions.

How to understand the inquiry function? Some scholars believe that the supervisory committee's exercise of inquiry powers can be divided into general inquiry powers and special inquiry powers, of which the former is the power to inquire disciplinary and ordinary violations (e.g. administrative violations), that is, disciplinary and administrative inquiry powers; while the latter is the power to inquire duty-related violation acts, that is, the power to inquire duty-related crimes.[128] This interpretation is reasonable to a certain extent, but it is not entirely accurate. First,

---

with the law. This not only expands the coverage of supervision and provides a legal basis for the supervisory committee to handle cases, but also ensures legality of the measures the discipline inspection commission applies to exercise inter-party supervision. The system of joint operation of party organs and state organs has a Chinese characteristic, but the specific manner in which it is to be done deserves in-depth study.

[126] Chen Weidong [117].

[127] Ma Huaide [118].

[128] Chen Guangzhong, Reform of the supervision system requires the initiation of a systematic project to amend the law, https://china.caixin.com/2017-01-17/101044638.html. Accessed: Jan 17, 2017.

the inquiry power of the supervisory committee is an integral power.[129] Upon the completion of the function transfer and integration, the supervisory committee exercises unified inquiry power in corruption cases, takes appropriate inquiry measures in cases of disciplinary violations, legal violations and suspected crimes, and makes decisions on substantive disposition or procedural transfer[130]; secondly, the basic positioning of the supervisory committee is that it is a specialized state supervisory organ rather than an investigative organ. Its investigative function is the exclusive function stipulated in the forthcoming National Supervision Law, which is not subject to the adjustment of the Criminal Procedure Law and does not have the attribute of investigative power.

How to understand the disposition function? The Pilot Decision states, "The supervisory committee inquires and decides on the disposition of duty-related legal violations and duty-related crimes, and for suspected duty-related crimes, it shall be transferred to procuratorial organs for public prosecution." As can be seen, the disposition functions of the supervisory committee are divided into substantive and procedural disposition functions. Since the supervisory committee operates jointly with the discipline inspection commission, substantive decisions on disciplinary violation and legal violation (ordinary legal violation) cases can be directly made, i.e., disciplinary and administrative punishments; However, for suspected duty-related crime cases, after inquiring the case, supervisory committee can only make procedural decision to transfer the case to the courts for judicial handling.

Among the 12 inquiry measures that can be taken by the supervisory committee, the detention measure deserves further study. We are not unfamiliar with detention measures. According to the People's Police Law, if certain conditions are met, the people's police can take the following measures to interrogate or detain suspects suspected of violating the law.[131] It is an administrative coercive measure designed to maintain public order. Under the new circumstances, the detention power will be given a new connotation[132] and will be exercised by the supervisory committee,

[129]This reform, which is being spearheaded by the CCDI, explicitly states that it handles disciplinary violations, legal violations and suspected criminal cases, rather than criminal cases, and it exercises inquiry power rather than investigative power. Although there may be a corresponding division of functions within the supervisory committee, it does not mean that the inquiry power it exercises has two different natures.

[130]The newly established supervisory committee mainly handles cases of disciplinary violations, legal violations and suspected crimes, and performs the functions of supervision, inquiry and disposition. Of these, substantive disposition is limited to cases of legal violations and disciplinary violations; it has no authority to dispose cases that are suspected of constituting crimes and those cases must be transferred to judiciary for handling.

[131]Article 9, paragraph 2, of the People's Police Law provides that "the detention of an interrogated person shall not exceed twenty-four hours from the time he or she is brought to the public security organ", which may be extended to forty-eight hours in special circumstances with the approval of the public security organs at or above the county level, and a record of the interrogation shall be kept.

[132]Based on past experience, the time limit for the discipline inspection commission to investigate a case is generally three months, and the time limit for the supervisory organ to investigate a case is generally six months. It may be extended, if necessary. Thus, the period of detention may be

so as to perform a function similar to that of a criminal coercive measure. By its nature, the detention measure is a special inquiry measure enjoyed by the supervisory committee, which is different from administrative coercive measures and criminal coercive measures. With the inclusion of the detention measure in the National Supervision Law, the previous "double regulation" and "two guidelines" methods may be replaced. The methods of handling cases will be further standardized and legalized in order to balance the dual value of combating corruption and safeguarding human rights and to demonstrate the principle that the party and the government operate within the Constitution and the law.

3.4.2 Key Issues to Be Addressed Once the Supervisory Committee is Established

With regard to the supervision system reform, it is necessary to study not only administrative and constitutional issues, but also issues of criminal procedure, in particular those contents relating to procuratorial power and the question of system linkage. As for supervisory committee, there has been considerable research by experts in administrative law, who have a good grasp of the constitutional and administrative law aspects of the supervisory committee. However, there may be some misinterpretations in the issues related to criminal proceedings, which need to be clarified.

3.4.2.1 The Procedural Positioning Issue of the Supervisory Committee in Handling Cases

If the power to investigate duty-related crimes is separated and exercised by the supervisory committee, is it still called the power to investigate duty-related crimes within the supervision system? Has there been any change in its connotation or denotation? And in what manner is it to be implemented and expressed? These are yet to be clarified by further research.[133]

We have noted that the 12 inquiry measures mentioned above all boil down to inquiry power rather than investigative power, and there are reasons for this: first, as noted above, the nature of the supervisory committee is that of a specialized national anti-corruption organ, not a criminal investigative organ, and it exercises inquiry power, not investigative power, in cases of disciplinary violations, legal violations

---

about three months, with the possibility of extension to six months upon approval. Explanation of "detention" measures by supervisory committees, https://www.360doc.com/content/16/1226/20/34701701_617876246.shtml. Accessed: Feb 13, 2017.

[133]Problems with the institutions and transfer of personnel of the procuratorates in the supervisory system reform, https://mp.weixin.qq.com/s/we_iD6C22CClyrXmS1mBRQ. Accessed: Jan 19, 2017.

and suspected duty-related crimes[134]; and second, in cases of suspected duty-related crimes, the architects of the reform position the relevant inquiry procedures as specialized supervision procedures, which are independent of criminal proceedings; thirdly, the law regulating and adjusting the supervision system is the forthcoming National Supervision Law, which has the status of a basic national law, while the Criminal Procedure Law obviously cannot regulate supervision activities. Therefore, in the basic context of the reform, the cases handled by the supervisory committees are not criminal cases, but "supervisory cases" of disciplinary violations, legal violations and suspected crimes. With this basic premise, the following questions will need to be answered:

When do criminal proceedings start? Since supervisory cases are independent of the proceedings, criminal cases can only be formally initiated when the supervisory committee transfers the case to procuratorial organs. Of course, whether the procuratorial organs will file a case depends on the specific results of the review, and those that fail meet the conditions for filing a case should be returned to the supervisory committee or the case will not be filed. Can the procuratorial organs directly decide to withdraw the case? The answer should be no, since the case has not yet proceeded to procedures and the procuratorial organ has no power to withdraw cases filed by the supervisory committee, nor can it exercise substantive decision-making power. Moreover, since the procuratorial organs no longer enjoy the power to investigate duty-related crimes, once they have decided to file a case, the case will immediately enter the review and prosecution process. This leads to a question that deserves profound consideration, that is, can there be no investigation procedure in criminal cases?[135]

Can lawyers intervene in the supervision process? Some scholars have argued that "since the inquiry activities involve investigation and is procedurally connected to the review and prosecution stage of the procuratorate, it shall allow the defense lawyer to intervene when the public officers are being inquired."[136] This view is questionable because it fails to recognize that the supervision procedures have different special characteristics from those of criminal procedures. It is obvious that the lawyer cannot intervene in accordance with the relevant provisions of the Criminal Procedure Law, unless he or she is authorized to do so by the National Supervision Law.

---

[134]It has been argued that "the powers of the supervisory committee are, in short, all the powers currently conferred on it by the Administrative Supervision Law plus the investigative power the Criminal Procedure Law gives to the procuratorial organs, and the investigative power is important power and function of the supervisory committee to perform the duty of inquiry". Wu Jianxiong, There are about 50,000 prosecutors transferred to the supervisory committee, and the procuratorates have supplementary investigative power, The Paper, http://mp.weixin.qq.com/s/usFupgIKJz_5P_VDDJr88A. Accessed: Jan 15, 2017. This view is obviously unfounded, as the special nature of the supervisory committee determines that the cases it handles are not criminal cases, but independent "supervisory cases", and it exercises inquiry power rather than investigative power.

[135]In private prosecution cases, it is true that there is no investigation stage, not even a review and prosecution stage. But what about public prosecution cases? Is it possible to follow the procedure of "case-filing, review and prosecution, and trial" after duty-related crimes enter the procuratorial organs? These questions are worth studying.

[136]Chen Guangzhong [119].

Otherwise, the lawyer can only intervene after the procuratorial organs have filed a case. The author does not oppose the intervention of lawyers, but rather interprets the current supervision system from an objective point of view. The author believes that, because of the supervision and inquiry procedures of the duty-related crime essentially replace the original duty-related crime investigation, the Constitution and the Criminal Procedure Law for the investigation stage of the power in defense should certainly apply to the inquiry stage. The legislation of the National Supervision Law should also clarify it.

Can supervisory committees take criminal coercive measures? Some scholars believe that "in the future, supervisory committees may use such means as criminal custody, arrest or even residential surveillance".[137] This view is also debatable. Under the new situation, a duty-related crime procuratorial department will be set up within the procuratorate to deal with the cases transferred by the supervisory committee. It will not only review whether or not to file a case, but will also consider whether or not to convert the detention measure into a criminal coercive measure, including the bail, residential surveillance, arrest, etc. Before the case proceeds to the criminal procedure stage, supervisory committees do not have the power to directly decide on the application of or apply for the application of criminal coercive measures, and the only option applicable is the special detention measure.

3.4.2.2 Effectiveness Issue of the Transfer of Evidence by the Supervisory Committee

The Pilot Project states that "a coordination and linkage mechanism between the supervisory committee and the judicial organs shall be established". The purpose of this "coordination and linkage mechanism" is to transform "supervisory cases" into "criminal cases", so that the evidence collected by supervisory committees during the inquiry of suspected duty-related crimes can be successfully used in criminal proceedings. From the basic idea of the reform design, in the process of handling cases of suspected duty-related crimes, the supervisory committees can collect evidence by implementing a series of measures, and the evidence collected through inquiry will in fact become the main basis for future prosecutions by procuratorial organs and court judgments. As mentioned above, the supervisory committee exercises inquiry power rather than investigative powers and the cases it handles are not criminal cases, so there is a question that cannot be avoided: generally speaking, the evidence on which the people's procuratorate initiates a prosecution and on which the court renders a verdict can only be collected or submitted through formal criminal proceedings, then since the inquiry procedure of the supervisory committee is independent of the criminal proceedings, can the relevant evidence it collects be directly considered criminal evidence? If not, can it be converted in a certain way?

[137] Ma Huaide's interpretation of the National Supervisory Committee, https://www.infzm.com/content/120901. Accessed: Jan 17, 2017.

The evidence collected by the supervisory committee, as a subject other than criminal proceedings, cannot be directly used as criminal evidence. According to the provisions of the Administrative Supervision Law and the Administrative Punishment Law, if a case inquired by a government supervisory department (administrative department) is suspected of being a crime, the case shall be transferred to judicial organs for handling in accordance with the law.[138] Although the two laws contain preliminary provisions on the division of jurisdiction and the mechanism for the transfer of cases, there is no legal basis for questions relating to the validity of the evidence collected by the administrative organs of the discipline inspection commissions after it has been brought into criminal proceedings and the treatments that should be taken by judicial organs. In this regard, the 2012 amendments of the Criminal Procedure Law contain a specific provision stating that "the physical evidence, documentary evidence, audio-visual materials, electronic data and other evidence gathered by administrative organs during administrative law enforcement and case investigation and handling may be used as evidence in criminal cases".[139] As a result, some of the physical evidence collected by the administrative organs can be used directly as criminal evidence. In the past, based on the special nature of embezzlement and corruption cases, their inquiry was generally first and foremost the responsibility of the discipline supervision organs, and relevant evidence was also collected mainly at this stage. However, because of the joint operation between discipline inspection commissions and supervisory committees, evidence collected by them is used directly as criminal evidence in the name of the administrative organs. There are no obstacles in the current system. Article 48, paragraph 3, of the Criminal Procedure Law stipulates that "the authenticity of evidence shall be confirmed before it can be admitted as the basis for making a decision or a verdict". "Confirmed" refers to the review by a judicial organ of the evidentiary capacity and probative value of the evidence through a legal procedure, so as to determine whether the requirements of legality and criminal evidentiary qualification have been met; "as the basis for the determination of a case" means that, it is used as the basis for determining the facts of the case, and the basis for making decisions and verdicts such as whether to transfer for prosecution and whether to prosecute.[140] So, can the newly established supervisory committee follow this approach to solve the problem of the transfer of evidence?

Obviously, the answer should be no. As mentioned above, the newly established supervisory committee is not an administrative or judicial organ, but an independent national supervisory organ, which has the attribute of a specialized national anti-corruption organ. Although the supervisory committee and the disciplinary inspection commission still jointly operate, the evidence transferred in the name of the supervisory committee is no longer "administrative evidence", but "supervisory evidence". The validity and transfer issue of the relevant evidence can no longer

[138] Article 44 of the Administrative Supervision Law and Article 22 of the Administrative Punishment Law.

[139] Article 52 of the Criminal Procedure Law.

[140] Lang Sheng ed. [120].

be governed by article 48, paragraph 3, of the Criminal Procedure Law. Unless the Criminal Procedure Law is amended, otherwise evidence transferred by the supervisory organs will again face "embarrassment" and will require review and transfer by the judicial organs.

3.4.2.3 Investigative Power Issue of Procuratorial Organs

After a case has been transferred by the supervisory committee, the procuratorial organs for duty-related crimes will review relevant evidence and materials, and handle the case according to the results of the review. For those who do not meet the conditions for filing the case or prosecution, although the case cannot be directly withdrawn, decisions can be made not to file the case or prosecute. However, can the procuratorial organs directly investigate or conduct additional investigations in cases where the facts of the case are unclear and the evidence is doubtful? This involves a series of questions about the procuratorial organs' power to investigate duty-related crimes.

1. The question of whether the procuratorial organ is still an investigative organ

The Pilot Decision states that the people's procuratorates in the pilot areas are responsible for investigating and dealing with corruption and bribery, dereliction of duty and the prevention of duty-related crimes. Those relevant functions are integrated into the supervisory committee, which investigates and makes decision on duty-related violations and duty-related crimes such as suspected corruption and bribery, abuse of power, dereliction of duty, rent-seeking of power, benefit transfer, irregularities for favoritism, as well as waste of national resources. For cases of suspected duty-related crimes, it will be transferred to procuratorial organs for prosecution in accordance with the law. What is even more striking is the content of Article 3 of the Pilot Decision, that is the provisions related to temporarily adjusting or suspending the application of several articles on procuratorial organs investigating cases that are directly submitted to them. From this, it can be seen that the investigative power conferred on the people's procuratorates by the Criminal Procedure Law with regard to the direct acceptance of cases has been entirely abolished. So far, out of four original functions of the procuratorial organs, namely, self-investigating, approval of arrests, prosecution and supervision, only three remain. According to some scholars, "the State Supervisory Committee will not exercise procuratorate's investigative, approval of arrests and prosecutorial powers. The inquiry power of the supervisory committee will not replace the investigative power of the procuratorate, and it is also different in nature from the investigative power".[141] This understanding is not entirely accurate, since: first, it has the merit of capturing the special position of the supervisory committee, recognizing that the inquiry power of the supervisory committee does not belong to investigative power in nature; secondly, there is a problem with

[141] Ma Huaide [88].

this view with regard to the question of criminal procedures as it believes that the procuratorates still enjoy investigative power.

There are also people within the procuratorial system who are studying the transference of investigative functions, and the author has learned of two views in the communication with them: one is that "the reform of the procuratorial system is aimed at embezzlement and corruption cases, and the Pilot Decision only integrates the anti-corruption, anti-graft, and corruption prevention functions into the supervisory committee, while the procuratorial organs still have investigative power in cases of duty-related violations"; and another view is that "although the anti-corruption, anti-graft, and corruption prevention function departments of the procuratorial organs have been transferred and integrated, they may exercise mobile investigative power in accordance with the relevant provisions of Criminal Procedure Law". It can be said that this is an issue deserving careful study. As duty-related crimes, malpractice and violations are realized in different ways, the former as passive inaction and the latter as active action. Although the Criminal Law makes a distinction between them, in judicial practice, both cases of malpractice and violations are investigated by the anti-graft department. Since the Pilot Decision has clarified that the anti-corruption and anti-graft functions of the procuratorate will be transferred and integrated to the supervisory committee, there is no valid reason for the procuratorial organs to reserve the investigative power for duty-related violation cases. It is true, however, that at present there are cases in which it is inappropriate for the supervisory departments to investigate crimes such as extortion of confessions through torture, corporal punishment and ill-treatment, and these cases should still be investigated by the procuratorial organs. As for the "mobile investigative power", it means, as stipulated in article 18, paragraph 2, of the Criminal Procedure Law, that "if cases involving other grave crimes committed by the State functionaries by taking advantage of their functions and powers need be handled directly by the People's Procuratorates, they may be placed on file for investigation by the People's Procuratorates upon decision by the People's Procuratorates at or above the provincial level". The "mobile investigative power" is in fact based on the procuratorial organs' power to investigate duty-related crimes, and is an extended rule based on investigative power. However, in a situation where the procuratorial organs have "lost their investigative power", this extended rule no longer exists, and as the saying goes, "where there is no skin, there will be no hair".

On the whole, the integration of the functions of the procuratorial organs in the investigation of duty-related crimes into the supervisory committee is reasonable. For a long time, there has been a major shortcoming in the procuratorial supervision in China: under the model of procuratorial supervision, the procuratorial organs assume both roles as the subject of investigation and the subject of investigative supervision, and self-investigative supervision has been reduced to self-supervision and consubstantial supervision.[142] After the reform of the supervisory system, the power to investigate cases of duty-related crime is exercised by the supervisory committee, while the procuratorial organs are only responsible for the review and

[142]Liu Jihua [122].

prosecution of cases. It has fundamentally changed the situation where procuratorial organs are "both the athletes and the referee", reflecting the obligatory value of "division of labor and restrictions", which is conducive to the smooth implementation of public prosecution and procuratorial supervision, and enhances the credibility of the rule of law in combating corruption.

2. The question of whether the procuratorial organs have supplementary investigative power

Article 171, paragraph 2, of the Criminal Procedure Law stipulates, "In examining a case that requires supplementary investigation, the People's Procuratorate may remand the case to a public security organ for supplementary investigation or conduct the investigation itself."[143] This article only provides for the return and supplementary investigation procedures for cases investigated by the public security organs, and there is no specific regulation about the return for supplementary investigations of cases of duty-related crimes. "In addition, the return of cases of duty-related crimes for supplementary investigation has combined investigation and prosecution integration and the leadership relation between the higher and lower levels of the procuratorial organs, which makes it particularly complex and controversial".[144] In this regard, Article 381 of the Rules for Criminal Procedure of the People's Procuratorate (for Trial Implementation) prescribes that, "After reviewing the case transferred to it by the investigation department of the people's procuratorate for review and prosecution, if the public prosecution department of the procuratorate considers that the facts of the crime are unclear, the evidence is insufficient, or that there is an omission of a crime or other suspects in the crime or under other circumstances that require supplementary investigation, it shall submit to the investigation department a written opinion on the supplementary investigation and return it with the case file materials to the investigation department for supplementary investigation; if necessary, it may also conduct self-investigation, and may request the assistance of the investigative department." Article 3 of the Pilot Decision of temporarily adjusting or suspending the application does not include Article 171 of the Criminal Procedure Law. Therefore, procuratorial organs still enjoy the power to conduct supplementary investigations in cases that the public security organs are responsible for investigating. With the establishment of the supervisory committee, the procuratorial organs are no longer investigative organs, nor do they retain any investigative powers in relation to

---

[143]This article is a provision on the supplementary investigative power of the procuratorial organs, which can be resolved in two ways: first, by returning it to the public security organs, which will conduct supplementary investigation; second, by self-investigation. The term "return for supplementary investigation" refers to that if the facts of the crime are unclear, and the evidence is insufficient, or there is an omission of a crime or other persons whose criminal responsibility needs to be pursued, and the conviction and sentencing of the suspect will be affected, such cases may be returned to the public security organs for supplementary investigation; "self-investigation" means that if there is only part of the evidence in the case that needs to be verified and it has the ability to investigate or if self-investigating is more conducive to the correct handling of the case, the people's procuratorate shall conduct its own supplementary investigation. Lang Sheng ed. [123].

[144]Su Hongwei and Feng Xingwu [124].

duty-related crimes, resulting in the automatic nullification of the provisions relating to investigative powers in cases of duty-related crimes. Then, in this new situation, from the point of view of criminal legislation, if after reviewing the case transferred by the supervisory committee, the procuratorial department for duty-related crimes finds that the facts are unclear and the evidence is insufficient, and that supplementary evidence is needed, does it have the power to conduct supplementary investigation? Is there any difference between this investigation and the investigation before the transfer for prosecution?

The procuratorial organs do not have investigative power in respect of criminal cases investigated by the public security organs, but they can exercise the power of supplementary investigation in accordance with the provisions of Article 171 of the Criminal Procedure Law. In practice, the procuratorial organs' power to conduct supplementary investigations is not dependent on the investigative power, but is a power derived from the public prosecution power. The supplementary investigation procedure is not a compulsory part of China's criminal procedure, but is initiated to make up the shortcomings of the investigative procedure. In the past, the subject responsible for the supplementary investigation in cases of duty-related crimes was the public prosecutor of the procuratorial organs, rather than investigators of the investigative department, the latter only participating when the case was returned for supplementary investigation. In China, prosecutors are given the status of neutral judiciary with the "objective duty"[145] to uphold judicial impartiality, and the public prosecution department's review and prosecution should ultimately satisfy the requirement of "clear facts and sufficient evidence". Therefore, in the course of the review and prosecution, if it is found that supplementary investigation is needed, the public prosecution department may conduct supplementary investigation on its own or return the case to the investigative department for supplementary investigation. Therefore, the removal of the procuratorial organs' power to investigate duty-related crimes will not affect the exercise of the relevant powers of the public prosecution departments, which shall enjoy the above-mentioned powers when reviewing and prosecuting cases.

3.4.3 Key Directions for Procuratorial Work in the New Circumstances

Under the new circumstances, the functions of the procuratorial organs in the investigation of duty-related crimes are integrated into the supervisory committee, and their main business is divided into three main areas, that is, examination and approval of arrests, review of prosecution and legal supervision. Among them, the examination and approval of arrests and the review of prosecution are procedural functions,

[145]The objective duty of the prosecutor means that he or she should be positioned as a neutral judiciary who "aims at truth and justice and acts in accordance with legality and objectivity". Chen Weidong [125].

while legal supervision is a supervisory function. For the above two functions, the procuratorial organs should "grasp them tightly with both hands".

3.4.3.1 Promote the Construction of Investigation and Prosecution Integration

As a result of the reform of the supervisory system, the procuratorial organs are no longer investigative organs, and the issue of the separation of investigative and procuratorial powers is an important topic involving the relationship between the prosecution and the police, which requires further in-depth study.

"Modern criminal procedure draws on the principle of the state and official prosecution of crimes (the ex officio principle) in the inquisitorial procedure, while retaining the medieval principle of no plaintiff, no judge (the principle of private prosecution). These two are linked with the principle of state prosecution and give rise to the position for public prosecutors: the prosecutor."[146] With the continuous refinement of the division of the procedural function, the investigative function is separated from the public prosecution function and is exercised directly or indirectly by the investigative organs. It can be seen that under the prosecution and police integration model, investigative power is the proper connotation of procuratorial power. In other words, investigative power is a derived power of procuratorial power, and prosecutors have natural investigative power, while the police are only entrusted with or instructed to exercise such power on their behalf. However, in China, separation of the police and prosecution is currently adopted, and investigative power and public prosecution power are two powers of different natures, so the investigative power does not necessarily derive from the public prosecution power. Therefore, if the structure of pretrial proceedings in China develops in the direction of the police and prosecution integration, then the procuratorial organs will inevitably acquire the power to investigate or command the investigation of criminal cases.

"The relationship between investigation and prosecution is not arbitrary, and it must reflect the basic requirements of the procedural rule."[147] The author pointed out in an article in 2002, "The basic function of the procuratorial organ is public prosecution, and the procuratorial power is essentially a public prosecution function. The judicial system should be reformed along the lines of the procuratorial organs being the public prosecution organs, and a pretrial system led by the public prosecution organ should be established with these organs at its core. Meanwhile, the current system of examining and approving arrests and other investigative measures should be reformed."[148] Fifteen years later, this viewpoint is still guiding the direction of the current judicial reform and also conforms to the basic requirements of the reform of the "trial-centered" procedural system for reasonable reform of pretrial

[146] Gustav Radbruch [111].

[147] Liu Jihua [127].

[148] Chen Weidong [128].

proceedings.[149] The key question is, how do we move in this direction? One of the major problems is the legal barrier. The Constitution and the Criminal Procedure Law provide for the principle of "dividing responsibilities, coordinating their efforts and checking each other" among the three organs, which divides the investigation, the prosecution and the trial into three distinct and separate stages and also ruptures the close relationship that should exist between the investigation and the prosecution. The future criminal procedural model should be structured according to the division between trial and pretrial proceedings. In pretrial proceedings, the predominance of public prosecution organs should be established. Public prosecution organs shall have the power to command and instruct the conduct of investigative activities for the purposes of the public prosecution. In this context, the main purpose is to give commands and instructions to the investigative organs and investigators in the collection and fixing of evidence, and to minimize the situation in which the results of the investigation are "inadequate" in judicial practice. Therefore, the next main task should be to further study the relationship between police and the prosecution in China and to promote the police and prosecution integration.

Of course, changes in the judicial system cannot be made overnight, and the elements of rule of law transformation need to be nurtured progressively through systematic evolution. In the absence of a judicial review mechanism, a rash reform of the police and prosecution integration would transform the sole investigative supervision subject into the investigation subject. It is very likely that this will "further weaken procuratorial supervision, and is inconducive to enhancing the legitimacy of the investigation".[150] As far as the current reform of the relationship between prosecution and police is concerned, it is a good choice to break the inherent model of "dividing responsibilities, and successive handling of cases" and to focus on the study of procuratorial intervention in the investigation. The early intervention of the procuratorial organs in investigation procedures to guide the collection of evidence is beneficial in playing a leading role in the pretrial proceedings and helps break through the "police-led" mode of investigation. Article 113 of the Draft of the Amendment to the Criminal Procedure Law, which was deliberated in the 22nd session of the Standing Committee of the 11th National People's Congress on August 30, 2011, was added specifically to stipulate that "the people's procuratorates may provide comments and suggestions on the investigation and evidence-collection activities in major cases filed and investigated by the public security organs such as intentional homicide". Although this provision was not retained in the 2012 Criminal Procedure Law, it reflects, to some extent, the importance attached by the legislator to the issue of procuratorial guidance in the collection of evidence. Therefore, this proposition deserves further study.

---

[149] Reform of pre-trial proceedings in a trial-centered context is as important as reform of trial proceedings. Chen Weidong [112].

[150] Long Zongzhi [88].

3.4.3.2 Advance the Reform of Litigation of Arrests

The "trial-centered" procedural system reform is a systematic project involving not only the reform of the trial process but also the reshaping of the power structure in the pretrial proceedings. With the advancement of the reform of the supervisory system, the procuratorial organs have been stripped of their power to investigate duty-related crimes, and among the remaining three basic functions, the one may be adjusted or stripped is the function of the examination and approval of arrests. As far as the author knows, back in 2012, when the Criminal Procedure Law was amended, the question of whether the power to approve arrests should be allocated to the court or to the procuratorate was given serious consideration at a high level. Although this function is still being performed by the procuratorial organs, it does not mean that the procuratorial organs can "get it done once for all". In fact, with the judicial review mechanism having become an important benchmark for the modernization of the rule of law, the transformation of China's criminal pretrial procedures is bound to follow this international trend.[151] Theoretically, in the long term, there is still a need for further research, rationalization, breakthroughs and consideration of the establishment of a Chinese-style judicial review system."[152]

In the Decision of the CPC Central Committee on Major Issues Pertaining to Comprehensively Promoting the Rule of Law (hereinafter referred to as the Decision), the Fourth Plenary Session of the 18th CPC Central Committee has proposed to "improve judicial supervision of judicial measures and investigative approaches that restrict personal freedom" in order to strengthen "judicial protection of human rights". It is noteworthy that the Decision uses the term "judicial supervision" instead of "legal supervision", which indicates that this model of supervision is different from the previous model of procuratorial supervision, and it is a "judicialized" or "litigation" supervision model. It is therefore believed that this will create room for reform in the future with regard to the establishment of a judicial review mechanism of investigative actions such as criminal coercive measures. It is also foreseeable that some important procedural decisions, including the examination and approval of arrests, will be exercised by the courts.[153] In these circumstances, where both opportunities and challenges exist, the procuratorial organs should "let go of their burden" and focus more on other work. In particular, it shall ensure the effective exercise of the legally mandated function of approval of arrests and to reform the arrest process so as to achieve the dual purpose of improving the quality of arrests and effectively safeguarding human rights. Among relevant reform measures, the "litigation of arrests" reform experiment is comparably notable.[154]

---

[151] According to Article 9 of the International Covenant on Civil and Political Rights, personal liberty is a fundamental right of criminal suspects and may not be arbitrarily deprived without judicial review.

[152] Fan Chongyi [96].

[153] Gao Yifei [53].

[154] In recent years, the Center for Criminal Procedure and Judicial Reform of Renmin University of China has been committed to promoting the reform of the litigation of arrest procedures, and

Obviously, the "litigation of arrests" is relative to the "administration of arrests". The current arrest procedure in China is strongly administrative in nature, and this "administrative punishment" has severely "dissimilated" the procedural function of arrests. In practice, abuse of arrest measures is not uncommon. Coupled with the "unification of arrest and detention", China's criminal arrest procedure is to a large extent contrary to the basic concepts of procedural justice and human rights protection. In the absence of the necessary system conditions and practical experience for granting judges the power of judicial review, prosecutors, who have the obligation of objective neutrality, shall take up a more active role in the reform of "litigation of arrests".

"When it comes to the litigation construction, the design of the procedure is far more urgent than the choice of the subject." However, in order to maximize the judicialization of the hearing process, the procuratorial organs should internally adopt a working mechanism of "separation of arrests and prosecution" and ensure the separation of the subject of the prosecution from the subject of the arrest. In order to alleviate the pressure on personnel brought about by the reform of the post system and to improve the efficiency of the handling of cases, some provinces and cities have carried out procuratorial reforms that integrate "arrests and prosecution". This method integrates the functions of review of arrests and prosecution into one and fundamentally undermines the legitimacy of the review of arrest process".[155] Procuratorial organs in China are a subject with special attributes, and their exercise of the power to examine and approve arrests and the public prosecution power have the natures of judicial and administrative powers respectively, which represent the values of neutrality and prosecution, respectively. If the prosecutor of the public prosecution organ is to be the subject of the review of arrests, it is likely to lead to a tendency towards prosecution in the arrest process, and the task of de-administration of review of arrests will be difficult to accomplish. Therefore, while paying attention to the reform of the arrest system, the procuratorial organs should actively seek a scientific and reasonable procedural design to avoid running counter to the direction of "litigation".

3.4.3.3 Improve Legal Supervision

Although the reform of the state supervisory system has had a significant impact and influence on the procuratorial organs, from the perspective of Constitution and the Criminal Procedure Law, there has been no change in the status and attributes of the procuratorial organ as a legal supervisory organ. Thus, the removal of the power to investigate duty-related crimes does not diminish the position of the procuratorial organs in the state legal system. However, "once the power of legal supervision is removed, the procuratorial organs can only become public prosecutors who assume

has carried out pilot work on the "litigation and judicialization of arrests" in Shanghai, Chongqing, Chengdu, Anhui and other places.

[155] Min Chunlei [133].

the prosecution function on behalf of the state".[156] In the current situation, the procuratorial organs should firmly grasp this important function of legal supervision as well as strengthen and improve their legal supervision work.

1. Scientifically explore and define the scope of supervision

Traditionally, procuratorial supervision was mainly concentrated in the area of procedural supervision, but with the advancement of the rule of law, especially as the Decision of the Fourth Plenary Session of the 18th CPC Central Committee has expanded the scope of procuratorial supervision, the legal supervision of the procuratorial organs has been extended from procedural supervision to non-procedural supervision. The Decision makes it clear that, when performing their duties, if a procuratorial organ discovers that an administrative organ has exercised its functions and powers or failed to exercise its powers in violation of the law, it shall urge the administrative organ to correct the situation. This point is relatively remarkable, and it gives the procuratorial organs a more direct and clearer basis for supervising administrative power. Some people interpret this supervision as "top-down supervision", that the legal status and supervision authority of the procuratorial organs have been enhanced and, in a sense, to be superior to that of the administrative organs. Regardless of whether this interpretation is correct or not, it is at least clear that the legal supervision of the procuratorial organs has been further enriched, and the legal supervision function has been further strengthened. At present, however, legal supervision by the procuratorial organs is still concentrated in the area of judicial power, and with regard to the supervision of administrative power, the relevant laws, regulations and reform practices are clearly inadequate.[157] Procuratorial organs are not only faced with the situation of being stripped of their powers, but also seem to be unable to grasp the new powers that have been endowed to them.[158] Therefore, while conducting in-depth theoretical discussions on this issue, a "reform plan" can be put forward at an appropriate time, which will be reported to the Standing Committee of the National People's Congress by the Supreme People's Court and the Supreme People's Procuratorate for approval and then launched on a pilot basis.

Another important question is whether the scope of procuratorial supervision can cover the State Supervisory Committee. In the author's view, this question does not need discussion and the answer is no. As mentioned above, the supervisory committee is neither a judicial nor an administrative organ, and even if the connotation of the legal supervision of the procuratorial organs has been extended from the previous procedural supervision to administrative supervision, supervisory committees are not the objects of the procuratorial supervision. Then, how should the powers of

[156] Chen Weidong [134].

[157] Wan Chun [135].

[158] The crux of the problem is not that the powers of the procuratorial organs have been curtailed, but that the legal powers they enjoy have not been effectively exercised. Just as Articles 47 and 115 of the Criminal Procedure Law entrust the procuratorial organs with the function of providing judicial remedies, in judicial practice, this function of the procuratorial organs is often "inactive" and does not play an effective part in restricting powers and remedying rights.

the supervisory committee be supervised? According to some scholars, "the powers of the supervisory committee will be supervised by external procuratorates, and it is necessary to establish an incremental mutual supervision relationship between the supervisory committee, the procuratorates and the courts".[159] "For cases transferred by the State Supervisory Committee to the procuratorates, if the procuratorate considers that it does not constitute a crime, it has the power to withdraw the case[160] or not to approve the arrest. This is a form of judicial supervision. The procuratorate has the power to exercise legal supervision over the decisions or measures taken by the State Supervisory Committee. This is also a form of judicial supervision."[161] These two views are debatable because they fail to recognize that: first, the supervisory committee is not the object of procuratorial supervision and, second, the concepts of "supervision" and "restriction" are confused.[162] In fact, there is no necessary link between the decision to prosecute or not made by the procuratorial organs and legal supervision, "Regardless of whether or not the procuratorial organs have the 'laurel' of legal supervisors, the law should endow it with the above-mentioned powers, as they are the most basic powers that a public prosecution service must have."[163]

2. Improve methods and ways of supervision

In the past, legal supervision did not have a well-formed organization and procedure for handling cases, and the its methods were somewhat arbitrary and unregulated. At a recent dialogue on supervisory reform held in Chongqing, the author mentioned the issue of the supervisory method reform. On the whole, although the establishment and adjustment of internal organs is not a key direction of procuratorial reform, the innovative path of "legal supervision case-handling organizations" may be a good choice for improving the methods of legal supervision. First of all, it is necessary to establish a sound case-handling organization. As legal supervision is not an individual act of the prosecutor, but is exercised by the procuratorial organs as representatives, the supervisory power should be exercised uniformly in the form of a case-handling organization. Second, inquiry thinking is used to handle the supervision of cases, so that the supervision matters can become cases, supervision clues can be inquired and details can be verified.[164] Once again, the approaches of supervision should be enriched. Procuratorial supervision can draw on the investigative approaches of

---

159Hao Tiechuan [136].

160As stated above, the procuratorial organ does not have the power to withdraw cases transferred to it by the supervisory committee, so there is something improper with this view.

161Ma Huaide [137].

162Restrictions are not the same as supervision. Supervision is a function that cannot be exercised by oneself, and it can only comment on the law enforcement actions of third parties. Meanwhile, supervisors themselves cannot exercise the disposition power of the supervision problems. Supervision only makes recommendations and organs with the power will correct it. It is contrary to basic legal principles for the procuratorial organs to assume the public prosecution function and at the same time exercise the legal supervision function.

163Chen Weidong [136].

164We can learn from the practice of Nanjing, Shanghai and other places where procuratorial organs and procuratorates have created a model for the implementation of legal supervision by interviewing, questioning, interrogation, freezing, retrieval and seizure mentioned in the Pilot Project of the Supervisory Committee, with a view to explicitly listing these powers in the Organic Law of the People's Procuratorates. These powers are very important and in fact play a role similar to that of coercive investigative measures in the Criminal Procedure Law.

In addition, it is necessary to establish a case-handling mechanism in which the procedural function and the supervisory function are appropriately separated. Although the procedural function and the supervisory function of the procuratorial organs are unified to the procuratorial powers conferred by the Constitution, "there are many differences between the two in terms of direction of power, conduct methods and procedural consequences."[165] The two functions are opposed in their attributes and cannot be compatible in the same subject. According to the general supervision rules, the supervisor itself cannot exercise any function, and cannot directly exercise the disposition power on supervisory matters[166]; it can only make comments and suggestions on the law-enforcement actions of third parties and organs with the power will correct it. It is contrary to the general supervision rules and basic legal logic to allow the procuratorial organs to exercise legal supervision while assuming the procedural function. For example, the investigative supervision department is responsible for the approval of arrests and at the same time supervises the case-filing and investigation activities. It is a combination of procedural and supervision functions. It is conceivable that, having assumed some responsibility for supervising the legality of the case-filing and investigation, if the procuratorial organs do not approve the arrest once the case has reached the stage of submitting an application for approval of arrests, isn't that equal to denying their own supervision work? This would place the investigative supervision department in a dilemma. In addition, if the public prosecution department exercises the function of trial supervision, does it mean that the prosecutor, as the accusing party, will have the power to overrule the court? Obviously, this is contrary to the basic procedural rules.[167]

It is therefore important to recognize the dichotomy between the two functions in the operation of the procuratorial power, and the reform of the procuratorial system should also ensure the separation of the two and avoid the problem of "conflicting roles" within institutions. Of course, the separation between the two functions is relative, not absolute. There are possibilities of interaction between different functional departments, for example, through the sharing of information and resources, a win–win situation can be achieved. Both the supervisory leads obtained by the public

issuing guidelines for the handling of cases under supervision, with separate files for cases of case-filing supervision and of investigation activity supervision, so as to ensure the success rate of case supervision.

[165]Chen Weidong and Cheng Yongfeng [139].

[166]Of course, the fact that the supervisor does not directly exercise the disposition power does not mean that supervision does not have a coercive effect; in fact, coercive means of supervision may be applied in the course of supervision, and the results of supervision have corresponding binding effects [137].

[167]Liu Jihua [141].

prosecution departments and the evidentiary gaps discovered by the supervisory departments are important information needed by the other side.

3. Strengthen the effectiveness of investigative supervision

After the establishment of the State Supervisory Committee, procuratorial organs no longer exercise investigative power, and the corresponding connotation of investigative supervision changes accordingly. Since the supervisory committee does not exercise investigative function and its investigative power is not the subject of procuratorial supervision, cases that the procuratorial organs are currently investigating and supervising are only the cases that the public security organs are responsible for investigating. This has ushered in new opportunities for the procuratorial organs' investigative supervision work: first of all, after the power to investigate duty-related crimes has been stripped away, investigative supervision work no longer has to face the skepticism of "consubstantial supervision and self-supervision"; secondly, procuratorial organs can put more energy into improving the effectiveness of investigative supervision. Of course, while opportunities are presenting themselves, investigative supervision work also faces considerable challenges, which need to be dealt with by the procuratorial organs in due course. According to the principle of "dividing responsibilities, which is a relay type of basic relationship between the public security organs for investigation and the procuratorial organs for prosecution,[168] China's investigation model belongs to the "police-led investigation model".[169] In this model, procuratorial organs cannot intervene in the investigation process. In addition to the lagging nature, investigative supervision also faces the difficulties of insufficient rigidity and lack of effectiveness, which should be solved by improving supervisory approaches and clarifying legal consequences.

It is necessary to strengthen supervision by enriching and improving the means of supervision. At present, supervision is mostly conducted in the form of an ex post facto written review, and prosecutors tend to correct illegal investigative acts orally. Often, such supervision receives no response and has no effect in correcting errors. Even if the procuratorial organs issue more formal and standardized opinions to the violation departments and personnel to correct the violations, the lack of legal consequences for non-implementation often results in a passive response on the part of the investigators. Illegal supervisory matters found should be dealt with differently according to their nature, and supervisory methods and approaches should be actively

[168]According to Article 135 of the Constitution and Article 7 of the Criminal Procedure Law of China, the People's Courts, the People's Procuratorates and the public security organs shall divide responsibilities, coordinate their efforts and check each other to ensure the correct and effective enforcement of law.

[169]According to Swedish scholar Brian Iselin, the relationship between the prosecution and the police is more typically embodied in the investigative model. The investigative models that exist in the world can be divided into three types: (1) the police prosecutor model, in which the police investigate crimes and are responsible for prosecuting them; (2) the prosecutor guidance model, in which the prosecutor plays a leading role in the criminal investigation activities; (3) the police-led model, where the police take the lead in the investigation but the prosecution of the case was transferred to the prosecutor. Brian Iselin [142].

explored to effectively strengthen the intensity of supervision. First, oral correction of violations shall be put in writing. For procedural flaws and minor violations of the law, in addition to oral notification of the correction, the investigative organs shall be reminded by regular written notification.[170] Second, a feedback system for correcting violations shall be established. For serious violations of the law, apart from the production of a formal and strict notice (opinion letter) to correct illegal violations, the supervised department should also be required to provide timely feedback on the status of corrective actions, which should not be left unattended.

Legal consequences of refusing to implement the supervisory opinions (notices) shall be clearly defined to ensure the implementation of decisions on the supervision of legal violations. Only in this way can the procuratorial organs' supervision of the correction of legal violations gain substantive binding force. This binding force is reflected in the fact that, once the relevant illegal investigative acts have been discovered by the procuratorial organs and corrective notices have been issued, the investigative organ and its related personnel, who are the object of the supervision, should respond to correct the mistake, or else there will be corresponding adverse consequences. Such adverse consequences or forms of responsibility may include: (1) for those who refuse to implement the supervision opinions of the procuratorial organs, the procuratorial organs may recommend that the public security organs and the supervisory organs to pursue responsibility for relevant personnel. In minor cases, corrections or administrative sanctions shall be implemented within the deadline; in serious cases where criminal responsibility should be pursued, the evidence of violations of the law should be transferred and pursuit of criminal responsibility should be recommended.[171] (2) The implementation of supervision of violations of the law is an important reference for the assessment of the quality of the handling of cases and the standardization of law enforcement by the police, and only in this way can the violators be urged to conscientiously carry out the supervision opinions or decisions. (3) When the smooth development of the case is concerned, the procuratorial organs shall recommend the organ with the power to replace the person handling the case.[172] The public security organs shall review the procuratorial recommendation for the replacement of the person handling the case, and if it is found that there is indeed a violation in the handling of cases and there is a need to replace the person handling the case, the violation of the law shall be promptly corrected and the relevant person replaced. Meanwhile, the results shall be reported back to the procuratorial organs in writing. It is only by clarifying the forms of responsibility from various aspects that the "cost of violating the law" of the investigators can be increased, so that they will be deterred from violating the law.

---

[170] "We have established two forms of supervision, regular reminders and corrective letters, which make it easy for investigators to accept and increase the rigidity of oral correction of violations." Zhou Bin [134].

[171] With the comprehensive reform of the supervisory system, cases of dereliction of duty or abuse of power occurring during the investigation process are no longer investigated by the procuratorial organs, but by the supervisory departments.

[172] Wan Chun [135].

3.5 Research on the Reform of Prosecutor's Responsibility System for Handling Cases

Reform of prosecutor's responsibility system for handling cases is an important element of the new round of judicial reform. The Decision of the Fourth Plenary Session of the 18th CPC Central Committee has also clearly proposed that "the responsibility system for handling cases by presiding judges, collegiate panels, chief prosecutors, and investigators in charge shall be improved, and it should be made clear that whoever handles the case is responsible for the case". In fact, as early as December 2013, the Supreme People's Procuratorate issued the Pilot Project Scheme on the Reform of the Prosecutor's Responsibility System for Handling Cases, and specific arrangements were made for the establishment of a pilot project on the reform of prosecutors' responsibility for handling cases, with the chief prosecutor system as the main component. From January to December 2014, in 17 procuratorates in 7 provinces, in order to ensure the independent and impartial exercise of procuratorial power by the procuratorial organs in accordance with the law, the procuratorial organs have piloted a prosecutor's responsibility system for handling cases, with highlighting the main status of prosecutors in handling cases at its core. The basis for this is establishing a case-handling organizational model with clear powers and responsibilities, close coordination, strong restrictions and efficient operation, and the focus is placed on implementing and strengthening the responsibilities of prosecutors in enforcing the law. In February 2015, the Supreme People's Procuratorate issued the Opinions on Deepening Procuratorial Reform (2013–2017 Work Plan) (hereinafter referred to as "the Opinions") to further clarify the need to "deepen the reform of the prosecutor's responsibility system for handling cases" in the Work Plan.

In the current the reform of the prosecutor's responsibility system for handling cases, the following issues need to be studied:

3.5.1 With Regard to the Functions and Powers of the Prosecutor Within the Post

It should be noted that this is a fundamental issue of how to define procuratorial power and its operation mechanism in the judicial reform. The question of procuratorial power and the power of trial are not the same. The operation of judicial power is relatively simple, and its operation mode and rules are arguably uncontroversial; however, this is not the case with the procuratorial power. As the settings of procuratorial organs in different countries of the world differ, the attributes of procuratorial power vary as well. Therefore, we cannot find any corresponding reference in the international perspective, especially since China's procuratorial power is unique in the world, how to define this power depends on our wisdom to explore the qualities of China's prosecutorial power. I believe this issue has not yet come to a clear and definite conclusion. Many situations are constantly being recognized in the reform and in the discussion. We have seen, for example, that after classified management, this round of reform has resulted in the creation of in-post and out-post prosecutors, auxiliary judicial personnel, judicial administrators, as well as the chief procurator and the procuratorial committee. In such a situation, what powers should be exercised by these different subjects? The procuratorial function is pluralistic, and different procuratorial functions exercise their powers in very different ways. For example, the power to review arrests is a judicial power, and the 2012 amendment to the Criminal Procedure Law gives the procuratorial organs the power to grant judicial remedies, which is a judicial power. However, self-investigation has a very clear administrative character, and the operation of the administrative power is not the same as the judicial power. What is the attribute of legal supervision? Should it be classified into the administrative or the judicial character, or is it a third attribute independent of judicial and administrative? These are issues that need to be well researched.

In general, there is one subject of procuratorates in handling cases, namely, the prosecutors, and all prosecutors are divided into in-post and out-post prosecutors through the reform. The most basic and most important subject of the exercise of powers by the procuratorial organs in handling cases is the in-post prosecutors. It should be noted that they have the right to independently exercise procuratorial powers in accordance with the law. According to the Opinions, except for cases of great importance and difficulty and those involving a large social impact, which require a decision by the chief procurator or a discussion and decision by the procuratorial committee, the prosecutors are vested with the power to independently exercise their prosecutorial powers and are, of course, accountable for their decisions. Chief procurators are very special and important in the operation of the procuratorial power in China. From the provisions of the Criminal Procedure Law, many powers of the procuratorates are given to the chief procurators, so what is the relationship between chief procurators' decisions and prosecutor's independent handling of cases?

Such a paradoxical and unifying relationship requires the chief procurators to perform their duties within the limits of their legally conferred authority and to take decisions in accordance with the law. Such decisions are not arbitrary, nor are they in any way without consequences. The decisions of the chief procurators should be incorporated into the legal system, and all decisions should be in writing; the prosecutors handling the cases shall obey the decision of the chief procurators, and the chief procurators are responsible for the consequences. Of course, the procuratorial committee is the highest decision-making organ of the procuratorates, and all major matters discussed and decided upon by it shall be implemented by both the chief procurators and the prosecutor handling the cases.

For different procuratorial functions, the methods adopted for this responsibility system for handling cases by prosecutors also vary. The operation of the investigative power of the anti-corruption self-investigation department is mainly an administrative case-handling method, and therefore the abolition of the administrative offices and the divisions in the hierarchical reform is inappropriate in self-investigating cases. This is because self-investigating cases are not handled by individual prosecutors; it is often a team working as a whole, from case-filing to the formulation of investigation plans, from arrest to evidence collection, especially in some major and difficult cases, where complex social relations and strong anti-investigation capabilities are involved. These cases cannot be handled by a single prosecutor. Therefore, the exercise of investigative powers requires teamwork and top-down unified command, and in the approval of arrests and prosecution, the main emphasis should be placed on the individual independence of the prosecutor handling the case.

Procuratorial organs in any country or region are composed of prosecutors, ancillary procuratorial personnel, and judicial administrators, which is an organic system. When we put the emphasis of the reform on the in-post prosecutors, we must not ignore the other two subjects, namely, auxiliary procuratorial personnel, and judicial administrators. It is important to address their position, responsibilities and remuneration. Auxiliary procuratorial personnel, as the name implies, are assistants to the prosecutors in their prosecutorial work, while the judicial administrators are responsible for the specific administrative affairs of the procuratorates. In the light of the Opinions, the functions and powers of the two are very clear, i.e., the auxiliary procuratorial personnel deal with matters of prosecutorial business, while the judicial administrators deal with matters of administrative affairs; therefore, the nature of their functions and powers must also be reflected in the management. In the case of auxiliary procuratorial personnel, their work should be accountable to the prosecutors and subject to the prosecutors' management, particularly in the case-handling team, auxiliary procuratorial personnel are accountable to the assigning prosecutor. On the other hand, judicial administrators deal with administrative affairs and are accountable to the chief procurators, deputy chief procurators, and heads of departments. Meanwhile, they are managed by the relevant leading cadres.

Generally speaking, auxiliary procuratorial personnel shall be distinguished from the civil service establishment, and the vocational perspective of the position is to be selected as a prosecutor. In some pilot areas, those who work as auxiliary procuratorial personnel for at least five years will be eligible for the selection as prosecutors. Those in the auxiliary procuratorial personnel hierarchy should be evaluated by separate rank and promotion criteria, and their remuneration should be set at a level lower than that of prosecutors but higher than that of judicial administrators. The length of service after being selected as a prosecutor shall also be taken into account, but the staffing shall be included in the prosecutor's hierarchy and evaluated on the basis of the criteria for prosecutors; those who fail to enter the post of prosecutors shall continue to be evaluated and promoted in their original capacity. Judicial administrators, on the other hand, are more complex, as some enter the procuratorial system through civil service examinations while others are publicly recruited by the procuratorial organs on a social basis. Judicial administrators who are civil servants and listed in the posts should be evaluated and promoted according to standards that are lower than those of auxiliary procuratorial personnel and higher than those of ordinary civil servants. They are no different from civil servants in administrative departments, except that they cannot occupy leadership positions in the procuratorial business departments; for those who are appointed as judicial administrators, since no promotion is involved, the appointing units shall determine their own criteria for evaluation and salary increase.

An assistant prosecutor is also essentially auxiliary procuratorial personnel. Unlike a former assistant procuratorial staff, assistant prosecutors cannot handle cases independently, and they provide only auxiliary support for the prosecutor's operational activities and carry out the tasks assigned to them by the prosecutors. The functional relationship between the prosecutors, the auxiliary procuratorial personnel and the judicial administrators is, in short: that the prosecutor manages and leads the corresponding auxiliary procuratorial personnel in carrying out their work, and the auxiliary procuratorial personnel are responsible to the corresponding prosecutors for their work; the chief procurator and the administrative director of the department command and manage the judicial administrators in dealing with administrative affairs, and judicial administrators are responsible to the head of their department and to the chief procurators.

3.5.2 Problems in the Operation of Chief Prosecutor System

Although the chief prosecutor system has demonstrated certain advantages and significance in theory and practice to varying degrees, there are also some knotty problems that cannot be overcome, which need to be faced and solved during the reform.

3.5.2.1 Lack of Clarity in the Relationship Between the Chief Prosecutor and the Head of the Administrative Department

In the process of deepening the reform of prosecutor's responsibility system for handling cases, after the failure of the reform of the principal prosecution prosecutor, the shift to the chief prosecutor is made in the hope that the transformation of the chief prosecutor's case-handing mode will lead to the clarification of the relationship between the prosecutors, the chief procurators and the procuratorial committee. However, in the process of reform, the "chief prosecutor" leads a group of prosecutors to form a case-handling organization, while the position and power of department heads are still retained. It appears to distinguish between procuratorial power and the procuratorial administrative matters that serve it, which further clarifies its internal operational mechanisms. In practice, however, the existence of a head of department with administrative functions between the chief prosecutor and the chief procurator makes it inevitable that, in the course of administration, these heads of departments will have some connection with the chief prosecutors and the cases for which they are responsible. All localities have further clarified the scope of authority of the two and the handling of disputes, for example, if the head of a department considers the decision made by the chief prosecutor to be inappropriate, he or she may express his or her own preference for the case, and some have further stipulated that his or her preference, together with the opinion of the chief prosecutor and the opinion of the joint conference of chief prosecutors, may be submitted to the chief procurator for his or her reference, and so on. However, the supporting systems are not particularly well developed at present, e.g., the traditional channels for administrative promotion remain unchanged, the specific scope of responsibilities is still vague. In these circumstances, the question of the relationship between the chief prosecutors and the heads of departments cannot be fully clarified. And once continuing for a long time, such a dual-regulation mode of operation can easily bring back the administrative management model and a kind of alienated three-tier examination and approval system; the chief prosecutors dare not or even unwilling to handle cases independently, and it returns to the old administrative pattern.[173]

3.5.2.2 Insufficient Prominence of Prosecutors as Subjects of Handling Cases

The Decision clearly states that "whoever handles the case is responsible for the case" and that, in the process of procuratorial reform, it should "focus on implementing and strengthening the responsibilities of prosecutors in enforcing the law" and "responsibilities for handling cases at all levels shall be clarified". In the course of the pilot project of the chief prosecutor, all pilot units have focused on clarifying the responsibilities of the "chief prosecutor". However, in the practice of the reform, the practice of creating prosecutors under the chief prosecutor needs further consideration. In fact, "under the chief prosecutor model, chief prosecutors do not personally handle all cases within the group, but they are ultimately responsible for all those cases; they need to exercise the necessary leadership and command within the group, while respecting the rudimentary independence of the prosecutors handling the cases". This reform is truly bewildering, as the prosecutors, who assume the role as the chief prosecutors, are expected to lead and command other prosecutors in the team to handle the cases, rather than handle the cases by themselves. While leading and commanding, they have to ensure the independence of the prosecutors being led or commanded in handling the cases, and meanwhile they have to be responsible for cases handled by prosecutors in their own teams. This takes us back to the starting point of the reform, where "the decision makers do not handle the case and case handlers do not decide".

In the deepening reform of prosecutor's responsibility system for handling cases, the prosecutor is supposed to return to the case and realize that the person handling the case decides and the person decides is responsible, but in the end, the prosecutor handling the case is still under the leadership and command of the "chief prosecutor". What this kind of leadership and command of the chief prosecutor means in China needs no further explanation, and there are concerns about whether the subject role of the prosecutors will be made visible.

[173]Zhang Dong [135].

3.5.2.3 Lack of Clarity in the Division of Responsibilities Between Prosecutors, the Chief Procurators and the Procuratorial Committee

Neither the Decision nor the Opinions clarify the responsibilities and powers of the prosecutors, the chief procurators and the procuratorial committee in the law enforcement and case handling. Even in the pilot project of some pilot provinces and municipalities, the responsibilities of the three are not clearly defined. This cannot help but produce a certain amount of confusion that, on the road to procuratorial independence, how the independence of prosecutors should be reflected? How should the principle of procuratorial integration be manifested? And how to embody the power of the procuratorial committee?

In the process of procuratorial reform, while pursuing procuratorial independence, we cannot neglect procuratorial integration. In the process of law enforcement and law enforcement, in addition to respecting the independence of the prosecutors, the command of the chief procurators should also be obeyed and the opinions of the procuratorial committee should also be emphasized. However, when there is a conflict among the three, how they should operate is a matter that needs to be sorted out, and yet the current chief prosecutor reform fails to give us any answers. Even in the practice of reform, the situation that has arisen is still a simple repetition of the same old formula. The main reason for this situation is that the establishment of the chief prosecutor does not truly reflect the procuratorial rules.[174] Rather than achieving the independence of the prosecutor, the chief prosecutor reform has made it more administrative.[175]

3.5.2.4 Strong Feature of Administrative Hierarchy in the Title of Chief Prosecutor

The title "chief prosecutor" has a strong administrative connotation. This is because the word "chief", whether through the regular dictionary or in everyday language in China, shows a strong administrative feature. In fact, the title "chief prosecutor" stems from a misunderstanding on our part. The term "chief prosecutor" is an imported term, derived from a translation of a foreign prosecutor's title. In Germany, the Chief Prosecutor is the agent of the Chief Procurator, and is responsible both for cases and for some administrative matters, but he does not have the power to decide on the cases handled by other prosecutors. The "chief prosecutor" system in Taiwan, China also has shortcomings. In addition to the title, the functions and powers exercised in its operation are also administrative powers to check and approve cases. In principle,

[174] At present, China's procuratorial organs implement a "three-tier review and approval system" that "procuratorial personnel undertake the case, the person in charge of the case-handling department reviews, and the chief procurator or procuratorial committee makes the decision. Zheng Qing [137].

[175] We need to guard against the formation of such a weak pattern in which a strong chief prosecutor leads a group of compliant prosecutors. Zhang Dong [136].

the handling of a case requires the approval and seal of the "chief prosecutor" to be effective. Therefore, scholars in Taiwan have long pointed it out that the "chief prosecutor" is nothing more than an "administrative staff" commanding and supervising prosecutors for the chief procurator. It is "empty" and "only used for seals".[176] This also means that it is clearly inappropriate for us to use the title "chief prosecutor", which has administrative overtones and deals with administrative affairs, to refer to prosecutors who specialize in handling cases and emphasize independence and autonomy.

3.5.3 Possible Advantages in the Operation of the System of Prosecutors in Charge

In our analysis of the reform of the chief prosecutor system, we believe that it is insufficient to enforce the case-handling responsibility system of "whoever handles the case is responsible for the case" and that it is even more impossible to demonstrate the independence of the prosecutors' position. Since this is a responsibility system for handling cases, responsibility should be linked to cases; since it is the prosecutors' responsibility for handling cases, responsibility should be linked to the prosecutor; if responsibility is to be pursued, it should be linked to the functions and powers.

In contrast to the reform of the chief prosecutor system, the author has always advocated the "system of prosecutors in charge" as the direction of procuratorial reform. The so-called "system of prosecutors in charge" is to recognize the independence of each prosecutor who undertakes a specific case, and the prosecutor undertaking a specific case is independent and autonomous in deciding the outcome of the case; each prosecutor undertaking a case is the "prosecutor in charge". Compared to the chief prosecutor system, the advantages of the system of prosecutors in charge are:

3.5.3.1 The Title "Prosecutors in Charge" is More Scientific and Reasonable

"The prosecutor in charge is a law enforcement position, rather than a duty, created by the procuratorial organs in response to the need to enforce the law; it is a seat of competence, not an institution; the power to decide on cases of the in charge derives from the provisions of the law and the authorization of the chief procurator."[177] In contrast to the "chief prosecutor", the title "prosecutors in charge" does not indicate a "leader" duty and has no administrative feature. This helps to eliminate administrative overtones within the procuratorial system. Moreover, the title "prosecutor in charge" can also cover all procuratorial operations, avoiding the weakness of a "principal

[176]Lin Shantian ed. [139].

[177]Zheng Qing [137].

prosecution prosecutor" only responsible for public prosecution. Therefore, from these two perspectives, the term "prosecutors in charge" is more scientifical and reasonable.

3.5.3.2 The System of Prosecutors in Charge Reflects the Nature of Personal Experience of the Prosecutors' Handling of Cases

Judiciary emphasized on personal experience, and only by personally experiencing the case is it possible to fully grasp the whole story of the case, correctly ascertain the facts and make right decision on that basis. In the operation of the procuratorial power, only by making the prosecutors handling the case to decide can they be motivated; only by making the prosecutors making the decision to be responsible can the prudence in the case handling process be ensured, and only by combining motivation with prudence can the quality of the handling of the cases be guaranteed and the efficiency be improved. In the system of prosecutors in charge, each prosecutor undertaking the case acts as the prosecutor in charge, being endowed with the power to decide the outcome of the case based on the inner conviction formed by one's own casework. There is no "chief prosecutor" or "department head" over the prosecutor in charge of the case to decide on the handling of cases. This eliminates the various administrative approvals or disguised administrative approvals that linger over the prosecutors, ensuring the personal experience of the judiciary, realizing the "let those who handle the case decide and those who decide be responsible", and conforming with the requirement of the principle of personal experience.

3.5.3.3 The Prosecutor in Charge Fundamentally Recognizes the Independence of Individual Prosecutors

The chief prosecutor is one of the few prosecutors selected to be granted independence and autonomy and to have command and supervision of the prosecutors in the team. Different from such functions and powers, under the system of prosecutors in charge, any prosecutor handling a case is a "prosecutor in charge", who can independently decide on the outcome of the case within the limits of the law and the authorization of the chief procurator. The prosecutor in charge is the title of the prosecutor handling the case rather than a duty and his function is to handle the case. Thus, the prosecutor in charge is able to give independence to each individual prosecutor as a whole.

3.5.3.4 The System of Prosecutors in Charge Has Weakened the Administrative Hierarchy Within the Procuratorial Organs

In the system of prosecutors in charge, when the prosecutors in charge handle cases, apart from those expressly stipulated in the law that must be decided or authorized by the chief procurator or the procuratorial committee, they have complete autonomy in the law enforcement and case handling. This harmonizes the relationship between the prosecutors in charge and the heads of the departments and abolishes the power of the heads of the departments to review cases; it can also weaken the administrative hierarchy within the procuratorial organs and liberate individual prosecutors from the complicated administrative hierarchy, so it is more in line with the direction of procuratorial reform.

3.5.3.5 Unity of Power and Responsibility Achieved Through the System of Prosecutors in Charge

"Let those who handle the case decide and those who decide be responsible" is the goal of procuratorial reform. This also means that the consistency of power, responsibility and interest shall be ensured. The unity of power, responsibility and interest is not only the pursuit of the construction of rule of law, but also the purpose of judicial reform. Under the system of prosecutors in charge, the one who really decides the outcome of the case is the prosecutor who personally handles the case, i.e. the prosecutor in charge. This completely realizes the goal of the prosecutorial reform of "letting those who handle the case decide and those who decide be responsible", and truly achieves the consistency of power and responsibility. This will help to motivate prosecutors in handling cases and lay the foundation for the specialization, professionalization and elite construction of the prosecutors' team.[178]

3.5.3.6 Case-Handling Organizational Form of the Prosecutors

The case handling team is a basic organizational form of the procuratorial organs in handling cases, and this issue has not been given sufficient attention in the past, nor has it been studied carefully. The current judicial reform raises this issue, which I think is very important. The current law has no specific provisions on the case-handling organization of the procuratorial organs, which is different from the courts. The trial organization of the court is very clearly written in the procedural law, that is the system of sole-judge proceedings and collegial system, plus the trial committee, while the procuratorate has none. This is why the reform of the procuratorates is so challenging, and there are many issues that need to be addressed from the beginning. In this round of reform, the court first proposes presiding judge, collegial case-handling responsibility system, which is very clear, but what about the procuratorate? Since it handles cases just as the court does, there must be an organizational form to handle cases. In the past case-handling organizational form of procuratorates, the prosecutors were the first persons to undertake a case, and then the case was reviewed at various levels, decided by the chief procurator or discussed and decided by the procuratorial committee. In such a highly administrative organizational form of the procuratorial organs, the subject position of the prosecutors is gone, and they are

178 Xu Hanming, Jin Xin et al. [141].

reduced to an implementer to follow the orders of superiors. In retrospect, we ask the following questions in the reform: Should there be a case-handling team or not? What should be the operation mode of the case-handling team? It depends on the actual needs of the procuratorial organs in handling cases, and generally speaking, most of the cases can be taken up independently by the in-post prosecutors.

In my view, for the organizational form of the procuratorial organs in handling cases, the first and foremost should be the prosecutor in charge, who corresponds to the presiding judge of the court. The prosecutors in charge have the power to decide on cases they undertake and exercise powers in accordance with the law and the boundaries of the power list; however, there are many cases in which one person cannot do the job, so two or more people are needed, which gives rise to a second form of procuratorial organs' handling of cases: the case-handling team. Therefore, I believe that the future case-handling organizational form of the procuratorial organs will be handling the cases in the form of the prosecutors in charge and the procuratorial team. This is the first time that I have explicitly put forward the idea of the "responsibility system of the procuratorial team in handling cases", which corresponds to the collegial panel system of the court as another form for the procuratorial organs to handle the cases. It is a form in which the case-handling team and the prosecutors in charge are included as the two main case-handling teams of the procuratorial organs. Of course, there are chief procurators and the procuratorial committee, but they are not normalized case-handling organizations. Instead, when the circumstances provided for by law arise, the decision is taken by the chief procurator or the case is referred to the procuratorial committee for discussion and decision.

How is this case-handling team constituted? In the courts, the composition of the collegiate panel is clear: in the first instance, the panel is composed of three persons; in the second instance, it is composed of three or five persons (in odd number); the responsibility system of the collegiate panel is also clear, that is, it is the responsibility of the persons who hold the majority view that make the judgement or decision, so it must be a majority number (odd number), and it may be three or five people. However, the case-handling team of the procuratorate is different, and I disagree with the view that in order to form a majority opinion, the case-handling team of the procuratorate must be composed of three persons. In many cases, two people will do. Who is going to make that decision? Two people. This is where I think the procuratorial power is special: in a case-handling team composed by two people, if the two are in agreement, they shall make a joint decision; if they disagree with each other, it shall be reported to the chief procurator to decide. If the chief procurator cannot decide, it shall be submitted to the procuratorial committee for discussion and decision. Whoever decides shall be responsible for it and the issue is settled.

So, should the case-handling team be fixed or not? At present, there are courts implementing "1 + 1 + 1" or " + N" case handling mode, and a fixed collegiate case handling mode is being implemented. I think the collegiate panels should be fixed. Although fixed panel has certain advantages, over time it will become homogeneous, and restrictions that shouldn't exist will be formed; Similarly, the procuratorial case-handling team must not be fixed. In the investigation stage, the case-handling team can be fixed, and must be so, because partners need to cooperate in the long-term, which makes it necessary for them to well understand the styles, characteristics and temperament of each other. However, this must not be fixed in the judicial practice of the procuratorates and the courts, since cases vary in types and need to be specific decided based on their natures. Therefore, my view is that the procuratorial case-handling team should be temporary, like the collegiate panel, which is formed for the case and dismissed upon its conclusion.

3.5.4 How to Supervise the Prosecutors in Correctly Performing the Procuratorial Functions and Powers in Accordance with the Law

The supervision of the in-post prosecutors shall be based on case supervision and internal supervision, and supplemented by conduct supervision and external supervision. In-post prosecutors need to be responsible for the quality of cases throughout their lives. This is not only a requirement of judicial responsibility, but also a core element for ensuring the quality of procuratorial services and should be given priority consideration. Conduct supervision, on the other hand, is a form of supervision of the misconducts of prosecutors in the course of handling cases, and is an important source of judicial responsibility. Internal supervision refers to the supervision of the procuratorates through the supervision of the prosecutors' conducts and the evaluation of the quality of cases. Since the operational conducts of prosecutors take place primarily within the procuratorial organs, it is practical to use internal supervision as the main supervision method. On the other hand, external supervision is conducted through methods including people's supervisors, the National People's Congress, the Chinese People's Political Consultative Conference and citizens' complaints. This is also an important supervision way.

Authorization and supervision are not problems in the same dimensions, and authorization does not lead to less effective supervision, while supervision does not lead to ineffective authorization. Although the elimination of the hierarchical review model has reduced one process for supervising the quality of cases in terms of the supervision methods, in general, due to the lifelong responsibility for handling cases, supervision and supervisory measures have not been substantively weakened. In order to ensure the effectiveness of supervision, it is necessary to design and improve the supervision mechanism itself. Specifically, it can be designed from three aspects: first, a mechanism for supervising the quality of cases, which can be based on three aspects of daily inspection, case supervision and discipline inspection supervision; second, direct supervision of cases by the chief procurator and procuratorial committee. Since the chief procurator responsibility system is implemented, chief procurator may at any time request an inspection of the conduct of the prosecutor's case and exercise supervision; Lastly, external supervision mechanisms such as the people's supervisors, the National People's Congress, and the Chinese People's Political Consultative

Conference should be maintained and improved so that both internal and external supervision can play an effective role.

3.5.5 Relationship Between the Independence of Prosecutors and Procuratorial Integration

Requiring prosecutors to independently handle the cases and assume responsibility does not imply the negation of procuratorial integration or the exclusion of the leadership of the chief procurators. In fact, the independence of prosecutors is still independence under an integrated procuratorial system and remains subject to the leadership of the chief procurator. However, based on the minimum guarantees of independence of prosecutors in handling cases, it is necessary to bring the leadership of the chief procurator under the rule of law, that is, to legalize the command of the chief procurator.[179] Specifically: first of all, the exercise of the chief procurators' command should be unified and it should be clarified that the command of the chief procurator should be made in writing and, if it is not possible to do so in a timely manner because of time constraints, it should be corrected afterwards as soon as possible. Secondly, the executor of the command is given the right to object to remind the chief procurator of the possible illegal and unreasonable aspects of the command. But objection does not mean that it is okay to not execute the command of the chief procurator. On the contrary, as long as the chief procurator commands, the relevant prosecutor must comply even if he or she objects. However, if it is subsequently proved that the command was erroneous and the prosecutor promptly objects to it, the prosecutor shall not be held responsible for the execution of an erroneous command. It should be pointed out that both the commands of the chief procurator and the objections of the prosecutor should be attached to the file. Lastly, the responsibility of the chief procurators for erroneous commands or commands given in violation of procedure should be clarified and a procedure for recourse should be established. This is conducive to the transparency and standardization of the operation of the procuratorial power, and will enhance the prudence of the commands issued by the chief procurator and avoid unnecessary interference.

There is no clear definition of the division of functions, responsibilities and authorization between the prosecutors and the procuratorial committee, nor is it found in the relevant legal norms. For example, Article 87 of the Criminal Procedure Law of China stipulates that "the chief procurator shall make the decision on a People's Procuratorate's examination and approval of the arrest of a criminal suspect. Major cases shall be submitted to the procuratorial committee for discussion and decision". Article 4 of the Regulations on the Procuratorial Committee of the People's Procuratorate provides that "the procuratorial committee shall discuss and decide on major

[179] Chen Weidong [142].

cases and other major issues.[180] However, it is unclear what is meant by "major cases". Such a definition is likely to leave the system open to inappropriate intervention by the procuratorial committee. Particularly in the actual judicial environment of China, prosecutors undertaking the cases are subject to the limitations of the current professional assessment and accountability system, or even to extrajudicial intervention or the influence of public opinions, and they often face enormous risks and pressure in the process of handling cases. Thus, it is more desirable that through the procuratorial committee, the adverse consequences can be transferred from being individual borne to being collectively borne by the procuratorial committee. If the scope of "major cases" discussed by the procuratorial committee is not well defined, the invisible function of the procuratorial committee as a safe haven for burden-sharing and risk-shifting will become more pronounced. This will fundamentally affect the effectiveness of the reform of the system of prosecutors in charge. Therefore, in the future reform of the prosecutors in charge, it is necessary to clarify the division of powers and responsibilities between the prosecutors and the procuratorial committee, in particular, to define the scope and limits of the procuratorial committee's discussion of cases.

References

1. Zhang, W. (2001). *Research on the basic category of law* (p. 19). Beijing: China University of Politic Science and Law Press.
2. Zhang, Z. (2007). *The study of the procuratorial power* (p. 243). Beijing: China Procuratorial Press.
3. Wu, J. (2011). Judicial value of procuratorial power and its improvement. *Chinese Criminal Science*, 10.
4. Zongzhi, L. (1999). On the nature of procuratorial power and revolution of procuratorial organs. *Law Science*, 10.
5. Chen, W. (2002). The reflection and reconstruction on the of procuratorial power. *Law Review*, 2.

[180] Article 4 of the Regulations on the Procuratorial Committee of the People's Procuratorate (2008 revision) provides that major cases and other major issues discussed by procuratorial committees are subdivided into eight items, namely: (1) deliberating and deciding on major issues relating to the implementation of national laws, policies and resolutions of the people's congresses and their standing committees at this level in the procuratorial work; (2) deliberating and adopting work reports, special reports and bills for deliberations by the people's congresses and their standing committees at this level; (3) summarizing the experience of procuratorial work and studying new situations and problems in procuratorial work; (4) the Procuratorial Committee of the Supreme People's Procuratorate deliberates and adopts interpretations of specific legal application issues in procuratorial work, as well as regulations, provisions, rules and measures relating to procuratorial work; the procuratorial committees of the people's procuratorates below the provincial level deliberate and adopt normative documents on procuratorial operations and management in the region; (5) deliberating and deciding on major, difficult and complex cases; (6) deliberating and deciding on cases or matters for review by the people's procuratorate at the next higher level.; (7) deciding on the withdrawal of chief procurators of people's procuratorates at this level and heads of public security organs; (8) other cases or matters to be brought before the procuratorial committee for deliberation.

8. Liu, L., Zhang, Z. et al. Research on the power of procuratorial organs, *Prosecution Review, 2*, 100–101.
9. Liu, L., Zhang, Z. et al., Research on the power of procuratorial organs, *Prosecution Review, 2*, 103–105.
10. Xie, P. (2000). On the nature of procuratorial power. *Law Science, 2*.
11. Zhen, Z. (2010). *On the comparative difference in procuratorial systems* (p. 161). Beijing: Law Press China.
12. Wei, W. (2008a). *Procuratorial systems in France and Germany* (p. 158). Beijing: China Procuratorial Press.
13. Wei, W. (2008b). *Procuratorial systems in France and Germany* (p. 169). Beijing: China Procuratorial Press.
14. Zongzhi, L. (2014). *On objective obligation of prosecutors* (p. 41). Beijing: Law Press China.
15. Li, M. (2010). *Study on the history of the Western procuratorial system—Origins and difference in types.* Beijing: Tsinghua University Press, 354-356.
17. Liu, J. (2012). The Chinese model of arrest review system and its reform. *China Legal Science*, 2.
18. Guangzhong, C., & Jie, C. (2007). An interpretation of justice and judicial organizations in Chinese-style. *China Legal Science*, 2.
20. Wang, G. (2008). *Wang Guiwu on procuration* (p. 167). Beijing: China Procuratorial Press.
22. Criminal Law Office of the Legislative Affairs Commission of the Standing Committee of the National People's Congress. (2008). *Description of the provisions of the criminal procedure law of the people's republic of China, legislative reasons and relevant provisions* (p. 242). Beijing: Peking University Press.
23. Weimin, Z., & Zhao, K. (2006). A survey and reconsideration of the investigation supervision system: Based on a positive study. Modern Law Science, 6.
24. Ji, M., & Shan, M. (2013). On dilemma and solution of criminal case-filing supervision. *Law Review*, 2.
25. Liu, J. (2014). The Chinese mode and reform of the system of supervision investigation. *China Legal Science*, 1.
26. Yuan, M., Hu, Y., & Tao, J. (2009, June 12). Concept of improving the mechanism for the criminal case-filing supervision. *Procuratorial Daily.*
27. Beijing Haidian District People's Procuratorate, "The Prosecution-Police Relations Project Group". (2006). Investigation and analysis on present situation and problems of procuratorial relationships. *People's Procuratorial Semimonthly*, 22.
28. Dongxiong, H. (1995a). *Study on criminal procedure law* (p. 98). Taibei: San Min Book Co., Ltd.
29. Huang , D. (1995b). *Study on criminal procedure law* (p. 106). Taibei: San Min Book Co., Ltd.
31. Zuo, W., & Zhao, K. (2006). A survey and reconsideration of the investigation supervision system: Based on a positive study. *Modern Law Science,* 6.
34. Wan, Y. (2010). On the Structural Change of Legal Supervision of Prosecutive Organ. *Legal Forum*, 1.
35. Huang, D. (1995c). *Study on criminal procedure law* (p. 106). Taibei: San Min Book Co., Ltd.
36. Xu, J. (Ed.). (1997). *Criminal procedure law (part 1)* (p. 186). China Legal Publishing House: Beijing.
37. Merryman, J. H. (1984). *The civil law tradition* (p. 149). Beijing: Knowledge Publishing House.
38. Chen, W., & Liu, J. (2000). Who has the power to arrest you—A discussion on the reform of China's arrest system (part 1). *Chinese Lawyer*, 9.
39. Chen, W., & Lu, E. (2004). A comparative analysis of power distribution in custody initiation and determination. *Legal Science,* 11.
40. Wang, X. (2012, March 12). Four major results of the reform of promoting the right of arrest a level higher. *Procuratorial Daily.*

41. Li, N. (2011, Aug 29). The supreme people's procuratorate reviews the "one-level promotion" reform of the duty-related criminal cases. *Legal Daily*.
43. Liu, J. (2006). Alienation and correction of the function of arrest. *Political Science and Law,* 3.
44. Liu, J. (2009). The term of criminal custody and examination of arrest shall be shortened. *Justice of China,* 3.
45. Chen, G. ed. (2002), *Criminal Procedure Law*. Beijing: Peking University Press, Higher Education Press, 83–84.
46. Cheng, R. ed. (1999). *Criminal procedure law*. Beijing: China Renmin University Press, 104.
47. Guangzhong, C. (2012). Overall strengthening of legal supervision of criminal procedure. *Legal Information,* Z1.
48. Chen, F. K., & Deng, S. (2014). The direction and path of legal supervision of the review of the death penalty. *Legal Science*, 7.
49. Chen, W., & Du, L. (2012). Procuratorial organs under special criminal procedures and their responses. *Journal of National Prosecutors College*, 3.
50. Chen, W. (2011). Building a special criminal procedure with Chinese characteristics. *China Legal Science*, 6.
51. He, W. (1997). On the problem of whether the prosecutor shall stand. *Legal Science*, 5.
52. Wang, J., & Sun, Y. (2001). Authority of judiciary and authoritarian judiciary. *Law Review*, 4.
53. Li, J. (2012). Deconstruction of the trial supervision function of the procuratorial organs. *China Legal Science*, 5.
54. Zhao, Y. (2013, Mar 25). The methods of the scope of legal supervision of the death penalty review shall be determined as soon as possible. *Legal Daily.*
55. Yuan, Q. (2014). Reflections and discussions on the establishment of criminal procuratorial organs. *People's Procuratorial Semimonthly*, 13.
56. Xu, Y. (2015, Jan 30). The "past and present" of criminal execution prosecution. *Procuratorial Daily.*
57. Yuan, Q. (2013). Procuratorial inspection patrol from the perspective of prison procuratorial work. *Procuratorial Daily*.
58. Shan, M. (2012). Problems and responses in the criminal execution supervision. *Political Science and Law,* 11.
59. Shang, A. (2013). Study on the system of execution procuratorial supervision of property penalties. *People's Procuratorial Semimonthly*, 18.
60. Nantong People's Procuratorate Research Group. (2015). Investigations and reflections on the execution supervision of compulsory medical treatment—A sample of the supervision of the suffocation of compulsory medical treatment by the procuratorial organs in N City. *The Chinese Procurators*, 11.
62. Zhou, W. (2013). Criminal execution procuratorial work: development of the procuratorial theories and practices of regulated places. *Journal of National Prosecutors College*, 4.
63. Li, G., Qi, Y., & Chen, W. (2015). Dilemmas and ways out: current status and reconstruction of criminal execution procuratorial work. *Journal of Beijing College of Politics and Law,* 4.
67. Zhang, Z. (2002). Some thinking about the supervision over the execution of punishment. *People's Procuratorial,* 6.
69. Weidong, C., & Sun, H. (2013). Building a Chinese-style complaint handling mechanism for detainees. *The Chinese Procurators*, 7.
70. Li, F., & Sun, H. (2014). Comparative study of complaint handling mechanisms for detainees. *Chinese Criminal Science*, 2.
71. Chen, W. (2009). Study on the system of inspection of places of custody. *People's Court Daily,* 6.
72. Wang, S. (2015). Methods of legal supervision and the amendment to the organic law of procuratorates. *Journal of National Prosecutors College*, 2.
73. Zhang, B. (2011). Basic issues and main points of view of amendment of the organic law of the people's procuratorates. *Journal of National Prosecutors College*, 6.

74. Xiaoqing, Z., & Zhang, Z. (2010). *Procuratorial science* (p. 427). Beijing: China Procuratorial Press.
75. Zongzhi, L. (2006). *Tutorial on the procuratorial system* (p. 99). Beijing: China Procuratorial Press.
76. Lian, Y. (2014). Positioning of the nature of procuratorial power under the vision of the connection of "two laws". *Exploration And Free Views, 2.*
77. Song, Y., & Lin, L.. (2016). Reflection on the internal operation mechanism of the prosecutorial power in the judicial reform. *Journal of Beijing Union University (Humanities and Social Sciences),* 1.
78. Zhou, Y., & Ye, Z. (2015). Analysis of some key issues of China's constitutional procuratorial system. *Journal of Sichuan Normal University (Social Sciences Edition),* 2.
80. Chen, W. (Ed.). (2012a). *Understanding and application of the provisions of the 2012 amendment of the criminal procedure law* (p. 37). China Legal Publishing House: Beijing.
81. Zhang, J. (2013). Jurisprudential analysis of the procuratorial function in criminal proceedings. *Jianghai Academic Journal,* 6.
82. Zhang, Z. (Ed.). (2009). *China procuratorial (Vol 18)* (p. 63). China Procuratorial Press: Beijing.
83. Wang, J., & Wang, Y. (2015). On procuratorial functions and internal institutions reform of the procuratorates. *Journal of National Prosecutors College,* 1.
85. Fan, C. (2010). Philosophical research on function of legal supervision. *People's Procuratorial Semimonthly,* 1.
86. Ge, L. (2013). Summary of the seminar on the amendment of the two major procedural laws and the improvement of the procuratorial system. *Journal of National Prosecutors College,* 1.
87. Miao, L. (2004). A study on the constitutionalizing of citizen's right to seek judicial protection. *China Legal Science,* 5.
88. Chen, W. (2002). The reflection and reconstruction on the of procuratorial power—An analysis with public prosecution power at its core. *Law Review,* 2.
89. Kaiju, S., & Fan, B. (1987). The status of letters and visits in administrative procedures. *Law Science,* 4.
90. Bifeng, Y. (1996). *Administrative law* (p. 222). Wuhan: Wuhan University Press.
91. Zhang, S. (1991). *Administrative law new theory* (p. 235). Beijing: Current Affairs Press.
92. Guo, D. ed. (1995). *Theory and practice of human rights.* Wuhan: Wuhan University Press, 699.
93. Lin, L. (1999). Study of basic theoretical issues of administrative remedies. *China Legal Science,* 6.
94. Xing, H. (2014). On the exceptions to the application of exhaustion of administrative remedies principles and their implications to China. *Legal Forum,* 2.
95. Dai, Y. (2007). Development and history of procuratorial science—Current situation and prospects of study. *People's Procuratorial Semimonthly,* 15.
96. Chen, W., & Cheng, Y. (2014). Key issues in the new round of procuratorial reform. *Journal of National Prosecutors College,* 1.
97. Chen, W. (2014). Study of the independent exercise of judicial organs in accordance with the law. *China Legal Science,* 2.
98. Chen, W. (Ed.). (2012). *Understanding and application of the provisions of the 2012 amendment of the criminal procedure law* (p. 37). China Legal Publishing House: Beijing.
99. Zhan, J. (2015). Institutional models of procedural remedies and adaptation. *China Legal Science,* 2.
100. Long, Z. (2013). Proper judicial reform of the way in which prosecutors handle cases. *Chinese Journal of Law,* 1.
101. Chen, W. (2011, Feb 23). Measures to resolve the contradictory roles of the procuratorial organs—Separation of the legal supervision function and procedural function. *Legal Daily.*
102. Gao, X. (2006). A tentative study of the function system of modern judicial power. *Study & Exploration,* 2.

103. Wang, L. (2015). On the current situation of the procuratorial judicial remedy function and the path to its realization-taking the amendment of the organic law of the people's procuratorate as a perspective. *Legal Forum,* 3.
104. Xiang, Z. (2013). The way forward for procuratorial reform in the new Era. *China Legal Science,* 5.
106. Wangm C., & Zhai, J., et al. (2016). Focus on the pilot reform of the national supervision system. *Fiscal Supervision,* 23.
107. Hao, T. (2017, Jan 18). Jurisprudential perspective on the establishment of supervisory committee, *Legal Daily.*
108. Xi, Z. (2016). National supervisory commission: The engine that ignites political reform. *China Newsweek,* 2.
111. Chen, W. (1999). Contingency and actuality: Thoughts on whether investigative powers are judicial powers. *Law Science,* 6.
112. Ma, H. (2016). Significance and main tasks of the state supervision system reform. *Journal of National Prosecutors College,* 6.
113. Lang, S. ed. (2012). *Amendment and application of the Criminal Procedure Law of the People's Republic of China.* Beijing: Xinhua Publishing House, 111–114.
116. Lang, S. ed. (2012). *Amendment and application of the Criminal Procedure Law of the People's Republic of China.* Beijing: Xinhua Publishing House, 307–310.
117. Su, H., & Feng, X. (2010). Empirical analysis on supplementary investigation on post crimes. *Chinese Criminal Science,* 8.
118. Chen, W. (2015). *Transformation and change: The procuratorial theory and practice in China.* Beijing: China Renmin University Press, 42.
119. Gustav, R. (1997). *Introduction to law,* Mi Jian, Zhu Lin (trans.). Beijing: Encyclopedia of China Publishing House, 122.
120. Liu, J. (2013). Reinterpretation of the prosecution and police integration model. *Chinese Journal of Law,* 6.
122. Chen, W. (2016). Trial-centeredness: The cornerstone of contemporary criminal judicial reform. *The Jurist,* 4.
123. Long, Z. (2000). On prosecution and police integration—And the relationship between prosecution and police in China. *Chinese Journal of Law,* 2.
124. Fan, C. (2010). Enhancing theoretical knowledge and grasping key points of supervision. *People's Procuratorial Semimonthly,* 3.
125. Min, C. (2016). Study on the litigation procedure of reviewing arrestment. *Law and Social Development Bimonthly,* 3.
127. Wan, C. (2014). Studying the decision to solve the legal supervision problem. *People's Procuratorial Semimonthly,* 22.
128. Hao, T. (2017, Jan 18). Jurisprudential perspective on the establishment of supervisory committee. *Legal Daily.*
133. Brian, I. (2006). The relationship between the prosecutor and the police under the comparative criminal justice perspective, Hou Xiaoyan (trans.). *People's Procuratorial Semimonthly,* 22.
134. Zhou, B. (2016, Mar 11). Comprehensive establishment of investigative supervisory procuratorial offices in public security organs. *Legal Daily.*
135. Wan Chun. (2010). Taking the chance of intensification of reform to promote capability and efficiency of investigation supervision. *People's Procuratorial Semimonthly,* 3.
136. Zhang, D. (2014). Reform of the chief prosecutor system should clarify the relationship between "integration" and "independence". *Law Science,* 5.
137. Zheng, Q. (2013). Some reflections on the chief prosecutor's responsibility system for handling cases—Taking the reform practice of Hubei Province procuratorial organs as a model. *People's Procuratorial Semimonthly,* 23.
139. Lin, S. ed. (2000). *Reform counterproposal of criminal procedure law.* Taipei: Angel Publishing House, p. 356.

141. Xu, H., & Jin, X. et al. (2013). The framework design and core elements of the responsibility system of prosecutors in charge—A study on the trial implementation of the responsibility system of prosecutors in charge under the leadership of the chief prosecutor general in Hubei Provincial procuratorial organs. *People's Procuratorial Semimonthly*, 19.
142. Chen, W. (2013, July 23). Procuratorial reforms within the context of the judicial reform. *Procuratorial Daily.*

Chapter 4
Theory and Exercise of the Power of Investigation

4.1 The Nature of Investigation Power and the Basic Principles of Investigative Activities

4.1.1 The Nature of the Right of Investigation

To explore and understand the nature of investigation power, we should first make clear the nature of police power. From the perspective of global legislation development, the police are responsible for criminal investigation activities, the collection of crime files and other things in the investigation stage. In China, the public security organ is the actor of criminal investigation activities. Although there are several other actors that are allowed to perform investigation according to law, such as the procuratorial organs, the national security agency, the military security departments and the prisons, the public security organ assumes the investigation responsibility of the vast majority of cases.[1] In addition to the investigation of criminal cases, public security organs also undertake a large number of public security management tasks. These functions correlates with each other, generating the police power.

The police's duty decides the power which they should be endowed with. The police of any country or region, regardless of the nature of their state institutions and regimes, all assume the basic duties of public security administration, maintaining public security, and preventing and investigating illegal and criminal activities. In addition to these, they may also undertake others, such as providing community service and first aid, helping people who are lost and the elderly and children. But this book only discusses the police's power of security management and criminal investigation. Therefore, the state must also give the police the powers to perform these duties above listed. For example, chapter two of the *Police Law of the People's*

[1] According to the Articles 3,4, and 290 of the *Criminal Procedure Law of the People's Republic of China*, the actors that have criminal investigation power in our country include the public security organs, the procuratorial organs, the national security agencies, the military security departments and the internal investigation departments of the prison.

W. Chen, *Reform and Development of Powers and Functions of China's Criminal Proceedings*, https://doi.org/10.1007/978-981-15-8431-2_4

Republic of China stipulates many functions and powers of the police. The individuals or organizations that violate the laws and regulations on public order administration or other public security administration may be subject to administrative coercive measures and administrative penalty. Persons who seriously jeopardize public security or pose threats to public security may be forcibly removed from the scene, detained according to law or other measures are taken as prescribed by law. According to this, these two powers of the police can be termed power of public security administration and the power of criminal investigation. The former clearly falls into the category of executive power, which has been agreed upon in both theoretical circle and judicial circle. However, there is still some divides on the nature of the police's criminal investigation power. Some think that it is a kind of the executive power, others argue that it is a part of the judicial power.

After the analysis of the essential characteristics of judicial power and executive power, we think that criminal investigation power is part of executive power. We have made a comparison between these two powers before and think that the judicial power is characterized by finality, neutrality, independence, passivity, exclusive or non-transferability.[2] As far as the criminal investigation power is concerned, its administrative attribute is obviously different from the feature of judicial power. Therefore, the reform to procedure and system in the investigation should be launched on the basis of understanding the nature of executive power of criminal investigation power.

First, the judicial power, in nature, is a kind of judgment power to decide a case and to render a judgment and determine the application of law, while the executive power is the executive power to carry the laws into effect in social life. The judicial power in a limited sense refers to the adjudicatory power to hear cases and render verdicts by state judicial organs so as to perform the function of judicial power. The judge's duty is to render judgement, the application and interpretation of the law is the example of the judgment. And the criminal investigation power, like the executive power in nature, also focuses on execution, that is, trying to bring as many criminals to stand trial by collecting solid and sufficient evidence in order to meet the goals of constitution and laws to maintain the social peace and order. There are obvious differences between judgment as the nature of judicial power and execution as the nature of executive power including investigation power. Although the process of trial entails court debate and out-of-court investigations, its purpose is to make reasonable, legal judgments. In the course of the investigation, investigators also need to make some judgments.[3] However, these activities also aim to gather evidence and prosecute. Moreover, the judgment, as a cognitive activity, requires that the judge can not make judgments based on priori knowledge or to achieve a certain goal. The actor of cognitive activity must remain objective and neutral, avoiding the undue influence of environmental factors. In the course of a trial, the judge can neither seek to prove

[2]Chen [9].

[3]For instance, whether there is a crime before the investigative procedure is officially started, criminal responsibility needs to be investigated, or whether to prosecute the cases in the course of investigation.

guilt nor innocence. The whole process of performance is to achieve a certain goal, and the goal itself is both the starting point and the end point of the performance activities. In the process of investigation, the goal of investigators is very clear—to collect criminal evidence and to arrest criminal suspects.

Second, in the aspect of value orientation, the judicial power focuses on justice, while the power of investigation centers on efficiency. Justice is the nature of judicature, and its connotation is to embody the fairness, equality and justice in the process and result of judicial activity. Judicial justice includes substantial justice and procedural justice. The former is the basic goal of judicial justice, and the latter is an important guarantee of judicial justice. In criminal proceedings, trials involve intense conflicts and confrontations between the power of the state and the rights of the individuals, so the disputes and conflicts can be settled only the judiciary can only ensure a fair and reasonable distribution of rights between the parties in action. Although efficiency can not be completely ignored in the trial activities, efficiency is minor compared with justice. The investigating organ is on the frontlines of the fight against crime. In order to evade the legal sanction, criminals often take all kinds of means to try to be arrested, destroy the crime scenes, threaten and induce witnesses to change their testimony and even kill witnesses and victims. So taking immediate action of investigation activities is essential to find the truth. Therefore, to maximize the efficiency of combating crime has always been the goal of the investigating organs in handling criminal cases.

Thirdly, in view of the exercise of power, various administrative characteristics make the power of investigation different from the judicial power. Firstly, the judicial power is passive, while the investigation power is active. For the judicial power, judicial organ passively accepts the request of the two parties to the conflict and follows the principle of no trial without complaint, so as to make a judgment on the conflict in a neutral and fair way. The goal of investigation is to collect criminal evidence and find the criminals. In order to find out the truth as soon as possible, once a criminal case needs to be investigated, the investigating organ must take steps to catch the suspect and collect evidence in a timely, accurate and comprehensive manner. Secondly, the judicial organ should be objective and neutral, while the investigating organ has the power to prosecute. The modern concept of rule of law requires that judges should not favor either the plaintiff or the defendant, but be objective and neutral. The modern criminal proceedings of the separation of prosecution and trial requires that the judge can only exercise the judicial power objectively and neutrally, but not perform the prosecution function with the attribute of executive power. The duty of investigation organ is to exercise the power of prosecution, focusing on collecting the evidence and material against the defendant, and making efforts to fight against crime. Thirdly, the exercise of judicial power is not subject to improper influence from other factors, while the exercise of the investigation power is restricted by the administrative management. In the design of system, the judge is an independent individual when exercising power and he has no superior except the law. The independence of the judiciary results from its impartial feature. As the types of crimes and criminals vary greatly, the investigating organs must make decisions as soon as possible in response to them, and to ensure that the decisions made in practice are promptly implemented. In order to achieve this goal, all countries adopt the system of chief responsibility system—only the supreme leader can exercise the decision-making power. Fourthly, the decisions made by the investigating officers are not like the finality of verdict rendered by the judiciary. The individual judgement made under the executive power is not a final decision, and the parties may lodge administrative reconsideration and administrative litigation. In criminal procedure, many decisions made by investigators are not viewed as the final results, but are examined by judicial review.

[4]Although some people don't agree with what we have discussed above, after analyzing the characteristics of the judicial power and comparing it with the investigation power, we still hold the view that the investigation power is a kind of the executive power in nature.

4.1.2 Principles of Investigation

4.1.2.1 Legality

According to Article 106(1) of the 2012 *Criminal Procedure Law of the People's Republic of China*, investigation means the special investigation activities and related compulsory measures carried out by the public security organs and people's procuratorates in accordance with the law in handling a case. In view of its nature, the investigating organs must follow the basic principle of legality during the investigation. In Britain, the rules of being ultra vires and invalid and natural justice are closely connected to legality. In the United States, the legality is embodied in the principles of fundamental rights and due process.[5] The two elements of the principle of legality in Germany are the supremacy of statutory law and basic elements of a legal system. In Japan, it includes the principles of priority of law, reservation of law and the judicial remedy. The executive branch must act to enforce the law.[6] The academic circles of administrative law in China generally discuss the principle of legality from two perspectives: priority of law and law reservation. They argue that any violation of administrative laws and regulations is an administrative illegal behaviour, and all the individuals that are against the administrative law should bear the legal responsibility.[7] In my opinion, the following points should be considered during an investigation according to the principle of legality of administrative law.

First, the power of investigation are established by law and granted according to law. Articles 3 of the *Criminal Procedure Law* provides that the public security organs shall be responsible for investigation, detention, execution of arrests and preliminary inquiry in criminal cases and the people's procuratorates shall be responsible for

[4]Liu [46].

[5]Mingyang [52]; Schwartz [63].

[6]Mingyang [51]; Jianmiao [39]; Vedel [73].

[7]Songnian [66]; Chonggao [23].

procuratorial work, authorizing approval of arrests, conducting investigation and initiating public prosecution of cases directly accepted by the procuratorial organs. Article 4 stipulates that state security organs shall, in accordance with law, handle cases of crimes that endanger State security, performing the same functions and powers as the public security organs. Article 290 provides that the security departments of the Army shall exercise the power of investigation with respect to criminal offenses that have occurred in the Army, crimes committed by criminals in prison shall be investigated by the prison, and the handling of criminal cases by the security departments of the Army and by prisons shall be governed by the relevant provisions of this Law. These provisions indicate that in addition to the above-mentioned actors, other organs, groups or individuals do not have the right to exercise these powers. The history of criminal procedure including its origin and development is the process of the state prosecuting agencies to commence a prosecution to replace private prosecution and self-relief. Private prosecution gradually evolved into the state prosecution. If a crime involves judicial intervention, a criminal proceeding will commence.[8] Investigation, as the beginning of criminal procedure, is a kind of process of using the public power to prosecute the crime. The inequality between the public power and the private rights, as well as the infringement of search activities and coercive measures on the personal rights and property rights of citizens, requires that the actors of investigation activities must be recognized by the state organs that have been authorized by law. The exclusivity of any other actors reflects the cautiousness on investigation power.

Second, the investigation must be carried out in compliance with the law. This means the application of the principles of priority of law and reservation of law in criminal investigation. These two principles are considered as the guidance for the investigative activities in both positive and negative ways. Priority of law in a broad sense was first proposed by Otto Meyer who argued that the law is the strongest force in the will of the state. In a limited sense, the priority of law is often regarded as the principle that determines the relationship between law and administrative legislation. The principle of reservation of law refers to the provisions of the constitution that lay restriction on the basic rights of the people. They are made by the legislature instead of the executive branch. Any administrative actions that are taken must comply with the law. This requires that the interrogation of criminal suspects, questioning of witnesses, inquest, examination, search, seal-up, seizure of physical evidence, documentary evidence, appraisal, technical investigative measures and coercive measures must be carried out in accordance with the law. The provisions of the Criminal Procedure Law and other laws concerning the applicable conditions, procedures, methods and time limits must be strictly implemented and no variation shall be made. Behaviors, such as extorting a confession by torture and illegal search, all violate the principle of legality of investigation. As for what is not provided for by law, it falls into the scope reserved by law, and the investigating organ shall not taken any other investigation measures and coercive measures on its own.

[8]Chen and Cheng [14].

Third, the investigation emphasizes the principle of procedural legality. The conflict between procedural and substantive value has been existing for a long time in the litigation. A consensus on procedural value has been reached by theoretical and practical researchers. The investigation, as the first step taken by investigating organs, processes the criminal procedure. The investigating organs collecting evidence and finding out the truth is to fulfill the prosecution function of the state. Therefore, the investigation should follow the spirit of litigation—the principle of procedural legality. The principle of legality of criminal procedure in the formal sense requires that any investigation of criminal responsibility must be carried out in accordance with the legal procedure, while this principle in the substantive sense not only requires that it should be carried out in accordance with the established procedure, but also requires that the procedure is the due process. Especially in the investigation stage where the court decision is not made on whether the criminal suspect is guilty or not, the investigation activities to restrict the suspect's rights should consider ensuring the smooth criminal procedure. "The history of liberty has largely been the history of the observance of procedural safeguards." To this end, legitimate procedural measures must be formulated in the law to regulate the conduct of criminal investigation activities. In addition, the investigation power must be exercised in strict accordance with the procedural provisions. It also embodies restricting the state power and guaranteeing the citizen's rights.

Finally, the investigation must be subject to supervision and remedy. One of the elements of the principle of legality is that the executive branch must act to enforce the law. In the process of investigation, the availability of monitoring and remedy is the inherent nature of its legality. Article 8 of the *Criminal Procedure Law of the People's Republic of China* gives the people's procuratorates the power of legal supervision over criminal proceedings. In the investigation stage, the People's procuratorates shall: (1) supervise the case filing of the public security organs; and (2) examine the cases investigated by them, to decide whether to arrest or prosecute offenders; and (3) monitor the legality of public security organs investigations. The *People's Police Law of The People's Republic of China* also provides for the monitoring over the administrative supervision organs, the higher-level organs of the people's police supervising the law-enforcement activities by the lower-level organs, and the public oversight on the police service in the performance of their duties. In addition, the law in the investigation allows the parties to take remedies, such as the parties having the right to demand withdrawal if an investigative officer has an interest in the case. During the investigation, it is essential to guarantee the right to defense of the criminal suspect, and the right of the defense lawyer to complain and apply for the change of the coercive measures. Any exercise of powers must be restricted, and remedies should be offered in the circumstances where any exercise of public power involves the restriction on civil rights. The regulation of oversight and remedy on investigation in our country's law demonstrates the principle of legality of investigation.

4.1.2.2 The Principles of Timeliness and Efficiency

The nature of the investigation requires that it must be timely and efficient. As an important component of criminal justice activities, investigation should considers both the punishment and protecting human rights. On the one hand, the principles of timeliness and efficiency can process an investigation smoothly and improve the performance; on the other hand, they are pivotal to respect and guarantee the human rights. The task of investigation is to gather evidence, find out the truth and catch the suspects, so as to provide reliable basis for fighting crime, preventing crime and ensuring the smooth proceedings.[9] As the criminals try to hide their crimes, they will hide and destroy the evidence against themselves. Influenced by the factors such as the environment, the difficulty in the investigation activities will gradually increase over the time.

The promptly investigation can collect evidence of the case and identify the criminal suspect in a timely manner. Such as the timely crime scene investigation can be as far as possible to prevent the negative effect of the destruction of the scene and evidence missing on the analysis of the case, the collection of evidence and the identification of investigative clues. Some characteristics and injuries of the victim and the criminal suspect may change from time to time due to the healing or unexpected circumstances. Failure to investigate in a timely manner will influence its authenticity and relevance of the evidence. Inaction and tardiness will allow for the concealment, destruction, falsification of evidence and the escape of the suspect. It is also necessary to take prompt actions to question the witnesses because their memories will fade away over time. In addition to timeliness, investigative activities must necessitate high efficiency. Timeliness is designed to collect perishable evidence, and high efficiency is the basic requirement for investigative activities. Some victims of criminal cases have generally suffered an injury, property damage, so early solving a case can help heal the victims' wounds. Some violent, drug-related crimes or other serious crimes have a lasting impact on society, so the principle of high efficiency of investigation activities can contain crimes, safeguard the interests of the victims and the public.

With the development of the concept of human rights protection, it has in criminal procedure brought greater attention in many countries. In the process of criminal legislation and judicial practice, emphasis is laid on it in our country. It is important to find out the truth in investigation, but the criminal procedure principle that no one may be found guilty without a court ruling makes the suspects be left with uncertainty, and it is common for innocent persons to be involved in the investigation. From the beginning of the investigation, the investigation measures of sealing up, seizure or freezing of assets or the coercive measures restricting the human rights are generally taken. In the process of investigation, the private property rights of the persons involved in the case are continuously restricted. The pronounced problem of pretrial detention in practice results to a large extent from the investigation. If criminal suspects can be detained in the investigation process, the investigating organs will be

[9] Chen [10].

unlikely to allow them to bail out. Sometimes they will be allowed the application for release on bail until the last day of detention. This is undoubtedly a serious violation of the private property rights of criminal suspects. By emphasizing the principle of high efficiency in investigation, it can help find more clues in a shorter time to complete the investigation as soon as possible and identify whether to prosecute or withdraw. This allows suspects who should not be held criminally responsible to be cleared of suspicion as soon as possible, and suspects who should be prosecuted to stand trial.

4.1.2.3 The Principle of Proportionality

In a modern country ruled by law, the principle of proportionality is the "king provision" of public law. It is a basic principle to be followed in adjusting the proportion between state rights and individual rights. This principle dates back to the Germany police act in the early nineteenth century. Its original meaning includes three sub-principles: the appropriateness of means in achieving goals, the necessity of the least damage caused by means, and the balance between the damage of means to individuals and the society interest of outputs, which is also called the principle of proportionality in a limited sense or the principle of balance. Since then, the principle of proportionality has gradually been introduced to the constitution, the criminal procedure and other public laws.[10] In criminal proceedings, in accordance with the criminal law and the criminal procedure, some offenders plead guilty and accept punishment in a minor case can be treated as innocent, such as not filing or withdrawing a case, not prosecuting or not prosecuting even, and acquittal. This can be regarded as an application of the principle of proportionality.[11] In addition, the specific legal actions and proceedings also involves it. There are two kinds of criminal cases: serious and minor. The principle of proportionality can only be met by adopting lenient measures and procedures for minor cases, and strict measures and procedures for serious cases. According to the situation of the defendant, there are differences in their personal danger or social danger. This principle can only be followed by using the lenient measures and procedures for cases with low-risk of personal danger, and strict ones for cases with high-risk of personal danger. The principle of proportionality of investigation power is also called the principle of relevance of investigation power. Although the investigation power with the nature of executive power must follow the principle of timeliness, efficiency and effectiveness, it must be strong enough to maintain social order, public safety and remove the actions that disrupt the society. However, the remit of the power of investigation must be proportionate to the capability of maintaining social order and public security and remove the actions disrupting the society, and its strength should be the minimum necessary to maintain public order. This is the principle of proportionality in the power of investigation.

---

[10] Yinzhong and Zuoli [83].

[11] Xiong [77].

The principle of proportionality in the power of investigation is also reflected in specific legal provisions. In accordance with Article 9 of the *People's Police Law of The People's Republic of China* and the *Regulations on the Cross-Examination of the Public Security Bureau,* in order to maintain public order, the police service, upon showing their police identification card, are allowed to take on-the-spot cross-examination and take measures against persons suspected of breaking the law or committing a crime. Only when the on-the-spot examination fails to identify the suspects of the illegal crime can they be brought to the public security bureau for further investigation and interrogation. Article 4 of the *Regulations on the Use of Firearms By the Police* in our country provides "trying to minimize casualties and property losses when stopping illegal and criminal activities", which indicates that the use of firearms and weapons by the police should also follow the principle of relevance. "The people's police may use coercive means to stop illegal or criminal behaviors; if necessary, they may use police weapons in accordance with the provisions of these regulations; if the use of police weapons fails to stop or they stop such behaviors without using weapons, which may lead to serious harmful consequences, they may use weapons in accordance with the provisions of these regulations", according to Article 2. Articles 7, 8 and 9 specify the police weapons used to subdue offenders, such as baton, tear gas, high-pressure water cannon and special riot control guns, and other weapons used for deterrent, like handcuffs, leg irons and ropes. The provisions on the criminal investigation power in *Criminal Procedure Law of the People's Republic of China* embody the spirit of the principle of proportionality in many ways. According to Article 117, for example, it requires that the summons or compelled appearance in court shall not last longer than 12 or 24 h depending on whether the cases are complicated, and it also requires ensuring the criminal suspect should be guaranteed with necessary food and rest. The chapter of compulsory measures in the general provisions describes the infringement of the right of various compulsory measures and the aim of investigation, and expounds different measures taken in different circumstances.

4.1.2.4 Principle of Judicial Control

The judicial control principle of investigation power means that the investigation power should be restricted by the judicial power to prevent it from going in the wrong direction in the exercise.[12] Although there are differences in the specific models, judicial control over investigation power is a common approach in countries under the rule of law. Judicial control can be divided into two parts: judicial authorization and judicial remedy. The former means that all civil rights-related activities carried out by investigating organs and officials must be authorized by a neutral agency that does not assume the responsibility of prosecution.[13] In Britain, the investigative measures, such as arrest, search or detention of suspects, must be reported to the

[12]Chen and Li [16].

[13]Chen and Li [17].

magistrate in advance with sound reasons, and can only be taken with the permission of the magistrate. In the United States, based on the constitutional due process, the police should first apply to a judge to make an arrest, search, seizure, wiretap and other compulsory investigative measures against a citizen, and a warrant may be issued only if they provide sound evidence and indicate that these measures are necessary. Judicial remedy means that if the suspect and his defender are not satisfied with the compulsory investigation measures, they may bring a suit before a law court or a judicial judge. The judicial police and the judge making the decision on compulsory measures shall prove the legality and legitimacy of them during the procedure.

There are three reasons for following the principle of judicial control in the investigation. First, it is essential to protect the rights of the defendant. Investigating organs often have an excessive obsession with investigating crimes, and this obsession is often make them prove the guilt of a criminal suspect by any kind of means. In this case, they are likely to infringe the personal rights and property rights of criminal suspects. Putting aside the circumstance where the defendant are innocent, those who have actually committed the crime and are supposed to be held criminally responsible are entitled to the right to due process. However, as far as the defendant are concerned, it is difficult for him to resist the public power, let alone in the hope that the investigation organs can protect their rights. Therefore, the investigation should be brought under the judicial control, because the judicial power with passive, neutral attributes can guarantee the rights of the defendant. Second, it is the result of the extension of the due process theory in the investigation procedure. theory of due process requires that no one be a judge during the trial for themselves and the voices of both parties should be heard. As this theory is applied in the investigation procedure, the investigation procedure involves the accuser, defendant and judge. The power to decide on measures involving civil rights, such as search, seizure, wiretap and arrest, is like adjudicative power and should be transferred from the procuratorial and police organs to courts or judges who are not responsible for prosecution. Third, this is the judicial final verdict principle in the criminal proceedings in the specific performance. The principle of judicial final adjudication means that there are many ways to solve social disputes, but the court exercising judicial power render authoritative verdict on the rights and obligations of the parties concerned in the name of the state. Once this it is in force, it is final and binding. In a case of public prosecution, only after investigation, prosecution and trial can the court make a final judgment of guilt or innocence. However, in the course of investigation, when it comes to whether compulsory investigative measures should be taken or the power of investigation may have an intense conflict with the rights of citizens, the investigating organ may make a decision on a matter involving the fundamental rights of citizens. But these can no be viewed as final judgments, and the judicial remedies should be offered to the defendant.

4.2 Criminal Investigation and Protection of Human Rights

In the process of criminal procedure, the exercise of the investigation power, especially the compulsory measures, often results in the infringement of the citizen's fundamental rights prescribed in the constitution. In order to prevent the abuse of investigation power and protect the citizens' rights, we should monitor the investigation. Therefore, establishing the investigation supervision system is out of dispute in the academia.[14] Nowadays, a variety of models of the investigation supervision system have been developed in the world. In addition to the oversight by the procuratorial organ, the supervision and control also come from the court and the lawyers of the defense.

4.2.1 Relationship Between Investigative Activities and Civil Rights and Interests

4.2.1.1 The Inevitable Restriction of Investigative Activities on Citizens' Rights and Interests

The initiative and expansibility of investigation power will inevitably lead to the restriction of civil rights. The administrative attribute of investigation power make it different from the judicial power characterized by passivity. The initiative means that it is incumbent upon the investigating organ to proactively discover the crime and investigate the case. The investigating organs in the investigation are given wider discretionary powers, and they, taking the goal as the compass, make the decision related to the interests of the people involved in the investigation procedure. This kind of initiative steps should not only be taken in some crimes that have already occurred, but also be carried out in those that have not yet been committed or are being committed, where the investigating organ may take some measures such as enticing investigation and monitoring.[15] In addition, the investigation power features expansibility. The investigative activity aims to solve the crimes, which can be easily found in the investigation model of "from person to case". The investigating organ tries to capture the criminal suspect after unearthing the clues, and then collects relevant information and finds the truth from the suspect. In the course of exercising the investigation power, investigative officers are likely to take the steps which are not expressly or vaguely prescribed in the law to achieve their goal, which will result in restricting the rights and interests of citizens.

[14]Liu [47].

[15]Chen [11].

4.2.1.2 Norms of International Conventions on Investigative Activities

In the twentieth century, especially after the World War II, the concept of human rights protection is getting greater attention, and the respect and protection of human rights has become an important part of international law. How to protect citizens' rights and interests from being infringed in investigation is essential to human rights protection. There are two main categories of convention about investigation. First, the United Nations General Assembly has passed a number of conventions concerning human rights protection, such as the *Universal Declaration of Human Rights*, the *International Covenant on Civil and Political Rights*, the *Convention against Torture and Other Cruel, Inhuman or Degrading Treatment or Punishment,* and *The Declaration of the Rights of the Child.* Second, relevant documents on criminal justice adopted by relevant organizations, such as the *United Nations Basic Principles on the Independence of the Judiciary*, the *Basic Principles on the Role of Lawyers*, and the *Standard Minimum Rules for Non-custodial Measures.* These documents not only require that investigative authorities of different countries provide minimum guarantees to participants in investigative activities, especially the defendant, but also ensure that people involved in the prosecution are given the right of action and the fairness in the proceedings.

Article 7 of the *International Covenant on Civil and Political Rights* prescribes that no one shall be subjected to torture or to cruel, inhuman or degrading treatment or punishment. Article 9 provides that arrest or detention in custody must be carried out in accordance with the grounds and procedures established by law, and that anyone who is arrested shall be informed of the reasons, brought promptly before a judge, and entitled to trial within a reasonable time or to release, and compensated in cases of unlawful arrest or detention. Article 10 stipulates that accused persons shall, save in exceptional circumstances, be segregated from convicted persons and shall be subject to separate treatment appropriate to their status as unconvicted persons. Accused juvenile persons shall be separated from adults and brought as speedily as possible for adjudication. The presumption of innocence and the right to silence are set out in Article 14(2&3).

The *Convention against Torture and Other Cruel, Inhuman or Degrading Treatment or Punishment* describes the term torture as "any act by which severe pain or suffering, whether physical or mental, is intentionally inflicted on a person for such purposes as obtaining from him or a third person information or a confession, punishing him for an act he or a third person has committed or is suspected of having committed, or intimidating or coercing him or a third person, or for any reason based on discrimination of any kind, when such pain or suffering is inflicted by or at the instigation of or with the consent or acquiescence of a public official or other person acting in an official capacity." It also provides that each State Party shall ensure that any statement which is established to have been made as a result of torture shall not be invoked as evidence in any proceedings, except against a person accused of torture as evidence that the statement was made. These provisions require the investigative authorities to treat the criminal suspect as the subject of criminal proceedings, and ensure that the criminal suspect shall not be subjected to mental and physical torture for the purpose of extorting a confession, nor shall he be subjected to any other treatment, or to other degrading treatment of human and human dignity during investigation. *Basic Principles on the Role of Lawyers* provides for the right of suspects to counsel at the investigative stage, such as Article 1, which states that all persons are entitled to call upon the assistance of a lawyer of their choice to protect and establish their rights and to defend them in all stages of criminal proceedings. Article 5 provides that governments shall ensure that all persons are immediately informed by the competent authority of their right to be assisted by a lawyer of their own choice upon arrest or detention or when charged with a criminal offence. Article 7 states that governments shall also ensure that all persons arrested or detained, whether or not criminally charged, have prompt access to a lawyer, no matter what the circumstances, no later than 48 h from the time of arrest or detention. Article 8 provides that all arrested, detained or imprisoned persons shall be provided with adequate opportunities, time and facilities to be visited by and to communicate and consult with a lawyer, without delay, interception or censorship and in full confidentiality. *Standard Minimum Rules for Non-custodial Measures* encourages states to be as active as possible in developing and monitoring alternative measures to pretrial detention as a last resort in criminal proceedings. If necessary, pretrial detention should not exceed the time required to "decide, at its discretion, to withdraw or prosecute" and should be carried out in a humane manner and on the basis of respect for the dignity of the humans. The suspect shall have the right to appeal the issue of pretrial detention to the judicial or other independent competent authority.

In addition, the issue of victims in the criminal proceedings suffering from unfair treatment has attracted more attention across the globe. The *Declaration of Basic Principles of Justice for Victims of Crime and Abuse of Power*, adopted by the United Nations General Assembly in 1985, provides for the victims' rights to access to justice and fair treatment, restitution, compensation, and assistance.

4.2.2 Respect for and Protection of Human Rights in China's Investigative Activities

As the concept of criminal procedure evolves in China, respecting and protecting human rights has become essential. Our government has signed a series of international conventions on the protection of human rights in the investigation process, such as the *International Covenant on Economic, Social and Cultural Rights*, the *International Covenant on Civil and Political Rights* and the *Convention against Torture and Other Cruel, Inhuman or Degrading Treatment or Punishment*. In addition, the amendment to the Criminal Procedure Law in 2012 makes the concept of respecting and safeguarding human rights implemented. Such provisions in the investigation stage mainly includes the protection of the right to defense, the prohibition of extorting a confession by torture, the strict regulation on the compulsory measures, and the strengthening of supervision over the investigation activities.

4.2.2.1 Protection of the Right to Defense

First, the current Criminal Procedure Law provides that a criminal suspect can entrust a defender during the investigation stage, but the previous law only allows a criminal suspect to hire a lawyer to provide legal assistance. This amendment clarifies the lawyer's status as a defender in the investigation, and protects the right to defense of the criminal suspect.

Second, the procedure of interview between offenders and their defense counsels is improved. If a defense counsel requests to meet with the criminal suspect or defendant in custody with practicing certificate, certification of law firm and power of attorney, the detention house shall arrange the meeting in a timely manner without permission, except in cases of crimes endangering state security, crimes involving terrorist activities and significant amount of bribes. This provision solves the long-standing problem of difficulty in meeting with defense counsels in the past. Moreover, it also provides that the criminal suspects should be visited by their defense attorney without interception.

Third, the exiting legal aid defense counsel system has benefited the criminal suspects in the investigation stage. Article 34 of the *Criminal Procedure Law* defines the people who need the legal aid as criminal suspects and defendants, which means that the legal aid which is only provided at the trial stage in the past has been extended to the entire process including investigation, prosecution and trial. The legal aid institutions that apply for legal aid and meet the requirements "should" assign lawyers to provide defense for them. The shift from word "may" to "should" reflects the obligation of the state to respect and protect human rights.

4.2.2.2 Scope for Enforcement of Compulsory Measures

Although the taking compulsory measures at the investigation stage can prevent the perpetrators from committing crimes again and endangering the public safety, and ensure the smooth progress of criminal proceedings, it also involves the deprivation and restriction of individual rights. Therefore, great attention needs to be given to how compulsory measures are taken. The revised *Criminal Procedure Law* in respect of compulsory measures not only takes into account the need to punish crimes in judicial practice, but also solves the problems in the enforcement of compulsory measures and strengthens the protection of citizens' rights.[16] It clarifies the conditions of arrest, the alternative measures to reduce detention and the prohibition of non-notification of family members following the imposition of coercive measures.

First, the conditions of arrest are clarified. Article 79 of the *Criminal Procedure Law* changes the previous "the criminal suspect or defendant shall be arrested if there is a risk that they endanger the society"into "the criminal suspect or defendant may commit a new crime; there is a real risk that the criminal suspect or defendant may endanger State security, public security or public order; the criminal suspect

[16]Lang [64].

or defendant may destroy or falsify evidence, interfere with the witnesses who give testimony or collude with others to make confessions tally; the criminal suspect or defendant may retaliate against the victims, informants or accusers; the criminal suspect or defendant tries to commit suicide or escape". Furthermore, it also provides that if there is evidence to support the facts of a crime, and the criminal suspect or defendant has committed a crime that is punishable by fixed-term imprisonment or severer punishments, but has intentionally committed a prior crime or has an unknown identity, the criminal suspect or defendant shall be arrested, and a criminal suspect or defendant who is released on bail pending trial or is placed under residential surveillance may be arrested if he or she commits grave violations of the provisions with respect to release on bail pending trial or residential surveillance. The above-mentioned specification of the conditions for arrest sets clear criteria for the enforcement of arrest as a compulsory measure by the investigating authorities, which helps to prevent arbitrary or unlawful arrests. In addition, it also provides the legal basis for arrests by the procuratorial authorities and compulsory measures by the public security organs.

Second, the alternatives to detention are developed. Article 72 of the *PRC Criminal Procedure Law* provides for circumstances of residential surveillance. residential surveillance can largely restrict individual liberty, so it is considered as an alternative measure to detention, and this law also sets out its applicable conditions which are different from those of release on bail pending trial. Articles 73 and 74 provide for residential surveillance in designated places. In order to avoid detaining criminal suspects and defendants in disguised form, which damages the protection of the legitimate rights and interests of the parties, provisions are made for the place of execution of residential surveillance at the designated residence, the notification of family members, the entrustment of a lawyer and the supervision of the people's procuratorate.[17]

Third, the requirement of notification of family members after the imposition of a coercive measure is clearly prescribed. In accordance with Articles 73 and 91 of the *Criminal Procedure Law*, family members shall be informed within 24 h of the enforcement of residential surveillance in designated place and of any arrest, unless notification cannot be processed. In addition, cases, where notification of family

[17] Article 73 of the *PRC Criminal Procedure Law* provides that "Residential surveillance shall be enforced at the domicile of a criminal suspect or defendant or at a designated place of residence if he/she has no fixed domicile. Where, for a crime suspected to endanger State security, crime involving terrorist activities and a crime involving significant amount of bribes, residential surveillance at the domicile of the criminal suspect or defendant may impede the investigation, it may, upon approval by the people's procuratorate or the public security organ at the next higher level, be enforced at a designated place of residence, provided that residential surveillance is not enforced in a detention house or a special venue for case investigation. Where a criminal suspect or defendant is placed under residential surveillance at a designated place of residence, his/her family shall be informed of the information related thereto within 24 h upon enforcement of residential surveillance, unless notification cannot be processed. Where criminal suspects and defendants under residential surveillance entrust defenders, Article 33 of this Law shall apply. People's procuratorates shall exercise supervision over the legality of the decision and enforcement of residential surveillance at designated places of residence."

members deems as impediments to investigation after detention, are classified as the crimes endangering the state security and involving terrorist activities. However, the family members of the detainee shall also be informed immediately after the impediment to the investigation is removed.

4.2.2.3 Prohibition of Extorting Confessions by Torture

Article 50 of the *Criminal Procedure Law* provides that judges, procuratorial personnel and investigators are strictly prohibited from extorting confessions by torture, collecting evidence through threats, enticement, deception or other unlawful means, or forcing anyone to provide evidence proving his/her own guilt. The *Rules for Criminal Procedure of the People's Procuratorate (for Trial Implementation)*, revised in 2012, deems the "extortion of confessions by torture" as "the use of corporal punishment or disguised corporal punishment or any other illegal means inflicting severe pain or suffering, physically or mentally, on the defendant so as to force him/her to make confession against his or her will", in which "any other illegal means" refers to methods involving a degree of illegality and compulsion against a criminal suspect that is equivalent to the use torture, violence or threats to exact a confession, and that compel a criminal suspect to confess against his will. In addition, the evidence collected by illegal methods such as extorting confessions by torture should be excluded or reinforced. Article 54 of the *Criminal Procedure Law* provides that confessions extorted from a criminal suspect or defendant by illegal means such as torture, testimony of witnesses and statements of victims collected by violent means, threat or other unlawful means shall be excluded, and physical evidence or documentary evidence that is not collected according to statutory procedures and is therefore likely to materially damage judicial justice shall be subject to correction or reasonable explanations, and shall be excluded if correction or reasonable explanations are not made. If an investigator collects evidence by illegal means and such act constitutes a crime, he or she shall be investigated for criminal responsibility according to law, and the victim shall have the right to damages.

4.2.2.4 Strengthening the Supervision of Investigation Activities

Article 115 of the *Criminal Procedure Law* gives the party concerned, his or her defender, the agent ad litem or an interested party the right to file a petition or complaint to a judicial organ if he/she is of the opinion the judicial organ or its staff members fail to order release from, or termination of, or alteration to, a compulsory measure upon expiry of the statutory time period, or fail to return the bond for bail with restricted freedom pending trial that shall be returned, or seal up, seize or freeze property irrelevant to the case at hand, or fail to terminate the sealing, seizure and freeze of property as required, or embezzle, misappropriate, privately divide, replace, or use in violation of relevant provisions the property that has been sealed up, seized or frozen. The party lodging the petition or compliant may appeal to the people's procuratorate at the same level if he or he has objections to the handling results. For a case accepted directly by a people's procuratorate, the party concerned may appeal to the people's procuratorate at the next higher level. The explicit provision has strengthened the procuratorial organ's oversight over the investigation, expanded the scope of the parties and interested parties' participation in investigation, and further protected the citizens' legal rights.

4.3 The Judicial Control of Investigation Power

"Success or failure in the fight against crime depends to a large extent on the ability to conduct investigation".[18] Because investigators "can find out the truth, catch the criminals, give criminal sanctions, and provide sufficient materials and basis for the prosecution of people's procuratorate and and trial of people's court" only through investigation.[19] The nature of investigation requires that the investigating organ must be given the power of compulsory disposition of persons or things—the power of investigation, such as summon by warrant, detention, arrest, search, and seize. However, most of these means involve citizens' rights. If there is absence of effective measures and or procedures to regulate the process, the exercise of the power of investigation may become the sword of Damocles threatening citizens' safety at any time, particular in the circumstance where the criminal suspects in criminal proceedings are prosecuted, and their legal right of action and safety are likely to be in the violations from violence by the state. As Justice Tannin of British House of Lords said that once the powers of social protection itself against criminals are abused, any tyranny must be "thrown in the towel".[20] Therefore, how to regulate the exercise of investigation power and prevent the investigating organs and officials from abusing the state power and violating the rights of citizens is essential to the modern investigative system.

The *Criminal Procedure Law*, after being revised in 1996 and 2012, has made significant progress in strengthening the protection of the rights of the defendant. The significant amendment of it in 1996 can be reflected in[21] (1) the clarification of the people's court's unified exercise of the right to conviction and the abolition of the system of immunity from prosecution; and (2) the regulation on the authorization, procedure and duration of the compulsory measures, and the clarification of the conditions for termination or changing compulsory measures; and (3) the abolition of the review of internment and introduction of a property bond system; and (4) the shift of lawyers' participation in proceedings to the investigative stage and the addition of provisions on legal aid and the assignment of a defence; and (5) the incorporation of the presumption of innocence. Established the principle of presumption of innocence.

[18]Boruchov [6].

[19]Chen et al. [7].

[20]Tannin [71].

[21]Xiuyun [78].

The amendment to this legal document further protects the rights of the defendant, which are showed in the (1) the prohibition of forcing the defendant to confess against his will and clarification of the exclusion of the unlawful evidence; and (2) the regulations that criminal suspects and defendants shall be taken to a detention house immediately after detention or arrest and that the interrogation of the detainees shall be carried out in the detention house; and (3) the requirements of censorship for the necessity of detention after arrest.

The above-mentioned reform is of far-reaching significance to ensure the defendant participation in the litigation. Especially the 2012 *Criminal Procedure Law* clearly prohibits the abuse of investigation power in judicial practice, such as extended detention, extorting confession by torture, obtaining evidence through illegal means, inappropriate compulsory measures. This abuse of power is ascribed to the major defects in the system of and relationship between the public security organs, procuratorates, courts established by constitution and Criminal Procedure Law of our country. Due to the lack of necessary judicial control over investigation powers, the entire investigation procedure has almost turned into a absolute "procedure of administrative judgement", and the accused is helpless when the accuser has the absolute power of the judge.[22] Although lawyers may intervene in advance and even participate in the proceedings as defenders at the investigative stage, there is in fact no substantive defence. That is because "if a prosecutor becomes a judge, he needs God as a lawyer"②.

This following mainly discusses the legal defects of the control model over the investigation power of procuratorial supervision in our country, its malpractices in the exercise, and the best practise of exercising investigation power in Western countries. In addition, the discussion on legitimacy of the judicial control mechanism of investigation power and the framework of this kind of mechanism are also included below, so as to regulate the exercise of investigation power, protect the rights of the defendant, and provide a train of thought for investigation procedure reform in our country.

4.3.1 The Judicial Control Model of Investigation Power in Western Countries

After making a comprehensive survey, it can be found that although there are differences in the concept of litigation and in the specific exercise of the investigation power in the major Western countries, most of them emphasize the involvement of judges in the investigation procedure so that the power of investigation is controlled by the judicial power, to prevent any misconducts. To sum up, the western countries generally control the investigation power through the following ways.

[22] Radbruch [57].

4.3.1.1 Judicial Authorization

The judicial authorization refers to a kind of authorization given by a neutral authority that does not assume the responsibility of prosecution to investigative bodies and officials to empower them to conduct activities involving civil rights. Otherwise, investigative agencies and investigators are not entitled to coercive means except in cases of flagrante delicto and emergencies. In the West, judicial police or prosecutors exercising investigation powers must apply in advance to a judge for arrest, search, seizure, interception, detention or other compulsory measures, and the judge will initiate a special judicial review procedure to determine whether the judicial authorization should be given. However, in some special circumstances, the investigative body and the investigators may also take matters into their own hands, but the offenders must immediately be brought before a judge or court.

In Britain, the police must make an application to the justice of the peace before they arrest, search or detain a suspect, and provide reasonable grounds. The police service are allowed to take these measure only after getting a warrant by a magistrate.

In the United States, according to the Due Process in the Constitution, the police should first apply to a judge to make an arrest, search, seizure, interception and other compulsory investigative measures against a citizen, and provide probable cause for the crimes to show the necessity to take investigative measure.[23] The judge will give the warrant if he or she thinks the this application satisfies the conditions prescribed by law.

Since the reform of criminal justice in Germany in 1974, judges no longer direct or carry out specific investigative activities at the investigative stage, and their function is primarily to issue a warrant upon application by a prosecutor or judicial police. According to the German *Code of Criminal Procedure*, judicial police and prosecutors are generally required to file an application for compulsory investigative measures such as arrest, detention, search, seizure, physical examination, and interception, and a warrant is issued after the court's review.

In Italy, the judicial police or the public prosecutor must first obtain the authorization from the examining magistrate for all compulsory investigative measures, such as searches, seizures, interception.

The investigation in Japan is divided into two parts: arbitrary and compulsory. Compulsory investigation should be, in principle, carried out according to the warrant issued by a judge. The methods of compulsory investigation prescribed by law include arrest, detention, seizure, search, inspection, identification and punishment, questioning witnesses, etc. Paragraph 1 of Article 197 of the Japanese *Code of Criminal Procedure* provides that for the purpose of investigation, necessary investigations may be carried out, but unless otherwise specified in this law, no compulsory measures may be imposed. It can be seen that the arbitrary investigation is taken as a principle, and the compulsory investigation can only be conducted on the special circumstances stipulated by the criminal procedure.

---

[23] Li [44].

The exception, of course, is the French pre-trial system by examining magistrates, who, according to French criminal law, have two functions: directing and leading the investigation of felonies and misdemeanor as well as approval of such compulsory investigative measures as detention, arrest and judicial control. The examining magistrates who has both the investigation power and the judicial power have long been criticized due to the abuse of power and lack of judicial control. Since the early 1990s, many French scholars have called for abolishing this system and taking away the investigation power of pre-trial judges to investigate felonies and misdemeanor. The decree which passed on 4 January 1993 took away their power, which, however, was granted again by the law enacted on 24 August 1993.

4.3.1.2 Judicial Remedy

[24]The judicial remedy means that in the proceedings, if the suspect and his defender have objection to the compulsory measures, they may bring a suit before a judicial organ or a judge. Both the judicial police and the judge who made the decision on compulsory investigation measures should prove the legitimacy of these measures.

In the United Kingdom, a detained person may apply to the police for bail or, if rejected, to the magistrate's court, which holds a hearing and makes a decision. If the application for bail is not accepted, the suspect may take his or her appeal to the high court. In addition, a suspect who has been wrongfully or unlawfully detained during the investigation may apply for writ of the Habeas Corpus of a supreme court. Once the tribunal has accepted the application, it will hold a hearing which both the prosecution and the defence participate in to decide whether the detention is legitimate.[25]

In Germany, a person detained in custody may not only apply to a judge at any stage for release, but may also apply directly to the German Constitutional Court for a hearing on the legitimacy of the detention.

In Italy, the accused and his defence have the right to apply to the court of the provincial capital where the examining magistrate is located for a review of the decision of the examining magistrate on compulsory measures relating to liberty, such as detention. If they are still unsatisfied with the results of the review, an appeal may also be lodged with the Supreme Court of Italy, which shall render the final decision.

In France, a suspect who has objection to a decision made by the pre-trial judge during a formal investigation has the right to appeal to the indictment review division of the court of appeal, which, after review, can set aside the decision of the pre-trial.

In Japan, a suspect has the right to lodge a quasi-protest against a judge's ruling on custody, bail, seizure or return of the seized property. An appeal can be lodged

---

[24]There are two differences between judicial authorization and judicial remedy. First, judicial authorization is carried out simultaneously, while judicial remedy is provided afterwards; secondly, the former is necessary, while the latter is not.

[25]Chen [8].

against judges of a summary court with the competent local court, or against other judges with the court at which they work, for setting aside or altering the decision.

After the collapse of the Soviet Union, the great changes have been made in strengthening the protection of the civil liberty in the criminal procedure of Russia. Article 11 of the *Criminal Procedure Code of the Russian Federation* provides that an arrested person shall have the right to appeal for judicial review of the legitimacy of his or her detention, and the decision of a judge to release a detainee made based on the outcome of judicial review shall be implemented without delay. In addition, the judicial review process has also been added to the current criminal procedure. The judge of the court in the place where the detainee is located shall, within three days after receiving an application from a citizen for judicial review, make a final judgement on the legitimacy of the detention in a closed court with the participation of the attorney-general, the defence, the detainee and his or her legal agent. At the end of the hearing, the judge will, depending on specific circumstances, make decisions on the withdrawal of custody and the release of the detainee or on the dismissal of the complaint.

4.3.1.3 Exclusionary Rule of Illegal Evidence

The illegal evidence refers to the evidence, including physical evidence and verbal evidence, which is obtained by illegal means or exceeding authority prescribed by law in the criminal procedure. Section 76 of the *Police and Criminal Evidence Act 1984* in Britain provides for the automatic exclusion of illegally obtained confessions of accused persons. As long as the physical evidence illegally searched and seized is related to the facts to be proved, it shall not be excluded in principle, and the judge shall have the right of discretion. But in the UK the fruit of the poisonous tree is allowed. Other evidence gained from excluded illegal evidence is admissible as long as it proves to be relevant.

Compared with the United Kingdom, the exclusionary rule of evidence in the United States is more widely and strictly adopted. The 4th amendment to the Constitution of the United States provides that evidence collected by illegal means shall not be used as evidence in criminal charges. For illegally collected physical evidence, the Federal Supreme Court established the exclusionary rule after studying many cases, and in 1961 the rule was applied to state criminal proceedings. After the 1980s, the Federal Supreme Court narrowed the scope of the exclusionary rule with "inevitable discovery exception" and "good faith exception". However, the court can exclude other evidence obtained by the police through illegal evidence, which means the fruit of the poisonous tree is applied.

Article 136a of the *German Code of Criminal Procedure* establishes the principle that illegally-obtained statements are admissible even with the consent of the accused. In Germany, evidence obtained by illegally means is handled according to the principle of weighing and balancing of interests. That means the evidence obtained through denial of of human dignity and freedom is admissible, but the former should yield to major crimes.[26]

Article 191 of the *Italian Code of Criminal Procedure*, as revised in 1988, provides the illegally-obtained evidence obtained by the police or the prosecutor is not admissible by a court or judge.

Both Article 38 of the *Constitution* and Article 319 of the *Criminal Procedure* in Japan stipulates that a confession obtained by illegally means may not be used as evidence. As for illegally obtained physical evidence, Japan, though influenced by the United States law, adopts the exclusionary rule in some circumstances. In order to find out the truth, it is only excluded when major crimes are committed.[27]

Article 50 of the *Constitution of the Russian Federation*, adopted on 12 December 1993, and Article 69 of the *Criminal Procedure Code of the Russian Federation* also specify the validity of illegally obtained evidence by providing that in administering justice it shall not be permitted to use evidence received through violating federal law.

In France, legislation and jurisprudence are also negative on verbal evidence obtained through torture and other illegal means. Of course, for countries, the control of judicial power over investigation power is also reflected in the fact that the court can make independent judgments on the conclusions of investigative agencies by means of open hearings, which means to reach an authoritative decision on whether the accused are guilty or innocent.

4.3.2 Theoretical Basis of Judicial Control Over Investigation Power

First, it is necessary to protect the rights of the accused. In criminal proceedings, the exercise of the investigation power may not only violate the rights of the accused, but also the rights of the victims and other participants. However, the protection of the rights of the victims and other participants can not base the criminal proceedings. This is because victims and other participants in the proceedings primarily play a role in assisting the prosecuting authority in finding out the truth, and their rights are unlikely to be violated unlawfully, whereas the rights of the accused to be prosecuted are most vulnerable to be violated by the unlawful acts of investigative bodies resulting from a desire to combat crime or hatred of crime. Therefore, how to protect the rights of the accused has become the focus of the investigation procedure in various countries. In fact, the protection of the rights of the accused in the criminal procedure is also the protection of the rights of all citizens. Because anyone can be suspected of committing a crime and be criminally prosecuted. But the accused can be either guilty or innocent. Based on the presumption of innocence, "society can not revoke his public protection

[26] Guangzhong [29].

[27] Guozhong [31].

as long as it can not be concluded that he has violated the contract that gave him public protection".[28]

However, the protection of the rights of the accusedfrom being violated by the investigation power can not be guaranteed by themselves, since no citizen, no matter how rich or how an important pose he or she holds, can be compared with the state in the respect of power; nor can investigative bodies and officials be relied upon to protect the rights of citizens, since they represent the interests of the state and their tasks in criminal investigations are mainly to find out the truth and to apprehend criminal suspects. It is impossible to take into account the protection of the rights of the accused in the investigation. In addition, his profession determines that he can not get rid of his psychological tendency to prosecute crimes, because when an extraordinary event occurs, it is natural for him to think that it may be a criminal case; when a suspect is found, he will try to prove that he or she is a criminal; when a criminal fact is established, he will speculate that there will be other crimes; when a misdemeanour crime is solved he will estimate that there will be more serious crimes; when a criminal is caught, he will try to find the accomplices".[29] Moreover, it is inappropriate for an official to engage in the defence of the national interest at some times, and in the maintenance of justice while neglecting the national interest at others.[30] Based on the above-mentioned, Western countries emphasize the intervention of the court or the judge in the investigative procedure, so that the investigative activities of the investigating organization are brought under the control of the judicial power to protect the rights of the citizens from infringement.

Second, it is the result of the extension of the due process theory in the investigation procedure. Due Process, as a concept, was proposed as early as the thirteenth century in the English Common Law, and has been extraordinarily widely accepted in the United States. It comes from theory of "Natural Justice" in ancient Roman times. At that time, in order to realize the natural justice, two basic points for the trial procedure were required: (1) iudex in sua causa—no man should be judge in his own case; and (2) audialre empartem—the opinions of both parties shall be heard.[31] However, there are reasons for the due process adopted in the Britain and American law and its development. According to the Japanese scholar Yasuhei Taniguchi, the development of justice in the Britain and American law is driven by three factors: the jury verdict and the litigant structure as its premise, the principle of precedent and the development of rule of equity.[32]

After the Second World War, as the comparative jurisprudence develops, the due process not only has been widely spread across the globe but also has been applied in the investigation. The justice of the investigation requires the intervention of the judicature in this process, which generates the investigation structure—a combination of the prosecution, the defense and the judge. This is because the decision-making

[28]Beccaria [1].

[29]Beccaria [2].

[30]Radbruch [58].

[31]Li [43].

[32]Ruihua [60].

power of compulsory investigative measures involving the rights and interests of citizens, such as search, seizure, interception and arrest, is essentially a power of judicial judgement. Once the above-mentioned compulsory measures are approved by the statutory bodies, the litigation rights and obligation proportionate to them will be defined accordingly. Whether it is applied properly or not is both related to the protection of suspects' rights and the justice in the prosecution. If the procuratorial and public security organs which conduct the investigation have the power to decide on the compulsory measures, it may result in this power unrestricted, and make the power be in contradiction with the prosecution function of the procuratorial and police organs. The investigating organs carry out the duty of prosecution in the criminal procedure, while the power of decision on the above measures falls within the category of judicial function. The bad situation where the functions of prosecution and trial are not separated may occur in the investigation when mixing them together, which is not in accordance with the requirements of due process. Due process is not understood differently by countries, but it is recognized that the differentiation of criminal procedural functions is essential to the due process. In the criminal proceedings, each main body has their own interest and hopes to meet the goals benefiting themselves through active actions. Moreover, each participant also fulfill the functions proportionate to their roles in this process. In the criminal proceedings, the procuratorial and police organs, as the main body of exercising the investigation power, are the specialist organs for prosecuting crimes set up by the state, carry out the criminal procedural activities, such as gathering evidence and apprehend the criminal suspects. As the executor of the defense function, the accused participate in activities such as application, defense and adducing evidence in the process. As the embodiment of justice, the court should be neutral between the prosecution and the defense, and make judgment on the controversial issues of parties. In order to make the criminal procedural functions explicit, in western countries the power to decide on the criminal procedural matters related to civil rights, such as search, seizure, interception and arrest, has been transferred from the procuratorial and police organs to a neutral court or judge who are not responsible for the prosecution and make a decision through a hearing. The procuratorial and police organs may, in a emergency situation specified under the law, carry out a compulsory investigation without a warrant, but they must immediately report to the judge or examining magistrate, who shall make a decision.

Third, this is how the "judicial final ruling" principle is reflected in the criminal proceedings. Disputes do not always have to be settled judicially. For example, the parties to a dispute may get it settled by means of conciliation, mediation or arbitration. However, in modern society, none of these methods has binding force, and the parties concerned can seek judicial protection in various ways. It is the courts exercising judicial power that make final authoritative decision, on behalf of the state, on the disputes involving the rights and obligations of the parties concerned. Once this conclusion is in force, it will bind upon both parties who are not allowed to apply to the court for a new trial and any individuals, private organizations or government agencies are unable to hear the case, nor do them have the right to alter the effective judgment already rendered by the court. After that, the parties concerned must carry out the final decision. In the criminal proceedings, the case(case of public prosecution) can be closed only after the investigation, prosecution and trial. However, despite the fact that only the judge can render verdict, the conflict between the prosecution and the defence does not occur only at the trial stage, nor is their dispute only related to the guilt or innocence of the accused and his criminal responsibility. Different from civil proceedings, criminal proceedings require the criminal cases to go through a complex pre-trial procedure before they enter the trial stage, in which the judicial police and the procuratorial department—the institutions responsible for prosecution—often needs to investigate the case, collect relevant criminal evidence and find the criminal suspect. Because of the need of criminal investigation, investigative agencies and investigators may use various compulsory measures such as search, seizure, interception and arrest. In this way, the conflict between the investigation power and the rights of citizens is likely to occur. On the one hand, in order to effectively prosecute crimes, the investigating organs will usually take the normal citizens as a relatively-confirmed criminal suspects; on the other hand, the accused not only try to make the outcome of the proceedings in his or her own favor, but also hope to be treated fairly and humanely in the process. Therefore, it is inevitable that there will be conflicts and even serious confrontation between the investigating agencies and the accused. The judicial police and the procuratorial department try to address such conflicts based on the rule of law. These organs, as the main bodies that exercise the investigation powers, although they may decide on procedural matters concerning citizens' rights in emergency situations, these decisions do not have binding force. The citizen concerned may also bring an action in a court in respect of a dispute over the procedure and the court shall make the final decision through legal procedures. The above-mentioned aspects are not completely separated, but they are inclusive, operative and competitive with each other. For example, the goal to drive the development of due process is mainly to protect the rights of the accused.

4.3.3 The Way to Control Investigation Power in Our Country and Its Defects

According to Article 106 of the *Criminal Procedure Law*, investigation refers to the special investigations conducted and relevant compulsory measures taken in accordance with the law by public security organs and people's procuratorates. The investigation refers to the interrogation of criminal suspects, the questioning of witnesses and victims, the inquest and examination, search, seal-up, seizure of material evidence and documentary evidence, expert appraisal and wanted orders, as stipulated in the Chapter 2 of Part II of this legal document. In judicial practice, there are also activities, such as identification and investigation. Compulsory measure refers to the restrictions on or deprivation of personal freedom as provided for by the public security organs and the people's procuratorates in their investigations according to the Chapter 6 of Part I, such as summon by warrant, release on bail pending trial, residential surveillance, detention and arrest.

Compared with the Western countries, the exercise of investigation power in our country is extremely unique. In our country, the judge is not involved in the investigation stage, so there is no judicial authorization and relief mechanism established by the neutral court or the judicial judge like the Western countries. Both the public security organs and people's procuratorates all are allowed to take initiate compulsory measures (The arrest by the public security organs has to be approved by the procuratorial organs, which also reflects the principle of judicial control. But the defects are obvious. This will be discussed in future due to the stylistic rules and layout of this book). Moreover, the criminal suspect who suffers from the violation by the investigation right has no right to seek judicial remedy from the court. Just like some scholars have pointed out that "judicial adjudication in China is only an activity of the court to determine the guilt or innocence of the accused, not the activity to judge whether the prosecution before trial is legitimate".[33]

Even though the judge does not participate in the investigation procedure in our country, both the Criminal Procedure Law and the judicial practice in our country hold the view that the investigation power should be appropriately controlled. It is believed that China's control of investigation powers is carried out in the following ways.

First, the investigation power should be controlled internally by the investigating organ. In China, both the public security officers and the prosecutors in charge of the investigation of a case must obtain the authorization or approval of the head of their organs when carrying out the investigation measures, and the latter must issue the relevant writ.

Second, the control over the investigation power and legal supervision of the people's Procuratorate's are the main approaches to control the investigation power in China. According to the constitution and the Criminal Procedure Law, the people's procuratorates are the legal regulatory organs of the country and have the power to oversee the investigation of the public security organs. This kind of legal supervision is embodied in the following aspects. First, the procuratorial organ has the power to carry out general supervision over the entire investigation process carried out by the public security officers. When the investigation is found illegal or improper, they can take it up with the public security organs. Second, it is reflected in the approval of the arrest. At the stage of investigation, arrest shall be approved or decided by the procuratorial organ. The public security organ must first submit an application for arrest to the procuratorial organ and provide the relevant report and case materials, in order to prove the necessity and legitimacy of the arrest, which is then examined by the procuratorial organ and a decision is made on whether or not to approve the arrest. If the people's procuratorate finds that the evidence submitted for application for the arrest is insufficient or non liquet, it may require a supplementary investigation by the public security organ. As an important way to control the investigation power,

[33] Ruihua [61].

the approval of arrest is of great significance to prevent the excessive and wrongful arrest and to ensure the arrest as a strict compulsory measure is taken according to law. Third, it is reflected in the prosecution. The public security organ investigates and concludes the cases transferred to the people's procuratorate for prosecution. If the conditions for prosecution are satisfied, the people's procuratorate shall initiate a public prosecution; if not, it shall make a decision not to prosecute and terminate the proceedings. In addition, if the people's procuratorate finds that the investigation by the public security organ has violated legal procedures, it may have the power to require the public security organ to make corrections or punish the person in charge. Fourth, the people's procuratorate can restrict the investigation activities carried out by the public security organ by excluding several kinds of verbal evidence obtained by illegal means. Article 65 of the *Rules for Criminal Procedure of the People's Procuratorate (for Trial Implementation)* provides that confessions of criminal suspects collected by illegal means such as extorting confessions by torture, witness testimony and statements of victims collected by illegal means such as violence and threats shall be excluded according to law and shall not be used as the evidence for application for arrest, approving or deciding to arrest, transferring for prosecution, or initiating public prosecution.

Finally, the People's Court can also restrict the investigation by excluding several kinds of illegal evidence in the trial stage. Article 102 of the *Interpretation of the Supreme People's Court Concerning the Implementation of the Criminal Procedure Law of the People's Republic of China* provides that after adjudication, if the existence of illegal means to obtain evidence proscribed by Article 54 of the Criminal Procedure Law is substantiated or cannot be ruled out, the evidence at issue shall be excluded.

The judicial control of the power of investigation in our country is much less stronger than that of the Western countries. It may play an important role in maximizing the functions of the public security organ, procuratorate and court to discover, substantiate and punish crimes. However, due to non-compliance with the requirements of the law of procedure, its defects include:

(1) Defects of procuratorial supervision can be found.
First, although the legal oversight of the prosecution service has a role to play in ensuring that the public security organ complies with its procedures, the public security organ, the procuratorate and the court all perform the function of prosecution in the criminal proceedings due to the design of the criminal justice system in which the three organs take different responsibilities but cooperate with and contain each other. They are intrinsically, necessarily and inseparably connected to each other, which makes it difficult for prosecutors to get rid of the psychological tendency to prosecuting criminals. Therefore, they often tend to not be just and stern to the public security organ in the respect of oversight, and the restrictions on its powers of arrest are also formalistic. Moreover, it is undoubtedly that the procuratorial organ should be positioned as the legal supervision organ of the state in the constitutional system and the criminal procedure of our country, whether from the perspective of the procedural legal principle or the system building of the state ruled by law.

Second, we can see from the above discussion that the procuratorial supervision is rather limited, and lack supporting measures, making the supervision becoming a mere formality. For example, if the procuratorial organ finds illegal means adopted by the police service in the investigation, it can only make a recommendation to correct it. If the public security organ ignores it, there is nothing the procuratorial organ can do about it. Although the people's procuratorate, in reviewing the prosecution, may refuse the three kinds of illegally-obtained evidence by the public security organ through the above five illegal means. However, due to the requirement of "cooperation principle" and the interference of various extra-legal factors, people's procuratorates seldom use this method in judicial practice. Moreover, a great deal of the work of the procuratorial organs in approving arrests and reviewing and prosecuting is to handle all written materials submitted by the investigation organs, so the illegal investigation activities can not be completely reported in the case files. Even if the criminal suspects and others report to the procuratorial organs that the police have committed such illegal acts as extorting a confession by torture and inducing confessions in the investigation, the procuratorial organs are unlikely to believe them if there is no sound evidence to prove it. Even if they believe them, it is actually hard to verify.

Third, the procuratorial organ may use any compulsory measure in cases under its own investigation. So who will oversee the overseer? "It is clear that legal supervision can not be performed by other prosecutors, since they all obey the orders of the head of the procuratorial organ, and the different prosecution functions of several prosecutors will eventually rest with the prosecutor-general alone".[34] In this way, the supervision of the procuratorial organ over the criminal cases investigated on their own has become nothing but empty talk.

(2) The defects of the investigative control model based on procuratorial supervision in practice.

The weak judicial control over the investigation power in our country and the fact that the current investigative control model which focuses on the procuratorial supervision and has some defects give rise to many problems in the investigation. "The entire investigation process is, so to speak, operated by the public security organ alone family in secret. Not only are there numerous illegal acts, but the judicial injustice is pervasive. Combined with the interference of various extra-legal factors, the investigation power has become an extra-legal privilege without any restriction."[35] "When the exercise of power is not constrained, it tends to cause tension and friction and hasty changes. In addition, in the social system of the unrestricted exercise of power, the strong tend to oppress or exploit the weak in society".[36] Practice has proved that the most of the illegal search, seizure, extorting a confession by torture and inducing confessions occur at the investigation stage. The criminal suspect now fear the investigation stage most. The investigation control model revolving around

[34]Guangzhong and Jiang [28].

[35]Chen and Yinzhong [21].

[36]Bodenheimer [5].

the procuratorial supervision in our country gives the opportunity to the abuse of power. It is not only a very dangerous system design, but also runs counter to our country's vision of building a socialist country under the rule of law. Because in a society ruled by law, "the crux of it is how to use and restrict public power reasonably and effectively."[37]

In a word, strengthening the control of investigation power to make the investigation meet the requirement of fairness has become the priority in the reform of criminal justice system of our country. In order to the prevent citizens' freedom, rights and privacy from being unreasonably restricted and deprived by investigation agencies, the judicial control mechanism is established to allow the neutral court to check and balance the investigation power, which reflects the basic law of the healthy operation of the investigation power. Therefore, we should learn from their best practice to reform our investigation procedure.

4.3.4 The Macro-Design of Judicial Control of Investigation Power in China

Justice and efficiency are the two main goals of reform to China's criminal justice, and these two goals can be achieved through building the judicial control mechanism of investigation power.

4.3.4.1 Judge[38]

For all compulsory measures involving citizens' rights and interests, such as arrest, detention, hold in custody, residential surveillance, release on bail pending trial, search, seizure and interception, a warrant is needed and issued by the judge who acts as a neutral third party involved in the investigation. If an emergency happens, the investigating organ may take the relevant compulsory measures on its own, but it must report to the judge immediately after taking them. After that, the judge shall make the relevant written decision after hearing the views of the investigators, the criminal suspect and their defenders. If a criminal suspect and his or her defender are not satisfied with the decision, they should be allowed to file a complaint about the legitimacy of the compulsory measures with the judge who originally imposed them, and the judge should hear the case in open court and make a decision. If permitted, the defendant can also be empowered with the right of appeal against the decision. This

[37] Yinzhong [82].

[38] With regard to the post design of "judge who grants a writ", I think that we can learn the best practices of other countries and design the post of full-time judges on duty in turns in the current court system to issue writs on compulsory investigation measures. They also receives complaints or appeals from citizens who are not satisfied with compulsory investigation measures.

puts the investigation on track of the "prosecution", so as to meet the requirements of procedural fairness.

4.3.4.2 The Current Criminal Justice System Should Be Adjusted to Build the Central Position and Neutral Image of Judicial Power

This requires the abolition of the "principle for the public security organ, the procuratorate and the court to take different responsibilities but cooperate with and contain each other" and "principle of procuratorial supervision", which are established by the Constitution and the Criminal Procedure Law of our country.[39] The biggest disadvantage of these two principles is that they undermine or destroy the authoritative status and neutral image that the judicial power should have in prosecution, making the public security organ the people's procuratorate and the court equal. Moreover, the court cooperation with the public security organ and the people's procuratorate also ruins the image of the court as a neutral judge in a modern country ruled by law. As a impartial judicial judge, the court should treat the state and the accused equally. The principle of cooperation among the public security organ, the procuratorate and the court leads to their functions confused. If such a court takes the judicial control over the investigation power, its performance is nothing but like the legal supervision by the procuratorial organ. In order to build the image of the court as a judicial judge and make the court be able to exercise independent judicial control over the investigation power, the reform should go far beyond the above two aspects, but these two issues are key to this reform.

4.3.4.3 The Systems of People's Procuratorate and the Public Security Organ Should Be Integrated and the Former Lead the Latter to Carry Out the Investigation

The establishment of the judicial control mechanism for the investigation power definitely restricts the means adopted by the people's procuratorate and the public security organ to fight crime. In order to ensure that the investigation by the public security organ and the procuratorial organ meet the requirements of procedural fairness and the goal of prosecuting criminals in an efficient way, a change needs to make in the relationship between these two organs. This is because "unscientific division of jurisdiction for the public security organ and procuratorial organ, overlapping establishment of departments, lack of competition mechanism and unreasonable procedures are found in the current Criminal Procedure Law, resulting in serious buck-passing and the judicial system wasting a large number of judicial resources in

[39] As for the legal and judicial defects about the two principles, please see Chen and Yinzhong [22]; Yinzhong [82]; Zongzhi [86].

the bad operation, and low efficiency in the proceedings."[40] If these issues are not addressed, it is hard to establish the judicial control mechanism. Even if it is built in such situation, it can not continuously operate. As for the integration of these two organs, we may take steps to: (1) weaken the investigation power of the procuratorial organ, and enable the procuratorial organ to direct, command and oversee the investigation and collection of evidence by the public security organ in the criminal proceedings to make the proceedings more accurate, authoritative, in order to ensure the process can be carried out efficiently; and (2) transfer the judicial police with investigative functions from the current public security management system to the procuratorial organ.[41]

4.3.4.4 It is Necessary to Reform the Existing System of Selecting and Appointing Judges to Make Them Be Social Elites

In order for the judiciary to become the patron of social justice and civil rights and to independently exercise judicial control over the investigative bodies subordinate to the government. "It is important that, while providing a enabling institutional environment for the independence of the judiciary, efforts should be made to turn the judiciary into a group capable of exerting counter-influence on the political community. Homogeneity and integration will ensure its unity, and good professional ethics and going beyond the social mores in a moderate way will improve the authority and effectiveness of its decisions. Only such an interaction with society can enable the judiciary to facilitate the social relations and drive the social development."[42] The current situation of judges in our country is really alarming. "About half of the judges in our country do not have a diploma of law school",[43] according to Zhou Dun and Zeng Zhuanwen, vice presidents of the Hunan High People's Court. This situation has become a major obstacle to the reform of China's judicial system. Therefore, we must launch a reform to current system of selecting and appointing judges. We can learn the best practices from civil law countries such as Japan in which law graduates take national judicial examinations and those who pass them receive judicial training before they are eligible to be nominated or appointed as judges, or from the United States and Britain where judges are selected from among the best lawyers. In addition, a limit must be set on the number of judges and an increase in their remuneration is required in order to give them greater respect and prestige and to attract more talents.

[40] Sun [67].

[41] Huai [35].

[42] Huai [35].

[43] He [32].

4.3.4.5 The Exclusionary Rule of Illegal Evidence Should Be Further Improved in Criminal Procedure Law so that the Judicial Power can Continue to Control the Legitimacy of Investigation Power at the Trial Stage

The Criminal Procedure Law was revised in 2012 to provide for the exclusionary rule of illegally obtained evidence. However, it still faces some problems, such as the understanding of illegal means such as extorting a confession by torture, the clues or materials provided by the defense when it proposes the exclusion of illegal evidence, and the importance of procedure of the exclusion of illegal evidence. These problems directly influence the effect of the exclusionary rule of illegal evidence. The exclusionary rule of illegal evidence on the basis of judicial practice should be further improved for the years to come.

4.3.4.6 Separation of Hold in Custody, Arrest and Detention

Compared with Western countries, the measures of hold in custody, arrest and detention carried out by our investigation agencies have not been separated in the criminal procedure in our country. Whether it is hold in custody or arrest, it will finally leads to detention. According to the common practice of Western countries, arrest is only used as a means to ensure the suspects and defendants can appear before the court. After arrest, the arrested person must be brought before a judge in a timely manner, who will decide on detention or release on bail and the detention period by way of a court session. Such a system of separation of arrest and detention ensures that detention has more legal conditions than arrest and is carried out in accordance with more stringent legal procedures, which prevent suspects from being vulnerable to unjust and unreasonable compulsory measures.[44]

Therefore, it is practical to separate hold in custody, arrest and detention in procedure in China, and the detention period should be decided by the court. Accordingly, the provisions of the Criminal Procedure Law relating to the approval by the prosecution service of the extension of the detention period and the power owned by the investigative service to calculate the detention period should be abolished.[45] Moreover, if a criminal suspect and his defence counsel are not satisfied with the decision on detention, they shall have the right to appeal, and the court that originally try the case shall give a ruling in a timely manner through a hearing. If the decision is not

[44] Ruihua [62].

[45] There are two circumstances in which the investigative service may, on its own initiative, calculate the period of detention: (1) if, during the period of investigation, a criminal suspect is found to have committed other major crimes, the time limit for holding the criminal suspect in custody for investigation shall be re-calculated as of the date of discovery of such other crimes; and (2) the identity of a criminal suspect shall be investigated if his/her identity is unknown due to his/her refusal to give a true name or address, in which case the time limit for holding the criminal suspect in custody for investigation shall be calculated as of the date when his/her identity is ascertained.

accepted, the suspect and his defence shall also have the right to appeal to a higher court, which shall make the final decision on the legitimacy the detention.

4.3.4.7 The Criminal Suspects and Their Defenders Should Be Given More Criminal Procedural Rights at the Investigation Stage

Because the defendant is less powerful than the prosecution, domineering over the weak by being strong is likely to happen if unchecked. According to Professor Merryman, the inequality of litigation rights and the secrecy of written procedures tend to create the danger of tyrannical regimes.[46]

However, it is far from enough to reform our investigation system and establish complete judicial control mechanism over investigation power. Moreover, the above-mentioned reform will not be accomplished in an action. This not only involves the reform to the China's judicial system, but the abilities of law enforcement officers should be improved, especially the law enforcement mindset. If the efficiency of fighting crimes is still regarded as the main goal of criminal proceedings, the legitimacy of the judicial control over investigation power is hard to prove. However, few modern countries under the rule of law regard the efficiency of fighting crime as their main goal, which is the symbol of democracy, humanity and justice in modern society.

4.4 The Balance Between Criminal Police Power and Civil Rights After the Revised Criminal Procedure Law

Whether the criminal police powers could be abused has been heatedly discussed when the Criminal Procedure Law was revised in 2012.[47] As a specific legal norm for prosecuting crimes, the Criminal Procedure Law involves the restriction and deprivation of civil liberties, which is closely related to the fundamental rights such as personal freedom and property rights stipulated in the Constitution. In a country under the rule of law, the criminal procedure is called "the law of application for the Constitution" and "the seismograph of the basic law of the state".[48] So, how

---

[46]Merryman [50].

[47]After the amendment of draft was published, the discussion on "secret arrest" caused by the measures such as the residential surveillance, detention, and notification of their families after arrest taken by the public security organ to the suspects or the defendants was triggered. I searched for the keywords of "secret arrest" and "criminal procedure" in the BAIDU search engine and found relevant results about 784,000. Search date: January 26, 2012.

[48]According to the German scholar Claus Roxin, such serious conflicts between the interests of the group and of the individual only happen in the criminal proceedings. This balance of interests in the law symbolically indicates that the Criminal Procedure Law acts as the seismograph of the basic law of the state in public affairs where the relationship between the state and the individual needs to be considered. Roxin [59].

to ensure a dynamic equilibrium between police power and civil rights protection, and to respond to public concerns about the abuse of criminal police power is a pronounced problem we face.

4.4.1 Two Key Points of Regulating the Criminal Police Power

Nowadays, the police is considered as the necessary tools for the state to maintain social order and ensure security. The criminals now are becoming more organized, intelligent and professional, so the public hope that the police can have enough power to fight crime and maintain social peace. At the same time, they are worried that increased criminal police power will, in turn, infringe upon their legitimate rights and interests. In criminal proceedings, "under certain conditions, the police power and the civil rights are in inverse proportion. That means the expansion of the police power leads to the reduction of the civil rights, and the abuse of the police power often deprive the citizens of civil rights."[49] Therefore, how to limit the criminal police power has become a matter of concern. In view of it, the Japanese scholar Taguchi Morikazu noted that the purpose of the criminal police power is to maintain social public order, and its exercise must follow (1) the principle of publicness which includes three sub-principles of inviolability of private life, residence and non-interference in civil affairs; and (2) the principle of police responsibility which means the police power is only exercised for the people that the police are responsible for; and (3) the principle of police proportionality that indicates the police function is only to maintain public order.[50] On this basis, some scholars in China have added the principle of police procedure—the exercise of police power should be exercised in strict accordance with the legal procedure.[51] Others argue that the principles of the exercise of police power include the legal principle, the limited principle, the procedure principle and the responsibility principle.[52] There is another perception that the exercise of criminal police power should follow the principles of law, responsibility, proportion and restriction.[53]

Although these scholars have different opinions on the principles of exercising criminal police power, they share the starting point—limiting the power. Because the criminal police power is a kind of public power, the investigating organ that exercises this power may take compulsory measures such as issuance of a warrant to compel the appearance, hold in custody, residential surveillance and arrest against the criminal suspect. "The lack of effective means of restraint or procedural regulations may endanger the safety of citizens at any time."[54] Therefore, "the government can

[49]Xingliang [75].

[50]Taguchi [70].

[51]Xingliang [76].

[52]Guicai [30].

[53]Xu [79].

[54]Chen and Li [18].

not abuse police power, or it will increase the risk of attack, making social order more difficult to maintain and resulting in even large-scale unrest".[55] In this regard, As Justice Tannin of British House of Lords said that once the powers of social protection itself against criminals are abused, any tyranny must be "thrown in the towel."[56] Therefore, the exercise of criminal police power must be regulated, so as to eliminate the public worry about its improper use. However, this is only one side of this problem. Another one is that the criminal police is an important force to maintain social security and stability, so it is necessary to give them new powers to enable them to fight harder against crimes and maintain public order, especially in transition where our country is facing pronounced social conflicts and rising crime rates. Therefore, in order to regulate the police power in the criminal proceedings, it is essential to clarify how to designate the police power from the perspective of authorization to meet the citizens' demand for social security. After that, it is appropriate to identify how to restrict the criminal police power from the angle of power limitation, in order to respond to the public's concerns about the abuse of police power.

One expert in judicial practical academia said that "the number of criminal offenses in our country is still rising, cases of vicious criminals taking heinous acts to kill innocent people and revenge on society happen from time to time, and criminal activities of the underworld forces are still quite rampant.[57] Therefore, in designating the criminal police power, the priority is how to fight more crimes and enhance the state's ability to control crime, so as to maintain social order, ensure that the public can live and work in peace and contentment and guarantee the human rights for the majority to greatest extent. As an important component of the police power, the criminal police power also characterizes executive power.[58] This means that the criminal police in criminal proceedings is on behalf of the state to prosecute persons suspected of committing crimes, and the individuals or agencies that exercise this power must obey the command and order of a superior. The administrative nature of the criminal police make the efficiency a key factor to consider, so that the police service can proactively prevent crimes and efficiently combat crimes. In this regard, Beccaria noted that the value of the timeliness of punishment is to use the connected concepts of punishment to suddenly awaken people from the lucrative crime activities that tempts them.[59] Therefore, the efficient criminal police power is not only beneficial in the fight against crimes, but also in the prevention of crimes and the fostering legal spirit and the maintenance of social order.[60] Therefore, the exercise of criminal police powers must be efficiency-oriented, and it is necessary to promptly initiate

[55]Becker and Becker [4].

[56]Tannin [71].

[57]Sun and Tong [69].

[58]Chen and Shi [19]; Yinmei [81].

[59]Beccaria [3].

[60]The Italian scholar Beccaria explains the value of the timeliness of punishment in the prevention of crimes and fostering legal spirit that the shorter the time between crime and punishment, the more clearly people bear in mind the two concepts of crime and punishment, so it is natural for people to regard crime as a cause and punishment as an inevitable result. Beccaria [3].

prosecution after discovering the facts of a crime, take requisite measures against persons and property associated with the crime according to the law, and collect and confirm evidence in a timely manner.

However, as a kind of executive power, the criminal police power has one-way coercive and domination power which is likely to violate the civil rights. Locke noted that of all the powers of the state, "the executive power is the most strongest, because it is the only power which can be exercised without going through procedure, and therefore it has a great deal of arbitrariness and space."[61] The criminal police power is even more expansionary and aggressive than other executive powers. Because the criminal police power includes the coercive power and technical investigation power against the citizens' personal rights and property rights in order to maintain public order and combat crimes.[62] In the aftermath of the terrorist attacks of 11 September 2001, the U.S. Senate and the House of Representatives passed the *Patriot Act* on 26 October 2001 in order to combat new type of crime such as terrorist crimes, the police are authorized to use appropriate technical means to prevent, detect and combat terrorist activities and terrorist crimes. While expanding the powers of the criminal police, the Act also provides the applicable procedures and conditions for the exercise of these powers, and the implementation is subject to oversight and inspection by the United States Congress.[63] Therefore, when designating the criminal police power, a special attention should be given to the protection of human rights in addition to the efficiency, so as to enhance the legitimacy of the exercise of criminal police power and strike a balance of fighting crime and protecting human rights. At present, the integration model of police and procurator and judicial review are the two main approaches to restrict the criminal police power.[64] The goal of these two models is to balance the authorization and control of criminal police power, and make the use of criminal police power in accordance with principle of proportionality or principle of relevance. That means the criminal police power must have enough coercive force to combat crime efficiently in order to maintain social order and ensure public safety; at the same time, criminal investigation measures, especially those that violate fundamental rights, must be proportionate to the crimes or harms under investigation.[65] These measure aimed at restoring public order should not be taken at the cost of depriving of any person of liberty and property.

---

[61] Locke [48].

[62] Chen and Shi [19].

[63] See website of U.S. Department of Justice (DOJ): https://www1justice1gov/archive/ll/highlights1htm, last visit time: 2001–10-02.

[64] To control the investigation power like the criminal police power, in addition to the integration model of police and procurator and judicial review, there are also exclusionary rule and procedural separation of hold in custody, arrest and detention.

[65] Herrmann [34].

4.4.2 An Analysis of the Revised Police Power in the Amendment to the 2012 Criminal Procedure Law

The revision of the criminal police powers in the 2012 Criminal Procedure Law includes two aspects. On the one hand, it grants new criminal police powers because of the new changes in crimes; on the other hand, according to the requirement of the state respecting and safeguarding the human rights in the Constitution, exercise of police power is limited. On the whole, this amendment is regarded by the judicial and academic circles as another leap in the development of the cause of human rights in our country, an initiative that focusing both fighting the crimes and protecting the human rights instead of paying attention to the fight against crime and punishment before,[66] the demand of punishing crimes and protecting the people under the new situation, a solution to the problems that urgently need to be solved in the current judicial practice, and the significant development and improvement of the criminal justice system of socialism with Chinese characteristics.[67] Although great progress and highlights has been made, there are also many disputes, especially over the criminal police powers.[68] Therefore, in order to improve the criminal police power, it is necessary to strike a balance between combating crime and protecting human rights.

4.4.2.1 Regulation on the Expansion of Criminal Police Power

The revision of the authorization of criminal police powers in the 2012 Criminal Procedure Law is reflected in two aspects. First, for complicated cases of grave circumstances where detention or arrest is necessary, summons or compelled appearance in court has been extended from 12 to 24 h according to the amendment under Article 117(2); second, the technical investigation and secret investigation is legalized. Article 148 stipulates that after putting a case on file, a public security organ may, based on the needs for criminal investigation, and after going through stringent approval procedures, employ technical investigation measures if the case involves crimes endangering State security, crimes of terrorist activities, organized crimes committed by groups in the nature of criminal syndicates, major drug-related crimes or other crimes seriously endangering the society. Article 151 provides that to ascertain the circumstances of a case, where necessary and subject to the approval of the person in charge of a public security organ, relevant personnel may be assigned to conduct an undercover investigation. These amendments are in response to the

[66]Han Yuanjun and Li Ying, Legal Expert Chen Weidong Gives An Exclusive Interview with Xinhuanet to Explain the Revision of the Criminal Procedure Law: Great Progress in All Aspects, https://news1xinhuanet1com/politics/2012lh/2012-03/11/c-1116362291htm, last visit time: March 22, 2012.

[67]Jianlin [38].

[68]Focus on the Amendment to the Criminal Procedure Law: Highlights and Disputes, *People's Daily*, September 14, 2011.

organized, intelligent, concealed crimes in the social transformation period of our country, and intensify crackdown on new types of crimes. However, according to the foregoing discussion on how to regulate the criminal police power, people may divide on understanding these provisions when they are implemented.

People may, for instance, understand duration differently in the subject of summons or compelled appearance in court. In judicial practice, it is possible to summon or compel a person to appear before investigator on the ground of suspicion of a crime and release him after the time limit, and then leverage these measures again because of suspicion of another crime or after the suspects being released a few hours later. Although Article 117(3) of the revised Criminal Procedure Law provides that a criminal suspect shall be guaranteed with necessary food and rest when he/she is summonsed or compelled to appear before investigators. However, there is no provision on the length of necessary rest. So the power of interpretation still be held in the investigation agency. As far as the legalization of technical investigations is concerned, the provisions of the 2012 Criminal Procedure Law have come in a abstract and general form, and how to implement properly is a problem we face. Its Article 148(1) provides that a public security organ should go through stringent approval procedures before conducting criminal investigation, but provisions of the "stringent approval procedures"and how to approve technical investigative measures can not be found in this legal document. In addition, if the technical investigative measures carried out fail to be in strict accordance with the approved types, applicable parties and time limits, or the materials obtained by technical investigation measures are not used for the investigation under Article 150, there is no provision on who should be held accountable.

In addition, in the process of amendment, the provisions concerning the non-notification of family members of criminal suspects within 24 h after the imposition of compulsory measures such as residential surveillance, criminal detention and arrest in specific circumstances, the public is worried about the legal abuse by the law enforcement agencies.[69] This is mainly because these provisions expand the scope of non-notification of family members, which is likely to result in the "secret detention" and doing harm to the protection of human rights.[70] The original purpose of the legislative amendment is to limit the criminal police power and to correct the behaviour that the investigation organs fail to notify the family members of the criminal suspects under the pretext of such notification hindering investigation not

[69]Suning, People's Daily comments on the Dispute over the Article 73 of the Criminal Procedure Law: Public Fears of Legal Abuse By Law Enforcement Agencies. See on PhoenixNet: https://news1ifeng1com/mainland/special/xingshisusongfa/content-3/detai-l2012-03/21/13334907-01shtml, last visit time: March 22, 2012.

[70]Some legal scholars argue that although the amendment is a big step forward, some of the provisions are still controversial. According to a survey on Sina Weibo, 97.2% of netizens expressed concern about the overhaul of the Criminal Procedure Law, 89.9 percent suggested the Article 73 of *Criminal Procedure Law(Draft Revision)* to be put on hold, 10.1 percent of people said that an immediate vote should be taken, 92.8 percent did not agree to adopt the *Criminal Procedure Law(Draft Revision)*. See Zhu Yi, The Concerns Raised by the Criminal Procedure Amendment. See on people.com.cn, https://yuqing1people1com1cn/gb/173696121html, last visit time: March 22, 2012.

be processed in order to conduct the cases investigating and solving efficiently. In addition, it also allows the non-notification if such notification cannot be processed or where the detainee is involved in crimes endangering state security or crimes of terrorist activities. However, in the criminal proceedings in China, there are already cases in which the investigating organs fail to notify the family members of the party concerned for various reasons, combined with the fact that the decide on whether the crime is major or notification hinders the investigation rests with the investigating organs, which make senses for the public fear the abuse of the criminal police power. In response to those concerns, Article 83 of the 2012 Criminal Law Procedure describes three circumstance in which the investigating organs are allowed not to notify the family members of the suspects within 24 h: detention, crimes endangering State security or crimes of terrorist activities, and the third one that such notification should be processed immediately after the circumstances impeding investigation has been eliminated.[71] Although some provisions limit the powers of the criminal police, it is not circumspect enough for the words used in the revised Criminal Procedure Law. As to how to understand the "notification hinders the investigation" under Article 83, and "notification can not be processed" under Articles 73, 83 and 91, the investigating organ still has high degree of discretionary power. Therefore, the absence of the mechanism to limit their powers or rights relief are likely to raise public concern.

4.4.2.2 The Main Provisions Restricting the Power of Criminal Police

The revision of limiting the criminal police power in the 2012 Criminal Law Procedure is reflected in six aspects. The criminal suspects are entitled to the right of defense at the investigation stage; the criminal suspects are required to be taken to detention house immediately after being held in custody or arrested, the interrogation after detention shall be conducted in the detention house; defense lawyers are entitled to meet with the suspects and defendants, and the meeting shall not be monitored; the relevant people's procuratorate shall still examine the necessity for detention; investigators may record or videotape the interrogation process where the criminal suspect is involved in a crime punishable by life imprisonment or capital punishment or in a otherwise major criminal case; illegally obtained evidence should be excluded. These provisions which restrict the power of criminal police embody the principles of equality of prosecution and defense, legal procedure and timely litigation in theory of criminal procedure. In addition, they will strengthen the protection of civil rights, especially the rights of criminal suspects and defendants, and helps to implement the constitutional provision of "the state respects and protects human rights" in criminal proceedings and facilitate the development of human rights protection in China.

It purpose is to restrict the criminal police power, but there are not provision of responsibilities and legal consequence for the abuse of the criminal police power, leading to some of the criminal procedure provisions limiting criminal police powers

[71]Minyuan [55].

impractical. For example, Article 37 of the 2012 Criminal Law Procedure provides that except in cases of crimes against state security, crimes of terrorist activity, and serious bribery crimes, a defense lawyer requests for a meeting with a criminal suspect or defendant under detention on the strength of the lawyer's practicing certificate, and the certification documents and letter of authorization issued by his/her law firm, or an official legal aid document, the detention house concerned shall arrange the meeting in a timely manner, no later than 48 h after receiving the request. And the meeting should not be monitored. However, there are no provisions of judicial relief for rights holders for violations such as the denial of access to lawyers by investigative authorities or detention house, the scheduling of meeting over 48 h or the monitoring of meeting, nor are any provisions of responsibilities for such violation. In addition, these provisions on access to attorney are to a great extent the same as those in the law on lawyers enacted in June 2008, due to the difficulties of implementing it.[72] Whether the 2012 Criminal Law Procedure can be implemented worries the public.

The exclusionary rule ofillegal-obtained evidence is most pronounced problem in the 2012 Criminal Law Procedure. Judicial practice shows that most wrongful convictions happen in the investigation.[73] In view of the acts of torture to extort a confession, they often occur when the suspects are taken out of the detention house for interrogation before or after they are transferred to the detention house. Article 83 provides that after being taken into custody, a detainee shall be immediately transferred to a detention house for detention within 24 h; Article 116 also provides that investigators shall interrogate a criminal suspect who has been transferred to a detention house for custody in the detention house; Article 54 further provides confessions extorted from a criminal suspect or defendant by illegal means such as torture, testimony of witnesses and statements of victims collected by violent means, threat or other unlawful means shall be excluded. Physical evidence or documentary evidence that is not collected according to statutory procedures and is therefore likely to materially damage judicial justice shall be excluded. The exclusionary rule of illegal evidence only contains the illegal means of obtaining evidence, but does not give a description of the illegal actors of obtaining evidence and illegal forms of evidence. Compared with its original version, the progress has been made in clarifying the consequences of excluding illegal verbal evidence, but illegal means of collecting evidence are not clearly defined. According to Article 54 of the 2012 Criminal Law Procedure, the illegal methods mainly include extorting confessions

---

[72] Since its implementation on 1 June 2008, lawyers are still denied access to their clients when they visit the detention house. In response to this issue, six organs, including the Beijing Municipal High People's Court, the Judicial Bureau and the Public Security Bureau, jointly promulgated the *Regulations on Lawyers' Meeting with Criminal Suspects and Defendants in Custody* (for trial implementation), using interim measures to solve this problem. By 2011, the issue had not been completely resolved. But at the National People's Congress and the Chinese Political Consultative Conference (Two Sessions) that year, a Guangdong deputy to the National People's Congress suggested the Standing Committee of the National People's Congress to resolve the problem. Chen and Wang [20].

[73] Some researchers note that most of the illegal search, seizure, extorting a confession by torture and inducing confessions in criminal proceedings happen at the investigation stage.

by torture, violence and threat, which corresponds to the crime of extorting confessions by torture or the crime of collecting evidence by violence stipulated in Article 247. However, there is no clear definition of what kind of illegal evidence collection methods means extorting confessions by torture or obtaining evidence by violence in the laws of out country. According to *Regulations on the Filing Cases of Dereliction of Duty and Infringement of Rights* by the Supreme People's Procuratorate of our country, the crime of extorting a confession by torture refers to the act of judicial officer who use corporal punishment or disguised corporal punishment to extort a confession from a criminal suspect or defendant, and the crime of obtaining evidence by violence refers to the behavior of judicial personnel to extort witness's testimony by violence.[74] However, the Regulation does not clearly define the corporal punishment, disguised corporal punishment and violence, and it only enumerates beating, binding, illegal use of weapons and other common illegal evidence collection methods such as freezing, hungering, sunburning and burning the suspects for a long time to collect evidences. Similarly, such inexplicit description can also be found in the relevant judicial interpretation and regulation documents of the Criminal Law Procedure. Such enumeration can help exclude the those enumerated situations in judicial practice. But it may have left out many important situations. It is possible for the investigators to use the non-listed methods before they are defined in law, such as the way of keeping the criminal suspect and defendant from sleeping.[75] Whether these methods of obtaining confessions or testimony are illegal was not clarified by the 2012 Criminal Law Procedure. Therefore, it could lead to abuse of criminal police power.

4.4.3 Proposals for Judicial Interpretation of the 2012 Criminal Procedure Law

As a procedural law, the implementation of Criminal Procedure Law is both for the realization process of substantive justice and procedural justice. This realization process is the process of building the authority of law. Max Weber noted that legal procedures are the appropriate means of rational choice and that fair and just procedural laws facilitated or are facilitating the establishment of authority of law.[76] Whether the criminal police power, which is at the front line of the fight against crime, is exercised according to the relevant procedure, is directly related to whether the provision that the state respects and protects human rights by the Constitution can be implemented in the criminal proceedings. From the analysis of the 2012 Criminal

[74]It was adopted at the 49th meeting of the Tenth Supreme People's Procuratorate on December 29,2005, and implemented on July 26,2006.

[75]Whether it is illegal or a form of extorting a confession by torture when the suspects and defendant are kept from sleeping, or not given timely treatment or water for illness, is not clearly defined in the law.

[76]Gong [26].

Law Procedure on criminal police powers above-mentioned, the key issue is that the police service are given enough powers but insufficient limits are put on the use of these powers.

Althoughimprovements need to be made for the 2012 Criminal Law Procedure, it is imperative to clearly define the criminal police powers to help the public security organ, the procuratorate and the court to improve or formulate judicial interpretations.[77] Scholars of this legal document should also proactively participate in the research and formulation of the judicial interpretation after its revision, or the exercise of criminal police power may be off the track of purpose of legislation in judicial practice.[78] As far as the specific regulations on the criminal police power are concerned, the judicial interpretation should be improved from the following two aspects.

4.4.3.1 Clarify the Meaning of the Terms

Legal language should be precise, especiallyfor the procedural law, as it is the norm for regulating people's behavior. Precision of language can make the procedure proceedings progress smoothly. However, the accuracy of legal language will lead to the disconnection between law and social development due to the complexity of the real world. If the legal provisions want to be made applicable widely for long time, legal words and expressions must ambiguous.[79] In view of this, the American scholar John Gibbons put forward the following ideas. Because these legal documents are so influential, it is important that they are phrased correctly; if they are over clearly defined, they may impose undue and unnecessary restrictions on our lives; if they are too loosely phrased, they may give credence to undesirable behaviour or lead to unexpected consequences; Precision does not mean extreme clarity, and ambiguity or flexibility can be used to some degree.[80] Therefore, based on the foregoing analysis, the improvements that can be made with regard to the precision of legal language in the provisions regulating the criminal police power in the 2012 Criminal Law Procedure include:

First, it is important to clearly interpret the expressions such as extorting confessions by torture and obtaining evidence by violence in Article 54 of the Criminal

---

[77] Sun Qian, deputy chief prosecutor of the Supreme People's Procuratorate, said on March 20, 2012, "the Supreme People's Procuratorate must do a good job in formulating the *Rules on the Criminal Process for People's Procuratorates*. The judicial interpretations that are made based on the CPL (1996) must be revised and improved so as to implement the new criminal procedure". Li [45].

[78] For example, after the Criminal Procedure Law was revised in 1996, *Regulations on the Procedure for Handling Criminal Cases by the Public Security Bureau, Rules on the Criminal Process for People's Procuratorates*, and *Interpretation of the Supreme People's Court Concerning the Implementation of the Criminal Procedure Law of the People's Republic of China* were respectively formulated by these three organs, making the renewed Criminal Procedure Law more practical.

[79] He [33].

[80] Gibbon [25].

Procedure Law. These two phrases are the exclusive legal terms of our country whose meaning is equivalent to torture in the world. According to Article One (1) of *Convention against Torture and Other Cruel, Inhuman or Degrading Treatment or Punishment*, "the term 'torture' means any act by which severe pain or suffering, whether physical or mental, is intentionally inflicted on a person for such purposes as obtaining from him or a third person information or a confession, punishing him for an act he or a third person has committed or is suspected of having committed, or intimidating or coercing him or a third person, or for any reason based on discrimination of any kind, when such pain or suffering is inflicted by or at the instigation of or with the consent or acquiescence of a public official or other person acting in an official capacity."[81] There are two key criteria for identifying whether a specific evidence-gathering act is torture. One criteria is the degree of seriousness, which means an act by which severe pain or suffering, whether physical or mental, is intentionally inflicted on the suspect, the defendant or the witness to obtain a confession or testimony from a witness, including, but not limited to the means of beating up, tying up, illegal use of weapons and prolonged freezing, starving, sunburning and burning; The second one is the identity of the actor. The actor of the above-mentioned acts is a public official or other person acting in an official capacity. Therefore, it is suggested that in formulating the provision of judicial interpretation of this Article, illegal evidence-collecting activities such as extorting confessions by torture and obtaining evidence by violence should be explicitly defined in accordance with the above-mentioned two standards, so as to make it more practical and avoid any possible loopholes.

Second, it is also important to clearly define the "necessary food and rest" in Article 117 of "A criminal suspect shall be guaranteed with necessary food and rest when he/she is summonsed or compelled to appear before investigators", in order not to leave the power of interpretation with the investigating organs and prevent disguised corporal punishment and ill-treatment in the process of the suspected being summonsed or compelled to appear before investigators. It is suggested that in formulating the provision of judicial interpretation of this Article, the "necessary food and rest" should be defined as "in any 24-h period, the cumulative time for summons or compelled appearance in court shall not exceed 12 h", or it may be stipulated that "the time for a criminal suspect to rest without disturb shall not be less than six hours during the intervals of two summonses or compelled appearances in court".

Third,it is also important to clearly define the "stringent approval procedures" in Article 148 that provides after putting a case on file, a public security organ may, based on the needs for criminal investigation, and after going through stringent approval procedures employ technical investigation measures. It is the best to enable the court to approve the technical investigation measures, because justices, as a neutral "third party" regarding the litigation, are very important to maintain the balance between investigation and defense, prevent the investigating organs from abusing their power, protect the legitimate rights of criminal suspects and defendants and to achieve the goal of criminal justice. However, as far as the current situation in China is concerned,

---

[81] Chen [12].

it is not possible for the court to make such kind of decision. This is mainly because that there is no justice of the peace in the existing law court system in China to exercise the approval power as in other countries. Therefore, it can not be solved only by revising the Criminal Procedure Law and by the court itself. One of the more feasible options in the formulating the provision learn from the practice of procuratorial organ reporting to the higher-level department for approval of arrest in cases of duty-related crimes. The Supreme People's Procuratorate issued the *Regulations on the Review and Decision of the People's Procuratorates at the Next Higher Level on the Arrest of Cases on File for Investigation by People's Procuratorates below the Provincial Level(trial implementation)* on September 2, 2009, which provides that cases on file for investigation by people's procuratorates below the provincial level, where it is necessary to arrest a criminal suspect, shall be submitted to the procuratorate at the next higher level for review and approval.[82] That means the investigating organs below the provincial level, in the cases where the technical investigation measures are needed, shall report to a higher-level department for approval.[83] In this way, the lowest level division of the approval power of technical investigation measures is the public security organ at the prefectural and municipal level, which can reduce the likelihood of the abuse of technical investigation measures, safeguard human rights, and will not undermine the efforts to fight against crime.

4.4.3.2 Clarity of the Consequences of Violating the Procedure

The exercise of criminal police power is theoretically restricted by procuratorial power, the restriction is less effective in judicial practice.[84] In addition to it, the fact that fewer powers to regulate the criminal police power are given by the Criminal Procedure Law and consequences of violating due process are rarely mentioned could cause the criminal police power to be abused and infringe upon citizens' freedom and other basic rights. In order to guarantee the dynamic equilibrium between the fight against crime and the protection of human rights, the exercise of criminal police power needs to be procedurally regulated. Apart from giving the parties concerned the relief right and investigating the related responsibility, it is more important to formulate the provision about the consequence of violating the legal proceedings. "The legal consequence in the procedural sense refers to the behavior and its result

---

[82]Starting from 2011, the reform that the review and arrest in the cases of duty-related crimes should be conducted and approved by the higher-level department would be launched in all procuratorial organs throughout the country. See Xu Ridan, *The Reform That the Review and Arrest in the Cases of Duty-Related Crimes Should Be Conducted and Approved by the Higher-Level Department Will Be Launched in All Procuratorial Organs in China,* Procuratorate Daily, January 14, 2011.

[83]If a procuratorial organ, in criminal proceedings, as an investigating organ, decides on the use technical investigative measures in anti-corruption, anti-malfeasance and other self-investigation cases, the approval procedure may be carried out with reference to the relevant documents issued by the Central Political and Legal Affairs Commission.

[84]The way of investigation and control, which is mainly based on procuratorial supervision, has shown the defects of the abuse of power in practice.

of the violation of the legal proceedings, which are not recognized or revoked in the proceedings, or should be negated, supplemented or amended legal provisions."[85] The purpose of clarifying the legal consequences is to highlight the relevant provisions of the Criminal Procedure Law that regulate how the powers of authorities are exercised, making them more authoritative and widely implemented. By doing so, the mindsets such as "pay more attention to the substantive law but less to the procedural law" and "attaching more importance to cracking down on crimes but less to the protection of rights" can be changed, to regulate the exercise of criminal police power, safeguard the legitimate rights of the participants in the proceedings and maintain the dignity of the criminal proceedings. Therefore, it is necessary to stipulate the legal consequences of violating the proceedings when formulating the provisions of judicial interpretation, and hang a "The Sword of Damocles" over the investigation organ, to implement the provisions of the 2012 Criminal Procedure Law that restrict the way in which criminal police powers are exercised. In view of clarifying the legal consequences, we should follow the protection of rights, regulations on functions and powers, integrity, appropriateness, coordination and other principles.[86] In view of the seriousness of the violation of statutory procedures in the exercise of criminal police powers, it is recommended that the relevant judicial interpretations provide for the following two circumstances in respect of the legal consequences of the violation.

The circumstances that can be corrected. This kind of legal consequence are mainly applicable for the minor violation of criminal procedure in the exercise of criminal police power. In respect of such violations, it is not necessary, in accordance with the principle of appropriateness, to invalidate proceedings already under way or to exclude evidence already obtained. However, in order to maintain the dignity of the proceedings, these minor infractions need to be corrected. If the family member is not notified or the lawyer is not allowed to meet with the suspects according to the time prescribed by law, the criminal suspect or the lawyer may submit a request to the People's Procuratorate at the same level, and the latter shall suggest to the investigating organ or the detention house that they should set it right. After that, these two organs should immediately notify the family members or arrange a meeting.

The situations that are deemed as invalid. Such kind of legal consequences are mainly directed at major violations of criminal procedure by investigating organs in the exercise of criminal police powers. For this kind of violation, the evidence collected can not be used in the proceedings according to the principle of protection of rights. As far as regulating criminal police power is concerned, there are mainly four circumstances. First, if a criminal suspect isn't guaranteed with necessary food and rest after he or she is summonsed or compelled to appear before court, the confession obtained this time is invalid; second, if a criminal suspect, after being detained or arrested, is not immediately brought to a detention centre, but is interrogated at the

---

[85]Minyuan [53].

[86]Some scholars in our country have summed up the principles of legal consequences in violation of proceedings into seven kinds: protection of rights, regulations on functions and powers, integrity, adequacy, appropriateness, coordination, and combination of law and discretion. ÛMinyuan [54].

office of the investigation organ, or is taken out of a detention house for interrogation after being brought there, the confession obtained from such interrogation shall be invalid; third, if the technical investigation measures are not carried out in strict accordance with the approved types, applicable parties and time limits, the evidence obtained shall be null and void; fourth, in the case of possible life imprisonment or death penalty, if no audio or video recording is made during the interrogation of a criminal suspect, the statement obtained from the interrogation shall be invalid. If the evidence obtained is deemed as invalid as a result of the above-mentioned violation of the statutory procedure in the exercise of the criminal police power, and the other legal evidence in the case is sufficient to bring the case to a conclusion, given the efficiency in combating crime and the protection of human rights, there is no need to start over the entire evidence-collecting procedure. If the existing evidence in the case is insufficient, the investigation organ may obtain other evidence in a way that is in compliance with the statutory procedure. If the evidence is still insufficient after the re-collection, the case should be dismissed.

4.5 Development and Regulation of Investigative Measures in Criminal Procedure Law

Under the new social situation, the rapid socio-economic development and the change of modus operandi unprecedentedly challenge the routine investigation methods. Under the ideal condition, the investigation should strike a balance between the two basic values—the efficiency of investigation and the protection of human rights. However, the commonly adopted investigation methods are less effective under this situation. How to respond to the increasing social demand of human rights protection and carry out investigation and control crime efficiently has become a major issue in the investigation. It is a problem in criminal investigation both home and abroad. Therefore, it is a common practice in most countries to allow the investigating organs to use special investigative means in addition to the commonly used ones.

The legalization of covert investigation is a common practice and one of the most defining trends in the development of the criminal procedure system in the past half century across the globe. There are three explanations for its legalization. First, the emergence of various types of invisible crime, the increasing number of crimes and more high-tech methods used to commit the crime make the commonly used investigation methods less and less efficient, and the demand of crime control is increasing rather than decreasing. All these require the investigation organ to respond effectively only by means of covert investigation. Second, because of the increasing perception of human rights protection, more regulated, open and demystified criminal procedures, the change of legal environment in which some conventional investigative methods that were "effective" work best in judicial practice and stricter control of conventional investigative methods, the covert investigation, as an alternative measure, has been greatly adopted. Third, the widespread use of covert investigation reflects a change in the methods of society control and the demand of social development. The formation of the industrial society, the stranger society, the pluralistic society and the mobile society has led to the failure of the traditional methods of social control. The methods of social control can only be changed from coercion to covert surveillance and deception in response to social changes and changes in human behavior patterns.

The practice that the technical investigation methods are used to investigate common criminal offenses has long existed in China's judicial practice, and it can also be found in the law.[87] But it was included in the Criminal Procedure Law. At the beginning of 2007, when the practical and academic scholars discussed the revision of the Criminal Procedure Law, I wrote an article to call for the focus on legalizing cover investigation.[88] At end of 2008, the new reform plan of the judicial system and working mechanism issued by the Central Political and Legal Affairs Commission include identifying the applicable bodies, scope and approval procedure of technical investigation and covert investigation measures. Four years later, the technical investigation was included in the Criminal Procedure Law revised in 2012, which verifies the importance of my appeal. Therefore, I am more convinced that any countries under the rule of law are attaching the importance to the balance of rights protection and crime control. If we tie the left hand of the police, we must release their right hand.

4.5.1 Legalization of Technical Investigation

4.5.1.1 Differentiation of Technical Investigation and Covert Investigation in Terms of Concept

Technical investigation and covert investigation can be understood from both academic and legislative levels.

On the academic level, technical investigation and covert investigation are not the same concepts, with the latter containing the former. It is believed that technical investigation is a kind of covert investigation. The covert investigation refers to the non-compulsory investigation which will be difficult or impossible to carry out or be carried out by means of concealment or deception under the condition that the relative person in the investigation knows about it. It mainly includes two kinds: undercover investigation and covert surveillance. The latter, surveillance-like

[87] Article 16 of the *People's Police Law of the People's Republic of China* provides that "after putting a case on file, a public security organ may, based on the needs for criminal investigation, and after going through stringent approval procedures, employ technical investigation measures."

[88] At that time, the direction of the reform of the police power was to further restrict the criminal police power on the basis of the Criminal Procedure Law in 1996. I was affirmative on the one hand but concern on the other hand that it is impossible to modernize the criminal procedure and manage it by law only through limits on their power even to greatest extent, as deducted by theory. See Weidong Chen, *Debate on Legalizing Covert Investigation*, https://www.legaldaily.com.cn/jdwt/content/2007-02/11/content_610118.htm?node=6158.

covert investigation, is known as technical investigation in China's judicial practice. After studying the history of covert investigation, it can be seen that the concept of covert investigation is extremely extensive. At the beginning, the undercover investigation was mainly conducted. Although the surveillance-like covert investigation existed, it didn't widespread until the industrial revolution that technology significantly advanced and was employed in criminal investigation. When it comes to the relationship between technical investigation and covert investigation, some scholars argue that "special investigation measures"—the covert investigation in a broad sense—should be collectively called investigation measures other than conventional measures. They also believe that the special investigative measures includes technical investigation and covert investigation in a narrow sense (undercover investigation and delivery under control).[89]

Different from the clear division in academic theory, the understanding of the relationship between technical investigation and secret investigation is more confused in the documents from the central government and even in the norms of national law. According to the a new round of reform scheme of the judicial system and working mechanisms issued by Central Political and Legal Affairs Commission in 2008, the technical and covert investigations are just juxtaposed without giving any differences between them. As a result, the Criminal Procedure Law adopted in 2011 was revised again. In the original discussion, both of these two investigation methods were not distinguished. Then the discussion draft attempted to specify the concept and types of technical investigation. There were two modification schemes. One is to define the technical investigation as "investigation measures of taking the technical means such as surveillance and communication to secretly photograph, record and videotape the citizen's residence and intercept their information sent over a computer network, to obtain the criminal evidence." The other is to define the technical investigation as "the technical investigation measures of taking the technical means such as surveillance, communication, secret photographing, recording, videotaping, intercepting the information of the computer network to collect the criminal evidence affect the citizens' right to freedom of communication, residence or privacy." No matter what kind of plan, it refers to the technical investigation measures in a narrow sense, emphasizing the use of technical means in the process of obtaining criminal evidence. The failure to differentiate technical investigation from the covert investigation does not accord with the inclusive relationship between the two in theory.

The draft amendment to the Criminal Procedure Law issued provides for two main types of means of covert investigation: covert surveillance and undercover investigation. Cover surveillance, known as technical investigation in Chinese context, refers to the use of technical means to secretly obtain information about citizens. Undercover investigation refers to the covert investigation methods characterized by deception and using humans as carriers, including informant, undercover, and enticing investigation. Identities are often changed in such investigation. Academics also call it undercover investigation. Technical investigation is also conducted in a

[89]Zhang [84].

secret way, so it falls into the category of covert investigation. The draft amendment equates undercover investigation with covert investigation, but there are not sufficient evidence to prove in logic, semantics and even in practice. This misconstrued understanding has also confuse the people in practical area about the relationship between technical investigation and covert investigation. According to the public security organ's interpretation of Criminal Procedure Law, the investigation with hidden identity is considered as covert investigation, also known as undercover investigation, which is also defined as "a method of investigation by specially selected investigators or other persons who, by hiding their original identity, lurk in the criminal organization or environment under investigation and, according to the law, secretly collect criminal evidence or intelligence".[90]

The expression of "technical investigative measures" is used in Chapter 2(8) of Part 2 in 2012 Criminal Procedure Law in order to distinguish them from conventional investigative measures. It can be seen from the contents of this section that technical investigation measures includes both covert surveillance using technical means, also understood as technical investigation, such as covert recording, videotaping and interception, and covert investigation methods including the investigation of hidden identity and the delivery under control, which should be theoretically classified as undercover investigation. In other words, this section contains both technical investigation and the covert investigation using manpower. However, the proposal to provide for the concept and specific types of technical investigation in the draft was finally dismissed. The legislature fails to clearly explain the differences between the technical investigation and covert investigation, but only gives provisions and authorization in general terms. All the investigation is the restriction and deprivation of civil rights. If the specific means are not explicitly described by law, it will clearly affect the implementation. Both technical investigation and undercover investigation in covert investigation are expressed only by giving concepts, which need to be further clarified, such as which means are included in technical investigation. Lack of specific definition indicates that the investigative authorities could be given many powers so that they are likely to use all means at their disposal to collect the citizens information and invade their privacy, which may lead to serious consequences.

In defining the technical investigation, two key characteristics should be considered: technology and secrecy. Human perception is extended or enhanced by means of certain technological equipment. Technical equipment is constantly updated. Technical investigation means must follow the natural law of continuous obsolescence and upgrading. Therefore, it is neither possible nor necessary for new types of means to be completely enumerated in law. Secrecy is in fact a central feature of all covert investigative techniques, it refers to all kinds of investigation methods that are carried out without the knowledge of the relative person, or, more specifically, those investigation measures that would be difficult to initiate once the relative person becomes aware of them. According to this standard, after-the-fact inquiry of communication information such as short message and call record, which is widely used in investigation, should not be regarded as technical investigation. The simultaneous interception

[90] Sun [68].

of short message or the location of mobile phone and computer, however, should fall into the category of technical investigation means.

4.5.1.2 Differentiation of Technical Investigation and Covert Investigation in Terms of Morality and Justice– from Proper Purpose to Lawful Means

In order to achieve the governance goals such as national security and political stability in sovereign states, it has long been the practice to adopt the technical investigation and covert investigation measures in the military and political struggle. High efficiency of criminal investigation is required by the social development and the crime control, so the technical investigation and the covert investigation measure have been introduced in the criminal proceedings, even causing intense disputes. From the policy-like, unpublished regulations to the explicit, open legal norms, the legalization of technical investigation and covert investigation also shows the legitimacy of its application in criminal investigation.

This legitimacy is reflected in the aspect that law enforcement agencies can collect information, which are difficult to gather by using other common investigative means, through covert surveillance such as telephone surveillance, interception, mail checking, tracking and location, or deception means including undercover, informants and enticement detection. It is effective in the following four aspects. First, the control on the emergence and spread of invisible criminal patterns requires the use of covert investigative methods to solve the cases involving weapons, smuggling, bribery and other trade-related cases that are difficult to handle through conventional investigation methods. Second, the fact that criminals use high-tech means to commit crimes also requires law enforcement to "give them some of his own medicine". Third, covert investigation is also a relatively low-cost means of law enforcement. Compared with the practice of collecting after-the-fact evidence retroactively, it is faster and more convenient to gather evidence through legal enticement investigation. In addition, it is also easier to obtain confession by telephone surveillance compared with the method of deploying many police forces to arrest and interrogate criminal suspects. Fourth, the evidence obtained by covert investigation is more convincing. The evidence obtained from on-the-spot arrest, combined with that collected through recording and videotaping, makes the defendant hard to deny.

Technical and covert investigations have all of these benefits, they were not legalized in an awkward situation until the Criminal Procedure Law was revised in 2012. First, these investigations are often carried out in a highly secret way. Sometimes even the prosecutors and judges handling the case, and the police and the case handlers other than the secret investigators have no idea about it, let alone the person under investigation. Second, the information obtained in such way usually can not be used as evidence, but only as clues to other evidence-gathering activities. Finally, the investigators will risk facing charges due to using unlawful means, because they are not clearly authorized by law to conduct such investigations which are only carried out in accordance with departmental rules and regulations. They are unsure of whether it is right to do so, coupled with the unclear boundary between legal and illegal methods, so they are placed in such boundary strip. The reason why we encounter the tough situation is that covert investigation appeared in China at the time of the founding of the People's Republic of China, during which it mainly used in the military struggle, the struggle between ourselves and enemies and the class struggle. Therefore, high confidentiality is required. Even though the covert investigation is allowed in the criminal investigation, we still carry the characteristic of high confidentiality.[91] Moreover, covert investigations are considered highly sensitive in our country because they involve too many political factors.

Even if we know that there must be some reason for the existence of something, it should be noted that the reasonableness is sometimes relative, or only in a certain period of time. As the modern rule of law is gradually established, the modernization and institutionalization of criminal procedure will make the rules of evidence more scientific and reasonable, so the current situation of secret investigation will change accordingly. On the over sensitive covert investigation, I think we should not avoid it but be brave to fight it out. Any sovereign state has the right to protect its national security and maintain the political stability and should defend their nations by all means. The United States, in the name of the defender of human rights, monitors one tenth of the 180 billion global phone calls each year. Of note, the national security affairs and the political stability affairs are quite different from the criminal justice matters, so we need to deal with it accordingly. Although the covert investigation is used to handle these matters above, it is internationally conventional to, based on different legal norms, authorize a covert investigation to sensitive matters by lifting some limits, and covert investigation methods in the criminal proceedings of the criminal justice system in a state, should consider the rule of law and human rights protection. The separation of the two is essential to the legalization of secret investigation.

4.5.1.3 The Perfection of the Regulations on the Technological Investigation

The legalization of secret investigation is the defining trend of social development, and people also are affirmative of its process. If the power of the investigating organs to adopt the measures of technical investigation and covert investigation can not be effectively regulated, it will definitely make the investigating organs more powerful, and infringe upon the rights of defendant. In 2012, a section titled "technical investigative measures" was added in the revised Criminal Procedure Law. In this section, the scope of application, the procedure for approval, the valid period, the procedure for extension, the procedure for execution, the restrictions on the use of materials obtained by technical investigative measures, the investigation of concealed identities, the controlled delivery and the special provision on the use of evidence gathered by technical investigative measures are all regulated. After studying these provisions,

[91] Lei [42].

I think that in addition to the above-mentioned regulations in these two investigations, the following three key issues still need to be further discussed.

First, the application scope of technical investigation measures should based on the demands in practice and follow the principle of "temper justice with mercy". According to law, there are two standards need to abide by in defining the scope of application of technical investigation: grave crimes and application only after case being filed. The former is one of the basic principles to manage the covert investigation by law, which is good to be identified. However, it is necessary to consider its feasibility and exception in investigation. Generally speaking, it tends to be formalistic for people to follow the first standard, because it is hard to judge whether some cases are major or not. Therefore, it is essential to detail provisions by clarifying the term of imprisonment to individual charges, to prevent the abuse of power. In strictly defining the scope of application, we should also take account into some special cases where the technical investigation is especially need. These special misdemeanour cases mainly refer to those that have significant influence on society and are of great concern to the local people. Once mishandled, such cases will be likely to cause civil disorder and social unrest. There are also some cases in which mobile phones and other communication devices are the objects to be stolen or destroyed, or used as tools to commit crimes against property. To detect such crimes, technical investigation means must be applied, regardless of the seriousness of the crime. The two exceptions mentioned above should be considered in the formulation of the principle of grave crimes. In addition, the application of technical investigation measures premising case filing reflects the spirit of strictly abiding by the standard. However, it is also pivotal to conduct prospective investigation or investigation before case filing in cases of endangering national security and terrorist crimes, because these two kinds of cases, crime prevention is more important than after-the-fact fight against crime in these two circumstances. The legislators need to realize that the regulation on the time point of "after filing a case" necessitates dividing the application of the technical investigation methods into two stages or two types—the evidence collecting method in the investigation and the information gathering method before filing a case—which are coexistent and interrelated.

Second, we should adhere to the principle of "last evidence that obtained by technical investigation measures to be used". The stipulation that the materials obtained in covert investigation can be used as evidence in the current Criminal Procedure Law shows a great progress because it solves the problem of evidence transformation that have beset the investigating organs for a long time. However, it can not be construed that such evidence can be used in all cases. It should be noted that materials obtained in covert investigations should be used until the last minute, in order to avoid or delay the consequences caused by the exposure of the methods and processes of such investigation, like counter-investigation methods and endangering the personal safety of investigators. In addition, the large amount of money spend on updating the database and technical equipment to store evidence can also be saved. In fact, the investigative techniques and evidence gathered by such way have always been allowed to use in special cases such as drug-related crimes and those where limited evidence is found. However, such cases are rarely seen. In most of the cases, the technical investigation means is mainly employed to find various clues to the investigation, rather than to collect the information for a verdict.

Finally, the approval procedure of technical investigation measures, as an important part of the control of investigation powers, should be made clear. However, it is not clearly defined in the current Criminal Procedure Law. The expression of "going through stringent approval procedures" does not restrict the investigation power and discourages the efforts to make the covert investigation managed by law. Therefore, lawmakers need to revise it. Without the approval procedure, the legislation of covert investigation will translate into the delegated legislation. If this one-dimensional legislation is not properly controlled, it will bring about a serious challenge to the citizen's right of privacy. In fact, the approval procedure is very strict, because the technical investigation is practically subject to a four-level internal approval mechanism. What's more important, specific practices should be explicitly described in the law so as to unveil the secrecy of this technical investigation, make this procedure open and transparent, embody the balance to control and grant the power to carry out the covert investigation.

4.5.2 Regulation and Development of Conventional Investigative Measure

4.5.2.1 Relationship Between Conventional Investigation Measure and Technical Investigation Measure

The conventional investigation measure and the technical investigation measure should not be adopted at the same time, with the former used in most of cases. As for the application of technical investigation measure, I think that it can be employed only when the conventional investigation measure can not or fail to work best. The main reasons are as follows.

First, on the level of the value embodied by the system, the technical investigation measures have pros and cons. Although the investigators with the technical investigation measures can effectively find criminal suspects and obtain clues and evidence, this kind of act involving enticement, deception and secret will label the dishonesty and dishonor on the state power. This also means that the investigators participate, directly or indirectly, in criminal activities in covert investigations carried out by means of inducement. And this kind of fight against crimes by any means is often frown upon. The more technical investigative measures are used, the more damages are made on the country's image.

Second, from the perspective of judicial input and output, although technical investigation can reduce the expenditure in the law enforcement, the acquisition and updating of technical equipment requires a large amount of judicial costs. In terms of of output, more restrictions are laid on the use of evidence obtained through technical investigation compared with the conventional investigation measures. Before the

Criminal Procedure Law was revised in 2012, materials obtained through technical investigation can not be used directly as evidence and could not be presented in court and they can only be used as a clue for investigation and evidence collection according to the*Regulations on Technical Investigation by the Ministry of Public Security*. However, they can be used as evidence if they have been transformed into a legal form of evidence by adopting the investigation measures prescribed by the Criminal Procedure Law.[92] The revised Criminal Procedure Law explicitly that the materials collected by investigation means "may be used as evidence", it also provides that "when necessary, judges may verify the evidence outside courtrooms".

Finally, in terms of harmful effects, we may encounter many challenges when taking technical investigation measures. These challenges could be caused by many aspects, such as by improper interference by technical means with the privacy of criminal suspects, defendants and persons not involved in cases, or by the covert investigations which may endanger personal safety of investigators if their identities are revealed. In addition, covert investigation involving informants and undercover may cause the investigators to have mental stress because they can not live a normal life in that circumstance. Moreover, some scholars argue that covert investigation will damage the right to a fair trial, and its "secrecy" will lead to the failure of both internal and external monitoring mechanism.[93]

4.5.2.2 Regulation and Development of Investigation and Interrogation

The fact of criminal juridical practice laying too much emphasis on the oral confession, the widely adopted investigation method of transforming confession to evidence and the imperfect procedure of investigation and interrogation has always led to an illegal act of obtaining evidence such as extorting a confession by torture and violation of rights of criminal suspects and defendants. Combined with the rapid social development and increasing complexity of crime, some stipulations on investigation and interrogation have not been adapted to the needs of actual investigation. In response to this, the Criminal Procedure Law was revised in 2012 to regulate the conduct of investigation and interrogation, while taking into account the need to extend the interrogation period under special circumstances.

The revised Criminal Procedure Law seeks to regulate investigative interrogation through the following ways.

First, regarding the place of interrogation, the detained and arrested persons shall be immediately taken into custody in a detention house, and the investigators shall interrogate the criminal suspects in the detention house after they are transferred to a detention center for custody, according to Articles 83, 91 and 116 (2) of the 2012 Criminal Procedure Law. This totally prevent the torture and other unlawful interrogation. According to previous studies, unlawful interrogation such as extorting a confession by torture often takes place in the interrogation places of the case

[92]Zhu [85].

[93]Lei [41].

handling organs. In the previous Criminal Procedure Law only described the place of interrogation for people who did not need to be arrested or detained, but did not specify the place of interrogation for criminal suspects who were in custody. According to the *Rules of Law enforcement by the Public Security Organ* in effect at that time, the interrogation of detained criminal suspects should in principle be carried out in the interrogation room of the detention house. However, it has been proved that it does not regulate investigation and interrogation in an effective way, and the interrogations conducted out of detention house and the unannounced interrogations are often found in the investigation. The possibility of unlawful interrogation, such as the use of torture to extort a confession, taking place outside the interrogation room of the detention house has also increased considerably. Compared with interrogation in interrogation rooms of investigation organs, interrogation in detention centers is more regulated. Especially since the "hide-and-seek event" (a suspect named Li Qiaoming was tortured to death in a detention house in 2009), great progress in recent years has been made in the management and protection of rights for the detainees in the detention house. Under the revised Criminal Procedure Law, the interrogation for a suspect in custody must be conducted in a detention house, which leave no chance for anyone interrogating suspects outside the detention houses, thus preventing torture and other unlawful interrogation.

Second, the revised Criminal Procedure Law gives lawyers the right to participate in the criminal proceedings with the legal status of a defender. Moreover, the new articles about the right of meeting and correspond with criminal suspects and the right of reviewing the files for the defense lawyer also play an important role in protecting the right to defense of the criminal suspect and other legitimate rights and even regulating the investigation and interrogation. After being revised in 1996, the Criminal Procedure Law provided that the defense lawyers can participate in the proceedings as early as at the investigation stage. The defense lawyers are not given the legal status of a defender, so they can only provide limited legal assistance to the criminal suspects. After being revised again in 2012, it provides that a criminal suspect shall be entitled to entrust a defender after he or she is interrogated for the first time by an investigating organ or as of the date on which compulsive measures are taken, provided that during investigation, the criminal suspect may only entrust a lawyer as his or her defender. In order to ensure the exercise of the right to defense of the criminal suspect during the investigation, the law also stipulates that the investigating organ shall inform the criminal suspects of such right to entrust a defender when they are interrogated for the first time by an investigating organ or as of the date on which compulsive measures are taken. In addition, the procedures for defense lawyers meeting with criminal suspects have also been simplified, such meetings are not allowed to be monitored and defense lawyers are given more powers to examine the case file materials. The above-mentioned new measures to safeguard the right to defence can regulate the exercise of the power of investigation and interrogation to some extent.

Third, recording and videotaping the investigation and interrogation are required in the revised Criminal Procedure Law in order to exert in-process control over these processes. After studying the Criminal Procedure Laws in the countries governed by the law, it can be seen that the investigation and interrogation are managed by the combination of ex ante and and ex post review and supplemented by in-process control. The ex ante review refers to judicial review, also known as writs doctrine; ex post review refers to the exclusion of illegal evidence. Compared with the presence of a lawyer during interrogation, recording and videotaping are more acceptable and therefore are more commonly used. The purpose of adopting these two measures in the processes of investigation and interrogation is to (1) supervise and regulate the investigation and interrogation by investing organs, which helps to prevent the unlawful interrogation such as extorting a confession by torture; and (2) to confirm and preserve the confession before the trial.[94] In addition, compared with the note-taking in the interrogation, the recording and videotaping can enhance the accuracy of the record and the efficiency of interrogation, protect the legitimate rights and interests of the criminal suspects and protect the investigators.[95] Because of this, Western countries generally adopt the recording and videotaping system during interrogation.[96] The addition of this system used in the interrogations in the Criminal Procedure Law demonstrates that it has been well recognized in judicial practice, especially in procuratorial practice over the years.[97]

---

[94]Chen [13]; Meijun [49].

[95]Meijun [49].

[96]Huang [36]; Meijun [49].

[97]The system of videotaping and recording during interrogation was first implemented in the People's Procuratorate of Zhejiang Province. Between 2000 and 2004, it adopted a progressive strategy, by using this system only in the anti-corruption and bribery cases and then in the major cases and all kind of cases, In 2004, a system of submitting videotaping and recording materials when a request is made for arrest and transferral of cases for examination before prosecution was developed in provincial and municipal people's procuratorates and some community-level procuratorates. After that, this system in Sichuan, Gansu, Jiangsu, Hubei and other places have been introduced. In 2005, the Supreme People's Procuratorate gave a directive requiring prosecutors across the country to progressively implement this system in the cases investigated by themselves. On November 1 of the same year, the 43rd Meeting of the 11th Procuratorial Committee of the Supreme People's adopted the *Provisions of the Supreme People's Procuratorate on Implementing Synchronous Audio and Video Recording throughout the Whole Process of Interrogation of Duty-related Criminal Suspects (for Trial Implementation)*, which further regulates this system. This provision, together with the subsequently issued "*Regulation on Technical Methods of the Supreme People's Procuratorate on Implementing Synchronous Audio and Video Recording throughout the Whole Process of Interrogation of Duty-related Criminal Suspects*, clearly defines the scope of application, applicable time and place and the relevant technical requirements of audio and video recording of the entire interrogation process, as well as how to save and use these materials. Compared with the active exploration by the procuratorial organ, the public security organ has been relatively slow in implementing this system. The head of the criminal investigation division of the Ministry of Public Security responded to the issue of audio-and video-recording in the interrogations raised in the press conference in 2006 by saying that "we will try to implement it especially in the murder and gang-related cases."(Huang [37].) In 2010, the People's Procuratorate of Zhengzhou and the Public Security Bureau of Zhengzhou jointly adopted the *Provisions of the Public Security Organ on Implementing Synchronous Audio and Video Recording throughout the Whole Process of Interrogation of Criminal Suspects (for Trial Implementation)*, providing that the public security organ should synchronously videotape and record the entire process of first interrogation of criminal suspects punishable by capital, severe punishment.

Finally, it is necessary to formulate the exclusionary rule of illegal-obtained evidence the procedure of investigation and interrogation to regulate the interrogation. The Criminal Procedure Law of 1979 and 1996 both provided that extorting confessions by torture and obtaining evidence by threats, enticement, deception and other illegal means are strictly prohibited, but exclusionary rule of illegal-obtained evidence and procedures were not clearly defined. The amendment to it includes the achievements of the earlier reform of the central judicial system and the two regulations on evidence proposed by the Supreme People's Court, the Supreme People's Procuratorate, the Ministry of Public Security, the Ministry of National Security and the Ministry of Justice, and defines the scope and procedure of the exclusionary rule. Therefore, the framework of exclusionary rule in our country is created, and the approaches for strict exclusion of verbal evidence and discretionary exclusion of physical evidence are developed. According to the revised Criminal Procedure Law, confessions of criminal suspects and defendants collected by illegal means such as extorting confessions by torture must be excluded, and such exclusionary rule is not only applicable at the trial period but throughout the whole proceedings including investigation, examination, prosecution and trial. In terms of case handing, the function of this ex post facto control mechanism is to exclude the confessions of the criminal suspect and the defendant obtained by illegal means such as extorting confessions by torturer. From the perspective of the criminal procedure system, the exclusionary rule provides a warning line for the conduct of investigation and interrogation, making organs concerned dare not cross it.

The purpose of the aforesaid new provisions on the investigation and interrogation is to regulate the investigation and safeguard the legitimate rights of the criminal suspects as well as protect the investigators, which also reflects the great progress made in the criminal procedure legislation in our country. However, it should also be noted that these provision are not perfect enough, and there are still more improvements to be made. In addition, to what extent these provisions can be implemented in judicial practice is yet to be identified. Taking the procedural rights of the defence lawyer in the investigation period as an example, the renewed Criminal Procedure Law grants the defence lawyer the legal status of defender in the investigation. Does it mean that they are given all the rights to defence of defender? In terms of recording and videotaping during interrogation, how to ensure the completeness of these materials and prevent not recording while torturing or torturing while not recording? With respect to exclusionary rule, how to understand other unlawful means in the expression of use of torture to extort a confession and other illegal means is directly related to the application scope of this rule. If these aspects are not clarified, the legal effect of these provisions of regulating the behavior of investigation and interrogation and protecting the legal rights of criminal suspects will be greatly reduced.

While regulating the interrogation, in view of the complexity of the crime circumstance and the fact that some of the practices adopted in previous judicial practice to obtain time for interrogation are no longer appropriate,[98] the revised Criminal Procedure Law relaxes some of the restrictions on investigative interrogation, such as prolonging the time for summons or compelled appearance in court to 24 h for complicated cases of grave circumstances where detention or arrest is necessary.

4.5.2.3 The Regulation and Development of Other Conventional Investigation Measures

Compared with the big changes of provisions in interrogation, few amendments are made to the provisions of investigation activities in the Criminal Procedure Law. These amendments are mainly reflected in the following aspects:

First, compulsory sampling is added in the Section of Inquest and Examination. The practice of compulsory collection of biological samples and information of victims and criminal suspects has long existed in the investigation, but compulsory sampling, which may violate the personal and privacy rights of the persons concerned, has not fallen within the category of provisions that need to be amended for ages, which extremely affects the protection of the rights of the persons concerned. Paragraph 1 of Article 130 provides that "fingerprints, blood, urine and other biological samples may be collected", thus incorporating compulsory sampling into physical examination. The current rules, of course, are still too principled and simple. When perfecting these provisions in the future, we should make clear regulations on the procedure and executing body of such compulsory sampling as well as how to use, store and destroy these biological samples and fingerprints.

Second, the scope to seal up and seize objects has been expanded. As the economic society and market economy develops, financial products such as bonds, stocks and funds are becoming important forms of value in financial market. The scope of the objects that need to be sealed up and seized should also be expanded. In the light of this new socioeconomic development, the Criminal Procedure Law has built the aforesaid new forms of property into the scope of seal-up and seizure, which embodies the constant improvement in this legal document.

---

[98]This refers mainly to the past cases in which the compulsory measures such as holding up interrogated person for cross-examination was used to solve the problem of insufficient time for interrogation after compelled appearance in court. Holding up interrogated person for cross-examination, also called continued cross-examination, is a kind of administrative compulsory measure stipulated by our country's law. In order to solve the problem of insufficient interrogation time after compelled appearance in court, such measure has been widely used in investigation for a long time, which enables the investigator to interrogate after investigation. The problem that the time of interrogation after compelled appearance in court is not enough is alleviated to a certain extent. However, since the adoption by the Ministry of Public Security in 2004 of the *Provisions on Continued Cross-Examination by Public Security Bureau*, such measure is less commonly adopted. On the one hand, the provisions of the punishment for abuse of such measure make the public security organs and the police think twice before using it; on the other hand, the approval procedures of such measure are extremely stringent, which make the police try to adopt is as less as possible. In this way, the problem of lack of time for interrogation after compelled appearance in court becomes more acute.

Third, the expert appraisal system is improved, which is mainly reflected in two aspects. First, the provision of "another expert verification for controversial medical appraisal of personal injury or medical appraisal of mental illness should be carried out by the hospitals designated by the provincial government" was removed from the Criminal Procedure Law, which allows more institutions to conduct such appraisal. This kind of institutions, of course, still need to be determined according to laws and regulations such as the *Decisions on the Administration of Judicial Expertise*. Second, the term of appraisal conclusion was replaced with expert opinion, making the legal evidence more consistent with the nature of the evidence.

4.6 Analysis on Converting the Evidence Collected by the Administrative Organs into Criminal Evidence

As a series of major reform documents were introduced, including the *Decisions of the Central Committee of the Communist Party of China on Major Issues concerning Comprehensively Deepening Reform* and the *Decisions of the Central Committee of the Communist Party of China on Major Issues concerning Comprehensively Advancing Governance by Law* adopted in November 2013 and October 2014 respectively, improving the cohesive mechanism between administrative law enforcement and criminal justice has been essential to judicial reform.

In fact, the key issue is how to use the evidence collected by the administrative organs in the criminal proceedings. Many changes have taken place, from the disputes with each side sticking to his own argument at the beginning to the unwritten rule of "evidence transformation", then to the requirements of transferring of evidence stipulated under the revised 2012 Criminal Procedure Law. Although this law resolves, to some extent, the problems on the connection of administrative law enforcement activities and the criminal justice activities, there are still many issues about use of evidence due to the inexplicit provisions of the existing laws and regulations and differences in the nature between these two activities. In view of this, it is necessary to theoretically conduct in-depth research on this issue.

4.6.1 Before and After the Revision of Criminal Procedure Law: From the Unwritten Rule of "Evidence Transformation" to the Statutory Provision of "Use of Evidence After Examination"

4.6.1.1 Before the Revision: The Emergence and Development of the Unwritten Rule of Evidence Transformation

The "evidence transformation" refers to the activity where the investigating organ adopts some means to convert some materials into legal evidence, because such materials do not satisfy legal conditions due to some factors such as the means of obtaining evidence, the actors of obtaining evidence, and the type of evidence. That's how the unwritten "rule of evidence transformation" emerged.[99] Before the Criminal Procedure Law was revised, there was little shortage of legal documents regulating the transfer of case files to the judicial organs by the administrative organs, such as, the *Provisions on the Transfer of Suspected Criminal Cases by Administrative Law Enforcement Agencies*, the *Provisions of the People's Procuratorates to Handle the Criminal Cases Transferred by the Administrative Law Enforcement Agencies* and the *Opinions on the Prompt Transfer of Criminal Cases by the Administrative Law Enforcement Agencies* adopted in 2001, 2001 and 2006, respectively, in order to make these two organ to cooperate in the fight against crime. These documents have a beneficial role in guiding the executive branch to effectively collect and confirm evidence and transfer it to judiciary. However, it should be noted that they mainly focus on instructing the administrative organs to collect evidence in the law enforcement according to statutory procedures and make it transferred to the judiciary. It is barely mentioned about how to convert the evidence transferred by the administrative organs into criminal evidence to be used as legal basis for conviction and sentencing. And this creates the opportunity to make the "rule of evidence transformation" in the judicial practice. Coupled with the failure of the previous Criminal Procedure Law to specify this issue, it has led to loophole in the legislation. However, the judiciary has to respond to it for the purpose of prosecuting crimes and safeguarding human rights.

Given the fact that the evidence is one of the core elements in the entire process of criminal prosecution, all matters and persons concerned must be proved by evidence, whether they are guilty or innocent, legal or illegal. In addition, the detection of criminal cases depends on the progress of socioeconomic development, especially the judiciary should realize from the frequent occurrence of economic crimes that cooperating with the executing organ in investigation is important. "Many criminal cases are investigated in accordance with the law by the administrative organs when they conduct law enforcement and investigation before being transferred to the criminal investigating organs. There are different perceptions about how to use the materials collected by the administrative organs during the investigation of a case in criminal

[99] Yi [80].

proceedings. If these materials can not be used as evidence in criminal proceedings, the judicial organs will find it extremely difficult in ascertaining the facts of the case and this will have deleterious effect on the fight against crime and the protection of human rights."[100] Therefore, the problem that whether the materials collected by administrative organs in the process of law enforcement can be used in criminal proceedings needs to be resolved as soon as possible.

In our country, the judicial organs have to deal with the matters concerning law enforcement of administrative organs while conducting criminal prosecution, because both "quality" and "quantity" elements are required to ascertain the fact of criminal offence, according to our criminal law. Many illegal acts do not satisfy the conditions of investigating the criminal liability, but they violate the administrative law. In the law enforcement, the administrative organs will transfer the cases that meet the conditions for investigating criminal responsibility, which becomes one of the main sources of cases for the judicial organs. In the case of administrative law enforcement and investigation, the evidence obtained by lawful means can be used as administrative admissible evidence to prove the behaviour of administrative organs. However, once one official of administrative organs breaks the administrative law and criminal law, there are two kinds of responsibilities he should take for his behavior. Then the criminal investigating bodies will collect and confirm the relevant materials when handling such criminal case. It is noted that this is a hypothetical scenario, but it is the laws and regulations of evidence that will determine whether these two kinds of responsibilities for a crime can be exchangeable.

However, this circumstance was not clearly defined by the original legal provisions, so the unwritten rule of transformation of evidence was made in judicial practice. It includes three kinds of practices. The first is the most simple and most direct way in which the evidence can be used directly, but the it is the judicial organs not the administrative organs that collect and confirm such materials. The second involves the change in the form of evidence. The statement of the administrative counterpart is transformed into the testimony of the witness, and the physical evidence is converted into the other forms of evidence, such as oral evidence, the record of investigation and examination. Sometimes in some cases where nothing is changed but the materials are just reorganized. The third is to act as an intermediary in the search for more probable evidence based on which further investigation is conducted to gather evidence that can be used in accordance with Criminal Procedure Law through the access to evidence, asking insiders and other means.

However, more attention need to be given to the harmful effect resulting from such practices. First, the legality of these practices is questioned. In the criminal proceedings, the requirements of investigating criminal liability are more stringent than those for investigating administrative liability and civil liability, and the system to allocate responsibility has to be found out. That makes how to make evidence admissible as required by the Criminal Procedure Law becomes the key to transforming the evidence of administrative liability into criminal liability. The judicial organs used what they think the most proper methods to admit the administrative law

[100] Lang [65].

enforcement evidence materials as the basis for investigation, prosecution, trial and verdict, which makes it hard for people to think that their behaviors in such practice are totally lawful. Second, in different regions or time, the standards and procedures that different organs use to transform evidence vary, leading to differences in the re-collected evidence. This contributes to different punishments for the same crime, undermining the justice of the judiciary. Third, the reason for developing legal, sound cohesive mechanism is that administrative law enforcement is mainly carried out by different administrative departments which are likely to keep the criminal acts that are beyond the purview of administrative law enforcement from being transferred to the judicial organs in the interest of their own departments (e.g. economic interests, political interests and doing someone a favor by pulling some strings). Such practice that administrative organs handle these cases on their own for their own benefit, to some extent, contributes to an increase in economic crimes, affecting the order of the socialist market economy.[101] The phenomenon of "investigating administrative liability instead of criminal liability" still persists, so it is in dire need of improve the cohesive mechanism between the administrative law enforcement and judicial behavior.

4.6.1.2 After the Revision: The Clearly-Defined Institutional Framework of "use After Investigation"

Nature of administrative crime, the imputation principle of administrative responsibility and criminal responsibility and the basic principle and value of the allocation of state power should be factored into converting administrative evidence into criminal evidence, and this practice should also be based on law and practical.[102] Therefore, how to properly deal with the evidence transformation and making administrative law enforcement and judicial behavior managed by rule of law has become the key to the revision of Criminal Procedure Law in 2012. Regarding the amendment to the Criminal Procedure Law, relevant departments held a special discussion on how to make documentary and physical evidence, obtained by the administrative organs during law enforcement and investigation of cases, admissible as required by Criminal Procedure Law. Article 15 of the *Amendment to Criminal Procedure Law (Draft for Comment)* issued by the Legislative Affairs Committee of the National People's Congress provides that "replace Article 45 with Article 51, and add a paragraph as the second paragraph: evidence such as physical evidence and documentary evidence collected by the administrative organ during the law enforcement can be used as evidence after judiciary verification."[103] Then the National People's Congress made amendments to the draft, which are mainly represented in the Article 52(2) of the

[101] Minyuan and Guo [56].

[102] Tian [72].

[103] *Amendment to Criminal Procedure Law(Draft for Comment),* https://news.qq.com/a/20110831/001104_5.htm,2015-02-21.

renewed Criminal Procedure Law providing that "The physical evidence, documentary evidence, audio-visual materials, electronic data and other evidence gathered by administrative organs during administrative law enforcement and case investigation and handling may be used as evidence in criminal cases", and Article 52(1) "The People's Courts, the People's Procuratorates and the public security organs shall have the authority to collect or obtain evidence from the units and individuals concerned. The units and individuals concerned shall provide truthful evidence". In addition, the provision that "Evidence involving State secretes, trade secretes or personal privacy shall be kept confidential" in Article 52(3) can be construed to safeguard organs concerned at the higher and lower levels respectively in Article 52(2). On the one hand, it can be seen from the law that providing truthful evidence and convenience to authorities is the legal obligation of every citizen and unit; otherwise, they may be held liable for administrative liability or criminal liability for violation of the law; on the other hand, not all evidence obtained by the executing organs is admissible as criminal evidence, which needs to prove the criminal entity responsibility or the criminal procedure responsibility.

4.6.2 Multi-Dimensional Discussion of Converting Evidence

4.6.2.1 On Theoretical Level: Discussion of Application of Rules Based on Legal Provisions

In 2012, the Article 52 of the Criminal Procedure Law was amended to address the long-standing unwritten practice of "evidence transformation", and clarify that evidence gathered by administrative organs may be used as evidence in criminal cases. In order to develop a better understanding of these amendments, it is necessary to be aware of the changes that matter both in theory and practice based on the nature of law, in addition to trying to keep the "evidence involving State secretes, trade secretes or personal privacy" confidential.

Different Types of Evidence Are Deal with According to Specific Circumstances When It Comes to Use

It can be seen from the Article 52 of the revised Criminal Procedure Law that the legislature adheres to the principle of "handling matters depending on specific circumstance" when proceeding with this Article, due to the differences in reacquisition and variability of different types of evidence. These are reflected in the following aspects.

First, not all kinds of evidence can be used. According to the provisions, only physical evidence, documentary evidence, audio-visual materials, electronic data, and other evidence can be used.

Second, it is difficult to clearly define how to use verbal evidence collected by the administrative organ. Verbal evidence includes confession, testimony and victim's statement. The procedure to collect the verbal evidence during law enforcement by the administrative organ is largely not strictly regulated. Compared with physical evidence, it is hard to use verbal evidence for verdict, so Article 52 does not provide for it.

Third, it should be noted that the records of investigation and examination and expert opinions can also be used under some circumstances. One the one hand, the record of investigation and examination is also a description, preservation and confirmation of facts, such as photographs and drawings at the scene; on the other hand, the expert opinions are in effect a kind of verbal evidence in nature. However, they may also be used as evidence in criminal cases after being "reinforced" by other evidence materials and examined by the court under the circumstances that verbal evidence can not be reproduced and replaced.

How to Comprehend the Meaning of "Other Evidence"

Article 52(2) of the 2012 Criminal Procedure Law makes it clear that tangible administrative evidence, which is objective and does not need to be re-collected, can be used as evidence in criminal cases, to improve the efficiency of the proceedings. However, it should be noted that, as stated above, the lawmakers only list four kinds of evidence including physical evidence, documentary evidence, audio-visual materials and electronic data instead of the others provided in Article 48. Although phrase of "other evidence" is given, it can not be construed as other kinds of evidence which are different in nature from the aforesaid four kinds. Therefore, only the tangible administrative evidence can be admissible as criminal evidence. So it is clear that verbal evidence, especially witness testimony, statements of victims and confession of criminal suspects can not be used either.

However, Article 64 of *Criminal Procedure Rules of the People's Procuratorates (for Trial Implementation)* describes how to empower themselves to deal with the confession of criminal suspects and testimony and statement of persons concerned in the criminal cases investigated on their own, which have broken the limits prescribed by legislation. It provides that if evidence of confession, testimony and statement can not be recollected because there is evidence to prove that the criminal suspects or the persons concerned have died, disappeared or lost their ability to testify or they have a long way to go to recollect them, such evidence can be used as evidence in criminal cases if the source of such evidence and the collection procedure are lawful and there is other evidence that can be used as corroborative evidence. This provision is an obvious ultra vires interpretation and should be invalidated. Moreover, in the judicial application, the newly published interpretation from the Supreme Judicial Court has no corresponding provisions. Even though the people's procuratorates believe that these verbal administrative evidence can be used as criminal evidence, there is no interpretation of the Supreme Judicial Court, and it is difficult to get through in the judicial proceedings.

Examination of Administrative Evidence for Its Being Admissible as Evidence in Criminal Cases

It is important to base the process of making administrative evidence admissible as evidence in criminal cases on exclusionary rule. The provision of Article 54 of the *Criminal Procedure Law* and other provisions provide that evidence that shall be excluded as found during investigation, examination before prosecution. Therefore, the investigating authorities also have the power to exclude illegal evidence in order to prevent it from being used as a basis for the opinions, decisions and judgments of the prosecution. In the later period of the examination before, particularly the trial period, judicial staff have the responsibility to examine. The initial purpose for administrative organ to collect evidence is to prove the legality of administrative behaviors such as administrative punishment. Although the documentary evidence, physical evidence, audio-visual data and electronic data can be used as evidence in criminal cases, such evidence should be reinforced or excluded in accordance with the provisions of the Criminal Procedure Law if the administrating organ collects these materials in an unlawful, improper way.

According to Article 65 of *Interpretation of the Supreme People's Court Concerning the Implementation of the Criminal Procedure Law of the People's Republic of China*, the evidence collected by administrative organs may be used as evidence in criminal proceedings or used as a basis for a verdict after being verified by the court, and if the collection procedures comply with legal and administrative regulatory requirements. Therefore, throughout the process of making the evidentiary materials transferred by the administrative organ admissible, it is necessary to verify such materials by the court. There may be applicable rules such as asking witness to appear in court at the trial. The court has the right to decide whether or not, when the defendant and his or her defender raise a doubt or file an application, to request the administrative organ that carries out the law enforcement to appear before the court to give an account of the law enforcement at that time and of the collected evidence. This is not only an important way to ensure the court to obtain accurate, truthful evidentiary materials, but also a basic means to protect the defendant's right to defense and other basic rights such as property rights.

Definition of Actors to Carry Out Administrative Law Enforcement

In the criminal proceedings, it is the law that defines who has the right to collect. During the administrative law enforcement, the actors to carry out administrative law enforcement character diversity and complexity according to the relevant administrative laws and regulations. It can be seen that a clear definition of such actors can ensure a smooth communication between the investigating organ and the administrative organ concerned. How to comprehend the actors that carry out "administrative law enforcement" and are responsible for "case investigation and handling" in the Article 52(2) of the revised Criminal Procedure Law is essential to solve this problem. In a nutshell, people who are able to carry out "administrative law enforcement" assume the responsibilities assigned by the laws and regulations governing administrative management, such as the departments of industry and commerce and quality inspection performing the obligation of market supervision, and the securities regulatory bodies fulfilling the duty of oversight over capital market. The phrase "case investigation and handling" refers to the investigation and handling of cases involving violations of administrative law and discipline according to law, such as department of industry and commerce investigating and handling cases of infringement of intellectual property rights, or the administrative supervision organs investigating and handling cases involving violation of administrative law.[104] In addition, it can be seen from Article 65(2) of the *Interpretation of the Supreme People's Court Concerning the Implementation of the Criminal Procedure Law of the People's Republic of China* and Article 64(4) of the *Criminal Procedure Rules of the People's Procuratorates (for Trial Implementation)* that, in addition to the administrative organs with law enforcement powers expressly provided for by law, the organizations that investigate and deal with cases of violating administrative law and discipline violations in accordance with the responsibilities assigned to them by laws and regulations belong to the administrative organs prescribed by the Criminal Procedure Law, that is, the organizations that exercise state administrative powers in accordance with laws and administrative regulations. Therefore, the evidentiary materials collected during the administrative law enforcement and investigation and handling of a case shall be deemed as the evidence collected by the administrative organ.

How to Comprehend the Phrase of "May Be Used as Evidence in Criminal Cases"

In order to save litigation resources and improve the efficiency of criminal proceedings, the Criminal Procedure Law clearly stipulates that certain types of evidence "may be used as evidence in criminal cases". This is in fact intended to avoid the circumstance that both the administrative law enforcement agencies and the criminal investigating agencies handle the same affairs. It is argued that this phrase can be interpreted differently because of diversity in the meaning of evidence, and it basically qualifies the administrative evidence as evidence used in criminal cases. However, I believe that it means qualifying the evidence collected by the administrative organ as evidence in criminal proceedings to prevent repetitive work done by the investigating organ. This consideration is based on some kinds of evidence whose characteristics will not be easily changed. Therefore, this phrase means that such evidence is admissible and no long gathered by the investigation organ. However, the investigating, procuratorial and judicial organs should examine such evidence before deciding whether it can be used as the basis for verdict in accordance with other provisions of this law. If it is examined as evidence that should be excluded or is not true, it can not be used for such purpose.② Therefore, the authorities concerned

---

[104]Lang [40].

need to review the evidence in the periods of criminal investigation, examination before prosecution and trial.

4.6.2.2 On the Practical Level: The Transfer and Use of Administrative Evidence

Some Issues on How to Safekeep Evidence

In addition to theoretical or legislative analysis of how to make the administrative evidence admissible as required by the Criminal Procedure Law, we should also need to discuss how to safekeep evidence during the process of transferring such evidence by the administrative organ to the judicial organ, especially how to keep it in the warehouse. Why safekeeping evidence is important in the process of evidence transferring because the parties that the administrative organ confronts with and the law enforcement climate are complicated. Sometimes a huge amount and volume of evidence is collected by the administrative organ during the law enforcement. In cases involving production and sale of counterfeit goods and selling fakes, for example, the transfer and safekeeping of evidence has always been a problem for administrative organ and judicial organ. A study conducted by me in the H district of G city shows the expenses on keeping evidence constitute a great share of the investigation outlay in the process of transferring evidence by the administrative organ to the judicial organ for criminal investigation. According to the head of the H district public security bureau, its unit usually spends about 400,000 yuan a year on keeping evidence. In W city, the public security organ, the people's procuratorate and the administrative organ will discuss who will pay for it, though they have not worked out the specific figures. It can be seen that this is a long-existing problem, and it always has an impact on the smooth transferring evidence or converting it into evidence used in criminal cases. There are three reason for it. First, as mentioned above, most of the crimes discovered in administrative law enforcement are economic crimes, and the evidentiary materials that need to be collected and confirmed are mainly commodities and raw materials. Second, the administrative organ, the public security organ, the people's procuratorate and the people's court rent their warehouses separately and no shared one is created. Third, there is no unified rules and regulations of management and procedure of transferring evidence, resulting in excessive costs incurred. So this is an important issue, especially where some evidence needs to be kept for a long period. Therefore, authorities concerned need to solve the problem of how to safekeep evidence and create a unified procedure in the process of administrative organ collecting evidence and transferring it to judicial organ.

During the survey, one judge suggested that the local method can be used to approach this problem. If the amount and volume of some evidence is large, such as fake medicine, the administrative law enforcement departments are allowed to destroy the drugs and take photos in accordance with the relevant provisions of the administrative law, and then only need to submit the materials such as photos and samples (including the verification of quantity) to the investigation organs. However, the judge also recognized that this is a written rule. According to the provisions of the Criminal Procedure Law on the transfer and safekeeping of evidence, the evidentiary materials used for conviction and sentencing must be transferred to the court during the trial, and cross-examined by the prosecution and the defense. If the administrative organs destroy the evidence before it being delivered, they are likely to be accused of destroying evidence. Although this practice is out of saving money and judicial resources, it should be thoroughly discussed.

Communication and Information Sharing Between Judiciary Organ and Administrative Organ

In addition to the problem discussed in the preceding paragraph, the relationship between the judiciary organ and administrative organ also matters. Due to the inherent differences between administrative law enforcement activities and judicial activities in terms of legal basis, rules and requirements of procedures and behaviors, the conflict between often arises. Especially in criminal judicial activities, stringent rules and requirements are made by law for the organs to carry out criminal prosecution. If these requirements are not met, they will be thought to break procedural rules and undermine the legal effects. This is an important factor in the criminal prosecution, which urges the investigating organs and the judiciary organ to attach great importance to the evidentiary materials to meet the statutory requirements of objectivity, relevance and legality. However, the administrative organ fails to raise enough awareness in the process of law enforcement and cases handling and investigating. Therefore, it is important for these two organs to understand and collaborate on each other's work.

The survey also shows that the judicial organ proactively communicates with the administrative organ concerned, including giving lecture and explaining to them about the norms of judicial activities, which helps them to take concerted action, reach consensus and reduce conflicts. For example, in City X, in order to enhance the effectiveness of judicial activities in food safety, drug safety and other areas, the procuratorial organs will regularly hold exchange and joint meetings with the departments, such as industry and commerce and quality inspection, to discuss how the administrative organ can properly collect and confirm evidence during law enforcement when it cooperate with judicial organ in the process of criminal prosecution. In city G, the public security organ exchanges opinions by discussing some typical cases, including experience gained and lessons learned, as well as strength that each administrative organ has in cooperation and matters to be considered. In the City W, the public security organ has established an information sharing mechanism with some administrative law enforcement agencies. In the event of a major case, it will instruct the coordinator of each administrative organs to collect, confirm and transfer evidence. But it can not participate in the handling of the case, and it plays a role in offering advice.

It should be noted that the above local methods or practices could help to have evidence collected and admitted in individual or partial cases, but they are not universally practical. This is because they are to some extend dependent on whether the local administrative organ is cooperative or not. In addition, these methods can not solve the ambiguity and uncertainty of provisions on the legislative level, and it is also doubted that if these local practices comply with the existing legal provisions. Therefore, there are still a number of issues that need to be resolved for the judicial organ and the administrative organ to communicate with and help each other.

Practical Approaches of Improving the Cohesive Mechanism of Converting Administrative Evidence into Evidence Used in Criminal Cases

1 Path of smooth evidence transferring

As judicial reform was vigorously launched, deepening the reform of the administrative law enforcement system and enforcing law in a strict, procedure-based, impartial and non-abusive way is the major aim of further promoting administration according to law and accelerating the building of a government under the rule of law. At the same time, it is not only necessary to emphasize that the investigating and judicial organs should maximize their functions, but also build a partnership between administrative organ and judicial organ in information sharing, notification of cases and transfer of cases at the judicial stage. They are all the multiple goals of the new round of judicial reform. Therefore, on the basis of the existing Criminal Procedure Law and the judicial interpretation, rules and the administrative regulation documents, we should legislatively renew the legal norm and totally understand the legal provisions and make the law more applicable to facilitate the transfer of cases and evidence. Aside from this, we are also supposed to take the opportunity of the new round of deepening the judicial reform to clearly define the how to cooperate and divide the scope of jurisdiction between the administrative law enforcement and judicial act. Moreover, it is pivotal to develop the reward and punishment mechanism and the accountability system to ensure both of these activities governed by rule of law.

2 Improving the standards and procedures for the transfer of cases

The differences between the administrative law enforcement organs and the criminal investigating organs in the collection of evidence in specific cases have become the main obstacles to the cooperation. It is a necessity to gradually explore and form a scientific and reasonable case transfer system for administrative organ and judicial organ on the practical level after discovering the existing problems, and such practice will provide basis to formulate legal norms on the legislative level. To be more specific, on the one hand, the communication and cooperation between the administrative law enforcement organ and the judicial organ underpins the establishment of the scientific transfer system. According to the practices aforesaid, the methods of joint meeting system, the case notification system and the intervention in advance are adopted in many regions, but they are not institutionalized. Therefore, it is important to use these methods in an institutionalized, procedure-based way during the reform. On the other hand, because of the differences in the scope of law enforcement, the types of cases involved and the procedures for handling them also vary greatly, so it is essential to coordinate the rules and regulations concerning evidence admitted, take into account both the needs of administrative law enforcement and judicial act, especially the circumstance where the cases are transferred to judicial proceedings. Therefore, at the stages of the collection, confirmation and transfer of evidentiary materials, it is pivotal to take ensuring the smooth running of criminal judicial activities as compass, and relevant standards and norms should be developed based on the needs of judicial act, which makes it necessary for the judicial organ to provide guidance to the administrative organ on some consideration of law enforcement and special requirements. However, it is inappropriate to request the administrative authorities to ascertain all the facts before transferring evidence. So there is a need to specify the criteria and conditions for transfer and to clarify the functional differences between these two organs. Furthermore, it is significant to avoid repetitive work and waste resources, and make the cohesive mechanism more transparent and practical.

3 Building a platform for information sharing

The information-sharing platform between administrative law enforcementorgan and judicial organ plays an important role in improving the efficiency of administrative law enforcement and cracking down on illegal and criminal acts. For example, Shanghai in 2005 took the lead in using modern technology, through the government affairs information network, to share information on administrative law enforcement cases, which makes the cooperation between the two organs more convenient, procedure-based, transparent and efficient, and forms a combination blow to crack down on and deal with crimes that undermine the market economic order. The popularization and application of the information sharing platbbform also provides a safeguard for strengthening the supervision of the procuratorial organs in filing a case, and preventing and correcting the practice of “substituting punishment with refine”.[105] From then on, more and more information platforms are created, which helps the coordination between the two organs.

To build a reasonable information sharing mechanism, there are three aspects that need to be considered. First, the administrative organ and judicial organ should reach an ideological consensus, that is recognizing the importance of information sharing mechanism in improving law enforcement, maximizing judicial resources and making law enforcement more authoritative. Second, it is also necessary to put forward practical ideas, have insufficient funds and personnel for operation, clearly define the scope of responsibility and specific working procedures, and seek coordination from watchdog agencies. Third, this kind of information platforms should be further expanded and connected nationwide, on the basis of the results

[105]Information Sharing Platform of Administrative Law Enforcement and Judicial Act Popularized by Shanghai, https://www.jcrb.com/n1/jcrb842/ca415770.htm,2015-03-24.

already achieved at the local level and the actual needs of law enforcement and judicial act, to establish an effective and prompt information exchange model. Therefore, it can be seen that building information sharing platform is of great significance, and it is a systematic engineering, which needs to be perfected with explicit and practical implementation rules and programs.

4. Maximize the role of the people's procuratorate in evidence admitted

The requirements of administrative law enforcement are different from those of criminal proceedings, so it is necessary to define the functions of procuratorial organs in evidence admitted, to prevent improper evidentiary materials from marring the running of proceedings. Therefore, the verification and supervision carry out by the procuratorial organ are exceptionally important in this process.

According to Article 64 of *Interpretation of the Supreme People's Court Concerning the Implementation of the Criminal Procedure Law of the People's Republic of China*, the people's procuratorate plays the role of the statutory review organ in the stage of transferring the evidentiary materials. It mainly review (1) physical evidence, documentary evidence, audio-visual materials and electronic data evidence collected by the administrative organ during the administrative law enforcement and investigation and handling of cases, and transferred in the name of this organ; and (2) expert opinions, records of crime scene investigation and examination collected by the administrative organ during the administrative law enforcement and investigation and handling of cases. At the same time, in order to protect the legitimate rights and interests of the administrative organ in transferring the corresponding cases, the people's procuratorial organ should also perform the role of legal supervisors. In accordance with Article 553 of the document, if an administrative law enforcement agency considers that a case should be filed for investigation by a public security organ but the latter has not done so, and such law enforcement agency has brought the matter to a people's procuratorate, the people's procuratorate should accept and review it. Where a people's procuratorate receives a complaint, reports or finds that an administrative law enforcement organ does not transfer a case involving a crime, the people's procuratorate shall issue procuratorial opinions to require the latter to transfer suspected criminal cases to the public security organ or the people's procuratorate within its jurisdiction.

Although Article 64 of this document aforesaid provides that only the evidence that is examined by the people's procuratorate to ensure it meets the statutory requirements can be admissible, it does not expound any practical procedures. This will confuse organs concerned, leading to ineffectiveness of such examination by procuratorial organ. So it is important to solve this inexplicit legal provisions. How to solve the problems brought about by these vague legislative provisions? The procuratorial organ should not only review evidence, but also perform the function of being a legal supervisor in the process of evidence admissible. Therefore, it is necessary to develop clearly-defined, practical work norms and codes of conduct to maximize the function of oversight according to law, in order to detect irregularities in the law enforcement and correct illegal or inappropriate actions.

4.7 The Function of Detention House from the Standpoint of Rule of Law

As a national criminal detention institution, detention house is essential to the criminal proceedings. Especially after the Criminal Procedure Law was revised in 2012 and many legal measures were added, the system of detention house as an important national power control mechanism to eliminate torture has been strengthened, making more burden laid on the detention house to protect human rights and this agency more important. This was followed by a new round of judicial reform, launched in 2013, which placed greater emphasis on the importance of rule of law in the social governance, and priorities such as the enactment of legislation on detention facilities were put on the agenda. At this critical point, I think that, against the background of judicial reform, it is necessary to, based on the primary concepts, identify some issues closely related to the legislation of detention house, especially how to define the functions of detention house. It is also pivotal to make new regulations compatible with the relevant provisions of the Criminal Procedure Law, and vigorously improve the detention house system during the judicial reform. This is a necessity for "respecting and protecting human rights" prescribed under the Criminal Procedure Law.

1. From edge to core: the function of detention house in the implementation of the revised Criminal Procedure Law

In China, detention house is an state criminal detention organ. It mainly detains three kind of persons: criminal suspects and defendants detained or arrested according to law, and criminals sentenced to death before execution, criminals sentenced to criminal detention or ones sentenced to fixed-term imprisonment but whose remaining term of imprisonment is less than three months before execution. It can be seen, from the proportion of different types of persons held in custody in detention house, that detention house in out country as the main place of detention before execution, plays a very important role in the criminal proceedings. It has three functions in this process: the primary function of ensuring the smooth running of criminal proceedings, the additional function of defending the society and the core function of protecting human rights. In fact, it is these functions that make detention house crucial in the proceedings. Especially the function of eliminating torture elevates its importance in human rights protection. This is why our country pays more and more attention to the detention house on theoretical and practical levels.

Therefore, to identify what role the detention house plays in the implementation and application of Criminal Procedure Law, it is important to develop a better understanding of the legal functions of this special functional institution. Moreover, a detailed knowledge of its multiple functions also lays a theoretical and perceptive foundation to determine of which organization it is under command during the new round of judicial reform

1.1 The Primary Function of a Detention House—Ensuring the Smooth Running of Criminal Proceedings

The purpose of the establishment by the state of a detention centre as a special institution is to ensure the smooth criminal proceedings, which enables the state, as the main actor of fighting crimes, to maximize its function of cracking down on crimes. As the renewed Criminal Procedure Law is implemented, it can be seen, from the detention house's responsibilities such as detaining dangerous criminal suspects and defendants for a long period of time, its involvement runs throughout the proceedings, including cooperating with the investigation organs and the procuratorial organs in interrogating the criminal suspects and the defendants, and with the judicial organs in the execution of sentence. It maximizes its functions in all stages including investigation, public prosecution, trial and execution.

The importance of the detention house to ensure the smooth criminal proceeding is reflected in the following aspects. First, in the case involving major crimes where criminals are sentenced to more than imprisonment and it is improper to impose non-custodial compulsory measures, detaining the criminal suspect and the defendant in the detention house can help the investigating organ to collect and confirm the evidence, and then provide the legal basis for the procuratorial organ to examine case files before public prosecution. Second, it also includes the detention of criminal suspects and defendants in order to prevent them from committing suicide or escaping. Aside from the humanistic care to prevent criminal suspects and defendants from committing suicide or self-harm, the death of them can affect the investigation of the cases, so such responsibility is an important component to ensure the smooth criminal proceedings, and is essential to the exercise of punishment power, the fight against crime and the maintenance of social stability. Third, the detention house, as a state organ that keeps the criminal proceedings running smoothly, also needs to ensure defenders can effectively carry out their defence role in the proceedings and participate in it according to law, such as the litigation activities of meetings and correspondence which are all arranged in the detention house. So it requires the detention house to cooperate, arrange and provide necessary assistance. However, some people fail to recognize it because they don't put it all in perspective. Therefore, it is necessary to raise the awareness in the future judicial reform and the enactment of legislation on detention house. This role of detention house is, of course, closely linked with the core function of the detention house to respect and protect human rights.

1.2 The additional function of the detention house—defending the society

The additional function of the detention house is the defense function for the purpose of preventing the criminal suspects and defendants from committing crimes again, endangering national security, public safety or social order. So it is necessary to detain such kind of persons, and they are detained in the detention house, observe some rules and regulations there, and are, to some extent, isolated from society. In this way, the likelihood of committing crimes and destroying evidence can be reduced or even eliminated due to the release of such people into society.

We can acquire more knowledge of this from the provisions of the application of compulsory measures such as detention and arrest in the Criminal Procedure Law. For example, Article 79 provides that the circumstance where it will not effectively prevent the dangers to the society caused by the concerned criminal suspect or defendant if he or she is released on bail pending trial, the criminal suspect or defendant shall be arrested in accordance with the law. Then a number of circumstances that could create such dangers are enumerated, such as where the criminal suspect or defendant may commit a new crime; or there is a real risk that the criminal suspect or defendant may endanger state security, public security or public order; or the criminal suspect or defendant may destroy or falsify evidence, interfere with the witnesses who give testimony or collude with others to make confessions tally. With respect to application of the initial detention, Article 80 also indicates, by way of enumeration, the intent of the legislation to control risk, such as the circumstances where if there is likelihood of his destroying or falsifying evidence or tallying confessions; or if he does not tell his true name and address and his identity is unknown; or if he is strongly suspected of committing crimes from one place to another, repeatedly, or in a gang, all of which are to reaffirm the important role that detention houses play in defending society.

1.3 Core function of detention houses—respecting and protecting human rights

In accordance with the provisions concerning respecting and protecting human rights in the Constitution and the revised new Criminal Procedure Law, the fundamental and core function of detention house is to protect human rights. And this function can be mainly reflected in two aspects. On the one hand, it needs to make sure that the detainees are guaranteed with basic necessities; on the other hand, it plays an important role in preventing extorting confessions by torture, which is connected with the provisions of the Criminal Procedure Law, such as exclusionary rule. In addition, when perform this core function, the detention house also tries to safeguard the right of lawyer to meet with criminal suspects and the right of criminal suspects and defendants to access to legal aid, and these efforts are recognized by the empirical research.[106]

1.3.1 The role of detention house in providing basic necessities for detainees

The detention house is a place where detainees are guaranteed with some basic necessities, such as food and water, accommodation, entertainment, medical treatment and epidemic prevention. One of its primary tasks is to guard the detained suspects and defendants and to manage and educate them. However, there is lack of knowledge of its role in judicial act for a long time both on theoretical and practical levels. The detention house and the issue of making it governed by rule of law—long-term neglected subject—did not get the attention of all sectors of society and

[106] Chen and Cheng [15].

academia until 2006 when we began to study on the reform of detention and inspection system.[107] Especially the unusual deaths in some detention houses in 2009 put this issue in the spotlight. That year marked the most critical evolution in the detention system in our country. Under the advocacy of the decision-making authorities, the reform on making detention house running more procedure-based began to set foot on the journey and achieved some preliminary results.[108] The reform initiative that was piloted in some detention houses to make them open to the public helps improve the living conditions of detainees. This move enables the public to develop a better understanding of the detention house. Although these facilities are open on a regular basis and in a controlled way, this activity gives the visitors a new perspective, because most of them were under the impression that the detention house was nothing but a high-wall and barbed wire place. In addition, they even made some suggestions on improving the living conditions of the detainees, which helps the local government departments to work on it by appropriation.

1.3.2 Great Effects of Detention House on Preventing Torture

It was commonly believed that it was less effective for the detention house to prevent torture, because most torture happens before criminal suspects being transferred to the detention house or after being taken out of it. However, people shift their opinion after the implementation of Criminal Procedure Law. Article 83(2) of this document provides that a detainee shall be immediately transferred to a detention house for detention within 24 h after being taken into custody, and Article 91(2) provides that an arrested person shall be immediately transferred to a detention house for custody, to ensure that the detention house is the only legitimate place of interrogation. This indicates that a burden has been placed on the detention house to prevent torture and safeguard the right to defence by this law. According to the provisions of this law, only the detention house can be the place where the interrogation is conducted after custody, so the detention house is of great significance in preventing illegal evidence collection and confirmation, and protecting legitimate rights and interests of detainees.[109]

In recent years, more attempts have been made to prohibit extorting confessions by torture and to prevent miscarriage of justice. In order to further improve China's laws and regulations against torture, especially how to protect human rights in a effective way in the criminal investigation period, it is necessary maximize the function of detention house in this regard. I believe that the detention house can be developed into a "safe harbor" after the extorting a confession by torture is largely prohibited after

[107]Pilot Reform of Inspection System of Detention House: Inspectors Checking to Eliminate Confessions by Torture. https://www.china.com.cn/aboutchina/txt/2009-02/02/content_17208310_3.htm,2015-03-25.

[108]The Reform Path to Break the Ice in Making the Law Enforcement of Public Security Organ More Procedure-Based, https://www.npc.gov.cn/npc/zgrdzz/2013-08/14/content_1802890.htm,2014-3-28;

NanFang Daily:Solidify the Reform Outcomes by Legislation, https://opinion.people.com.cn/n/2014/0515/c1003-25020641.html,2015-03-28.

[109]Gu [27].

strengthening and adopting the supervision mechanism over the detention house. This has been evidenced by the empirical research on detention house.[110]

2. Discussion of Which Organ Should Manage the Detention House in the New Round of Judicial Reform

There are many importantissues concerning the detention house that need to be discussed and solved. The most pronounced one is what kind of management system should be adopted in the detention house and which organ should manage it. In recent years, theorists and all sectors of society have been arguing that having detention house managed under the judicial organ instead of the public security organ is the only solution to it. Because they think the fact that both of detention house and investigating departments under the public security organ will be likely to result in "cooperation"between them in an inappropriate way, thus violating the basic rights of the detainees.[111] They actually advocate the separation of detention and investigation. If this matter is properly handled, it doesn't matter which of the two organs manage it. However, based on the current situation of criminal justice in China, this advocacy should not be built into legislation. In order to improve the detention system, it is necessary to select and adopt the most context-specific management system through some programs of pilot reform during the deepening judicial reform.

2.1 The separation of detention from investigation should not be built into legislation of detention house

Extorting a confession by torture, extended detention, bullying in prisons, and digging deeper into crimes are the four malpractices in the current detention house system. Do these problems result from the integration of investigation and detention—both investigating organ and detention house are under the public security organ? If the investigation and custody are separated, some problems including those listed-above can be solved? In effect, we can seek response from legislation of detention house and which organ directly manages it. The latter sparks concern on the drafting of the law. However, people engaging in theory and practice are divided on the system of position of detention house. Although the legislation is still in the process of drafting, there is great divide in the community as to whether the management system of detention house should be changed. Over the past decade, the idea of separating detention house from the public security organ and placing them under the judicial organ is increasingly popular. From the social context when it was put forward, it was a solution to solve the problems existing in the detention house at that time. Since the "hide-and-seek event", authorities concerned have been trying to solve these problems, such as preventing the "cooperation" in investigation and detention, improving the living condition of detainees, and strengthening the protection of the rights and interests of the detainees, after the management mechanism was significantly perfected. Changing the system has become a costly proposal and no one knows in which direction it goes.

---

[110]Chen and Cheng [15].

[111]Xie [74].

It can be seen from the practice and change in the detention house that inaccurate role positioning for this agency is the root cause of the above four malpractices. It is usually regarded as an appendage of investigating organ, and its function to serve this organ. Some people even think it is supposed to digging deeper into the crimes, which is also an manifestation of the detention house serving the investigation organ. However, the non-neutrality of detention house is the source of all kinds of malpractices.[112] Some people argue that the integration of investigation and custody is the root of all problems. I think that such integration just an symptom of the underlying problem, while the non-neutrality of the detention house is the culprit, which is not only caused by this kind of combination but also by its role positioning. Even if the custody and investigation are separated, the above problems can not be solved as long as the detention house is viewed as a vassal of the investigation organ and can not be as a neutral institution. On the contrary, even if such integration exists, as long as the role of the detention house is re-positioned as a neutral actor in the litigation and scientific and well-conceived system are adopted, problems such as four malpractices above-mentioned can all be solved. The significant progress, made in the protection of human rights in detention facilities over the years, is a testament to this. In addition, there are also some problems, such as bullying in prisons, which is attributed to the mismanagement not the system of detention house.

The practice of the reform of detention house in the past five years exposes that many problems in detention house result from mismanagement, which can be solved by the innovation of management mechanism without changing the system. The underlying causes of the lack of neutrality in detention facilities is what more people concern. However, it is noted that even we change the system, we are still not free of interference from the localism. In fact, bringing the detention house under the judicial administrative department can not address the core issues of local judicial practice. Therefore, from the current situation of criminal justice, the separation of custody and investigation should not be included in the legislation of detention house.

There are also some other reasons in addition to what are discussed above.

First, creating a neutral detention house is what the public, including the Ministry of Public Security, really want. In order to achieve neutrality, the proposal of being a neutral actor in the litigation made by the detention house system in recent years is a solution to the "integration of investigation and detention".[113] This concept emphasizes the function of detention house as a neutral actor in the criminal proceedings to ensure the equal protection of both the prosecution and defense, instead of only being cooperative with investigating organ and as a second battleground in the fight against crime. In fact, this is to a large extent a correction of its previous function of "digging deeper into the crimes". Therefore, to promote the reform to make the detention house neural, it is necessary to expand efforts to strengthen some existing mechanisms that restrict the illegal investigation, and make ridding the detention

[112] See Xie [74], for details on the function of digging deeper into the crimes for detention house.

[113] Re-Position the Detention House as a Neural Actor in the Criminal Proceedings in the First Law of Detention House Drafted by the Ministry of Public Security, https://www.cnprison.cn/bornwcms/Html/fl_shzx/2014-04/29/4028d117459b68a80145ad8f68dc17de.html,2015-03-27.

house of the function of "digging deeper into the crimes" as an indicators of its performance assessment.

Second, the role positioning of detention facilities should be specified in the ongoing drafting of detention house law in accordance with the Criminal Procedure Law revised in 2012. The detention house will also be the pre-trial detention institution to ensure the smooth progress of the criminal proceedings by supervising and detaining the criminal suspects and defendants according to law and protecting their legitimate rights and interests. Other than those, the detention facility has no other litigation function. It can be seen that the security and non-abusive law enforcement are the basic goals for the detention house to performs the legal duties. Therefore, each system and the rule should be designed based on the role positioning and basic goals of the detention house in the law drafting. Only doing so can we ensure that the legislation will go in the right direction

2.2 A feasible plan for the reform of which institution the detention house should under the command of

In terms of this issue, we should take into account both the situation in our country and the foreign practice. The findings of the comparative law study show that it is extremely rare for detention facilities to be part of the public security organ. In most countries, the detention house is administered by the ministry of justice or the ministry of law.[114] However, judicial administrative department is very different from those in western countries in many aspects, such as function, remit, personnel size. Therefore, whether it is effective to copy foreign practices is yet to be confirmed. Especially given to the fact that detention houses are set up on a county basis in our country, whether the grass-roots judicial organ can handle more onerous and complicated tasks than prison management is an important question that needs to be answered.

Based on the above reasons, there are two following reform proposals that I present for legislation.

First, if thedetention house is still under the management of public security organ, lawmakers should create a most stringent system of separation of investigation and detention, to ensure that detention house is neutral in investigation, prosecution and trial. Laws such as the Criminal Procedure Law also emphasizes its role as distinct from investigating organs, such as strengthening its role in safeguarding the litigation rights of detainees and the function of supervision and restriction over the handling of cases, especially the investigating act, by the investigating organ. In addition, reducing the burden on it to reform criminals will make this proposal more viable.[115] In this regard, the public security organs have carried out the work in supervision,[116] but they still need to expand efforts and improve effectiveness. Especially as to the

[114]Gao and Chen [24].

[115]Xie [74].

[116]Unscramble the Supervision of Public Security Organ with Rationality and Trust, https://www.legaldaily.com.cn/bm/content/2010-05/26/content_2155388.htm?node=20737,2015-03-27.

issues such as whether the separation of investigation and detention will impact the detection rate,[117] how to effectively solve them is the key to the reform proposal.

Second, a more thorough reform is to establish a relatively independent general administration of detention, so as to achieve relative independence in the establishment and system. The goal of reform plan is a bit more ambitious, but not unattainable. Although small changes will be made in personal size and management, it can bring out revolutionary institutional changes. The plan will increase the cost of reform, but it could improve working mechanisms and effectiveness in the judicial administrative departments.[118]

3. Functions and legislation of detention house

Therole positioning of detention house and of which organization it is under command are central to the legislation of detention house. The Criminal Procedure Law, since *Decision on the Revision of the Criminal Procedure Law of The People's Republic of China* was reviewed and adopted by 11th National People's Congress in 2012, was implemented for more than five years. The revision of the law is focused on punishing crimes and protecting human rights, and whether it is effectively implemented always makes the people in theoretical and practical sphere concerned. I hold the view that the effective implementation of the renewed Criminal Procedure Law requires not only new provisions to instruct the judicial staff to carry out their work, but also needs the corresponding laws and judicial systems. Those two should go hand in hand and must be given high priority by the legislature. When the Two Sessions was on the verge of adopting the revised Criminal Procedure Law at the beginning of 2012, I called on the legislature, the practical departments and all sectors of society to start working on the making, revision and abolition of the supporting laws after its adoption. At this point, the drafting of the law on detention houses has been put on the legislative agenda of the National People's Congress, and the State Council is leading the initiative.[119] Given the important role of the detention house plays in the entire process of criminal procedure, I believe that it is a wise move to formulate the detention house law in the judicial reform.

One of the goal of the establishment of the law on detention house is to clearly define its legal status: a pre-trial detention institution to ensure the smooth progress of criminal proceedings by detaining and overseeing the criminal suspects and defendants according to law and protecting their legitimate rights and interests. Other than that, it is not given any litigation power. I think formulating the detention house law is the most important matter at this point. In the light of the spirit of emphasizing judicial reform and respecting judicial laws at the third and fourth plenary sessions

[117]Fruitlessness to Promote the Reform of Separation of Investigation and Detention Which Affects the Detection Rate, 'bhttps://news.eastday.com/c/20101129/u1a5578667.html,2015-03-28.

[118]Chen Weidong, TaruSpronken. *Three Approaches to Combating Torture: Procedural Sanctions, Prevention in Places of Detention and Improvement of Police Interrogation Skills*, p. 160–161, Beijing: China Legal Publishing House.

[119]The State Council Leading the Initiative to Draft the Law on Detention House with Experts based on the Standard of the United Nations. https://news.sohu.com/20141125/n406373742.shtml,2015-01-03.

of the 18th Central Committee of the Communist Party of China, I argue that the best way to reform the central judicial system and working mechanism is to, instead of making amendments to the existing regulations on detention facilities, enact a law. The reasons are listed as follows.

3.1 The establishment of the law of detention house is essential for the perfection of the socialist legal system with Chinese characteristics

At the Two Sessions in 2011, Chairman Commissioner Wu Bangguo announced that a socialist legal system with Chinese characteristics had been established, but perfecting the supporting laws and regulations is a tremendous job. I think that the establishment of the law of detention house is an important step to improve the legal system. As we all know, the detention house is an important place to ensure the smooth progress of criminal proceedings, which is not only related to the protection of the fundamental rights of citizens, but also related to the implementation of several primary systems of the Criminal Procedure Law. The law of detention house is an important supporting law. The practice that we make an extra regulation to regulate how it is made is neither in line with the requirements of the legislative law, nor far from meeting the requirements of the socialist legal system with Chinese characteristics. The prison law, which is also a supporting law of the Criminal Procedure Law, was enacted two decades ago, and that the community correction law is now being formulated. To balance the legal system, it is inappropriate to adopt another regulation to regulate such a major legal matter.

3.2 The establishment of a law on detention houses is paramount to ensure the smooth implementation of the new Criminal Procedure Law

The revision of the new Criminal Procedure Law has involved some changes about the detention facilities, highlighting its role of detention facilities in ensuring the smooth running of proceedings. According to the revised Criminal Procedure Law, it is can be found that the detention house should arrange the meeting for lawyers, interrogation must be carried out in detention house, the detention period for major and complicated cases should be extended, and burden placed on it to execute the criminal punishments is reduced. These new provisions increase its responsibilities, which means this institution needs to to improve its management. Therefore, it is necessary to enact a law on detention house to implement the provisions of the Criminal Procedure Law. If its legal hierarchy remains unchanged, it is hard for it to participate in the litigation activities of procuratorate and court. Only amending the regulations of detention house can not many important litigation systems and norms be embedded. The procuratorial supervision of resident procurators, measurement of penalty, the duration of proceedings and the management of detention, for example, only can be regulated by law and not by administrative regulations of the State Council.

3.3 The establishment of the law of detention house is important to regulation of detention in the new era

The establishment of the law of detention house is the best way to solidify the achievements of the reform of regulation by the public security organ in recent years. According to my in-depth study on the recent reform of detention houses, significant progress has been made in regulation over detention houses after the "hide-and-seek event". Moreover, the introduction and implementation of a host of innovative reform measures have considerably strengthened the management of detention houses, enhanced the safeguarding of the rights and interests of the detainees, and explored many best practices, and many of these reforms are even trailblazing globally. The time is ripe for the enactment of the law on detention house. Only legislation can we solidify the best practices, further respect and protect human rights prescribed under the Constitution, acknowledge the fruits of detention house's endeavour in human rights protection and continue to push forward with it.

3.4 The establishment of the law of detention house is pivotal to manage the detention house in a scientific and procedure-based way

China's regulations on detention house have not been amended for 24 years since its implementation, and its legislative idea and words and expression are far from meeting the requirements of the current rule of law. Moreover, with the deepening of the reform of detention houses of the Ministry of Public Security, many deep-seated and institutional shortcomings have been exposed, which include the following aspects. First, the legal hierarchy of the regulations is relatively low, and they do not meet requirements of the Constitution and the legislative laws. They are also incoherent with the functions of the detention house and its important position in the protection of human rights. Second, the legal ideas are outdated in the document, which can be reflected by the presumption of guilt. Third, the role of the detention house is mis-positioned. It is taken as the institution providing service for the investigating organ, making it less neutral. Fourth, there is lack of the regulatory mechanism over the detention house, making the protection of the personal rights, living conditions and litigation rights of the detainees less guaranteed. Issues such as these need to be addressed through legislation, because many are difficult to be solved by the public security organ alone, such as the role positioning of detention house, budget and staffing and its participation in the litigation activity. To improve the management level of the detention house, only through legislation can we make substantial progress.

In a nutshell, the most important significance of changing the regulations of detention houses into a law is that it is consistent with spirit of the law-based governance. According to the provisions of the legislative law, the system of restricting personal freedom should adopt the principle of legal reservation—it can only be stipulated by law. It is obviously inconsistent with the spirit of the law-based governance to manage the detention house by the State Council using administrative regulations, which also deviates from the goal of strengthening the law-based governance in China. Therefore, this move is consistent with the spirit of the law-based governance, and elevates the legal hierarchy, makes the detention house free from the constraints of sectoral interests and makes provisions more scientific and rational. In addition, this initiative also helps to mobilize our country's resources to further strengthen the protection of detainees' litigation rights and improve their living condition. For example, more funds are needed to reform the detention house, which can not be provided by public security organ alone but requires cross-departmental collaboration.

4. Future Projection of Detention House

From a macro perspective, the achievements that have been gained from the implementation of the Criminal Procedure Law is only a good start, because many indirectly related provisions, such as the protection of civil rights, legal aid and even those that seem irrelevant to the enforcement of the law, for instance, audio and video recordings, evidence collection and confirmation, need more studies to be conducted to expand the functions of detention house in the implementation of the Criminal Procedure Law.

The introduction of the law of detention house is not only expected by the public, and is also the prerequisite for the detention house to fulfill its duties. This is the need to respect and protect human rights as required by the Constitution and the Criminal Procedure Law, and is also consistent with the goal of law-based governance in China as set out at the Third Plenary Session of the 18th Central Committee of the Communist Party of China.

There are some suggestions that I made to promote the reform of the detention house in the future. First, a custody and regulation system open to the public needs to be established, allowing them to visit the detention house at any time. This system can not only enhance the public regulation over the detention house, but also help the detention house and the law enforcement agencies to send a positive signal to the society and gain the trust of the public. Second, it is important to separate the detention house and the investigating department on the interest level, abolish evaluation indicator of the detention house for digging deeper into the crimes, and ensure it to carry out its role in a safe and non-abusive way, so as to make the lawsuit procedure process smoothly. When it is at the time of a more deepening social reform, the detention house can be separated from the public security organ, to make the detention house more neutral. Third, in the internal regulation over detention house, it is better to use scientific methods to prevent bullying in prison; in the external regulation, it is necessary to identify the regulatory powers of resident prosecutors, and develop an independent medical examination system and a mechanism for investigating complaints lodged by detainees.

References

1. Beccaria, C. (1993). *On Crime and Punishment* (p. 44). Beijing: Encyclopedia of China Publishing House.
2. Beccaria, C. (1993). *On crime and punishment* (p. 188). Beijing: Encyclopedia of China Publishing House.
3. Beccaria, C. (2003). *On crimes and punishments* (F. Huang, Trans.) (p. 45). Beijing: China Fangzheng Press.

4. Becker, H. K., & Becker, D. L. (1991). *World police & paramilitary forces* (Z. Liu, Trans.) (p. 5). Taiyuan: Shanxi People's Publishing House.
5. Bodenheimer, E. (1992). *Jurisprudence: The Philosophy and Method of the Law* (p. 321). Shanghai: Shanghai People's Publishing House.
6. Boruchov, H. N. (1985). *The scientific basis of interrogation in Pretrial* (p. 1). Beijing: Mass Publishing House.
7. Chen, W., et al. (1983). *The functions of procuratorial supervision* (p. 122). Beijing: Mass Publishing House.
8. Chen, R. H. (2000). *Frontier issues in criminal procedure* (p. 290). Beijing: China Renmin University Press.
9. Chen, W. (2002). Reconstruction and reflection of procuratorial power in China. *Legal Studies* (2).
10. Chen, W. (2008a). *Study on Criminal Procedure Law* (p. 219). Beijing: China Renmin University Press.
11. Chen, W. (2008b). *Study on Criminal Procedure Law* (p. 362). Beijing: China Renmin University Press.
12. Chen, W. ed. (2008). *A comparative study of Chinese and European efforts to prevent torture* (p. 6). Beijing: Peking University Press.
13. Chen, Y. (2009). On the safeguard mechanism of videotaping and recording system in the interrogation. *Contemporary Law Review* (4).
14. Chen, W., & Cheng, L. (2004). Outline of the legality of criminal procedure. *Legal Science* (1).
15. Chen, W., & Cheng, L. (2014). An empirical study on the implementation of the criminal procedure in detention house. *Journal of Political Science and Law* (4).
16. Chen, W., & Li, F. (2000). *Studies on Judicial Control of investigation power,* no. 6. Political Law Forum.
17. Chen, W., & Li, F. (2000). *Studies on Judicial Control of investigation power,* no. 6, Tribune of Political Science and Law.
18. Chen, W., & Li, F. (2000). Study on the integrated model of investigation and inspection. *Tribune of Political Science and Law* (6).
19. Chen, W., & Shi, XZ. (2003). The principles of the design and control of the police power. *Journal of Shandong Public Security College* (5).
20. Chen, X., & Wang, F. (2011, March 2). Voices of deputies: difficulties in meeting with lawyers still exist. *Guangzhou Daily.*
21. Chen, W., & Yinzhong, H. (1999). Study on the integrated model of investigation and inspection. *Legal Studies* (1).
22. Chen, W. Yinzhong, H. (1999). Study on the integrated model of investigation and inspection. *Chinese Journal of Law* (1).
23. Chonggao, W. (1992). *Introduction to administrative law* (pp. 9–11). Beijing: China University of Political Science and Law Press.
24. Gao, Y., & Chen, L. (2012). China's reform to make detention house neutral. *Criminal Science* (9).
25. Gibbon, J. (2007). *Forensic linguistics: an introduction to language in the justice system* (W. Ding, Y. Li et al., Trans.) (p. 45). Beijing: Law Press.
26. Gong, X. (1980). *Judicial systems in western countries* (p.155). Beijing: Peking University Press.
27. Gu, Y. (2013). Re-positioning of the functions of detention house—analysis based on the revised criminal procedure law. *Contemporary Law Review* (4).
28. Guangzhong, C. (1998). Jiang, W. editor-in-chief: *On Procedural Law Series*, vol. 1 (p. 241). Beijing: Law Press.
29. Guangzhong, C. ed. (2000). *UN Criminal Justice Norms and China's Criminal Legal System* (p. 265). Beijing: China University of Politic Science and Law Press.
30. Guicai, P. (2009). On the legal regulation of the exercise of police power in China. *Contemporary Law Review* (4).

31. Guozhong, W. (1999). The conception of the exclusionary rule of illegal evidence in China. *People's Procuratorate* (10).
32. He, W. (1998). *The philosophy of the judicial system* (p. 22). Beijing: China University of Political Science and Law Press.
33. He, J. (2009). On the unity and standardization of legal language. *Journal of Renmin University of China* (1).
34. Herrmann, J. (1995). *German code of criminal procedure* (Li Changke, Trans.). Beijing: China University of Political Science and Law Press.
35. Huai, M. (1994). Influence on Judges. *Chinese Journal of Law* (3).
36. Huang, B. (2006). *On the structure of investigation* (p. 355). Beijing: Publishing House of People's Public Security University of China.
37. Huang, B. (2006). *On the structure of investigation* (p. 357). Beijing: Publishing House of People's Public Security University of China.
38. Jianlin, B. (2012, March 16). The significant development of the criminal justice system of socialism with Chinese characteristics. *Procuratorate Daily.*
39. Jianmiao, H. (1993). *Comparative studies on the administrative law of ten countries* (pp. 114–115). Beijing: China University of Political Science and Law Press.
40. Lang, S. (2012). *Revision and application of the criminal procedure law of the People's Republic of China* (p. 120). Beijing: Xinhua Publishing
41. Lei, C. (2008). Controversy and risk analysis in covert investigations. *Journal of Jiangsu Police Institute* (9).
42. Lei, C. (2011). A study of the macro issues of covert investigation legislation. *Tribune of Political Science and Law* (5).
43. Li, X. (1997). *On the structure of criminal procedure* (p. 55). China University of Political Science and Law Press.
44. Li, Y. (1999). *American Criminal Justice System for probable cause.* Beijing: China Law Press.
45. Li, N. (2012, March 21). Supreme procuratorate clears the way for the implementation of the new Criminal Procedure Law. *Legal Daily.*
46. Liu, J. (2012). Chinese model and reform of the system of arrest and censorship. *Chinese Journal of Law* (2).
47. Liu, J. (2014). The Chinese model and the reform of the investigation supervision system. *China Legal Science* (1).
48. Locke, J. (1964). *The second treatise of government* (p. 92). Beijing: Commercial Press.
49. Meijun, X. (2003). Study on videotaping and recording system in the interrogation. *Criminal Science* (6).
50. Merryman, J. H. (1984). *The civil law tradition* (p. 152). Beijing: Knowledge Publishing House.
51. Mingyang, W. (1989). *Administrative law of France* (pp. 196–198). Beijing: China University of Political Science and Law Press.
52. Mingyang, W. (1995). *U.S. Administrative law* (pp. 115–116). Beijing: China Legal Publishing House.
53. Minyuan, W. (1994). On the consequence of the violation of the criminal proceedings. *China Legal Science* (3).
54. Minyuan, W. (2007). Principles of providing for legal consequences of violation of criminal proceedings. *The Jurist* (4).
55. Minyuan, W. (2012, March 22). Notification of family members after detention is a basic requirement of the principle of safeguarding human rights. *Procuratorate Daily.*
56. Minyuan, W., & Guo, H. (2009). An empirical study on the connection between administrative law enforcement and criminal justice. *Journal of National Prosecutors College* (2).
57. Radbruch, G. (1997a). *Introduction to Jurisprudence* (p. 121). Beijing: Encyclopedia of China Publishing House.
58. Radbruch, G. (1997b). *Introduction to Jurisprudence* (p. 101). Beijing: Encyclopedia of China Publishing House.
59. Roxin, C. (2003). *German code of criminal procedure* (Wu Liqi Trans.) (p. 13). Beijing: China Law Press.

60. Ruihua, C. (1997). *Principles of criminal trial* (p. 27). Beijing: Peking University Press.
61. Ruihua, C. (1997). *Principles of criminal trial* (p. 235). Beijing: Peking University Press.
62. Ruihua, C. (1999). Comparative study of criminal investigation structure. *Tribune of Political Science and Law* (5).
63. Schwartz, B. (1967). *Administrative law*. Boston: Little Brown and Company.
64. Sheng, L. (2012). *Revision and application of the Criminal Procedure Law* (p. 7). Beijing: Xinhua Press.
65. Sheng, L. editor-in-chief. (2012). *Revision and application of the criminal procedure law of the People's Republic of China* (p. 119–120). Beijing:Xinhua Publishing House.
66. Songnian, Y. (1988) *A course in administrative law* (pp. 40–42). Beijing: China University of Political Science and Law Press.
67. Sun, Y. (1998). Review and prospect of investigation studies in 1997. *The Jurist* (1).
68. Sun, M. (2012). *New criminal procedure interpretation and practical guide to public security organ* (p. 324). Beijing: Publishing House of People's Public Security University of China.
69. Sun, Q., & Tong, J. (2011, November 1). Thoughts on several issues concerning the revision of the criminal procedure. *Procuratorate Daily*.
70. Taguchi, M. (2000). *Japanese code of criminal procedure* (D. Liu, & L. Zhang et al., Trans.) (p. 37). Beijing: Law Press.
71. Tannin, T. D. (1999). *Process of law* (p. 36). Beijing: Law Press.
72. Tian, H. (2014). The imputation procedure of administrative crime and its evidence transformation. *Journal of Peking University (Philosophy and Social Sciences)* (2).
73. Vedel, G. (1984). *Droit administrative*.
74. Xie, Y. (2010). The system of preventing personal danger to detainees. *Law Science Magazine* (7).
75. Xingliang, C. (2002). Limitation and decentralization: police power in the perspective of criminal rule of law. *Science of Law* (1).
76. Xingliang, C. (2002). Limitation and decentralization: police power in the perspective of criminal rule of law. *Legal Science* (1).
77. Xiong, Q. (2016). Theoretical Review and institutional improvement of leniency in pleading guilty. *The Science of Law* (10).
78. Xiuyun, B. (1998). On the protection of the rights of criminal defendants. *Jurist* (3).
79. Xu, Z. (2006). Reasonable design of criminal police power in the angle of rule of law. *Hebei Law Science* (6).
80. Yi, W. (2011). Critique of the rule of evidence transformation. *Political Science and Law* (1).
81. Yinmei, W. (2007). On the legal attribute of police power and reform of designation. *Political Science and Law* (2).
82. Yinzhong, H. (1999). Query on procuratorial power. *Journal of Renmin University of China* (3).
83. Yinzhong, H., & Zuoli, X. (2004). The Principle of proportionality from the perspective of constitutional government. *Studies in Law and Business* (6).
84. Zhang, J. (2012). The grant and restriction of special investigation powers: an analysis of the relevant provisions of the revised criminal procedure law. *ECUPL Journal* (5).
85. Zhu, X. (2004). On the application o technical investigation in the investigation of duty-related crimes. *Journal of National Prosecutors College* (1).
86. Zongzhi, L. (1991). On some "Side Effects" of the principle of coordination and restriction and prevention. *Peking University Law Journal* (3).

Chapter 5
What Theory of Right of Defense is and How to Perfect It

5.1 Theory of the Right to Defense

In criminal proceedings, there are three fundamental litigation functions, including trial, prosecution and defense which are performed by the court, the procuratorial organ and the defendant, respectively, and none of them is allowed to carry out more than one roles. The judicial organ, the prosecution organ and the defender are the actors in the criminal proceedings, and they fulfill their functions to process the procedure. To this end, they must be given certain rights. To be specific, in criminal proceedings, the courts have judicial power to hear and adjudicate cases; the procuratorial organ have the power to prosecute offences and charge them to the courts; and the defendant has the right to defence, and make rebuttal of the charges. The judicial power and power of prosecution are a kind of the state power in essence, featured by state compulsion. The right of defense, granted to the criminal suspect and the defendant, does not belong to the state power. Therefore, the right of defense, judicial power and power of prosecution fall into different categories, with different attributes and on different levels, so they can not be compared with one another. The judicial organ, the prosecution organ and the defender are the actors in the criminal proceedings and form a triangle structure to process the procedure, so the right of defense, judicial power and power of prosecution are correlated with each other. In this sense, it is important to study the basic theoretical issues of them in criminal proceedings. Based on the previous research results, the nature and attribute of the judicial power and power of prosecution are given adequate attention. As for the right of defense, the scholars in academic arena often focus on more specific issues, such as the time when the defendant can entrust the defender, what litigation rights the defender are entitled to, the obstacles encountered by the defendant and his defender in exercising the litigation rights, how to ensure the exercise of the right of defense. However, few scholars have discussed theoretical issues of the right of defense in terms of its essential attribute and characteristics. The foundation of fundamental theoretical research in turn affects the definition of right of defense and its protection by legislation and judicial practice.

W. Chen, *Reform and Development of Powers and Functions of China's Criminal Proceedings*, https://doi.org/10.1007/978-981-15-8431-2_5

In theory, the concept of the right of defense is usually used in a broad sense and a narrow sense. In a narrow sense, the right of defense refers to the right to exculpation, explanation, justification of the defendant to refute the charges by presenting his own materials and statement on the basis of facts and law to prove he is innocent, or his crime is minor, or his punishment can be mitigated or criminal responsibility can be exempted. In a broad sense, the right of defense includes not only the abovementioned rights, but also other rights, such as the right of petition and the right of appeal, and sometimes all the litigation rights the defendant is entitled to are called the right of defense. I believe that the concept of the right of defense should be used in a narrow sense, otherwise we can not fully understand the nature and characteristics of the right of defense. This book discusses the right of defense on its narrow sense level.

1. The right of defense is the natural right of human beings

The right of defense, a civil right established in the constitutions and criminal procedure laws in all countries, has received more and more attention. So to speak, a country's law on the right of defense reflects how much emphasis the government lays on the civil rights and its protection. However, the right of defense in essence does not exist as a legal right, but as a natural right of human beings. It is the a natural defense, refutation and even the right to resist when an individual faces investigation, criticism, oppression.

From thestandpoint of nature, man is the only creature that has the subject consciousness and thinking ability which others do not have, so they also have a distinctive dignity. The recognition of human right of defense is the recognition of human dignity. The Italian scholar Giovanni Pico Della Mirandola once said that man is his own master, and his only goal is to eliminate limits, be free, choose his own fate, and weave his own laurel or chains of shame with his own hands.[1] The Austrian jurist Messner distinguished the first natural law from the second, holding that the first natural law is absolute and an unalterable and unconditional natural law which must be obeyed, and its most universally acceptable principle is to respect the rights of everyone and to avoid injustice. In this principle, the integrity of the human life and body should be highly respected. These rights are the fundamental human rights, such as the right of freedom of conscience, the right of freedom of religion, right of life, right of personhood and right of marriage.[2] Maritain, a French scholar, holds that man is both acts as an individual and as a person. The former is derived from the material and the latter from the spirit. The basic characteristic of any civilization is to respect human dignity. Man is also an animal and an individual, but also different from those. He is an individual who holds himself in hand by his intelligence and his will, and has spiritual super-existence through knowledge and love. This means that in the human body there is a soul which is a spirit, the root of personality. Values, freedoms and rights of human are derived from the divine order of nature. The fundamental rights, stipulated in the natural law are enjoyed by human beings naturally, are equal to and superior to the rights stipulated in the written law

[1]Eugenio Garin [1] and Yang Zhengwan [2].

[2]Lu Shilun [3].

and the agreements between governments, are universally acknowledged valid rights which do not need to be granted by the secular society, and can not be revoked or belittled under any circumstances. Maridan argued that the rights of man to existence, freedom and the pursuit of improving livelihood are the rights prescribed by natural law. According to this law, some human rights are absolutely inalienable and some are basically inalienable. Natural human rights are based on human nature, which of course can not be lost by anyone, so it can not be alienable. But that doesn't mean they naturally reject any restrictions. All human beings share a common humanity and are a kind of creature with intelligence. A man in action knows what he is doing and can decide what he is after. In addition, a man has a nature which enables him to achieve the objectives which human nature requires. Such an order or arrangement, which human reason can discover, is established by the power of human nature. Human will must act upon in order to bring itself into harmony with the essential and necessary ends of mankind. Unwritten law or natural law is nothing more than this". In terms of ontology, natural law is the ideal procedure for the action of man, a watershed between proper and improper action and between just and unjust action. It depends on the nature or essence of man and the unchanging necessity that rooted in such nature or essence. The rule of natural law is based on the essence of man, and the primary purpose of human nature is to keep the existence of man as a survivor as well as the existence of the world related to him. A man is entitled to the right to existence.[3] The British scholar John Finnis proposed that right means a kind of claim, which results in a mutual logical relationship. The right itself may divide into the natural right and the legal right, with the latter based on the former.[4] Roch made it clear that equality, life, liberty, and property are the natural rights of the individual, and that those whose natural rights are violated have the right to retaliate, punish, and resist, and bring attention to his self-defence and resistance. In Jean-Jacques Rousseau's view, to safeguard human nature is to safeguard human qualification as a human being and to defend natural rights.[5]

So to speak, according to the philosophy of the natural law school, everyone is entitled to some unchangeable, inalienable and inviolable natural rights, such as the right to life, the right of personality, the right of property. Some Chinese scholars, when discussing the thoughts of Hugo Grotius, Baruch Spinoza, Roch, Voltaire, Jean-Jacques Rousseau and other natural law theorists since late Middle Ages, commented they resolutely declare the natural characters such as equality, freedom, autonomy, self-respect and self-defense which a man has as their rights. According to this, since such natural characters are nature, the right of nature is natural right and vice versa. Because such right derives from of nature, man is born with them. Since natural rights are regulated and controlled by the transcendent authority—natural law, natural rights exist beyond the actual law and are inalienable. Nature is owned by all, and represents the basic character of man, so the rights of nature are common to all.

[3]Lu Shilun [4].

[4]Lu Shilun [5].

[5]Xia Yong [6].

Therefore, natural rights or rights of nature are human rights.[6] In the early Western thoughts of human rights, the important view of natural freedom emphasizes dignity and autonomy. Chinese scholars have pointed out that it includes four interrelated characters which are reflected in man in nature: selfish, dignified, rational with ability of self-determination and choice, and able to resist all insults.[7] On this basis, everyone has the right, according to his own nature, to defend these fundamental rights. When these rights are violated, as a man who can make his own decisions, he has the right to defend himself instinctively through defense, rebuttal, and resistance. A man who can make his own decisions has the freedom of will, that is, he has the freedom of thinking, the freedom of choice and the freedom of decision. That is to say, an individual who can make his own decisions is the subject, not the object, acting on his own reason and willingness, not the instrument by which the other subject achieves some purpose. Immanuel Kant argued that no one has the right to use others only as an instrument to meet his own subjective ends, and human beings should be treated as an end in themselves.[8] Being one's own master is manifested not only in man's free will, but also in his freedom of speech. A man can be called a human being with dignity and be called a real human being only when he has the right to speak and the freedom of expression. Moreover, the freedom of expression is human's physiological and psychological instinct and natural reaction. To recognize the freedom of expression is to affirm and value human nature and human dignity. If man's inner freedom of will can not be expressed by words, then he can not be thought to have autonomy and subjectivity.

It is the desire of man that drive him to live and to be free. Desire is an essential component of human existence and an objective necessity. Normal people have biological and social attributes. They have biological basic material needs and sociological material and spiritual needs. The criminal procedure aims to solve the conflict between the state and the individual who suffers from being convicted, sentenced and put into prison by the state apparatus, so his natural reaction, in order to live and be free, is to defend his rights and interests and human dignity to the best of his ability by defending and refuting the accusation and prosecution to exculpating himself. As for the accused in criminal proceedings, his basic desire is to try not to be investigated, prosecuted, tried and found guilty, sentenced and so on. These are his instinctive desires and needs as a human being with normal mind and thinking. Moreover, due to the natural instinct of a normal person to live and to be free, the accused in criminal proceedings will not only instinctively justify and explain their actions, but also refute the charges and accusations, and try to figure out a way or tactic of defense and refutation. The difference between human needs and animal needs is that animal needs only respond selectively to the material, energy and information elements on which it depends, and human responds to those elements on which he depends. On the basis of this response, man will develop an action plan

[6]Xia Yong [7].

[7]Xia Yong [8].

[8]Edgar Bodenheimer [9].

and program to take steps to meet his needs.[9] The natural instinct of a normal-mind individual in the face of investigation, rebuke, accusation and oppression is to defend and refute the accusation and resist the oppression and so forth. The accused, as a normal individual with the ability of thinking and rationality as others, will pursue the maximization and optimization of his own interests based on his situation in criminal proceedings, to try not to be prosecuted, tried and detained by the state. In fact, to recognize the individual's natural right of defense in the face of prosecution and accusation is to recognize that the human is an end rather than a tool, that is, to recognize the human autonomy and subjectivity.

In criminal proceedings, the recognition and respect for human dignity and subjectivity are also reflected in the right given to the accused to participate in the proceedings as an actor and to express their views in the face of rebuke, accusations and even state criminal compulsory measures against him. According to the view of natural justice, to respect the dignity and subjectivity of an individual means to respect his right to participate in the process of dispute settlement, to decide whether to be a part of criminal procedures to influence the final decision. Such subjective rights are required by natural law and must be respected by the state and society, and they can not arbitrarily be deprived in the interests of the state or of society, unless there is probable cause and due process. In addition, procedural justice also requires that the two sides of the dispute should participate equally in the settlement of the dispute. As such, the criminal suspect and the defendant, as the accused, shall have the right to have dialogue and confrontation with the state organs as the prosecuting party on an equal footing, and shall have the right to defend and refute the charges against them, the right to receive information about the charges against him or her and to have a say in the proceedings. Therefore, when facing the rebuke and accusation, behavior such as defense, refutation and resistance is human's natural and instinctive reaction, and is his or her inalienable fundamental right. The right of defense of the criminal suspect and the defendant in the criminal proceedings is a kind of natural right, which is the moral right that the accused should be entitled to as a human and is indispensable and inalienable.

2. The right to defense is a legalized natural right

The right of defense first exists as a natural right of man. However, the natural right and the legal right are not the same, and the right is not only limited to the legal right. Some scholars in our country pointed out that the most basic meaning of right is that a person should or can get results of action or inaction taken by others or society. This is a kind of justice idea that can be supported by morality and custom. It indicates a kind of social life principle, which is not necessarily created or maintained by law. Where there is an order of social life, there is a link between rights and obligations. Right exists without law. The legal right is only one form in which right exists. Aside from it, there are the moral right and the customary right. Moral rights mean the existence of an idea, supported by moral principles in philosophy and religion. The customary right means the existence of a fact, supported by the established rules of

[9] Wang Weiguang and Guo Baoping [10].

life. Moral rights can be viewed as legal rights and customary rights can be elevated to legal rights, but they can exist independently of the law.[10] There are not only legal rights and obligations, but also moral and social rights and obligations. In the process of the formation of law, other kinds of rights and obligations are often recognized as legal ones and are supported and safeguarded by the state. Legal rights refer to the legal means which, permitted by the law and guaranteed by the legal obligations of others, the rights holders use to realize their own interests.[11] In human social stratification, law, as an important norm regulating social relations, has advantages and values that other norms do not have. Both moral rights or customary rights can not be safeguarded by the state unless they are recognized by national laws. As the German scholar Rudolf Stammler commented that rules of law, once established, are binding, whether citizens are willing to abide by them. Customs and practices merely have citizens to get used to obeying them, but they are not compulsory. The rule of law contains an inviolate element. This means that, as long as these rules are valid, they are strictly binding not only on those citizens who are subject to them, but also on those who have been entrusted with their formulation and promulgation. There has been a great deal of theoretical research on this issue, and there is no need to go into details.[12] On this basis, we can draw a conclusion that the natural rights and moral rights of defense, refutation and resistance, which a man should have to deal with accusations or charges, can not be recognized as legal rights until they are legalized. After that, they can be implemented in the criminal proceedings and safeguarded by the citizens, the judicial staff and the entire community.

The national legal system is grounded in the empirical knowledge of human society. There is no rules at the beginning based on which to decide what kind of right of defense should be given to citizens, including the way of exercising it and the system to safeguard it. It is developed and formed in the development of human society. From the standpoint of natural justice, the accused in criminal proceedings have the right to defend themselves. However, this natural right was suppressed when the defense system was not established back then. There were no mechanisms, procedures and means by which the accused could exercise this natural, moral right. Only after the right has been officially recognized by national law which clearly defines it, including the mechanisms and procedures for exercising it, this right has become a legitimate right of defense with coerciveness. So is the case of the right of defense, it was recognized first by the national law, and established, then expanded and strengthened. This is actually relation to the link between natural law and positive law.

Regarding the relationship between natural law and positive law, Messner pointed out that natural law represents the power to formulate positive law, which in turn, directly or indirectly, relies on natural law. It means the validity of positive law comes from the legal power represented by natural law.[13] Maritain believed that

---

[10]Xia Yong [11].

[11]Shen Zongling [12].

[12]Edgar Bodenheimer [13].

[13]Lu Shilun [14].

society composed of people with personalities. Human dignity precedes society. Law must exist as a rational order, and natural law is a divine rational order. Natural law is the philosophical or rational basis of human rights. It is the natural law that lays down our fundamental obligations and rights. Maritain also argued that it is not the rational knowledge, nor knowledge gained from conceptual judgments based on which human reason comes to know natural law, but based on the knowledge acquired from human nature and inclinations, which is an inexplicit but necessary knowledge from the common nature of man. As for positive law, it refers to a set of customary or statutory law that is valid in a given society, and it is inferior to natural law because it exists depending on natural law and is an extension natural law. Natural law is immutable and universal in the nature of things. Positive law is valid only in certain society, and it changes as society develops. In addition, natural law is based on human nature and inclinations, while positive law is grounded in rational judgment.[14] According to the Italian legal philosopher Giorgio Del Vecchio, the ideal of law is the idea of natural law. Natural law is the standard by which the positive law is evaluated and its justice is measured. Respect for the autonomy of human personality is the basis of justice. The justice should base the personality and personal autonomy. Everyone can ask his countrymen not to see him as just a tool or an object. Human evolution has contributed to an increasing recognition of human autonomy, and thus to the implementation of natural law and and ultimate triumph.[15] The German scholar Stammler pointed out that the concept of law is the delivery of justice. The ideal of society is to build a society of free will. Stammler summarized some necessary requirements of "just law" from his social ideal, and argued that to achieve this social ideal, the legislator must bear in mind four basic principles. First, a person's will should never be oppressed by the arbitrary power of any other person; second, every legal requirement must be presented based on the fact that the person to whom the obligation is owed may have his or her human dignity; third, the members of the legal community may not be arbitrarily excluded from the group; fourth, the power of control granted by law can be considered legitimate only under the circumstance where the person affected by the law may have his or her human dignity. The essence of what Stammler calls "the principles of respect and participation" is that each member of society should be seen as an end in itself, not as an object of the arbitrary will of others. No one should see others merely as a means to an end.[16]

Although some viewpoints of natural law scholars are notright, they are ideological limited. The idea that national laws should respect the natural rights of human beings should be valued. As the German jurist Gustav Radbruch argued, in order for a law to carry out it role, it must satisfy certain absolute requirements. The law recognizes individual freedom, and the state completely denies law of individual rights is absolutely wrong law.[17] The purpose of the state is to improve welfare of its own

[14]Lu Shilun [15].

[15]Edgar Bodenheimer [16].

[16]Edgar Bodenheimer [17].

[17]Edgar Bodenheimer [18].

citizens, make them live in happiness, respect their nature, ensure their well-ordered life and maintain social stability. The law is not only used to settle disputes and encourage justice to deter violence, but to act as a neutral to protect both sides and not allow either side to suffer losses and eliminate unfairness.[18] Therefore, in terms of the relationship between natural law and positive law, national law must respect and recognize the natural rights enjoyed by individuals, such as human dignity, right of defense. It can be found from the laws of all countries that much attention is given to human subjectivity, dignity and autonomy, which was reflected in some international conventions. According to the preamble to the Universal Declaration of Human Rights, adopted by the United Nations in 1948, "whereas recognition of the inherent dignity and of the equal and inalienable rights of all members of the human family is the foundation of freedom, justice and peace in the world". In addition, the preamble of International Covenant on Civil and Political Rights adopted in 1966 reaffirmed it—"considering that, in accordance with the principles proclaimed in the Charter of the United Nations, recognition of the inherent dignity and of the equal and inalienable rights of all members of the human family is the foundation of freedom, justice and peace in the world". Article 10 of this document provides that "all persons deprived of their liberty shall be treated with humanity and with respect for the inherent dignity of the human person". All these show that modern law recognizes and respects human dignity and other natural rights. The right of an individual to a defense against a complaint is also officially recognized in these international legal documents. Article 14 of this document provides that "in the determination of any criminal charge against him, everyone shall be entitled to the following minimum guarantees, in full equality: to have adequate time and facilities for the preparation of his defence and to communicate with counsel of his own choosing; ... To be tried in his presence, and to defend himself in person or through legal assistance of his own choosing".

In addition to theory of natural law that needs the national law to recognize the individual's right of defense, the nature of the criminal procedure also requires such right to be given to people. In the modern criminal procedure, the litigation functions are carried out by different organs or actors, and a triangle structure with parties of prosecution, defense and trial is formed. The recognition of the defendant as a participant in the criminal proceedings means that the defense function is indispensable. Otherwise, the triangular structure may not be created. It is people's deepening understanding of objective law of criminal proceedings that enables the criminal suspect and the defendant to be part of the proceedings. In criminal proceedings, the accused is the person who is suspected of committing a crime by evidence and should be investigated for criminal responsibility. From the perspective of social value orientation, the accused are often vulnerable to public reprimanding and are thought to be morally and legally punished. In addition, according to the mainstream value orientation in a society, the state combating crimes is legitimate. Therefore, the defendant who is charged of committing crime by the state and the organs of the state to fight crime are on an unequal footing. In terms of maintaining national

[18]Xia Yong [19].

security and social stability, combating, deterring and preventing crime is one of the goals of legislation to maintain social order and safeguard the rights and interests of the state, society and citizens, because the primary goal of ruling class's in establishing the state and maintaining its regime is to ensure the stability and security of the community. Therefore, under the censure of both morality and law, the rights and interests of the criminal suspect and the defendant who are suspected of committing crimes are likely to be, whether in national legislation or in judicial act, neglected, excluded and even violated. Moreover, prosecutorial and judicial organs that fight crimes are backed by their powerful state with forces and resources, so there is a considerable disparity in power between them and the criminal suspects and defendants. They are in fact disadvantaged people "oppressed" by the state power, under which they are considerably degraded. Therefore, their interests are vulnerable to be ignored, suppressed or even infringed by legislators, judicial officers and the public. In this structure of litigation power and rights, the lawmakers must see to it and try to regulate the state power by establishing criminal procedure institutions which can restraint the power of prosecution and trial to effectively prevent the expansion and abuse of the judicial power, so as to keep the defendants from becoming "mutton for punishment" in the criminal trial. Therefore, the right of defense should be given and established by law, which is adapted to the requirements of the idea of natural law and separation of litigation functions and the restriction on power.

3. The right to defense is in essence a right of active defense

In the preceding part, we have discussed that the right of defense refers to the right to exculpation, explanation, justification of the defendant to refute the charges by presenting his own materials and statement on the basis of facts and law to prove he is innocent, or his crime is minor, or his punishment can be mitigated or criminal responsibility can be exempted. This definition reflects its characteristics. It is a kind of defense right and also an active defense right which is exercised by active action.

On the one hand, the right of defense is a kind of defense right which is exercised in a clear response to the charge against the accused. In fact, the defense rights of criminal suspects and defendants in criminal proceedings are the rights that they have in order to offset and eliminate the effect of the prosecution's accusation when facing the criminal charges against them. In modern criminal proceedings, the accused are entitled to many defense procedural rights, including the right of defense which is undoubtedly the most important one. In terms of the essence of the criminal proceedings, it is a prosecution initiated by the state organs against an individual—the criminal suspect and the defendant, and is one of the manifestations of social conflicts. Some even compare it to a battle between the state and its citizens. The entire process of criminal proceedings goes like this. The investigating organ of the state first files a case against a person on the ground that he is suspected of committing a crime. After that, if the criminal suspect is considered to be criminally liable, the case is transferred to the procuratorial organ for review which initiates the prosecution against a person whose conduct constitutes a crime to the judicial organ that will convict and sentence him according to law and make him bear due legal responsibility. In such battle, the state is the initiator, and the procuratorial organ is the leader that launch this offensive. The criminal suspect and the defendant only passively participate in the criminal proceedings because of the investigation and prosecution of the state organs. As the accused in criminal proceedings, what the criminal suspects and defendants most want is to try to exculpate themselves and prove that they are innocent, their crime is minor, or punishment can be mitigated or criminal responsibility can be exempted. In this sense, the right of defense of the criminal suspect and the defendant has a clear and specific response and is passive. It can be said that it if the procuratorial organ does not initiative a prosecution, there is no defense or interpretation for accusation, let alone the right of defense and exercise of it. Although the defense act is passive, it is in response to the charge by the prosecution. The procuratorial organ play a dominant role in the criminal proceedings, so the defense act of the accused is defensive, not offensive. The right of defense, the natural right for human, is in essence a kind of instinctive defensive right of human beings. It is, in fact, an instinct of man, which has been discussed above. Due to the human nature to seek advantage and avoid disadvantage, a man, when his or her rights are violated and adversely affected, will use whatever means are available to him or her to resist such accusations, to prevent any infringement of rights or negative impact.

On the other hand, the right of defense can be exercised only by the active activity of the accused, so it is is a kind of active defense right. From theoretical definition, it can be found that the right of defense is in a clear response to the charge filed by the prosecution. The accused must take action to explain his conduct, weaken or refute the accusation. According to the provisions of our country's law, what the accused only can do to defend themselves is to exculpate and justify his conducts by providing evidence or materials and using legal means to prove that he is innocent, his crime is minor, or punishment can be mitigated or criminal responsibility can be exempted. It can be seen from this that when the accused is exercising his right to defence, he must take action to make it happen. In other words, when the criminal suspect and the defendant are defending and exculpating themselves, they have to articulate their opinions on the case to authorities concerned by providing some supporting evidential materials. Therefore, in this process they take action rather than inaction.

In contrast to this active behavior, the criminal suspect and the accused in criminal proceedings may also be passive about the accusation of the prosecution—keeping silent. The attitude that they take toward the charge by keeping silent and refusing to answer the questions of the prosecution is also a way of self-protection and defense against. In many countries nowadays, for the purpose of protecting human rights, respecting human dignity, restricting state power, the criminal suspects and defendants are entitled to the right to remain silent, which is called the right to silence. In my opinion, the right to silence is a kind of passive defense right, which is exercised by the inaction of the accused, while the right of defense, to the contrary, is exercised by the citizen taking action. They complement each other and are two crucial components of the defense rights of the criminal suspect and the defendant.

In the evolution process of the criminal procedure, the defense system has been created and developed, and under such system the accused in criminal proceedings can defend themselves and entrust others to defend themselves. This is because some criminal suspects and defendants find it difficult to protect their rights through their own active actions and give well-founded reasons to explain and justify their conducts, due to lack of legal knowledge, education level, capability, difficult situation and restricted personal freedom, and the fact that the right of defense can only be exercised by taking initiative. The establishment of the defense system provides many supporting measures, which vary greatly in different times and countries, for the exercise of the right of defense by criminal suspects and defendants. Nowadays, to make sure the active defense right can be exercised and safeguard the right of the accused, the minimum standard for an internationally recognized defence system includes: (1) the right of the accused to have prompt access to aid from a lawyer and meeting with a lawyer; and (2) the right to access to government legal aid; and (3) the right of defenders to consult, excerpt and reproduce the case file materials; and (4) the right of defenders to collect and investigate relevant evidence; and (5) the right of defenders to express opinions to prosecutorial organs and judicial organs; and (6) the right of defense attorney to be present during the interrogation of a criminal suspect by an investigating organ and so forth. From the above, it can be seen that many right are given to defender. However, the core of the defence system in effect is to make sure the accused can exercise the right of defence and effectively participate in the litigation. Although China's defense system is relatively complete, it still needs to be improved based on this standard. We should fully understand the essence of the right of defense—making sure the active defense right of the criminal suspect and the defendant can be exercise, perfect and innovate the defense system of our country and follow the principle of protecting human rights in criminal procedure.

4. Characteristics of the right to defence

As one of the three primary functions in criminal procedure, defense plays an equally important role as prosecution and trial. However, the judicial power and and the power of accusation are state compulsory powers granted to the state organs according to law, and they share the same nature to some extent. Compared with them, the right of defense is a right, not a power. According to what we have discussed above, I think that the right of defense, as a civil right recognized by law, has six characteristics.

First, it is inalienable. Defence is first and foremost a natural right of man. In human society, as long as we recognize that man is an end rather than an instrument, and has autonomy and subjectivity, we should respect his dignity, ability to decide on his own destiny and his right to speech, expression, justification and refutation in the face of prosecution and accusation. The right of defense is the natural right of human being, and it is an inalienable fundamental right, which has been explained in detail in the preceding part. Although the right to defence, as a natural right, must be recognized and granted by law before it is turned into a legal right and supported and safeguard by the state, it does not mean that it can be taken away under the guise of the law. From what we discussed about the relationship between natural law and positive law, we know that the lawmakers of a state will not act arbitrarily in legislation and will take into account many factors. They should treat any member of society as an end in itself, not as an object which the state arbitrarily imposes its will upon, and should not treat individuals as instruments for the purpose of ruling and deprive others of their dignity. In addition, the triangle structure of criminal procedure also requires that the right of defense can not be deprived, or it will collapses, becoming a inquisitorial system and losing its meaning.

Neither legislation nor the judicial organ can, in any way, deprive a person of his or her right of defense. During judicial activity, judicial organ, under various pretexts, interferes with and restricts the exercise of the right to defence or even deprives criminal suspects and defendants of it. For example, sometimes they are not allowed to defend themselves or exculpate themselves. Those that try to do so will be seen as being dishonest, or refusing or unwilling to admit their crimes. Some organs even prohibit or limit the time for statements by defendants and their defenders during trial, regardless of whether their statements is relevant to the case. Such practices should be prevented, because they are a denial of the right to a defence.

Second, it is non-transferable. In addition its inalienability, the right to defence is also non-transferable, because it is relative to personal status. As is known to all, civil rights can be divided into property rights and personal rights. Property rights, featured by property interest, can be transferred and inherited among civil legal subjects according to law. However, personal rights, characterized by an individual, is an inalienable right and can not be transferred or inherited, for instance, the right of life, name, image and reputation which belong to personality right, and the right of marital autonomy and the right of honor that fall into the category of identity right. Although the right to defence is not a kind of civil rights, and it is a legal right granted and confirmed by law, it, as a natural right coming from human nature, dignity and autonomy, is tied to who you are. Therefore, just as the right to vote and to be elected, it is is not transferable between legal subjects as property rights are.

It should be noted that the non-transferability of the right of defense does not mean that the right holder can not entrust others to exercise it. To make sure it can be effectively exercised, the defense system has been established in all the countries across the globe, including the one that enables the criminal suspect and the defendant to entrusts others to exercise it. Although the defender has acquired independent litigation right in the criminal procedure as the defense system and the lawyer system are gradually perfected, the defense right is in essence given to the accused. The defender is only entrusted or designated to assist him in exercising this right, and can not be regarded as the right holder.

Third, it is a right that can be waived. The right of defense shares some characteristics of other rights—it can be waived. Although it, as a fundamental right, is inalienable and non-transferable, the accused in criminal proceedings can sit passively for his final ruling. He is allowed to waive the right of defense, wholly or partially. Because it comes from the personal autonomy and bases the respect and recognition of it, an individual can either actively exercise this right or voluntarily waive it.

On this very note, when a suspect or defendant who has reached the age of 18 years and has full capacity for civil conduct decides voluntarily to waive the right to defence, including the right to defend himself or to entrust the defense to another person, no one is allowed to interfere. According to the existing judicial interpretation of the

Supreme People's Court, if a defendant refuses to accept the lawyer assigned by the court or refuse to retain another another lawyer designated to defend him, the court will disapprove it.[19] This provision is not only in contradiction to the fact that rights can be waived, but also difficult to be implemented. For example, in April 2001, when the Chongqing Municipal Court heard the major robbery and murder case, the principal culprit Zhang refused to entrust a defender and insisted on refusing the defender appointed by the court to defend him. Finally, the case was decided in the absence of a defender. This shows that it is not practical and feasible if we fail to respect and recognize the characteristics of the right of defence.

Fourth, it is exercised in a targeted response way. As discussed above, defence is the opposite of prosecution, based on which the former exists. The right of defense is usually exercised by the defendant who exculpate and justify his conducts by providing evidence or materials and using legal means to prove that he is innocent, his crime is minor, or punishment can be mitigated or criminal responsibility can be exempted. As can be seen, the defense targets the charge and relevant information against him. The criminal procedure starts from the prosecutorial organ investigating cases. The prosecution is offensive, and the accused exercise the right of defense just in response to it. Therefore, the right of defense is a kind of defense right and self-defense right of the accused, and it targets the charge.

In this context, when the statements and expressions of the criminal suspect, the defendant and his or her defender are not relevant to the case, they can not be deemed to have properly exercised the right to a defence. The authorities in charge of the case may stop them from giving statements in due course, to bring them back on the track of the procedure and improve the litigation efficiency. The interruption and stopping of the statements of the accused and his or her defender in such circumstances can not be regarded as a denial of the right of defense.

Fifth, it is exercised in an active way. As discussed above, the right of defense refers to the exculpation, explanation, defense and rebuttal of the accused against the charges to prove that he is innocent, his crime is minor, or punishment can be mitigated or criminal responsibility can be exempted. Therefore, this right can only be exercised through these behaviors. If the accused, in the face of prosecution and accusation, does not respond and exercise his right of defense in an active way, but instead remains passive and silent, this is deemed as a failure to exercise such right and a waiver of it. Therefore, the right of defense of the accused can only be exercised through their active defense.

Sixth, it is vulnerable to be violated. The right of defense is a kind of right, not a power. Unlike the state power which is compulsory, so it is difficult to ensure it can be effectively exercised. Moreover, the right itself is vulnerable to be violated by the state power, and citizens only exercise the right of defense when facing criminal prosecution. The accused, who are often deemed as criminals or major suspects, are morally disadvantaged and often draw rebuke of public opinion. In addition, since the power of prosecution is the opposite of the right of defense, the intense conflict is

---

[19] Article 45 of *Interpretation of the Supreme People's Court Concerning the Implementation of the Criminal Procedure Law of the People's Republic of China.*

often seen between them. As a state power, the right of defense is usually perceived as being just in cracking down on and punishing crimes. Therefore, the right of defense is likely to be infringed under the pretense of fighting crime.

In a nutshell, in the legislation of criminal procedure, we should consider various systems and rules to ensure the right of defense can be effectively exercised, so as to prevent it from being violated by the state power, especially the power of prosecution and judicial power. For example, a presumption of innocence system can be established to increase the burden of the prosecutorial organ to provide more proof, or a system for defense lawyers to be present for interrogations may be created to strengthen the regulation over the investigating activities, or an evidence disclosure system can be developed for the prosecution and the defense to enable the defendant to provide adequate information against charge.

5.1.1 Conclusion

Nowadays, the defense system has become an indispensable part of the national legal construction, and the protection of the right of defense is also an essential to national law. Since the right of defense is a legal right which is gradually established from the natural right, there is no unified rules for its establishment. However, this does not mean that the it can be created at will. Rather, it is necessary to base its establishment on the characteristics of natural rights, the gains scored through human long-term endeavour, the requirements from the international community.

The right of defense is a citizen's right to defend and rebut when facing prosecution and accusation. In order to ensure it can be effectively exercised, in addition to enactment of law, there must be supporting systems and rights. In this regard, legislation should be grounded in nature and characteristic of the right of defense to improve the relevant systems and norms. After a long period of exploration and efforts, the minimum international standard on the right of defense has been developed. Any law-based countries should try to make their right of defense meet this standard. For example, to protect the rights and interests of the accused from being violated and constrain the state power, it is pivotal to adopt the presumption of innocence. Besides the right of the accused to defend himself, he should also have the right to entrust others to defend himself, and ask for legal assistance as soon as he is charged. The government shall provide free, effective legal aid to persons in need. The defender should be entitled to the right to consult, excerpt and reproduce case files, meet with his client, investigate and collect evidence. The lawmakers who engage in legislation to protect the right of defense in China should not only consider the characteristics of the right of defense, but also consult and adopt the minimum standards of relevant international legal documents.

5.2 The Litigation Right of Defense Lawyer and Its Institutional Guarantee in the Prosecution-Defense Procedure

1. Lawyer's defense—Institutional foundation of the prosecution-defense procedure

As we enter the twenty-first century, great progress has been made on the path to make criminal procedure more modernized and democratic. As a symbol of the modernized, democratic criminal procedure, lawyer defense system has gradually developed and become the bedrock of modern criminal procedure. In particular, under the adversary system, the lawyer-defense system, as one of the important part of the criminal judiciary to keep the proceedings fair and ensure its smooth running, underpins the efficient, sound criminal judicial system. As the foundation of the prosecution-defense procedure, the lawyer defense practically improves the justice, the essence of judicial act, in the criminal proceedings.

1.1 System of defense by lawyer bases the balance between prosecution and defense

The key to the prosecution and defense procedure is to make them balanced. Under the system of prosecution and defense procedure, public prosecution system has evolved and become sound. The public security organ, responsible for investigating cases and collecting evidence, and the prosecutorial organ, accountable for initiate prosecution, combine into a strong prosecution. Its power to prosecute crimes has been greatly strengthened. In addition, it has played an active role in the exercise of the state's power of punishment, and, as a party to the proceedings, has its own incomparable advantages to the defendant. It the defense, as its opposing party, is not given need rights, this will cause great disparity in the power between them and undermine the fairness of the criminal procedure. It can be said that the sound procuratorial and investigative system is the foundation of the public prosecution system, and the perfection of the lawyer defense system not only base the protection of the rights of the accused, but also underpin the balance between prosecution and defense to achieve fairness of criminal procedure and justice system.

Defense lawyer, as a person providing private legal aid, is the essential part to balance the power between the prosecution and the accused, and the guarantee to make the accused equally armed as the prosecution in the criminal procedure. The defendant, who is deprived of liberty and lack of legal knowledge, may be disadvantageous in the procedure, so it is difficult for him to effectively exercise the right of defense. Without the assistance of defence counsel, their legitimate rights and interests will not be fully safeguarded. Only with the legal assistance can the accused exercise the right of defense and articulate his opinions against the charge to realize the fairness of procedure system. It is hard to imagine how the accused could have been given a fair trial without the assistance of his defender. With the independent litigation status and rights, lawyers can help the defendants who are unable to exercise their right of defense, which greatly enhances their defense ability. The defense lawyer reveals the facts of the case against the accusation to try to perform the defense function in the criminal procedure. There is no doubt that the system of defense by lawyer is the institutional guarantee to balance the power between the accused and the prosecution.

System of defense by lawyer has become the cornerstone of the modern criminal justice system, and the right to access to legal advice has also become an important part of the protection of the rights of the accused. In modern countries, the right to access to legal advice is built into the law and even the constitution as an important right of the defendant. According to the Sixth Amendment to the United States Constitution, an accused person has the right to be assisted by a lawyer to defend himself. Moreover, another important system in the prosecution-defense procedure is the disclosure of evidence which needs to be carried out by the defender. It can be said that without the participation of defense lawyers, the prosecution-defense procedure will lose its foundation and meaning.

Thesystem of defense by lawyer underpins the prosecution-defense procedure and helps to realize the fairness of justice system. The more functions the defence counsel maximize, the more fair the trials can be. This can be explained by an old Chinese saying—both sides must present their opinions. In the countries where the system of prosecution and defense is well-established, the defense system has been quite perfect. First, there is a high level of participation of defence counsel. In Japan, for example, 97.1% of the defenders were appointed in the first instance cases in local courts in 1993, of which 34.7% were entrusted and 63.7% were appointed. Moreover, 96.9% were also hired in summary courts, with 15.7% entrusted defenders and 81.2% designated defenders.[20] It can be seen that in Japan, the designated defense represents a greater share of the criminal defense.[21] Many states have even invalidated proceedings without the participation of defence counsel. If, in the United States, this right is not effectively granted to or guaranteed for the accused during the trial, the defense of the accused against charges and the imposition of a sentence, it will constitute a major violation of constitutional rights and result in the automatic annulment of any conviction against the accused or the reopening of proceedings. Second, the well-established system of defense by lawyer is reflected in the wide range of litigation rights given to lawyers, which enables to play an active role in criminal proceedings.

1.2 The system of defense by lawyer enables the judicial neutrality

Another primary characteristic of the prosecution-defense procedure is that the judge, including the jury is neutral and can stay calm to render impartial judgment. The neutrality is the premise to realize the fairness of the criminal procedure and even the justice system, and is based on the balance between prosecution and defense. The judge is considered as the person who ascertains the truth and implements the law. The quality of the his or her judgement depends on the degree to which the case is investigated by both sides.

---

[20]Nishihara Haruo [20].

[21]Liu Lixian and Xie Pengcheng [21].

The equality of the status of the prosecution and the defense, equal litigation rights given to them, and the offensive and defensive activities are essential to the judicial neutrality. Only when both sides effectively perform their functions can the judge gives a fair trial. The neutrality is based on the balance of power between both sides and the equality of rights they are entitled to. Only when two sides are well-matched can they confront each other on an equal footing, the neutrality be realized, and the judge's impartial judgment be based on sufficient legal basis. In particular, the active defence activities of lawyers against the charges makes more truth in favor of the defense in the criminal proceedings revealed, provides more legal basis for the judges' judgement and ensures its quality. In short, the system of defense by lawyer is the cornerstone of the prosecution-defense procedure. If such system is not well-established, the confrontation between two sides is less effective and the judge is likely to render a impartial judgement. It must be fully recognized that the such system plays an irreplaceable role in keeping the normal operation of the prosecution-defense procedure.

2. The reform of the prosecution-defense trial procedure in China and the lack of the rights of defense lawyers

In 1996, a new trial procedure system was established, based on the separation of prosecution and trial and adversarial system. This is a big revamp to the criminal procedure in China. The new trial procedure has retained certain functions and powers of the judge, but it undoubtedly characterizes the active evidence-providing and counterarguments by the prosecution and the defense. This system comprises the evidence-providing, cross-examination and argument of both sides, which are verified by the court, aiming at effectively combining the inquisitorial system and adversarial system. It reflects the pursuit of litigation science and democracy, which is the trend of trial procedure reform in China. It has been established, but the prosecution, defense and trial can not maximize their functions due to lack of effective institutional guarantee. Therefore, an important and long-term task is to make the prosecution and the defense are well-matched in power during the reform. Such problem of imbalance is extremely acute. The capacity of defense is relatively weak, making it impossible to confront the prosecution and lay the foundation for the prosecution-defense trial procedure. In legislative and judicial activities, we need to place more emphasis on this kind of balance, which is both essential to the procedural justice and the substantive justice.

At present, the level of participation of defenders in criminal cases in China is not high. It is worrying that only 30% of the cases are statistically heard with the involvement of defenders, which gets in the way of realizing the fairness of justice system. The defense and the prosecution are not well-matched in our country. Some defendants are at distinct disadvantage from being "interrogated" by both the public prosecutor and the judge in the court. This situation makes it difficult to guarantee the fairness of the trial. In summary cases, the level participation of the defence was even lower. In such cases where the public prosecutor did not appear in court, so a single judge directly tries the defendant using evidence. This practice improves the efficiency, but the right of defense is not effectively exercised without the legal aid from the defender, which will ultimately undermine the fairness of justice system. The right to access to the legal aid from defense counsel given to the defendant helps to balance the power between the prosecution and the defense, make the reform a success, improve the fairness of judgement and make the law effectively implemented. In addition, it is also a necessary measure to protect the constitutional rights of the accused. Faced with the challenges, we need to proactively develop the system of defense by lawyer and improve the legal aid system via various means, so that all criminal defendants can enjoy the right to obtain the assistance of lawyers. This is particularly important for the effective operation of the prosecution-defense trial procedure and the justice of the litigation, and it is also what we are striving for.[22]

In addition to getting defense lawyers involved, it is also important to define what kind of rights given to them and the role they play, which determines whether the trial procedure of prosecution and defense can operate smoothly. In this context, right of defense was further improved by the criminal procedure law in 2012. The revamp includes that the right of defense can be exercised at the investigating stage. Moreover, the law also perfects the right of lawyer to meet clients, expands the right to consult case files, extends the scope of legal aid, reduces the professional risks of lawyers and provides more measures to remove the impediment to the fulfillment of their duties, in order to realize the balance of both sides. Although this amendment to the defence system is of great significance, some important rights are still not granted to the defense lawyers, their personal freedom is not effectively guaranteed and procedural rights are extremely vulnerable to infringement. These problems are still a huge obstacle to the smooth running of the trial procedure.

First, there is still a need for interpretation of the provisions concerning the right of meeting. The difficulty in meeting clients is solved by criminal procedure law revised in 2012, which is one of important part of this revision and can be reflected in the following aspects. First, the meeting procedure has been streamlined, and a defense lawyer can request for a meeting with a criminal suspect or defendant under

---

[22]It is necessary to perfect the legal aid system after the establishment of the trial procedure of prosecution and defense in China. Although the Constitution and the criminal procedure law do not clearly provide that the accused are entitled to the right to access to the legal aid from lawyer, there is an increasing demand for legal aid from the suspects and the accused with the enhanced law-based governance and the protection of civil rights. Article 34 of the Criminal Procedure Law provides that With respect to a criminal suspect or defendant who is vision, hearing or speech impaired, or who is punishable by life imprisonment or capital punishment has not entrusted a defender, or a criminal suspect or defendant who has not entrusted a defender due to financial difficulties or other reasons, the people's court shall inform a legal aid agency to designate a lawyer as his or her defender. However, the people's court rarely appoints lawyers for the latter. Without the help of lawyers, the disparity in power between the prosecution and the defense become more serious, and we can not maximize the function of the prosecution-defense trial procedure system, undermining the fairness of judgement. In our country, the criminal defense system now is far from playing its role due to the bias of thoughts of judicial officials, lack of legal legal awareness of citizens and their financial difficulties. This will also inevitably hinder the reform of the prosecution-defense trial procedure.

detention on the strength of the lawyer's practicing certificate, and the certification documents and letter of authorization issued by his or her law firm, or an official legal aid document. Second, prompt action is taken to arrange the meeting. The detention house concerned shall arrange the meeting in a timely manner, no later than 48 h after receiving the request. Third, more things that the attorney is allowed to do during the meeting. A defense lawyer shall be entitled to verify relevant evidence with the criminal suspect or defendant from the date on which the case is transferred for examination before prosecution. Fourth, it applies to more people—the criminal suspect and the defendant under residential surveillance. However, there are still many issues relating to the right that need to be clarified. Does this right belong to defense lawyer or criminal suspect? Since the meeting is required to be arranged in a timely manner by law, why there is a delay of "no later than 48 h after receiving the request"? Is it justifiable to restrict the meeting in the case of "a crime involving significant amount of bribes"? What are the specific things that can be done during the investigation stage? Does it include verification of evidence? How to take judicial remedy about undue restriction or deprival of meeting right? How to acquire the right of correspondence? These are the questions that remain unanswered after the 2012 revision of the criminal procedure law, and such problems will also arise in judicial activity.

Second, it is difficult to exercise the right to investigate and collect evidence. It is a long-standing problem that it is difficult for lawyers to investigate and obtain evidence in our country's criminal procedure, partly due to legislation. Article 41 of the Criminal Procedure Law provides that defence lawyers may, with the consent of the witnesses or other units and individuals concerned, collect information pertaining to the current case from them and they may also apply to the people's procuratorate or the people's court for the collection and obtaining of evidence, or request the people's court to inform the witnesses to appear in court and give testimony. In addition, it also provides that with permission of the people's procuratorate or the people's court and with the consent of the victim, his close relatives or the witnesses provided by the victim, defence lawyers may collect information pertaining to the current case from them. Although the legislation gives lawyers the right to investigate and collect evidence, some of its provisions make it hard to be exercised. First, whether the lawyers have such right at the investigation stage is controversial. Article 36 of this legal document provides that during the investigation period, a defense lawyer may provide a criminal suspect with legal aid, file petitions and complaints on the suspect's behalf, apply for alteration of the compulsory measures, find out from the investigating organ the offense of which the criminal suspect is convicted and the information pertaining to the case, and offer his or her opinions. However, it makes no mention of the right of lawyers to investigate and collect evidence, and whether lawyers can exercise this right under Article 41 is controversial in theory and practice. Second, this right is difficult to be effectively implemented. The lawyers can investigate and obtain evidence, they practically can not exercise this right if the witness does not agree to testify. Moreover, they have to gain the permission of the people's procuratorate or the people's court and with the consent of the victim, his close relatives or the witnesses provided by the victim, producing more obstacles to the exercise of this right and also providing legal basis for the people who refuse the lawyer's investigation. Therefore, these provisions are seriously flawed and unpractical. The law does not provide legal consequences for witnesses who do not testify. Many citizens meet the obligation to testify only for the judicial organ, but not for the lawyers. In addition, there are risks associated with lawyers investigating evidence. Once lawyers have collected evidence that is not in the favour of the investigating organ, they may be detained or even sentenced by the investigating organ or the procuratorial organ for the crime of perjury or interference with of evidence-collecting, and risks losing their jobs. This causes great concerns about evidence-gathering concerns at the investigation period, leading to little evidence collected and and undermining the quality of defense.

Third, little attention is given to the right to apply to the people's procuratorate and the people's court to collect and obtain evidence, and to apply to the People's Court to notify witnesses to testify. If lawyers have difficulties in obtaining evidence due to the restriction of their right to investigate, they may apply to the court or the procuratorate for the collection of evidence. But this can not help the defense counsel to obtain sufficient evidence, because their request is not given enough attention. Especially when applying to the procuratorial organs for evidence collection, they are less cooperative. Defence counsel applied to the tribunal for witnesses to be notified of their appearance, which is sometimes not taken seriously, resulting in the deprival of the right of defense.

Fourth, the rights of counsel are limited and not respected by the court at the trial stage. Taking part in court investigation and court debate are important activities for defense lawyers to play their role. In a court trial, the defence lawyer has the right to present evidence, cross-examine the prosecution's evidence, inquire about information from witnesses and argue with the prosecution. Some judicial officials, however, think that lawyers in criminal proceedings only try to avoid the responsibility for the accused, and some even believe that they know much more about cases than the lawyers do. Therefore, they have contempt for lawyers, who are considered to have no role to play in the proceedings, leading in some circumstance to a lack of respect for the rights and dignity of lawyers by the judicial officials.[23]

Fifth, the right to personal liberty of defence counsel is seriously threatened. Because of insufficient evidence collected by the lawyers in the investigation stage

[23]On January 10,1997, the Taiyuan Intermediate People's Court conducted a public retrial of the "2–26" major case requested by the Shanxi Provincial High People's Court and tried the defendant about the remaining crime undiscovered. When the adversary procedure began, the defense speech was first delivered by Ms.Li, the first defender of the defendant, and then by Mr.Liu, the second defender for the second round of defense. During the defense speech, Mr.Liu was interrupted three times by the presiding judge who even did not allow him to speak. Then, the presiding judge opened the case file to read out the testimony against Mr. Liu's defense opinions, and then a debate between the judges and the defense lawyers began. When the presiding judge finished his testimony and asked the Ms.Li if she had any arguments, she said in response to the judge's refusal to let Mr. Liu finish his speech that it was the lawyers' duty to make the facts clear and how they can fulfill their duty without making their speech. She was then interrupted by the presiding judge who asked the court police to get her out of the court. Then she was immediately forced out of the court by two court police, indicating that her right of defense and the right to debate in court were deprived.

and the obstacles to evidence collection, it is hard for them to maximize their functions. In addition, the procuratorate, as a regulator with great power, makes the prosecution and the defense far from being well-matched. The right of approval and deciding on arrest by the procuratorial organ enables it to send defense lawyers to prison on many charges, such as "perjury". The public prosecutors could not "defeat" the defense lawyer in court, because the evidence could not hold water. Once challenged by the defense, they can hardly keep calm. So they often confront their opponents by power rather than litigation rights. As a result, some lawyers who just walk out of the court or are even in the court are brought to the procuratorate by force and then arrested under the false pretence of "questioning". The lack of protection of the personal freedom of lawyers and the absence of immunity from trial speech have exposed defence lawyers to serious professional risks and the possibility of being held criminally liable if they are not careful. This will inevitably cause the defense functions to be significantly reduced, and make the power of prosecution and defense unbalanced. In addition, this also makes the lawyers less motivated in handling criminal case. Many lawyers are unwilling to handle these cases, resulting in the decreased defense rate in criminal cases and damaged defense system. We are now facing severe challenges. This runs counter to the law-based governance and democracy in China, so we must try to address these problems.

The above-mentioned problems makes it difficult for defense lawyers to maximize their functions, which results in lawyers' unwillingness to undertake their defense work. This will compound the yet-to-be-improved defense system in our country and also considerably restricts the function of the prosecution and defense trial procedure.

3. The improvement of the litigation rights of defense lawyers in China

There are mainly two problems of the lawyer's defense system in China. On the one hand, there are too many obstacles to the exercise of the lawyer's rights; on the other hand, the lawyer's practice can not be guaranteed by law, causing lawyers unwilling to deal with the defense.

Perfecting the system of lawyer"'s defense is not only essential to establish the modern democratic procedure regime, but also to strengthen the protection of human rights and building a socialist law-based country. The lawyer defense system is an important part of the modern criminal procedure system. The sound lawyer defense system underpins the modern criminal procedure system which sustains a country ruled by law. We must establish the criminal defense system, especially the lawyer defense system in a law-based way, and we are not supposed to bias this system. Instead, we need to recognize its importance. Especially in the prosecution—defense trial procedure, the right of defense lawyer and the role they play determine the normal operation of criminal justice system and can realize the value of security and freedom of criminal procedure. To this end, we need to engage them in more parts of criminal proceedings, give the rights needed for them to effectively play their protective role and provide various guarantees for the exercise of their rights. From the point of view of the prosecution-defense trial procedure, the following rights should be given to the defense lawyer.

3.1 The involvement of a defense lawyer in the investigation stage and the related rights

It is commonly seen that lawyers participate in the entire process of criminal proceedings as defenders in most countries. The common law countries have given the defense lawyers the right to be present when the criminal suspects are interrogated by investigators, and they are provided with adequate protection. In the United States, defense lawyers enjoy a wide range of rights to be present in the investigation process, including investigation, interrogation and arraignment stages. The right of defense counsel to be present should not be constrained for the purposes of the investigation. The right to be present when investigators interrogate criminal suspects and the right to meet with criminal suspects are granted to lawyers. There is no limit on the number and time of meetings, and the suspect and the lawyer have the right to meet without being monitored. In the UK, lawyers can go to the police station at any time to talk to suspects, or they can do so in private over the phone. The fact that lawyers can perform their functions as defenders from the beginning of an investigation not only assist the accused in exercising their right of defense, but also help themselves to carry out the defense work in an effective way.

The criminal procedure allows lawyers to participate in the investigation phase. From the date of the first interrogation of the criminal suspect by the investigating authorities or of the coercive measures taken against him, a lawyer can meet with a criminal suspect as a defender, but the lawyer at this stage has no right to investigate and collect evidence, or to be present for questioning. Without the right to investigate and collect evidence, the evidence in favor of the criminal suspect may be lost at this stage, causing difficulties to the defense in the trial stage. In order to effectively protect the right of defense of criminal suspects, the legislation need to, in accordance with the common international practice, grant defense lawyers the rights including the right to be present during interrogation, the right to investigate and obtain evidence, and the right to apply for the preservation of evidence. These rights should be protected by developing guarantee system.

In a nutshell, the defense system should be implemented in the investigation procedure. The participation of defense lawyers in the investigation stage is necessary, which is not only to prevent the investigation organs from violating the suspects' rights of personal freedom and procedural rights, but also to collect evidence in time manner or apply for collection of evidence. Moreover, it also prevents the one-sidedness of the evidence collection of the investigation organ, to ensure the timely collection of the evidence in favor of the criminal suspect, and make adequate preparations for the defense activities in the court trial stage.

3.2 Refinement of the right of defense lawyers to investigate and collect evidence

Defense lawyer actively fulfilling the defense functions is reliant on the cross-examination of the prosecution evidence and necessary to evidence collection in favor of the accused. Therefore, the right of lawyers to collect evidence should be expanded to lay a foundation for defense lawyers to investigate and collect evidence and effectively perform their defense functions. The investigation and collection of evidence by the defense, carried out in sync with the investigation and collection of evidence by the investigating organ, is an integral part of the prosecution-defense trial procedure. According to the current criminal procedure law, defense lawyers may collect materials relevant to the case from witnesses or other relevant entities and individuals with their consent. Moreover, they can also collect these materials from the victims or their close relatives or witnesses provided by the victims, but only with their consent and with the permission of the People's Procuratorate or the People's Court. This to a large extent limits the exercise of right of defense counsel to investigate and collect evidence, making it become a right in name only. This can be attributed to the large disparity in such right between investigating organs and lawyers and misconceived criminal procedure structure. In order to address these problems, we need to perfect the right of investigation and collection of evidence. For example, we need to put the lawyer's application for investigation and collection of evidence under the jurisdiction of the court, restrict the discretion of its approval, and introduce the system of investigation order to ensure the application for right to investigate and collect evidence, and reduce and remove legislative discrimination and restrictions on defense lawyers taking evidence to make sure they exercise this right without being interfered with.

3.3 The right to apply for evidence preservation

Defence lawyers who are unable to collect evidence have the right to apply to the court, which shall examine the application and make a decision as soon as possible. The court may set up a special examining department for the application of evidence preservation. If the evidence needs to be collected and preserved, the court need take measures in a timely manner to prevent the damage to or loss of evidence and the difficulties in collection caused by the delay in time. During the investigation stage, defense lawyers have the right to apply to the public security organ and procuratorial organ for evidence collection and preservation. If these organs fail to do so in a timely manner, defense lawyers have the right to apply to the court.

3.4 Participation in court investigation and the protection of the right of defense in court

We should perfect the procedure of adducing evidence and cross-examining, establish the cross-examining mechanism for witnesses, experts and investigators and the cross-examining system for other evidence, to regulate the procedure of court debate. The judge should ensure the right of defense lawyer to debate and the latter should abide by the order of the court. In addition, the judge should support and protect, rather than restrict, the routine defense act of them. It is strictly forbidden to infringe upon the freedom and safety of the defense lawyers, charge them and throw them out of court or even to detain, arrest or investigate their legal responsibility at will.

3.5. The protection of the rights of personal freedom and to practice law of the defense lawyers

The personal freedom and the right to practice law are essential for the defense lawyer to fulfill duties. Therefore, the immunity should be given to them. The law provides the lawyer with the right not to be prosecuted when he offers the legal opinion to the client or makes the statement and defense in court. If the law provides the immunity and tries to protect it, this will largely avoid the above-mentioned practice risks. Article 20 of the *Basic Principles on the Role of Lawyers* adopted by United Nations provides that "lawyers shall enjoy civil and penal immunity for relevant statements made in good faith in written or oral pleadings or in their professional appearances before a court, tribunal or other legal or administrative authority." This right has been recognized in many countries. Before 1996, our country's law on lawyer and the related law did not make it clear about the immunity. The first sentence of paragraph 2 of Article 37 of the Law on lawyers revised in 2012 provides that "lawyers shall not be held liable for the comments or opinions related to defense in tribunal." It is the first time to make it clear that the immunity is given to lawyers in court. It is important to note that such immunity is limited. Defense counsel shall not make the abuse of it. Thus, the second sentence of the same paragraph provides that "except for statements that endanger national security, maliciously defame others or seriously disturb the order of the court". Legislation can ensure the exercise of immunity through reasonable restriction, which not only enable the lawyers to exercise all litigation rights and perform their duties, but also ensure the fairness of litigation process and judicial system. Moreover, it can be seen from the Article 20 of of the *Basic Principles on the Role of Lawyers* that immunity can also be used in the trial stage, so our legislation should make the immunity cover the trial stage.

4. Reform and improvement of relevant systems

4.1 Making the public prosecutor a litigant

As the reform of the prosecution-defense trial procedure in China, we come to know that the status of the procuratorial organ must be redesigned and the reform entails the introduction of adversary system. As the party who fulfills the prosecution function, it is self-evident that prosecution of crime is its important mission. However, this should not make its impartiality in prosecution less important. Both of them need to be taken seriously. Moreover, its neutrality can not be seen qualified as a regulator over the judgement in the court. According to the psychology, it is impossible for actor to assume the roles of both a litigant and a regulator.

In the prosecution-defense trial procedure, the prosecution and the defense should be treated equally and armed with the equivalent rights. Otherwise, the unequal footing will destabilize the procedure and undermine the fairness of justice system. In order to innovate the procedure in China, we must establish the principle of equal litigation status and rights between prosecution and the defense. To this end, we need to redesign the relationship between the prosecutor, the defender and the judge, and make the responsibilities of prosecution and judgement divided, the prosecutor and the defender well-matched as well as the judge neutral. Some people think that the functions of prosecution and supervision can be separated, with the former fulfilled by the public prosecutor in court and the latter performed by other internal departments of procuratorial organs. This assumption is impractical. First, the integrated system of the procuratorial organs and fact that the lower-level ones are submissive to higher-level ones makes it hard to turn this vision into reality, because the internal departments is hardly independent. Second, the structure with additional regulatory organization set up in addition to the original three parties in the criminal procedure is neither fish nor fowl, because it is not rational and impartial. It must be noted that the normal operation and fairness of criminal justice system must also rely on its own scientific framework, which should comprise the division of responsibility of prosecution and judgement, the balance of power between the prosecutor and the defender, and the impartiality of judge, the division and effective performance of the three functions of prosecution, defense and judgement.

In the process of this reform, the public prosecutor needs to be defined as a litigant on an equal footing with the defender. Moreover, making the court hold the central place in the criminal procedure is essential to create scientific procedure system, realize the fairness and meet the needs of prosecution-defense trial procedure. Taking the public prosecutor as one of the litigants is not in any way to dwindle its role in the proceedings, but to redefine the relationship between the public prosecutor and the defense in the trial procedure.

4.2 Respect the defense opinions and the right to practice law of defense lawyers

The division of responsibilities of prosecution and judgement is central to innovate the prosecution-defense trial procedure. As a judge who render a judgement, the impartiality is the essence of this job. Therefore, the judge should be neutral and shouldn't bias or even discriminate against defence lawyers. The equal status of the prosecutor and defender is the foundation of this procedure. As an important actor to perform the defense function, the defense lawyer independently exercising the right of defense and fulfilling duties according to law is seen as a bedrock of this kind of procedure. This is because without the participation of lawyers with specialized legal knowledge and defence experience, a adversary system can not be developed between the two parties. The judge should not lean toward the prosecution and should treat the two parties equally and listen to their opinions. This is extremely important for impartial judgment, prosecution-defense trial procedure and fairness of justice system.

However, the judges' prejudice against lawyers do exist to a certain extent, and they do not value their procedural rights. They will absolutely approve the application submitted by the public prosecutor for a postponement of the trial because of the need for additional investigation, but are unwilling to do so when the defence lawyers file applications for re-identification, notification of new witnesses to appear in court and the taking of new evidential materials. This unequal treatment will, to some extent, restrict or deprive the defendant's right of defense.[24] This attributed to the traditional

[24] Article 223 of the *Interpretation of the Supreme People's Court Concerning the Implementation of the Criminal Procedure Law of the People's Republic of China* provides that "during the court trial, if the procurator believes the case needs further investigation and suggests deferment of the

inquisitorial mind set of the judges and their failure to recognize the importance of the lawyer's defense to the trial.

Judges must recognize how important it is to innovate the prosecution-defense trial procedure and treat both sides equally so as to make them participate in the procedure on an equal footing and ensure the fairness of judgement. In addition, they need to realize that both sides maximizing their functions can make the judgement more impartial. As the party to fulfill the defense function, the lawyers must ensure that they try their best to perform their duties while participating in the criminal procedure. As such, defence lawyers must be given the same procedural rights as prosecutors and some fundamental rights, otherwise they will not be able to carry out their work effectively and the defence system will just exist in name only. The procedural rights of defense lawyers primarily refer to the rights to bring in witnesses and present evidence in court, make a request to summon new witness to testify in court or to collect new evidence or conduct new forensic examination or crime scene investigation, cross-examine the witnesses and evidence of prosecutor and debate on an equal footing with the prosecutor. Therefore, the judge need to treat both sides equally and give them equal procedural rights.

4.3 Improvement of the management system and self-discipline of lawyers

It can be found that some defense lawyers do not abide by professional ethics and the rules to practice law, and even engage in illegal acts to impede judicial activities. We must regulate the practice of lawyers, and punish them, if necessary, for illegal evidence collection and misconduct, which is essential to ensure the operation of the defense system and the fairness of justice system.

Regulate the practice of defense lawyers entails the refinement of the lawyer management system. It is worth noting that the provision of perjury by a defender was added to Article 306 of 1997 criminal procedure law. The defense system is established to ensure the justice and fairness, which demonstrates the democracy of developing legal systems. This provision that the defense lawyers are held criminally liable for perjury will affect the effective of the defense system and allow the law enforcement officials take advantage of it for vengeance. In short, this provision runs counter to the purpose of the defense system and hinders the development of the lawyer's career. In this way, people will lose confidence in the defense system,

adjudicative procedure, the collegial panel shall consent. Suggestion to deferment shall not be submitted to court for more than twice". Article 222 of this legal document also provides that "during the court hearing, to request the court to summon witness to testify in court or to collect new evidence or conduct new forensic examination or crime scene investigation, parties and their defenders or litigation advocates shall provide the name of the witness concerned and the place where the evidence is held in custody, indicate the fact that is expected to prove and explain the reasons for new forensic examination or crime scene investigation. The court shall grant the request, if it is considered necessary, and announce that the court hearing will be deferred". The retention and exercise of certain powers by the judges are necessary to prevent delays of the procedure and to make it efficient. However, the different treatment by the tribunal and its failure to give a convincing reason about rejection of the request is likely to raise doubts about its impartiality.

making this system develop in an unsound way. Therefore, I think that this provision should be repealed.

It is also necessary to punish the lawyers who do not abide by the rules of practicing law and impede the judicial activities. I think it is important to enable the bar association or court to take disciplinary action against lawyers, so that they can discipline themselves. Therefore, we need to perfect the lawyer management system to realize self-management, self-restraint and self-regulation.

As to how to ensure that lawyers can practice law in accordance with the law, lawyers should be granted the rights they are entitled to in the performance of their duties on the one hand and the disciplinary system of lawyers should be strictly enforced on the other hand. But the disciplinary action against lawyers are not supposed to be taken by the prosecutorial organ. The lawyer management and the control over the judicial administrative department should be strengthened. We also need to regulate the management of lawyers for lawyer self-discipline. As an unofficial force, lawyer is an important force to resist public right and protect private right, and is an integral part of law-based governance. However, the lawyer system does not exist for quite long time in China, so it will take some time for the lawyer to effectively maximize their functions. The implementation of the unified judicial examination system, as well as the development and maintenance of the judicial research and training system and the judicial professional ethics in the future, is paramount to the communication among prosecutors, judges and lawyers, and mutual understanding and trust, which helps to redefine the relationship among them in the prosecution-defense trial procedure.

5.3 Discussion of the Right to Meet with Criminal Suspects Under Detention Based on the Article 37 of Criminal Procedure Law

March 14, 2012, the *Decision on Amendment to the Criminal Procedure Law* was adopted by the 5th Session the 11th China's National People's Congress, aiming to extensively revise this law.[25] The amendment or addition of articles on the right of defense and its related regulations amounts to 25, covering the role positioning of defenders, the stage at which they can participate in the proceedings, the right to meet with criminal suspects and consult case file materials and legal aid. Among all the revised articles, the amendment of Article 37 concerning the right to meet with criminal suspects is so important that it solves the long-standing problem of criminal defense in China, which can be reflected in four aspects. First, the meeting procedure has been streamlined, and a defense lawyer can request for a meeting with a criminal suspect or defendant under detention on the strength of the lawyer's practicing certificate, and the certification documents and letter of authorization issued by his

[25]Compared to 1996 Criminal Procedure Law, the new revision expands the Law from 225 to 290 articles, adds 66 ones, revises 90 and deletes 1.

or her law firm, or an official legal aid document. Second, prompt action is taken to arrange the meeting. The detention house concerned shall arrange the meeting in a timely manner, no later than 48 h after receiving the request. Third, more things that the attorney is allowed to do during the meeting. A defense lawyer shall be entitled to verify relevant evidence with the criminal suspect or defendant from the date on which the case is transferred for examination before prosecution. Fourth, it applies to more people—the criminal suspect and the defendant under residential surveillance.

It can be seen from what we discussed above that the Article 37 is extremely essential to ensure the exercise of the right to meet with criminal suspects. However, can this article answer all the questions of this right? Is it perfect enough that there is no need to make interpretation? I think there are still four issues regarding this article that need to be clarified and interpreted by jurists in order to implement the legislative intent. First, does this right belong to defense lawyer or criminal suspect? Second, since the meeting is required to be arranged in a timely manner by law, why there is a delay of "no later than 48 h after receiving the request"? Is it justifiable to restrict the meeting in the case of three kind of crimes? Third, what are the specific things that can be done at the meeting during the investigation stage? How to apprehend monitoring and the right to correspond? Fourth, how to take up judicial remedy about undue restriction or deprival of meeting right? I will give answers to these four questions, including the holder of this right, the principle and exception of the exercise of this right, things that are allowed to be done during the meeting and the way in which they are done, and the legal remedy that can be taken up against the violation of such right.

1. The holder of the right of meeting

The 2012 criminal procedure law makes a separate article for the right of meeting, which is different from the old version in which the right of meeting and the right to consult case files were under one article. In addition, the previous provision thata criminal suspect can hire a lawyer to provide legal assistance during the investigation was altered into the one that a criminal suspect can entrust a lawyer as a defender, so the first sentence of Article 37(1), provides that defense lawyers may have meeting and correspondence with criminal suspects or defendants who are under detention, and the second sentence includes the difference of the procedure in meeting the criminal suspects and the defendants for the defense lawyers and other defenders.[26]

[26]Prior to the amendment to the Criminal Procedure Law in 2012, lawyers did not have the status of defenders at the investigation stage and were therefore unable to exercise the right of meeting and the right to consult case files. Article 36 of the 1996 Criminal Procedure Law provides for these two rights in two separate paragraphs for examination before prosecution stage and trial stage, respectively. Article 36, Paragraph 1, provides that, a defense lawyer may, from the day on which the people's procuratorate begins to examine and prosecute the case, consult, make abstracts of or reproduce the indictment and technical appraisal materials of the case, may meet and correspond with the crime suspect in custody. Any other defender, with permission of the people's procuratorate, also may consult, make abstracts of or reproduce the aforesaid materials, and meet and correspond with the crime suspect in custody. Article 36, paragraph 2, provides that a defense lawyer may, from the day on which the people's court accepts to hear the case, consult, make abstracts of or reproduce

It seems that there is no need for more discussion about the Article 37(1), because it was revised based on separation and consolidation of previous provisions. However, I think an in-depth discussion is need to answer the first question above—does this right belong to defense lawyer or criminal suspect?

The reason why the first issue concerning the right of meeting is the most important is that it is closely related to the legislation for such right. It determines whether such right is restricted from the perspective of the right of defense or the right of lawyer to practice law, and what kind of legal remedies are taken against the violation of this right. It is therefore necessary to respond first to the first question.

It can be seen from the Article 37 that the subject of the sentences therein is defense lawyer, and word "may" means that this article is an enabling legal norm. The right applies to criminal suspects and defendants under detention. According to what is said, the holders seem to be defense lawyers and defenders. Is that really the legislative intent ? If it is, can we infer that the lawyer who is the right-holder can give up the right? If a suspect or A defendant under detention requests to meet with a lawyer, is the lawyer allowed to refuse to do so? Is the exercise of this right by a lawyer the prerequisite for a criminal suspect or a defendant under detention to obtain assistance from a lawyer or to meet with a lawyer? Is the exercise of this right by lawyers rather than criminal suspects? This is clearly contrary to the nature of the right of defense and the legislative intent. Therefore, we must make it clear that who this right should belong to. Does it belong to defense lawyers or the accused under detention? Or is it shared by both?

Since the right ofmeeting is an important part of the right of defense, it is necessary to discuss who this right should belong to based on the right of defense. From the nature of the right of defense, it exists as a natural right of human beings, so it is a natural right of defense, refutation and even resistance when an individual faces investigation, accusation and oppression. However, this natural right can not be seen as a right of defense in modern society until it is legislated. After that, it can be mandatory and a legislated right.[27] International conventions and the constitutions of many countries including China stipulate that the right of defense is a kind of fundamental constitutional right of the accused. Article 125 of the Constitution provides that the defendant shall have the right to access to defence. It's only few words, but it's a lot to take in. First, the persons entitled to defense are the defendants who refers to criminal suspects and defendants therein. Second, it can be known from "have the right to obtain defence" that the defendants can not only defend themselves but also ask others, especially the lawyers, for help.[28] Emphasizing the right of access to

---

the materials of the facts of the crime charged against in the case, may meet and correspond with the defendant in custody. Any other defender, with permission of the people's court, also may consult, make abstracts of or reproduce the aforesaid materials, and meet and correspond with the defendant in custody.

[27] Chen Weidong [22].

[28] According to what is implied, it means that the defendants can defend themselves or, what's more important, they have the right to access to legal assistance rather than that they can only defend themselves. The first draft of the 1954 Constitution provided that "The defendant shall have the right of defence", which was later amended to "The accused shall have the right to access to defence".

defence does not mean it denies the accused's right to defence, but to ensure the right of defense can be exercised effectively, to close the gap between the accused and the state procuratorial organs in terms of information, knowledge and resources with the assistance of lawyers with legal expertise so as to implement the adversarial system and make the judgement impartial. According to the Criminal Procedure Law,[29] an investigating organ shall, from the date of the first interrogation of a criminal suspect or the imposition of compulsory measures, inform the criminal suspect of his or her right to entrust a defender, and the accused has the right to entrust a defender at any time, and in a particular case or situation, the people's court, the people's procuratorate and the public security organ concerned shall inform a legal aid agency to designate a lawyer as his defender. It can be seen from the relevant provisions of this law that the accused has the right to choose his defender, refuse to accept a defender or entrust his defence to another defender, except the case of mandatory defence. Therefore, the right of defense without the doubt belongs to the accused, whether we discuss it based on the Constitution or the Criminal Law Procedure. To a lawyer, he has the status of a defender only because he is entrusted or appointed, and the law gives him this right to defend on the basis of his status as a defender. So does the right of meeting—one right deriving from the right of defense.

In my opinion, the right of meeting should be enjoyed by the defendant under detention, then followed by the lawyer. It includes two ways of exercising the right, right of the defendant to meet with a lawyer and the right of a lawyer to meet with a criminal suspect. In this context, the above-mentioned problems are resolved. When the accused in custody requests to see a lawyer, the lawyer may not refuse to do so. Moreover, the detention house or the case-handling authority is obliged to inform the lawyer and arrange for the meeting. This right for the defendants is more important for the lawyers. The exercise of the right by the lawyers helps the defendants exercise this right, in order to ensure they can access to defence stipulated by the Constitution. I thinks that the reason that the defense lawyer are taken as the actors in Article 37 is that this wording is only a kind of legislative technique, not the manifestation of legislative intent. In fact, it has laid a solid foundation for the explanation of the restriction of this right and legislation on what kind of legal remedies can be taken against the violation of such right.

2. The principles and exceptions of the exercise of the right of meeting

The right of access of the accused to a defence lawyer is one of the most important fundamental rights of the accused, whose personal freedom is restricted, to be assisted by a lawyer. In addition, it also bases the protection of the right of defence stipulated

---

Liu Shaoqi, a communist leader who served as vice president of the Chinese Communist Party, said during the constitutional conference at the time that although it was hard to ensure the defendants have the right to acquire defence, they still need to be given such right. He also added that some individuals found it difficulty in articulating their opinions and asked the court for help which could find someone, but it didn't need to be a lawyer. Therefore, this article emphasizes that defendants are entitled to the right to obtain the help from others. See Political Research Group of the Standing Committee of the National People's Congress [23].

[29]See 2012 Criminal Procedure Law, Article 33, paragraphs 1,2, and Article 34.

by the Article 125 of the Constitution. Such right should be given full of respect without monitoring. However, it is important to ensure the exercise of the right of meeting and resolve conflicts caused by different interests, such as the conflicts between this right and right of investigation, the management system of the detention house and the preservation in criminal procedure. These conflicts are the reasons for restricting the right of meeting. However, what is the principle of the exercise of this right? And under what circumstances it is justified to lay restriction on such right? Which restrictions are legitimate? What principles should be formulate to restrict this right? These issues are the focus of this book and should be considered for the legislation for the exercise of such right.

2.1 Legislative Evolution of the exercise of the right of one meeting

The exercise of the right of meeting at the pre-trial stage in China has gone through a tortuous course from prohibition to multiple restrictions, and then to free meeting, to special restrictions now. In 1979, the criminal procedure only granted defendants access to a lawyer at the trial stage, because the accused could only entrust a lawyer to defend himself at the trial stage. Between 1979 and 1996, the criminal suspects detained at the pre-trial stage in our country did not enjoy the right of meeting.

The 1996 Criminal Procedure Law allows the defendants to entrust defenders at the review before prosecution stage, and allows them to hire lawyers during the investigation. Accordingly, criminal suspects under detention have been given the right to meet with defence counsel during the review before prosecution state, and even may meet with counsel who is not in the capacity of defence counsel during the investigation stage. However, cases involving state secrets must be approved by the investigating authorities before the meeting can be arranged. Moreover, the investigation organ may, according to the circumstances and needs of the case, send officers to the scene to monitor the meeting. This is the stage with multiple restrictions—approval and monitoring of the meeting according to actual situation. The judicial activities after 1996 shows that the expansion of the right of meeting in legislation has finally become a judicial problem. The approval system of lawyers meeting with criminal suspects has changed from exceptional to common practice, and the presence of officers to monitor the meeting has emerged as necessary, making it difficult to have effective communication between the suspects and the lawyers. This practice in effect restricts the right of meeting and even make it exist in name only, which is far from the legislative intention for the right by the Criminal Procedure Law, and seriously violates the right of defense of the accused protected by Constitution.

The Lawyers Law of the People's Republic of China was revised in 2007, but this much-maligned issue has not been largely resolved. Article 33 provides that as of the date of first interrogation of or adoption of a compulsory measure on a criminal suspect by the criminal investigative organ, an authorized lawyer shall have right to meet the criminal suspect or defendant and learn information related to the case, by presenting his lawyer's practicing certificate, certificate of his law firm and power of attorney or official legal aid papers. A lawyer who meets a criminal suspect or defendant shall not be under surveillance. According to this, the impediment to the right of meeting seems to have been removed completely by the Lawyers Law. In any case, as long as the lawyers provide the document above, they are allowed to meet the criminal suspects at any time without interference. Under this legislation, it is the "free meeting" stage for the accused. Although, this legal document was perfected, the investigating organs still do what they used to do under the pretext that it does not say so in the criminal procedure law. Therefore, the right of meeting was not literally established based on the refinement of the lawyers law.

It wasn't until 2012 when the provision that a meeting without being monitored can be arranged with the three kinds of documents listed-above in the Lawyers Law was built into the Criminal Procedure Law. Since then, the difficulty in exercising the right of meeting has been largely addressed. In addition, the Criminal Procedure Law provides that during the investigation period for crimes endangering State security, involving terrorist activities or involving significant amount of bribes, defense lawyers shall obtain the approval of investigating organs before they meet with the criminal suspects. This actually lays restrictions on the exercise of this right, so I call this period "special restriction" stage.

2.2 Principle of the right of meeting: no later than 48 h

The Article 37, Paragraphs 2 and 3, of 2012 Criminal Procedure Law sets out the principles and exceptions for the exercise of the right of meeting by the accused and the defence, respectively. The Paragraph 2 provides that "where a defense lawyer requests for a meeting with a criminal suspect or defendant under detention on the strength of the lawyer's practicing certificate, and the certification documents and letter of authorization issued by his/her law firm, or an official legal aid document, the detention house concerned shall arrange the meeting in a timely manner, no later than 48 h after receiving the request". Whereas, Article 96 of 1996 Criminal Procedure Law provides that "when a lawyer meets a crime suspect already taken into custody, personnel from the investigating organ may, in light of the circumstances of the case and needs, be assigned to be present. With respect to a case involving State secrets, a lawyer intending to meet the crime suspect already taken into custody shall seek the approval from the investigating organ". The biggest difference is the organ which is responsible for arranging the meeting. It provides that the detention house arranges it in 2012 Criminal Procedure Law, while this work is carried out by the investigating organ stipulated by the 1996 version of this legal document. It seems to make small changes, but the meeting arrangement system is altered. According to the 1996 Criminal Procedure Law, the investigating organ has the right to decide whether or not the meeting can be arranged and when it should be arranged, and whether or not to send officers to present. It can be seen that the right of meeting for the accused is restricted by the expansion of power of investigation. The power of investigation over the right of meeting is the value preference of the legislation at that time. It also indicates that the cart is placed before the horse. However, the 2012 version of this document get it right and provides that the meeting is arranged by the detention house, which means the meeting arrangement system is changed. The detention house is just a detention institution and has no powers to forbid or restrict the meeting, and a lawyer may request a meeting with the three kinds of documents. Compare with the right of meeting of the accused and the defence lawyer, it is the duty rather than the power of the detention house to arrange such meeting. The requirement of presenting the certificates or documents is more of showing qualifications, and does not mean that the detention house has the right to disapprove.

This can be proved by "the detention house concerned shall arrange the meeting in a timely manner, no later than 48 h after receiving the request" in the latter part of Article 37(2). However, why there is a delay of "no later than 48 h" under the principle of arranging the meeting in a timely manner? In my opinion, the legislators mainly consider the following two factors. First, the detention house is not well equipped.[30] Due to the limited space and resources, it is impossible for the accused to meet the defender at any time. Therefore, the time, place and way of meeting depends on the actual condition of the detention house. According to research, since the Criminal Procedure Law was promulgated in 2012, there is still a serious shortage of meeting rooms for lawyers, although detention houses across the country have stepped up efforts to improve facilities to ensure the meeting can be arranged without any delay.[31] When problems arise such as insufficient meeting rooms, the meeting definitely can not be arranged in a timely fashion. Second, there is "physical limitation".[32] It happens when a request to meet the criminal suspect by the lawyer comes at the time of investigation, such as when the criminal suspect in the detention house is brought to the scene for search, inquest and examination, or is being questioned by the investigation organs. At this time, the criminal suspect can not cooperate with the investigation and meet the lawyer at the same time. Therefore, it is impossible to arrange the meeting in a timely manner in order to ensure the smooth running of the investigation.

However, the "physical limitation" invites a question that it is justified to postpone the meeting to ensure the smooth running of investigation when it happens. In fact, this legislative preference can also be seen in Article 33 of the Criminal Procedure Law, which provides that "a criminal suspect shall be entitled to entrust a defender after he/she is interrogated for the first time by an investigating organ or as of the date on which compulsive measures are taken". In the absence of the provision to allow the lawyer to be present in the criminal procedure, Article 33 implies that the meeting can only be arranged after the first interrogation, which is likely to leave the accused at a disadvantage. Generally speaking, there is little possibility for most suspects to hire defence lawyer prior to their first interrogation, let alone the opportunity to meet with him to consult with him on their situation and related rights. The investigating

[30]The detention house is, of course, also affected by force majeure, such as power outages or emergencies (e.g. prison breaks), but such exceptional cases are not universal enough to be discussed in this book.

[31]Chen Weidong and Cheng Lei [24].

[32]"Physical limitation" refers to the circumstance where the suspect is being questioned, or need to be present for on-site investigation and examination, and therefore they can not be available for the meeting. See Hirano Ryuichi [25]. Quoted from Li Minghong: A Review of the Draft of China's Criminal Procedure Law on the Lawyer's Meeting with Criminal Suspects Based on Japanese Law and Human Rights Conventions, Chen Yuncai [26].

organ is likely to obtain a confession against the suspect at this time when the criminal suspects are panic with little knowledge of defending himself. Therefore, legislative preference for power of investigation is not well-conceived.

There is no doubt that the most intense conflict between right and power happens in the investigation period. The battle is drawn between the right of meeting and the power of investigation from the first interrogation carried out or compulsory measures taken. The meeting with a defence lawyer is the prerequisite of obtaining the assistance of a lawyer for a suspect who has lost his personal freedom as a result of compulsory measures such as detention, arrest and residential surveillance. Defense lawyers tell the accused how to deal with the interrogation and protect their legitimate rights and interests with their expertise. However, it should not noted that besides the protection of human rights, it is equally important to ascertain the facts of a crime and punish the crime in the criminal procedure, which are based on the smooth investigation. Therefore, although the right of meeting is totally over the power of investigation according to the Constitution, it is practically not true. Therefore, it is pivotal to address the conflict between them in the investigation period.

This issue also baffles other countries, so we can find solution from an extraterritorial system similar to our criminal procedure system or defence system. As professor Lin Yuxiong said, comparative law can help people develop consciousness of finding problems. By comparison, domestic law may focus on issues that have never been addressed, or come up with solutions that have never been presented to some problems.[33] The designated interview procedure as defined in Article 39(3) of the Code of Criminal Procedure of Japan is similar to the arranged interview procedure in our country. Alongside that, the solution of grand court to this conflict between the investigation power and the right of meeting provides a best practices for China's legislation and for the perfection of China's right of meeting.

Article 39(1) of the Japanese Code Of Criminal Procedure provide that "the accused or the suspect in custody may, without any official being present, have an interview with, or send to or receive documents or articles from defense counsel or prospective defense counsel"; Article 39(1) provides that "a public prosecutor, public prosecutor's assistant officer or judicial police official may, when it is necessary for investigation, designate the date, place and time of the interview or sending or receiving of documents or articles prescribed in paragraph (1) only prior to the institution of prosecution; provided however, that such designation must not unduly restrict the rights of the suspect to prepare for defense." The Article 39(1) formulates the principle that the suspect is given the right to meet with defense counsel at any time, and the Article 39(3) makes an exception that the time and place of the interview may be postponed for the purpose of investigation, without prejudice to the right of the suspect to prepare for defense.

We need to find some precedents to clarify "when it is necessary for investigation". The judgment of "Ando Case" by the Supreme Court of Japan in 1999 provides best practice for addressing the conflict between the power of investigation and the right

[33] Yuxiong Lin [27].

of meeting.[34] The Grand Court said that "it is justified to exercise the power of investigation because of or for the purpose of exercising the power of punishment according to the constitution, and the right of communication between the criminal suspect and the defender, which is born with the constitution, is not totally over the power of punishment or the power of investigation; in order to exercise the right of investigation, it is also necessary to interrogate the suspect whose personal freedom is restricted, which is allowed according to the constitution; so we need to make the exercise of right of interview and the power of investigation not conflict with each other". This means that the right of interview is taken as a priority by principle, and it is not an absolute right and may be restricted by the power of punishment or investigation. The Grand Chamber of the Supreme Court added that "when an investigation agency and a defender make a request for an interview with a suspect, such interview should be arranged at any time". The phrase that "when it is necessary for investigation" in Article 39(3) applies to cases where the interview would suspend the investigation, creating big problem. Where the above-mentioned conditions are met and the interview is designated, it should be interpreted that the investigation agency shall, as soon as possible and by agreement with the defender, designate the date of the interview and take measures to enable the suspect to prepare for defense.[35] The legal reasoning regarding the above decision can seen as an explanation for why the meeting is postponed in the preceding part.

Alongside that, "Uchida Case" in 2000 provide basis for the perfection of the right of meeting in our country. Regarding this case, the Supreme Court of Japan, in addition to reaffirming the above-mentioned gist of the judgment of "Ando Case", declared the importance of the first interview after arrest for the first time and gave a detailed explanation about the restrictions over the first interview by saying that the arrest of a criminal suspect and the first meeting of a defender are among the most important purposes of selecting a defender for a suspect who is physically restrained, as well as the opportunity to get suspect to be questioned by the investigating authorities after the arrest, and a timely-arranged interview was especially important for the defense preparation of a criminal suspect.[36] I think that such practice can be learned by us to refine and protect the right of meeting in our country. Under the current situation where the right to the presence of defenders during interrogation is not prescribed by the criminal procedure law, the interview before interrogation is of

[34]Lawyers A and B wanted to meet the criminal suspects detained in the detention room of the police station for attempted intimidation, but were rejected nine times by the police who managed the detention room. Meanwhile, they were requested to obtain the approval of the prosecutor and to submit a file containing the date of the interview. Therefore, the rights and interests of lawyers to meet with criminal suspects were violated. Then damages were claimed by the Fukushima Prefecture and the central government according to the State Compensation Law. See also from the Lord Chancellor's Interpretation of Communication Rights– a Commentary on the Amendment to Article 34 of the Code of Criminal Procedure(No.654), *The Taiwan Law Review*, 2011(5).

[35]*Precedents by the Supreme Judicial Court of Japan*, 24 March, Heisei 11(1999), Volume 53, No. 3, p.514.

[36]*Precedents by the Supreme Judicial Court of Japan*, 13 June, Heisei 11(2000), Volume 54, No. 2, p.1635.

great significance to ensure the legality of interrogation procedure, prevent extorting a confession by torture, protect the procedural and substantive rights of criminal suspects and ensure the truthfulness of statements. Therefore, I argue that the right of interview should be over the power of investigation when the time conflict happens between the first interrogation and interview. It should be stipulated that that if a criminal suspect requests to meet with a lawyer at the time of the first interrogation, the investigating organ should immediately give way to the interview and ensure that they can obtain legal assistance through meetings with defence counsel prior to the first interrogation.

According to the provision of the right of meeting in the Article 37(2) of the Criminal Procedure Law, it can be seen that the interview can arranged after three required documents are provided and is allowed to be postponed due to the less well-equipped detention house and physical limitation. Ensuring that a criminal suspect or a defendant can meet with a defense lawyer is an important part of the constitutional protection of fundamental human rights. Therefore, it can not be forbidden, but adjustments to when the interview is arranged and how long it lasts are allowed to be made.[37] Therefore, the meeting can be postponed, but no later than 48 h. In my opinion, the first interview should be valued over the first interrogation and can not be delayed in order to protect the right of first interview of the defendant under detention.

2.3 The Exceptions for right of meeting: three kinds of crimes

Under the principle of freedom of meeting, the postponing of an interview on the grounds of physical limitation should be subjected to strict procedure. As to the exception for the interview prescribed in Article 37(3) of the Criminal Procedure Law, we need to find legitimate explanation for it from legislation, in order to restrict the right of meeting in an reasonable way. Before that, we need to discuss the following three issues: What are the investigating organs allowed to restrict the exercise of right of meeting when it comes to the three kinds of crimes? Is it right to have the investigating organ to approve such meeting? Does the measures of restriction conform to the principle of proportionality?

According to the references,[38] I think the reasons for restricting the right of meeting during the investigation are to maintain the order in the detention house,[39] and ensure that people strictly abide by the criminal procedure in order to prevent abuse of such right.[40] However, some laws do not bases this principle. Defenders and their right of communication can be restricted due to the particularity of the

---

[37]Lin Yushun [28].

[38]Chen Xuequan [29], Chen Yuncai [30], Lin Yuxiong [31], Wu Junyi [32], Cai Qiuming [33].

[39]It is incumbent upon the detention house to maintain the order, prevent the detainees from escaping and committing suicide and ensure their safety, so it is necessary to take preventive measures for the meetings of the accused and the defenders.

[40]The protection of criminal procedure and the prevention of abuse of rights refer to the restriction for preventing the abuse of the right of meeting to destroy, falsify evidence, interfere with the testimony of witnesses and hinder the smooth progress of criminal procedure.

facts of the punishable acts. For example, the Sect. 129a of the German Penal Code provides that the right of communication of defender can be restricted if the accused is suspected of establishing a terrorist organization. In addition, such restriction can also be found in the Sect. 148II of the German Criminal Code.[41]

This argument has also beensupported by the European Court of Human Rights, which ruled in 2001 on the Case of Erdem Against Germany.[42] It is about the restriction on the right of meeting in the case of offenses relating to terrorist activities, and the court concluded unanimously that Germany had not violated Article 8 of the European Convention on Human Rights.[43] It can be seen from this judgement that the particularity of the facts of the punishable acts is recognized as a reason for restricting the right of meeting. However, the reason why Germany won the lawsuit is that the security measures provided by German legislation for the restriction of meeting conform to the principle of proportionality, which will be discussed in detail later.

Therefore, there are someforeign judicial precedent and theories to support the argument that particularity of the facts of the punishable acts can be seen as a reason for restricting the right of interview. In addition, the China's legislators, in the revision of the Criminal Procedure Law 2012, define crimes endangering State security, involving terrorist activities or involving significant amount of bribes as three major crime cases in which the right of meeting is restricted, in order to maintain national and public security.[44] Here is a question: why is the bribery crime counted as a factor that restrict the right of interview if the focus of legislation is to, in the view of state interests, improve the ability of crime control. So how to interpret "crimes involving significant amount of bribes" is the key to understand the legislative intent.

The "crimes involving significant amount of bribes" is a legal term created by the criminal procedure law in 2012 and cannot be found in the substantive criminal law. According to the Criminal Procedure Rules of the People's Procuratorates (for Trial), the cases are seen as crimes involving significant amount of bribes in any of the following circumstances: (1) where the amount of the suspected bribery crime is over 500,000 yuan and the circumstances of the crime are serious; and (2) where the case has a major social impact; and (3) where the state interests are seriously damaged. According to the interpretation of the Supreme People's Procuratorate, why this kind of crime is seen as an element that restrict this right is because such crimes are special and can cause serious consequences and great social impact and damage the state interests. So this crime is seen as serious as crimes endangering State security and involving terrorist activities. Does it mean that all cases under the

[41]Wu Junyi [32].

[42]Cai Qiuming [33].

[43]Article8–right to respect for private and family life Everyone has the right to respect for his private and family life,his hone and his correspondence.There shallbe nointerference by a public authority with the exercise of this right except such as is in accordance with the law and is necessary in ademocratic society in the interests of national security,public safety or the economic well-being of the country,for the prevention of disorder or crime,for the protection of health or morals,or for the protection of the rights and freedoms of others.

[44]Lang Sheng [36].

jurisdiction of the intermediate people's court can be seen as special crimes to restrict this right[45]? This interpretation can hardly hold water. Therefore, I think we need to find the legislative intent from the criminal procedure law.

After studying the revised Criminal Procedure Law, it can be found that it provides special criminal procedures for some kinds of crimes. The crimes that the criminal suspects, who are placedunder residential surveillance at a designated place of residence, commit in Article 73 are the same as those that can seen as the reasons to restrict the right of interview in Article 37. The cases endangering State security or involving terrorist activities are recognized as the ones that are under the jurisdiction of the intermediate people's court in Article 20, and Article 83 also stipulates that the family of the detainee is allowed not to be notified of the detention within 24 h after the detention if the detainee is involved in these two kinds of crimes and such notification may hinder the investigation. In addition, the two crimes are also mentioned as exceptions in Article 62 that provides that protective measures shall be taken for personal safety of the witnesses, experts or victims or their close relatives and in Article 148 which stipulates that technical investigation measures can be employed if the case involves these crimes. After studying these kinds of crimes and special provisions, it can be found that there are two characteristics. First, most of the "special provisions" restrict the rights of the participants in the proceedings, especially the criminal suspects, and the case-handling organs have discretionary power. Second, except for trial jurisdiction, "special provisions" apply to the investigation period, and most of them only apply to this period.[46] Therefore, we can know from the above two characteristics that the aim of provisions which stipulate special provisions apply to the investigation period, or the restriction of rights or the expansion of powers is to ensure the smooth running of investigation, protect the criminal procedure and prevent the abuse of power, which are discussed aforementioned.

According to theparagraphs 4 and 5 of Article 49 of the Regulations on the Procedures for the Handling of Criminal Cases by the Public Security Organ (hereinafter referred to as the "Regulations of the Ministry of Public Security"),[47] "impeding the investigation" is seen as the reason to disapprove the meeting, which shows the purpose of restricting the right of meeting. These stipulates that if the Public

[45]Article 20 of the Criminal Procedure Law provides that intermediate people's courts shall have the jurisdiction as courts of first instance over the following criminal cases: (1) Cases endangering State security or involving terrorist activities; and (2) Cases of crimes punishable by life imprisonment or capital punishment.

[46]Zhang Pinze [37].

[47]The paragraphs 4 and 5 of Article 49 of the Regulations on the Procedures for the Handling of Criminal Cases by the Public Security Organ provides that when a public security organ does not approve a meeting, it shall notify the defense attorney in writing and explain the reason. When the circumstances that would impede the investigation or might reveal state secrets are gone, the public security organ shall approve the meeting.

If there are any of the following, it is considered "impeding the investigation" as used in this article: (1) might destroy or fabricate evidence, harass witness or collude on testimony; and (2) might lead to the suspect hurting themself, killing themself or fleeing; and (3) might lead to a co-criminal in the same case escaping or hampering the investigation; and (4) the suspect's family are implicated in the crime.

Security Bureau does not approve the meeting, it shall notify the defense attorney in writing and explain the reason. When the circumstances that would impede the investigation or might reveal state secrets are gone, the public security organ shall approve the meeting. If there are any of the following, it is considered "impeding the investigation": (1) might destroy or fabricate evidence, harass witness or collude on testimony; and (2) might lead to the suspect hurting themself, killing themself or fleeing; and (3) might lead to a co-criminal in the same case escaping or hampering the investigation; and (4) the suspect's family are implicated in the crime. The reason why the right of interview is restricted by "obstruction of investigation" lies in the fact that the investigating authorities are worried that when the defense lawyers exercise the right of interview, they may cross the line to ask something unrelated to the case, such as instigating suspects to destroy and fabricate evidence, commit suicide or escape, which hampers the smooth running of criminal proceedings and make evidence collection and detection more difficult.

However, this seemingly legitimate reason is logically questionable. Article 79 of China's Criminal Procedure Law provides that the criminal suspects or defendants are arrested if they may destroy or falsify evidence, interfere with the witnesses who give testimony or collude with others to make confessions tally or tries to commit suicide or escape. These circumstances are also seen as impeding the investigation. If the suspect has already been detained for a reason to prevent his conduct from impeding the investigation, why is the right of interview further restricted for the same reason? The assumption in paragraphs 3 and 4 of the Regulations of the Ministry of Public Security is that such right is likely to be abused by defense lawyer to instigate the suspects and his or her family members implicated in the crime to hamper the investigation. Taking exceptions as normal, laying restrictions on the right of interview based on presumption and lawlessness and expanding the power of investigation will seriously infringes the right of defense of the accused and shake the foundation of the judicial system, like killing the goose that lays the golden eggs. To say the least, even if defense lawyers engage in illegal activities, we can still hold them accountable under Article 42 of the Criminal Procedure Law and exclude them from ongoing criminal proceedings, and suggest the criminal suspects or help them to find another defense lawyer, rather than restrict such right through legislation.

The legislativeintent of "special provisions" for special crimes such as "crimes involving significant amount of bribes" in Criminal Procedure Law and its related judicial interpretation in our country can be explained by the Enemy Criminal Law proposed by German scholar Jackobs.[48] There are mainly three ways in which Enemy Criminal Law is applied in criminal procedure. First, the misdemeanors and felonies are classified into two types to highlight the extreme danger of felonies, and then restrictions are laid upon the litigation rights of felons. Second, in the view of the utilitarianism, priority should be given to the interests of the investigation and prosecution

[48]Enemy Criminal Law, seen as opposed to citizen criminal law, refers to treating a specific dangerous criminal as a "source of danger" in criminal legislation and judicature, and it means "flawed stability". The criminals are classified according to whether they have reason and personality and treated differently by legislation and justice. The Enemy Criminal Law and the Citizen Criminal Law constitute "the two ends of one world". See Jacobs [38].

authorities. So it is necessary to restrict the lawyer's right to help others, the right of personal freedom and the right of privacy to improve the efficiency of the investigation when it comes to the crimes involving terrorist activities, organized crimes committed by groups in the nature of criminal syndicates, drug-related crimes and the like. Third, it is also important to recognize that both Citizen Criminal Law and Enemy Criminal Law need to be implemented. So legislating separately according to the different types of cases in the same criminal procedure is required.[49] The reason they share the same concept it that Enemy Criminal Law is closely related to our country's political stance(maintaining stability, anti-terrorism, anti-corruption) and the utilitarianism (ensuring the smooth running of investigation and maintaining the order of detention house) in the process of creating legislation.

The legislative intent under the influence by Enemy Criminal Law is more likely to violate the fundamental rights guaranteed by the Constitution. So we need to find out whether it is legitimate to do so. Why German won the lawsuit of Case of Erdem Against Germany judged by the European Court of Human Rights is because that the guarantee measures provided by German legislation for the restriction of rights conform to the principle of proportionality. First, with regard to the circumstances where restrictions are laid, the German Criminal Code defines the particularity of the facts of the punishable acts only as crimes suspected of being committed by terrorist organizations. Second, in terms of the means to use such restrictions, the principle of examination by a neutral judge is applied to correspondence and materials exchanged between the defense lawyers and suspects. The judge is not only not involved in the case, but also has the duty to keep it confidential. German law has created many procedures and systems for people to apply for the restrictions on the fundamental rights, making the restriction of the right of interview conform to the principle of proportionality. However, on the one hand, there is no clear definition of crime involving significant amount of bribes, one the special crimes, in the Criminal Procedure Law of China. If we handle cases according to *The People's Procuratorates' Rules of Criminal Procedure*, powers will be likely to be abused in practice. The expression that "the alleged amount of the bribery is more than 500,000 Yuan" can be construed that anyone who is charged with the amount of bribery is over 500,000 yuan is all suspected, which will "expand the scope of this kind of crime" and probably seriously infringe upon the right of interview of criminal suspect. On the other hand, our law stipulates that the investigating organ that bears the obligation of prosecution has the power to approve such restrictions. This means that it is difficult for the investigating authorities to neutrally examine the grounds for permission and to make a decision on whether or not to grant permission for the meeting. Finally, the Criminal Procedure Law does not clarify a time limit on the restriction of this right, which may result in the deprivation of this right instead of the restriction of it.

As to the exceptions for the exercise of the right of meeting in our country, the legitimate reasons, the agencies that make the decision on restrictions and the proportionality of the restriction means all need to be discussed. Because of the

[49] Shanshan Chen [39].

ambiguity and abstractness of the relevant terms in Article 37, paragraph 3, of the criminal procedure law, it is necessary to give some interpretations. For example, the date is specified in *The People's Procuratorates' Rules of Criminal Procedure.* Article 46, Paragraph 3, stipulates that "people's procuratorates shall permit the defense attorney to meet with criminal suspects before the investigation terminates in especially serious bribery cases", which ensures the interview can be arranged before the end of the investigation. However, it is not clarified by Regulations of the Ministry of Public Security, which provides that when the circumstances that would impede the investigation are gone, the public security organ shall approve the meeting, which facilitates the investigation by the investigating authorities, but creates risk for violation of the right of interview. Therefore, I think that it is necessary to limit the restriction on the right of interview, making the restriction of the right of interview conform to the principle of proportionality.

3. What can be done during the meeting and the way to do it

The first sentence of Article 37, paragraph 4, of the Criminal Procedure Law stipulates that a defense lawyer shall be entitled to inquire about the case and provide legal advice during the meeting with a criminal suspect or defendant under detention and may, from the date on which the case is transferred for examination before prosecution, verify relevant evidence with the criminal suspect or defendant. Three are mainly three kinds of things that defense lawyers are allowed to do. First, they can inquire about the case from the accused, for example, by listening to the statements and justifications of the criminal suspects or defendants so as to make a preliminary judgment of the case. Second, the can give legal advice by providing information to the criminal suspects or defendants to let them know what kind of situation they are in, for example, by telling them about legal provisions relating to the charges against them and his procedural rights. In addition, they are allowed to know which stage of the criminal procedure the case is at and ask whether the rights were violated or a request to lodge a complaint on behalf of the criminal suspects or defendants is needed. Third, they can verify evidence after the stage of examination before prosecution. Defense lawyers may check the files and the relevant materials obtained after investigation and evidence collection with criminal suspects and the defendants to determine whether they are true or not.

Both the meeting between the defendants and defense lawyers about filing petition andcomplaints against the violation of rights and prosecution of the investigative organs and preparation for substantive defence by inquiring about the case and verifying the evidence are what the defendants and defense lawyers can do during the interview to make defence effective. The extent to which the procedural and substantive defense are carried out depends on the trust built between the defendants and the defense lawyers, because the relationship is special. The defense system will become less effective if such trust doesn't exist.[50] Two components are needed to build this kind of trust. First, the defendants do not be afraid of getting into trouble about what they said to the defense lawyers. Second, the defendants and lawyers do not have

[50]Mototeru [40].

to worry about the interference from the public power during the communication. The first component, which is not discussed in this book, relates primarily to the privilege of defense lawyers. The second one is the legislative basis for the right of interview, which allows them to create a space in which they can communicate case-related information without being interfered by public power. In the form of space, it can be based on a "three-dimensional space" or "medium", such as paper letters, e-letters, phone calls and video calls.[51] This concept can be found in the newly-added second sentence of the 4th paragraph of Article 37 of the Criminal Procedure Law of China, which provides that the meeting between the defense lawyer and the criminal suspect or defendant shall not be monitored. This means that the interview shall not be monitored, authorities shall not send personnel to be present and no secret recordings is allowed.[52] This provision is praised by the practical researchers, and all detention houses have detached monitoring devices or turning off the recording in the meeting room to ensure that communications between lawyers and detainees are not monitored and recorded.[53]

Here is one question: can the second sentence of the 4th paragraph of Article 37 above-mentioned be construed as interviews that may be within sight but not within hearing? The principle that interview can be within sight but not within hearing was created during the case of S V. Switzerland by the European Court of Human Rights on the right of defendants under detention to meet with their lawyers.[54] Such protective measure is taken to maintain the order of detention house, so as to avoid lawyers taking the opportunity of meeting to give the suspects some prohibited items. It is legitimate because this kind of surveillance is on what they do, not what they say. This principle is widely adopted in China. Since the implementation of the Criminal Procedure Law in 2012, the practice that personnel are sent to monitor the interview is prohibited. Some monitoring devices are still left in the meeting room, but the detention house has turned off the recording during the interview, which is under the surveillance of prison guards, in order to prevent the lawyer from giving any prohibited items to the detainees, and maintain the order of detention house instead of monitoring what they say. However, it is important to keep certain distance to ensure that they lawyers and suspects can talk freely.

In addition to the way in which the interview is arranged above, there is another way—communication via medium, which can be found in the Article 37 which stipulates the right ofcorrespondence. The right of correspondence, like the right of interview, aims to ensure the free and secret communication between the defendant and the defense lawyer. However, the two kinds of rights are provided in Article 37, Paragraphs 1 and 5, of the Criminal Procedure Law, without any specific provisions on the exercise of the right of correspondence. So this right is yet to be interpreted.

---

[51] Wu Junyi [41].

[52] Lang Sheng [42].

[53] Wei Dong Chen [43].

[54] ECHR,Sv.Switzerland,1991,Series Ano.220,48:"Interviews between the prisoner and his legal adviser maybe within sight but not within hearing,either director in direct,of a police or institution official."

With the advent of the information age and the popularization and application of electronic and network technology, it is more convenient to exchange information in the form of email, audio and video than the paper letters. Therefore, it is necessary to give the interpretation of the right of correspondence to clarity the ways of communication through network medium. Criminal suspects and defendants in custody can not communicate with the outside world at any time by means of mobile phones or the internet, as others do, but they can be offered landline phone and computer to communicate with lawyers via video and voice calls, so as to avoid the possibility of some prohibited items being hidden in the paper letters during interview. As such, the right of correspondence is an important right with more interpretations given. If such is exercised through paper letter, what kind of measures can be taken to prevent any prohibited items from being hidden without unpacking the package of letters. The principle that letters can be opened but not read was created during the case of Campbell and Fell V. U. K by the European Court of Human Rights.[55] Prison staff open, but do not read, letters on the spot in front of the accused and check if anything unrelated is attached to give them privacy, which is a good example for us to follow.

4. Judicial remedy for infringement of the right of interview

Effective and substantive defence requires an increase in access to legal aid and kinds of defence activities as well as some checks and balances and judicial remedy mechanisms, when the right of defence has been infringed unlawfully or improperly by state organs, such as failure to inform the defendants of the rights they are entitled to and improper restrictions on the interview and correspondence between the defendant and the defender, in order to ensure this right is exercised effectively.[56] This is the principle that right and judicial remedy co-exist. There are mainly two ways in which the investigative organ infringes the right of interview. First, the illegal postponement or deprivation of the exercise of the right of interview result in the failure to arrange the meeting in a timely manner or to provide a opportunity of communication between suspects and lawyers. Second, the restrictions, such as the interception of interviews and the opening of correspondence, are used to prevent the accused from communicating freely and secretly with his defence counsel or to obtain information for the investigative authorities. This may lead to the three harmful consequences, including (1) inadequate defensive preparation resulting from failure to arrange to meeting or arrange it in a timely manner; and (2) statement against the defendant himself due to deprivation of the exercise of the right of interview; and (3) obtaining information from interview as evidence in preparation for prosecution. The exclusionary rule can be applied for the relief for last two kinds of damages. However, this rule is only applicable to the confession obtained by illegal methods such as extorting confession by torture, so I propose to include statements obtained in the way of violation of the right of defence. However, exclusionary rule is only an ex post facto remedy method. When the right of interview is violated, it is important to restore the right as soon as possible so that lawyers have sufficient time to prepare

[55]ECHR,Campbell and Fell v.U.K,1984,SeriesAno.80.

[56]Chen Yuncai [44].

their defence. Article 47 of the Criminal Procedure Law provides that a defender or agent ad litem shall be entitled to file a petition or bring a complaint to the people's procuratorate at the same or the next higher level if he or she is of the opinion that the staff members of relevant authorities have hindered his or her lawful exercise of the litigation rights.[57] However, it also provides that people's procuratorate shall notify relevant organs to make correction if the authenticity of petition or complaint is confirmed, which shows that it is not compulsory. If the relevant authorities do not make correction, the issue of the restoration of the violated rights will remain unresolved. Therefore, I propose to substitute the word order for notify, in order to remedy the right of interview in an effective way.

5. Conclusion

When a criminal suspect is deprived of his liberty, isolated from the outside world, upset and has little knowledge of information, he needs the help of a lawyer in order to prepare for defense. Therefore, the right of meeting is extremely important for the accused to obtain the legal aid from a lawyer. It also helps prevent the illegal investigation activities and ensure the trial judicial. The revision of the right of interview in Criminal Procedure Law is a highlight, but there are still many provisions to be interpreted. After the Article 37 is interpreted and analyzed based on cases of Japan and Germany to find our legislative intent and solutions to problems, a conclusion is drawn as follows.

First, the first holder of the right of interview is the defendant under detention, then the defense lawyer.

Second, based on the principle of arranging the interview in a timely manner, a postponement of no more than 48 h is allowed due to less well-equipped detention house and physical limitation, but the first interview should prioritize the first interrogation. As for the three types of special crimes in which circumstances the meeting is subject to restriction, although particularity of the facts of the punishable acts can be seen as a reason for such practice in the view of state interests, but it is less acceptable for the crime involving significant amount of bribes. After studying all the special provisions of the Criminal Procedure Law covering special crimes, it can be found that the reason for restricting the right of interview can still be summed up as hindering investigation. However, this reason is illegitimate because of its illogicality, inappropriateness for the investigating organs to give permission and the disproportionality of the restriction means. Therefore, I think that the judicial interpretation should be given to make the restriction means conform to the proportionality principle.

Third, in order to ensure the detained criminal suspects and defense lawyers can talk freely about case-related information, we are supposed to help them build trust

[57] A defender or agent ad litem shall be entitled to file a petition or bring a complaint to the people's procuratorate at the same or the next higher level if he/she is of the opinion that the relevant public security organ, people's procuratorate, people's court or its staff members have hindered his/her lawful exercise of the litigation rights. The said people's procuratorate shall review the petition or complaint in a timely manner, and notify relevant organs to make correction if the authenticity of petition or complaint is confirmed.

by creating a space without being interfered by public power, including creating a a "three-dimensional space" within sight but not within hearing of personnel of authorities and creating principle that letters can be opened but not read and giving interpretation of different kinds of correspondence.

Fourth, the exclusionary rule is used to exclude the confession obtained by restricting the right of interview and judicial remedies should be provided. In addition, defendants shall be entitled to file a petition or bring a complaint to the people's procuratorate about the violation of their right of interview to restore such right.

5.4 Guarantee of the Right of Consulting Files and the Establishment of a System for Disclosure of Evidence in China

1 The Evolution of Legislation on the Protection of the Right of Consulting Files in China's Criminal Procedure Law

The right of consulting files, one of the most important rights enjoyed by the defense, enables a defense lawyer to consult, excerpt and reproduce the case file materials in the proceedings so as to obtain sufficient information before the trial and ensure the right of defense can be exercised at the trial stage. This right is so important that it was built into the 1979 Criminal Procedure Law, which provides that the defendant shall have the right to receive a copy of the indictment of the people's procuratorate 7 days before the court session, and shall be informed that a defender may be entrusted or appointed if necessary and the defence lawyer has access to the materials of the case.[58] In accordance with the provisions of 1979 Criminal Procedure Law, defence lawyers are not allowed to exercise the right of consulting files until 7 days before the court session. Although the defence lawyers may not conduct a comprehensive study of the case file for a well-prepared defence, they can get enough information of the case because the case file materials transferred to the court from the people's procuratorate include all the evidence collected during the investigation and prosecution. Therefore, the right of consulting files was, without controversy, granted to the defense lawyer before 1996.

In order tocreate an adversarial system, the provision of case file materials that need to be transferred in the 1979 criminal procedure law was revised in 1996, by substituting "a list of evidence, name list of witness and photocopies and photos

[58]See Articles 29 and 110 of the 1979 Criminal Procedure Law. Article 29 provides that a defense lawyer may consult the case file materials, meet and correspond with the defendant under detention, and other defenders, with the permission of the people's court, may also get more information of the case and meet and correspond with the defendant under detention. Article 110, paragraph 2 (b), provides that a copy of the indictment of the People's Procuratorate shall be delivered to the defendant no later than 7 days before the court session and the defendant shall be informed that he has the right to entrust defender or, if necessary, people's procuratorate shall designate a lawyer as his defender.

of major evidence"for "all case file materials". As for the other evidence, it will be produced by the prosecution in court and will be cross-examined by the defence. The new trial system implements the principles of presenting evidence by prosecution and defense, cross-examination, and debate, supported by verification by the court, which combines the merits of adversarial system system and the inquisitorial system.[59] The main purpose of the reform is to prevent the judge from prejudging, maximize the function of court hearing, and make the court adversarial. The 1996 criminal procedure Law moved up the time for lawyers and other defenders to participate in criminal proceedings in order to ensure that the defense and the prosecution are on an equal footing, and a new provision that defence lawyer has the right to investigate and obtain evidence and to apply to the people's procuratorate and people's court for the obtaining and collecting evidence at both the prosecution and trial stages was added. However, legislators have ignored a crucial issue: the fact that the case file materials which need to be transferred are not as many as before, to some extent, avoids the preconceptions of judges, but has significantly limited the right of the defence to consult the case files. According to Article 36 of the 1996 Criminal Procedure Law, lawyers may consult the indictment and technical appraisal materials of the case at the examination before prosecution stage. At the trial stage, the lawyer may consult the materials of the facts of the crime charged against in the case. According to Article 150, the files provided by the public prosecution organ include only the indictment, a list of evidence, name list of witness and photocopies and photos of major evidence. However, lawyers are not actually allowed to consult all these materials. The prosecution often only provides a list of evidence. For example, only a list of witnesses, but no testimony of witness are provided, and only materials that prove guilty or heavy offense, but no exculpatory or extenuating evidence are provided.[60] Before the trial began, the defense lawyers were unable to consult many evidential materials of the case, making it difficult for the lawyers to be well prepared for the defense. If the prosecution in court presented some evidence that had not been transferred to the court before, the defense would make no adequate defense. The problem that the lawyers find it difficult in consulting case file materials results in

[59]Chen Weidong [45].

[60]The practice of "concealment of evidence" by the prosecution that can be widely found results from the provisions of Article 283 of *The People's Procuratorates' Rules of Criminal Procedure*, which came into effect on January 18,1999. It provides that when the people's procuratorate transfers a case for prosecution, it is the case-handling officer who determines what kind of materials are seen as main evidence based on this article and the value of each material in a specific case. The main evidence is the evidence that proves the defendant guilty and can be used for conviction and sentencing. The main evidence includes: (1) the evidence that is important for many other kinds of evidential materials in the indictment; and (2) the evidence that is important for more than one type of evidential materials; and (3) the evidence of legally prescribed circumstances of sentencing, such as voluntary surrender, meritorious service, recidivism, suspension of sentence, attempted crimes and self-defense. Where the main evidence is documentary evidence, written records of witness testimony, victim's statement, defendant's confession and defense, and investigation and examination, only those parts that prove that the defendant constitutes a crime may be photocopied, and only the conclusion of expert testimony may be copied reproduced.

a one-man show for the prosecution and makes the adversarial system designed by the 1996 Criminal Procedure Law being merely a formality.

In response to the issues created by the 1996 Criminal Procedure Law, it was revised and reinstated the system that case file materials shall be transferred before trial in 2012. This legal document also stipulates that a defense lawyer may, from the date on which the relevant people's procuratorate begins to examine the case for prosecution, consult, excerpt and reproduce the case file materials, which expands the scope of what the lawyers can do to the files materials. It also repealed the provision that what the lawyers can do about the case files at the prosecution stage and the trial stage separately. Such reform make both sides on an equal footing in the proceedings and enables the defense to get adequate information about the case file materials at the prosecution and trial stages so as to be well prepared for proof-providing, cross-examination and debate in the trial and prevent him from being placed in a disadvantage.

However, the provision of the right of consulting case file materials in 2012 Criminal Procedure Law needs to be refined, because there are still a lot of questions about this right to be answered. What should the defender do when he finds that evidence in favour of the suspect or the defendant has not been included in the case file materials? Does the defendant have the right to consult the files and how to exercise it? Are the materials of video and audio recording of interrogations and evidentiary material collected through the technical investigation are allowed to be consulted? In addition, it should be noted that 2012 Criminal Procedure Law provides that the defender is obliged to offer three types of evidence to the authorities concerned.[61] What are the legal consequences if the defendant does not inform the authorities of such kinds of evidence? This kind of problems need to be solved. The common law system and the civil law system respectively provide us with two kinds of systems to further improve the right of access to the case materials according to the differences of their litigation procedures. One is disclosure of evidence in common law system; the other one is the right of consulting case file materials in civil law system. We will discuss next about which is more suitable for our country.

2. The comparative advantage of discovery system and the way to go for China

2.1 The comparative advantage of discovery system

For the protection of the right of access to the case materials, the common law countries adopt the system of disclosure of evidence, while the civil law countries adopt the system of giving the right of consulting case materials because of the different litigation procedures. Although these two system play similar role in ensuring that the defense could get adequate information, they are different in the following aspects.

[61] Article 40 of the 2012 Criminal Procedure Law provides that where a defender has gathered evidence showing that the criminal suspect concerned was not at the scene of the crime, has not reached the age for assuming the criminal liability, or is a mentally challenged person who is not required by law to assume the criminal liability, the defender shall inform the relevant public organ and people's procuratorate of such evidence in a timely manner.

First, they have different legal intents. The disclosure of evidence in common law system aims to limit the judge's access to evidence before trial but the prosecution and the defence are aware of the evidence, while the other one adopted by civil law system is that the judge is fully aware of the evidence so as to prepare to preside at the court hearing, and the defense is prepared for the trial with the evidence he is aware of.

Second, the disclosure of evidence is a two-way system that allows the prosecution and defense to exchange information, while system of giving the right of consulting case materials is a one-way system that the defense is allowed to consult what the prosecution provides. Under the latter system, on the one hand, judges must be allowed to access all case materials before and at the trial, or else it will results in the failure of the operation of the trial procedure of the inquisitorial system; on the other hand, the defense has less impact on the proceedings and enjoy the "privilege" to consult case materials.

Through the comparison between the two systems, we can find that the disclosure of evidence has the following advantages.

First, it prevents the judge from prejudging. This system is designed to enable both sides to make good preparation for the trial, while the other system in the civil law countries is aimed to enable the judges to access the files before the trial to prepare for it, which does not prevent the judge from prejudging and make the judgment less judicial.

Second, it discloses the evidence to the greatest extent. Under the system of consulting case materials, the defence is not usually required to present evidence to the prosecution. The disclosure of evidence requires both sides to disclose evidence, which enables both of them to examine the evidence in the case in a comprehensive manner, especially the evidence that helps the prosecution to know about the defence and to prevent being caught unprepared or unnecessary litigation.

2.2 The necessity of establishing system of disclosure of evidence in China

In the context of China's system, it is important to establish the system of disclosure of evidence to protect the right of the defense to know the natural choice. The reasons are as follows.

First, the 1996 Criminal Procedure Law makes a comprehensive revision of the criminal proceedings, including clarifying the functions of the prosecution, the defense and the judge, weakening the judicial investigating power of judges, expand the powers of the prosecution and the defense on the hearing of court, which shows that adversary system is gradually established. From the inquisitorial system to adversary system is what the reform of criminal procedure is aimed at. In 2012, the provision of "respecting and protecting human rights" was built into the renewed Criminal Procedure Law and was guaranteed by a series of regulations. This further demonstrates the protection of the human rights of the accused under the adversary system, a better understanding of the status of the accused, the democracy and worldwide litigation proceedings and international norms. This makes us firmly believe that the adversary system is the way to go.

Second, the 2012 Criminal Procedure Law further improves the defense system, guarantees the right to practice as a lawyer, and expands the scope of legal aid. Given that more rights are given to the defense to investigate and obtain evidence, the defense is asked to disclose three kinds of special evidence to the prosecution, which shows that we are try to make the both sides on an equal footing and to make the adversary system a reality.

Third, an impartial procuratorate is essential to the exercise of the right to consult case file materials in the civil law countries. In our country, the laws stipulate that prosecutors and investigators must collect all kinds of evidence that can prove the innocence or misdemeanour of the criminal suspect and the defendant according to the legal procedure. However, it should be noted that Chinese and US prosecutors share the same function to collect evidence to prove the defendant's guilt. Therefore, the system of disclosure of evidence is suitable for our country.

In addition, there is another important reason to implement this system. Italy and Japan, the two countries that first choose the mixed development path, provide practices for us to revamp our criminal procedure. The fact that they change their system from consulting case files to disclosing evidence show that the latter system can help protect the right of the defense to consult case files.

3. The framework of establishing system of disclosure of evidence in China

3.1 Subject of evidence disclosure

The subject of evidence disclosure refers to the person who is obliged to disclose evidence and the has the right to know about the evidence in the process of evidence disclosure. Therefore, the defense and the prosecution are the two main actors. The prosecutor is without question the subject for the prosecution, but whether the subject for the defence includes other defenders and defendants who do not entrust any defenders in addition to lawyers. Should the judges participate in the process? If so, what kind of role do they play?

3.1.1 Whether the defendant who does not entrust a defender is a subject of evidence disclosure

The implementation of the evidence disclosure involves the negotiation and confrontation between the prosecution and the defence, and is important for the defence to make good preparation, and it is also technically demanding. The countries where this system is adopted often require the participation of a lawyer who is also seen as the main participant. However, due to the fact that few defendants entrust lawyers and limited legal aid that they can access in China, the condition that the lawyers are asked to participate is often not satisfied. Therefore, how to implement this system under the circumstance where defendants do not entrust lawyers is one of the problems that need to be solved.

In our country, there are two kinds of defendants that do not entrust defense lawyers: the ones who do not entrust defenders and those who defend themselves. For the first kind of defendants, Article 38 of the Criminal Procedure Law stipulates that "A defense lawyer may, from the date on which the relevant people's procuratorate begins to examine the case for prosecution, consult, excerpt and reproduce the case file materials. Other defenders, with permission of the people's procuratorate or people's court, may also consult, excerpt and reproduce the above-mentioned materials." It can be seen that other defenders also have the right to access these files. Some restrictions are laid on the way in which the other defenders access the case file materials in order to ensure that such practice is under the oversight of judicial department concerned, and such limit is only necessary if the access to the files is likely to result in collusion or impediment to the proceedings. If there is no impediment to any proceedings, the people's procuratorate and the people's court shall permit other defenders to have the same right to access files as lawyers. Therefore, the status of other defenders is basically equal to that of lawyers, which indicates that other defenders can also represent the defendants at the evidence disclosure.

As for the second kind of defendants, whether they can be seen as the actor to participate in the evidence disclosure, and how to carry out such procedure are the problems that need to be solved. The only material that these defendants can see before the trial is the indictment which only includes a list of the types of evidence without any details. Aside from whether the defendants have evidence awareness, they, when receiving an indictment, can only make objections against the charges. In this context, the defense of the defendant, who knows nothing about the details of evidence, is just an argument without evidence at the trial. How can they cross-examine the evidence presented by the prosecution? How can they be well prepared for the defense? How can their evidence be convincing? This will bring harm to the right of defense and the trial. From the perspective of legal principle, the defendant should be entitled to the right to access case files, and this right is essential for the defendants to exercise the right to know and the right of cross-examination. Obtaining legal assistance from a lawyer only ensure that the defendant can make a good preparation for the trial, but can not be used as the restriction on the exercise of right by the defendant. Otherwise, this practice will break the principle of equal protection and even cause people to misunderstand that lawyer right is more important that the defendant right. Therefore, the defendant that does not entrust defenders is of course the actor of evidence disclosure.

However, two problems may occur if defendants that do not entrust a defense lawyer is taken as the subject of evidence disclosure. First, the lack of legal knowledge and evidence awareness of the defendant makes the evidence disclosure less effective. Second, practices that impede the judicial procedure may happen, such as retracting confession, colluding, even destroying and falsifying evidence.[62] To solve the two problems, I think a detailed list of evidence need to be made on the basis of the investigation files by the procuratorial organs, and details should be given for the main evidence in the list. The people's court may, when serving a copy of the indictment

[62]As for the second problem, the investigating authorities may be over-anxious. According to the Criminal Procedure Law, the defenders can only access the files at the stage of examination before prosecution, so they can enjoy this right at this stage when the investigation is over and the evidence is fixed. If the evidence is true and included in the case file, it is very difficult for them to impede the proceedings by retracting confession.

to defendants, serve the list of evidence to them at the same time which includes the details such as the where the evidence is gathered and facts that need to be proved, so as to achieve the purpose of evidence disclosure. At the same time, if defendants asks for a comprehensive review of the case file, we can use technical means to reproduce the evidence relevant to the case, such as presenting the case file to the accused in electronic form, in order to prevent them from destroying and falsifying the evidence.

3.1.2 Whether judges should participate in the disclosure of evidence

Since the adversarial system is being established in China, it seems justified for the trial judge to be involved in the system of evidence disclosure in order to prevent the trial from being a formality, make the judgement judicial and avoid prejudgment. However, this does not mean that judges other than the ad litem judges can not play a role in this procedure. As we all know, the right without being guaranteed is equivalent to no right at all, and the system of disclosure of evidence without dispute adjudication and relief mechanism is difficult to operate effectively, making it hard to realize the right to know. Although the court, as a third party for the prosecution and the defence, is not suitable as the subject of disclosure of evidence, it can make decisions by using authority of command in litigation and jurisdiction to ensure the smooth running and the realize the right to know about the evidence. For example, in pre-court meetings, disclosure of evidence can be presided over by a non-ad litem judge who rule on disputes arising from the procedure; in a court hearing, the party in breach of the rules of disclosure of evidence should be punished accordingly and the other party is given appropriate relief.

3.2 The rules of evidence disclosure system

Before drawing up rules on the evidence disclosure system, it important to identify it is an one-way discovery or two-way evidence disclosure system. I think that two-way disclosure is more in line with the development trend of modern disclosure system and China's legislative basis and practice. First, both judicial justice and efficiency are essential to the modern criminal procedure. In order to improve the quality of court hearing and the efficiency of litigation, some countries are reforming the system of disclosure of evidence. For example, the renewed laws of United Kingdom and the United States stipulate that the defense also need to disclose evidence to the prosecution. Second, Article 40 of the Criminal Procedure Law requires the defense to present evidence to the prosecution that the criminal suspect concerned was not at the scene of the crime, has not reached the age for assuming the criminal liability, or is a mentally challenged person who is not required by law to assume the criminal liability, which lays foundation for the implementation of the two-way disclosure. Finally, the newly-added provision in this legal document to protect lawyers' right to defense will give them more rights to obtain evidence in the future. Therefore, both the prosecution and the defense have the obligation to disclose the evidence to each other against the backdrop, so as to ensure judicial fairness and trial efficiency.

However, it should be noted that the two-way disclosure only indicates that both sides have the obligation to disclose evidence, and does not mean that the two sides share the same obligation. Whether they have the same obligation determines what kind of rules to be made. We hold that the prosecution should bear more disclosure obligation than the defense, which means a two-way unequal evidence disclosure system should be adopted. This helps to make both sides "on an equal footing". There are main three reasons. First, aside from the fact that the defendants who do not entrust lawyers can not confront the prosecution, those who have lawyers to defend them can not be compared with the police force specialized in investigation activities and the prosecutors with various kinds of compulsory investigation powers in the aspects of promptness and ability to investigate and collect evidence. Therefore, this disparity determines the implementation of unequal disclosure in our country. Second, although our country has established the right for the criminal suspect and the defendant who can not be compelled to testify against themselves, but this right has been compromised by the "obligation of telling the truth". Therefore, it is easy for the prosecution to collect a large amount of evidence of criminal suspects and defendant's confession. Under the circumstance where the defense has already provided the prosecution with the most important verbal evidence, it is reasonable to ask the prosecution to disclose more evidence. Third, Article 2 of China's Criminal Procedure Law provides that criminals are punished and innocent people are protected from criminal prosecution, which means that the public prosecutors who exercises the right of prosecution on behalf of the state assume the roles of both "one party" to prosecuting the crime and "public interest representative" to enforce laws impartially. Therefore, these roles make the prosecution bear more responsibilities than the defence in the system of evidence disclosure.

In a nutshell, in accordance with the principle of two-way unequal disclosure, different rules are drawn up as below about what can kind of evidence subject to disclosure by the defense and the prosecution respectively.

3.2.1 The prosecution's disclosure

First, the statutory disclosure of evidence refers to those that the prosecution want to present in the trial. The prosecution should also open file first, which is mandatory. According to Article 38 of the Criminal Procedure Law, a defense lawyer may, from the date on which the relevant people's procuratorate begins to examine the case for prosecution, consult, excerpt and reproduce the case file materials. Because most of the evidence presented by the prosecution in court has been included in the case file, what the defense is allow to access can be seen as the materials that the prosecution should disclose. It should be noted that the right to access the case file materials herein is different from the that in the civil law system mentioned above. The former is a way to carry out the disclosure procedure, and such way can make the case file opened to the greatest extent. This is called open file in the United States which is the is the most effective mechanism in the evidence disclosure system. According to the provisions of Article 38, what the defender can access is the evidential material and litigation documents that can prove the criminal suspects guilty or not and the severity of the crime and are transferred by the investigating organs to the procuratorate and those from procuratorate to the court.[63]

Second, the evidence that need to be disclosed at the request refers to the evidence that is not intended to be used by the prosecution in court, but should be disclosed if it is requested by the defense. The right to access the case file materials is the best way of disclosure, but the evidence presented by the prosecution should not be limited to that presented during the trial, but should also include what is not intended to be used during the trial, and need to be disclosed at the defense's request. When a defender meets with a criminal suspect or defendant, consults a file and investigates a case, it may be found that the evidence of innocence or misdemeanour collected by the investigating organ or the procuratorate has not been transferred with the case because it is not accepted or for other reasons. According to Article 39 of the Criminal Procedure Law, the defender shall be entitled to apply with the people's procuratorate or the people's court concerned to obtain such evidence. The defense may of course request the prosecution to present such evidence.

Second, the exception to file opening to the defense. If evidence that involves state secrets and the disclosure of some evidence may cause severe damage to the investigation of other cases, for example, the discovery of evidence in a technical investigation, such evidence may not be disclosed to the defense. This is the restriction laid by the prosecutor after weighing the interests between the state interest and the defendant.[64] However, it is the court that determines whether the evidence involves state secrets or whether the disclosure of some evidence may cause severe damage to the investigation of other cases. If the prosecution is of the opinion that the evidence should not be opened, it shall apply with the court for immunity, and the court shall decide whether to open it or not. If the court decides not to open it, it shall mark the level of secrecy and make it the case materials filed separately.

Finally, as towhat kind of evidence subject to disclosure by the prosecution, there are several special types of evidence that need to be further discusses. First, whether all witness statements referred to in the case file need to be presented to the defence. This is also one of the most controversial issues among the scholars. The focus is whether the disclosure of testimony, names and addresses of witnesses will exert pressure on the prosecution witness, causes the witness to change testimony, and endanger the safety of the witness. Some states have made it clear that statements made by witnesses to the prosecution or the defence are not subject to mandatory disclosure to the other party.[65] This rule, on the one hand, ensure that a witness on both sides of the case would not change statement in some way by the other before the trial, and, on the other hand, ensure that the national courts would adopt the principle

---

[63] Lang Sheng [46].

[64] Yinghui, Wei Xiaona [47].

[65] Rule 16 of the United States Federal Rules of Criminal Procedure provides that, except as specifically provided by law, statements made to the prosecution by government witnesses or prospective government witnesses are not subject to government's disclosure; Statements made by or on behalf of the government or defence witnesses, or the statement intended by the prospective government witnesses or defence witnesses, to the defendant, attorney or agent of the defendant are not information disclosed by the defendant.

of the principle of directness and verbalism in their proceedings. The witness's testimony that is seen as the basis of verdict can only be cross-examined by both parties in the court, and the written testimony is only an exception with legal reasons. However, so few witnesses appear in court in our country and the principle of conveyance of whole dossier was reinstated in 2012 Criminal Procedure Law, so judges are very likely to determine the facts of the case according to the written testimony. In such circumstances, it would be difficult for the defence to make effective defense preparations if the prosecution did not present its own witness statements. Therefore, the testimony of witnesses whom the prosecution does not want to appear in court must be presented to the defence, and that, in the event of an objection to the testimony of such witnesses, the prosecution witness must be required to appear before the court and be cross-examined by both the prosecution and the defence in order to confirm the evidence for a decision. In addition, witness protection in special cases can not be ignored. For witnesses who need protection, only their testimony, excluding their names, addresses, units and other personal information, can be disclosed. Second, the provision that recording or videotaping shall run throughout the interrogation process is added to the 2012 Criminal Procedure Law.[66] This procedure not only can preserve and fix the criminal suspect's confession, but also regulate the investigation and protect the defendant's rights. Moreover, whether the audio and video recording materials obtain from the system are legal evidence, and whether they should be transferred along with the case,[67] whether recording materials are subject to disclosure are all what we need to discuss in this chapter. Before that, it is necessary to

---

[66]In 2005, the Supreme People's Procuratorate issued the *Provisions of the Supreme People's Procuratorate on Implementing Synchronous Audio and Video Recording throughout the Whole Process of Interrogation of Duty-related Criminal Suspects (for Trial Implementation)*, and a well-conceived plan was put forward to implement it. On December 4, 2006, the General Office of the Supreme People's Procuratorate issued the *Workflow* for *Supreme People's Procuratorate on Implementing Synchronous Audio and Video Recording throughout the Whole Process of Interrogation of Duty-related Criminal Suspects (for Trial Implementation)* and the *Regulations on System for Supreme People's Procuratorate on Implementing Synchronous Audio and Video Recording throughout the Whole Process of Interrogation of Duty-related Criminal Suspects (for Trial Implementation)*, which regulate how to carry out this procedure. As of October 1, 2007, this procedure had been, by and large, implemented by procuratorial organs across the country according to the legal documents above. Therefore, 2012 criminal Procedure Law established the system and Article 121 stipulates that investigators, when interrogating a criminal suspect, may record or videotape the interrogation process, and shall do so where the criminal suspect is involved in a crime punishable by life imprisonment or capital punishment or in a otherwise major criminal case. Recording or videotaping shall run throughout the interrogation process for the purpose of completeness.

[67]Since this Provisions was implemented in 2005, some investigating departments do not transfer the audio and video recordings or only transfer part of them to the defendant. Therefore, the renewed Criminal Procedure Law shall make it clear that the recording materials shall be transferred with the case files. However, the legislators dodged this issue. In the draft amendments drafted by the Legislative Affairs Commission of the Standing Committee of the National People's Congress, it was stipulated that the audio and video recordings should be made in two copies synchronously, one to be transferred along with the case files, the other to be archived for reference and kept safely. After discussion and departmental coordination, the regulation was removed from the draft amendment submitted to the Standing Committee of the National People's Congress at its 22nd meeting in August 2011. See Chen Weidong [48].

discuss whether the recording materials fall within the category of evidence. If they are seen as evidence, we can identify whether they are subject to disclosure. If this procedure is only considered as a means of monitoring interrogations,[68] this kind of evidence should not be subject to disclosure. We believe the functions for the system of audio and video recording include (1) preserving and fixing the statement of the criminal suspect and regulating the investigation; and (2) preventing the extortion of confession by torture and protecting the rights of the defendant. For the first function, the recording materials are are better than the interrogation record which is also a method to fix the statement because of the diversity of information, the completeness of recording and the recreating of the interrogation.[69] So such recording materials to preserve and fix criminal suspect statement are legal evidence, same as the statement from the criminal suspect. For the second function, the audio–video recording materials, which can prove whether the investigating organs violate the law or even commit a crime during the interrogation, are also seen as evidence. Therefore, these audio-visual recording materials as legal evidence are of course to be transferred in its entirety with the case files and disclosed to the defense. Third, whether the evidence from technical investigation is subject to disclosure. Although it is not clarified in he 2012 Criminal Procedure Law, Article 20 of *Provisions of the Supreme People's Court, the Supreme People's Procuratorate, the Ministry of Public Security, the Ministry of State Security, the Ministry of Justice, and the Legislative Affairs Commission of the Standing Committee of the National People's Congress on Several Issues concerning the Implementation of the Criminal Procedure Law* provides that if the materials of technical investigation are used as evidence, the legal document approving the adoption of technical investigation measures shall be attached to the case files; and defense lawyers may consult, excerpt and reproduce them according to law, and may present them to the court in the trial. Therefore, the technical investigation materials are subject to disclosure. However, in view of the particularity of the evidence of technical investigation, when the evidence of technical investigation may endanger the personal safety of an individual, involve state secrets or disclosure of such evidence may reveal the investigative secrets or seriously damage the business secrets or personal privacy, the prosecution shall first take protective measures and technical methods to ensure that the disclosure is carried out in the way of without reveal the identity of the persons concerned.

---

[68]At the beginning of the implementation of the procedure, the Supreme People's Procuratorate declared that it can help (1) fix key evidence; and (2) prevent the suspect from retracting his confession and lodge a false accusation against the case-handling police officer; and (3) find new leads by in the case by recreating the trial process; and (4) draw lessons from the past, and strengthen the training of police officers through practice. Therefore, it can be seen that an see that synchronous audio and video recording is a means of monitoring interrogation to prevent torture to extort a confession and prevent a suspect from retracting his confession or lodging a false accusation against the case-handling police officer, so these recording materials can not be used to prove the facts of the case and such materials can not be taken as evidence. Zheng Gaojian [49].

[69]Chen Yongsheng [50].

3.2.2 The defense's disclosure

First, all evidence presented by a defence lawyer at a trial should in principle be presented to the prosecution. On the one hand, with respect to the discovery of exculpatory evidence for a suspect or defendant, and exculpatory evidence is not limited to the evidence showing that the criminal suspect concerned was not at the scene of the crime, has not reached the age for assuming the criminal liability, or is a mentally challenged person, as stipulated in Article 40 of the Criminal Procedure Law, also includes other evidence that does not constitute the alleged offence. On the other hand, the evidence that subject to disclosure also include the materials about circumstances of sentencing and discretion on sentencing.

Second, whether the records of the interview between the defense lawyers and the criminal suspects or the defendants are subject to disclosure. These records are what they talk about and may include some secrets and even evidence against the suspects or defendants. In addition, according to newly added provision in the 2012 Criminal Procedure Law, defense lawyers will not be monitored when they meet with criminal suspects or defendants. When the conversation between them is strictly confidential, it is not appropriate to disclose these records.

Third, whether the defense lawyer should present his defense opinions to the prosecution. Advocates argue that since the prosecution has made available to the defense an indictment containing facts of the charges, opinions on prosecution and the basis, the defense should also do so. However, I disagree with it. The materials that are subject to disclosure should be evidence, so the materials, such as defense opinions obtained through the reasoning of lawyers based on the facts of the case, evidence, laws and his expertise, should not be disclosed. Of course, the defense is allowed to submit his defense opinions to the procuratorate at the stage of examination before prosecution and present its arguments of defence to the prosecution before the trial, but he is not obliged to do so.

3.3 The procedure of evidence disclosure system

3.3.1 Prior to prosecution: informal disclosure procedure

The procedure of evidence disclosure involves how, when, where it is carried out and who to preside over it. To protect the defence's right to know, disclosure of evidence is an ongoing process that can take place at all pre-trial stages. Therefore, it is necessary to discuss it in different stages to make it more clear. At the investigation stage, the defense should have the right to know about the crucial investigation and the evidence produced. The prosecution must, for example, base the decision of detention on certain evidence, which the defence can learn of through pre-trial proceedings. The defense can also open its file to the prosecution through the procedure of hearing defense attorney opinions, so the disclosure at the investigation stage is often incidental to detention and other procedures. At the stage of examination before prosecution, defense lawyers can go to the special places set up by the people's procuratorate to consult, excerpt and reproduce the case file materials, and the disclosure at this stage can be carried out in an informal way according to the decision made by the both sides. When to carry it out can be determined by the public prosecution department in a timely manner upon the defense's application and there is no need for an officer to preside over it. Furthermore, the access of the defense to the case file materials presented by the prosecution is how the procedure works, and the defense may present the evidence in its possession to the prosecution.

It should also be noted that there are two kinds of free disclosure. The first is the disclosure of evidence with the participation of the defence. In such case, the defense is allowed to become aware of the relevant evidence by accessing the case file materials, and thereafter to meet with the defendant in a timely manner to present and verify such evidence to the defendant, and the prosecution in the agreed time should opened files to the defense.[70] The second is the disclosure of evidence without a defense. As mentioned above, the list of evidence transferred by the procuratorate shall be exhaustive. When a copy of the indictment is served on the defendant, the court also provides the list of evidence to hear his opinions on the prosecution's evidence.

3.3.2 After prosecution: formal disclosure procedure

The disclosure of evidence is a continuous process, but its formal procedure is conducted after the prosecution and before the trial. This is because the functions of this procedure are to prevent the defense from being caught by little knowledge of the evidence presented by the prosecution and guarantee the right of the defense to know so as to make the trial impartial. But such functions are based on the fact that a trial needs to be conducted, or else it is unnecessary to disclose evidence if it is not even determined whether the case needs to be prosecuted or whether the trial needs to be conducted. Therefore, the formal procedure of disclosure takes place after the prosecution and before the trial.

The formal disclosure of evidence, I think, can be arranged in the pre-trial meeting. Article 182, paragraph 2, of 2012 Criminal Procedure Law establishes pre-trial meeting system with Chinese characteristics. It is not only because the evidence disclosure system and pre-trial meeting system share the features of fairness and efficiency, but also one of the functions of the pre-trial meeting—credibility—is consistent with the purpose to conduct evidence disclosure. The credibility function is to ensure the prosecution and the defense are well-equipped, the defense can have

---

[70] Article 49 of The People's Procuratorates' Rules of Criminal Procedure (Provisional), promulgated on November 22, 2012, stipulates that The case management department shall make timely arrangements for defense counsel or other defenders with the permission of the people's Procuratorate, to consult, extract and duplicate case files, and the prosecution department shall provide the case files materials. If due to the public prosecution department's work or other factors arrangements cannot be promptly made, an explanation shall be given to the defender and the public prosecution shall cooperate in arranging for the files to be read within three business days. The reading, copying and reproduction of case file materials shall be conducted in special venues established by the people's procuratorate. When necessary, the people's procuratorate may appoint staff to assist at the venue. Defenders copying case materials may do so by means of photocopy or photography, and the people's procuratorate will only collect necessary work capital. The people's procuratorate shall reduce or waive the feels for reproducing case file materials for defense counsel handling legal aid cases on the basis of the specific case circumstances.

access to all the prosecution's case files and evidence, including the evidence for and against the defendant.[71] China's pre-trial meeting provides a procedural platform to connect the examination before prosecution with the trial. Many systems can be c on this platform. Therefore, it can be seen from the expression of "other trial-relevant issues" in Article 182(2) that the evidence disclosure system can be carried out. Furthermore, the date, place, presiding officer and what should be disclosed for the formal discovery of evidence after the indictment can be determined according to the procedure of the pre-trial meeting. According to the Criminal Procedure Law, judges may convene a meeting with the public prosecutor, the parties concerned, the defenders and the agents ad litem. The date of disclosure is when the pre-trial meeting is hold, and it should be carried out at the people's court. As for the presiding officer of the pre-trial meeting, he or she shall be a judge who hear a case according to the current regulations. However, I think it is better to have a judge who file a case to undertake this task in order to avoid the prejudgment. ②With regard to what should be disclosed, since most of the evidentiary material is available to the defence through informal discovery at the stage of examination before prosecution, the files that should be opened by the prosecution to the defence are mainly the evidence gathered after the indictment and that not included in the case files but need to be disclosed upon the defense's request. What the defense should disclose is the evidence showing that the criminal suspect concerned was not at the scene of the crime, has not reached the age for assuming the criminal liability, or is a mentally challenged person who is not required by law to assume the criminal liability. It should be noted that there are two reason to arrange the procedure of discovery of evidence in the pre-trial meeting. First, it can help sort out the main materials. During the pre-trial meeting hold by judges, both sides can screen the case files through the disclosure procedure to identify the main evidence and disagreement, which makes judges to focus on the disputes in the trial. Second, it can help to solve the disputes arising from discovery of evidence before prosecution. If the parties fail to reach an agreement on such issues as the date of evidence discovery and what should be disclosed, the court does not have the power to settle them at the stage of investigation and examination before prosecution, but they can be addressed by judges in the pre-trial meeting.

3.4 Relief measures of evidence disclosure system

Although the disclosure system has been introduced, what the judiciary authorities should do if a party to the prosecution and defense presented evidence in court, which had not previously disclosed. This will result in consequences from breaking the rules of disclosure and some relief measures need to be taken. Criminal case, different from civil case, concerns citizen's personal freedom and life safety, so both parties must be scrupulous in choosing evidence. Moreover, the reasons for the failure of the prosecution or the defence to present evidence in compliance with the rules of disclosure vary. If the innocent person or the offender is wrongfully convicted because some evidence is not allowed to be presented at trial, it will negatively affect the fight the judicial organs' against crime and the protection of human rights, as well

[71] Weidong Chen and Du Lei [51].

as their authority. For example, in cases where the defendant is in fact innocent, it is, of course, unjust to convict and sentence him if the defense counsel fail to produce in a timely manner evidence that prove him innocent. Therefore, it is illegitimate to not allow the undisclosed files to be presented at trial.

After examining the systems of other countries where the discovery of evidence is implemented, it can be found that some evidence that is not disclosed is allowed to be presented in the trial according to actual situations. For example, Article 16 of the United States Federal Rules of Criminal Procedure provides that if the court, at any time, notices that a party fails to comply with the rule, it may order that party to permit the discovery or inspection, or grant an adjournment, or deny discovery, or grant other appropriate relief, or specify its time, place and manner or prescribe other just terms conditions. Based on these practices, when the system of discovery of evidence in our country is established, the following relief and sanctions can be taken if the rule of discovery is broken. First, the court can order the party who fails to comply with the rule to continue disclosing evidence to the other party. Second, the court may grant a request by one party to adjourn the proceedings on the ground that the other party has broken the rule of discovery. Third, the court may, according to actual situations, prohibit the production or use in court of evidence that has not been disclosed.

4. The supporting systems for the effective operation of the evidence discovery system

The failure to establish adversarial system by 1996 Criminal Procedure Law results from the repeal of the system of transferring all case file materials replaced by system of transferring the copy of the major evidence and failure to create guarantee mechanism. This can not solve the long-standing problem—court hearing is a mere formality, but create new one—difficult in access case files. In order to avoid establishing such system that attend to one thing and lose another, the system of discovery of evidence in our country needs a series of supporting systems. However, we only discuss several major systems in this part. In order to make the system of evidence discovery work effectively, the following two systems, I think, should be improved: legal aid system and witness protection system.

4.1 Improvement of the legal aid system

In the countries where the system of discovery of evidence isimplemented, lawyers are required to participate in discovery of evidence. However, the problem that few defendants entrust defenders need to be addressed. Although we have discussed the ways before for the defendant who has no defendants to realize his rights to access files and to know, it is very difficult for the defendant to exercise his rights effectively when facing the highly technically demanding discovery of system, and the court trial will remain a mere formality. Therefore, it is important to enable more defendants to entrust defenders, and the legal aid system is the only way to solve this problem. The

2012 Criminal Procedure Law expands the scope of legal aid,[72] but it still falls below the minimum standards required by the *International Covenant on Civil and Political Rights*,[73] nor can it be compared with that in law-based developed countries. This is because it is restricted by the current legislation, the insufficiency of the legal aid funds and the unequal distribution of the funds. Therefore, on the basis of ensuring the effective operation of the legal aid system of 2012 Criminal Procedure Law, it is important to expand the scope of legal aid according to the actual situation, such as expanding it to the extent to which it can be applied in the first instance cases of normal court procedure, continue to increase financial support for legal aid and enable more criminal suspects to present evidence effectively with the help of defense lawyers.

4.2 Improvement of the witness protection system

The prosecution and the defence are likely to interfere with the testimony of the witness due to the discovery of evidence, so the information subject to disclosure is absolutely significantly reduced in the absence of effective protection for the witness, and it is also difficult to achieve the desired effect of solving disputes between the two sides through the discovery of evidence.[74] Therefore, the witness protection system has always been a supporting system that all countries must create when they adopt the evidence discovery system. The provision of witness protection system is added in the 2012 Criminal Procedure Law,[75] clarifying what kinds of witnesses are

---

[72]According to 1996 Criminal Procedure Law, if the criminal suspect or defendant is a person who is vision, hearing or speech impaired or minors or commit a crime punishable by capital punishment, a lawyer shall be designated as his or her defender. However, two kinds of criminal suspects or defendants who are a mentally challenged persons but have not lost entirely the ability of recognition or the ability to control their conducts and who commit a crime punishable by life imprisonment are added to the group of people that shall receive legal aid in 2012 Criminal Procedure Law. In addition, it also provides that a criminal suspect or defendant who has not entrusted a defender due to financial difficulties or other reasons, the criminal suspect or defendant himself or herself or his or her close relatives may file an application with a legal aid agency which may designate a lawyer as his or her defender where the application satisfies the conditions for legal aid services, which regulates legal aid.

[73]Article 14 of the *International Covenant on Civil and Political Rights* provides that in the determination of any criminal charge against him, everyone shall be entitled to the following minimum guarantees, in full equality: To be tried in his presence, and to defend himself in person or through legal as sistance of his own choosing; to be informed, if he does not have legal assistance, of this right; and to have legal assistance assigned to him, in any case where the interests of justice so require, and without payment by him in any such case if he does not have sufficient means to pay for it.

[74]Sun Changyong [52].

[75]Article 62 of 2012 Criminal Procedure Law provides that with regard to crimes endangering State security, those involving terrorist activities, organized crimes committed by groups in the nature of criminal syndicates, drug-related crimes and the like, if the personal safety of the witnesses, experts or victims or their close relatives is threatened due to their testimony in lawsuits, the people's courts, people's procuratorates and public security organs shall adopt one or more of the following protective measures: (1) Keeping confidential the real names, addresses, employers and other personal information of the aforesaid persons; (2) Adopting measures to avoid the actual

protected, what protective measures can be taken and that witnesses may apply for protection. The scope of witness protection, the specific measures taken to protect witnesses and the right of application for witness protection have been established. At the very least, the new provisions would ensure that legitimate restrictions can be laid on the disclosure of personal information of witnesses upon one party's request prior to a hearing, and the public authority may protect the witness according to a specific case or an application. The above measures can minimize the shortcomings of the system of discovery of evidence, but they are not designed to completely restrict the discovery of evidence, thus ensuring the effective operation of the system of discovery of evidence.

5.5 The Current Situation and Realization of Defense Lawyer's Right to Investigate and Collect Evidence

The 1996 Criminal Procedure Law was an attempt to transform the criminal procedure from an inquisitorial system to adversarial system. In order to make the prosecution and the defense on an equal footing in the court trial, it is necessary to equally equip them with rights. Therefore, the 1996 Criminal Procedure Law also granted lawyers the right of interview, the right of accessing case files and the right to investigate and gather evidence. However, giving more rights makes it difficult to realize them, including difficulty in meeting with suspects or defendants, accessing case files and investigating and obtaining evidence. The 2012 Criminal Procedure Law solves some of these problems at the legislative level, including the difficulty in meeting with defendants and accessing case files, but the provisions of the lawyers' right to investigate and collect evidence remain unchanged.[76] However, compared with the difficulty in meeting with defendants and accessing case files, difficulty in investigating and obtaining evidence is the obstacle that hamstrings the development of China's criminal defense system. This is because justice is actually the stage where the evidence should be presented, and most of the cases are not "legal disputes" in the

appearance or true voice of those who appear in courtrooms for testimony; (3) Prohibiting certain persons from having contact with the witnesses, experts, victims and their close relatives; (4) Adopting special measures to protect the personal and residential security of the aforesaid persons; and/or (5) Other necessary protective measures. A witness, expert or victim who is of the opinion that his/her personal security or the personal security of his/her close relatives is in danger due to his/her testimony in lawsuits may apply for protection with a people's court, people's procuratorate or public security organ. Relevant entities and individuals shall provide cooperation when people's courts, people's procuratorates or public security organs take protective measures pursuant to the law.

[76] Although Article 33 of the 2012 Criminal Procedure Law provides that criminal suspects are entitled to entrust lawyers as their defenders at the investigation phase and provisions of Article 42 reduce lawyers' professional risk to a certain extent, it can be seen from the Article 41 that the meaning for the provision of investigation and collection of evidence is pretty much the same as before.

first place, but "disputes on facts".[77] If this impediment can not be removed and the defense counsel can only collect the evidence in favour of the suspect or the defendant or find out the questionable points from the materials provided by the prosecuting authority by exercising the right to interview and the right to access the case files, but do not have the right to investigate and collect evidence to verify such evidence or to obtain new evidence, they will be "unable to make bricks without straw". In view of this, we will discuss the current situation of the right of investigation and collection of evidence in China and pinpoint the problems so as to find a way to realize such right.

1. The current situation and issues of defense lawyer's right of investigation and collection of evidence

1.1 Ambiguities in legislation of the right of investigation and evidence collection in the investigation stage

Article 33 of the 2012 Criminal Procedure Law provides that criminal suspects are entitled to entrust lawyers as their defenders at the investigation phase, but what's more important is what rights lawyers should enjoy in this stage no matter whether the position of defender is ceremonial or not.[78] In this respect, another issue is whether the lawyer with the status of "defender" can exercise the right of investigation and evidence collection in the investigation stage.

Article 33, paragraph 1, of the 2012 criminal procedure law provides that a criminal suspect shall be entitled to entrust a defender after he or she is interrogated for the first time by an investigating organ or as of the date on which compulsive measures are taken; Article 41 provides that defence lawyers may, with the consent of the witnesses or other units and individuals concerned, collect information pertaining to the current case from them and they may also apply to the People's Procuratorate or the People's Court for the collection and obtaining of evidence, or request the People's Court to inform the witnesses to appear in court and give testimony. We can, of course, presume from these provisions that defense lawyers have the right of investigation and collection of evidence during the investigation stage. However, this right is not mentioned in Article 36 specifies rights defense lawyers are entitled to in this stage. Does this Article 36 enumerate all rights? This ambiguity makes it hard to identify whether lawyers have this right in the investigation stage.

We can figure it out through logical interpretation to identify itslegislative intent. After we think about it from the perspective of the whole criminal procedure system, we will find that failure to give the right to investigate and collect evidence to defense lawyers would render ineffective some of the new provisions closely related to the investigation and collection of evidence, such as the new added Article 40 which

[77]Liu Pinxin, An Analysis of the Problem of Defense Lawyers' Investigation and Collection of Evidence In China—on Establishing a Balanced System of Investigation and Collection of Evidence Chen Weidong, which is referenced by Chen Weidong [53].

[78]Wang Haiyan, Guangping [54].

stipulates the duty of defense lawyers to present three types of evidence to the prosecution by providing that where a defender has gathered evidence showing that the criminal suspect concerned was not at the scene of the crime, has not reached the age for assuming the criminal liability, or is a mentally challenged person who is not required by law to assume the criminal liability, the defender shall inform the relevant public organ and people's procuratorate of such evidence in a timely manner. Three types of evidence concerning criminal suspects and the duty to inform the relevant public organ and people's procuratorate mentioned above indicate this Article applies to the defender at the investigative stage and the examination before prosecution stage. In addition, if a lawyer does not have the right to investigate and collect evidence at the investigative stage, how can he obtain these three types of evidence and how can he inform the prosecution authorities? For example, Article 159 provides that an investigating organ shall listen to the opinions of a defense lawyer prior to closing the investigation of a case. These opinions include not only investigation procedure information, but also substantial evidence which prove the suspect guilty or innocent or the severity of crime. However, these opinions can not be groundless and must be supported by evidence before they can be accepted by the investigation organs. If defense lawyers are not entitled to the right of investigation and collection of evidence at the investigation stage, how can the procedure of listening to the opinions of a defense lawyer carried out? What's more convincing, Article 86, paragraph 2, of the 2012 Criminal Procedure Law provides that the people's procuratorate may question witnesses and other litigation participants, and listen to opinions of defense lawyers during the course of examining and approving the arrest. It shall hear the opinions of the defense lawyers if they have so requested. Furthermore, it can be seen from Article 79 that the criminal suspect or defendant shall be arrested if there is evidence to support the facts of a crime and he or she has committed the crime punishable and such crime will endanger the society. Therefore, defense lawyers need to present the evidence to support their opinion that arrest should not be approved, or else their opinions will be rejected. In conclusion, if we do not give lawyers the right to investigate and collect evidence during the investigation phase, the above-mentioned systems will be reduced to a mere attempt, which runs contrary to the legislative intent. So Article 36 does not list all the activities that the defence lawyer can participate during the investigation. In other words, Article 36 is not inclusive of Article 41.[79] The right to investigate and obtain evidence provided for in Article 41 should be construed as a right enjoyed by lawyers at the investigation stage. In short, at the legislative level, lawyers have the real right to investigate and collect evidence instead of being hamstrung by the ambiguity of what is stated in 1996 Criminal Procedure Law.

1.2 The difficulty in exercising the right to investigate and collect evidence

After securing the lawyers' right to investigate and collect evidence in the investigation stage, we find that it is hard for them to exercise it according to the current

[79] Wan Yi [55].

provisions of the law, because the contents of Article 41 of the 2012 Criminal Procedure Law are pretty much the same as before. It provides that "Defence lawyers may, with the consent of the witnesses or other units and individuals concerned, collect information pertaining to the current case from them and they may also apply to the People's Procuratorate or the People's Court for the collection and obtaining of evidence, or request the People's Court to inform the witnesses to appear in court and give testimony. With permission of the people's procuratorate or the people's court and with the consent of the victim, his close relatives or the witnesses provided by the victim, defence lawyers may collect information pertaining to the current case from them". Thus the problem is still unsolved, and the obstacles to the exercise of such right are as follows:

1.2.1 Obstacle to investigate and collect evidence

Lawyers have the right to investigate and obtain evidence on their own and to apply for such practice, but the law places multiple obstacles to the exercise of the both rights. In this regard, the criminal procedure law clearly stipulates that defence lawyers shall collect evidence on their own with the consent of witnesses or other relevant units and individuals. However, the legislative restrictions become obstacles to evidence collection by lawyers. Due to the traditional ideas of litigation and the imperfect witness protection system, people in our country are reluctant to get involved in litigation. They worry a lot about testifying for the criminal suspect and the defendant who are opposed to the state public authority. Based on the results of some empirical research, defense lawyers often meet with a refusal when they obtain evidence from state agencies, such as public security organs, industrial and commercial administration, real estate management departments, and from non-governmental functional departments such as banks, telecommunications, post offices, hospitals and properties.[80] The lawyer could do nothing about it. The same is true of collecting evidence from lay witnesses, and it is even more difficult to obtain evidence from victims and the witnesses they provide. According to the criminal procedure law, with permission of the people's procuratorate or the people's court and with the consent of the victim, his close relatives or the witnesses provided by the victim, defence lawyers may collect information pertaining to the current case from them. However, the existing laws and judicial interpretations do not specify under what circumstances the people's procuratorates and the people's court may or may not grant permission. Thus, the power is entirely under the subjective control of these two authorities, so this restraint reflects the extreme inequality between the prosecution and the defence.

Lawyers can instead apply to the People's Procuratorate and the People's Court for investigation and collection of evidence when they meet with a refusal. Under Article 41(1) of the Criminal Procedure Law, defence lawyers may also apply to the People's Procuratorate or the People's Court for the collection and obtaining of evidence, or request the People's Court to inform the witnesses to appear in court and give testimony. This provision can be construed as additional interpretation to the collection and obtaining of evidence by defence lawyers. However, the provision

[80]Chen Ruihua [56].

is yet to be implemented. It is difficult for defence lawyers to practically collect and investigate evidence from procuratorate and court. Because if the court approve such request, it needs to carry out this procedure by itself. Due to lack of personnel and money in China now, it is also difficult for the court to meet the requirement of defense lawyers.

1.2.2 Unexpected risks from evidence investigation

Besides the obstacles to the investigation and collection of evidence created by Article 41 of the criminal procedure law that prevent defence lawyers from obtaining evidence, Articles 42 and 306 provides that giving false testimony by defence lawyers shall be subject to the legal liability, which makes them afraid to collect evidence, because there are not only insurmountable obstacles in the way of accessing evidence, but also the pitfalls hidden in it.

It cannot be denied that that Article 42 of the 2012 Criminal Procedure Law does reduce some of the professional risks faced by defense lawyers compared to 1996 Criminal Procedure Law. For example, the original subject "defense lawyer and other defender" is replaced with "defense lawyer or any other person". In addition, the two main modifications are reflected in two aspects. First, intimidating or inducing witnesses to giving false testimony are not strictly subject to the legal liability. Second, rules are made for defenders and lawyers if they violate the provisions. The above-mentioned amendments aim to prevent retaliation by investigating and case-handling authorities against the professional practice of defence lawyers by introducing the principle of refusal. The prompt notification to law firms or bar associations will enable the defenders involved to receive assistance in a timely manner. It also, to a certain extent, reduces the possibility of retaliation by the public power.

However, reducing the risk does not mean eliminating the risk. The above amendments only reduce the pitfalls and provide the possibility of relief. As long as Article 306 is not repealed, it will be difficult to eliminate the professional risks of lawyers. Although most of the lawyers prosecuted for "impeding testimony" have not been convicted, the investigating organs charge them for this reason to deprive them of personal freedom and make them unable to practice the law. Therefore, the investigating organs retaliate lawyers on some level. Faced with the risk during the investigation and collection of evidence, how can lawyers not be afraid? All the above legislative restrictions, obstacles and risks make it hard for lawyer to exercise the right to investigate and obtain evidence.

2. The analysis of the causes of the difficulties for lawyers to investigate and collect evidence

2.1 Unequivalence between power and right

Pretrial procedure, as thepreliminary stage of public prosecution trial procedure, is also the stage where intense conflict may happen between state power and individual rights. So how the powers and rights are given is directly related to whether the judgement is impartial, and whether a country's criminal procedure law can protect human rights and punish criminals. At the pre-trial stage, the power of investigation for the investigator is a counterpart to the right of evidence collection and investigation for the lawyer in China. The purpose of them is to obtain evidence and reveal the truth. However, both of them are opposed to each other. The investigators are acting for the state to perform prosecution. They protect human rights, but their mission is to fight against crime. The mission of lawyers is to protect the legal rights of the defendant and avoid being prosecuted. Therefore, the power of investigation and the right of investigation and evidence collection in the pre-trial stage are exercised under the circumstance where they conflict with each other. Equivalence between the power and the right will helps these two actors to achieve their purposes. As the English judge Lord Devlin once said that the best way to get to the truth is to have the parties to search the facts which will prove the truth, and then both parties present all the material which they have obtained. He also stated that two biased seekers start from the ends of the field, and what they miss is far less than what an altruistic seeker who starts from the middle of the field misses.[81] In fact, however, there is a distinct difference between the two due to the nature of the actors' competence, especially in the pre-trial stage in China.

First, the power of investigation for investigators is compulsory, while the right of investigation and evidence collection for lawyers is non-compulsory. The investigation power reflects the national will, and the investigators, relying on the state organs and backed by compulsory measures, exercise the state power, so the power-based investigation and evidence collection must be mandatory. It is mainly reflected in the compulsory measures. In order to ensure that the public security organ and the people's procuratorate handle criminal cases in a timely and effective manner, investigators are allowed to use all kinds of investigative means, such as interrogation of criminal suspects, interrogation of witnesses and victims, investigation, inspection, experiment, search, identification, technical investigation. In addition, the above investigative means can be protected by compulsory measures. On the contrary, the right of defense lawyers to investigate and collect evidence is right-based, and it reflects the will of individuals and is an extension of the procedural rights of criminal suspects and defendants. It is exercised by relying only on private actors and non-compulsory with measures limited to the questioning of witnesses, victims or their relatives. When the subject of the investigation does not cooperate, there are no compulsory measures. The only relief is to apply with the people's procuratorate and the people's court concerned to collect and obtain evidence, and this measure is difficult to be approved under the situation described above. According to the 2012 Criminal Procedure Law, the People's Courts, the People's Procuratorates and the public security organs shall have the authority to collect or obtain evidence from the units and individuals concerned. The units and individuals concerned shall provide truthful evidence, and defence lawyers may, with the consent of the witnesses or other units and individuals concerned, collect information pertaining to the current case from them. It also provides that investigators may question a witness at the scene, his or her employer's premises, his or her domicile or a location designated by

[81] Mike McCawley [57].

the witness. Where necessary, the witness may be notified to provide testimony at a people's procuratorate or a public security organ. Compared with options available to investigators regarding the location of questioning a witness, defence lawyers can conduct interviews only at locations agreed to by the witnesses. Thus, there is a great disparity between the compulsory power and non-compulsory right of investigation and evidence collection.

Second, investigators take the initiative to exercise the investigation power, but lawyers exercise the right of investigation and evidence collection passively. The initiative of investigation power means that although the initiation of investigation acts is a response to criminal acts, it does not consider the will of citizens, including victims, except for private prosecution cases involving minor crimes, and it is exercised by the state organs acting actively in accordance with laws.[82] In addition, because it is the prosecution that should provide the evidence that prove the defendant guilty in the public prosecution case, it naturally needs to proactively collect evidence, otherwise it will bear the risk of losing the case. However, a lawyer's right to investigate and obtain evidence is based on the entrustment of a suspect or the assignment of a legal aid agency. This is because only after a lawyer becomes a defender and obtains the right to defend can he have the right to investigate and obtain evidence provided for by law, and the will of the witness and the victim must be factored in the process of collecting evidence. Therefore, compared with the initiative to exercise the investigation power by state organs, lawyers exercise the right of investigation and evidence collection in a passive way.

Third, thepower of investigation is exercised much earlier than the right of evidence investigation and collection. The priority of the power of investigation depends on the objective law of litigation. Except the case of private prosecution, investigating organs initiate the prosecution. Concretely speaking, once the investigating organ discovers or receives a report, information or charge against a crime or a criminal suspect, it shall promptly examine and place on record and investigate the criminal fact that is subject to criminal prosecution. As for the right of evidence investigation and collection, the earliest time when a lawyer can participate in a litigation is from the date of the first interrogation or compulsory measures taken by the investigative organ, so there is a time difference in the exercise of the power and the right. In addition, it is extremely important for investigators to take action in a timely manner, because investigation is efficiency-oriented.[83] Edmond Feigal, a French famous criminologist, said that the first hours of an investigation are of inestimable importance and lose timing is to lose truth.[84] The priority of investigation power not only depends on the objective law of litigation, but also on the necessity of the provision of evidence and the interest of investigation. On the one hand, the investigator's duty of collecting evidence is to prove whether the suspects are guilty or not, sot he investigating organ must find, discover and fix the evidence in time to

[82]Long Zongzhi [58].

[83]Xie Youping [59].

[84]La Berdin [60].

prove the fact of crime. On the other hand, in order to ensure the investigation activities are carried out in an effective way and prevent the damage or loss of evidence caused by improper intervention, investigating organs must restrict the intervention of subjects other than themselves. Therefore, this leads to the priority of investigation power over the right of evidence investigation and collection.

Fourth, investigators collect evidence in a more comprehensive way than defence lawyers. Article 113 of Criminal Procedure Law provides that with respect to a criminal case which has been filed, the public security organ shall carry out investigation, collecting and obtaining evidence to prove the criminal suspect guilty or innocent or to prove the crime to be minor or grave. According to this provision, our investigators have the obligation to investigate and collect evidence in a fair and comprehensive way, and they not only need to collect the evidence that can prove the criminal suspect's guilt, but also to obtain evidence that prove them innocent or the crime is minor. However, the defense lawyers do not collect evidence in a comprehensive way. According to Article 35 of this legal document, the responsibilities of a defender shall be to present, in accordance with facts and the law, materials and opinions proving that the criminal suspect or defendant is innocent or the crime involved is a petty offense, or the criminal suspect or defendant is eligible need for a mitigated punishment or exemption from the criminal liability. Therefore, the evidence that defense lawyers collect is just favorable to the criminal suspect.

Which is stronger can be seen from what we discuss above. It is self-evident that the investigation of evidence at the pretrial stage relies more heavily on the investigation power than the defense lawyer's right of evidence collection and investigation. On the way of revealing the truth, the expanding investigation power makes it hard for this right to be exercised. The inequality will result in violation of the rights of the defendant and even run counter to the truth and justice.

2.2 Ill-conceived litigation structure

In addition to the properties of right and power that lead to the disparity between them, the ill-conceived pre-trial litigation procedure in our country actually exacerbates this situation, making it more more difficult to exercise the defense lawyer's right of investigation and evidence collection. Before we start discussion, we need to introduce two kinds of criminal procedure structures: horizontal structure and vertical structure. The structure of criminal procedure is part of theory of criminal procedure, which originated from the West,[85] and our structure of criminal procedure is built on Japan's.[86] The structure of criminal procedure can be divided into horizontal

[85]Hessmann, a western European scholar, who divided the criminal procedure system into three categories in the 1880s and 1890s. In the 1950s, American Carl Loewe proposed the internal model and the external model. In 1964, American criminologist Herbert Packer constructed two criminal procedure models. In 1974, American law sociologist Goldstein put forward the adversarial and inquisitorial systems. See Huang Bao [61].

[86]The earliest monograph on the structure of criminal procedure in China is *Theory on the Structure of Criminal Procedure* by Li Xinjian, which is based on the research of Japanese scholars. Since then, there have been more studies on the litigation structure from different perspectives,

structure and vertical structure.[87] The former refers to the legal relationship among the prosecution, the defender and the judge in the entire procedure, so this structure focuses on mutual constraints among the three parties. The latter refers to the legal relationship and status of the three parties in the entire criminal procedure, and the relationship between the pretrial procedure and the trial procedure should be part of the vertical structure, so this structure emphasizes the mutual restriction between procedures, especially the restriction of trial procedures on pre-trial procedures. From the perspective of litigation structure, difficulty in realizing the right of investigation and evidence collection attributes to the ill-conceived horizontal structure and vertical structure.

2.2.1 Ill-conceived horizontal structure

Before the 1996 criminal procedure law was revised, the legislative and judicial organs follow the principle of crime control regarding the criminal procedure, which was reflected in the pre-trial and trial procedures basing the inquisitorial system. Therefore, in the horizontal structure of the pre-trial or the trial stage, the accused is not in a principal position and the defense is regarded as the "dissident" in opposition to the power of the state, while the prosecution has the intimidating power and the judge is given the investigation power. The last two parties implement the criminal law, punish crimes and maintain social stability. Therefore, the structure of criminal procedure in which the prosecution, the defense and the judge condition each other was not built before 1996.

After the 1979 Criminal Procedure Law was overhauled in 1996, it highlighted the trial stage in the horizontal and introduced part of adversary system in the court trial. The new trial system implements the principles of presenting evidence by prosecution and defense, cross-examination, and debate, supported by verification by the court, which combines the merits of adversarial system system and the inquisitorial system.[88] The main purpose of the reform is to prevent the judge from prejudging, maximize the function of court hearing, and make the court adversarial, so a triangular structure in which the defense and the prosecution are on an equal footing and the judge could render impartial decision. However, this litigation structure is not applied in the pre-trial stage where there is not a neutral party. In the absence of a neutral judge, the defence has to turn to the public security organ and the procuratorate for help when he or she find it difficult to exercise his or her rights and needs to seek relief. In addition, it will be more hard to realize the right to defense in the case

including *Comparison on Criminal Procedure Structure* by Xu Youjun, *Value and Structure—A Dual Analysis of Criminal Procedure* by Zuo Weimin, *Ideal Structure and Realistic Structure of Criminal Procedure* and *Analysis of Efficiency of Criminal Procedure Structure*by Ma Guixiang, Liang Yuxia's doctoral dissertation titled *Legitimacy of Criminal Procedure* and Wang Haiyan's doctoral dissertation titled *Evolution of Criminal Procedure Model.*

[87]Chen Ruihua [62].

[88]Chen Weidong [45].

where the accuser serves as judge.[89] This situation results in the failure to connect the pre-trial procedure where two parties participate with the trial procedure where three parties participate in our country. It can be seen from fact that the three rights granted to lawyers by the 1996 criminal procedure law eventually turn into three problems. When it is difficult to obtain evidence and to make both parties on an equal footing in the pretrial stage, procedure of evidence presenting and cross-examination can only be "castle in the air", which finally led to failure of the reform of trial procedure in 1996.

Although the 2012 Criminal Procedure Law, to some extent, addresses the difficulties in meeting with criminal suspects and accessing case files to make the defense more adversarial at the pretrial stage, the evidence, whether obtained through interviews or access to case files, can only constitute negative defense based on the evidence already collected by the prosecution, far from being comparable to the positive defence based on evidence collected through power of investigation and collecting evidence collection. What's even worse, it is hard for the defense to seek relief from being restricted to exercise his or her right to investigate and collect evidence with litigation structure in which only two parties participate without an impartial judge. Therefore, it is necessary to revamp the litigation structure at the pre-trial stage before establishing the well-set "triangle" structure at the trial stage.

2.2.2 Ill-conceived vertical structure

A basic principle of clear division of responsibilities, mutual coordination and mutual restraint to define the relationship among the public security organ, procuratorate and court in our country was established by the 1979 Criminal Procedure Law, and was built into the Constitution in 1982. Since then, it has not been amended even through the Criminal Procedure Law was revised twice. This principle has also established the vertical structure of the criminal procedure characterized by responsibility, cooperation and condition in our country. Compared with the reform of horizontal structure, the academic scholars in our country have criticized this vertical structure a lot. Some even call it "line-production-like" litigation structure. Some scholars even joke it as dinner cooking, serving, and eating.[90] The reason for the metaphor is that the line-production-like litigation structure that is changed from the one characterized by responsibility, cooperation and condition completely deviates from purpose to create the vertical structure—the constraint of trial procedure on pre-trial procedure. What's worse, it centers around the "investigation"stage, resulting in a investigation-based litigation structure, which also makes it difficult for judicial organ to oversee the investigation. Therefore, it leads to absence of impartial judicial organ at the pretrial stage, the expanding investigation power of the investigating organ and the weakening defense lawyer's right of investigation and evidence collection. In addition, the judicial function at the trial stage depends on all kinds of evidence obtained by

[89] If the accuser is the judge, only God can serve as a defender. Gustav Radbruch. An introduction to Jurisprudence. Mi Jian, Zhu Lin trans., p.121, Beijing: Encyclopedia of China Publishing House, 1997.

[90] Chen Weidong [64].

the investigating organ with its investigation power, and the role of defense lawyer to carry out investigation and evidence collection has long disappeared.

3. The approach to realize the right of lawyers to investigate and collect evidence

The disparity between state power and individual rights hobbles the efforts to realize the lawyers' right to investigate and obtain evidence. This persistence of the problem will exist until such gap can be narrowed by improved litigation structure and legislation. After conducting an in-depth study, we find out two causes to make the lawyers' right to investigate and obtain evidence difficult to be exercised. The first cause, which is the inequality between right and power, can be solved by constraining power and strengthening right; the second cause, which is the ill-conceived litigation structure, can be addressed by reconstructing the horizontal structure and correcting the vertical structure.

3.1 Strengthen lawyers' right to investigate and collect evidence

3.1.1 Strengthen lawyers' right to investigate and collect evidence

The implementation of the 2012 criminal procedure law shows us that difficulty in exercising the right investigation and evidence collect can not be solved by legislation only. The right-based investigation and evidence collection relies heavily on the cooperation from the witnesses, and the right to apply for investigation and evidence without relief and guarantee system can only depend on the self-management of the people's procuratorates and the people's court. Therefore, in order to address this issue, it is necessary to provide the guarantee and relief for the realization of the right and restrict the public power, or the newly established rights will be in name only.

Many scholars attribute the difficultyin obtaining and investigating evidence to the mechanism for the consent of the person under investigation established by the criminal procedure.[91] This mechanism needs to be corrected according to Article 35, paragraph 2, of *Law of the People's Republic of China on Lawyers*, which provides that when a lawyer investigates to collect evidence for a case on his own, he may, on the strength of his lawyer's practice certificate and the papers issued by his law firm, inquire of the unit or individual concerned about the legal matters which he has undertaken to handle. According to the provision, when lawyers conduct investigations and collect evidence from witnesses, victims and other units and individuals concerned, they are no longer required to obtain their consent nor are they asked to apply in writing to the people's procuratorate or the people's court and obtain their consent.[92] But this provision can not solve the problem once and for all. As mentioned above, the lawyer's right to investigate and collect evidence is not mandatory because of its nature, so it is impossible to acquire self-relief by itself. More importantly, can we deprive or restrict the witness or the victim's right to refuse to testify with the lawyer's right of Investigation and evidence collection? According to

---

[91] Guan Yu [65], Wang Haiyan and Hu Guangping [66].

[92] Guan Yu [65].

criminal procedure laws across the globe, witnesses are under an obligation to testify before a judge, but not before a lawyer, and even the police generally can not compel an informed person to provide information about the case. Ordinary people have the "moral obligation", but no "legal obligation" to do so.[93] Therefore, we believe that the legislative intent of removal of the phrase "with the consent of the entities or individuals concerned" is to prevent the refusal of the person under investigation to provide relevant evidence to lawyers for this reason. But in fact, it does not change the fact that a lawyer needs the consent of the witness before conducting investigation and evidence collection. Since we can not change the nature of the right, we may as well turn our attention to the realization of the right to apply for investigation and evidence, and explore how to make the application for investigation and evidence by a lawyer constrain the judiciary authorities. In the case of action of judiciary authorities, what relief can be provided to lawyers and whether some systems can be introduced to ensure that the right to apply for investigation and evidence collection can be realized in a more effective way. In this regard, there are some suggestions as follows.

First, the lawyers' application for the right to investigate and collect evidence should be handled by people's court. According to Criminal procedure Law in China, lawyers applying to the people's procuratorate for investigation and collection of evidence is against the criminal procedure rules. Because the procuratorial organ, as a party to the prosecution, should not be given his power due to the conflict of interests in litigation. Otherwise, it will violate the principle of "balance between prosecution and defense".[94] When the decision to approve the application of such right is made by the people's court, it also shows that a neutral third party can participate in the pre-trial stage to correct the imbalance between prosecution and defense and the ill-conceived litigation structure at the pre-trial stage.

Second, discretionary power of the people's court toapprove an investigation and evidence collection should be restricted to some degree. China's Criminal Procedure Law and relevant judicial interpretations do not specify what conditions should be met in applying for investigation and collection of evidence, and the court should agree to send personal for investigation and collection of evidence. Furthermore, there is no provision for the circumstances in which an application for investigation and collection of evidence should be rejected, nor for the remedies available to a lawyer if he or she is refused.[95] Section 244 of the German Code of Criminal

[93] Mike McConville [68].

[94] Chen Weidong et al. [69].

[95] Article 51 of the Interpretation of the Supreme People's Court Concerning the Implementation of the Criminal Procedure Law of the People's Republic of China provides that when a defense lawyer applies to the court for permission to gather or submit evidence or require a witness to testify in court after requesting such information regarding the case from a witness, individual or relevant entity and the witness, individual or relevant entity refuses to cooperate, if the people's court deems it necessary, permission shall be granted to the defense lawyer's request. The expression of "if the people's court deems it necessary" gives the court non-restricted discretionary power, leading to the consequence that people's court may refuse or even ignore an application by a lawyer for any reasons.

Procedure specifies the circumstances in which a court rejects an application for taking of evidence an application to take evidence may be rejected only if the taking of such evidence is superfluous because the matter is common knowledge, if the fact to be proved is irrelevant to the decision or has already been proved, if the evidence is wholly inappropriate or unobtainable, the application is made to protract the proceedings or if an important allegation which is intended to offer proof in exoneration of the defendant may be treated as if the alleged fact were true. This provision provides a best practice for us, and we also provide clear rules for the rejection of lawyers' applications for taking evidence in order to restrict the people's court's discretion. In addition, in order to ensure that lawyers' right to investigate and obtain evidence is realized in a timely manner, it is not only necessary to limit the time for the people's court to decide whether or not to give its consent,[96] but also to regulate how long the investigation and evidence collection by the personnel of the people's court will last to avoid delaying the realization of the right of lawyers to take evidence. In addition, the decision not to grant and not to grant this application after reconsideration, should be made in writing and the reasons for the refusal should be given. More importantly, relevant remedies should also be given to lawyers. Specifically speaking, the law should give lawyers the right to apply to a court or a higher court for review of a decision not to give consent. If lawyers have the evidence to prove that the people's court rejects the application without just cause and the evidence in favor of the defendant is not presented in court, an appeal may be filed to the court of first instance for the reason that the people's court may break the procedure rules prescribed by law and may undermine a fair trial. If the court of second instance does think so, it can overturn the original judgment and order a retrial and request the court of first instance to provide relevant evidence.

Finally, the system of investigation orderneeds to be introduced to guarantee the realization of the right to apply for investigation and evidence collection. We have to take into account the fact that the rejection of lawyers' applications for the right to investigate and collect evidence by courts, to a great extent, results from the enormous amount of judicial resources processing them and pressure that courts face in this procedure. To solve this problem, we can introduce an investigation order system. The system was first used in civil litigation. Shanghai municipal government began to try out the investigation order system in the first intermediate court in 1996 to address the difficulty in investigation and collection of evidence in civil litigation, and then implemented it in all courts of the city in 2001 when it comes to civil litigation.[97] From what we have learned about the current situation, some units, such as banks, securities companies, industrial and commercial executive branches, real

[96] Article 51(2) of the Interpretation of the Supreme People's Court Concerning the Implementation of the Criminal Procedure Law of the People's Republic of China provides that the decision to approve or allow an application filed by a defense attorney shall be made and communicated to the defense lawyer by the people's court within five days; reasons shall be provided if the people's court decides not to approve or allow the application.

[97] Qiao Xianzhi [70].

estate management departments, public security organs that were reluctant to cooperate before, are willing to help after lawyers produce an investigation warrant.[98] Therefore, some scholars suggest that the introduction of this system in criminal proceedings will help to correct the shortcoming of self-investigation and application for investigation, which makes the investigation and evidence collection of the defense lawyers supported by the court and does not bring more burden on it.[99] An investigation order is actually given to lawyers who apply with the court for investigation and collection of evidence. After the court examines and approve this application, it does not collect evidence by itself, but authorizes the lawyer to investigate and collect evidence from relevant units and individuals by issuing an investigation order. However, the system investigation order has not been adopted by the legislature. Article 8 of the *Provisions of the Supreme People's Court, the Supreme People's Procuratorate, the Ministry of Public Security, the Ministry of State Security, the Ministry of Justice, and the Legislative Affairs Commission of the Standing Committee of the National People's Congress on Several Issues concerning the Implementation of the Criminal Procedure Law* provides that where a defense lawyer applies to a people's procuratorate or a people's court for gathering or submission of evidence, and the people's procuratorate or the people's court deems it necessary to investigate and gather evidence, the people's procuratorate or the people's court shall gather or require submission of evidence, and may not issue an investigation approval decision in writing to the lawyer to allow the lawyer to gather or require submission of evidence. The reason for creating this provision is that the legal duty and power of the judicial organs, procuratorial organs and investigating organs to ascertain the facts of the case, collect all kinds of evidence that can may prove whether criminal suspects or defendants are guilty or innocent, or whether cases involve serious criminal offenses or not, or whether the judgement for convicting and sentencing criminal suspects or defendants is impartial, and the organs concerned are also not authorized to delegate the investigation powers granted by Law to lawyers to exercise.[100] In fact, when the court grants the lawyer an investigation order, it does not give the investigation power to the lawyer, but uses it to ensure the realization of the lawyer's right to investigate and collect evidence which is not mandatory and needs cooperation from the persons under investigation. The reason why they are willing to cooperate is that the court-issued order is seen as deterrent, but not compulsory. After what we have discussed above, it can be seen that the system of investigation order can be considered a practical approach to realize the right of the investigation and evidence collection of the defense lawyers in the future.

3.1.2 Repeal of Article 306 of Criminal Procedure Law

Article 16 of the *Basic Principles on the Role of Lawyers* established by United Nations provides that Governments shall ensure that lawyers (a) are able to perform all of their professional functions without intimidation, hindrance, harassment or

[98] Jiang Anjie [71].

[99] Chen Ruihua [72].

[100] Wang Shangxin [73].

improper interference; (b) are able to travel and to consult with their clients freely both within their own country and abroad; and (c) shall not suffer, or be threatened with, prosecution or administrative, economic or other sanctions for any action taken in accordance with recognized professional duties, standards and ethics. However, the lawyers in China conduct investigation and evidence collection with three swords of Damocles—intimidation, hindrance, threat—hanging over their head, which is reflected in the Article 306 of *Criminal Law of the People's Republic of China.* Both lawyers and academics have strongly advocated the repeal of this provision for the following reasons.

First, there is discrimination against the subject of crime. The 1996 Criminal Procedure Law allowed lawyers to participate in the investigation stage. In order to prevent lawyers from interfering with the investigation, a charge of destroying and falsifying evidence against lawyers can be filed. Are lawyers the only subjects to take evidence? Are they only the ones who may break the rules of taking evidence? However, this is not the case. Investigators have far more access to witnesses than lawyers, and they are more likely to "destroy, falsify evidence or hinder testimony" with their power. In addition, their illegal evidence collection creates more hindrance to the discovery of the truth of the case than what the lawyers did.[101] Why only lawyers can be charged against in this regard according to Article 306 of Criminal Procedure Law?

Second, the statement of guilt is ambiguous. According to Article 306 of the Criminal Law, lawyer will be charged from: (1) destroying, falsifying evidence: and (2) assisting parties concerned in destroying, falsifying evidence; and (3) threatening, luring witnesses to contravene facts. The third one is so ambiguously described. First, how to prove that lawyers threaten, luring witnesses to contravene facts. The witnesses are likely to change their testimony due to bad memory and other reasons, so it is not appropriate to create this provision. Second, how to demonstrate lawyers falsify evidence. If this an not be proved, how to find a lawyer guilty of perjury? Third, if the testimony of the witness to the investigating organ is false, but to the defense lawyer is true, is it determined by the investigating organ? If not, who should make this decision? Fourth, is it fair that only lawyers, but not witnesses, are being investigated for criminal responsibility? Fifth, is it deemed as luring rather than falsifying if lawyers only ask some leading questions? The ambiguity of the provision, which is most frequently used by the judicial organs to investigate lawyers' criminal responsibility, creates space for their discretion.

Finally, this Article blurs the line between professional ethics violations and criminal conduct. The provisions in Article 42 of the Criminal Procedure Law can not

[101] In the case of Xu Xianglin from Yao Ling village who was misjudged for killing his wife Zhang Zaiyu, villagers, including Ni Leping, Ni Xinhai and Nie Maiqing, had seen Zhang Zaiyu after this happening, so they circulated a petition to prove that Zhang Zaiyu did not die. However, this evidence did not verified by the investigating authorities. Instead, it brought bad luck to the witnesses who signed the petition. These villagers were taken into the detention house by the public security organ that forced them to admit that the evidence was false, which reflects that the investigative authorities had violently threatened the witnesses. See Record of Presumption of Guilt for "Wife Killing" Case in Hubei Province [74].

be seen as a measurement for criminalization, but only a norm for regulating the practice of law. If lawyers are investigated for criminal responsibility due to professional ethics violation, such practices must result in gravity of the circumstances, serious consequences and a major social impact. If not, the provisions will absolutely make more lawyers suffer from this ill-conceived legislation.[102] Therefore, the provisions of Article 306 of the *Criminal Law of the People's Republic of China* should be repealed. For the lawyers who obtain evidence in an illegal way or impede the proceedings, they shall be investigated first by the local judicial organ. In the case of offenses, the local judicial organ shall give administrative punishment to lawyers or the Bar Association punish them in accordance with the rules of the Bar. In order to prevent retaliation, the case of offenses need to be handled by an investigating organ other than the investigating organ handling the case undertaken by the defender pursuant to Article 42 of the 2012 Criminal Procedure Law. The law applied to lawyers shall be the same as that to any other person who participates in or is related with criminal proceedings, including persons of the investigation and control authorities, as stipulated in Article 307 of the Criminal Law.[103] Furthermore, Article 307 already contains what is described in Article 306. By repealing Article 306 to remove the sword of Damocles hanging over the head of the lawyers, they can take evidence move smoothly instead of being afraid of it. By doing so, the legitimate rights and interests of criminal suspects and defendants can be safeguarded in a more effective way.

3.2 Reconstructing and adjustment of litigation structure

The realization of a right depends not only on what it contains and how to measure it, but also on its litigation structure. Otherwise, ill-conceived litigation structure would fail to play its role no matter how well right is designed. Because the well-designed right is hard to restrict the state power in this structure, it will become the "castle in the air", so will the lawyer's right of investigation and collection of evidence. Therefore, it is very important to reconstruct and correct the litigation structure of our country.

3.2.1 Reconstruction of the horizontal structure

According towhat we have discussed above, the flawed "linear" structure with prosecution and defense at one end at the pre-trial stage fails to make both parties on an equal footing due to the huge disparity between the right of the defense and the

---

[102]Tian Wenchang and Chen Ruihua [71].

[103]Article 307 of Criminal Law provides that whoever stops with violence, threat, bribe, and other methods a witness to testify or instigates others to make false testimony is to be sentenced to not more than three years of fixed-term imprisonment or criminal detention; when the circumstances are severe, to not less than three years but not more than seven years of fixed-term imprisonment; whoever assists the parties concerned in destroying or falsifying evidences is to be sentenced to not more than three years of fixed-term imprisonment or criminal detention if the circumstances are severe; any judicial personnel committing the crimes as stated in the previous two paragraphs is to be severely punished.

power of the prosecution. In the proper sense, as an important stage of criminal procedure, the structure of the pretrial stage should be designed based on nature of the procedure, and a neutral judge is needed between the prosecution and the defense to correct any imbalance. Otherwise, the disputes arising from the serious confrontations between the prosecutor representing the power of the state and the defender representing the right of citizenship in criminal pre-trial proceedings can not be settled impartially. This will shake the foundation of proceedings, resulting in a predator–prey system.[104] Based on this idea, both common law system countries and civil law countries have introduced review mechanism and placed the power of investigation under the control of judicial power to create balance between the two parties. These attempts are to protect human rights and build well-conceived litigation structure, in order to realize the law-based pre-trial litigation procedure.

A "triangle" litigation structure should be built on the basis of "linear" structure, and it is necessary to create a position of neutral judicial officer in the pretrial stage. On the one hand, the judicial officer is responsible for handling the application of the mandatory investigation and issuing an order to regulate the investigation act and protect the rights of the suspect; on the other hand, the judicial officer deals with the defence's complaint about the illegal investigation act, and listen to both sides to make decisions on whether the investigation is legal and whether the evidence obtained should be excluded. In this sense, the judicial power is more of a hidden protective force in the pre-trial stage. When there is the possibility or necessity that the investigation power interferes with the civil rights and freedoms, the judicial power appears from "backstage" to "front stage". The judicial power is used to restrict the power of investigation so as to avoiding the weakening of defense right due to the over-expansion of the power of investigation, and create more space for the defense to exercise its right of investigation and evidence collection. These efforts aim to stabilize the triangle litigation structure and make the court trial run in a more efficient and fair way.

3.2.2 Adjustment of the vertical structure

Although the principle of principle of clear division of responsibilities, mutual coordination and mutual restraint has been criticized by scholars, it is difficult to abolish this principle because it has been built into the Constitution. Therefore, it is better to adjust the relationship among public security organ, procuratorate and court in the vertical structure, and change from doctrine of separate regulation on investigation and evidence collection, examination and prosecution and judgment to the trial-centered doctrine. In other words, the new procedure is trial-centered; investigation and prosecution are the activities to prepare and initiate trial; execution is to enforce a court judgment.[105] In this regard, it it necessary to weaken the role of the public security organ to restrict the court trial by investigating the case files, emphasizing the principle of directness and verbalism in the court trial, and strengthen the restriction of the court on the public security organ. Therefore, we need to reconstruct

[104]Chen Weidong [72].

[105]Zhang Jianwei [73].

horizontal structure, make a impartial judicial officer in charge of the pre-trial stage and perfect the exclusionary rule of illegal evidence.

4. Conclusion

In any developedcountries with good legal system, what people expect is not a right in name only, but an effective right, that is, a right accessible to all.[106] However, the right of defense lawyers to investigate and collect evidence in China is such a right in name only which is difficult to be exercised. In order to solve this problem, we need to do more than just expand the meaning and dimension of the right, More importantly, we need to reconstruct and adjust the litigation structure, to make the rights exercised effectively. These are all the suggestions in this book to realize the right to investigate and obtain evidence.

References

1. Garin, E. (1998). *Italian humanism.* Li Yucheng trans., Beijing: Joint Publishing Company, p.71.
2. Yang, Z. (2002). *A study of criminal victims* (p. 71). Beijing: People's Public Security University of China Press.
3. Lu, S. (2000a). *The schools of modern western laws* (p. 27). Beijing: Encyclopedia of China Publishing House.
4. Lu, S. (2000b). *The schools of modern western laws* (p. 37). Beijing: Encyclopedia of China Publishing House.
5. Lu, S. (2000c). *The schools of modern western laws* (p. 57). Beijing: Encyclopedia of China Publishing House.
6. Xia, Y. (1992a). *The origin of the concept of human rights* (p. 133). Beijing: China University of Political Science and Law.
7. Xia, Y. (1992b). *The origin of the concept of human rights* (p. 132). Beijing: China University of Political Science and Law.
8. Xia, Y. (1992c). *The origin of the concept of human rights* (p. 102). Beijing: China University of Political Science and Law.
9. Bodenheimer, E. (1999). *Jurisprudence: The philosophy and method of the law.* Deng Zhenglai trans., Beijing: China University of Political Science and Law, p.77.
10. Wang, W., & Guo, B. (1988). *Social interests* (p. 39). Beijing: People's Publishing House.
11. Xia, Y. (1992). *The origin of the concept of human rights* (p. 14). Beijing: China University of Political Science and Law.
12. Zongling, S. (Ed.). (1994). *Jurisprudence* (p. 386). Higher Education Press: Beijing.
13. Bodenheimer, E. (1999). *Jurisprudence: The philosophy and method of the law.* Deng Zhenglai trans., Beijing: China University of Political Science and Law, p.172.
14. Lu, S. (Ed.). (2000a). *The schools of modern western jurisprudence* (p. 29). Encyclopedia of China Publishing House: Beijing.
15. Lu, S. (Ed.). (2000b). *The schools of modern western jurisprudence* (p. 37). Encyclopedia of China Publishing House: Beijing.
16. Bodenheimer, E. (1999a). *Jurisprudence: The philosophy and method of the law.* Deng Zhenglai trans., Beijing: China University of Political Science and Law, p.175.

[106]Mauro Cappelletti [74].

17. Bodenheimer, E. (1999b). *Jurisprudence: The philosophy and method of the law*. Deng Zhenglai trans., Beijing: China University of Political Science and Law, p.173.
18. Bodenheimer, E. (1999c). *Jurisprudence: The philosophy and method of the law*. Deng Zhenglai trans., Beijing: China University of Political Science and Law, p.177.
19. Xia, Y. (199). *The origin of the concept of human rights* (p. 32). Beijing: China University of Political Science and Law.
20. Nishihara, H. (1997). *The formation and characteristics of Japanese criminal law*. Li Haidong et al. Trans., p.447, Beijing: China Law Press and Japan Chengwen Tang, 1997.
21. Liu, L., & Xie, P. (2000). *Trends in overseas judicial reform*. p.170, Beijing, China Fangzheng Press.
22. Chen, W. (2005). *The path of procedural justice*, Vol. 1, p. 375 to 384, Beijing: Law Press China.
23. Political Research Group of the Standing Committee of the National People's Congress. (1996). *Interpretation of the constitution law of people's republic of China*, pp. 277 to 278, Beijing: China Legal Publishing House.
24. Chen, W. & Cheng, L. (2014). An empirical study on the implementation of the criminal procedure in detention house. *Journal of Political Science and Law, 4*.
25. Hirano, R. (1958) *Criminal procedure*, p. 105, Tokyo.
26. Chen, Y. (2010). *Memoir of the symposium on criminal justice and international human rights conventions*, pp.219, Taipei, Taiwan, Tunghai University's Law Department.
27. Lin, Y. (2012). Criminal procedure and International Human Rights Part II, pp. 157 to 158, Taipei: Yuanzhao Publishing Co. Ltd.
28. Lin, Y. (2010). *Fundamental human rights and judicial reform* (p. 18). Taipei: New Xuelin Publishing Co., Ltd.
29. Chen, X. (2011). Study on reasonable restriction of the right of lawyers to meet with criminal suspects during investigation. *Modern Law Science, 9*.
30. Chen, Y. (2010). Interpretation (No.654) and right of unrestricted communications. *The Taiwan Law Review, 5*.
31. Lin, Y. (2008). Right of Correspondence between defendants under detention and lawyers—comparison and analysis between European law and Chinese law. *Taiwan Environmental and Land Law Journal, 1*.
32. Wu, J. (2006). Study on the right of communication between the defender and the accused through interviews and correspondence. *The Taiwan Law Review, 10*.
33. Cai, Q. (2005). The right of communication between defendants under detention and lawyers — comments on the judgment of the European court of human rights in the case of erdem against Germany. *Taiwan Environmental and Land Law Journal, 6*.
34. Lang, S. (2012). *Interpretation of criminal procedure law of the people's republic of China* (p. 73). Beijing: Law Press China.
35. Zhang, P. (2013). Comments on the "special provisions" on terrorist crimes. *Journal of National Prosecutors College, 7*.
36. Jacobs. (2003). Citizen criminal law and enemy criminal law, Xu Yuan trans., *The foundations and limits of Criminal Law: A Collection of Hong Fuzeng*, pp. 17–18, Taipei, Xuelin publishing, 2003.
37. Chen, S. (2012). Revision of criminal procedure law under the influence of enemy criminal law. *Oriental Law, 4*.
38. Mototeru. (2012). Criminal procedure and International Human Rights II, 130 PP. Taipei.
39. Wu, J. (2009). On the defender, Pp. 149–152, Taipei, Canon Publishing Culture Co. Ltd.
40. Lang, S. (2012). An interpretation of the criminal procedure, 76 PP. Beijing, Law Press.
41. Wei Dong, C. (2014). Cheng Lei: A study on issues related to the implementation of the criminal procedure in detention centers. *Political law series, 4*.
42. Chen, Y. (2011). Interpretation (No.654) and right of unrestricted communications. *The Taiwan Law Review, 5*.
43. Chen, W. (2005). *Litigation rights of defense lawyers and the guarantee system in prosecution-defense trial procedure, The Path of Procedural Justice* (Vol. 1, p. 428). Beijing: Law Press China.

44. Lang, S. (2012). *Interpretation of the criminal procedure Law*, pp. 77–78. Beijing, Law Press China.
45. Wei Xiaona, Y. (2014). Jurisprudence and design of evidence disclosure system. *Criminal Science, 4.*
46. Chen, W. (2012). *Interpretation and application of 2012 criminal procedure law* (p. 229). Beijing: China Legal Publishing House.
47. Zheng, G. (2009). Basic thoughts on the identification of evidence in the case of defendant's retraction of confession. *Gansu Social Science, 1.*
48. Chen, Y. (2009). The mechanism to ensure the implementation of audio-visual recording system of interrogation, Contemporary Law Review, *4.*
49. Weidong, C., & Du, L. (2012). The framework of the pretrial conference system and its application — Review of article 182, Paragraph 22, of Criminal Procedure Law. *Zhejiang Social Sciences, 11.*
50. Sun, C. (2005). *Exploring due procedure: A treatise on criminal procedure law* (p. 429). Beijing: China Legal Publishing House.
51. Weidong, C. (2004). *Legal system building from the perspective of 3R—Proceedings of the Sino-American symposium on lawyers' defense function and judicial justice*, p.424, Beijing: China Procuratorial Press.
52. Haiyan, W., & Guangping, H. (2013). An analysis of whether the defense lawyers have the right to investigate and obtain evidence in the investigation from the perspective of hermeneutic of law. *Law Science Magazine, 11.*
53. Wan, Y. (2013). A critique of misinterpretation of criminal procedure law—an analysis based on the criminal defense system. *Tribune of Political Science and Law, 3.*
54. Chen, R. (2014). Three ways of Investigation and Collection of Evidence by Defense Lawyers. *Studies in Law and Business, 1.*
55. McCawley, M. (1999). The value of adversary system and pretrial criminal procedure. *An introduction to Chinese and English law* by The British Council, p. 120, Law Press China.
56. Long, Z. (2001). Human rights protection in investigation procedure. *Peking University Law Journal, 4.*
57. Xie, Y. (2007). From governance to rights protection: reconstruction of the structure of criminal proceedings in China, *Jianghai Academic Journal, 3.*
58. Berdin, L. (1986). *Essays in criminal investigation*, Li Ruiqin trans., p. 69, Beijing: People's Publishing House.
59. Huang, B. (2006). Origin and concept of criminal procedure models, *Journal of South-Central University for Nationalities(Humanities and Social Sciences), 6.*
60. Chen, R. (2005). *Problems of criminal procedure* (p. 326). Beijing: China Renmin University Press.
61. Chen, W. (2005b). *The path of procedural justice* (Vol. 1, p. 508). Beijing: Law Press China.
62. Guan, Y. (2008). *Lawyer's defense in criminal pre-trial procedure*, p.246, Beijing, Law Press China.
63. Wang, H., & Hu, G. (2013). An analysis of the right of defense lawyers to investigate and collect evidence in the stage of investigation—From the perspective of legal hermeneutics, *Law Science Magazine, 11.*
64. McConville, M. (2001). Criminal justice: An introduction to the criminal justice system in England, *British criminal procedure law(selected works)*, China University of Political Science and Law trans., p.15, Beijing: China University of Political Science and Law Press.
65. Weidong, C., et al. (2004). *Investigation report on the protection of the litigation rights of defense lawyers and the discovery of evidence, The Legal System of Lawyers from the Perspective of "3R"–a Collection of Essays on the Symposium on Lawyers' Defense Function and Judicial Justice in China and The United States by Chen Weidong*. Beijing: China Procuratorial Press.
66. Qiao, X. (editor-in-chief). (2002). *Evidence System and Judicial Application in China*, p.148, Beijing: Law Press China.

67. Jiang, A. (2012, June 21). Hot topic on establishing the system of investigation order, *Legal Daily* (5th ed).
68. Chen, R. (2014). Three ways of investigation and collection of evidence by defense lawyers, Studies in Law and Business, *1*.
69. Wang, S. (2013). Interpretation of the Provisions of the Supreme People's Court, the Supreme People's Procuratorate, the Ministry of Public Security, the Ministry of State Security, the Ministry of Justice, and the Legislative Affairs Commission of the Standing Committee of the National People's Congress on Several Issues concerning the Implementation of the Criminal Procedure Law, p.43. Beijing: China Legal Publishing House.
70. Hubei Province. (2005). *Wenzhou Liao Wang, 5*.
71. Tian, W., & Chen, R. (2013). *The best practices of criminal defense in China: A dialogue between Tian Wenchang and Chen Ruihua (Revised and* (Enlarged, p. 323). Beijing: Beijing Huilin Printing Co., Ltd.
72. Weidong, C. (2005). *The path of procedural justice* (Vol. 1, p. 106). Beijing: Law Press China.
73. Zhang, J. (2014, June 20). The nature and appearance of trial-centered doctrine, *People's Court Daily*.
74. Cappelletti, M. (2000). *Fundamental sstigation*. Xu Xin trans, p.50, Beijing: Law Press China.

Chapter 6
Other Rights of Litigants in Criminal Procedure

6.1 Discussion on the Rights of Crime Victims

Victim refers to a person whose personal right, property right or other legitimate rights and interests have been infringed upon by criminal acts. There must be a victim or victims in a crime. Before the state and the law were established, the victim has a wide range of rights to punishment onto the offender. With the emergence of the state, the state organs are given the state power, and the victims could only turn to them for help when they were violated by crimes, and could no longer have the right of private revenge. Aside from the crimes that infringe individual rights and interests, the acts that violate the legal interests of the state and society are also seen as committing crimes. The trial and punishment of the criminals are also carried out and executed by the state organs. In addition, the dispute between the offender and the victim gradually turns into a dispute between the offender and the state, which has unconsciously weakened the role of the victim who is the party concerned only serves as a witness in criminal proceedings. Then, as human rights protection is strengthened, people come to realize that are more injustice is caused by protection of the rights of the defendant than by the concern of the rights of the victims. Therefore, more studies have been conducted on the rights of the victims.

6.1.1 Theoretical Analysis of the Rights of Victims

6.1.1.1 The Concept of Criminal Justice and the Model of Victim Participation in Litigation

Limited attention was paid to the victims by many countries in the criminal proceedings before. They only server as the prosecution witnesses, and have little impact on criminal proceedings. The criminal offence is generally regarded as the infringement of the legal interests of the state by the criminals, and the criminal procedure is seen

W. Chen, *Reform and Development of Powers and Functions of China's Criminal Proceedings*, https://doi.org/10.1007/978-981-15-8431-2_6

as the prosecution of the crime by the state and the antagonism between the accuser and the defender. Since the 1960s, due process model has been widely adopted in the United States. The American scholar Packer summed up the values as two models of criminal procedure: Crime Control Model and Due Process Model.[1] The former focuses on controlling crime, and its core value is efficiency. "The model, in order to operate successfully, must produce a high rate of apprehension and convictions, and must do so in a context where the magnitudes being dealt with are very large and the resources for dealing with them are very limited. There must then be a premium on speed and finality. Speed, in turn, depends on formality and on uniformity; finality depends on minimizing the occasions for challenge. The process must not be cluttered up with ceremonious rituals that do not advance the process of a case", according to Packer when he discussed about the Crime Control Model.[2] Therefore, what is important for the criminal procedure is to solve the case and carry out the prosecution the trial in an efficient way and prevent the red tape from encumbering the attempts to achieve our objective. The latter focuses on the establishment of due process to protect the rights of the defendant, and its core value is to prioritize the defendant. "The aim of the process is at least as much to protect the factually innocent as it is to convict the factually guilty. It is a little like quality control in industrial technology; tolerable deviation from standard varies with the importance of conformity to standard in the destined uses of the product. The Due Process Model resembles a factory that has to devote a substantial part of its input to quality control. This necessarily cuts down on quantitative output", according to Packer according to Packer when he discussed about Due Process Model.[3] That means, under this model, more attention will be paid to the protection of the rights of the defendants, and therefore many procedures will be created to prevent the state from prosecuting them, so as to ensure that their rights will not be unduly infringed upon. However, it would also reduce the output of those legally found guilty. Packer regards these two models as the two extremes in criminal litigation activities, and here can not be more models than these two.

This theory caused a sensation in the academic circle at that time, and some scholars even criticized it. Beloff proposed that there is a third model of criminal process: Victim Participation Model.[4] Because Packer did not foresee that the victim would participate in the procedure. According to Packer's theory, the victim's participation causes impact, to varying degrees, on the criminal procedure and the entity. This can not be deemed as the Crime Control Model or Due Process Model, which can not be explained using Packer's theory. Packer argued that criminal procedure is only a confrontation between the state and the defendant and there is not third party value involved. With the development of society, people gradually realize the importance of protecting the rights of victims. Therefore, victims are allowed to participate in the procedure and given some rights, which makes Packer's theory fail

---

[1]Packer [1].

[2]Yu and Guo [2].

[3]Yu and Guo [3].

[4]Beloof [4].

to work. Therefore, Beloof thinks that it is only to introduce the third mode—Victim Participation Model, can explain this value, which at its core is "victim first". "For a victim model to be useful, there needed to be a consensus in law that the values underlying the victims' roles are genuine and significant. This consensus in law now exists, as reflected in modern laws that create rights of participation for victims of crime in all fifty states and the federal government, and in historic traditions of victim participation that have endured to the present day. However, because victim participation does not rest on the values underlying the Crime Control and Due Process Models, the two models cannot facilitate an understanding of victim participation", according to Beloof. So this theory is not a replacement for Packer's two models, but a complement to it. Therefore, the value of victim first, like the values of efficiency and the defendant first, exists in all stages of criminal proceedings and they check and balance each other. Beloof shows the uniqueness and usefulness of the value of victim first by analyzing the application of the three value in the six stages of criminal procedure, including reporting a crime, investigating a crime, initiate a prosecution, court trial, sentencing and appeal. Therefore, the victim participation model is essential to the completeness of models of criminal proceedings.

6.1.1.2 Procedural Justice Bases the Victim's Rights

The procedural justice is generally regarded as the theoretical basis of the protection of the rights of the defendant. In addition, it is also the foundation of the protection of the rights of the victims. The procedural justice is a term to denote natural justice in English legal system. The principle of natural justice is the core of the British rule of law and the original form of procedural justice. This principle includes two key points: (1) no one may serve as a judge in his or her own litigation cases; and (2) the judge shall hear the statements of both parties when making the decision. The latter, also known as the principle of case hearing from the accused and accuser, means that a judge must make a decision after having the opinions heard from both parties interested. Otherwise, his or her decision will not be justified, and therefore has no legal effect.[5] According to the second key point, a judge must have the opinions of both parties interested heard in order to arrive at a fair decision. In criminal proceedings, the original parties should be the victim and the defendant. Although it is the state, no longer victim, who prosecutes the defendant, the opinions and feelings of the victims can not be expressed by the national prosecution organ. Therefore, in criminal proceedings, the judge must listen to the victims interested to render a fair decision and ensure that the facts found are close to truth and verdict is what justice represents. Before this, due to the lack of the protection of the rights of the defendant, we paid more attention to the protection of the defendant's right to participate in the proceedings but ignored such right of the victims.

The victim is the aggrieved party a criminal case. Delegating the power of prosecuting the case to the state does not mean that the state can fully understand and

[5] Chen [5].

represent the interests of the victim. We have established due process to safeguard the interests of the defendant in order to prevent the state from abusing its power in criminal proceedings. Similarly, in order to prevent the prosecution organ from ignoring the victim's claims, certain procedures should be developed to ensure the realization of the victim's legitimate rights. Therefore, under the jurisdiction of the state, the victims are supposed to be allowed to communicate with the state prosecution organs and the defendant to restrict state power and abuse of it.

Procedural justice has its own value, which is different from the value of substantive justice. Procedure is the link through which individual and state can exchange ideas, the way to realize individual rights and the effective means to restrict state power. Through the establishment of legitimate legal procedure, individuals and the state can have a talk on an equal footing so as to make a fair decision. As the saying goes: Justice should not only be done but should manifestly and undoubtedly be seen to be done. This is also the value of procedural justice. The rights of the parties to participate in the process can be safeguarded through the procedure people can see, so as to achieve the justice. However, due to our previous neglect of the procedural rights of the victims who are supposed to be a party to the lawsuit, many decisions are rendered without hearing the opinions of the victims. The improper establishment of criminal procedures even cause some victims to be "violated" again, which is undoubtedly unjust. Some scholars have summarized the connotation of procedural justice as the following three points: (1) the rights of the parties shall not be reduced without due process; and (2) action against the rights of the parties must be carried out in accordance with the law, and their rights must be safeguarded by procedures; and (3) when the rights of the parties are violated illegally, especially when they are violated by state power, it is necessary to provide them with legal remedies. 40 Pages, Ph.D. Dissertation, China University of Political Science and Law, 2005.[6] The above three points show the demand of procedural justice for the protection of the rights of the parties, and the victims who should be one of the parties should be protected as well. Therefore, we need to take into account the victim's rights and the construction and perfection of its guarantee system for these right when we make laws.

6.1.1.3 The Status of the Victim in Criminal Proceedings

Modern criminal proceedings are more about the balance between the interests of the defendant, the victim and the state. It is necessary to identify the relationship between the victim and other subjects of rights before getting to know the status of the victim in criminal proceedings. The public prosecution organ and the defendant had been deemed as both sides of the criminal proceedings before. Whether the victim is seen as the other party depends on whether the victim has different demands and plays a different role from those of the public prosecution organ and the defendant. In other words, whether the victims participate in the proceedings and have an independent status in the proceedings helps to realize justice.

---

[6]Zhang [6].

The Victim and the Prosecution Organ

Crime is generally considered to have two characteristics: the infringement of the social legal interests and the infringement of the victim's personal legal interests. The reason for the prosecution by the state is that the individual legal interest is also a part of the social legal interest. However, it can be seen from the past that the demand of the public prosecution organ is not completely the same as the victim's. In addition, the victim not satisfied with the final decision happens from time to time. This is because the goal of the prosecution organ is to punish crimes and protect the human rights of the accused, but not to pay attention to the victim's demands including revenge and compensation.[7] This problem can be found in three occasions. First, when the defendant is the perpetrator, the judgement can not be made due to various reasons given by the staff of the state prosecution service, such as the exclusion of key evidence because of obtaining it in an illegal ways, and the victim has to alive with the consequences caused by the fault of the state organs. Second, the victim may not wish to punish the accused because of his special relationship with the accused, such as relatives and friends, or may wish to give them less severe punishment than the prosecuting authority; or the victim detests the defendant, thinking that the prosecution organ should give more severe punishment than it has already given. Third, the crime may cause material damage or mental blow to the victim, so he or she often claims compensation in addition to the claim, which is the same as that of prosecution organ, for punishment on the criminal suspect. The amount of such compensation depends on how much the victim hates the suspect. In these three cases, if the participation and influence of the victim is completely excluded from the proceedings, the victim is likely to be dissatisfied with the final judgment of the court, resulting in the decline of the prestige of the court. This is because the state has failed to protect the interests of the victims by using its power of prosecution, in some cases it has violated the rights and interests of the victims. Therefore, in order to achieve the justice-based goal, it is pivotal for victims to participate in the lawsuit, and them ligation rights and status, make them become the litigants in the proceedings and exercise their rights.

Victim and Defendant

The confrontation between the victim and the defendant turns into the confrontation between the state and the defendant after the state initiate the prosecution and punish the crime. With the development of society, it is found that criminal procedure is not necessarily antagonistic procedure, nor should it take confrontation as the ultimate goal, but should pay attention to the settlement of disputes, restore social order, have the defendant to forgive the victim through restorative justice in order to help the defendant return to society as soon as possible. This new concept of justice naturally includes the victim into the criminal procedure system and makes it play an extremely

[7]Li [7].

important role. By participating in the proceedings, the victim can better understand the acts of the national prosecuting authority (such as discretionary non-prosecution) on the one hand and get compensation through reconciliation with the defendant. The defendant may also beg for forgiveness from the victim for reduction of the criminal punishment. The state prosecuting authority can also reduce the workload of prosecution and improve the efficiency of prosecution because of the defendant's guilty plea. In fact, although the victim and the defendant are the two sides of the confrontation, they are also the parties to settle the dispute. As the saying goes: it is better for the doer to undo what he has done. Of the settlement of the contradiction. The victim, as the party involved in the criminal proceedings, not only can meet their own needs, but also help to restore the social order.

The people of the country want a criminal justice system that helps to realize justice and they believe that the victims of crime should be at the heart of the system, according to Britain White Paper on Judicial Reform.[8] Based on what we have discussed above, it can be see that the victim's participation in the criminal procedure not only generates different demands from those of the prosecution organ, but also can help to resolve disputes and restore social order because of his or her special relationship with the defendant. Therefore, it is what the justice calls for to engage the victims in the criminal procedure and make them be the party concerned.

6.1.2 United Nations Basic Principles on the Protection of the Rights of Victims

6.1.2.1 Discussion About the Declaration of Basic Principles of Justice for Victims of Crime and Abuse of Power[9]

In order to better safeguard the rights of victims, *Declaration of Basic Principles of Justice for Victims of Crime and Abuse of Power* (hereinafter referred to as the Declaration) was adopted by General Assembly resolution 40/34 of 29 November 1985. The basic principles guaranteeing the rights of victims are established in the form of legal document. The Declaration consists of 21 articles in Parts A and B, 17 articles in part A for victims from crime and 4 articles in Part B for victims from abuse of power.

---

[8]Law Policy Research Office of the Supreme People's Procuratorate [8].

[9]The contents in this part are quoted from *Declaration of Basic Principles of Justice for Victims of Crime and Abuse of Power.* UN website https://www.un.org/zh/documents/view_doc.asp?symbol=a/res/40/34.

Victims of Crime

According to the Article 1 of victims of crime, "victims" means persons who, individually or collectively, have suffered harm, including physical or mental injury, emotional suffering, economic loss or substantial impairment of their fundamental rights. According to the Article 2, the term "victim" also includes, where appropriate, the immediate family or dependants of the direct victim and persons who have suffered harm in intervening to assist victims in distress or to prevent victimization, regardless of whether the offending party has participated in the criminal proceedings. In addition, four rights are given to victims: access to justice and fair treatment, restitution, compensation and assistance.

Access to Justice and Fair Treatment

Article 4 provides that victims are entitled to access to the mechanisms of justice and to prompt redress for the harm that they have suffered. According to Article 5, victims can obtain redress through formal or informal procedures that are expeditious, fair, inexpensive and accessible and should be informed of their rights in seeking redress.

Articles 6 and 7 respectively specify the requirements for the two procedure. Article 6(a) provides that if the victim seeks redress through formal judicial and administrative processes, victims must be informed of the relevant circumstances of the case; Article 6(b) stipulates that victims the views and concerns of victims are allowed to be presented and considered at appropriate stages of the proceedings where their personal interests are affected; Article 6(c) provides that victims should be provided with proper assistance; Article 6(d) provides that measures should be taken to protect victims' privacy and ensure their safety; Article 6(e) stipulates that victim should be granted awards without delay; Article 7 provides that informal mechanisms for the resolution of disputes, including mediation, arbitration and customary justice or indigenous practices, should be utilized where appropriate to facilitate conciliation and redress for victims.

Restitution

This part is about who should made restitution and what should be restituted. "Offenders or third parties responsible for their behaviour should, where appropriate, make fair restitution to victims, their families or dependants. Such restitution should include the return of property or payment for the harm or loss suffered, reimbursement of expenses incurred as a result of the victimization, the provision of services and the restoration of rights", according to Article 8. It can be seen that not only offenders but also third parties responsible for their behaviour should make fair restitution to victims, and restitution can be made in several ways and forms.

Article 9 provides that governments should review their practices, regulations and laws to consider restitution as an available sentencing option in criminal cases, in addition to other criminal sanctions. It can be seen that restitution is considered as an available sentencing option in criminal cases so as to ensure the victims can secure the right to get restitution.

Articles 10 and 11 are about the who should made restitution and what should be restituted in cases of substantial harm to the environment and public officials committing crime.

Compensation

Article 12 provides that when compensation is not fully available from the offender or other sources, States should endeavour to provide financial compensation to (a) victims who have sustained significant bodily injury or impairment of physical or mental health as a result of serious crimes; and (b) the family, in particular dependants of persons who have died or become physically or mentally incapacitated as a result of such victimization. According to Article 13, other funds may also be established to ensure the compensation to victims.

Assistance

Article 14 provides that victims should receive the necessary material, medical, psychological and social assistance through governmental, voluntary, community-based and indigenous means, and Article 15 stipulates that victims should be informed of the availability of health and social services and other relevant assistance and be readily afforded access to them. In order to obtain better assistance, Article 16 provides that police, justice, health, social service and other personnel concerned should receive training to sensitize them to the needs of victims, and Article 17 provides that attention should be given to those who have special needs when services and assistance are offered to victims.

Victims of Abuse of Power

What the victim means is different from the one we have defined above. "Victims" means persons who, individually or collectively, have suffered harm, including physical or mental injury, emotional suffering, economic loss or substantial impairment of their fundamental rights, through acts or omissions that do not yet constitute violations of national criminal laws but of internationally recognized norms relating to human rights. The Declaration does not give more details than Article 19, which provides that states should consider incorporating into the national law norms proscribing abuses of power and providing remedies to victims of such abuses. In particular, such remedies should include restitution and/or compensation, and necessary material, medical, psychological and social assistance and support.

The principles set forth in the Declaration have further promoted the legislation and improvement of victims' rights in the world and makes people protect victims according to this. We should also strengthen and perfect the legislation and practice of the protection of the victims' rights as soon as possible.

6.1.2.2 Protection of Special Victims by the Guidelines on Justice in Matters Involving Child Victims and Witnesses of Crime

Guidelines on Justice in Matters Involving Child Victims and Witnesses of Crime (hereinafter referred to as the Guidelines), was adopted by the United Nations Economic and Social Council in 2005 to realize justice in matters involving child victims and witnesses of crime (Article 1). "Child victims and witnesses" denotes children and adolescents, under the age of 18, who are victims of crime or witnesses to crime regardless of their role in the offence or in the prosecution of the alleged offender or groups of offender (Article 9). They are entitled to the right to be treated with dignity and compassion (Articles 10–14), the right to be protected from discrimination (Articles 15–18), the right to be informed (Articles 19–20), the right to be heard and to express views and concerns (Article 21), the right to effective assistance (Articles 22–25), the right to privacy (Articles 26–28), the right to be protected from hardship during the justice process (Articles 29–31), the right to safety (Articles 32–34), the right to reparation (Articles 35–37) and the right to special preventive measures (Articles 38–39).

Unlike the victims discussed above, more attention should be paid to special victims, such as children. In addition, there are the protection of the rights of the victims from the multi-stakeholder crime, the protection of the rights of female victims in special cases, and so on. The Guidelines provides basis for the improvement of China's juvenile criminal proceedings.

6.1.3 The Legislation and Perfection of the Victim's Rights in China

6.1.3.1 The Current Situation of Legislation on the Rights of Criminal Victims in China

Victim refers to a person whose personal right, property right or other legitimate rights and interests have been infringed upon by criminal acts. In China, the victim has three kinds of roles because of the different ways in which they participate in the criminal procedure: the private prosecutor in the private prosecution case, the plaintiff in the criminal incidental civil case and the litigant who takes part of the function of prosecution in the case of public prosecution. No matter which kind of role they play, the victim is one party of this case, enjoys the rights of other parties, and fulfills the relevant obligations.

In 2012, some of the rights of victims in the Criminal Procedure Law was amended and improved. The rights of victims in criminal proceedings in China mainly include (1) the right to complain against crimes that victims are given at the stage of filing a case where the accuser's right to safety and privacy is also given; and (2) the right to remedies from the decision not to file a case through which the victims can apply for reconsideration to the decision-rendering organ, or to request the people's procuratorate to exercise the power to file a case and oversee; and (3) the right to be informed of and the right to dissent from the expert opinions used as evidence by the investigative organs; and (4) the right to apply for withdrawal; and (5) the right to entrust an agent to participate in the proceedings; and (6) the right to express opinions in the examination before the prosecution in which the people's procuratorate reviews the prosecution, the opinions of the victims and their agents ad litem shall be heard and recorded, and the written opinions submitted by the victims and their agents ad litem shall be attached to the volume; and (7) the right of appeal and the right of direct prosecution against the people's procuratorate's decision not to prosecute; and (8) the right of the parties to reconcile in some cases; and (9) the right to participate in the proceedings at the trial stage(the victim has the right to be informed of the hearing, the right to present opinions in court, the right to question, the right to apply for witnesses, expert witnesses, the right to appear in court, the right to participate in the debate); and (10) the right of appeal to the procuratorial organ and the right of appeal to the effective judgment; and (11) the right to initiate private and incidental civil proceedings.

6.1.3.2 The Problems of the Legislation on Victim's Rights in China

Although the criminal procedure law gives the rights to the criminal victims since 1996, the victim's rights have not been paid enough attention in our country. Furthermore, the protection of the victim's rights has been strengthened by this legal document, but the victim's rights and protection for them in our country need more attention, compared with the protection of the defendant's rights. According to the current legislation and the United Nations basic principles on the protection of the rights of victims, the main problems for victim's rights in China are as follows.

Legislative Issues in Pre-trial Proceedings

The first problem exists in the case-filing stage. Article 108(3) of the Criminal Procedure Law stipulates that the public security organ, the people's procuratorate or the people's court shall accept all reports, complaints and information. If the public security organ or the people's procuratorate decides not to file a case, victims may apply for reconsideration in accordance with the law, or may also request the people's procuratorate to exercise the power of supervision on the filing of a case in such case, or they may bring a private prosecution before the court. However, the protection for the victims' right to bring a private prosecution before the court is limited when the public security organ and the people's procuratorate do not file the case for some illegitimate reasons and the victims bring a private prosecution before the court. "Cases in which the victim has evidence to prove that the defendant should be investigated for criminal responsibility according to law for acts that infringe upon his or her personal and property rights, and the public security bureau or the people's procuratorate shall not investigate the defendant for criminal responsibility" is the third kind of cases of private prosecution provided by Criminal Procedure Law. The victim's private prosecution is attributed to the decision of the public security organ or the people's procuratorate not to file a case. In the case of the decision based on illegitimate reasons, it is difficult for the victim to obtain written documents, and thus can not initiate a private prosecution. Moreover, according to the law of our country, the public security organ or the people's procuratorate are given great discretionary power in filing a case. Article 107 of the Criminal Procedure Law provides that the public security organs or the people's procuratorates shall, upon discovering facts of crimes or criminal suspects, file the cases for investigation within the scope of their jurisdiction. It is the two organs that decide whether there are facts of a crime or a criminal suspect, and there is not enough redress for the victim in this regard.

The second problem exists at the investigation phase. Since our country adheres to the principle of discovering the true facts, there is a possibility to bring additional hard to victims, such as keeping asking them for details of cases (e.g. sexual assault), having them to repeatedly talk about their painful experience and media report and public opinion on the cases. The law to protect this right to the victim has not been made in China.

The third problem can be found in the examination and prosecution stage. Although the victim's rights of expression and the ways to seek remedies are provided at this stage, it is the procuratorate to decide whether to give victims these rights or remedies or not. After the procuratorate decide not to initiate the prosecution, the victim may file a complaint or a private prosecution. When a victim files a private complaint, the people's court should accept it. The law stipulates that the people's procuratorate shall transfer the relevant case materials to the people's court, but the law does not stipulate whether the victim has the right to access these materials. In judicial practice, the judiciary often refuses the victims of private prosecution cases to consult the case files on the grounds that the law does not clearly provide for them, making it difficult for the victims to know the details the case.[10] If the procuratorate or the court does not allow the victim to access these materials for this reason, it places the victim at a disadvantage. The law has clearly stated that the burden to provide proof in the case of private prosecution lies on the victim, but it is very difficult for the victim to obtain evidence without the right to access the files. In this case, can a victim's agent ad litem have the same access as the defendant's defender to the files at the examination and prosecution stage? Article 44 of the Criminal Procedure Law provides that a victim in a case of public prosecution, his legal representatives or close relatives, and a party in an incidental civil action and his legal representatives shall, from the date on which the case is transferred for examination before prosecution, have the right to entrust agents ad litem. Article 56 of the Rules of Criminal Procedure of the People's Procuratorate (for trial implementation) provides that if, with the permission of the people's procuratorate, an agent ad litem can consult, excerpt or reproduce the case file materials according to Articles 47–49. In other words, the victim's agent ad litem can only be involved in the examination and prosecution stage

[10]Chen and Xiao [9].

during the proceedings, and does not have the right to access the files until he or she obtains the permission. In judicial practice, if the law stipulates that an agent ad litem has to apply for the access to case files, it means that it is hard for him or her to get such permission. Unlike defenders who have access to case files at the examination and prosecution stage, victims may not be aware of the materials obtained at the investigation stage and the materials used to review the prosecution, because these materials are only accessible after the approval of the prosecution service. The law also does not specify the right of the victim to remedies if the prosecution does not approve it.

Legislative Aspects of the Trial Proceedings

The victim's right to participate in the criminal proceedings is very extensive, including the right to be informed of the hearing, the right to present opinions in court, the right to question, the right to apply for witnesses, expert witnesses, and the right to participate in the debate. Such full participation in the proceedings can reflect the subject status of the parties, but the victims, as the parties, do not have the right to appeal relief of the criminal part of the sentence, and can only apply to the procuratorial organs for protest, the decision-making power rests entirely with the prosecution, which is incompatible with the victim's status as a party.

In addition, there are few criminal cases under which victims can bring an incidental civil action, which hobbles their efforts to realize the right to obtain financial compensation. Article 99 of the Criminal Procedure Law provides that where the victim has died or lost his/her capacity for civil conduct, his/her statutory representative or close relative shall be entitled to bring an incidental civil action. Article 138 of the *2013 Interpretation of the Supreme People's Court Concerning the Implementation of the Criminal Procedure Law of the People's Republic of China* provides that a victim who suffers material loss as a result of a criminal violation of their personal rights or as a result of property damage by a criminal offender, shall have the right to file a incidental civil action during a criminal prosecution. This means that victims can get compensation only in the case of crimes involving violation of personal rights and the damage to property. For the increasing number of economic crimes, the victims can not bring an incidental civil action and get compensation, especially in the cases of multi-stakeholder crime economic crimes. This is because there many often too many victims in such crime. Failure to enable victims to get compensation is likely to result in disorder.

Legislative Issues in Remedy Proceedings

Article 241 of the Criminal Procedure Law stipulates that a party or his legal representative or his close relative may present a petition to a people's court or a people's procuratorate regarding a legally effective judgment or order, however, execution of the judgment or order shall not be suspended he parties, their legal representatives and close relatives may appeal to the people's court or the people's procuratorate against a legally effective judgment or order, but the execution of the judgment or order can not be suspended. In other words, whether or not to initiate a trial supervision procedure to correct a wrong case depends on the decision of people's court or people's procuratorate. The victim, as a party to the procedure, only has the right of appeal against an unfair judgment. If people's court or people's procuratorate do not initiate trial supervision procedure, victims have no other means of redress.

Legislative Issues in Special Proceedings

Procedures for Criminal Cases Committed by Minors

As cited above in the *Guidelines on Justice in Matters Involving Child Victims and Witnesses of Crime*, our country has also begun to attach importance to the procedures for criminal cases committed by particular groups, such as minors. Chapter One of the Special Procedures of the Criminal Procedure Law provides for procedures for criminal cases committed by minors, which is a great improvement. However, most of the provisions in this chapter are to protect the special rights of minor suspects and defendants. As for the rights of minor victims, only one provision that paras 1, 2 and 3 shall apply where minor victims or witnesses are questioned is found in para 5 of Article 270. It can be seen that no provisions related to other stages than the trial and interrogation stages. In addition, the difference between the victim, criminal suspect or defendant is not clarified. Addition harm is likely to be caused to victims, but not to the criminal suspect or defendant, by questioning them. Keeping asking them about details of cases, especially the sexual assault, will cause more additional harm to the minors than the adults.

Procedures for Reconciliation Between Parties Concerned in Cases of Public Prosecution

Chapter Two of the Special Procedures of the Criminal Procedure Law provides plays a role to better protect the victim's right to obtain the financial compensation, but it also has some shortcomings. According to Article 277 of the Criminal Procedure Law, the parties may reach reconciliation agreements in the cases involving crimes prescribed under Chapters 4 and 5 of the Special Provisions of the Criminal Law that arise out of private disputes, which are punishable by fixed-term imprisonment of no longer than three years and the cases of crimes of negligence which are punishable by a fixed-term imprisonment of no longer than seven years, except for crimes of malfeasance. In that case, the parties are not allowed to reach reconciliation agreements in the cases involving crimes which are prescribed under those two chapters and punishable by fixed-term imprisonment of over three years. Victims, as analyzed above, can not obtain compensation by bringing an incidental civil action in the property crime. If the validity of the reconciliation is not recognized, it is unreasonable that the victim can not get compensation in the case of serious crime.

6.1.3.3 Suggestions on the Improvement of the Protection of the Rights of the Victims in China

Based on the discussion about the problems of the protection of the victims' rights in China above, suggestions will be made to improve the protection of the victims' rights in China with respect to four aspects, so as to maximize the functions of the victims and realize fairness and justice.

Pretrial Proceedings

First, more ways for victims to seek remedies should be provided if case is not filed at the case-filing stage. For example, the public security organ and procuratorate should provide a receipt of a report in writing, whether or not the case is eventually filed. As long as the victim reports a case, this document must be available as evidence that the victim has reported a case to the two organs. Moreover, in the case of long-term non-decision on whether to file a case, victims may seek judicial remedy from the court on this basis, or the court may issue a notice to the two organs to request them to make a decision on whether to file a case within a time limit, or give victims the right of private prosecution.

Second, the law for victim's right in the investigation stage to be protected from being hurt again should be made. While there may be concerns that this right may lead to greater difficulty or less efficiency in solving cases, victims are often the ones who are most eager to solve cases as soon as possible and they will certainly do their utmost to cooperate with the public prosecution authorities. So it doesn't make the case-solving less efficient. The victim's rights should be taken into account in addition to efficiency. Such regulations on the public security organ and procuratorate to solve the case in a more appropriate way are designed to prevent the state power from violating the rights and interests of the victims. Moreover, this right of the victim should be allowed to be exercised in the entire criminal procedure.

Third, a legal aid system should be established at the review and prosecution stage to ensure that victims can exercise their rights on an equal footing with other parties and avoid the occasion that their little knowledge of law will make it difficult for them to realize their rights. At the investigation and examination before prosecution stages, the victim should be entitled to the right of being informed of proceedings and the victim and his agent ad litem should also be given the right to access the case files, so as to better protect the victim's right to initiate private prosecution when the procuratorial organ makes a decision not to prosecute.

Trial Proceedings

As mentioned above, victims participate in criminal proceedings to "revenge" and get financial compensation. In order to enable the party to be a better role player and meet his desire for "revenge", the victim should be given the right of appeal which can be exercised not only in the criminal proceedings in order to avoid the situation where the procuratorate does not demurrer for a variety of reasons but the case meets the condition. Victims who can not obtain financial compensation may apply for compensation which can be given in cases of death or serious injury caused by violent crimes. More kinds of criminal cases in which the victims can bring incidental civil action should be added to ensure the victim can obtain the reasonable compensation.

Remedy Procedures

The remedy mechanism for criminal misjudged case, including reporting mechanism and correction mechanism, should be established on the basis of the best practices of two law systems in this regard, to make the remedy for misjudged case a procedure-based, long-term-operated procedure.[11] Establishment of a social assistance system that attracts the public attention can help victims return to a normal life as soon as possible from the disorder caused by the criminal act.

Special Procedures

Procedures for Criminal Cases Committed by Minors

Based on the *Guidelines on Justice in Matters Involving Child Victims and Witnesses of Crime*, a law should be made to safeguard the right of the victim minor. In addition, provisions should distinguished from those for minor criminal suspect and defendant.

Procedures for Reconciliation for Parties in the Case of Public Prosecution

The scope of application of the procedure for parties to make reconciliation should be expanded, such as making it applicable to non-violent property offenses. In cases of less serious crimes, such as those with a sentence of no more than three years' imprisonment, the prosecution may be granted the power of discretion not to prosecute if the defendant makes promise to give compensation in the case of serious crimes, the punishment may be reduced accordingly depending on the circumstances of compensation, rather than the current lenient punishment. In this way, we can enable the criminal suspect and the defendant to be more likely to give compensation and ensure the realization of the victim's right to compensation.

---

[11] Chen [10].

6.2 From Physical Evidence to Testimony of a Witness—The Perfection of the Criminal Witness System in China

The evidence system is an important part of the criminal procedure system, and also a key guarantee system to ensure the criminal cases can be solved in an impartial way. The lawsuit is evidence-based. The criminal proceedings are carried out by collecting evidence and finding the facts of the case. If there is something wrong with evidence collection, such as using the wrong collection method and adopting the improper evidence rules, it will be easy to make a case misjudge, which will undermine the impartiality. In the criminal procedure of our country, although there have been many judicial interpretations in recent years, improvement still needs to be made to such interpretations. The 2012 Criminal Procedure Law overhauled its rules of evidence.

With respect to the amendments concerning the evidence system in Criminal Procedure Law, five adjustments can be found in Article 57 (relevant investigators or other personnel appear before the courtroom to make explanations), Article 62 (measures to protect the witness, Article 63 (allowance for the witness), Article 187 (provisions for the witness, police and expert witnesses appear before the court) and Article 188 (people's court may compel the witness to appear and allow the witness not to appear before the court). These are newly added articles, which shows the efforts of the legislature to solve various problems in the process of witness testimony in criminal trial by improving the law. In the evidence system, the rules of what kinds of evidence should be collected, how to using evidence to prove guilty or innocent and who should provide evidence are objective, while the opinions provided by the witness, an important participant of the lawsuit, are subjective. Therefore, lawmakers need to develop a scientific procedure for the witness to participate in the criminal proceedings by taking into account the thoughts of people and the behavior norms. In the past, the rules of witnesses' participation in criminal proceedings were loosely defined, making them unpractical and the witnesses unwilling or afraid to testify. This affects the smooth running of the criminal proceedings. The effective participation of the witness in the criminal procedure can help establish the foundation of the adversarial system in China, safeguard the right of the defendant to cross-examine, and help the court to get to know the he facts of the case to make a fair decision. The amendment of the witness system by the Criminal Procedure Law marks the initial establishment of the criminal witness testimony system in China and significant progress has been made in a more procedure-based witness system.

6.2.1 The Perfection of the System of Witness Appearing in Court

6.2.1.1 The Rules of a Witness's Testimony in Court

Article 47 of the 1996 Criminal Procedure Law stipulated that the testimony of witnesses must be questioned and cross-examined in the courtroom by the public prosecutor, the victim, the defendant and the defenders, should the testimonies of witnesses of all sides have been heard and verified can they be used as the basis for settling the case. Although the word "examination" implies that the witness should be present, the ambiguity of this legal document makes the cross-examination in court trial focus on the written testimony. Article 141 of the Interpretation of the Supreme People's Court Concerning the Implementation of the Criminal Procedure Law states that a witness shall appear before court to give evidence and enumerates the exceptions to the rule. However, there are no more specific provisions to ensure its implementation, either physically or procedurally. The non-appearance of witnesses has led to direct use of witness statements which are provided before trial in court hearings, which not only frustrates the judges who want to examine the validity and the truth of witness testimony by the presence of witnesses in court, but also makes the legislator's expectation of enhancing the adversarial system and preventing the court hearing from being a mere formality come to naught.[12] A series of adjustments were made to the Criminal Procedure Law in 2012 to address this issue, such as Article 187, para 1, which first defines the cases in which a witness should testify in court.

A witness shall give evidence in court and three conditions must be met. First, the public prosecutor, the party concerned or the defender have any objection to the witness' testimony. The purpose of the witness testifying in court is to help realize the right of cross-examination of the prosecution and the defense and find out whether testimony is false. If both sides agree on the content of the testimony, there is not need for the witness to testify in court. Second, the testimony of the witness has a significant impact on the conviction and sentencing. This condition is given after taking into account the limited judicial resources of our country and the attitude of the public towards testifying. No country has the judicial resources to bring all criminal witnesses before the court, and this is particularly true in our country. On the one hand, once the witness appears in court, it involves a series of problems, such as trial time, witness protection, compensation for appearing in court. On the other hand, traditional wisdom has it that people are unwilling to appear in court as a witness because they fear of being retaliated and jeopardizing their relationship with others. It is a good solution to use limited resources to help the witness to appear before court to help find out the truth. The people who have significant impact on conviction and sentencing refer to the witness to the occurrence of the case or the main or even the

[12] Chen [11].

only witness who have impact on conviction and sentencing, separately or jointly.[13] Third, the people's court considers it necessary for a witness to testify. The court shall have the final decision as to whether it is necessary for the witness to appear in court after considering all the factors.

In addition, in the case of persons who are unable to appear before a court for objective reasons, such as serious illness, severe mobility difficulties, the remoteness of their residence from the place where the court is to be held and the lack of access to transportation, as well as the fact that they are unable to return to their home country for a short period abroad, the supreme people's court has made exceptions through judicial interpretation. As technology advances, people who can not appear in court for justified reasons can testify by video and other means. Video testimony here should be understood as testimony by means of remote instant messaging rather than through the playback of pre-recorded video files.

6.2.1.2 Establishment of Compulsory Witnesses Attendance System

The court may compel a witness who should appear in court but refuses to do so without just cause to appear, and may take certain compulsory measures. Article 188 of the Criminal Procedure Law provides for the compulsory measures to compel a witness to appear. In the past, although witnesses were required by law to testify in court, the absence of compulsory measures and legal liability for a witness who refuse to testify without just cause made it difficult for the prosecution, the defence and the court to compel the witness to appear in court, this is also a major reason for the low attendance rate of witnesses. On the one hand, the establishment of compulsory witnesses attendance system can make the witness fulfill his obligation to appear in court and establish the authority and solemnity of law. On the other hand, the law to compel witnesses to testify can also make the witness no longer fear that they hurt the relationship with others by doing so. Now the witnesses can say that they have to do so because it is what the law prescribes.

In order to compel a witness to appear in court, some conditions must be met. First, there is the necessity of requiring the witness to testify as prescribed by Article 187 of the Criminal Procedure Law and the court shall notify the witness. Second, the witness is not the defendant's spouse, parents, children. Third, the witness has no justified reasons for not being able to testify. After confirming these three conditions are met, the people's court may issue an order to have the witness to be compelled to appear by the court police.

In addition to compelling the witness to appear in court, the people's Court may discipline or detain the witness depending on the extent to which the witness does not comply with his or her obligation to appear in court. Instances of non-compliance with the obligation to testify in court include refusal to appear in court without good cause and refusal to testify after the hearing. While courts are empowered by law to take more stringent measures to improve the attendance of witnesses, they should

[13] Lang [12].

be careful of using them. There are many reasons, subjective and objective, that witnesses refuse to testify in court. Both the court and the prosecution and defense parties should cooperate with each other to enlighten the witnesses, take measures to protect witnesses and encourage the witnesses to testify.

Article 188(1) of the Criminal Procedure Law stipulates that while the people's court may compel a witness to testify in court, it makes it clear for the first time that the spouse, parents and children of the defendant may be exempted from compulsory attendance at court. The reason for the exception is that "it is not appropriate to compel him to appear in court because of his status. Forcing spouses, parents, and children to testify against the accused in court is likely to jeopardize the relationship with family members and harm the social harmony".[14] It is important to note that the law does not exempts these three kinds of persons from the obligation to testify, but from appearing in court at the trial stage. In the Bo Xilai case, for example, Bo Xilai repeatedly asked Bo Gu Kai Lai to testify. However, under this article, the court can not compel her to appear if she does not want to, and testimony was only be made by showing footage in this case.

6.2.2 Improvement of the System of Expert Witness Appearing in Court

It has been a serious problem that the witness, including the expert who is seen as a kind of witness in a broad sense, does not appear in court and the attendance rate is low. The expert, as the party who gives opinions, shall appear in court to face cross-examination of his or her opinions. The absence of an expert witness in court results in the expert opinion being used directly in court, which not only frustrates the judges who want to examine the validity and the truth of witness testimony by the presence of witnesses in court, but also makes the legislator's expectation of enhancing the adversarial system and preventing the court hearing from being a mere formality come to naught. To solve this problem, the renewed criminal Procedure Law has clarified the circumstances where the expert must appear in court to testify and the procedural consequences caused by non-attendance.

If the public prosecutor, the party or the defender, or the agent ad litem have any objection to the expert testimony and the people's court deems it necessary for the expert witness to appear in court, the expert shall appear before court. Unlike the conditions under which a witness must testify in court, the expert's presence in court does not result from an expert's opinions having material impact on the conviction and sentence, but from the disagreement with the opinions between the prosecution and defense and the people's court deeming it necessary. In such case, the expert witness shall fulfill his obligation to testify in court. The provisions of Criminal Procedure Law are different from those of Civil Procedure Law. In criminal proceedings, the people's court decides whether the expert should appear in court

[14] Lang [13].

based on the disagreement with the opinions between the prosecution and defense. In civil proceedings, if the parties have any objection to the expert opinions, the expert shall testify in court; if the parties have no objection, but the court deems it necessary, the expert shall also appear in court. The criminal procedure's provisions on the conditions under which expert witnesses may appear in court accommodate both fairness and efficiency. The fact that the law gives the people's court the power of discretion in this matter shows respect for our country's long-existing tradition of criminal procedure.

The fulfillment of the obligation needs to be encouraged by responsibility. The renewed Criminal Procedure Law for the first time stipulates the legal consequences for the expert witness not to testify in court. If, as notified by the people's court, the expert witness refuses to appear in court to give evidence, the expert opinion shall not be used as the basis for deciding the case. This is a procedural sanction. The design of this provision is similar to the way in which exclusionary rules are adopted to prevent illegal evidence collection. In order to ensure the reliability of the expert opinion, it is important to encourage the party who gets supported by the expert opinion to convince the expert witness to appear before court by not accepting the expert opinion.

The updated Criminal Procedure Law stipulates that the witness should appear in court but not in court, and the content of compulsory appearing in court, admonishing and even detaining, but the new criminal procedure law has no similar provisions for the expert, except that the expert's opinion will not be adopted if he refuses to appear in court. If the expert witness refuses to testify in court without proper reasons, the People's Court shall inform the executive branch or the relevant departments. In accordance with Article 13 of the Decision of the Standing Committee of the National People's Congress on the Administration of Expert Testimony, hereinafter referred to as the Decision on Expert Testimony, if the expert refuses to appear as a witness in court upon notification of people's court in accordance with the law, the Ministry of Justice of the Government of the People's Republic of China at the provincial level shall impose a penalty of suspending the business in expert testimony for not less than three months and not more than one year; if the circumstances are serious, the registration shall be revoked.

The Criminal Procedure Law has added procedural sanction to expert witness appearing in court, which indicates the development trend for the system of witness appearing in court. In addition, Article 63 of the Criminal Procedure Law provides that a witness shall be entitled to allowance for his/her performance of the obligation of giving testimony and such allowance shall be guaranteed, but it does say so for the experts. The reason for the expert witness to charge fee is that he or she provides the service, and the expert witness should get paid for this because some manpower and material resource are used. This charge does not include the remuneration for appearance before the court.

6.2.3 The Investigators' Statements and Testimony Before the Court

In accordance with the Criminal Procedure Law, anyone who knows the circumstances of a case, except for persons with people with physical and mental disabilities or the young who are unable to distinguish between right and wrong and to express correctly, is qualified as a witness in criminal proceedings. In the criminal procedure, the case includes not only the substantive facts, but also the procedural facts. In the usual context, we tend to consider the persons who know the substantive facts as the witnesses, but exclude the witness who knows the procedural facts. The person who is most likely to access the procedural facts is the investigator. In the past, few ordinary citizens appear in court to give evidence, let alone the investigators who are bureaucracy-oriented. With improvement of the law-based criminal procedure, efforts are made to prevent the trial from being a mere formality and to avoid the occurrence of misjudged and unjust cases, which all help to refine the witness system. Investigators testifying in court has become a significant improvement in the criminal procedure to improve its witness system. Articles 57 and 187 of the Criminal Procedure Law respectively provide for the appearance of investigators in court to give testimony on procedural facts concerning the legality of the collection of evidence and on substantive facts concerning the witnessing of crimes in the exercise of their functions.

"Where there exists no evidentiary support for the legality of the evidence gathering means, the people's procuratorate may request the people's court concerned to notify relevant investigators or other personnel to appear before the courtroom to make explanations. The people's court may, at its own discretion, notify relevant investigators or other personnel to appear before the courtroom to give explanations. Relevant investigators or other personnel may also take the initiative to request an appearance before the courtroom for an explanation. Relevant personnel shall also appear before courtroom if so notified by the people's court", according to Article 57 of the Criminal Procedure Law. As part of the exclusionary rules, this article incorporates the contents of Article 7 of the *Regulation on Certain Issues of Exclusion of Unlawful Evidence in Criminal Cases*. The public prosecutor bears the burden to prove the legality of the evidence. As for way of proof, the most common situation in the past about taking the confession of the defendant, for example, was that the defendant is claimed to be extorted by torture, and the investigating organ would often provide a written "statement of the case" in response. This "statement of the case" is often difficult to overturn as long as the it is complete in form. In fact, the means of torture are varied and hidden. The "statement of the case" alone is clearly not enough to prove legality. The presence of the interrogators, who are questioned by the court and cross-examined by the accused, absolutely can help to find out if the evidence is legal in a fast and efficient way. In addition to interrogators, anyone who participates in and is aware of the collection of evidence has the obligation to testify in court when necessary, such as investigators taking material evidence, police officers in detention house, witnesses during searches. It is important to note that the presence of investigators in court is not the primary means of proving the legality of evidence. The phrase of "where there exists no evidentiary support for the legality of the evidence gathering means" refers to the fact that the court, after public prosecutor providing records of interrogations, audio and video recordings of interrogations, records of medical examinations in detention houses, records of searches and investigations, still have doubts about the legality of the evidence.

Article 57 of the Criminal Procedure Law states that people's court concerned should notify relevant investigators to appear before the courtroom to "make explanations" to prove the legality of the evidence rather than "give evidence". It is believed that the presence of investigators in court to make explanations does qualify as the presence of witnesses in court. The main reason is that the investigators are acting on behalf of the investigating authorities for the prosecution, not for themselves, and that the statements made are not witness testimony.[15] I thinks that this idea results from misunderstanding the function of the exclusionary rules. The procedure of exclusionary rules is relatively independent from the procedure of court investigation and debate in the court trial, and its purpose is to find out whether the collection of evidence is lawful or not. It investigates the procedural facts and reflects the value of criminal procedure. The investigator's explanation of evidence collect is to provide evidence to prove the legality of evidence, and he is a witness in a broad sense. After the investigators give testimony, they also need to be cross-examined by the defendant in order to fulfill their obligations as witnesses.

Article 187, para 2, of the Criminal Procedure provides for the police to testify as witnesses. This Article is different from Article 57. The police officers, as witnesses as prescribed in this Article, should follow the rules of witness testimony and are entitled to relevant rights and perform official duties.

It is new for investigators to testify in court, which means more things to be done by investigating organs and procuratorial organs. To implement this system smoothly, relevant measures need to be developed. First, investigators should enhance their professional quality. On the one hand, the exclusionary rules procedure can urge the investigators to exercise the power of investigation and use investigative means in accordance with the law; on the other hand, they have to make preparations both in psychology and capacity to give evidence. Through the survey on the investigators' appearance in court, some researchers found that the investigators who are as witnesses to appear in court could not make clear explanations, making it difficult for the judges to get a clear picture of what happened in the case. In some cases, this procedure even turns out to be meaningless.[16] Investigative organs should provide training for investigators in testifying in court when they face new circumstances. Second, protective measures should also be offered to them. Investigators who serve as witnesses when giving evidence are more likely to risk their personal safety in cases involving mafia-style crimes, crimes against state security, and serious violent crimes. In addition, relevant provisions on witness protection shall be applied equally. When evidence is cross-examined by means of technical investigation, protective measures

[15]Zhu [14].

[16]Maran [15].

shall be adopted to avoid the exposure of the applied technical measures and the true identity of such personnel, in accordance with the provisions of Article 152 of the Criminal Procedure Law. Furthermore, as long as investigators testify truthfully in court and even the testimony is against the prosecution and the investigating organ, the unit where they work shall not retaliate against them. Even if it is related to his illegal evidence-gathering behavior, it is the evidence-gathering behavior, not the testimony behavior, that should be investigated for legal responsibility.

6.2.4 The Improvement of the Guarantee System for Witness Testimony

6.2.4.1 Methods of Witness Protection

The people's court, the people's procuratorates and the public security organ may take protective measures according to the specific circumstances of the case and their respective power. In addition, the law gives the witness, expert witness, the victim and their close relatives the right to apply for such protection.

Article 62 of the Criminal Procedure Law defines what kinds of protective measures that may be taken. The persons, including witnesses, expert witnesses, victims and their close relatives who are threatened by personal safety because of testifying in proceeding, should be given protective measures. The proceedings here contain trial, investigation and prosecution stages. The protective measures should be used in the cases involving crimes endangering State security, those involving terrorist activities, organized crimes committed by groups in the nature of criminal syndicates, drug-related crimes and the like. These kinds of cases prescribed by law all pose great danger to society and criminal suspects use cruel means to commit crimes, which make witnesses, victims and expert witnesses more vulnerable to retaliation. We can also know from common sense that the witnesses are likely to be retaliated in the cases involving violent crimes and duty-related crimes. Therefore, in deciding whether to take protective measures, the judicial organ should not only convict a criminal suspect of a crime, but also investigate the circumstance of a case and use the term "the like" properly in the law. "Special protective measures may be taken if danger created by crimes to society and the threaten faced by the witnesses, expert witnesses and victims are comparable to those of above-mentioned four kinds of crimes", according to the legislator's interpretation. It is not scientific to determine the degree of the harm of crime to the society according to whether some cases meet certain conditions.[17] In criminal proceedings, there is a variety of things that can pose threat to witnesses and others. This depends on the attitude of the party whose interests are impaired by the testimony of a witness, regardless of what charge is against the defendant. This danger may be created by the suspect, the defendant's associates, relatives, or the prosecution because the witness has given testimony in

[17] Lang [16].

favour of the suspect or the defendant. Therefore, when witnesses seeking protective measures, the organ with such responsibility should consider what kinds of threaten witnesses may be exposed to. A large number of judicial resources, of course, will be used for protective measures. The lawmakers may take into account the actual situation when they create these provisions, but it is the way to go.

Protective measures mainly includes: (1) keeping confidential the real names, addresses, employers and other personal information of the aforesaid persons; and (2) adopting measures to avoid the actual appearance or true voice of those who appear in courtrooms for testimony; and (3) prohibiting certain persons from having contact with the witnesses, experts, victims and their close relatives; and (4) adopting special measures to protect the personal and residential security of the aforesaid persons and other necessary protective measures. This is the first time that the law clearly enumerates the methods of protection, thus making the witness protection system practicable, which is a great progress made in improving the witness system. The protective measures will be updated according to how this system is implemented. In the implementation of these special protection measures, it is necessary to coordinate the relationship with the protection of the defendant's basic procedural rights. The right of being informed, the right of being present, and the right of cross-examination, for example, should be safeguarded after taking measures to avoid the actual appearance or true voice of the witness.[18] In order to improve this system, it is necessary to learn from foreign best practices to keep introducing protective measures, such as the provision of change of identity for witnesses and the provision of accommodation.

6.2.4.2 Compensation for Witness

Article 63 of the Criminal Procedure Law for the first time clarifies the allowance for witnesses and provides that a witness shall be entitled to allowance for his or her performance of the obligation of giving testimony in terms of transportation, accommodation and catering expenses incurred thereby and the allowance granted to witnesses for giving testimony shall be included into the business expenses of judicial organs and be guaranteed by the public finance of people's governments at the same level. The testimony of a witness is the performance of his obligations to the state through his conduct. The loss caused to the witness by the act of giving evidence should be made up by the state. In addition, the unit at which the witness works shall not deduct his salary due to his testimony, because the unit has the responsibility to support witness testimony and cooperate with the judicial organs in handling the case. It should be noted that the allowance provided for by law is not only for his or her performance of the obligation of giving testimony in court, but also for the expenses incurred as a result of his testimony at various stages of the proceedings, and such allowance shall be given by the authorities handling the case at that stage.

[18] He [17].

System of compensation for witness is supported by the state transfer, and it difficult to define how and how much to compensate the witness. It may be made clear that such allowance granted to witnesses is a kind of compensation rather than remuneration. Compensation shall be given according to the actual expenses of the witness, including transportation, accommodation and catering expenses. How much the witness spend in the testimony depends on the different economic development levels in different areas of our country, so it is hard to for lawmakers to set a standard. Even where the compensation standards set by the case-handling authorities are based on local per capita income, there are often cases where witnesses are from other cities or countries and can not get full compensation. We should take into account this situation. The allowance is not what the witness comes to testify in court for. The function of the compensation system should be viewed objectively, and it shows the respect of the judicial system to the witness.

6.2.5 Other Problems

6.2.5.1 The Validity of the Testimony of the Witness Who Does not Appear in Court

The perfection of the witness system in Criminal Procedure Law directly aims at improving the low rate of witness appearing in court which has existed for a long time in China. On the one hand, it defines the cases in which the witness should testify in court. On the other hand, the court is empowered to compel the witness to appear in court and punish him, so as to urge him to appear. As for the supporting measures, a witness protection system should be established to get the "fear of retaliation" out of the mind of witness; the salary of the witness should not be deducted during his testimony, and the expenses should be paid so as to eliminate the worries of the witness. All these measures can help increase the attendance of witnesses. However, the law does not specify whether the testimony of a witness who has not appeared in court can be excluded, and it is up to the judge to determine this according to the circumstances of the case and other evidence.

This problem results in the no procedural consequences prescribed for the non-attendance of witnesses and could easily lead to the failure of the entire system of ensuring the attendance of witnesses. This is like a series of exclusionary rules of illegal evidence in order to prevent the use of torture. The Criminal Procedure Law has always taken a clear stand against extorting confessions by torture, which is, however, often seen due to the lack of practicable system to restrict such misconduct and supporting measures. The methods of restraining extorting a confession by torture includes using money to recording the entire interrogation process and build "isolated" interrogation rooms, or making law to regulate interrogation time, place and methods. However, the most effective measure is to exclude the confessions obtained by illegal means, regardless of whether the confession is true, so as to get this means out of the mind of investigators. If a witness who is supposed to appear does not appear for interrogation and his or her written testimony can not serve as a basis for conviction and sentence, there is no doubt that this will prompt the party who brings the witness before the court to either actively urge the witness to appear before the court, or require authorities concerned to reformulate provisions of lawsuit or defense. One of the many reasons for the low rate of witnesses appearing in court is that the public prosecution, which bears the burden of proof, uses a large number of written testimony, which makes it impossible for the defendant to cross-examine the evidence effectively and exercise the right to defence. If the testimony of a witness who does not appear in court can not be admitted, there is no doubt that this will have a huge impact on the prosecution.

If the expert witness refuses to testify in court, the expert opinion shall not be used as the basis for deciding the case. The absence of a similar provision for witnesses may come down to the fact defendants in serious crimes are prevented from evading justice due to insufficient evidence to charge them, so as to enable authorities concerned to try their best to fight against crimes. It may take some time to establish a complete system of exclusion of written testimony, or even a system of "fruit of the poisonous tree". More importantly, we need to keep following the principle of directness and verbalism through the appearance of witnesses in court. Where written testimony is still used at this point, the people's court should perform strict scrutiny of written testimony. For the written testimony of a witness who has not appeared in court as a witness, the opinions of the procurators appearing in court, the defendants and their defenders shall be heard, and a comprehensive judgment shall be made on the basis of other evidence. If there is an inconsistency in the written testimony of a witness who has not appeared in court and it can not be excluded and there is no other evidence to prove the inconsistency, it can not be used as a basis for deciding a case.

6.2.5.2 Immunity from Testifying

Article 188 of the Criminal Procedure Law provides that the people's court may compel the witness to appear, unless the witness is the spouse, parent or child of the defendant. After its implementation, people consider it as a "tolerating and concealing between kinfolks" system and even an "immunity from testifying obligation", which make lawmakers a little disappointed.

This is a human-based article which pays attention to the emotional care of the defendant and his family, avoiding the awkward situation of "place righteousness above family loyalty" in the court. It is believed that this reflects the change of orientation of social value. The national interest and social interest are no longer seen as over everything, and more attention are paid to protect the family.[19] However, this rosy view ignores the appearance in court prescribed by the law. The core value of the "tolerating and concealing between kinfolks" in traditional Chinese culture or the "right of exemption from testifying for relatives" in modern legal context is that relatives should not be forced to make statements against each other. This is for the

---

[19]Zhang [18].

sake of maintaining people's ethical principles and values. Article 188 of the Criminal Procedure Law states that relatives may not be compelled to testify, but it doesn't provides that relatives are allowed not to testify. A relative of the defendant, who has knowledge of the facts of the case and is cognitively and judicially competent, is still required to testify at the investigation and prosecution stages, even if his testimony is against the defendant. This clearly demonstrates that the state and social interests are all that matter and the procedure is fact-finding oriented.

The purpose of not compelling the specific relatives of the defendant to testify in court is to avoid the testimony which is not in favour of the defendant to harm the family relationship. This is clearly about the prosecution's case for a witness appearance. If the witness is not willing to appear in court, the defendant can not in any way make him appear. It is clearly difficulty for the defendant to exercise the right cross-examination and the right to defense. For the defendant, cross-examination in court may enable the defendant to get the information in his favour. In this regard, the protection of maintaining the family relationship should be seen less important than the protection of the defendant's procedural rights. The fact that the important witnesses are allowed not to appear in court to be questioned by multiple parties is in the favour of the prosecution, which reflects the fact that this article still emphasizes the primacy of the interests of the state and of society.

Although it may have been true that Article 188 avoids confrontation between relatives in court and shows the "tolerating and concealing between kinfolks", there is hardly the case of "immunity from obligation to testify" manifested in this Article. As stated earlier, this Article absolves the obligation to appear in court, but not to testify. If we want to give such immunity, not only close relatives, but also others, such as doctors, lawyers, religious persons, who should also be exempted from the duty of testimony due to their obligations from professions to keep information confidential.

6.2.5.3 Accomplice as a Witness in the Joint Offense

Due to the increasing number of joint crime cases, we often encounter a problem that whether the co-defendant is qualified as a witness. In my opinion, this issue should be discussed depending on the three kinds of actual situations below:

First, the co-defendant is an accomplice, which is the most common situation. I think that the defendant and the witness in this situation have completely different status in criminal proceedings, enjoy and fulfill different rights and obligations, bear different legal consequences, so they disqualified as witnesses. Firstly, the joint offender in such cases has a common criminal intent and should be charged in the criminal proceedings. It is obviously inappropriate if a part of the confession of the defendant is taken as "the confession of the defendant" and a part as "the testimony of the witness". Secondly, the defendant and the witness have different rights and obligations because the co-defendant is the party of the case and the witness is a party other than the party litigant. The most significant difference is that the witness must tell the truth or it will constitute perjury, but it doesn't say so for the defendant. It is known to all that leniency should be shown to those who confess, and severity should not be imposed upon those who resist. Thirdly, if one defendant serves as a witness to prove the guilt of another defendant, this is actually proving his own guilt. It shifts the burden of proof to the defendant.

Second, the co-defendant is not an accomplice, but is implicated in the crime. Such situation can be found in the cases where criminals are harbored and an accomplice in the first crime also commits the second crime alone. In such cases, when the defendant who harbors criminals and the defendant who commits the first crime state the crime which they do not commit, co-defendants are not interested parties and do not prove their guilt in an indirect way, so they are qualified as witnesses and their statement can be seen as testimony.

Third, the co-defendant is an accomplice who have been tried separately or sentenced before others. As the name implies, co-defendant is charged and tried at the same time. The joint offenders who have been tried separately and participate in the proceedings of other have different status from the co-defendants, so they are entitled to the same rights and perform the same obligations as the witness.

In order to effectively combat corruption, criminal and terrorism-related crimes and improve the capacity to deal with the increasingly complex forms of crime, we need to consider implementing the system of tainted witness with immunity while creating the provision of "no one shall be compelled to prove his guilt" in the criminal procedure law and requiring "truthful answer". The testimony from perpetrators who are involved in criminal acts and have key evidence in some major and serious cases may of great help to fight against crime thoroughly. The current system of voluntary surrender and meritorious service can only help to expose other crimes. The system of tainted witness may encourage the accomplice in a joint crime to be the "prosecution witnesses" to help combat crime.

6.2.5.4 Participation of Eyewitness in Criminal Proceedings

A criminal eyewitness is a person who testifies to the investigative acts of investigators during the investigation stages of inquest, examination, search, seizure and identification. This is explicitly prescribed by the Criminal Procedure Law and its judicial interpretations. A criminal eyewitness observes, supervises and testifies to particular criminal proceedings. Observation is the eyewitness's first-hand experience of the means and process of obtaining evidence from investigators. Supervision does not mean that the witness has the right to "give opinions" on the investigators' evidence collection, but by doing so, the witness, as a neutral party, can participate in the investigation where no one other than investigators involved before to prevent their abuse of power. The role of the witness is manifested in two aspects. First, the eyewitness signs the investigation records and confirms his participation in the investigation and that the investigation is carried out in accordance with the law; second, when the legality of the source of evidence is in doubt in the court hearing, he can explain to the court.

In the past, the eyewitness's role to testify in the investigation usually ended with his signature on the records. Now, as the sanction measures are strengthened by the Criminal Procedure Law, especially the application of the exclusionary rule of illegal obtained evidence, another way for the eyewitness to prove the legality of the investigation has become increasingly important. Article 54 of the Criminal Procedure Law provides that physical evidence or documentary evidence that is not collected according to statutory procedures and is therefore likely to materially damage judicial justice shall be subject to correction or reasonable explanations, and shall be excluded if correction or reasonable explanations are not made. The Public Prosecution organ bears the responsibility to prove the legality of evidence collection. When the records of investigation is in doubt, the public prosecutor may require the collegiate bench to notify the investigators and the eyewitness to appear before the court to make a statement.

There are two issues to be clarified. First, the eyewitness should be one of the participants in the proceedings prescribed in Article 106 of the Criminal Procedure Law. A participant in the proceedings is a citizen or a unit other than the personnel of state organs who take part in the proceedings, and he participates in the proceedings in accordance with the law and enjoys certain rights and assumes some obligations. The law gives the eyewitness the right to participate in the witness activity and play his role in it. On the one hand, he has the right to witness the investigation in person, sign the records and request an appearance before the courtroom for an explanation; on the other hand, he has the obligation to explain the investigation. Article 67 of the *Interpretation of the Supreme People's Court Concerning the Implementation of the Criminal Procedure Law of the People's Republic of China* excludes the personnel or hired persons from public security and judicial organs who carry out crime scene investigations, inspections, searches, seizures, or other powers in criminal proceedings as eyewitnesses Second, the rules for the eyewitness to appear before the court should be made on the basis of the rules for the witness. The question whether eyewitness is witness is basically the same as whether the investigator appearing before the court to give an explanation is seen as testifying. The answer depends on the perspective from which you perceive it. Different perspectives affect the content of the answers. In this regard, the key is how we look at the procedural trial. I it part of the trial? Is procedural fact deemed as case fact? To be more specific, is the procedure of exclusion of illegally-obtained evidence independent during the trial or relatively independent? I think that "yes" is the answer to all these questions. Evidence is the basis of making substantive judgment. Investigating the legitimacy of evidence reflects the value of this procedure, which is the development trend of our criminal procedure and human rights protection system. Eyewitness gets to know the facts through witness activity and plays an irreplaceable role of proof, making them equally important as the witnesses. Although we still take the substantive fact as the standard to determine the qualification of the witness according to the criminal procedure law, the rule on eyewitness' and the investigator's testimony should be improved compared with the rule on witness.

6.3 The Criminal Procedure's Right of the Expert in the Criminal Procedure Law

Expert appraisal refers to the activities in which the expert uses technology or expertise to make identification and judgement about certain special problems in proceedings and to provide expert opinions. As the society develops, there is an increasing forms of evidence and the certain special problems are various and involve many subjects. Appearing in court is giving evidence, as the saying goes. Expert appraisal is carried out through scientific means to interpret the contents of evidence, which is important for the judge to find out the facts of the case and convict and sentence the criminals in an impartial way. The expert, as the main player in appraisal, is playing an increasing important role in proceeding. Furthermore, more problems are exposed in this appraisal. The Criminal Procedure Law was overhauled in 2012, which is manifested in the refined rules relating to appraisal and updated regulations on the activities of experts in the proceedings. In addition, the "expert conclusion" in the categories of evidence was revised as "expert opinion". It also clarifies the circumstances under which the expert will testify in court, provides protective measures for the experts and establishes a supporting system for proceeding for "persons with expertise".

6.3.1 The Litigant Status of the Expert Witness

According to Article 106 of the Criminal Procedure Law, an appraiser is one of the participants in the criminal proceedings. The appraiser is not a party, but a participant in the proceedings who has no interest in the case, like the legal representative, the agent ad litem, the defender, the witness, the interpreter and so on. The appraiser does not assume the independent litigation obligation, and he plays a role in assisting the authorities to ascertain the facts of the case. Article 144 of the Criminal Procedure Law stipulates that when certain special problems relating to a case need to be solved in order to clarify the circumstances of the case, experts shall be assigned or invited to give their appraisal.

In the Western countries, especially in the common law countries, the legislation and theory on evidence regard appraiser as expert witness and expert opinion as witness testimony. In the legal system of these countries, the appraiser is only a kind of expert witnesses. Anyone with expertise in a particular area who can help the court the jury to solve special problems is an expert. For example, teachers who have been teaching for many years may act as expert witnesses in cases involving teaching and learning, and drivers with long experience in driving may give their professional opinion on facts involving traffic. In other words, in these countries people are deemed as expert witnesses because they maintain certain kinds of knowledge. These expert witnesses are entrusted by one of the parties to testify before the court and have the same status as other witnesses. The validity of his testimony is not as influential as the expert opinions used in our country. The adoption of this model in common law countries is mainly because of the adversarial system used in these countries. The prosecution and the defense, on an equal footing, invite their own expert witnesses to help them in the proceedings. The judge remains neutral in this procedure, and both parties condition each other and maximize their litigation functions to ascertain the facts of the case.

In civil law countries, the appraiser is generally regarded as the judge's assistant. In France, a judicial appraiser is a professional technical person who, under the instructions of a judge, gives an opinion on facts that needs to be found out through professional knowledge and verified through a complex investigation.[20] German scholars regard appraisers as persons entrusted by judges to present empirical reports on specific issues or to use their expertise to work on the materials provided by the court in order to assist it in its awareness-raising activities.[21] Under this concept, the judge has the right to appoint and employ appraisers. In addition, the appraiser must be neutral and has to withdraw if necessary. The appraiser system originates from the litigation model of inquisitorial system in civil law countries. The judge is the main actor to proactively discover the truth in the lawsuit. When he is faced with a problem that he can not solve because of his limited knowledge, he needs the help of the appraiser to find out the truth. The appraiser under this circumstance is free from the influence of the prosecution and the defense, and carries on the appraisal work neutrally, so the appraisal features impartiality and the authority. However, the drawback is that the defense can not participate in the appraisal process, so it is difficult to effectively cross-examine the appraisal. When a judge makes a mistake, it's hard to correct it in time.

The expert witness system in our country is similar to the one in the civil law countries. It distinguishes the witness from the expert. The important differences between expert witness and witness, expert opinion and witness testimony are as follows:

(1) Witnesses can not be chosen or replaced because they are determined by the case itself. The expert witness is appointed or hired by the public security organ or the judicial organ according to the needs of the case, and can either be chosen or replaced, and a new appraisal or a supplementary can be organized if necessary.
(2) The testimony of a witness is a statement of the facts of the case to the authorities and persons concerned. Expert does not know the facts of the case beforehand, and gives opinions on some specific issues of the case after analysis, so as to ascertain the facts of the case. If the expert knows the facts of the case beforehand, he should serve as a witness, not an expert witness.
(3) A witness does not need to have expertise to testify. Anyone can be a witness if he is able to distinguish between right and wrong and to express himself clearly, and the expert must have the relevant expertise and skills.
(4) All those who have information about a case shall have the duty to testify and can act as a witness, and there is no need for the witness to withdrawal. This is

[20]Xu [19].

[21]Fan [20].

not the case for the expert who can demand withdrawal in some situations, for example, where he or a close relative of his has an interest in the case.

(5) In order to provide scientific conclusions, the expert witness may request to get more information about the facts of the case or to consult the case file materials. When several expert witnesses make a joint appraisal, they may discuss with each other and write the appraisal report together. However, witnesses are not allowed to get more information about the case, and the law clearly stipulates that the interrogation of witnesses should be conducted on an individual basis and that discussion among witnesses is prohibited, so as not to influence each other and lead to misrepresentation.[22]

6.3.2 A Summary of the Rights and Obligations of an Expert Witness

An expert is a litigant participant engaged or appointed by the judicial organ to give a written expert opinion on a particular issue of the facts of the case by suing his expertise and skills. As a professional with expertise and skills, an expert witness is only managed by the Ministry of Justice, but also constrained by the litigation system. Therefore, the rights and obligations of the expert witness can be divided into two kinds: the rights and obligations of practicing and the rights and obligations of litigation.

The experts' rights to perform their duties refers to the rights they shall be entitled to in the activities of judicial expertise. These rights are built into some laws and regulations as the *Decisions on the Administration of Judicial Expertise* by Standing Committee of the National People's Congress and the *Measures for the Administration of the Registration of Expert Witnesses* by the Ministry of Justice.

Article 21 of the *Measures for the Administration of the Registration of Expert Witnesses* gives experts the rights to (1) get information and consult materials needed for the appraisal, and to question the parties and witnesses; and (2) request client to provide reference materials and samples free of charge; and (3) participate in the appraisal activities which are deemed necessary; and (4) refuse to perform the appraisal that is illegal, does not meet the relevant requirements or falls out of the registered business scope; and (5) refuse to answer questions that are not relevant to the appraisal; and (6) disagree; and (7) receive the pre-service training and education; and (8) get paid legally. Article 22 of this legal document enumerates nine obligations to be fulfilled by judicial experts.

In the criminal proceedings, in order to ensure the expert witness can given the scientific appraisal opinions, the law gives him the following litigation rights. First, they are allowed to consult the case file materials related to the appraisal matters and participate in the investigation and examination with the consent of the investigators and judges. Second, when there are more than two expert witnesses for the same

[22]Chen [21].

special issue, they may jointly give appraisal opinions, or they may separately provide their own appraisal opinions. Third, if the expert witness thinks that the personal safety of himself and his close relatives is in danger as a result of testifying in the proceedings, he may apply to the judicial organ for protective measures.

While enjoying the litigation rights, the expert witness should also assume litigation obligations to (1) withdrawal; and (2) appear in court and answer the questions about the appraiser's opinion according to law; and (3) provide the details and results of appraisal completely and honestly; and (4) not conceal, falsify opinions or intentionally provide false appraisal opinions, and bear legal responsibility.[23]

6.3.3 *Improvements to the Rights and Obligations of the Expert Witness in the 2012 Criminal Procedure Law*

6.3.3.1 Obligation of an Expert Witness to Testify in Court

According to the principle of directness and verbalism, evidence should be cross-examined before it can be used as the basis for ascertaining facts, conviction and sentencing. The appraisal opinion, as a kind of evidence, must comply with the requirement of this principle. An expert witness, as the producer of an expert opinion, shall appear in court to accept cross-examination of the expert opinion. However, the non-attendance of witnesses and the low attendance rate have been a serious problem in the criminal procedure in China. Such problem can also be found in the testifying of the expert witness, as one of the witnesses in the broad sense.[24]

The trial procedure regulated by the 1979 Criminal Procedure Law is a written procedure. As a result of the evidence-judging doctrine and the file transfer system, the basis of the trial generally comes from the confession and other written evidence provided by the investigating organs, and there is not need for expert witnesses, witnesses and other witnesses to testify in court. After the implementation of the Criminal Procedure Law in 1996, the model of prosecution-defense trial procedure has been preliminarily established. Article 156 of the 1996 Criminal Procedure Law provides that The public prosecutor, the parties and the defenders and agents ad litem may, with permission of the presiding judge, put questions to the witnesses or expert witnesses. It can be seen that the expert witness has the obligation to appear in court for questioning during the trial. Article 144 of the *Interpretation of the Supreme People's Court Concerning the Implementation of the Criminal Procedure Law of the People's Republic of China* further clearly stipulates that the expert witness shall appear in court to give evidence. In 2005, the Standing Committee of the National People's Congress issued the *Decisions on the Administration of Judicial Expertise*, which further stipulated that f the parties have objections to the expert opinions in

[23]Wang [22].

[24]Weidong [23].

litigation, the expert shall give evidence in court upon notification by the people's court according to law, and it also provides that those who, upon notification by the people's court, refuse to appear in court as witnesses, shall be punished according to law. It can be seen that the expert's obligation to testify in court is prescribed by the law.

Why theexpert witness is still unwilling to appear in court? Some scholars argue that although the importance of experts' appearance in court to testify has been recognized, a scientific and practicable system needs to be developed to support this procedure. No substantive and procedural provisions are found in the 1996 Criminal Procedure Law and its Interpretation of the Supreme People's Court Concerning the Implementation of the Criminal Procedure Law to ensure the implementation of expert testimony in court. This causes the expert not to perform the obligation of appearing in court to testify. The crux of the problem is that the expert witness's litigation status, the right of cross-examination and the right of getting paid after testifying in court are not clarified.[25] What's worse is that the expert who should appear in court does not bear any legal liability, which makes the system of expert witness appearance in court merely a formality.

The absence of an expert witness in court results in the expert opinion being used directly in court, which not only frustrates the judges who want to examine the validity and the truth of witness testimony by the presence of witnesses in court, but also makes the legislator's expectation of enhancing the adversarial system and preventing the court hearing from being a mere formality come to naught. In order to solve this problem, the renewed Criminal Procedure Law has overhauled the system of witnesses and expert witnesses appearing in court to testify.

The renewed Criminal Procedure Law specifies the circumstances under which an expert witness must appear in court to testify. A witness shall appear before a people's court to give testimony where the public prosecutor, the party concerned or the defender or agent ad litem has objections to the testimony of a witness, and the people's court deems it necessary to ask the witness to appear before the court. Unlike the conditions under which a witness must testify in court, the expert's presence in court does not result from an expert's opinions having material impact on the conviction and sentence, but from the disagreement with the opinions between the prosecution and defense and the people's court deeming it necessary. In such case, the expert witness shall fulfill his obligation to testify in court. The provisions of Criminal Procedure Law are different from those of Civil Procedure Law. In criminal proceedings, the people's court decides whether the expert should appear in court based on the disagreement with the opinions between the prosecution and defense. In civil proceedings, if the parties have any objection to the expert opinions, the expert shall testify in court; if the parties have no objection, but the court deems it necessary, the expert shall also appear in court. The criminal procedure's provisions on the conditions under which expert witnesses may appear in court accommodate both fairness and efficiency. The fact that the law gives the people's court the power

[25]Li [24].

of discretion in this matter shows respect for our country's long-existing tradition of criminal procedure.

Responsibilities should be given to the expert witnesses to urge them to fulfill their obligations. The renewed Criminal Procedure Law clearly stipulates the legal consequences for the expert witness not to appear in court. If, upon notification by the people's court, the expert witness refuses to appear in court, the expert opinions shall not be used as the basis for deciding the case. This is a procedural sanction. The design of this provision is similar to the way to exclude illegally-obtained evidence to prevent the use of illegal means to collect evidence. In order to ensure the reliability of the expert opinion, it is important to encourage the party who gets supported by the expert opinion to convince the expert witness to appear before court by not accepting the expert opinion.

This provision was not added in the Criminal Procedure Law until the second review to this draft was conducted. Before that, there was no difference in the provisions for expert witness and witnesses on this matter. "*Decisions on the Administration of Judicial Expertise* issued by the Standing Committee of the National People's Congress has clearly stipulated legal liability for the behavior of expert witnesses who do not fulfill their obligation to testify in court, so it is unnecessary to built it into the Criminal Procedure Law", according to Li Shishi, deputy director of the Law Committee of the National People's Congress when the second review to the draft was conducted. If the expert witness refuses to testify in court without proper reasons, the People's Court shall inform the executive branch or the relevant departments. In accordance with Article 13 of the *Decision of the Standing Committee of the National People's Congress on the Administration of Expert Testimony*, if the expert refuses to appear as a witness in court upon notification of people's court in accordance with the law, the Ministry of Justice of the Government of the People's Republic of China at the provincial level shall impose a penalty of suspending the business in expert testimony for not less than three months and not more than one year; if the circumstances are serious, the registration shall be revoked.

After such modification, the obligations and liabilities of expert appearing in court has been improved. The question of expert witness appearing in court is at the heart of expert witness participating in criminal proceedings, and the perfection of this system involves other matters such as the right of expert witness to be protected.

6.3.3.2 Right to Be Protected

The expert witness gives opinions to help ascertain the facts of the case. In many cases, such opinions concerning DNA, human testimony and physical evidence are important to solve the case. When the expert opinions place one party at disadvantage, the expert may be retaliated. This is more likely to happen when the expert witness is called to testify. The state is under an obligation to provide the expert witness with adequate protection measures to prevent false statements made by him out of fear of retaliation, which may undermine the realization of procedural and substantive justice. The renewed Criminal Procedure Law has improved the guarantee of witnesses' rights and established a witness protection system that is more complete than that of the 1996 Criminal Procedure Law. It clarifies that expert witnesses shall be protected by the state.

Article 62 of the Criminal Procedure Law provides for five special protective measures, including (1) keeping confidential the real names, addresses, employers and other personal information; and (2) adopting measures to avoid the actual appearance or true voice of those who appear in courtrooms for testimony; and (3) prohibiting certain persons from having contact with the witnesses, experts, victims and their close relatives; and (4) adopting special measures to protect the personal and residential security; and (5) other necessary protective measures. The last provision is a miscellaneous provision which ensure the exercise of the right of expert witnesses and their close relatives to be protected by the state.

If an expert witness thinks that his personal safety or that of a close relative is in danger as a result of testifying in the proceedings, he may apply to the judicial organ for protection. This provision gives the expert witness the right to apply for protection. The judicial organ may take one or more protective measures if, after examination, it deems it necessary to take such measures. The judicial organ can absolutely also take protective measures on its own initiative when it finds out there is a danger.

6.3.3.3 The Establishment of the System for "Persons with Specific Expertise"

The purpose of the expert to appear in court for being questioned is to help the judge to confirm the legitimacy, authenticity and scientificity of the expert opinions, which shows the principle of directness and verbalism and realize the right of the parties to cross-examine. Therefore, the expert to testify in court is important, formally and substantively. However, what the expert testimony turns out is not entirely satisfactory. The Public prosecutor, the defendant, the defender or the judge may not have the knowledge of the rationale, methods, results and evaluation of the appraisal, so they can't ask some pertinent questions to the expert opinions. In this way, the expert's appearance in court becomes a formality and can not produce the effect of cross-examination. The expert witness may also feel that his opinions are less convincing through cross-examination, so he persuades the referee to admit them. This will definitely discourages the expert witness to appear in court. Some scholars deem it as the right of the expert witness to be questioned.[26] It means that when the expert witness appears in court to give evidence, he has the right to ask the adverse party to question the important part of the expert opinions and raise questions about the technology, rationale, methods and other aspects of the special problems.

From the perspective of the responsibility to give evidence, if the party who bears the burden of proof can not provide convincing evidence, he will accept responsibility for the negative results of such action. As for the right to be questioned, it is neither

[26] Li [25].

necessary nor feasible for the expert witness to ask the other party to raise questions, but it does reflect the tricky problem to be solved. In criminal proceedings, appraisal is a part of the investigation, and only the investigating organ can carry out this procedure. The expert witness, the criminal suspect or the defendant can only apply for additional appraisal or reappraisal after the appraisal has been completed, because this activity is organized by the investigating organ. During the trial, if the defendant is unable to ask pertinent questions about the expert opinions because of lack of expertise, he can only accept the views expressed in the expert opinions and can not fully exercise his right to defense. If the judge is unable to understand and assess the expert opinions, the professionals and technical personnel may become the main actors in the making the decision, which makes it difficult to find out the truth and leads to misjudged case.

The renewed Criminal Procedure Law established a system for "persons with specific expertise" to provide judges and the prosecution and the defense with certain professional assistance in response to expert opinions. Article 192(2) provides that the public prosecutor, the parties and the defenders, and the agents ad litem may apply to the court to notify a person with specific expertise to appear before the court and render an opinion on the expert opinions given by the expert witness. The term of "persons with specific expertise" has been used since 2002 *Provisions of the Supreme People's Court Concerning Evidence in Civil Proceedings* and the *Rules of Supreme People's Court Concerning Evidence in Administrative Proceedings.* The absence of an evidence-based regulation or law in criminal proceedings may be one reason why the system for "persons with specific expertise have been established late.

The participation of "persons with specific expertise" in criminal proceedings can be very helpful. First, the other party can question, weaken the authenticity of or even negate the expert opinions through this procedure. The party submitting the expert opinions may, with the help of persons with specific expertise, further explain the opinions, so as to make them convincing and admissible. Second, the presence of persons with specific expertise to discover problems in expert testimony can provide a basis for judges to screen expert opinions and make scientific judgments in order to ensure a fair trial. Third, this system can raise the awareness of responsibility of expert witness and play a key role in the production of expert opinions as a way to make the opinions more scientific. Finally, this can reduce the occurrence of repeated appraisal to a certain extent, save litigation resources and improve the efficiency of the trial.[27]

The establishment of the system of "persons with specific expertise" is a highlight in the Criminal Procedure Law, but some improvements still need to be made. For example, it should clarify the status of persons with expertise in criminal proceedings. Article 106 of the Criminal Procedure law provides the provisions for the litigant participant, but not for this kind of persons. They should fall into the category of litigant participants because they participate in the activities where they have the right to attend the criminal court hearing, express their own opinions on the expert opinions

[27]Lang [26].

and have an impact on the criminal proceedings, which help move the proceedings along forward. This may be clarified in the future by the judicial interpretation.

A question relating to the status of persons with expertise in the proceedings is whether they should be neutral or represent the interests of the party who invites them to appear before the court to present their views on the expert opinions. From the law alone, different interpretations can be drawn. First, the public prosecutor or parties to find their own persons with expertise to assist them in their proceedings by inviting them to appear before the court. In such cases, these persons are appointed by the defense or the prosecution and the costs are borne by either of the parties, so they are supposed to represent the interests of that party. They should not and can not be expected to be neutral, but they shall not deliberately distort the facts and mislead the judge. Once such a violation of professional ethics occurs, they should bear legal liability according to the seriousness of the conduct. Second, the public prosecutor or the parties do not look for the persons with expertise, but apply to the court when necessary, and the court will select the such persons to present their views on the expert opinions. People with expertise in such situations should of course remain objective and neutral. These two models have their own advantages. The criminal procedure law and its judicial interpretation do not make it clear that which model shall be used. I think that people are supposed to a proper one based on specific circumstances.

The system of "persons with specific expertise" is newly established thing in criminal procedure, and it needs to be tested by judicial practice and perfected gradually. These persons assist the parties in questioning the experts on special problems and are given the legal guidance of the judge to ensure the objectivity and scientificity of the expert opinions. This helps the judges in finding the facts of a case involving special issues so as to improve the quality and efficiency of the court's cross-examination and promote the realization of procedural and substantive justice. However, it is doubtful whether the new system will be practical.[28] Persons with expertise appearing before the court to present their views on the expert opinions mainly respond to the doubts about the existing expert opinions, and they only need to ask questions without having to answer any questions. After hearing the expert opinion, the judge can know if there is something wrong with the expert opinion. But how to draw a conclusion on the expert opinions may baffle the judge again. This may reduce the possibility that the judge misjudges the case by only hearing the expert opinions, but it does not ensure that the judge can make a correct judgement of the expert opinions. In addition, giving expert opinions is highly professionally demanding, especially in the case involving personal injury. Different professionals may have different conclusions, which, however, are not all incorrect. When the expert and the person with specific expertise confront with each other at the court, the difference of opinions will lead to the disagreement about the expert opinions again, thus causing "repeated appraisal". This will make the system designers hoping to save litigation resources and improve the efficiency of litigation come to nothing.

[28]Zhang [27].

Although the court has the power to decide on this issue, it is very difficult for the judge to decide whether to perform re-appraisal.

6.3.3.4 The Right to Charge Fees for Appearing in Court

In order to improve the attendance of witnesses, the provisions of allowance and guarantees for witnesses to testify were created in the Article 63 of the 2012 Criminal Procedure Law. The Article stipulates that A witness shall be entitled to allowance for his/her performance of the obligation of giving testimony, and where the witness is an employee of an entity, the entity shall not deduct his/her salary, bonus and other benefits directly or in a disguised form. However, such allowance for experts who also has to testify in court was not included.

The right of expert witness to charge fees has long been prescribed by law. Article 15 of the *Decisions on the Administration of Judicial Expertise* stipulates that the items and standards of charging fees for judicial appraisal shall be determined by the competent department of the Ministry of Justice under the State Council. In addition, the *Measures for Administration of Charging Fees for Judicial Expertise* stipulates how to charge fees for judicial expertise in different circumstances. However, there is no such provision of fees charged for the expert witness to testify in court. Article 13 of the Measures only states that the costs of transportation, accommodation and lost earning incurred by a judicial expert as a witness in court are not included in the scope of the fees to be charged for judicial expertise. Such fees are collected by the People's Court in accordance with the standards set by the state and then handed over to the judicial expertise institution, but there aren't legal documents specifying what the standards are and from whom the fees are collected.

There is no doubt that fees should be charged by and allowance should be given to the expert witness for giving testimony in court. The reason for the expert witness to charge fees is that he or she provides the service and gives opinions on the special problems, and the expert witness should get paid for this because some manpower and material resource are used. This charge does not include the remuneration for appearance before the court. This is not included in the Measures and not all proceedings need expert testimony in court, so it is inappropriate to charge the fess in advance. But when an expert has spent time and put efforts in attending court to give testimony, he or she should be entitled to be paid for the time he or she spends in providing such service.

China's criminal procedure system has always identified expert testimony as one of the means of investigation, and the investigating organ holds the power to initiate this procedure. In addition, the judicial expertise institution is usually set up by the investigating organ. Therefore, the cost has in fact been borne by the state. The state may be deemed to have covered the expenses of expert witness appearing in court as a witness, by establishing judicial expertise institution in the investigating organs, purchasing equipment and instruments, and paying the personnel.

The cost of presence of persons with specific expertise to express their views in court now seems to be paid by the party who invites them. As mentioned above, the opinions of persons with specific expertise who charge fees from one party are more likely to be in favor of such party.

6.3.4 Conclusion

The battle between the demon—increasing complexity of cruel means to commit crimes and the justice—continuous advance of investigation technology is nonstop. Judicial expertise plays an increasingly important role in the process of finding out the facts, so more scientific rules are needed to make it work best. As the core of the appraisal, the expert witness not only needs sufficient room to display his talent, but also needs the well-conceived system to prevent the risk. Although the appraisal system was refined by two major procedural laws in 2012, some improvements still need to be made through learning from practice, coordination and communication between different departments.

6.4 Interested Parties in the Special Procedure for Confiscating Illegal Gains

One of the major tasks of criminal procedure law is to punish crimes. In criminal proceedings, in order to ensure the smooth execution of judgments in the future, the investigative organs usually, in addition to restraining or depriving criminal suspects of their personal freedom, also seal and seize the related property and documents, and at the same time recover all the illicit money and goods of the suspects; especially for corrupt crimes, restricting both the personal rights and property rights of criminal suspects is of equal importance. However, the Criminal Procedure Law of China, which was put into force in 1979, has been characterized as "putting the punishment of criminals in the first place", since there are fewer provisions in this Law that provide for the confiscation of the possessions and properties of criminal suspects and defendants. With the rapid socio-economic development, China has seen new circumstances and new changes in its criminal judicial practice. The lack of detailed and adequate provisions can hardly respond to the public call for fighting corruption, nor can it meet the country's need to combat violent and terrorist activities.[29]

In view of this, in the Criminal Procedure Law revised in 2012, a new provision for the "procedure for confiscating the illegal gains of criminal suspects and defendants that escape or die" was added into the "Special Procedures" chapter. Such a forward-looking procedure, which was yet tested by judicial practices, stirred heated discussions among both legal scholars and practitioners while this Law was revised

[29] Chen [28].

and after it was enacted.[30] Most studies in this regard center on the roles of the procuratorial organs and the people's courts, rather than care about the interested parties—another important participant in the confiscation procedure. The author holds that the confiscation procedure of illegal gains is of vital importance for citizens' private property right, so there must be a powerful guarantee for preventing this procedure from being abused. Although this procedure requires the efficiency of proceedings, it is a non-administrative procedure subject to judicial review. As such, we cannot place one-sided emphasis on the unilateral role of the party that applies for confiscation, that is, we cannot only rely on the professional and objective prosecutors to safeguard the legitimate operation of this procedure, the correct way to understand and apply this procedure is to ensure the interested parties who might be affected to be entitled to joining in the adversary proceeding with the prosecutors, so that the judges can hear all parties and make a decision according to law.

6.4.1 Litigation Status of "Interested Parties"

"Interested parties" are a new role that came into being after the "procedure for confiscation of illegal gains" was added into the revised Criminal Procedure Law. But the role positioning of interested parties is yet defined in the law. According to Article 106 of the Criminal Procedure Law, which was free from any change in this round of revision, interested parties do not belong to "parties" or "participants in the proceedings". Without positioning in criminal procedure, the proper functioning of interested parties is sure to be affected. In order to further explore the role of interested parties in the proceedings, their relationship between parties or participants in the proceedings and their status in criminal procedure must be clarified in the first place.

"Participants in the proceedings" and "parties" are in a relationship between including and being included. Generally, participants in the proceedings are divided

[30] Since the implementation of the revised *Criminal Procedure Law*, the judicial organs across China began to apply the "procedure for confiscating illegal gains". For example, the procuratorial organs in Shangrao City of Jiangxi Province, Zhongshan City of Guangdong Province, and Wenzhou City of Zhejiang Province applied for confiscating the illegal gains to the local people's courts of the criminal suspects who are accused of committing the crime of corruption and now are absconding abroad, those who were accused of committing the crime of corruption but now are deceased, and those who were are accused of committing the crime of illegal fundraising but now are deceased, respectively. Something should be pointed out is that when Wenzhou People's Procuratorate was confiscating the illegal gains in the illegal fund-raising crimes, it violated the provisions of the *Criminal Procedure Law* for the applicable scope of the confiscation procedure. See the details about these cases in Shangrao Daily, *Announcement of the Intermediate People's Court of Shangrao City, Jiangxi Province*, https://paper.srxww.com/srrb/html/2019-10/09/content_2402132.htm; People.cn, Zhongshan of Guangdong: *First Application for Confiscation of Illegal Gains in Corruption Cases*, https://legal.people.com.cn/n/2013/0418/c188502-21184412.htm; Eastday.com, *Wenzhou People's Procuratorate Applied for Confiscation of Illegal Gains, Setting a Precedent in Zhejiang Province*, https://news.eastday.com/eastday/13news/auto/news/china/u7ai705393_K4.html.

into parties and other participants according to their different status in the proceedings. Among participants in the proceedings, parties are those that have a direct interest in the outcome of a case, exert a great influence on the criminal proceedings, and they are either in a status of prosecution or defense in the proceedings.[31] Specifically, parties include victims, private prosecutors, criminal suspects, defendants and the plaintiffs and defendants in incidental civil actions. The common feature of these subjects is that they have a direct interest in the outcome of a case, and their rights and interests are in an unstable state due to the lawsuit. Parties have a wide range of rights in the proceedings; by exercising these rights, they exert a stronger influence on the proceedings and settlement than other participants.

"Other participants in the proceedings" include legal representatives, agents ad litem, defenders, witnesses, expert witnesses and interpreters. Participants of this kind have no direct interest in the outcome of a case. Although they also have certain rights and obligations in criminal procedure, they cannot play a major procedural role in starting, operating and terminating the proceedings. The main purpose of their participation in the proceedings is to provide assistance to a party (such as legal representative, agent ad litem and defender), furnish evidence for the proceedings (such as witness and expert witness), or help the proceedings proceed smoothly (such as interpreter). These participants do not have any independent functions in the proceedings.

According to the announcement of the Supreme People's Court, interested parties involved in the procedure for confiscation of illegal gains may apply for participation in the proceedings since they claim ownership of the properties that are under application for confiscation. An interested party is allowed to entrust an agent ad litem, and make a statement, produce evidence, cross-examine and defend himself during a court hearing. An interested party has the right to appeal or protest the result of judgment.

Regarding the procedural acts of interested parties, they have a relatively wide range of procedural rights according to law. From a substantive point of view, the participation of interested parties has a significant impact on the case, and the outcome of the lawsuit concerns their interests. They somewhat resemble the parties in criminal procedure. Interested parties can provide evidence, cross-examine, make a statement and conduct self-defense during a court hearing, and appeal or protest the result of judgment, which fully demonstrate their independence in the proceedings. But their participation is not to provide assistance for the smooth progress of the court hearing. Therefore, the author believes that interested parties could be substantially categorized as participants in the proceedings, enjoying both litigation status and corresponding rights, but in the meantime undertaking certain obligations.

[31] Song [29].

6.4.2 Scope of Interested Parties Involved in Litigation

In the procedure for confiscation of illegal gains, the scope of "the properties under application for confiscation" includes "the illegal gains and other properties involved in a case that should be recovered in accordance with the provisions of the Criminal Law". In reference to Article 509 of the Interpretation on the Application of the Criminal Procedure Law of the People's Republic of China, "the properties under application for confiscation" are defined as the "properties and their fruits obtained from the commitment of criminal acts, and the prohibited goods illegally possessed by the defendants, as well as their private properties for committing crimes". In view of this, anyone who is legally interested in these properties should be a participant in the procedure for confiscation of illegal gains. Two types of subjects are set out in the Criminal Procedure Law and the afore-said Interpretation: one is the criminal suspects and the near relatives of the victim, and the other is other interested persons who claim ownership of the properties under application for confiscation.

The near relatives of the criminal suspects and the defendants refer to their husband, wife, father, mother, son, daughter, and siblings, etc. The near relatives of the criminal suspects and the defendants may be the co-owner or heir of the properties of the criminal suspects and the defendants. So their ownership or inheritance of the concerned properties is about to be directly affected if these properties are confiscated. Despite of these near relatives, the persons who are legally interested in the properties under application for confiscation are also eligible to participate in the confiscation process. Article 513 of the above Interpretation defines "legally interested" as a claim of ownership, which applies to the case where the properties used for committing the crime were borrowed or stolen by the suspects. So the real owners of these properties may claim for their return during the confiscation process.

6.4.2.1 Necessity of Near Relatives and Interested Parties to Participate in Litigation

Literally, anyone who is legally interested in the properties under application for confiscation is an interested party. So, what about Article 281(2) of the Criminal Procedure Law is modified as "interested parties have the right to apply for participation in the proceedings or entrust agents ad litem to do so on behalf of them? That is, there should be special reasons for distinguishing near relatives from other interested parties.

In terms of legal norms, the most significant difference between near relatives and other interested parties is reflected in the way of participating in the proceedings. Other interested parties, instead of near relatives, must provide evidence to prove that they are owners of the properties under application for confiscation, so that they will have necessity and legitimacy to apply for participation in the proceedings. In contrast, for the near relatives of the criminal suspects or the defendants, a proof of their relationship is enough for them to participate in the proceedings. The near relatives seems naturally to have the necessity and legitimacy to participate in the properties confiscation process, why is that? Isn't it true that the formal difference should mean a substantial difference?

Now that the near relatives can participate in the proceedings without providing materials related to the properties under application for confiscation, they are ought to have some non-property interests in this regard since they are one of the interested parties, so they have the necessity to participate in the proceedings. Regarding the content of the court hearing, the court mainly investigates whether the suspects have committed the crime and fail to appear before the court and whether the properties under application for confiscation should be recovered, which are prescribed in Article 515 of the Interpretation.

After the prosecutor presents the relevant evidence, the interested parties will make a statement, present the evidence and cross-examine it. In short, their focus is on the facts of the crime and the properties involved. The statement made by the interested parties should be in line with the scope of the court investigation. For the interested parties other than the near relatives, since their participation in the proceedings is to claim for the ownership of the properties involved in the case, they can only make a statement on the properties in the court, provide evidence and participate in the debate. For the near relatives, if they do not claim on the properties, then their statement will only be about the criminal facts.

The procedure for confiscation of illegal gains is a procedure for disposing of objects which is independent of the criminal responsibility judgment of the persons being accused. As the group that has the closest relationship with the suspects or the defendants, near relatives can speak for their own interests (claim for property right) in the confiscation procedure, and "explain" the criminal behaviors of their relatives (the suspects or the defendants), which makes it meaningful for them to participate in the procedure for confiscation of illegal gains. The content of this kind of participation is similar to the exercise of the "right to defense". Even if the near relatives do not claim for property right, they may explain the sources of the concerned properties to the court based on some information in their hands, and also explain the criminal acts of their relatives involved in the case, in order to help the court ascertain the facts of the case. It is not the exercise of the right to defense, because the criminal suspects and the defendants are the only subject of the right to defense. It is based on their authorization that defense lawyers can help them defend themselves. In the special confiscation procedure, the criminal suspects or the defendants cannot appear at the court or they are already deceased, then their right to defense can neither be exercised by themselves nor by others with their authorization; accordingly, their near relatives' explanation of the criminal facts and behaviors is not to defend the criminal suspects or the defendants. In terms of objective effects, the involvement of near relatives in the confiscation procedure may explain the circumstances of the crime on behalf of the criminal suspects or the defendants.

In practice, especially in the corruption cases where the criminal suspects or the defendants have fled, the investigative organs cannot find them or cannot arrest them even if they know where they are hiding, but the near relatives of these criminal suspects or the defendants are often aware of their whereabouts. If the near relatives are entitled to participating in the proceedings, they may help the investigative and procuratorial organs to track the suspects' relevant situations and pleas, and even create a communication channel between the two sides. It is especially valuable for solving the cases where the corrupt officials have fled abroad, and for bringing them to justice. In addition, the property confiscation procedure has lower requirements for the near relatives of criminal suspects or the defendants to participate. According to the interpretation of the judiciary, even if the participation of the near relatives is not for objecting to the property confiscation or for commenting on the criminal behaviors of the suspects or defendants, but for tracking the progress of litigation, the people's court should still hold a hearing, but simplify the proceedings appropriately.[32]

In view of this, among the participants in the special confiscation procedure, the scope of the "interest relationship" of near relatives is quite loose. This kind of "interest relationship" can be expressed as a claim for property right, a concern about the property disposal and conviction of their criminal relatives, or only an inquiry of the case trial due to their family relationships.[33] To empower the near relatives to participate in the confiscation procedure, it may to some extent "rebalance" the justice imbalance due to the absence of the suspects or the defendants in this procedure.

6.4.2.2 Necessity of Other Interested Parties to Participate in the Proceedings

Near relatives can easily participate in the proceedings, while other interested parties can only do so on the grounds of "claiming ownership" of the properties that are under the application for confiscation, is that too strict for them? When claiming for property ownership, which is the strongest poverty-related claim, it is necessary for all interested parties to participate in the proceedings, which needs not to be repeated. However, the legal interest relationship includes not only the property right represented by ownership, but also the creditor's right. If there are any interested parties that have a creditor's right with respect to the properties under the application for confiscation, can they apply for participation in the confiscation procedure? There is a view that the scope of properties to be recovered (which applies the confiscation procedure) includes the properties and their resulting fruits obtained by the defendants in committing a criminal act, as well as the prohibited items in their illegal possession and their private properties for committing the crime. These properties are in essence not legally owned by the defendants, and should be turned over to the treasury or returned to the victims; they cannot be used to repay the debts of the defendants. Therefore, it is of no practical significance for the legitimate creditor of

[32]Xiang [30].

[33]In an announcement made by the Intermediate People's Court of Shangrao City, Jiangxi Province on March 11, 2013 concerning the case of Li XX, the participation of interested parties in the proceedings was stated as "if the near relatives of the suspect Li XX and other interested parties claim ownership of the above properties..." Literally, this announcement limits the scope of near relatives' participation in the proceedings to the claim of property ownership, which is different from the Supreme People's Court's interpretation.

the criminal suspects or the defendants to participate in the proceedings, and they are not allowed to participate in the special procedure.

The author believes that the logic of the above view is worth scrutinizing, because the view that "it is unnecessary for the creditor interested parties to participate in the confiscation procedure" uses the results to reverse the process, that is, it presupposes that the "properties involved in the case must be recoverable", thus denying the necessity of the participation of the creditor interested parties. Before the judgment of the confiscation is made, the properties under the application for confiscation (excluding prohibited articles) should be regarded as the legitimate properties of the criminal suspects or the defendants according to the principle of "presumption of innocence". As for the creditor interested parties of the criminal suspects or the defendants, they cannot directly claim ownership of the properties under the application for confiscation, but they are likely to realize their creditor's right considering the properties owned by the criminal suspects or the defendants. If the suspects' properties are confiscated, it will weaken their solvency, and in turn affect the realization of the creditor's right. The creditor interested parties have no idea of the sources of the debtors' properties, and they only care about whether their creditor's right can be realized, not the guilt or innocence of the debtors. Once the debtors' properties are confiscated by the court, it will be more difficult for the creditor to realize their creditor's right and defend their private interests. In this regard, creditors are of course major interested parties. For the purpose of realizing their creditor's right, the creditors subjectively hope to maintain the debtors' solvency, which will objectively prompt them to participate in the property confiscation procedure and raise a plea against the confiscation applicant. In order to achieve this goal, creditors are motivated to provide evidence and make a statement in court. If the court dismisses the application for property confiscation, it protects its own interests objectively.

Under this circumstance, the creditor interested parties play a similar role with the near relatives that do not claim for property right, that is, they neither argue they are owners of the confiscated properties nor do they agree that these properties should be confiscated, so they are objectively defending the interests of the criminal suspects or the defendants who cannot be present at the confiscation procedure. However, because of the system design of the current confiscation procedure, there is no room for the interested parties other than close relatives to issue such a claim.

Under the framework of the existing system, if the creditor interested parties participate in the confiscation procedure, it seems that they can only appear in court as witnesses who are aware of the facts of the case, so that they explain the relevant criminal behaviors and properties. The prosecutor and near relatives can give evidence in the court hearing, and they can support their views by asking witnesses to appear in court or showing witness testimony. However, when there are no near relatives or ownership interested parties applying to participate in the proceedings, the people's court may decide not to open a court session; then the procedural structure only consists of judge and applicant, and no one else has the opportunity to participate in the procedure for confiscation of illegal gains. "Heed only one side you will be benighted", which may lead to errors in the ruling on property confiscation. The creditor interested parties shall be allowed to attend the hearing, since "listen to both sides and you will be enlightened".

6.4.2.3 Expand the Scope of Interested Parties

As part of the criminal procedure, although the confiscation procedure has its special background, it should still follow the principle of "due procedure" to the greatest extent possible, and safeguard the interests of absent criminal suspects and defendants. In order to achieve this goal, everyone who knows something about the facts and property matters of the case should have the opportunity to participate in the confiscation procedure. Considering the special role of near relatives in this procedure, it is necessary to distinguish them from other interested parties, while other interested parties, in the opinion of the author, should be deemed as "third party" like the one in civil procedure.

The "third party" in civil procedure refers to the participants in the proceedings who file an independent lawsuit against the plaintiff or the defendant in the proceedings that are already started, or who claim for independent interests after being introduced by the plaintiff or the defendant in the proceedings, or who assist one of the two parties in the debate for their own benefit.[34] On the basis whether they have an independent claim to the object of procedure under dispute, the third party in civil procedure is divided into a third party with independent claim and a third party without independent claim.

The third party with independent claim is allowed to file an independent claim on all or part of the object of procedure of the pending case, while the third party without independent claim cannot file an independent claim on the object of procedure between the two parties in the proceedings, but he has legal interest in the outcome of the case. The "legal interest" here and "independent claim" are in a relationship between including and being included. But the scope of "independent claim" in civil procedure, including both property right and creditor's right, is much larger than the scope of interested parties in the special criminal confiscation procedure. The "interest" claimed by the third party without independent claim is more like an indirect interest, such as the relevant interests in the lawsuit of subrogation and revocation.

A similar structure also exists in the procedure for confiscation of illegal gains. This is a special procedure where the properties under the application for confiscation are taken as the object of procedure, and the two parties involved in the proceedings should be the procuratorial organ and the criminal suspects or the defendants. However, due to the absence of the criminal suspects or the defendants, the proceedings become an "action against the object" by the plaintiff who has filed for the confiscation application. Those who are interested in the object of procedure except the litigants are a "third party" in the special criminal confiscation procedure. Among

[34] Jiang and Xiao [31].

them, the party claims ownership of the properties under the application for confiscation, which is analogous to "the third party with independent claim", is called "ownership interested party". He neither agrees with the application for confiscation of properties, nor believes that the properties should belong to the criminal suspects or defendants; he participates in the proceedings to fight for the ownership of his properties. The interested party that claims a creditor's right is analogous to "the third party without independent claim". The reason why the creditor interested party participates in the proceedings is that the property confiscation may prevent them from realizing their creditor's right, so they have a legal interest in the results of judgment. The purpose of their participation in the proceedings is to provide evidence and make a statement at the court to prevent the confiscation of the properties of the criminal suspects or the defendants. Objectively speaking, the participation of creditor interested party in the proceedings may help the criminal suspects or the defendants to safeguard their property interests.

Regarding the ownership interested party and the creditor interested party, the specific content of their procedure participation right is different due to their different purposes in participating in the proceedings. The ownership interested party intends to get their properties back, while the creditor interested party strives for non-confiscation of the properties. Therefore, the ownership interested party should make a statement on "whether the properties under the application for confiscation should be recovered" during the trial, and give evidence that they are the owner of the properties proposed to be recovered. The creditor interested party may make a statement and provide evidence on whether the criminal suspects or the defendants have committed relevant criminal acts to pursue other claims other than the ownership claim. If the ownership interested party and the creditor interested party are concurrently involved in the same case, then the latter may confront the former in order to retain the properties of the criminal suspects or the defendants for paying the debt.

6.4.3 Safeguard the Procedure Participation Right of Interested Parties

The direct target of the procedure for confiscation of illegal gains is the properties of the criminal suspects and the defendants who cannot appear before the court. Since the criminal suspects or the defendants cannot appear before the court, they cannot explain and distinguish the properties involved in the case. Therefore, the investigative organ can only take corresponding measures for the properties according to its own judgment. Such kind of one-way measures will inevitably lead to improper handling of the properties not involved in any case. It is possible that the interested parties do not directly control the properties involved in the case or do not know the use of these properties since they are lent or leased. Moreover, considering the relative confidentiality at the investigation stage, the interested parties may have no idea that their properties are involved in criminal activities. In order to protect the property right of interested parties, the potential right holders should be notified to participate in the property confiscation procedure in advance.

6.4.3.1 Extraterritorial Experience: Notification in the US Civil Confiscation Procedure

The civil confiscation procedure in the United States is an "action in rem". Civil confiscation is not premised on conviction, the law enforcement agencies only need to provide civil "preponderance of the evidence" to prove the relevant properties "constitute, originate or derive from the proceeds of crime directly or indirectly", so that they can seize, freeze or confiscate these properties even if they fail to meet the criminal standard of "excluding reasonable doubt".[35] This type of confiscation is simple and easy for law enforcement agencies to implement and raise the efficiency in handling cases. But the improvement of efficiency has limited citizens' defense opportunities, and tends to infringe upon their property right. Given this, the United States Civil Asset Forfeiture Reform Act (2000) has strengthened procedural guarantees for all aspects of civil confiscation.

When implementing the notification procedure, the law enforcement agencies shall, in the name of the government and in accordance with law, issue a written notification to interested parties for seizing their properties no later than 60 days after the seizure. If the case is transferred to a federal agency by a state government or a state-level law enforcement agency, the written notification should be issued within 90 days after the seizure. After the properties are seized, there may be the circumstances where the identity or interest of the interested partied cannot be confirmed. If the identity of the interested parties can be confirmed before the confiscation decision is made, a written notification shall be issued to them within 60 days after the confirmation.[36] If the law enforcement agency or the court has reason to believe that issuing a written notification may endanger the safety of others, or the informed parties may evade litigation, destroy evidence, interfere with witnesses or carry out other conducts that hinder litigation, then the period for issuing such notification may be extended.[37]

The purpose of the above procedure is to protect the rights of the interested parties to know and to participate in the procedure to the greatest extent possible, and to prevent civil confiscation from becoming tools of law enforcement agencies. To highlight the importance of this notification procedure, the law enforcement agencies that violate this procedure shall be subject to the procedural sanctions as prescribed by law. If the government fails to issue a written notification to the owners of seized properties within the prescribed time limit, the seizure must be released immediately, and these properties will be exempted from another civil confiscation procedure.[38]

[35]He [32].

[36]18U.S.C.§983(a)(1)(A).

[37]18U.S.C.§983(a)(1)(D).

[38]18U.S.C.§983(a)(1)(F).

Interested parties may file a claim to the properties in writing to the court within the prescribed time limit. The deadline for making such a claim is generally no earlier than the 35th day upon their receipt of the notification letter. Such claims made by interested parties should include at least the confirmation of the items of the claimed properties, the claimed interests and the promise to be punished for perjury if they make false claims.[39] The government generally responds to such claims made by interested parties within 90 days. If the government fails to do so on time or proposes a criminal procedure that involves the confiscated properties, the seizure must be ceased immediately, and these properties will be exempted from another civil confiscation procedure.

6.4.3.2 Notification for the Procedure for Confiscation of Illegal Gains in China

According to the provisions of the Criminal Procedure Law, in order to guarantee the interested parties to participate in the procedure for confiscation of illegal gains, the people's court shall, after accepting the application for confiscating illegal gains submitted by the people's procuratorate, make public an announcement with a period of validity no less than six months, reminding those who are legally interested in the properties under the application for confiscation to apply for participating in the proceedings. During the period of the announcement, interested parties may file an application with the people's court to participate in the procedure for confiscation of illegal gains.

Announcement of the People's Court and Direct Notification

The Criminal Procedure Law incorporates the service of notification system in civil proceedings, that is, as long as the period of notification of expires, regardless of whether the interested parties have learned the content of the notification, they are deemed to do so according to law, and the people's court has fulfilled the legally prescribed obligation to inform. The traditional method of public announcement is to publish it on newspapers that are distributed nationwide and on the bulletin boards of the people's courts. Although these traditional announcements have achieved the effect of "publicity" to a certain extent, they are now hard to achieve substantial effect with the development of the times and increased population mobility. Therefore, the Interpretation of the Supreme People's Court requires that such announcements can be posted and published in the place of crime, residence and real estate of the criminal suspects or the defendants when necessary. More than that, the people's court should make full use of modern emerging communication means to publish announcement on official websites, official micro-blogs, and other new media to fully protect citizens' property right.

---

[39] 18U.S.C.§983(a)(2)(C).

According to Article 512(3) of the Interpretation of the Supreme People's Court, if the people's court has obtained the contact information about the near relatives and other interested parties of the criminal suspects or the defendants, it shall directly inform them of the content of the announcement by telephone, fax, email, etc., and make relevant records. Interested parties are not directly notified to participate in the proceedings, but the content of the announcement, because these interested parties who are known to the court are no more than those that may have any interest in the case. Whether there is indeed any interest and whether they will claim for their rights, it is at the discretion of the informed party.

Identification of Interested Parties

Being informed of the relevant information about the interested parties, the people's courts shall give credit for the investigative organs (including the public security organs and the investigative offices of the people's procuratorates) and the procuratorial organs which investigate the situation of the interested parties. In the course of investigating the facts of a case, the investigative organs need to probe into the origin and flow of the properties involved in the case, which may contain some information about the subjects of the properties. In addition, in the investigative activities, when the investigative organs intend to take measures to seal up or detain the properties involved in a case, they have to find out whether these properties belong to a third party. The investigative organs are of course the subject that investigates the interested parties.

As an applicant for confiscation of properties, the procuratorial organ has the obligation to provide evidence to the court to prove that the relevant properties are the properties involved in the case and should be confiscated. The main form for the procuratorial organ to bear the burden of proof is to submit an application for confiscating illegal gains to the court. According to the Article 526 of the Criminal Procedure Rules of the People's Procuratorates (for trial), the main content of the application should include the names, addresses, contact information and requests of the near relatives and other interested parties of the criminal suspects and the defendants. With regard to the submissions of confiscation of illegal gains transferred by the public security organ to the procuratorial organ, they shall contain the situation about the relevant interested parties, and the procuratorial organ may investigate these interested parties by itself if necessary. As such, the procuratorial organ is also the subject with the obligation to identify interested parties.

Interested Parties Apply for Participating in the Proceedings

When near relatives, as interested parties, apply with the court to participate in the proceedings, they only need to provide identification materials. In contrast, the interested parties other than near relatives have to provide evidence showing they have certain interest in the properties under the application of confiscation. The ownership interest parties shall provide evidence that the properties under the application of confiscation belong to them. When examining the evidence materials of interested parties, the people's court only conduct procedural examination. Interested parties can participate in the proceedings in person or entrust agents ad litem to participate in the proceedings on their behalf.

Even if interested parties fail to apply to participate in the proceedings during the announcement period for various reasons, their participation right cannot be denied only because of expired announcement. The announcement period is essentially different from the scheduled period or the limitation of action in civil procedure. The "announcement period" here does not have any legal effect in eliminating rights or depriving someone's right to win a lawsuit. Moreover, being unable to participate in the confiscation procedure in time, the right owners will find their property right fully infringed. Apparently, the value of right protection exceeds the value of litigation efficiency based on a time limit. In addition, Article 283 of the Criminal Procedure Law stipulates that "if there is indeed something wrong with the property confiscation of the criminal suspects or the defendants, these properties shall be returned or compensated". In the proceedings, interested parties may claim for rights and present evidence and apply to participate in the proceedings, if they are ignored simply because of expired announcement, it will inevitably lead to the correction in the future, which is not conducive to the efficiency of litigation. Article 513(2) of the Interpretation of the Supreme People's Court urges the interested parties to file the application during the announcement period, so as to exercise their rights in a timely manner. But Article 513(3) stipulates that as long as they can make reasonable explanations and give the evidence to prove that they are the owner of the properties under the application for confiscation, the people's court shall allow them to participate in the proceedings. If they do not know their legitimate properties have been confiscated until the ruling is made, then corrections shall be made through the trial supervision procedure according to Article 283 of the Criminal Procedure Law.

6.4.3.3 Participate in the Pre-trial Preparation Procedure

The start time of the procedure for confiscating illegal gains should be at least the time when the people's procuratorate submits the application for confiscating illegal gains to the people's court. If interested parties expect to participate in the proceedings, they have to wait until the people's court accepts their application for the participation. The criminal proceedings of the investigative and procuratorial organs have been going on prior to the start of the confiscation procedure.

Before submitting to the people's procuratorate the opinions for confiscating illegal gains, the public security organ shall conduct an open investigation on the illegal gains and the properties involved in the case of the criminal suspects or the defendants, with a focus placed on finding out the existing properties of the criminal suspects or the defendants who have absconded or who are already deceased, distinguishing their personal properties, family properties and common properties, and assessing the value of their securities such as stock, bond and bill of exchange.

By the time for filing the application, the procuratorial organ should have obtained almost all of the above information, and made preparations for the imminent procedure for confiscating illegal gains. But for interested parties, they may have no idea that their relevant properties are confiscated until they see the announcement issued by the people's court.

While preparing for participating in the proceedings, interested parties may encounter the problems such as limited time and insufficient information, which affects their substantial participation in the proceedings. The author believes that, on the one hand, after approving the application of interested parties to participate in the confiscation procedure, the people's court should guarantee that they have both time and means to make necessary preparations; and on the other hand, the investigative and procuratorial organs shall, during the investigation of the properties involved in the case, listen to the opinions of interested parties, and allow them to take part in the whole process of sealing, seizing and freezing the properties when necessary. The results of the property investigation shall be disclosed to the interested parties, which may help them learn about the scope, type and quantity of the confiscated properties and get prepared to respond to any lawsuit.

6.4.3.4 Legal Aid in Confiscation Procedure

In the special confiscation procedure, the purpose of the interested parties' participation in this procedure is to confront the procuratorial organ which attempts to apply for the confiscation of the properties to which they claim for right, and strive to defend their own properties. This confrontation may either succeed or fail. Any failure will indicate the property loss of the interested parties, and may cause a significant adverse impact on their life. Therefore, there shall be objective guarantee that the interested parties can fully take part in some activities to defend their own interests. For the interested parties, they are about to confront the procuratorial organ which is backed up by the state power, their abilities to investigate and obtain evidence are not on an equal footing. Based on the concept of "equality of arms", when interested parties are unable to fully exercise their right to participate substantially in the special confiscation procedure due to their own conditions, the competent state organs should provide aid to them. It is no doubt unjust if they are unable to hire a lawyer to help them and have to lose the lawsuit with their own properties confiscated. In reference to Article 34 of the new Criminal Procedure Law, "the criminal suspects" are added into the scope of the objects to receive legal aid. However, whether the interested parties that expect to participate in the procedure for confiscation of illegal gains could obtain legal aid when they need help, there is no legal provision in this regard. Looking at the civil procedure system, according to Article 10 of the Regulations on Legal Aid promulgated by the State Council in 2003, even if the interested parties claim for the properties involved in the case, they are unlikely to receive any legal aid.[40]

---

[40]According to Article 10 of the Regulations on Legal Aid, the situations where the interested parties are entitled to applying for legal aid are as follows: request state compensation according to

In the US Civil Asset Forfeiture Reform Act of 2000 there are special institutional arrangements for the above issue. First, for the claimants who are unable to hire a lawyer due to financial difficulties, if they have received legal aid from a designated lawyer in criminal proceedings related to this, then the court may agree that this lawyer will continue helping them act for the civil confiscation procedure. But the court should investigate whether the claimants really have an interest in the properties under the application for confiscation, and whether their participation is for good faith instead of interference with the proceedings. Secondly, if the properties under the application for confiscation are the main residence of the economically difficult claimants, the court should designate a lawyer to provide legal aid to these claimants upon their application.[41]

From the perspective of guaranteeing citizens' legal property right, it is necessary to provide legal aid to interested parties in the procedure for confiscation of illegal gains. Citizens should not suffer losses when they are attempting to protect their legitimate rights. Interested parties are passively involved in this resource-consuming procedure activity. From another perspective, if the procuratorial organ mistakenly initiates the confiscation procedure, thus causing the interested parties to spend time and money for this purpose, the state should undertake the corresponding obligation in providing them with legal aid. After the revision of the Civil Procedure Law and the Criminal Procedure Law, the Ministry of Justice issued the Opinions on Further Promoting Legal Aid Work in April 2013, which pointed out that it is necessary to expand the coverage of legal aid and adjust the scope of supplementary items for legal aid in a timely manner, accelerate the establishment of a dynamic adjustment mechanism for the scope and standards of legal aid, and safeguard the procedural rights of the criminal suspects and the defendants according to law. The Opinions put forward an open interpretation of legal aid matters and objects. China shall include the legal aid for interested parties into the statutory scope of legal aid services based on its economic and social conditions.

6.4.4 How Interested Parties Provide Proof in Confiscation Procedure

The details of the confiscation procedure in Article 515 of the Interpretation of the Supreme People's Court are designed in reference to the first-instance procedure of public prosecution cases, the first-instance procedure of civil actions and the hearing procedure of administrative cases. According to this article, the main content of

---

law; receive social insurance treatment or minimum living security treatment; receive pensions or relief; pay alimony or child-support payments; pay labor remuneration; and claim for civil rights and interests for doing boldly what is righteous. The reason for mentioning civil procedure is that there is still controversy about the nature of the procedure for confiscating illegal gains. However, with a view to the current legal regulations, no matter whether it is a civil or criminal lawsuit, interested parties cannot obtain legal aid in times of difficulty.

[41] 18U.S.C.§983(b).

the court trial is "whether the criminal suspects or the defendants have committed corruption and bribery crimes or the major crimes such as terrorist activities, and they have been wanted for one year and cannot appear before the court, or whether they are already decreased", and "whether the properties under the application for confiscation should be recovered according to law". Revolving round these two main contents of the court trial, the substantial participation of interested parties in the confiscation procedure is reflected in making a statement, giving evidence and cross-examining evidence, and joining in debates, while the central part is giving evidence and cross-examining evidence.

6.4.4.1 Burden of Proof

The Criminal Procedure Law does not specify the burden of proof for the special confiscation procedure. According to Article 49 of the Criminal Procedure Law, in public prosecution cases, the people's procuratorate shall bear the burden to prove the guilt of the defendants, which has all along been a consistent criminal justice practice in China. There is no law that defines the people's procuratorate should bear the burden of proof in special procedures. Special procedures are still an integral part of the criminal procedure, but compared with the ordinary procedures of public prosecution cases, each special procedure differs in the application subject, trial object and trial method, etc. Even so, it does not deny the burden of proof needs to be borne by the people's procuratorate, and Article 49 of the Criminal Procedure Law of course applies to special procedures. Article 535 of the Criminal Procedure Rules of the People's Procuratorates (for trial), clarifies the procuratorate's burden of proof in the confiscation process; in other words, interested parties do not bear the burden of proof.

There is a view that under certain circumstances, if it can be directly presumed that a property is derived from a criminal act, then the burden of proof can be reversed to the interested parties, that is, interested parties should also bear the burden of proof under certain conditions.[42] The reason for this view is that corruption and bribery crimes and terrorist crimes are relatively hidden, and it is very difficult for the procuratorial organs to fully bear the burden of proof. Based on considerations of fairness, criminal policy, and ease of proof, it is reasonable to invert the burden of proof. The author believes that the defect of this view is that it makes a mistake in the object of reversion of burden of proof. It is true that letting the procuratorial organs bear the burden of proof borne entirely is not conducive to recovering illegal gains, so the issue of reversion of burden of proof is worth discussing. But the focus of the issue is whether the criminal suspects or the defendants need to bear part of the burden of proof, rather than the interested parties. The reason why interested parties participate in the proceedings is to fight for their own interests; they are neither the "spokespersons" for the criminal suspects or defendants or the perpetrators of the suspected criminal acts, so they cannot and should not know the legitimate

---

[42] Xue [33].

sources of the properties involved in the case. It is obviously improper to require interested parties to bear the burden of proof belonging to the criminal suspects or the defendants.

6.4.4.2 Objects of Proof

When the near relatives and other interested parties of the criminal suspects or the defendants participate in the confiscation procedure, they are not going to replace the criminal suspects or the defendants who cannot appear before the court to exercise their right to defense, nor they are about to provide evidence as witnesses for the case. Rather, they put forward their own claims on the properties under the application for confiscation, supplemented by relevant evidence. Regardless of the special family relationship between the criminal suspects or the defendants and their near relatives, the Criminal Procedure Law and its related judicial interpretations only allow them to claim for the ownership of the properties under the application for confiscation. It is unquestionable that the ownership claim will confront the confiscation application, but the key is that whether the claim for "legal ownership" can counter against the confiscation application.

The illegal gains in criminal cases may exist in many different forms. Paragraphs 4, 5 and 6 of Article 31 of the United Nations Convention against Corruption list three main forms, including "converted illegal gains", that is, to convert direct criminal proceeds into other properties such as buying real estate with stolen money; "mixed illegal gains" means mixing illegal with legal gains; "profit gains", that is, the properties derived from the convention or mixing of proceeds of crime generate new gains. These three kinds of properties evolved from illegal gains are all properties that the United Nations Convention against Corruption requires to be confiscated, but their existence is shown in a legal form, so that interested parties can claim ownership of them. If interested parties are only required to provide the "evidence that the properties belong to them", these case-related properties may be exempted from being confiscated. In addition, interested parties may be in either of the following two situations: one is that all of their properties are used by others for criminal purposes, and the other is that the goods or proceeds used by others to commit crimes have become their own properties. In both situations, interested parties have the right to the confiscated properties. Whether such property right can resist confiscation, it depends on specific situations. In the illegal gains confiscation procedure of China, only ownership is prescribed in general, and no distinction is made in this regard.

The problems involving the protection of third-party properties also exist in the US civil confiscation procedure. In U.S. laws, this third-party act against the government's seizure of properties is known as "Innocent Owner Defense".[43] This refers to "a situation where the owner (such as the owner of real estate or money) claims that

[43] Chu and Lian [34].

the properties were confiscated due to the wrongful conduct or negligence of others when using his properties, but the owner did not know or did not agree".[44]

The basic conditions applicable to the "Innocent Owner Defense" are as follows: First of all, the owner needs to prove that he has obtained the property right when the criminal act occurred, which is the case that "all of his properties are used by others for criminal purposes". Secondly, the owner claims that he is unaware of the occurrence of the criminal act that leads to the confiscation of his properties, or despite knowing the occurrence of the criminal act, he has done everything he can to prevent it. For the latter, the law requires innocent owners to promptly report to law enforcement agencies that an illegal act is imminent or has already occurred, and to prevent the illegal act in a timely or good faith manner, including taking reasonable measures to prevent wrongdoing after consultation with law enforcement agencies.[45] It can be seen that this provision stipulates a higher standard of obligations for "innocent owners", that is, owners must take active measures to prevent illegal use of properties by others.

For the circumstances where property right is acquired after a property-related criminal act occurs, the applicable conditions for the "Innocent Owner Defense" will be different: First, the claimant must be a bona fide purchaser or seller, and has paid or received reasonable consideration. Second, the claimant does not know or has reasonable grounds to believe that the properties are unlikely to be confiscated due to a criminal act.[46] If the above conditions are met, the court should determine that the "Innocent Owner Defense" is effective, thereby preventing the confiscation act by the law enforcement agencies. It should be noted that if the object is contraband, such as drugs or smuggled goods, the owner shall not claim the defense.

The "Innocent Owner Defense" in the US civil confiscation procedure distinguishes the different relationships and different causes between the third party and the properties involved in the case, as well as the different handling approaches. This plays an important role in safeguarding the interests of third party in the property confiscation procedure, and can be used as a reference for perfecting the protection of the rights of interested parties in China's illegal gains confiscation procedure.

The current system only requires proof of ownership to defend against confiscation, which is imperfect. The people's court should also investigate whether the sources of the properties under the application for confiscation are involved in a criminal act. It should also be a focus of the investigative and procuratorial organs when they are investigating the case-related properties. For interested parties, filing a proof of ownership with the court is not sufficient to counter the application for confiscation, and evidence must also be provided to prove the legality of the sources of the properties. If the properties under the application for confiscation are found to be illegal gains, but interested parties claim to enjoy their legal ownership because of good faith acquisition, they should also provide evidence that they did not know or

[44] Garner [35].

[45] 18U.S.C.§983(d)(2).

[46] 18U.S.C.§983(d)(3).

should not know that the properties were illegal gains when accepting their transfer, and they have paid a reasonable consideration.

6.4.4.3 Criteria of Proof

Article 516 of the Interpretation of the Supreme People's Court stipulates that the confiscation can only be determined if the people's court believes that "the facts of the case are clear and the evidence is true and sufficient" after hearing, which is consistent with Article 53 of the Criminal Procedure Law. This is not only a consistent tradition of China's criminal procedure, but also meets the general requirements of procedural justice. This criterion is applicable to the procuratorate, it seems too stringent if applicable to the claim of interested parties. Although interested parties claim property ownership in the criminal confiscation procedure, their pursuit for property protection is more like a civil action. When interested parties claim for the right to the properties under the application for confiscation, they bear the burden of proof, and the criterion of proof can meet the criterion for preponderance of the evidence in civil action.

References

1. Packer, H. L. (2013). The two models of criminal procedure. In L. Genlin (Trans.), P. Yu & Z. Guo (Ed.), *Contention and speculation: A selection of classic papers on the models of criminal procedure* (pp. 3–50). Beijing: Peking University Press.
2. Yu, P., & Guo, Z. (Ed.). (2013). *Contention and speculation: A selection of classic papers on the models of criminal procedure* (p. 10). Beijing: Peking University Press.
3. Yu, P., & Guo, Z. (Ed.). (2013). *Contention and speculation: A selection of classic papers on the models of criminal procedure* (p. 13). Beijing: Peking University Press.
4. Beloof, D. E. (2013). A third model of criminal process: The victim participation model. In: Z. Guo (Trans.), P. Yu & Z. Guo (Eds.), *Contention and speculation: A selection of classic papers on the models of criminal procedure* (pp. 190–216). Beijing: Peking University Press.
5. Chen, R. (1998). An outline of procedural justice. *Proceedings Law Review*, Issue 1.
6. Zhang, J. (2005). *Research on the rights of criminal victims* (p. 40). Ph.D. thesis, China University of Political Science and Law.
7. Li, F. (2013). Protection of the rights of criminal victims based on meeting the desire for revenge. *Tribune of Political Science and Law*, Issue 5.
8. Law Policy Research Office of the Supreme People's Procuratorate (Trans. & Ed.). (2003). *Justice for all—Report on British judicial reform* (p. 1). Beijing: China procuratorial Press.
9. Chen, W., & Xiao, L. (2013). A study on several issues concerning the protection of the rights and interests of victims in the new criminal procedure law. *Oriental Law*, Issue 2.
10. Chen, W. (2013). Criminal misjudged cases: From case remedy to system remedy. *Procuratorate Daily*, May 9.
11. Chen, W. (2007). A study on the system of witnesses appearing in court to testify in criminal cases. *Journal of Shandong Police College*, Issue 2.
12. Lang, S. (2012). *Revision and application of the criminal procedure Law* (p. 335). Beijing: Xinhua Publishing House.
13. Lang, S. (2012). *Revision and application of the criminal procedure law of the People's Republic of China* (p. 337). Beijing: Xinhua Publishing House.

14. Zhu, X. (2013). Investigators appear in court to make explanations does not qualify as testifying in court as witness. *People's Procuratorial Semimonthly*, Issue 16.
15. Maran, Z. B. (2014). Police on the witness stand as a witness—Investigation and research on the investigator testifying in court . *Nomocracy Forum*, Issue 2.
16. Lang, S. (2012). *Revision and application of the criminal procedure law of the People's Republic of China* (p. 137). Beijing: Xinhua Publishing House.
17. He, T. (2007). Conflict and trade-off between witness protection and the fundamental rights of the defendant. *Criminal Science*, Issue 3.
18. Zhang, J. (2012). Tolerating and concealing between kinfolks and placing righteousness above family loyalty—On the relationship between revision of criminal procedure law and traditional culture. *Journal of Hubei Polytechnic Institute*, Issue 1.
19. Xu, J. (2006). *On the reform of the judicial expertise system*. Beijing: China procuratorial Press.
20. Fan, C. (2001). *Introduction to judicial expertise* (p. 254). Beijing: Law Press.
21. Chen, W. (2012). *Criminal procedure law* (p. 130). Beijing: China Renmin University Press.
22. Wang, X. (2013). *Criminal procedure law* (p. 65). Beijing: China Renmin University Press.
23. Weidong, Z. J. (2012). *Lecture on the new system of the criminal procedure law* (p. 106). Beijing: People's Court Press.
24. Li, X. (2012). An analysis of the difficulties for expert witness testifying in court. *Journal of Renmin University of China*, Issue 3.
25. Li, X. (2012). Appraisal system under the new procedural law. *Chinese Journal of Forensic Sciences*, Issue 6.
26. Lang, S. (2012). *Revision and application of the criminal procedure law of the People's Republic of China* (p. 344). Beijing: Xinhua Publishing House.
27. Zhang, L. (2014). On the litigation function of the expert witness system—An analysis of the first judicial cases after the implementation of the renewed criminal procedure law. *Hebei Law Science*, Issue 3.
28. Chen, W. (2012). On the procedure of pre-judgment property confiscation in the new criminal procedure law. *Legal Forum*, Issue 3.
29. Song, Y. (2011). *Criminal procedure law* (p. p56). Beijing: China Renmin University Press.
30. Xiang, B. (2013). *Understanding and application of the supreme people's court's interpretation on the application of the criminal procedure law of the People's Republic of China* (p. 435). Beijing: China Legal Publishing House.
31. Jiang, W., & Xiao, J. (2011). *Civil procedure law* (p. 136). Beijing: China Renmin University Press.
32. He, F. (2007). *Study on criminal confiscation: From the perspective of international law and comparative law* (p. 76). Beijing: Law Press· China.
33. Xue, W. (2013). The procuratorate bears burden of proof in the special confiscation procedure for illegal gains. *Journal of Henan Institute of Education*, Issue 6.
34. Chu, D., & Lian, H. (2014). A close view of the "innocent owner defense" in the United States. *Journal of Beijing University of Aeronautics & Astronautics (Social Sciences Edition)*, Issue 2.
35. Garner, B. A. (2009). *Black's law dictionary* (p. 483). Beijing: West Publishing Company.

Postscript

Powers and rights are the two main lines running through the entire criminal procedure. The powers of investigation, prosecution and adjudication are state powers, while the parties, participants in proceedings, their legal representatives, defenders, and agents exercise the rights of individual citizens. To a certain extent, criminal procedure is the interweaving, restriction and balance of state power and individual citizen rights.

From criminal legislation to criminal justice, the allocation and operation of powers and rights represent the level of criminal law and human rights protection in a country. Since the end of the 1970s when China enacted the Criminal Procedure Law, the country organized two rounds of revision to this law respectively 1996 and 2012. It is an indisputable fact that the overall level of rule of law and human rights protection has been continuously improved in China. The development trend of criminal legislation and justice is advancing in the direction of further restricting state power and expanding citizens' rights. Several rounds of judicial reforms during this period have continuously promoted this trend. In this context, how to further deepen the study of powers and rights in criminal procedure, especially under the circumstance that judicial reforms increasingly concern about this issue, becomes more urgent and necessary. Our research must be problem-oriented and based on the shortcomings of the criminal procedural power, norms of rights and judicial practices. And we must propose practical solutions for advancing the ongoing judicial reform.

In recent years, I have published some texts in newspapers and magazines, and discussed the relevant issues in the book *Road to Procedural Justice* published by Law Press China, but they are scattered and not systematic. In today's view, the materials at that time have become outdated and are not compatible with the rapid development of judicial practice. After two years of conception and composition in 2016 and 2017, my book *The Change and Development of the Powers and Functions of Criminal Procedure in China* is finally unfolded in front of everyone.

W. Chen, *Reform and Development of Powers and Functions of China's Criminal Proceedings*, https://doi.org/10.1007/978-981-15-8431-2